Java: An Eventful Approach

Java: An Eventful Approach

Kim B. Bruce
Pomona College

Andrea Pohoreckyj Danyluk
Thomas P. Murtagh
Williams College

PEARSON
Prentice
Hall

UPPER SADDLE RIVER, NEW JERSEY 07458

Library of Congress Cataloging-in-Publication Data
CIP Data Available

Vice President and Editorial Director, ECS: Marcia Horton
Senior Acquisitions Editor: Tracy Dunkelberger
Editorial Assistant: Christianna Lee
Executive Managing Editor: Vince O'Brien
Managing Editor: Camille Trentacoste
Production Editor: Irwin Zucker
Director of Creative Services: Paul Belfanti
Art Director: Maureen Eide
Cover Designer: Suzanne Behnke
Cover Illustration: Fireworks, Photodisc Collection / Getty Images, Inc.
Managing Editor, AV Management and Production: Patricia Burns
Art Editor: Xiaohong Zhu
Manufacturing Buyer: Lisa McDowell
Marketing Manager: Pamela Hersperger
Marketing Assistant: Barrie Reinhold

© 2006 by Pearson Education, Inc.
Pearson Prentice Hall
Pearson Education, Inc.
Upper Saddle River, NJ 07458

Pearson Prentice Hall® is a trademark of Pearson Education, Inc.

Printed in the United States of America

ISBN 0-13-142415-7

Pearson Education Ltd., London
Pearson Education Australia Pty. Ltd., Sydney
Pearson Education Singapore, Pte. Ltd.
Pearson Education North Asia Ltd., Hong Kong
Pearson Education Canada, Inc., Toronto
Pearson Educación de Mexico, S.A. de C.V.
Pearson Education-Japan, Tokyo
Pearson Education Malaysia, Pte. Ltd.
Pearson Education, Inc., Upper Saddle River, New Jersey

To my wife, Fatma.   – Kim

To my children, Stephan and Katya, and my husband, Andrew.   – Andrea

To my wife, Fern.   – Tom

Contents

13 General Loops in Java   338

14 Arrays   354

18 Exceptions   505

19 Streams   527

List of Figures

Preface

Java-based introductory course provides new challenges to instructors and students. While Java is simpler than C++, the fact that Java is an object-oriented language with a significant number of standard libraries adds both new complexities and opportunities.

This introductory computer science text provides a new approach to teaching programming in Java that combines several interesting features:

1. an objects-first approach to programming,
2. the intensive use of object-oriented graphics,
3. the use of concurrency early,
4. the use of event-driven programming from the beginning.

At first glance, this list of topics might seem overwhelming for an introductory text, but the synergy of these features results in a surprisingly effective introduction to programming using Java, especially when presented with the help of a library, objectdraw, that we have developed.

0.1 Target Audience

The primary target audiences for this text are first-year computer science majors, other college and university students interested in programming, and students taking high school advanced placement courses in computer science. In particular, this text covers the AP A exam material.

0.2 For the Student

0.2.1 Mysterious Buzzwords

We began this preface by listing some of the special features of this text that we find particularly exciting. Specifically, we said that the text provides:

1. an objects-first approach to programming,
2. the intensive use of object-oriented graphics,

3. the use of concurrency early,
4. the use of event-driven programming from the beginning.

At this point you're probably wondering what all of these buzzwords mean.

Java is an example of an *object-oriented* programming language. Just as there are many different types of spoken languages, there are many different computer programming languages. The object-oriented languages are simply one class of languages. Because programming languages differ from each other in many ways, it stands to reason that they should not all be taught in the same way. Since Java is object oriented, we have aimed to present it in a manner that is appropriate for that language paradigm.

From the beginning of the text, you will learn how to write programs that involve simple graphics—rectangles, ovals, and lines, for example. You will even learn to write programs that create graphical animations, using mechanisms for *concurrency*. We find that both students and instructors enjoy writing programs that involve interesting, albeit simple, graphics. In addition to being fun, graphics are very concrete. When a program involves drawing and manipulating graphical objects in a window, you can actually see what the program is doing. We find this helpful for the beginning programmer.

We also introduce *event-driven programming* early. While you probably haven't heard the term "event-driven programming", you're almost certainly familiar with it. If you've interacted with a computer by pulling down menus, clicking on icons, and dragging items with a mouse, you've interacted with event-driven programs. The programs you will learn to write will allow a user to interact with them through mouse movements, buttons, scroll bars, and so on.

0.2.2 How to Read This Book

Practice is an extremely important component of learning to program. Therefore, we have provided many opportunities for you to practice as you read this text. Each chapter contains embedded exercises that will allow you to check your understanding. Read with a pencil and paper beside you, so that you can do these short exercises as you go along. In addition, at the end of each chapter you will find chapter review exercises as well as programming problems. Working through the review exercises will help you determine whether you have understood the major concepts introduced in the chapter. Once you feel comfortable with these, try the programming problems. The more you do, the better you'll know Java.

0.3 For the Instructor

0.3.1 Special Features of This Text

A Graphics Library for the Objects-First Approach

We have adopted the use of graphics for our first examples and have constructed a truly object-oriented library of graphics classes. There are several reasons we believe that graphics provide a good setting for introducing object-oriented programming.

First, graphics are good examplars of objects. Graphics classes (e.g., framed and filled rectangles and ovals) provide good examples of objects because they have state (their location and dimensions) and a useful collection of methods that go well beyond methods that just get and set instance variables. Second, the graphics classes in our objectdraw library provide excellent visual feedback for novice programmers. When a graphics object is created, it appears on the screen immediately. When a graphics object in our library is moved or resized, the picture on the screen changes immediately. As a result, if a program contains a logical error, that error is immediately visible on the screen. Third, graphics provide motivating examples. With graphics, very simple programs can become much more interesting to students. Moreover, once animations are introduced, it is easy to provide fun and interesting examples well before the introduction of arrays. Finally, graphics persist in the course. Rather than introducing a set of example objects and then discarding it, an instructor can use the graphics library throughout the course.

Our objectdraw library not only provides the graphics classes, it also provides a WindowController class that extends JApplet by installing a DrawingCanvas in the center of the window. DrawingCanvas is an extension of JComponent that keeps track of the objects on the canvas and redraws them whenever necessary. This reduces the complexity of using graphics for novice programmers.

Event-Driven Programming

Some authors have argued for an event-driven approach in an introductory course because "real" programs that students use every day operate in an event-driven way. In students' use of computers they rarely see programs that respond to line-by-line text input. Thus event-driven programming is more motivating for students.

We believe there are several other pedagogically important advantages to an event-driven approach in an introductory course. One very important advantage is that students get experience writing methods from the beginning. Moreover, the methods tend to be very short.

In our library, we provide an environment in which novices learn to program by defining simple mouse-event-handling methods. For example, our onMouseDrag method is similar to standard Java's mouseDragged method, except that it has a simpler parameter. Because it is called repeatedly while the mouse is being dragged, very interesting programs can be constructed without using loops. This use of event-driven programming allows us to postpone the discussion of loops until after we discuss the definition of classes, while still presenting interesting examples to students.

Students get experience writing methods and using parameters by writing methods with fixed names and numbers of parameters, simplifying the introduction of these concepts. For example, all of our mouse-handling methods take a single Location parameter representing where the mouse is when the event occurs. Students become accustomed to using these formal parameters inside the associated method bodies. At the same time, students use actual parameters in the graphics commands.

This experience in writing event-handling methods with well-specified names and signatures, as well as the experience of writing code to send messages with actual parameters to graphic objects, makes the transition to designing and writing classes and their methods easier for students. Students still need to work to understand the "how" and "why" of parameter passing, but they will have seen and written many examples. That helps students in writing and understanding their own classes.

Objects-First

The combination of graphics and event-driven programming supports our objects-first approach. Students see example programs using objects from the graphics library starting from the first chapter of the text. Examples contain code to create new graphics objects and send messages to them. Moreover, the programs are extensions of the WindowController class.

Because the WindowController class of our library is an extension of Java's JApplet class, students need not begin with the static main method, and then have to learn about the differences between static and nonstatic methods. Instead they write instance methods that respond to mouse events. Thus students are introduced to using objects and writing their own methods from the first chapter of the text.

In the sixth chapter, students learn how to write their own classes. This chapter occurs before the introduction of loops, and just after the introduction of conditional statements. Our approach using event-driven programming allows us to construct and use interesting classes at this early point in the text.

Concurrency Early

We found that when examples are properly chosen to avoid race conditions, concurrent programming is conceptually easy for students to understand. After all, the world is concurrent, so there is nothing unnatural to students in having several threads executing concurrently. Moreover, many applications are much easier to program using concurrency rather than as a single thread.

We have provided a class ActiveObject in our library that supports using and managing threads. From a student's point of view, the primary difference between the ActiveObject class that we provide and the built-in Thread class is that we provide a variant of the sleep method that does not throw exceptions. As a result we are able to introduce concurrency in Chapter 9 of the text, before our discussion of exceptions. Behind the scenes, we also manage threads so that when a program (or applet in a web page) terminates, all threads will be terminated gracefully.

0.3.2 Why Introduce a Library?

We have chosen to introduce a library to support our approach, because it reduces syntactic and conceptual complexity early in the text. While we depend on the library early, it is not our intention to teach a different style of programming than that normally supported by Java. Our philosophy is to provide support early, but to also teach students the "right" way to program in Java.

A possible obstacle to using event-driven programming early in Java is the number of language and library features that must be introduced in order to handle events. For example, one would have to introduce listeners, interfaces, Java events, and so on. Moreover, if a class is to implement, for example, MouseListener, then it must implement all of the mouse-listening methods, even if only one is needed in the program.

Our library reduces this complexity as the WindowController class from the library implements both of the mouse listener interfaces. It also provides event-handling methods that take the Location of the mouse, rather than a more general MouseEvent. The advantage of getting a Location (a library type representing a point on the screen, but using doubles rather than integers) is that the useful information is immediately available, rather than requiring the programmer to extract it first. Finally, with our library, students only need to write the event-handling methods that they actually use in their program.

In Chapter 11 we teach students about standard Java GUI components. In conjunction with this we also teach students the standard Java event model. Students learn to associate listeners with user interface components and to write methods to handle the generated events. Thus they do learn how to program without using our library, but at a time when they are better equipped to understand the needed concepts.

As we noted above, introducing threads without using our library would require a discussion of exceptions before being able to pause a thread. Moreover, the exception that must be handled with the `sleep` method is a very bad first example of exceptions, as there is generally not much to do to handle it. Because we think exceptions can be better motivated later in the course (for example, in discussing I/O) and because they involve the complexity of inheritance and subtyping, we designed our library to enable us to postpone the discussion of exceptions. We do not use the library as an excuse to avoid teaching key components of Java. Instead we use it to provide a more pedagogically sound approach to presenting the various concepts introduced.

0.3.3 Supplementary Materials for Instructors

Supplementary materials are available on-line for instructors at http://eventfuljava.cs.williams.edu. These materials include the objectdraw library, a rich collection of sample programs and laboratory assignments that use the library and that are coordinated with the text, and detailed lecture notes.

The sample programs include those already in the text as well as a large collection of additional examples. The supplementary examples are rich and varied and add a great deal to the overall presentation of the material in the text. In some cases the additional programs stress (and therefore reinforce) certain dependencies. (This is in direct contrast to the way in which we wrote the text, where we attempted to minimize dependencies wherever possible.) Many of the additional examples involve `ActiveObjects` and, more specifically, animation. These do not always serve as the best types of examples in a text, as a book is a static medium, but they can be used extremely effectively by the instructor in a classroom or laboratory setting.

0.4 Flexibility for the Instructor and Student

In this text we have aimed to provide maximum flexibility for the reader. We expect the reader to cover the core introductory material in Chapters 1, 2, 3, 4, 6, 7, and 9. These chapters introduce the objectdraw library, conditionals, classes, `while` loops, and concurrency. Chapters 5 and 8 provide additional details about the topics introduced in Chapters 3 and 6. As well, they introduce strings and the topics of declaration and scope. While they are important, these chapters can be covered later, if desired.

Optional sections in all of the chapters, marked with an asterisk (*), can also be skipped.

The remainder of the text presents topics in the order in which we cover them in our course. We have found this order to work very well. However, as remarked earlier one of our goals was to avoid topic dependencies as much as possible, so that instructors could tailor their courses as appropriate for their students and their institutions. Figure 0.1 shows the ways in which Chapters 10–19 depend upon each other. Note that, in particular, recursion (and recursive data structures) and arrays can be presented in any order. It is also possible to cover inheritance before either recursion or arrays.

In addition to the dependencies shown in Figure 0.1, it is important to note that later chapters assume knowledge of GUI to a limited extent. In particular, examples in these later chapters make use of `JTextFields` and the `setText` and `getText` methods.

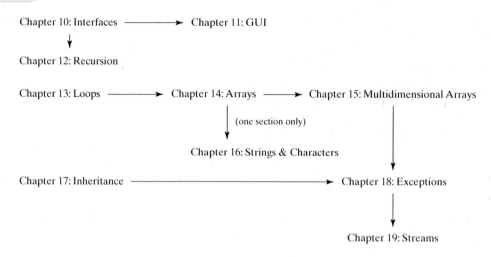

Chapter 10: Interfaces ⟶ Chapter 11: GUI

Chapter 12: Recursion

Chapter 13: Loops ⟶ Chapter 14: Arrays ⟶ Chapter 15: Multidimensional Arrays

(one section only)

Chapter 16: Strings & Characters

Chapter 17: Inheritance ⟶ Chapter 18: Exceptions

Chapter 19: Streams

Figure 0.1   Chapter dependencies after core introductory topics

Chapter 20. "Searching and Sorting", is an advanced topic and assumes knowledge of arrays and recursion. The sections on search do, however, give both iterative and recursive versions of the algorithms presented.

The second half of Chapter 21, "Introduction to Object-Oriented Design", assumes that students are familiar with both recursion and arrays. However, the first half of that chapter assumes nothing beyond familiarity with the core chapters, 1–9. If desired, the reader could work through the design unit in two stages, covering the first half after the core introductory material and the second half after the more advanced topics.

Finally, it is important to note that this text is not meant to be a complete reference on the Java programming language. We have strived to present the elements of the language at a level that is appropriate for a beginner. Some of the chapters in the second half of the text, for example, provide introductions to important concepts, without necessarily providing details on the level that an advanced student might require. Our goal is to give students a firm footing, with the expectation that they will develop a deeper and more complete understanding of the language later, as they gain more experience.

0.5   Additional Practical Information

We have included a great deal of additional useful material in several appendices to the book. The first appendix provides style guidelines for programming. While there are fairly standard conventions followed by Java programmers, some issues of style are obviously subjective. Students should note that their instructors might provide their own guidelines.

The next appendix provides a summary of the classes and methods available in the objectdraw library. In the third appendix, we take the reader through the process of navigating the documentation for Java APIs. An API (Application Programming Interface) specifies the details a programmer must know to use the resources a library provides. We go through parts of the API for the objectdraw library, but as the documentation for many APIs follows a standard format, the reader should then be able to read other API documentation as well.

The transition from our library to standard Java is quite straightforward. The final appendix summarizes for the reader the standard Java equivalents for many of the features in the library.

0.6 Acknowledgements

This book would not have been possible without help and feedback from many people. First we thank our Williams College faculty colleagues, Barbara Lerner, Jim Teresco, Steven Freund, and Stacia Wyman, who were willing to teach with the sometimes very sketchy notes and not always stable library that we provided. Hundreds of Williams students enthusiastically met the challenge of learning a new way of approaching computer science using our materials as they developed over the last few years. Special thanks go to our undergraduate teaching assistants, many of whom worked hard to learn new material and helped make it seem easy to the students. A number of other Williams students worked with us in developing the library, writing up lab and homework problems and their solutions, testing the library, and designing the web pages for our course materials. These students include Peter Applegate, Jing Cao, Brendan Dougherty, Marcus Duyzend, Cheng Hu, Jonathan Kallay, Krishna Kannan, Christine Osterman, and Ashok Pillai.

A very important part of developing our materials was getting feedback from faculty at other institutions who used our materials in their own classes. While there are too many testers to list them all here, we single out the following for their very helpful feedback on the text and materials: Barbara Adler, Mary Courtney, Chris Haynes, David Housman, Lonnie Fairchild, James Taylor, and Douglas Troy. Special thanks to Chris Nevison for using the objectdraw library in his short courses for high school Advanced Placement Computer Science teachers.

The outside reviewers engaged by Prentice Hall provided very thoughtful comments on this text. While we did not follow all of their advice, their detailed feedback resulted in many improvements and clarifications in the text. The reviewers include: Chris Haynes of Indiana University, Richard Albright of Goldey-Beacom College, Henry A. Etlinger of Rochester Institute of Technology, Carlos A. Varela of Rensselaer Polytechnic Institute, Richard E. Pattis of Carnegie Mellon University, Ron Zacharski of New Mexico State University, Trudy Howles of Rochester Institute of Technology, Mark Williams of Lane Community College, Mary Courtney of Pace University, Mary Ann May-Pumphrey of De Anza College, David Housman of Goshen College, Lawrence C. Petersen of Texas A & M University, Mark A. Holliday of Western Carolina University, Gavin T. Osborne of Saskatchewan Institute of Applied Science and Technology, and Adel S. Elmaghraby of University of Louisville.

We are especially grateful to our editors from Prentice Hall, Petra Recter, who signed us up, Kate Hargett, who took over after Petra moved to a new division, and who gave birth to her first child about the time we sent this manuscript off into the publisher's arms, and Tracy Dunkelberger, who saw this project through to completion. We are also grateful to our production editor, Irwin Zucker.

We hope you enjoy using this book as much as we have enjoyed developing this approach to an introductory course. We appreciate receiving comments and suggestions on this text and the associated materials. Contact information is available on our web page:

http://eventfuljava.cs.williams.edu

1

What Is Programming Anyway?

*M*ost of the machines that have been developed to improve our lives serve a single purpose. Just try to drive to the store in your washing machine or vacuum the living room with your car and this becomes quite clear. Your computer, by contrast, serves many functions. In the office or library, you may find it invaluable as a word processor. Once you get home, slip in a DVD and your computer takes on the role of a television. Start up a flight simulator and it assumes the properties of anything from a hang glider to the *Concorde*. Launch an mp3 player and you suddenly have a music system. This, of course, is just a short sample of the functions a typical personal computer can perform. Clearly, the computer is a very flexible device.

While the computer's ability to switch from one role to another is itself amazing, it is even more startling that these transformations occur without major physical changes to the machine. Every computer system includes both hardware, the physical circuitry of which the machine is constructed, and software, the programs that determine how the machine will behave. Everything described above can be accomplished by changing the software used without changing the machine's actual circuitry in any way. In fact, the changes that occur when you switch to a new program are often greater than those you achieve by changing a computer's hardware. If you install more memory or a faster network card, the computer will still do pretty much the same things it did before but a bit faster (hopefully!). On the other hand, by downloading a new application program through your Web browser, you can make it possible for your computer to perform completely new functions.

Software clearly plays a central role in the amazing success of computer technology. Very few computer users, however, have a clear understanding of what software really is. This book provides an introduction to the design and construction of computer software in the programming language named Java. By learning to program in Java, you will acquire a useful skill that will enable you to construct software of your own or participate in the implementation or maintenance of commercial software. More importantly, you will gain a clear understanding of what a program really is and how it is possible to radically change the behavior of a computer by constructing a new program.

A program is a set of instructions that a computer follows. We can therefore learn a good bit about computer programs by examining the ways in which instructions written for humans resemble and differ from computer programs. In this chapter we will consider several examples of instructions for humans in order to provide you with a rudimentary understanding of the nature of a computer program. We will then build on this understanding by presenting a very simple but complete example of a computer program written in Java. Like instructions for humans, the instructions that make up a computer program must be communicated to the computer in a language that it comprehends. Java is such a language. We will discuss the mechanics of actually communicating the text of a Java program to a computer so that it can follow the instructions contained in the program. Finally, you have undoubtedly already discovered that programs don't always do what you expect them do to. When someone else's program misbehaves, you can complain. When this happens with a program you wrote yourself, you will have to figure out how to change the instructions to eliminate the problem. To prepare you for this task, we will conclude this chapter by identifying several categories of errors that can be made when writing a program.

1.1   Without Understanding

You have certainly had the experience of following instructions of one sort or another. Electronic devices from computers to cameras come with thick manuals of instructions. Forms, whether they be tax forms or the answer sheets for an SAT exam, come with instructions explaining how they should be completed. You can easily think of many other examples of instructions you have had to follow.

If you have had to follow instructions, it is likely that you have also complained about the quality of the instructions. The most common complaint is probably that the instructions take too long to read. This, however, may have more to do with our impatience than the quality of the instructions. A more serious complaint is that instructions are often unclear and hard to understand.

It seems obvious that instructions are more likely to be followed correctly if they are easy to understand. This "obvious" fact, however, does not generalize to the types of instructions that make up computer programs. A computer is just a machine. Understanding is something humans do, but not something machines do. How can a computer understand the instructions in a computer program? The simple answer is that it cannot. As a result, the instructions that make up a computer program have to satisfy a very challenging requirement. It must be possible to follow them correctly without actually understanding them.

This may seem like a preposterous idea. How can you follow instructions if you don't understand them? Fortunately, there are a few examples of instructions for humans that are deliberately designed so that they can be followed without understanding. Examining such instructions will give you a bit of insight into how a computer must follow the instructions in a computer program.

First, consider the "mathematical puzzle" described below. To appreciate this example, don't just read the instructions. Follow them as you read them.

1. Pick a number between 1 and 40.
2. Subtract 20 from the number you picked.
3. Multiply by 3.
4. Square the result.
5. Add up the individual digits of the result.
6. If the sum of the digits is even, divide by 2.
7. If the result is less than 5 add 5, otherwise subtract 4.
8. Multiply by 2.
9. Subtract 6.
10. Find the letter whose position in the alphabet is equal to the number you have obtained ($a = 1$, $b = 2$, $c = 3$, etc.).
11. Think of a country whose name begins with this letter.
12. Think of a large mammal whose name begins with the second letter of the country's name.

You have probably seen puzzles like this before. You are supposed to be surprised that it is possible to predict the final result produced, even though you are allowed to make random choices at some points in the process. In particular, this puzzle is designed to leave you thinking about elephants. Were you thinking about an elephant when you finished? Are you surprised we could predict this?

The underlying reason for such surprise is that the instructions are designed to be followed without being understood. The person following the instructions thinks that the choices he or she gets to make in the process (choosing a number or choosing any country whose name begins with "D") could lead to many different results. A person who understands the instructions realizes this is an illusion.

To understand why almost everyone who follows the instructions above will end up thinking about elephants, you have to identify a number of properties of the operations performed. The steps that tell you to multiply by 3 and square the result ensure that after these steps the number you are working with will be a multiple of nine. When you add up the digits of any number that is a multiple of nine, the sum will also be a multiple of nine. Furthermore, the fact that your initial number was relatively small (less than 40) implies that the multiple of nine you end up with is also relatively small. In fact, the only possible values you can get when you sum the digits are 0, 9, and 18. The next three steps are designed to turn any of these three values into a 4, leading you to the letter "D". The last step is the only point in these instructions where something could go wrong. The person following them actually has a choice at this point. There are four countries on Earth whose names begin with "D": Denmark, Djibouti, Dominica, and the Dominican Republic. Luckily, for most readers of this text, Denmark is more likely to come to mind than any of the other three countries (even though the Dominican Republic is actually larger in both land mass and population).

This example should make it clear that it is possible to *follow* instructions without understanding how they work. It is equally clear that it is not possible to *write* instructions like those above without understanding how they work. This contrast provides an important insight into the relationship between a computer, a computer program, and the author of the program. A computer follows the instructions in a program the way you followed the instructions above. It can comprehend and complete each step individually but has no understanding of the overall purpose of the program, the relationships between the steps, or the ways in which these relationships ensure that the program will accomplish its overall purpose. The author of a program, on the other hand, must understand its overall purpose and ensure that the steps specified will accomplish this purpose.

Instructions like this are important enough to deserve a name. We call a set of instructions designed to accomplish some specific purpose, even when followed by a human or computer that has no understanding of their purpose, an *algorithm*.

There are situations where specifying an algorithm that accomplishes some purpose can actually be useful rather than merely amusing. To illustrate this, consider the standard procedure called long division. A sample of the application of the long-division procedure to compute the quotient 13042144 / 32 is shown below:

```
            407567
      32 )13042144
         128
         ___
          242
          224
          ___
          181
          160
          ___
          214
          192
          ___
          224
          224
          ___
            0
```

Although you may be rusty at it by now, you were taught the algorithm for long division sometime in elementary school. The person teaching you might have tried to help you understand why the procedure works, but ultimately you were probably simply taught to perform the process by rote. After doing enough practice problems, most people reach a point where they can perform long division but can't even precisely describe the rules they are following, let alone explain why they work. Again, this process was designed so that a human can perform the steps without understanding exactly why they work. Here, the motivation is not to surprise anyone. The value of the division algorithm is that it enables people to perform division without having to devote their mental energies to thinking about why the process works.

Finally, to demonstrate that algorithms don't always have to involve arithmetic, let's consider another example where the motivation for designing the instructions is to provide a pleasant surprise. Well before you learned the long-division algorithm, you were probably occasionally entertained by the process of completing a connect-the-dots drawing like the one shown in Figure 1.1. Go ahead! It's your book. Connect the dots and complete the picture.

A connect-the-dots drawing is basically a set of instructions that enable you to draw a picture without understanding what it is you are actually drawing. Just as it wasn't clear that the arithmetic you were told to perform in our first example would lead you to think of elephants, it is not obvious, looking at Figure 1.1, that you are looking at instructions for drawing an elephant. Nevertheless, by following the instructions "Connect the dots" you will do just that (even if you never saw an elephant before).

This example illustrates a truth of which all potential programmers should be aware. It is harder to devise an algorithm to accomplish a given goal than it is to simply accomplish the goal.

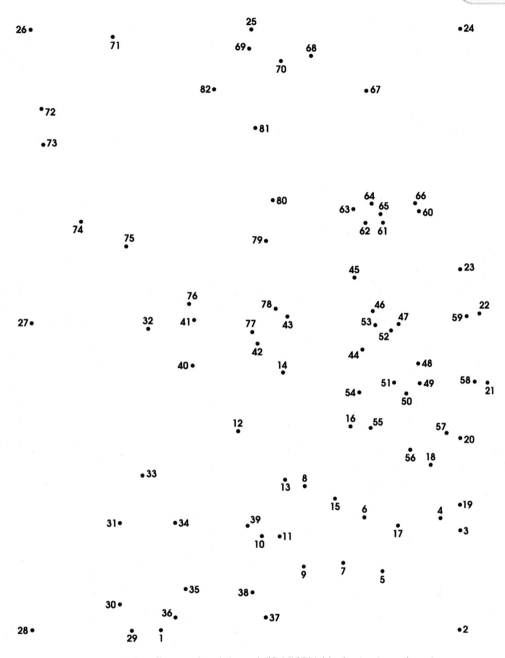

Figure 1.1   Connect dots 1 through 82 (©2000 MonkeyingAround.com)

The goal of the connect-the-dots puzzle shown in Figure 1.1 is to draw an elephant. In order to construct this puzzle, you first have to learn to draw an elephant without the help of the dots. Only after you have figured out how to draw an elephant in the first place will you be able to figure out where to place the dots and how to number them. Worse yet, figuring out how to place and number the dots so the desired picture can be drawn without ever having to lift your pencil from the paper can be tricky. If all you really wanted in the first place was a picture of an elephant, it would be easier to draw one yourself. Similarly, if you have a division problem to solve (and you don't have a calculator handy) it is easier to do the division yourself than to try to teach the long-division algorithm to someone who doesn't already know it, so that he or she can solve the problem for you.

As you learn to program, you will see this pattern repeated frequently. Learning to convert your own knowledge of how to perform a task into a set of instructions so precise that they can be followed by a computer can be quite challenging. Developing this ability, however, is the key to learning how to program. Fortunately, you will find that as you acquire the ability to turn an informal understanding of how to solve a class of problems into a precise algorithm, you will be developing mental skills you will find valuable in many other areas.

1.2   The Java Programming Language

An algorithm starts as an idea in one person's mind. To become effective, it must be communicated to other people or to a computer. Communicating an algorithm requires the use of a language. A program is just an algorithm expressed in a language that a computer can comprehend.

The choice of the language in which an algorithm is expressed is important. The numeric calculation puzzle that led you to think of Danish elephants was expressed in English. If our instructions had been written in Danish, most readers of this text would not understand them.

The use of language in a connect-the-dots puzzle may not be quite as obvious. Note, however, that we could easily replace the numbers shown with numbers expressed using the Roman numerals I, II, III, IV, . . . , LXXXII. Most of you probably understand Roman numerals, so you would still be able to complete the puzzle. You would probably have difficulty, however, if we switched to something more ancient like the numeric system used by the Babylonians or to something more modern like the binary system that most computers use internally, in which the first few dots would be labeled 1, 10, 11, 100, 101, and 110.

The use of language in the connect-the-dots example is interesting from our point of view because the language used is quite simple. Human languages like English and Japanese are very complex. It would be very difficult to build a computer that could understand a complete human language. Instead, computers are designed to interpret instructions written in simpler languages designed specifically for expressing algorithms intended for computers. Computer languages are much more expressive than a system for writing numbers like the Roman numerals, but much simpler in structure than human languages.

One consequence of the relative simplicity of computer languages is that it is possible to write a program to translate instructions written in one computer language into another computer language. These programs are called *compilers*. The internal circuitry of a computer usually can only interpret commands written in a single language. The existence of compilers, however, makes it possible to write programs for a single machine using many different languages. Suppose that you have to work with a computer that can understand instructions written in language A but you want to write a program for the machine in language B. All you have to do is find (or write) a program written in language A that can translate instructions written in language B into equivalent instructions in language A. This program would be called a compiler for B. You can then write your programs in language B and use the compiler for B to translate the programs you write into language A so the computer can comprehend the instructions.

Each computer language has its own advantages and disadvantages. Some are simpler than others. This makes it easier to construct compilers that process programs written in these languages. At the same time, a language that is simple can limit the way you can express yourself, making it more difficult to describe an algorithm. Think again about the process of constructing the elephant connect-the-dots puzzle. It is easier to draw an elephant if you let yourself use curved lines than if you restrict yourself to straight lines. To describe an elephant in the language of connect-the-dots puzzles, however, you have to find a way to use only straight lines. On the other hand, a language that is too complex can be difficult to learn and use.

In this text, we will teach you how to use a language named Java to write programs. Java provides some sophisticated features that support an approach to programming called object-oriented programming that we emphasize in our presentation. While it is not a simple language, it is one of the simpler languages that support object-oriented programming.

Java is a relatively young computer language. It was designed in the early 90s by a group at Sun Microsystems. Despite its youth, Java is widely used. Compilers for Java are readily available for almost all computer platforms. We will talk more about Java compilers and how you will use them, once we have explained enough about Java itself to let you write simple programs.

Our approach to programming includes an emphasis on what is known as *event-driven programming*. In this approach, programs are designed to react to *events* generated by the user or system. The programs that you are used to using on computers use the event-driven approach. You do something—press the mouse on a button, select an item from a menu, etc.—and the computer reacts to the "event" generated by that action. In the early days of computing, programs were started with a collection of data all provided at once and then run to completion. Many textbooks still teach that approach to programming. In this text we take the more intuitive event-driven approach to programming. Java is one of the first languages to make this easy to do as a standard part of the language.

1.3   Your First Sip of Java

The task of learning any new language can be broken down into at least two parts: studying the language's rules of grammar and learning its vocabulary. This is true whether the language is a foreign language, such as French or Japanese, or a computer programming language, such as Java. In the case of a programming language, the vocabulary you must learn consists primarily of verbs that can be used to command the computer to do things like "**show** the number 47.2 on the screen" or "**move** the image of the game piece to the center of the window." The grammatical structures of a computer language enable you to form phrases that instruct the computer to perform several primitive commands in sequence or to choose among several primitive commands.

When learning a new human language, one undertakes the tasks of learning vocabulary and grammar simultaneously. One must know at least a little vocabulary before one can understand examples of grammatical structure. On the other hand, developing an extensive vocabulary without any knowledge of the grammar used to combine words would just be silly. The same applies to learning a programming language. Accordingly, we will begin your introduction to Java by presenting a few sample programs that illustrate fundamentals of the grammatical structure of Java programs, using only enough vocabulary to enable us to produce some interesting examples.

1.3.1   Simple Responsive Programs

The typical program run on a personal computer reacts to a large collection of actions the user can perform using the mouse and keyboard. Selecting menu items, typing in file names, pressing buttons, and dragging items across the screen all produce appropriate reactions from such programs. The details of how a computer responds to a particular user action are determined by the instructions that make up the program running on the computer. The examples presented in this section are intended to illustrate how this is done in a Java program.

To start things off simply, we will restrict our attention to programs that react to simple mouse operations. The programs we consider in this section will only specify how the computer should respond when the user manipulates the mouse by clicking, dragging, or moving the mouse within the boundaries of a single window. When one of these programs is run, all that will appear on the display will be a single, blank window. The programs may draw graphics or display text messages within this window in response to user actions, but there will be no buttons, menus, scrollbars or the like.

As a first example, consider the structure of a program which simply draws some text on the screen when the mouse is clicked. When this program is run, a blank window appears on the screen. The window remains blank until the user positions the mouse cursor within the window and presses the mouse button. Once this happens, the program displays the phrase

    I'm Touched

in the window as shown in Figure 1.2. As soon as the user releases the mouse, the message disappears from the window. That is all it does! Not exactly Microsoft® Word®, but it is sufficient to illustrate the basic structure of many of the programs we will discuss in this text.

Such a Java program is shown in Figure 1.3. A brief examination of the text of the program reveals features that are certainly consistent with our description of this program's behavior. There is the line

    new Text("I'm Touched", 40, 50, canvas);

which specifies the message to be displayed. This line comes shortly after a line containing the words "on mouse press" (all forced together to form the single word onMousePress) which

Figure 1.2 Window displayed by a very simple program

```
import objectdraw.*;
import java.awt.*;

public class TouchyWindow extends WindowController {

    public void onMousePress( Location point ) {
        new Text( "I'm Touched", 40, 50, canvas );
    }

    public void onMouseRelease( Location point ) {
        canvas.clear();
    }

}
```

Figure 1.3 Our first Java program

suggest when the new message will appear. Similarly, a little bit later, a line containing the word onMouseRelease is followed by a line containing the word clear, which is what happens to the window once the mouse is released. These suggestive tidbits are unfortunately obscured by a considerable amount of text that is probably indecipherable to the novice. Our goal is to guide you through the details of this program in a way that will enable you to understand its basic structure.

1.3.2 "Class" and Other Magic Words

Our brief example program contains many words that have special meaning to Java. Unfortunately, it is relatively hard to give a precise explanation of many of the terms used in Java to someone who is just beginning to program. For example, to fully appreciate the roles of the terms import, public, and extends one needs to appreciate the issues that arise when constructing programs that are orders of magnitude larger than we will discuss in the early chapters of this text. We will attempt here to give you some intuition regarding the purpose of these words. However, you may not be able to understand them completely until you learn more about Java. Until then, we can assure you that you will do fine if you are willing to regard just a few of these words and phrases as magical incantations that must be recited appropriately at certain points in your program. For example, the first two lines of nearly every program you read or write while studying this book will be identical to the first two lines in this example:

```
import   objectdraw.*;
import   java.awt.*;
```

In fact, these two lines are so standard that we won't even show them in the examples beyond the first two chapters of this text.

The Head of the Class

Most of your programs will also contain a line very similar to the third line shown in our example:

```
public class TouchyWindow extends WindowController
```

This line is called a *class header*. The programs you write will contain a line that looks just like this except that you will replace the word TouchyWindow with a word of your own choosing. TouchyWindow is just the name we have chosen to give to our program. It is appropriate to give a program a name that reflects its behavior.

This line is called a class header because it informs the computer that the text that follows describes a new class. Why does Java call the specification that describes a program a "class"? Java uses the word class to refer to:

> A set, collection, group, or configuration containing members regarded as having certain attributes or traits in common. (From the *American Heritage Dictionary*)

If several people were to run the program shown above at the same time but on different computers, each would have an independent copy of the program described by this class. If one person clicked in the program's window, the message "I'm Touched" would only appear on that person's computer. The other computers running the same program would be unaffected. Thus, the running copies of the program form a collection of distinct but very similar objects. Java refers to such a collection of objects as a *class*.

Using Software Libraries

The class header of TouchyWindow indicates that it extends something called Window-Controller. This means that our program depends on previously written Java instructions.

Programs are rarely built from scratch. The physical circuits of which a computer is constructed are only capable of performing very simple operations like changing the color of a single dot on the screen. If every program were built from scratch, every program would have to explicitly describe every one of the primitive operations required to accomplish its purpose. Instead, libraries have been written containing collections of instructions describing useful common operations like drawing a line on the screen. Programs can then be constructed using the operations described by the library in addition to the operations that can be performed by the basic hardware.

This notion of using collections of previously written Java instructions to simplify the construction of new programs explains the mysterious phrases found in the first two lines of our program. Lines that start with the words import inform Java which libraries of previously written instructions our program uses. In our example, we list two libraries, java.awt and objectdraw. The library named java.awt is a collection of instructions describing common operations for creating windows and displaying information within windows. The initials "awt" stand for "Abstract Windowing Toolkit". The prefix "java." reveals that this library is a standard component of the Java language environment used by many Java programs.

The second library mentioned in our import specifications is objectdraw. This is a library designed by the authors of this text to make the Java language more appropriate as an environment for teaching programming. Recall that the class header of our example program mentions that TouchyWindow extends WindowController. WindowController refers to a collection of Java instructions that form part of this objectdraw library. A WindowController is an object that coordinates user and program activities within the window associated with a program. If a program were nothing but a WindowController, then all that would happen when it was run would be that a window would appear on the screen. Nothing would ever appear within the window. Our TouchyWindow class specification extends the functionality of the WindowController by telling it to display a message in the window when the mouse is pressed.

Getting Braces

The single open brace ("{") that appears at the end of the class header for TouchyWindow introduces an important and widely used feature in Java's grammatical structure. Placing a pair consisting of an open and closing brace around a portion of the text of a program is Java's way of letting the programmer draw a big box around that text. Enclosing lines of text in braces indicate that they form a single, logical unit. If you scan quickly over the complete example, you will see that braces are used in this way in several parts of this program, even though it is quite short.

The open brace after the `public class TouchyWindow...` line is matched by the closing brace on the last line of the program. This indicates that everything between these two braces (i.e., everything left in the example) should be considered part of the description of the class named TouchyWindow. The text between these braces is called the *body* of the class.

► EXERCISE 1.3.1

Write the class header for a program called HiMom. ❖

1.3.3 Discourse on the Method

The first few lines in the body of the class TouchyWindow look like:

```java
public void onMousePress( Location point ) {
    new Text( "I'm Touched", 40, 50, canvas );
}
```

This text is an example of another important grammatical form in Java, the *method definition*. A method is a named sequence of program instructions. In this case, the method being defined is named onMousePress and within its body (which is bracketed by braces just like the body of the class) it contains the single instruction:

```java
new Text( "I'm Touched", 40, 50, canvas );
```

In general, the programmer is free to choose any appropriate name for a method. The method name can then be used in other parts of the program to cause the computer to obey the instructions within the method's body. Within a class that extends WindowController, however, certain method names have special significance. In particular, if such a class contains a method which is named onMousePress, then the instructions in that method's body will be followed by the computer when the mouse is depressed within the program's window. That is why this particular program reacts to a mouse press as it does.

The single line that forms the body of our onMousePress method:

```java
new Text( "I'm Touched", 40, 50, canvas );
```

is an example of one of the primitive commands provided to display text and graphics on a computer's screen. It specifies that the phrase

```
I'm Touched
```

should be displayed on the canvas, the portion of the computer's screen controlled by the program, at a position determined by the *x* and *y* coordinates (40,50). The components of an instruction like this that tells the computer to display information on the screen are quite important. By changing

Figure 1.4   Changing the information displayed in the window

them you can display a different message or make the message appear in a different position on the screen. For example, if we replaced the body of our onMousePress method with the line:

```
new Text( "How Touching", 0, 80, canvas );
```

the program would display a different message in a different location as shown in Figure 1.4. Accordingly, you cannot simply view these components of a Java program as a magical incantation. Instead, we must carefully consider each component so that you understand its purpose. We will begin this process in Section 1.5.

The remainder of the body of the TouchyWindow class contains the specification of a second method named onMouseRelease:

```
public void onMouseRelease( Location point ) {
      canvas.clear();
}
```

As with onMousePress, the body of this method contains the instructions to be followed when the user performs a particular action with the mouse—releasing the mouse button. The instruction included in this case tells the computer to clear all graphics that have been displayed in the program's drawing area, named canvas.

Other special method names (onMouseMove, for example) can be used to specify how to react to other simple mouse events. We will provide a complete list of such methods in Sections 1.6.1 and 1.6.2.

There are a number of additional syntactic features visible in these method definitions that it is best not to explain in detail at this point. First, the method names are preceded by the words public void. For now, think of this as another magical incantation that you simply must include in the first line of almost every method definition you write. After the method names, the words Location point appear in parentheses. Like public void, you should be sure to include this text in the header of each method you define for a while. To make this part of the method header a bit less mysterious, however, we can give you a clue about its meaning. You might imagine that in many programs the instructions that respond to a mouse press would need to know where the mouse was pointing. In the next chapter, we will see that the Location point portion of such a method definition provides the means to access this information.

1.4 Programming Tools

Writing a program isn't enough. You also have to get the program into your computer and convince your computer to follow the instructions it contains.

A computer program like the one shown in the preceding section is just a fragment of text. You already know ways to get other forms of textual information into a computer. You use a word processor to write papers. When entering the body of an email message you use an email application like Eudora® or Outlook®. Just as there are computer applications designed to allow you to enter these forms of text, there are applications designed to enable you to enter the text of a program.

Entering the text of your program is only the first step. As explained earlier, unless you write your program in the language that the machine's circuits were designed to interpret, you need to use a compiler to translate your instructions into a language the machine can comprehend. Finally, after this translation is complete you still need to somehow tell the computer to treat the file(s) created by the translation process as instructions and to follow them.

Typically, the support needed to accomplish all three of these steps is incorporated into a single application called an *integrated development environment* or IDE. It is also possible to provide separate applications to support each step. Which approach you use will likely depend on the facilities available to you and the inclination of the instructor teaching you to program. There are too many possibilities for us to attempt to cover them all in this text. To provide you with a sense of what to expect, however, we will sketch how two common integrated development environments, BlueJ and Eclipse, could be used to enter and run the TouchyWindow program. These sketches are not intended to provide you with the detailed knowledge required to actually use either of these IDEs effectively. We will merely outline the main steps that are involved.

The IDEs we will describe share several important properties:

* Implementations of both IDEs are available for a wide range of computer systems including Windows systems, MacOS, and Unix and its variants.
* Both IDEs are available for free and can be downloaded from the Web.

They also differ in major ways. BlueJ was designed by computer science faculty members with the primary goal of providing a Java development system for use when teaching students to program. Eclipse was developed to meet the needs of professional programmers.

Just as it is helpful to divide a book into chapters, it is helpful to divide large programs into separate text files describing individual components of the program. Within a Java IDE, the collection of text files that constitute a program is called a project. In fact, most Java IDEs expect all programs, even programs that are quite small, to be organized as projects. As a result, even though our TouchyWindow program is only ten lines long and will definitely only require one text file, the first step performed to enter and run this program using either Eclipse or BlueJ will be to use an entry in the application's "File" menu to create a new project.

The IDE will then display a number of dialog boxes asking for information about the project we wish to create. Among other things, we will be asked to specify a name for the project and to select a location in our computer's file system to store the file(s) that will hold the text of our program.

Once a project has been created, the IDE will display a window representing the state of the project. The window Eclipse would present is shown in Figure 1.5 and the window BlueJ would present is shown in Figure 1.6.

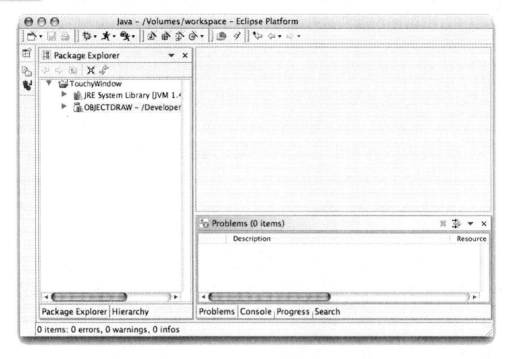

Figure 1.5   An Eclipse project window

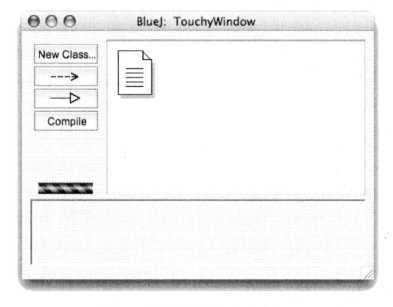

Figure 1.6   A BlueJ project window

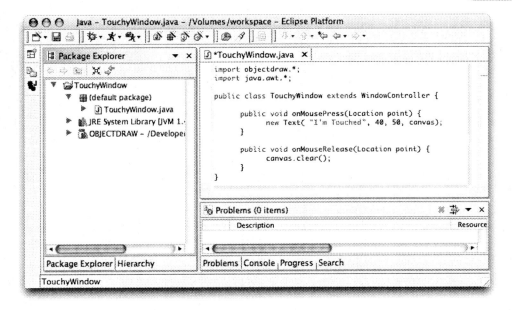

Figure 1.7   Entering the text of TouchyWindow under Eclipse

The next step is to tell the IDE that we wish to create a new file and enter the text of our program. With BlueJ, we do this by pressing the "New Class…" button seen in the upper left of the window shown in Figure 1.6. With Eclipse, we select a "New Class" menu item. In either case, the IDE will then ask us to enter information about the class, including its name, in a dialog box. Then the IDE will present us with a window in which we can type the text of our program, much as we would type within a word processor. In Figures 1.7 and 1.8 we show how the windows provided by BlueJ and Eclipse would look after we ask the IDE to create a new class and enter the text of the class. Eclipse incorporates the text entry window as a subwindow of the project window. BlueJ displays a separate text window.

In both the BlueJ project window and the BlueJ window holding the text of the TouchyWindow class there is a button labeled "Compile". Pressing this button instructs BlueJ that we have completed entering our code and would like to have it translated into a form the machine can more easily interpret. Under most Java IDEs, compiling your code will produce files storing a translation of your instructions into a language called Java virtual machine code or byte code. After this is done, we can ask Java to run our program by depressing the mouse on the icon that represents the TouchyWindow class within the BlueJ project window and selecting the "new TouchyWindow" item from the pop-up menu that appears. BlueJ will then display a new window controlled by the instructions included in our program. When the mouse is pressed in this window, the words "I'm touched" will appear, as shown in Figure 1.9.

With Eclipse, compiling your program and running it can be combined into a single step. You first create what Eclipse calls a *run configuration*. This involves specifying things like the size of the window created when your program starts running. We will not discuss the details of this process here. Once you have created a run configuration, you can compile and run your program by pressing an icon displayed at the top of the Eclipse window that is designed to look like a human runner. Like BlueJ, Eclipse then displays a new window in which you can interact with your program.

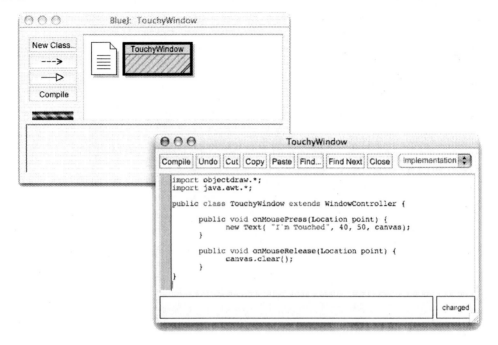

Figure 1.8   Entering the text of TouchyWindow under BlueJ

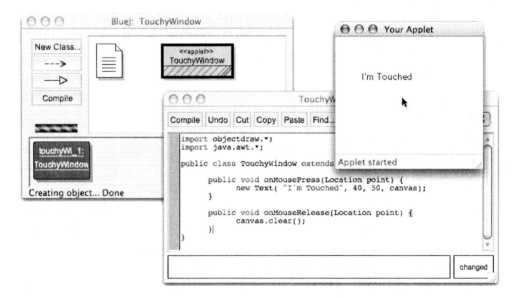

Figure 1.9   Running a program under BlueJ

In this discussion of how to enter and run a program we have overlooked one important fact. It is quite likely that you will make a mistake at some point in the process, leaving the IDE confused about how to proceed. As a result, in order to work effectively with an IDE you need some sense of what kinds of errors you are most likely to make and how the IDE will react to them. We will return to this issue after we teach you a bit more about how to actually write Java programs.

1.5 Drawing Primitives

1.5.1 The Graphics Coordinate System

Programs that display graphics on a computer screen have to deal extensively with a coordinate system similar to the one you have used when plotting functions in math classes. This is not evident to users of these programs. A user of a program that displays graphics can typically specify the position or size of a graphical object using the mouse to indicate screen positions without ever thinking in terms of x and y coordinates. Writing a program to draw such graphics, however, is very different from using one. When your program runs, someone else controls the mouse. Just imagine how you would describe a position on the screen to another person if you were not allowed to point with your finger. You would have to say something like "Two inches from the left edge of the screen and three inches down from the top of the screen." Similarly, when writing programs you will specify positions on the screen using pairs of numbers to describe the coordinates of each position.

The coordinate system used for computer graphics is like the Cartesian coordinate system studied in math classes but with one big difference. The y axis in the coordinate system used in computer graphics is upside down. Thus, while your experience in algebra class might lead you to expect the point (2,3) to appear below the point (2,5), on a computer screen just the opposite is true. This difference is illustrated by Figure 1.10, which shows where these two points fall in the

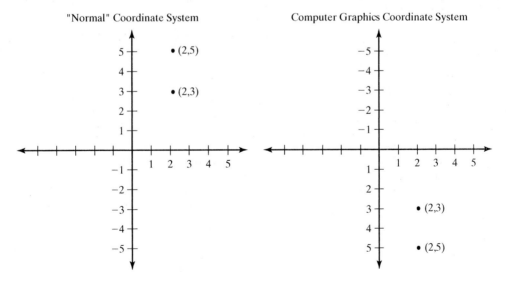

Figure 1.10 Comparison of computer and Cartesian coordinate systems

I'm touched

Figure 1.11   Text enlarged to make pixels visible

normal Cartesian coordinate system and in the coordinate system used to specify positions when drawing on a computer screen.

The graphics that appear on a computer screen are actually composed of tiny squares of color called *pixels*. For example, if you looked at the text displayed by our `TouchyWindow` program with a magnifying glass you would discover it is actually made up of little black squares as shown in Figure 1.11. The entire screen is organized as a grid of pixels. The coordinate system used to place graphics in a window is designed to match this grid of pixels in that the basic unit of measurement in the coordinate system is the size of a single pixel. So, the coordinates (30,50) describe the point that is 30 pixels to the right and 50 pixels down from the origin.

Another important aspect of the way in which coordinates are used to specify where graphics should appear is that there is not just a single set of coordinate axes used to describe locations anywhere on the computer's screen. Instead, there is a separate set of axes associated with each window on the screen and, in some cases, even several pairs of axes for a single window.

Rather than complicating the programmer's job, the presence of so many coordinate systems makes it simpler. Many programs may be running on a computer at once, and each should only produce output in certain portions of the screen. If you are running Microsoft Word at the same time as Adobe Photoshop, you would not expect text from your Word document to appear in one of Photoshop's windows. To make this as simple as possible, each program's drawing commands must specify the window or other screen area in which the drawing should take place. Then the coordinates used in these commands are interpreted using a separate coordinate system associated with that area of the screen. The origin of each of these coordinate systems is located in the upper left corner of the area in which the drawing is taking place rather than in the corner of the machine's physical display. This makes it possible for a program to produce graphical output without being aware of the location of its window relative to the screen boundaries or the locations of other windows.

In many cases, the area in which a program can draw graphics corresponds to the entire interior of a window on the computer's display. In other cases, however, the region used by a program may be just a subsection of a window or there may be several independent drawing areas within a given window. Accordingly, we refer to a program's drawing area as a canvas rather than as a window.

In interpreting your graphic commands, Java will assume that the origin of the coordinate system is located at the upper left corner of the canvas in which you are drawing. The location of the coordinate axes that would be used to interpret the coordinates specified in our `TouchyWindow` example are shown in Figure 1.12. Notice that the coordinates of the upper left hand corner of this window are (0,0). The window shown is 165 units wide and 100 units high. Thus the coordinates of the lower right corner are (165,100). The text is positioned so that it falls in a rectangle whose upper left corner has an *x* coordinate of 40 and a *y* coordinate of 50.

The computer will not consider it an error if you try to draw beyond the boundaries of your program's canvas. It will remember everything you have drawn and show you just the portion of these drawings that falls within the boundaries of your canvas.

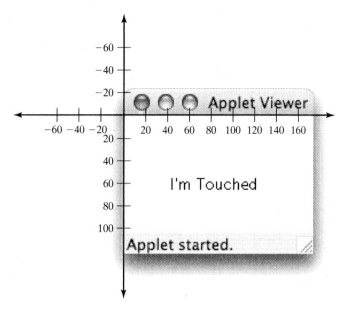

Figure 1.12   A program window and its drawing coordinate axes

➡ EXERCISE 1.5.1

Rewrite the line of code in onMousePress *of class* TouchyWindow *so that it now displays the message "Hello" 60 pixels to the right and 80 pixels down from the top left corner of the window.*   ❖

1.5.2   Constructing Graphic Objects

The line

```
new Text( "I'm Touched", 40, 50, canvas );
```

used in our example program's onMousePress method is called a *construction*. Whenever you want to display a new object on the screen, you will include a construction in your program. The general syntax for such a command includes:

* the word new, which informs the computer that a new object is being constructed;
* the name of the class of object to be constructed; and
* a list of coordinates and other items describing the details of the object. These extra pieces of information are called *actual parameters* or *arguments*. The entire list is surrounded by parentheses, and its elements are separated by commas.

After the parameter list, Java expects you to type a semicolon. This semicolon is not part of the construction itself but is a more general aspect of Java's syntax. Java requires that each simple command we include in a method's body be terminated by a semicolon, much as we terminate sentences with periods in English. For example, the other command which appears in the TouchyWindow program:

```
canvas.clear();
```

also ends with a semicolon. Most phrases that are not themselves commands, such as the headers of methods, do not end with semicolons.

The parameters required in a construction will depend on the class of the item being constructed. In our example program, we construct a Text object. Text is the name for a piece of text displayed on the screen. The first parameter expected in a Text construction is the text to be displayed. In this example, the text we want displayed is:

```
I'm Touched
```

We surround this text with a pair of double quote marks to tell Java that we want exactly this text to appear on the screen. The next two values specify that the text be indented 40 pixels from the left edge of the drawing area and that the text be placed immediately below an imaginary line 50 pixels from the top of the drawing area.

The last item in the list of parameters to the Text construction, the canvas, tells the computer in which area of the screen the new message should be placed. In your early programs, there will only be one area in which your program can draw, and the name canvas will refer to this region. As a result, including this bit of information will seem unnecessary (if not tedious). Eventually, however, you will want to construct programs that display information in multiple windows. To provide the flexibility to construct such programs, the primitives for displaying graphics require you to include the canvas specification even when it seems redundant.

Several other types of graphical objects can be displayed using similar constructions. For example, to display a line between the corners of a canvas whose dimensions are 200 by 300, you would write:

```
new Line( 0, 0, 200, 300, canvas );
```

The line produced would look like the line shown in the window in Figure 1.13. In this construction, the first pair of numbers, 0,0, specifies the coordinates of the starting point of the line (the upper left corner of your window) and the pair 200,300 specifies the coordinates of the line's end point (the lower right corner).

Similarly, to draw a line from the middle of the window, which has the coordinates (100,150), to the upper right corner, whose coordinates are (200,0), you would say:

```
new Line( 100, 150, 200, 0, canvas );
```

Such a line is shown in Figure 1.14.

Using combinations of these construction statements, we could replace the single instruction in the body of the onMousePress method shown above with one or more other instructions. Such a modified program is shown in Figure 1.15.

The only differences between this example and TouchyWindow are the name given to the classes (CrossedLines vs. TouchyWindow) and the commands included in the body of the onMousePress method. The modified program's version of onMousePress includes two commands in its body which instruct the computer to draw two intersecting, perpendicular lines. The drawing produced is also shown in the figure.

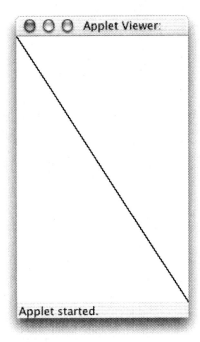

Figure 1.13   Drawing of a single line

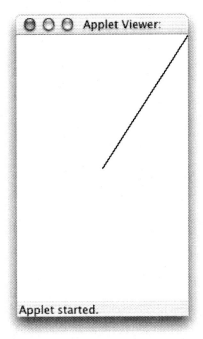

Figure 1.14   A line from (100,150) to (200,0)

```
import objectdraw.*;
import java.awt.*;

public class CrossedLines extends WindowController {

    public void onMousePress( Location point ) {
        new Line( 40, 40, 60, 60, canvas );
        new Line( 60, 40, 40, 60, canvas );
    }

    public void onMouseRelease( Location point ) {
        canvas.clear();
    }

}
```

Figure 1.15   A program that draws two crossed lines

There are several other forms of graphics you can display on the screen. The command:

```
new FramedRect( 20, 50, 80, 40, canvas );
```

will display the outline, or frame, of an 80-by-40 rectangular box in your canvas. The pair 20, 50 specifies the coordinates of the box's upper left corner. The pair 80, 40 specifies the width and height of the box. If you replace the name FramedRect by FilledRect to produce the construction

```
new FilledRect( 20, 50, 80, 40, canvas );
```

the result will instead be an 80-by-40 solid black rectangular box.
   The command:

```
new FilledOval( 20, 50, 80, 40, canvas );
```

will draw an oval on the screen. The parameters are interpreted just like those to the FilledRect construction. Instead of drawing a rectangle, however, FilledOval draws the largest ellipse that it can fit within the rectangle described by its parameters. To illustrate this, Figure 1.16

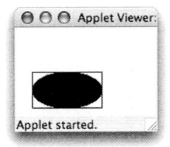

Figure 1.16 A FilledOval nested within a FramedRect

shows what the screen would contain after executing the two constructions

```
new FramedRect( 20, 50, 80, 40, canvas );
new FillOval( 20, 50, 80, 40, canvas );
```

The upper left corner of the rectangle shown is at the point with coordinates (20, 50). Both shapes are 80 pixels wide and 40 pixels high.

Other primitives allow you to draw additional shapes and to display image files in your canvas. A full listing and description of the available graphic object types and the forms of the commands used to construct them can be found in Appendix B. For now, the graphical object types Text, Line, FramedRect, FilledRect, FramedOval, and FilledOval will provide enough flexibility for our purposes.

➡ EXERCISE 1.5.2

Sketch the picture that would be produced if the following constructions were executed. You should assume that the canvas associated with the program containing these instructions is 200 pixels wide and 200 pixels high.

```
new Line( 0, 100, 100, 0, canvas );
new Line( 100, 0, 200, 100, canvas );
new Line( 200, 100, 100, 200, canvas );
new Line( 100, 200, 0, 100, canvas );
new FramedRect( 50, 50, 100, 100, canvas );
```

➡ EXERCISE 1.5.3

Write a sequence of Line and/or FramedRect constructions that would produce each of the drawings shown below. In both examples, assume that the drawing will appear in a 200-by-200-pixel window. For the drawing of the three-dimensional cube, there should be a space 5 pixels wide between the cube and the edges of the window in those areas where the cube comes closest to the edges. The rectangle drawn for the front face of the cube should be 155 pixels wide and 155 pixels high. The two visible edges of the rear of the cube should also be 155 pixels long.

a.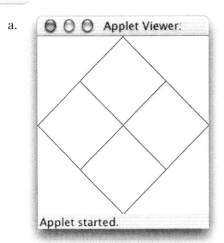

b.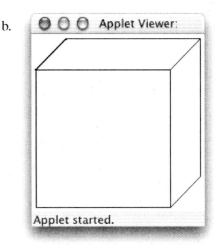

1.6 Additional Event-Handling Methods

In our examples thus far, we have used the two method names onMousePress and onMouseRelease to establish a correspondence between certain user actions and instructions we would like the computer to follow when these actions occur. In this section, we introduce several other method names that can be used to associate instructions with other user actions.

1.6.1 Mouse-Event-Handling Methods

In addition to onMousePress and onMouseRelease, there are five other method names that have special significance for handling mouse events. If you include definitions for any of these methods within a class that extends WindowController, then the instructions within the methods you include will be executed when the associated events occur.

The definitions of all these methods have the same form. You have seen that the header for the onMousePress method looks like:

```
public void onMousePress( Location point )
```

The headers for the other methods are identical except that onMousePress is replaced by the appropriate method name.

All of the mouse-event-handling methods are described below:

onMousePress specifies the actions the computer should perform when the mouse button is depressed.

onMouseRelease specifies the actions the computer should perform when the mouse button is released.

onMouseClick specifies the actions the computer should perform if the mouse is pressed and then quickly released without significant mouse movement between the two events. The actions specified in this method will be performed in addition to (and after) any instructions in onMousePress and onMouseRelease.

onMouseEnter specifies the actions the computer should perform when the mouse enters the program's canvas.

onMouseExit specifies the actions the computer should perform when the mouse leaves the program's canvas.

onMouseMove specifies the actions the computer should perform periodically while the mouse is being moved about without its button depressed.

onMouseDrag specifies the actions the computer should perform periodically while the mouse is being moved about with its button depressed.

➡ EXERCISE 1.6.1

Write the method header for the onMouseMove *method.*   ❖

➡ EXERCISE 1.6.2

Write a method that draws a filled square on the canvas when the mouse enters the canvas. The square should be 100 by 100 pixels with the upper left corner at the origin.   ❖

➡ EXERCISE 1.6.3

Write a complete program that will display "I'm inside" when the mouse is inside the program's window and "I'm outside" when the mouse is outside the window. The screen should be blank when the program first begins to execute and should stay blank until the mouse is moved in or out of the window.   ❖

1.6.2 The begin Method

In addition to the seven mouse-event-handling methods, there is one other event-handling method that is independent of the mouse. This is the method named begin. If a begin method is defined in a program, then it is executed once each time the program begins to execute.

The form of the definition of the begin method is slightly different from that of the mouse-event-handling methods. Since there is no point on the screen associated with this event, Location point is omitted from the method's header. The parentheses that would have appeared around the words Location point are still required. Thus, a begin method's definition will look like:

```
public void begin() {
    ...
}
```

The begin method provides a way to specify instructions the computer should follow to set things up before the user begins interacting with the program. As a simple example of this, consider how we can modify our TouchyWindow program to improve its rather limited user interface. When the current version of the program runs, it merely displays a blank window. Now that you are familiar with the program, you know that it expects its user to click on the window. The program, however, could make this more obvious by displaying a message asking the user to click on the window when it first starts. This can be done by including a command to construct an appropriate Text object in a begin method.

```
import objectdraw.*;
import java.awt.*;

public class TouchyWindow extends WindowController {

    public void begin() {
        new Text( "Click in this window.", 20, 20, canvas );
    }

    public void onMousePress( Location point )  {
        canvas.clear();
        new Text( "I'm Touched", 40, 50, canvas );
    }

    public void onMouseRelease( Location point ) {
        canvas.clear();
    }

}
```

Figure 1.17   A simple program with instructions

The code for this improved version of TouchyWindow is shown in Figure 1.17. In addition to adding the begin method, we have added the invocation canvas.clear(); to onMousePress so that the instructions will be removed as soon as the user follows them.

1.7   To Err Is Human

We all make mistakes. Worse yet, we often make the same mistakes over and over again.

If we make a mistake while giving instructions to another person, the other person can frequently figure out what we really meant. For example, if you give someone driving directions and say "turn left" where you should have said "turn right", chances are that they will realize after driving in the wrong direction for a while that they are not seeing any of the landmarks the remaining instructions mention, go back to the last turn before things stopped making sense and try turning in the other direction. Our ability to deal with such incorrect instructions, however, depends on our ability to understand the intent of the instructions we follow. Computers, unfortunately, never really understand the instructions they are given, so they are far less capable of dealing with errors.

There are several distinct types of errors you can make while writing or entering a program. The computer will respond differently, depending on the type of mistake you make. The first type of mistake is called a *syntax error*. The defining feature of a syntax error is that the IDE can detect that there is a problem before you try to run your program. As we have explained, a computer program must be written in a specially designed language that the computer can interpret or at least translate into a language which it can interpret. Computer languages have rules of grammar just like human languages. If you violate these rules, either because you misunderstand them

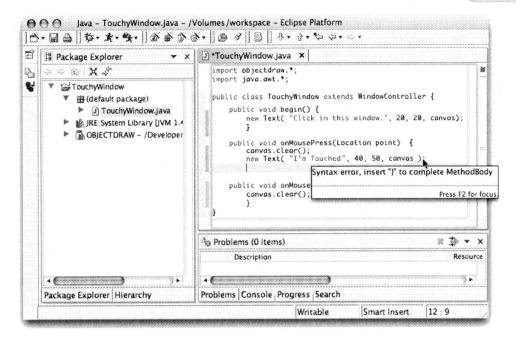

Figure 1.18   Eclipse displaying a syntax error message

or simply because you make a typing mistake, the computer will recognize that something is wrong and tell you that it needs to be corrected.

The mechanisms used to inform the programmer of syntactic errors vary from one IDE to another. Eclipse constantly examines the text you have entered and indicates fragments of your program that it has identified as errors by underlining them and/or displaying an error icon on the offending line at the left margin. If you point the mouse at the underlined text or the error icon, Eclipse will display a message explaining the nature of the problem. For example, if we accidentally left out the closing "}" after the body of the onMousePress method while entering the program shown in Figure 1.17, Eclipse would underline the semicolon at the end of the last line of the method. Pointing the mouse at the underlined semicolon would cause Eclipse to display the message "Syntax error, insert '}' to complete MethodBody" as shown in Figure 1.18.

The bad news is that your IDE will not always provide you with a message that pinpoints your mistake so clearly. When you make a mistake, your IDE is forced to try to guess what you meant to type. As we have emphasized earlier, your computer really cannot be expected to understand what your program is intended to do or say. Given its limited understanding, it will often mistake your intention and display error messages that reveal its confusion. For example, if you type

```
canvas.clear;
```

instead of

```
canvas.clear();
```

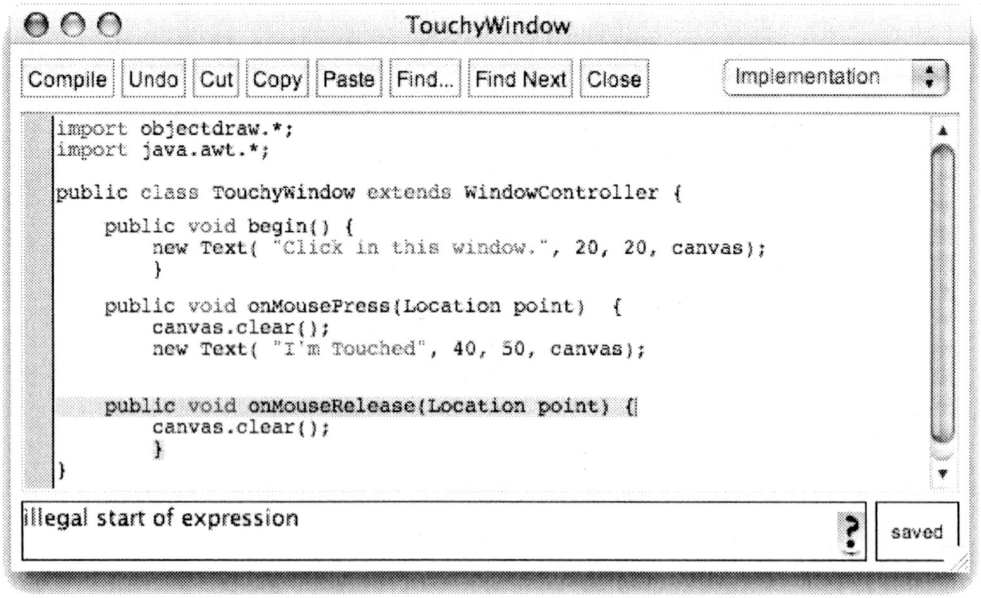
TouchyWindow
Compile
Undo
Cut
Copy
Paste
Find...
Find Next
Close
Implementation
import objectdraw.*;
import java.awt.*;
public class TouchyWindow extends WindowController {
public void begin() {
new Text("Click in this window.", 20, 20, canvas);
}
public void onMousePress(Location point) {
canvas.clear();
new Text("I'm Touched", 40, 50, canvas);
public void onMouseRelease(Location point) {
canvas.clear();
}
}
illegal start of expression
?
saved

Figure 1.19 BlueJ displaying a syntax error message

in the body of the `onMouseRelease` method of our example program, Eclipse will underline the word "clear" and display the message "Syntax error, insert 'AssignmentOperator ArrayInitializer' to complete Expression." In such cases, the error message is more likely to be a hindrance than a help. You will just have to examine what you typed before and after the position where the IDE identified the error and use your knowledge of the Java language to identify your mistake.

BlueJ is more patient about syntax errors. It ignores them until you press the Compile button. Then, before attempting to compile your code, it checks it for syntactic errors. If an error is found, BlueJ highlights the line containing the error and displays a message explaining the problem at the bottom of the window containing the program's text. Figure 1.19 shows how BlueJ would react to the mistake of leaving out the closing brace at the end of `onMousePress`. Note that different IDEs may display different messages and, particularly in the case where the error is an omission, associate different points in the code with the error. In this case, Eclipse flags the line before the missing brace, while BlueJ highlights the line after the error.

A program that is free from syntax errors is not necessarily a correct program. Think back to our instructions for performing calculations that was designed to leave you thinking about Danish elephants. If, while typing these instructions, we completely omitted a line, the instructions would still be grammatically correct. Following them, however, would no longer lead you to think of Danish elephants. The same is true for the example of saying "left" when you meant to say "right" while giving driving directions. Mistakes like these are not syntactic errors; they are instead called *logic errors*. They result in an algorithm that doesn't achieve the result that its author intended. Unfortunately, to realize such a mistake has been made, you often have to understand the intended purpose of the algorithm. This is exactly what computers don't understand. As a result, your IDE will give you relatively little help correcting logic errors.

As a simple example of a logical error, suppose that while typing the onMouseRelease method for the TouchyWindow program you got confused and typed onMouseExit instead of onMouseRelease. The result would still be a perfectly legitimate program. It just wouldn't be the program you meant to write. Your IDE would not identify your mistake as a syntax error. Instead, when you ran the program, it just would not do what you expected. When you released the mouse, the "I'm Touched" message would not disappear as expected.

This may appear to be an unlikely error, but there is a very common error which is quite similar to it. Suppose that, instead of typing the name onMouseRelease, you typed the name onMooseRelease. Look carefully. These names are not the same. onMooseRelease is not the name of one of the special event-handling methods discussed in the preceding sections. In more advanced programs, however, we will learn that it is sometimes useful to define additional methods that do things other than handle events. The programmer is free to choose names for such methods. onMooseRelease would be a legitimate (if strange) name for such a method. That is, a program containing a method with this name has to be treated as a syntactically valid program by any Java IDE. As a result, your IDE would not recognize this as a typing mistake, but when you ran the program, Java would think you had decided not to associate any instructions with mouse-release events. As before, the text "I'm Touched" would never be removed from the canvas.

There are many other examples of logical errors a programmer can make. Even in a simple program like TouchyWindow, mistyping screen coordinates can lead to surprises. If you mistyped an *x* coordinate, as in

```
new Text( "I'm Touched", 400, 50, canvas );
```

the text would be positioned outside the visible region of the program window. It would seem as if it had never appeared. If the line

```
canvas.clear();
```

had been placed in the onMousePress method after the line to construct the message, the message would disappear so quickly that it would never be seen.

Of course, in larger programs the possibilities for making such errors just increases. You will find that careful, patient, thoughtful examination of your code as you write it and after errors are detected is essential.

1.8   Summary

Programming a computer to say "I'm Touched" is obviously a rather modest achievement. In the process of discussing this simple program, however, we have explored many of the principles and practices that will be developed throughout this book. We have learned that computer programs are just collections of instructions. These instructions, however, are special in that they can be followed mechanically, without understanding their actual purpose. This is the notion of an algorithm, a set of instructions that can be followed to accomplish a task without understanding the task itself. We have seen that programs are produced by devising algorithms and then expressing them in a language that a computer can interpret. We have learned the rudiments of the language we will explore further throughout this text, Java. We have also explored some of the tools used to enter computer programs, translate them into a form the machine can follow, and run them.

Despite our best efforts to explain how these tools interact, nothing can take the place of actually writing, entering, and running a program. We strongly urge you to do so before proceeding to read the next chapter. Throughout the process of learning to program you will discover that it is a skill that is best learned by practice. Now is a good time to start.

1.9 Chapter Review Problems

EXERCISE 1.9.1

Here is a sample class header:

```
public class Hangman extends WindowController
```

Explain what is meant by the following words from the above line:

a. `class`
b. `Hangman`
c. `extends`
d. `WindowController`

EXERCISE 1.9.2

Consider the point located at coordinates (100,100). What are the coordinates of the following points in the computer graphics coordinate system?

a. *40 pixels* **down** *and 30 pixels to the* **left** *of (100,100)*
b. *60 pixels* **up** *and 10 pixels to the* **right** *of (100,100)*
c. *35 pixels* **up** *and 45 pixels to the* **left** *of (100,100)*
d. *20 pixels* **down** *and 50 pixels to the* **left** *of (100,100)*
e. *80 pixels* **down** *and 15 pixels to the* **right** *of (100,100)*

EXERCISE 1.9.3

Sketch the picture that the following lines of code would produce. Assume the window is 200 pixels wide and 200 pixels high.

```
new FramedRect( 20, 20, 160, 160, canvas );
new Line( 20, 180, 100, 20, canvas );
new Line( 100, 20, 100, 180, canvas );
new FilledOval( 100, 100, 80, 80, canvas );
new Line( 180, 100, 100, 100, canvas );
```

1.10 Programming Problems

➤ EXERCISE 1.10.1

Learn how to enter and run a program using the tools available to you by entering the TouchyWindow *program discussed in this chapter. Once you are able to enter the program:*

* *Enter smaller or larger values where we had used the numbers 40 and 50 and see how the behavior of the program changes when run.*
* *Interchange the bodies of the two methods so that the construction appears in* onMouseRelease *and the* canvas.clear *is in* onMousePress. *How does the modified program behave?*   ❖

CHAPTER 2

What's in a Name?

An important feature of a programming language is that the vocabulary used can be expanded by the programmer. Suppose you want to draw a line that ends at the current position of the mouse. The actual location of this point will not be determined until the program you write is being used. To talk about this position in your program you must introduce a name that will function as a place holder for the information describing the mouse's position. Such names are somewhat like proper names used to refer to the characters in a story. You cannot determine their meanings by simply looking them up in a standard dictionary. Instead, the information that enables you to interpret them is part of the story itself. In this chapter, we will continue your introduction to programming in Java by discussing how to introduce and use such names in Java programs. In addition, we will introduce additional details of the primitives used to display graphics.

2.1 Naming and Modifying Objects

Constructions like:

```
new Line( 200, 200, 300, 300, canvas );
```

provide the means to place a variety of graphic images on a computer screen. Most programs that display graphics, however, do more than just place graphics on the screen. Instead, as they run, they modify the appearance of the graphics they have displayed in a variety of ways. Items are moved about the screen, buttons change color when the mouse cursor is pointed at them, text is highlighted, and often items are simply removed from the display. To learn how to produce such behavior in a Java program, we must learn about operations that change the properties of objects after they have been constructed. These operations are called *mutator methods*, based on the nonbiological meaning of the word "mutate", to change or alter.

2.1.1 Mutator Methods

Just as each class of graphical objects has a specific name which must be used in a construction, each mutator method has a specific name. The names are chosen to suggest the change associated with the method, but there are some subtleties. For example, there are two mutator methods that can be used to move a graphical object to a new position on the screen. They are named move and moveTo. The first tells an object to move a certain distance from its current position. The second is used to move an object to a position described by a pair of coordinates, regardless of its previous position.

With most mutator methods, including move and moveTo, the programmer must specify additional pieces of information that determine the details of the operation applied. For example, when you tell Java to move an object, you need to tell it how far. The syntax used to provide such information is similar to that used to provide extra information in a construction. A comma-separated list of values is placed in parentheses after the method name. Thus, to move an object 30 pixels to the right and 15 pixels down the screen one would say:

```
move( 30,15 )
```

While the use of a mutator method shares portions of the syntax of a construction, there are major syntactic and conceptual differences between the two. A construction produces a new object. Hence, each construction begins with the word new. A mutator method is used to modify an already existing object. Accordingly, the word new is eliminated and must be replaced with something that indicates which existing object should be modified. To make this clear, let us consider a simple example.

Many programs start by displaying an entertaining animation. With our limited knowledge of Java, we can't yet manage an entertaining animation, but we can, with a bit of help from the program's user, create a very simple animation. In particular, we can write a program that displays a circle near the bottom of the canvas and then moves the circle up a bit each time the mouse is clicked. With a bit of imagination, you can think of the circle as the sun rising at the dawn of a new day.

Without knowing anything about mutator methods, you should be able to imagine the rough outline of such a program. Basically, from the description it is clear that the program needs to construct a FilledOval in its begin method. It is also clear that the program will need to define an onMouseClick method that uses the move mutator method. You don't know enough to write this method yet. The fact that onMouseClick will be used, however, should tell you a bit more about begin. If the user of our program needs to click the mouse to get it to function, then, just as we did in our improved version of TouchyWindow, we should include code in begin to display instructions telling the user to do this. So, your first draft of a begin method might look something like:

```
public void begin() {
    new FilledOval( 50, 150, 100, 100, canvas );
    new Text( "Please click the mouse repeatedly", 20, 20, canvas );
}
```

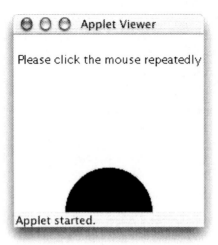

Figure 2.1   An oval rises over the horizon

This code will produce an image like that shown in Figure 2.1. In an effort to make it look like the sun is rising over the horizon, the oval is positioned so that its bottom half extends off the bottom of the window, leaving only the top half visible. Of course, it might help your imagination if the "sun" were yellow, but we will have to wait until we learn a bit more Java before we can fix that.

Now, consider how we would complete the program by writing the onMouseClick method. To make an object move directly upward, we need to use the move method specifying 0 as the distance to move horizontally and some negative number for the amount of vertical motion desired, since *y* coordinates decrease as we move up the screen. Something like:

```
move( 0, -5 );
```

might seem appropriate. The problem is that if this is all we say, Java will not know what to move. In the version of the begin method above, we construct two graphical objects, the filled circle and the text displaying the instructions. Since they are both graphical objects, we could move either of them. If all we say is move, then Java has no way of knowing which one we want moved.

To avoid ambiguities like this, Java won't let us simply say move. Instead we have to tell a particular object to move. In general, Java requires us to identify a particular object as the target whenever we wish to use a mutator method. You have already seen an example of the Java syntax used to provide such information. In our first example program, when we wanted to remove a message from the screen, we included a line of the form:

```
canvas.clear();
```

clear is a mutator method associated with drawing areas. The word canvas is the name Java gives to the area in which we can draw. Saying canvas.clear() tells the area in which we can draw that all previous drawings should be erased. When we tell an object to perform a method in this way, we say we have invoked or applied the method. Alternately, we might say that we sent a clear message to the canvas.

In general, to apply a method to a particular object, Java expects us to provide a name or some other means of identifying the object, followed by a period and the name of the method to be used. So, in order to move the oval created in our `begin` method, we have to tell Java to associate a name with the oval.

2.1.2   Instance Variable Declarations

First, we have to choose a name to use. Java puts a few restrictions on the names we can pick. Names that satisfy these restrictions are called *identifiers*. An identifier must start with a letter. After the first letter, we can use either letters, digits, or underscores. So, we could name our oval something like `sunspot`, `oval2move`, or `ra`. Case is significant. An identifier can be as long (or short) as you like, but it must be just one word (i.e., no blanks or punctuation marks are allowed in the middle of a identifier). A common convention used to make up for the inability to separate parts of a name using spaces is to start each part of a name with a capital letter. For example, we might use a name like `ovalToMove`. It is also a convention to use identifiers starting with lowercase letters to name variables to help distinguish them from the names of classes and constants.

We can use a sequence of letters, numbers, and underscores as an identifier in a Java program even if it has no meaning in English. Java would be perfectly happy if we named our box `e2d_iw0`. It is much better, however, to choose a name that suggests the role of an object. Such names make it much easier for you and others reading your code to understand its meaning. We suggested earlier that you could think of the display produced by the program we are trying to write as an animation of the sun rising. In this case, `sun` would be an excellent name for the oval. We will use this name to complete this example.

There are two steps involved in associating a name with an object. Java requires that we first introduce each name we plan to use by including what is called a *declaration* of the name. Then, we associate a particular meaning with the name using an *assignment statement*. We discuss declarations in this section and introduce assignments in the following section.

The syntax of a declaration is very simple. For each name you plan to use, you enter the word `private` followed by the name of the type of object to which the name will refer and finally the name you wish to introduce. In addition, like commands, each declaration is terminated by a semicolon. So, to declare the name `sun`, which we intend to use to refer to a `FilledOval`, we would type the declaration:

```
private FilledOval sun;
```

With the declaration of `sun` added, the contents of the program file for our animation of the sunrise might begin with the code shown in Figure 2.2.

The form and placement of a declaration within a program determines where in the program the name can be used. This region is called the *scope* of the name. In particular, we will want to refer to the name `sun` in both the `begin` and `onMouseClick` methods of the program we are designing. The declaration of names that will be used in several methods should be placed within the braces that surround the body of our class, but outside any of the method bodies. Names declared in this way are called *instance variables*. We recommend that instance variable declarations be placed before all the method declarations. The inclusion of the word `private` in an instance variable declaration indicates that only code within the class we are defining should be allowed to refer to this name. The `public` qualifier that we included in method declarations, by way of contrast, indicates that the method is accessible outside of the class.

```
import objectdraw.*;
import java.awt.*;

public class RisingSun extends WindowController {

    private FilledOval sun;

    public void begin () {

        ...
```

Figure 2.2   Declaring sun in the RisingSun program

The declaration of an instance variable does not determine to which object the name will refer. Instead, it merely informs Java that the name will be used at some point in the program and tells Java the type of object that will eventually be associated with the name. The purpose of such a declaration is to enable Java to give you helpful feedback if you make a mistake. Suppose that after deciding to use the name "sun" in our program we made a typing mistake and typed "sin" in one line where we meant to type "sun". It would be nice if when Java tried to run this program it could notice such a mistake and provide advice on how to fix the error similar to that provided by a spelling checker. To do this, however, Java needs the equivalent of a dictionary against which it can check the names used in the program. The declarations a programmer must include for the names used provide this dictionary. If Java encounters a name that was not declared, it reports it as the equivalent of a spelling mistake.

2.1.3   Assigning Meanings to Variable Names

Before a name can be used in a command like:

```
sun.move( 0, −5 );
```

we must associate the name with a particular object using a command Java calls an *assignment statement*. An assignment statement consists of a name followed by an equals sign and a phrase that describes the object we would like to associate with that name. As an example, the assignment statement needed to associate a name with the oval that represents the sun in our program is:

```
sun = new FilledOval( 50, 150, 100, 100, canvas );
```

In this assignment statement, we use the construction that creates the oval as a subphrase to describe the object we want associated with the name sun. When we use a construction as an independent command, as we have in all our earlier examples, the only effect of executing the command is to create the specified object. When a construction is used as a subphrase of an assignment, on the other hand, execution of the command both creates the object and associates a name with it.

Ordering is critical in an assignment. The name being defined must be placed on the left side of the equal sign while the phrase that describes the object to which the name refers belongs on the right side. This may be a bit nonintuitive, since Java must obviously first perform the construction described on the right before it can associate the new object with the name on the left, and we are used to processing information left to right. Java, however, will reject the command as nonsense if we interchange the order of the name and the construction.

Java will also reject an assignment statement that attempts to associate a name with an object that is not of the type included in the name's declaration. The declaration included in Figure 2.2 states that sun will be used to refer to a FilledOval. If we included the assignment

```
sun = new FilledRect( 50, 150, 100, 100, canvas );
```

in our program, it would be identified as an error, because it attempts to associate the name with an object that is a FilledRect rather than with a FilledOval.

Given this introduction to associating names with objects, we can now show the complete code for a "rising sun" program. It appears in Figure 2.3. It includes examples of all three of the basic constructs involved in using names: declarations, assignments, and references.

* The declaration:

```
private FilledOval sun;
```

appears at the beginning of the class body.
* An assignment of a meaning to a name appears in the begin method:

```
sun = new FilledOval( 50, 150, 100, 100, canvas );
```

* A reference to an object through a name appears in onMouseClick:

```
sun.move( 0, −5 );
```

2.1.4   Comments

In the complete version of the program, we introduce one additional and very important feature of Java, the *comment*. As programs become complex, it can be difficult to understand their operation by just reading the Java code. It is often useful to annotate this code with English text that explains more about its purpose and organization. In Java, you can include such comments in the program text itself as long as you follow conventions designed to enable the computer to distinguish the actual instructions it is to follow from the comments. This is done by preceding such comments with a pair of slashes ("//"). Any text that appears on a line after a pair of slashes is treated as a comment by Java.

The program we are writing seems a good example in which to introduce comments. Although the program is short and simple, it is not clear that someone reading the code would have the imagination to realize that the black circle created by the program was actually intended to reproduce the beauty of a sunrise. The Java language isn't rich enough to allow one to express nontechnical ideas in code, but we can include them in comments. We include some general guidance on using comments to make your programs easier to read and understand in Appendix A.

The class declaration in Figure 2.3 is preceded by three lines of comments. If we have multiple lines of comments, we can write them a bit more simply by starting the comments with a "/*" and ending them with "*/" as follows:

```
/* A program that produces an animation of the sun rising.
   The animation is driven by clicking the mouse button.
   The faster the mouse is clicked, the faster the sun will rise. */
```

```
import objectdraw.*;
import java.awt.*;

// A program that produces an animation of the sun rising.
// The animation is driven by clicking the mouse button.
// The faster the mouse is clicked, the faster the sun will rise.
public class RisingSun extends WindowController {

    private FilledOval sun;        // Circle that represents the sun

    // Place the sun and some brief instructions on the screen
    public void begin() {
        sun = new FilledOval( 50, 150, 100, 100, canvas );
        new Text( "Please click the mouse repeatedly", 20, 20, canvas );
    }

    // Move the sun up a bit each time the mouse is clicked
    public void onMouseClick( Location point ) {
        sun.move( 0, -5 );
    }

}
```

Figure 2.3   Code for rising sun example

Many programmers prefer to format multiline comments as follows:

```
/* A program that produces an animation of the sun rising.
 * The animation is driven by clicking the mouse button.
 * The faster the mouse is clicked, the faster the sun will rise.
 */
```

While Java only considers the initial "/*" and final "*/", the "*"s at the beginning of new lines make it easier for the reader to see that it is part of a comment.

2.1.5   Additional Mutator Methods

There are several other operations that can be applied to graphical objects, once we have the ability to associate names with the objects. For example, as we mentioned earlier, there is a mutator method named moveTo which moves an object to a specific location on the screen. There are also two methods named hide and show which can be used to temporarily remove a graphical item from the screen. We can use these three methods to extend the behavior of our RisingSun program.

First, the version of the program shown above becomes totally uninteresting after the mouse has been clicked often enough to push the filled oval off the top of the canvas. Once this happens, additional mouse clicks have no visible effect. It would be nice if there was a way to tell the program to restart by placing the sun back at the bottom of the canvas. Second, as soon as the user starts to click the mouse, the instructions asking the user to click become superfluous. Worse yet, at some point, the rising sun will bump into the instructions. It would be nice to remove them from the display temporarily and then restore them when the program is reset.

All we need to do to permit the resetting of the sun is to add the following definition of the onMouseExit method to our RisingSun class.

```
public void onMouseExit( Location point ) {
    sun.moveTo( 50, 150 );
}
```

With this addition, the user can reset the program by simply moving the mouse out of the program's canvas. When this happens, the body of the onMouseExit method will tell Java to move the sun oval back to its initial position.

Making the instructions disappear and then reappear is a bit more work. In order to apply mutator methods to the instructions, we will have to tell Java to associate a name with the Text created to display the instructions. As we did to define the name sun, we will have to both declare the name we wish to use and then incorporate the creation of the Text into an assignment statement.

An obvious name for this object is "instructions". If this is our choice, then we need to tell Java that we plan to use this name by adding a declaration of the form:

```
private Text instructions;
```

to the beginning of our class. We also need to add an assignment of the form:

```
instructions = new Text( "Please click the mouse repeatedly",
                         20, 20, canvas );
```

to the begin method to actually associate the name with the text of the instructions.

It is worth noting that it is sometimes helpful to split a long command into several lines, as we have done in presenting this assignment statement. It can make your code much easier to read and understand. Using multiple lines for one command like this is perfectly acceptable in Java. It is the semicolon rather than the end of a line that tells Java where a command ends. You can split an instruction between two lines at any point where you could type a space except within quoted text. You will also find that the use of indentation and blank lines can make groups of related commands stand out to the reader. These issues are discussed further in Appendix A.

The pair of mutator methods named hide and show provide the means to temporarily remove a bit of graphics from the display. To make the text disappear when the mouse is clicked, we include an instruction of the form:

```
instructions.hide();
```

in the onMouseClick method. Each time the mouse is clicked, the instructions will be told to hide. Of course, once they are hidden, telling them to hide again has no effect. Note that even though hide expects no parameters, Java still expects us to include the parentheses that would surround the parameters.

When the program is reset, the instructions should reappear. To do this, we would include an instruction of the form

```
instructions.show();
```

in the onMouseExit method. The complete text of this revised program is shown in Figure 2.4.

The hide method should only be used when an object is being removed from the canvas *temporarily*. If an object is being removed permanently—that is, you know that your program will never use the show method to make the object reappear—another method

```
import objectdraw.*;
import java.awt.*;

// A program that produces an animation of the sun rising.
// The animation is driven by clicking the mouse button.
// The faster the mouse is clicked, the faster the sun will rise.
public class RisingSun extends WindowController {

    private FilledOval sun;          //  Circle that represents the sun
    private Text instructions;       //  Display of instructions

    // Place the sun and some brief instructions on the screen
    public void begin() {
        sun = new FilledOval( 50, 150, 100, 100, canvas );
        instructions = new Text( "Please click the mouse repeatedly",
                                 20, 20, canvas );
    }

    // Move the sun up a bit each time the mouse is clicked
    public void onMouseClick( Location point ) {
        sun.move( 0, -5 );
        instructions.hide();
    }

    // Move the sun back to its starting position and redisplay
    // the instructions
    public void onMouseExit( Location point ) {
        sun.moveTo( 50, 150 );
        instructions.show();
    }
}
```

Figure 2.4   Rising sun program with reset feature

named removeFromCanvas is more appropriate. The removeFromCanvas method irreversibly removes a graphical object from the display. There is no way to put an object that has been removed in this way back on the display. When hide is used, the system must save information needed to display the object in case the show method is invoked. This consumes space in the computer's memory. Using removeFromCanvas instead allows the system to totally remove information about the object from the computer's memory.

2.1.6   Exercises

In the exercises below, we ask you to consider how to write a program displaying a diamond that appeared to grow a bit each time the mouse was clicked. The following constructions will produce a drawing of the initial diamond shape desired if executed in a program whose canvas is 200 by 200 pixels.

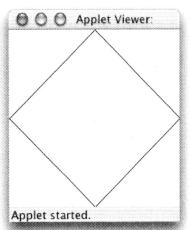

```
new Line( 0, 100, 100, 0, canvas );
new Line( 100, 0, 200, 100, canvas );
new Line( 200, 100, 100, 200, canvas );
new Line( 100, 200, 0, 100, canvas );
```

   The complete program we have in mind won't actually make the diamond grow. Instead, all it will do is move each of the four lines drawn by the constructions a bit closer to the corner closest to the line each time the mouse is clicked. For example, each time the mouse is clicked, the line in the upper left corner of the window will be moved one pixel to the left and one pixel up, so that it ends up closer to the upper left corner of the window. The line that starts in the upper right quarter of the window, on the other hand, will be moved one pixel to the right and one pixel up with each click of the mouse. If this is done, after a number of clicks, the display will look like the picture shown below. The four lines won't be any longer than they were at the start, but they will appear to be part of a bigger diamond than was originally drawn, a diamond that is too big to fit in the window.

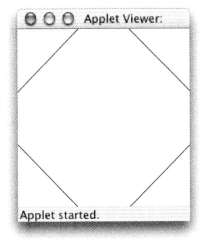

➡ EXERCISE 2.1.1

Before we can move one of these lines or any other graphical object, we must first associate a name with the object. A list of possible names that might be used to refer to the line of the diamond shape drawn by the construction

```
new Line( 200, 100, 100, 200, canvas );
```

is shown below. For each name, indicate whether it would be:

* **invalid** *according to Java's rules for forming names,*
* **inappropriate** *as a name for this particular line, because it would not help a person working with the program remember the purpose of the name or it does not conform to Java's naming conventions, or*
* **appropriate** *as a name for this particular line.*

In each case, briefly explain your answer.

3rdLine	thirdLine	line3
Leftlower	lower right line	lowerLeft
southEast	S.E.	south-east

➡ EXERCISE 2.1.2

Suppose that you selected the instance variable names leftToTop, topToRight, rightToBottom, *and* bottomToLeft *to describe the four lines that form the diamond. Show the declarations required to introduce these names in a Java program.*

➡ EXERCISE 2.1.3

Assuming that the names leftToTop, topToRight, rightToBottom, *and* bottomToLeft *had been chosen to describe the four lines that form the diamond and that they had been declared appropriately, show how the constructions shown above would be turned into assignment statements that both created the* Lines *and associated the names listed with them. In which methods should these commands be placed if you want the lines to appear in their initial positions as soon as the program is started?*

➡ EXERCISE 2.1.4

Assuming that the names leftToTop, topToRight, rightToBottom, *and* bottomToLeft *had been declared appropriately and associated with the lines of the diamond using assignment statements, show the statements required to invoke the move method on each line to move the line closer to the nearest corner of the program's window. Each line should be moved one pixel horizontally and one pixel vertically. In which method should these commands be placed if you want the lines to move each time the mouse is clicked?*

➡ ⌐ EXERCISE 2.1.5

Assuming that the names leftToTop, topToRight, rightToBottom, *and* bottomToLeft *had been declared appropriately and associated with the lines of the diamond using assignment statements, describe the effect the following statements would have on the lines each time they were executed. In addition, sketch the contents of the window after these lines were executed 100 times.*

```
leftToTop.move( 0, 1 );
topToRight.move( 0, 1 );
rightToBottom.move( 0, -1 );
bottomToLeft.move( 0, -1 );
```

2.2 Nongraphical Classes of Objects

We have seen how to construct graphical objects of several varieties, associate names with them, and apply methods to these objects. All of the objects we have worked with, however, have shared the property that they are graphical in nature. When we create any of these objects, they actually appear somewhere on the computer's screen. This is not a required property of objects that can be manipulated by a Java program. In this section we will introduce two classes of objects that are related to producing graphics but do not correspond to particular shapes that appear on your screen.

2.2.1 The Class of Colors

So far, all the graphics we have drawn on the screen have appeared in black. Black is the color in which graphics are drawn by default. To add a little variety to the display, we can change the color of any graphical object using a mutator method named setColor. As an example, it would certainly be an improvement to make the sun displayed by our RisingSun program appear yellow or any other more "sunlike" color than black.

It is quite simple to make this change. All we have to do is add an invocation of setColor to our begin method. The revised method would look like:

```
public void begin() {
    sun = new FilledOval( 50, 150, 100, 100, canvas );
    sun.setColor( Color.YELLOW );
    instructions = new Text( "Please click the mouse repeatedly",
                             20, 20, canvas );
}
```

The setColor method expects us to include a parameter specifying the color to be used. The simplest way to specify the color is to use one of Java's built-in color names. We chose yellow for our sun, but if we wanted a more dramatic sunrise we could have instead used Color.ORANGE or even Color.RED. Java provides names for all the basic colors including

`Color.BLUE`, `Color.GREEN`, and even `Color.BLACK` and `Color.WHITE`.[1] Of course, there are too many shades of each color to assign a name to every one. Accordingly, Java provides an alternative mechanism for describing colors.

We have seen that names in Java can be associated with objects like the drawing area (`canvas`) or graphical objects we have created. You might suspect that if a color can be associated with a name, it might be thought of as an object. In this case, you would be right.

What properties do colors share with the other classes of objects we have seen? First, they can be constructed. Just as we have been able to say `new FilledRect(...)` to create rectangles, we can construct new colors. This is how Java gives us access to the vast range of colors that can be displayed on the typical computer screen. If we want to set the color of our sun to something not included in the small set of colors that have names, we can describe the particular color we want by saying:

```
new Color(...)
```

as long as we know the right information to use in place of the dots between the parentheses.

When we want to construct a new color for use in a program, we must provide a numerical description of the color as parameters to the construction. Java uses a system that is fairly common for specifying colors on computer systems. Each color is described as a mixture of the three primary colors: red, green and blue.[2] The mixture desired is specified by giving three numbers, each of which specifies how much of a particular color should be included in the mixture. Each of the numbers can range from 0 ("use none of this particular primary color") to 255 ("use as much of this color as possible"). The numbers are listed in the order "red, green, blue". So "0, 0, 0" is black, "255, 255, 255" is white, "0, 255, 0" is solid green, and "255, 0, 255" is a shade of purple. If you wanted to make the `sun` purple, you could construct the desired color by saying:

```
new Color( 255, 0, 255 )
```

`Color`s are objects. Therefore, just as you can associate names with objects such as FilledOvals, you can associate names with `Color`s. If you wanted to use the color purple in a program, you might first declare an instance variable named "purple" as:

```
private Color purple;
```

Then, in the `begin` method you could associate the name with the actual color by saying:

```
purple = new Color( 255, 0, 255 );
```

You could then make the sun purple by replacing the `setColor` used to make the sun yellow by:

```
sun.setColor( purple );
```

---

[1] In early versions of Java, the names used for colors used lowercase letters. For example, the name `Color.red` was used instead of `Color.RED`. These names are still supported, but their use is discouraged. Throughout the text, we will use the capitalized versions of color names.

[2] If you thought the primary colors were red, yellow, and blue, you aren't confused. Those are the primary colors when mixing materials that absorb light (like paint). When mixing light itself (as in flashlight beams or the light given off by the phosphors on a computer screen), red, blue and green act as the primary colors. Mixing red and blue lights produces purple. Mixing red and green produces yellow. Mixing all three primary colors together produces white.

It is worth noting that it is not actually necessary to introduce a new name to use a color created using a construction. When we use the `setColor` method, we have to provide the color we wish to use as a parameter to the method, but we can describe the desired color in several ways. In particular, we could make the sun purple by simply saying

```
sun.setColor( new Color( 255, 0, 255 ) );
```

The construction describes the color just as well as the name `purple` from Java's point of view.

In general, wherever Java allows us to identify an object or value by name, it will accept any other phrase that describes the equivalent object or value. This applies not just to names used to describe parameter values but also to names used to indicate the object we wish to alter.

⟹ EXERCISE 2.2.1

Write a method that creates a red oval when the mouse is clicked. The oval should be 100 pixels in width and 75 pixels in height and should appear 50 pixels down from the top of the canvas and 50 pixels in from the left of the canvas.   ❖

2.2.2 The Location Class

As we have seen, we can turn a triple of numbers into a single object by making a new `Color`. We can turn pairs of numbers into objects by constructing an object of another class called `Location`. In the construction of a `Location`, two numbers are provided as parameters. These numbers are treated as coordinates within the graphical coordinate system. The construction produces an object that represents the position on the screen described by the specified coordinates. The name `Location` should sound familiar. It is part of the thus far unexplained notation (`Location point`) that appears in the headers of all mouse-event-handling methods. Once we introduce this class of objects, we can explain the function of this notation in method declarations.

To construct a new `Location` object you simply say something like:

```
new Location( 50, 150 )
```

replacing the parameters "50, 150" with the coordinates of whatever point you are trying to describe. A line containing just this construction would have no effect on the behavior of a program. Nothing appears on the screen when a `Location` is created, and if no name is associated with an object when it is created you can never refer to it later. It is far more likely that one first would declare a name that can refer to `Location` objects by typing something like:

```
private Location initialPosition;
```

and then associate the name with an actual coordinate pair through an assignment of the form:

```
initialPosition = new Location( 50, 150 );
```

The real worth of `Location`s comes from the fact that they can be used to take the place of typing a pair of numbers to describe a point in the coordinate system when writing a construction for any of the graphical classes we have described or invoking a method that requires a coordinate pair such as `moveTo`. For example, the instruction used to construct the sun in our `RisingSun` program looks like:

```
sun = new FilledOval( 50, 150, 100, 100, canvas );
```

Assuming that the declaration of `initialPosition` shown above is added to the `RisingSun` class and that the assignment:

```
initialPosition = new Location( 50, 150 );
```

is included in the `begin` method, then the construction for the sun could be replaced by:

```
sun = new FilledOval( initialPosition, 100, 100, canvas );
```

Similarly, the instruction used to reposition the sun in the `onMouseExit` method:

```
sun.moveTo( 50, 150 );
```

could be revised to read:

```
sun.moveTo( initialPosition );
```

These changes would not alter the behavior of the program, but they would make it easier to read. A human looking at your program is more likely to understand the purpose of the `moveTo` written using `initialPosition` than the one that uses "50, 150". In addition, this approach makes the program easier to change. If you wanted to run the program using a larger screen area, the coordinates for the starting position would need to be changed. In the version of the program written using the name `initialPosition`, only one line would have to be altered to make this change.

Like the graphical objects we introduced earlier, `Location` objects can be altered using mutator methods. There is a mutator method for `Location`s named `translate` that is very similar to the `move` method associated with graphical objects. Both `translate` and `move` expect two numbers specifying how far to travel in the *x* and *y* dimensions of the graphical coordinate system. The difference is that when you tell a graphical object to `move`, you can see it move on the screen. When you tell a `Location` to `translate`, nothing on the screen changes. A `Location` object describes a position on the screen, but it does not appear on the screen itself. Accordingly, translating a `Location` changes the position described by the `Location`, but it does not change anything already on the screen. The effect of the `translate` only becomes apparent if the `Location` is later used to position some graphical object.

To clarify how `translate` works, consider the sample program shown in Figure 2.5. Each time the mouse is clicked, this program will draw a pair of thick, perpendicular lines. The first lines drawn will intersect at the upper left corner of the window. With each click, the lines drawn will be placed to the right and below the preceding lines, so that the window is eventually filled with a grid pattern.

The program includes two `Location` variables named `verticalCorner` and `horizontalCorner`. If you examine the declaration of these variables, you will see that Java allows us to define several variables of the same type in a single declaration by listing all the names to be declared separated by commas. It is appropriate to use this form of declaration only when the names declared together have related functions. In this case they do. Each of these names describes the `Location` at which one of a pair of `FilledRect`s will be drawn when the user clicks the mouse.

In its `begin` method, this program creates two `Location` objects that both describe the point at the origin of the coordinate system, the upper left corner of the canvas. One of these objects is associated with the name `verticalCorner` and the other with the name `horizontalCorner`.

```
import objectdraw.*;
import java.awt.*;
// A program that uses the translate method to draw a
// grid of thick black lines on the canvas
public class DrawGrid extends WindowController {

    // The corners of the next two rectangles to draw
    private Location verticalCorner, horizontalCorner;

    // Set Locations to position first pair of lines at upper
    // left corner of the canvas
    public void begin() {
        horizontalCorner = new Location( 0, 0 );
        verticalCorner = new Location( 0, 0 );
    }

    // Draw a pair of lines and move Locations so that the next
    // pair of lines will appear further down and to the right
    public void onMouseClick( Location point ) {
        new FilledRect( verticalCorner, 5, 200, canvas );
        new FilledRect( horizontalCorner, 200, 5, canvas );

        verticalCorner.translate( 10, 0 );
        horizontalCorner.translate( 0, 10 );
    }
}
```

Figure 2.5   An application of the translate method

Although they are created to describe the same position initially, two distinct objects are needed because they will be modified to describe different locations using the translate method in other parts of the program.

The names assigned to these two Locations reflect the way they are used in the program's other method, onMouseClick. Each time the mouse is clicked, this method creates two long, thin rectangles on the screen. The rectangle created by the first construction in onMouseClick is a long vertical rectangle. The position of its upper left corner is determined by the Location named verticalCorner. The other rectangle is a long horizontal rectangle and its position is determined by the Location named horizontalCorner.

Since both of the Locations initially describe the upper left corner of the canvas, the first time the mouse is clicked, the rectangles created by the execution of the first two lines of onMouseClick will produce a drawing like that shown in Figure 2.6.

The last two commands in onMouseClick tell the Location objects named verticalCorner and horizontalCorner to translate so that they describe new positions on the screen. verticalCorner is changed to describe the position 10 pixels to the right of its initial position. horizontalCorner is translated 10 pixels down from its initial position. When these commands are completed, nothing changes on the screen. The program's window will still

Figure 2.6   Display after one click

Figure 2.7   Display after second click

appear as shown in Figure 2.6 after they have been performed. The Locations will describe new positions, but the two rectangles will remain where they were initially placed, even though the Locations were used to describe their positions when they were constructed.

The next time the mouse is clicked, the two constructions at the beginning of onMouseClick are performed based on the translated positions of the two Locations. Accordingly, the vertical rectangle created will appear a bit farther to the right and the horizontal rectangle will appear a bit farther down the screen, as shown in Figure 2.7. After these rectangles are created, the last two lines of the method will shift the Locations used farther to the right and down the screen, so that the rectangles produced by the next click will appear at the correct locations.

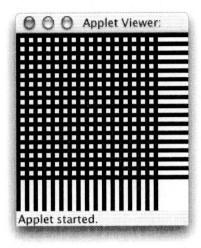

Figure 2.8 Display after many clicks

This process will be repeated each time the mouse is clicked. After about 15 additional clicks, the window will be nearly filled with a grid of lines, as shown in Figure 2.8. Just a few more clicks will complete the process of filling the screen.

2.3 Layering on the Canvas

Now that we can set the color of a graphical object, we could actually make a much prettier picture for our rising sun program. We could add a blue sky, some white clouds and even a bit of green grass. Better yet, given that the figures in this text are not printed in color, instead of the sun we can draw the moon with a light gray cloud passing in front of it and a dark gray sky behind it. The picture we have in mind is shown in Figure 2.9.

To construct this picture we must declare variables to refer to the sky, moon, and cloud:

```
private FilledOval moon, cloud;
private FilledRect sky;
```

Then we must construct the desired objects:

```
sky = new FilledRect( 0, 0, 300, 300, canvas );
moon = new FilledOval( 50, 50, 100, 100, canvas );
cloud = new FilledOval( 70, 110, 160, 40, canvas );
```

and finally set their colors appropriately:

```
sky.setColor( new Color( 60, 60, 60 ) );
moon.setColor( Color.WHITE );
cloud.setColor( Color.GRAY );
```

Figure 2.9   Tonight's forecast: Partly cloudy

The parameters "60, 60, 60" provided to the Color construction used to set the color of sky describe a dark shade of gray.

Suppose we changed this code by reordering the assignment statements in which the objects are created so that the moon is created after the cloud, as in:

```
sky = new FilledRect( 0, 0, 300, 300, canvas );
cloud = new FilledOval( 70, 110, 160, 40, canvas );
moon = new FilledOval( 50, 50, 100, 100, canvas );
```

This will change the picture drawn so that it resembles the one shown in Figure 2.10. The moon and the cloud still overlap, but now part of the cloud is hidden behind the moon rather than the other way around.

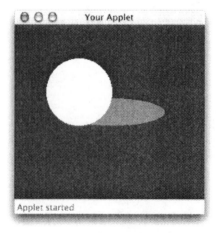

Figure 2.10   Tonight's forecast: Partly moony?

The canvas views the collection of objects it has been asked to display as a series of layers. When a new object is created, it is placed in a layer above all the older objects on the canvas. When two objects overlap, the object on the lower level will be partially or completely hidden by the object on the upper level. In the code to produce Figure 2.9, the moon was created before the cloud and therefore was drawn as if it were underneath the cloud. In the revised code, the moon was created last and therefore was drawn as if it were above the cloud.

None of the methods we have considered so far changes this layering. Changing an object's color or moving it will not change the way in which it is drawn when it overlaps with other objects. If we included code to move the moon shown in Figure 2.9 as we could move the sun in our RisingSun program, the moon would move vertically on the screen, but it would still remain on a layer below the cloud. It would therefore appear to slide upward while remaining behind the cloud. Even the hide and show methods preserve this ordering. If we show an object that has been hidden, it will reappear underneath the same objects that were above it before it was hidden. In particular, it does not appear at the top level as if it had just been created.

There are, however, several methods that enable a programmer to rearrange the layering of objects on the screen. The methods sendForward and sendBackward move an object up or down one layer. The methods sendToFront and sendToBack move an object to the top or bottom of all the layers drawn. Thus, if we had created the picture shown in Figure 2.9 and then executed either the command

```
cloud.sendBackward();
```

or the command

```
moon.sendToFront();
```

the picture displayed would change to look like Figure 2.10.

2.4 Accessing the Location of the Mouse

In the header of every mouse-event-handling method we have included the phrase Location point in parentheses after the name of the method. Now that we have explained what a Location is, we can explain the purpose of this phrase. It provides a means by which we can refer to the point at which the mouse cursor was located when the event handled by a method occurred. Basically, within the body of a mouse-event-handling method that includes the phrase Location point we can use the name point to refer to a Location object that describes where in the canvas the mouse was positioned.

As a simple example, we can write a variant of our very first example program TouchyWindow. This new program will display a bit of text on the screen when the mouse is pressed, just like TouchyWindow, but:

1. it will display the word "Pressed" instead of the phrase "I'm Touched",
2. it will place the word where the mouse was clicked instead of in the center of the canvas, and finally
3. it will not erase the canvas each time the mouse is released

The code for this new example is shown below.

```
import objectdraw.*;
import java.awt.*;

// A program that displays the word "Pressed" wherever
// the mouse is pressed
public class Pressed extends WindowController {
    public void onMousePress( Location point ) {
        new Text( "Pressed", point, canvas );
    }
}
```

Note that the name `point` is used in the construction that places the text "Pressed" on the screen. It appears in place of an explicit pair of *x* and *y* coordinates. Because `point` is included in the method's header, Java knows that we want the computer to make this name refer to the location at which the mouse was clicked. Therefore Java will place the word "Pressed" wherever the mouse is pressed.

You may have noticed that the phrase `Location point` is syntactically very similar to an instance variable declaration. It is composed of a name we want to use preceded by the name of the class of things to which the name will refer. All that is missing is the word `private`. In fact, this phrase is another form of declaration known as a *formal parameter declaration*, and a name such as `point` that is included in such a declaration is called a *formal parameter name* or simply a *formal parameter*.

As in instance variable declarations, we are free to use any name we want when we declare a formal parameter. There is nothing special about the name `point` (except that we have used it in all our examples so far). We can choose any name we want for the mouse location as long as we place the name after the word `Location` in the header of the method. For example, the program shown in Figure 2.11, which uses the name `mousePosition` as its formal parameter instead of `point`, will behave exactly like the version that used the name `point`.

```
import objectdraw.*;
import java.awt.*;

// A program that displays the word "Pressed" wherever
// the mouse is pressed
public class Pressed extends WindowController {
    public void onMousePress( Location mousePosition ) {
        new Text( "Pressed", mousePosition, canvas );
    }
}
```

Figure 2.11   Using a different parameter name

Another important aspect of the behavior of formal parameter names like mousePosition and point is that each parameter name is meaningful only within the method whose header contains its declaration. To illustrate this, consider the program shown in Figure 2.12. This program displays the word "Pressed" at the current mouse position each time the mouse button is pushed, and it displays the word "Released" at the current mouse position each time the mouse is released. The onMousePress method in this example is identical to the corresponding method from the Pressed example except for the word it displays and the name chosen for its formal parameter. The onMouseRelease method is also quite similar to the earlier program's onMousePress.

Suppose now that we wanted to write another program that would display the words "Pressed" and "Released" just as in the UpsAndDowns example, but would also draw a line connecting the point where the mouse button was pressed to the point where the mouse button was released. A snapshot of what the window of such a program would look like right after the mouse was pressed, dragged across the screen, and then released is shown in Figure 2.13.

Given that the UpsAndDowns program has names that refer to both the point where the mouse button was pressed and the point where the mouse button was released, it might seem quite easy to modify this program to add the desired line-drawing feature. In particular, it probably seems that we could simply add a construction of the form:

```
new Line( pressPoint, releasePoint, canvas );
```

to the program's onMouseRelease method.

THIS WILL NOT WORK!

Because pressPoint is declared as a formal parameter in onMousePress, Java will not allow the programmer to refer to it in any other method. Java will treat the use of this name

```
import objectdraw.*;
import java.awt.*;

// A program that displays the words "Pressed" and
// "Released" where the mouse button is pressed and
// released.
public class UpsAndDowns extends WindowController {
    public void onMousePress( Location pressPoint ) {
        new Text( "Pressed", pressPoint, canvas );
    }

    public void onMouseRelease( Location releasePoint ) {
        new Text( "Released", releasePoint, canvas );
    }
}
```

Figure 2.12 A program to record mouse-button changes

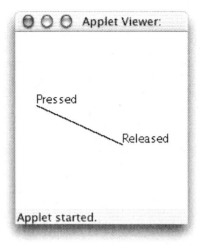

Figure 2.13   Connecting the ends of a mouse motion

in onMouseRelease as an error and refuse to run the program. In general, formal parameter names cannot be used to share information between two different methods.

If we want to share information about the mouse location between two event-handling methods, we must use formal parameters and instance variables together. We have already seen that instance variables can be used to share information between methods. In the RisingSun example, the begin method created the oval that represented the sun and the onMousePress later moved the oval. This was arranged by associating the name sun with the oval.

In order to write a program to draw a line between the points where the mouse was pressed and released, we will have to associate an instance variable name with the Location where the mouse was pressed. This variable will then make it possible for onMousePress to share the needed information with onMouseRelease. We will choose firstPoint as the name for this variable.

As always, we will have to add both a declaration and an assignment involving this new instance variable. Accordingly, the completed program will look like the code shown in Figure 2.14.

When the mouse is pressed, the assignment

```
firstPoint = pressPoint;
```

associates the name firstPoint with the Location of the mouse. This assignment is interesting in several ways. It is the first assignment we have encountered in which the text on the right side of the equal sign is something other than the construction of a new object. In the general form of the assignment statement, the text on the right side of the equal sign can be any phrase that describes the object we wish to associate with the name on the left. So, in this case, rather than creating a new object, we take the existing Location object that is named pressPoint and give it a second name, firstPoint. Immediately after this assignment, the Location that describes the mouse position has two names. This may seem unusual, but it isn't. Most of us can also be identified using multiple names (e.g., your first name, a nickname, or Mr. or Ms. followed by your last name).

This assignment also illustrates the fact that a name in a Java program may refer to different things at different times. Suppose when the program starts you click the mouse at the point with

```
import objectdraw.*;
import java.awt.*;

// A program that displays the words "Pressed" and "Released"
// where the mouse button is pressed and released while connecting
// each such pair of points with a line.
public class ConnectTwo extends WindowController {

    private Location firstPoint;
    // The location where button was pressed

    // Display "Pressed" when the button is pressed.
    public void onMousePress( Location pressPoint ) {
        new Text( "Pressed", pressPoint, canvas );
        firstPoint = pressPoint;
    }

    // Display "Released" and draw a line from where the mouse
    // was last pressed.
    public void onMouseRelease( Location releasePoint ) {
        new Text( "Released", releasePoint, canvas );
        new Line( firstPoint, releasePoint, canvas );
    }
}
```

Figure 2.14 A program to track mouse actions

coordinates (5,5). As soon as you do this, onMousePress is invoked and the name firstPoint is associated with a Location that represents the point (5,5). If you then drag the mouse across the screen, release the mouse button, and then press it again at the point (150,140), onMousePress is invoked again and the assignment statement in its body tells Java to associate firstPoint with a Location that describes the point (150,140). At this point, Java forgets that firstPoint ever referred to (5,5). A name in Java may refer to different objects at different times, but at any given time it refers to exactly one thing (or to nothing if no value has yet been assigned to the name).

In fact, the values associated with most instance variables are changed frequently rather than remaining fixed like the variable in our RisingSun example. To illustrate the usefulness of such changes, we can write a simple drawing program.

Complex drawing programs provide many tools for drawing shapes, lines, and curves on the screen. We will write a program to implement the behavior of just one of these tools, the one that allows the user to scribble on the screen with the mouse as if it were a pencil. A sample of the kind of scribbling we have in mind is shown in Figure 2.15. The program should allow the user to trace a line on the screen by depressing the mouse button and then dragging the mouse around the screen with the button depressed. The program should not draw anything if the mouse is moved without depressing the button.

Figure 2.15 Scribbling with a computer's mouse

The trick to writing this program is to realize that what appears to be a curved line on a computer screen is really just a lot of straight lines hooked together. In particular, to write this program, what we want to do is notice each time the mouse is moved (with the button depressed) and draw a line from the place where the mouse started to its new position. Each time the mouse is moved with its button depressed, Java will follow the instruction in the onMouseDrag method. So, within this method, we want to include an instruction like:

```
new Line( previousPosition, currentPosition, canvas );
```

where previousPosition and currentPosition are names that refer to the previous and current positions of the mouse. The trick is to also include statements that will ensure that Java associates these names with the correct Locations.

Associating the correct Location with the name currentPosition is easy. When onMouseDrag is invoked, the computer will automatically associate the current mouse Location with whatever name we choose to use as the method's formal parameter name. So, if the header we use when declaring onMouseDrag looks like:

```
public void onMouseDrag( Location currentPosition )
```

we can assume that the name currentPosition will refer to the location of the mouse when the method is invoked.

Getting the correct Location associated with previousPosition is a bit trickier. Think carefully for a moment about the beginning of the process of drawing with this program. The user will position the mouse wherever the first line is to be drawn. Then the user will depress the mouse button and begin to drag the mouse. The first line drawn should start at the position where the mouse button was depressed and extend to the position to which the mouse was first dragged. This situation is similar to the problem we faced when we wanted to draw a line between the point where the mouse was depressed and the point where the mouse was released. The position at which the mouse button is first depressed will be available through the formal parameter of the onMousePress method, but we need to access it in the onMouseDrag method because this is the method that will actually draw the line. We can arrange for onMousePress to share the needed information with onMouseDrag by declaring the name previousPosition as an instance variable and including an appropriate assignment in onMousePress to associate this name with the position where the mouse button is first pressed.

Given this analysis, we will include an instance variable declaration of the form:

```
private Location previousPosition;
```

and then write the following definition for onMousePress:

```
public void onMousePress( Location pressPoint ) {
    previousPosition = pressPoint;
}
```

We also know that the onMouseDrag method must contain the Line construction shown above and that its formal parameter should be named currentPosition. So, a first draft of this method would be:

```
public void onMouseDrag( Location currentPosition ) {
    new Line( previousPosition, currentPosition, canvas );
}
```

Unfortunately, if we actually use this code, the program will not behave as we want. For example, if we were to start near the upper left corner of the screen and then drag the mouse in an arc counterclockwise, hoping to draw the picture shown below on the left, the program would actually draw the picture shown on the right.

The problem is that we are not changing the point associated with previousPosition as often as we should. In onMousePress, we tell the computer to make this name refer to the point where the mouse is first pressed, and it continues to refer to this point until the mouse is released and pressed again. As a result, as we drag the mouse, all the lines created start at the point where the mouse button was first pressed. Instead, after the first line has been drawn, we always want previousPosition to refer to the mouse's position when the last line was drawn. To do this, we must add the assignment statement:

```
previousPosition = currentPosition;
```

at the end of the onMouseDrag method, yielding the complete program shown in Figure 2.16.

```
import objectdraw.*;
import java.awt.*;

// This program allows its user to draw simple lines on the screen
// using the mouse as if it were a pencil
public class Scribble extends WindowController {

    private Location previousPosition; // Last known position of mouse

    // When the mouse button is depressed, note its location
    public void onMousePress( Location pressPoint ) {
        previousPosition = pressPoint;
    }

    // Connect current and previous mouse positions with a line
    public void onMouseDrag( Location currentPosition ) {
        new Line( previousPosition, currentPosition, canvas );
        previousPosition = currentPosition;
    }
}
```

Figure 2.16   A simple sketching program

➠ EXERCISE 2.5.1

Explain why the assignment statement is still needed in onMousePress *as shown below, even though* previousPosition *is always updated in* onMouseDrag:

```
public void onMousePress( Location pressPoint ) {
    previousPosition = pressPoint;
}
```

2.6   Summary

In this chapter we explored the importance of the use of names to refer to the objects our programs manipulate. Instance variable names were used to share information between methods, and formal parameter names provided a means to pass information from outside the program into a method body. We saw that these names had to be declared before we could use them in a program, and, in the case of instance variable names, that we had to use an assignment statement to associate each name with a particular object.

We learned more about displaying simple graphical objects on our program's canvas and learned how to modify the properties of these objects using mutator methods. In addition, we learned that the notions of "objects", constructions, and mutator methods in Java extend to types of objects such as Colors and Locations that are not themselves visible on our screen.

In case you did not notice, the last example program we discussed, the Scribble program, was different from most of the other examples in one important regard. It actually is (at least part of) a useful program. This reflects the fact that the features we have explored are fundamental to the construction of all Java programs. With this background, we are now well prepared to expand our knowledge of the facilities Java provides.

2.7 Chapter Review Problems

➡ EXERCISE 2.7.1

Revise TouchyWindow *so that the* Text *object has a name. Create the* Text *object in the* begin *method, but don't show it unless the mouse is pressed. Change the* onMouseRelease *method so that it does not use the* canvas.clear() *command, but hides the text when the mouse is released.*   ❖

➡ EXERCISE 2.7.2

Suppose that in the Scribble *class you want to clear the contents of the canvas if the mouse exits the window. Write the appropriate method to do this.*   ❖

➡ EXERCISE 2.7.3

What is wrong with the following line of code?

```
message = Text( "Welcome to Hangman v1.0", 60, 60, canvas );
```
                    ❖

➡ EXERCISE 2.7.4

Write a program that draws a filled 20-by-20 square at the mouse location each time the mouse is pressed. When the mouse is released, the frame of the square should remain. The user should then be able to press again to create a new filled square at a new location that will leave a frame when the mouse is released.   ❖

➡ EXERCISE 2.7.5

What is an instance variable and what are the two important steps needed to create it before being able to use it?   ❖

➡ EXERCISE 2.7.6

Modify Scribble *so that everything drawn in the window is red instead of black.*   ❖

➡ EXERCISE 2.7.7

Look at the two pieces of code. Do they produce the same or different outcomes? If the outcomes are different, explain the difference.

a. i. public void onMouseClick (Location point){
```
        new Text ( "Hello.", point, canvas );
}
```
   ii. public void onMouseClick (Location clickPoint){
```
        new Text ( "Hello.", clickPoint, canvas );
}
```

b. *Assume* clickPoint *is an instance variable of type* Location *that has been initialized in a* begin *method.*
   i. public void onMouseClick (Location point){
```
        point = clickPoint;
        new Text ( "Hi", clickPoint, canvas );
}
```
   ii. public void onMouseClick (Location point){
```
        clickPoint = point;
        new Text ( "Hi", clickPoint, canvas );
}
```

2.8   Programming Problems

EXERCISE 2.8.1

Write a simple program that does the following:

* *When the program begins, a red square with a black frame is drawn. Each side of the square is 60 pixels, and the square is located 70 pixels from the right and 60 pixels down from the top left corner.*
* *When the mouse is clicked, the square turns blue.*
* *When the mouse exits the window, the square disappears.*
* *When the mouse re-enters the window, the square reappears and is once again red.*

EXERCISE 2.8.2

Write a program called DrawRect. *The program should display the frame of a rectangle when the mouse is pressed. The rectangle should be 100 by 100 pixels with the upper left corner at the point where the mouse was clicked. When the mouse is dragged, the frame should move with the mouse, with the upper left corner of the rectangle always following the cursor. When the mouse is released, the rectangle should be filled in so it is no longer just a frame.*

EXERCISE 2.8.3

a. *Write a simple program called* Measles *with these features:*

* *When the program begins there should be a message telling the user "Measles: Click to catch the disease!"*

⁕ *When the user clicks the mouse, a red dot should form at the location where the mouse was clicked. Make the diameter of the dots 5 pixels. The introductory message should no longer be visible.*

⁕ *When the mouse exits the window, the user should be cured. Thus all the spots should disappear and a message saying "You have been cured!" should appear.*

⁕ *When the mouse re-enters the window, the original message should reappear.*

Hint: *Hidden items are also removed from the canvas when you clear it.*

b. *Modify your code from part (a) so that the spot is centered at the point where the mouse was clicked.*

CHAPTER 3

Working with Numbers

$\mathscr{I}$n the preceding chapter, we used numbers extensively to manipulate graphical objects. They were used to specify coordinates, dimensions, and even colors. While we used numbers to describe what we wanted to do to various graphical objects, we did not do much of interest with the numbers themselves. Numbers are of critical importance to Java. Just as Java provides operations to let us work with graphical objects, it provides operations to let us work with numbers. In this chapter we will explore some of these operations. We will see how to obtain numerical values describing properties of existing objects, how to perform basic arithmetic computations, how to work with numeric variables, and how to display numeric values.

3.1 Introduction to Accessor Methods

When we perform a construction of the form

```
new Location( 50, 150 )
```

we combine two numbers to form a single Location object. There are many situations where it is useful to do the opposite. That is, we have a Location object and want to access the numerical values of the *x* and *y* coordinates associated with that location.

Suppose, for example, that we decided to change the RisingSun program so that, rather than having to click the mouse to move the sun, the user could simply drag the mouse up and down and the sun would follow it. The desired behavior is similar to the way in which the scrollbars found in many programs react to mouse movement. If you grab the scroll box displayed in a vertical scrollbar you can move the scroll box up and down by moving the mouse, but you cannot move the scroll box to the left or right. Similarly, in the program we have in mind, even if the mouse is dragged about in spirals, the circle that represents the sun should only move straight up and down so that its *y* coordinate is always the same as the *y* coordinate of the mouse's current position.

In this new version of RisingSun, which we will name ScrollingSun, we need to replace the onMouseClick method from the previous version with an onMouseDrag method of the form:

```
public void onMouseDrag( Location mousePosition ) {
    sun.moveTo( ... );
}
```

The question is: What should we provide as parameter information to the moveTo method?

We want the sun to move to the position in the canvas whose *x* coordinate is the same as the sun's initial *x* coordinate, 50, and whose *y* coordinate is equal to the *y* coordinate of the mouse. We can handle the *x* coordinate by simply typing 50 as the first parameter to the moveTo method. The hard part is providing the *y* coordinate of the mouse's position.

The Location object named mousePosition certainly contains enough information to determine the *y* coordinate of the mouse. Java lets us ask the Location object to provide this information through a mechanism called an *accessor method*. Like the mutator methods discussed in the preceding chapter, a small collection of accessor methods is associated with each class of objects. Objects of the Location class support two accessor methods, getX and getY.

To use an accessor method we write a name that refers to the object that is the target of the request followed by a period, the name of the method to be applied, and a parenthesized list of parameter values. So, to position the sun appropriately in the onMouseDrag method, we should say:

```
sun.moveTo( 50, mousePosition.getY() );
```

You should observe that this notation for using accessor methods is identical to the notation used for mutator methods. In particular, in the case that no parameters are provided, you still need to include a set of empty parentheses after the name of the method.

The complete text of the revised program is shown in Figure 3.1. With the exception of the substitution of the onMouseDrag method for the onMouseClick method, the only difference between this program and the one shown in Figure 2.3 is that the instructions displayed by the begin method have been modified.

Accessor methods are also associated with objects of the graphics classes introduced in the last chapter. The location and dimensions of a graphical object can be accessed using methods named getX, getY, getWidth, and getHeight. Like the methods discussed above, these accessor methods provide numeric information about an object. In addition, there are accessor methods associated with graphical objects that provide other forms of information. There is a method named getColor that returns the Color of a graphical object. Similarly, getLocation returns a Location object describing an object's current position.

```
// A program that produces an animation of the sun rising and setting.
// The animation is driven by dragging the mouse.
public class  ScrollingSun extends WindowController {

    private FilledOval sun;       //  Circle that represents the sun

    // Place the sun and some brief instructions on the screen
    public void begin() {
        sun = new FilledOval( 50, 150, 100, 100, canvas );
        new Text( "Drag the mouse up or down", 20, 20, canvas );
    }

    // Move the sun to follow the mouse's vertical motion
    public void onMouseDrag( Location mousePosition ) {
        sun.moveTo( 50, mousePosition.getY() );
    }

}
```

Figure 3.1   Program to make the sun scroll with the mouse

EXERCISE 3.1.1

Is the translate *method of the* Location *class an accessor method? Why or why not?*   ❖

EXERCISE 3.1.2

What is the difference between an accessor method and a mutator method? What can an accessor method do that a mutator method cannot?   ❖

3.2   Accessing Numerical Attributes of the Canvas

In the last chapter, to keep things simple, we assumed that we knew the size of the windows in which our programs would run. For example, the DrawGrid program presented in Section 2.2.2 draws a grid like the one shown in Figure 3.2. The bars in this grid are created by constructions of the form:

```
new FilledRect( verticalCorner, 5, 200, canvas );
new FilledRect( horizontalCorner, 200, 5, canvas );
```

placed within the program's onMouseClick method. The vertical rectangles created by these constructions are 200 pixels tall and the horizontal rectangles are 200 pixels wide. The resulting drawing looks fine if the window is exactly 200 by 200, which is the window size we showed in the figures that illustrated the drawings the program would produce, but it would not look right if the window was larger. If the window was wider, we would want the program to draw wider horizontal rectangles. If the window was taller, we would want taller vertical rectangles.

Figure 3.2   Drawing produced by the DrawGrid program

When we write a program, we cannot be certain of the size of the window in which it will run. The size of the window is not determined by our Java code. For the types of programs discussed in this text, the window size is determined by specifications written in a different language, HTML or Hypertext Markup Language, the language used to describe the content of Web pages.

Given that the canvas size is unpredictable, it would be best to write programs that determine the actual size of the canvas while running and adjust the objects they draw accordingly. We have seen that the canvas provides a mutator method named `clear`. It also supports two accessor methods named `getWidth` and `getHeight` which allow a program to determine the dimensions of the

---

We mentioned above that the actual window size used by our programs is determined by a specification written in the language used to construct Web pages, HTML. The programs we have been writing are all examples of what are called *applets*. They are Java programs that can be embedded within the contents of a Web page. A fragment of HTML that could be used to include our DrawGrid program in a Web page is shown below:

```
<applet archive="JavaClasses.jar"
        code="DrawGrid.class"
        width=200 height=200>
</applet>
```

If a web browser was used to visit a web page whose HTML description contained this specification, our DrawGrid program would be displayed in a 200-by-200-pixel rectangle within the larger web browser window. If the person who constructed the web page had instead included the specification

```
<applet archive="JavaClasses.jar"
        code="DrawGrid.class"
        width=400 height=300>
</applet>
```

then the program would be displayed in a 400-by-300-pixel region. Even if the environment you use to write Java programs does not use a Web browser to run your programs, it probably does depend on a file containing at least a fragment of HTML like the one shown above to decide how big the window your program runs in should be. The key thing to note is that the individual who writes the HTML gets to specify the width and height of the program's canvas.

drawing area. Like the getX and getY methods associated with Locations, these methods do not expect any parameter values. To produce a version of DrawGrid that would work correctly in any size canvas, we would simply replace the occurrences of the number 200 in the constructions shown above with appropriate uses of accessor methods to obtain the following code:

```
new FilledRect( verticalCorner, 5, canvas.getHeight(), canvas );
new FilledRect( horizontalCorner, canvas.getWidth(), 5, canvas );
```

➠ EXERCISE 3.2.1

Write the begin *method for a program that draws an X through the canvas using the* getHeight *and* getWidth *accessor methods of the canvas.*   ❖

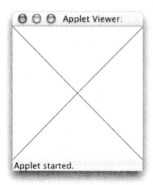

3.3   Expressions and Statements

It is important to observe that accessor methods serve a very different function than do mutator methods. A mutator method instructs an object to change in some way. An accessor method requests some information about the object's current state.

Simply asking an object for information is rarely worthwhile by itself. We also need to tell Java what to do with the information requested. We would never write an instruction of the form:

```
mousePosition.getY();
```

Such an instruction would tell Java to ask the Location named mousePosition for its *y* coordinate but make no use of the information. Instead, we use accessor methods in places within a program where Java expects the programmer to describe an object or value. For example, an accessor method can be used to describe a parameter to a construction as in

```
new FilledOval( 10, mousePosition.getY(), 2, 2, canvas );
```

or to describe the parameters for another method, like moveTo.

This notion of a phrase that describes an object or value is important enough to deserve a name. Such phrases are called *expressions*. We have already seen several different sorts of phrases that Java recognizes as examples of expressions.

Where numeric information is needed, we have often explicitly included the numbers to use by typing *numeric literals* like "50" and "150" as in the invocation

```
box.moveTo( 50, 150 );
```

In other situations, *accessor method invocations* have been used to describe numeric values as in

```
box.moveTo( 50, point.getY() );
```

Where non-numeric information was needed, we have either used a *construction* to create the needed information as in

```
sun.setColor( new Color( 200, 100, 0 ) );
```

or provided a *name* that was associated with the desired object as in

```
sun.setColor( purple );
```

Thus, numeric literals, instance variable names, constructions, and invocations of accessor methods can all be used as expressions.

In any context where it is necessary to describe an object or value, Java will accept any of the forms of expressions we have introduced. In a context where Java expects the programmer to describe a Color, we can equally well use a name associated with a Color, a Color construction, or an invocation of the getColor accessor method. Java is, however, picky about the type of value described by an expression. In a context where Java expects us to provide a Color, we can't provide an expression that describes a number or a Location instead.

Not all phrases found in a Java program are expressions. The invocation of a mutator method such as:

```
sun.move( 0, −5 );
```

is an example of a phrase that is not an expression. This phrase contains subparts that are expressions, the numeric literals 0 and −5, but is not an expression itself because it does not describe a value. Instead, this phrase instructs Java to perform an action. Such phrases are called *instructions* or *statements*. Statements instruct Java to perform actions that either produce output visible to the user or alter the internal state of the computer in a way that will affect the future behavior of the program. The body of each method we define in a Java program must be a sequence of statements.

We have seen three types of statements at this point. The invocation of a mutator method, such as

```
sun.move( 0, −5 );
```

is one type of statement. The second type is the assignment statement. It instructs the computer to perform the action of associating a name with an object or value. Note that the phrase on the right side of an assignment must be an expression.

The third type of statement we have encountered is the construction. We have used instructions like:

```
new Text( "Pressed", mousePosition, canvas );
```

to place graphics on the canvas. We have already stated, however, that a construction is an expression. Which is it? It is both. A construction like the one shown above describes an object.

Therefore it can be used in contexts where expressions are required. At the same time, the construction of a graphical object involves the action of changing the contents of the display. Accordingly, the construction by itself can be viewed as a statement.

There are constructions that merely describe an object without having an associated action that affects any aspect of the state of the program. For example,

```
new Location( 10, 20 );
```

It does not make much sense to use such a construction as a command, because a program that contained such a command would behave the same if the command were removed. Java, however, does not prevent the programmer from writing such nonsense. In fact, Java will allow the programmer to use many kinds of expressions as if they were commands by simply placing semicolons after the expressions. In a sensible program, however, the only expressions we have introduced so far that make sense as commands are constructions of graphical objects.

➡ EXERCISE 3.3.1

Which of the following statements could actually be useful in a program and which could not? Explain.

```
a. sun.getColor();
b. new Text( "Hello", point, canvas );
c. new Color( 60, 60, 60 );
d. myLocation = new Location( 50, 50 );
```

3.4 Arithmetic Expressions

Sometimes it is very useful to describe a numeric value to Java by providing a formula to compute the number. For example, to describe the *x* coordinate of a point slightly to the left of the current mouse position we might say something like:

```
mousePosition.getX() - 10
```

Java allows the programmer to use such formulae and calls them *arithmetic expressions*. As an example of the use of arithmetic expressions, we can make some additional improvements to our ScrollingSun program.

Using arithmetic expressions involving the getWidth and getHeight methods of the canvas, we can revise the ScrollingSun program so that it adjusts the size and position of the circle that represents the sun based on the size of the canvas. To maintain the proportions used in the original program as shown in Figure 3.3:

⁕ the diameter of the circle should be half the width of the canvas,
⁕ the left edge of the circle should fall one-quarter of the width of the canvas from the edge of the canvas,
⁕ initially, the top of the circle should be placed so that half the circle is visible above the horizon. To do this, the top of the circle should be half of its diameter above the bottom of the canvas.

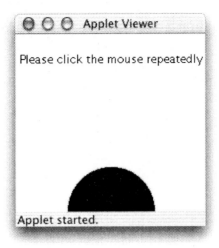

Figure 3.3 The sun rises over the horizon

It would also be appropriate to center the text of the instructions horizontally on the canvas. The indentation of the text from the left edge of the canvas should be equal to that on the right side. So, it should be half of the difference between the width of the text and the width of the canvas.

Each of these verbal descriptions can be turned into a formula, which can then be used in the program. The diameter of the circle, which is the value that should be specified as the width and height in the `FilledOval` construction, would be described as

```
canvas.getWidth()/2
```

The *x* coordinate value for the left edge of the circle would be given by the formula

```
canvas.getWidth()/4
```

The *y* coordinate for the top of the circle would be described as

```
canvas.getHeight() - canvas.getWidth()/4
```

Finally, the *x* coordinate for the left edge of the instructions should be

```
( canvas.getWidth() - instructions.getWidth() ) / 2
```

The complete `ScrollingSun` program using such formulae is shown in Figure 3.4. In most cases, we have simply replaced a number used as an expression by the appropriate formula. The only slight complication is the code to center the text. We cannot use the `getWidth` method associated with the `Text` object until it has been constructed. So, when we construct the `Text`, we just use 0 as its *x* coordinate value. Then, once it exists, we use the `getWidth` method to figure out how big it is. Finally, we use `moveTo` to place the `Text` where it belongs.

The arithmetic expressions shown in the preceding examples use only two of the arithmetic operators, subtraction and division. It is also possible to use multiplication and addition. The symbols used to indicate addition, subtraction and division are the standard symbols from mathematics: +, −, and /. Multiplication is represented using an asterisk, *. Thus, to say

```
// A program that produces an animation of the sun rising and setting.
// The animation is driven by dragging the mouse.
public class ScrollingSun extends WindowController {
    private FilledOval sun;      // Circle that represents the sun
    private Text instructions;   // Display of instructions

    // Place the sun and some brief instructions on the screen
    public void begin() {
        sun = new FilledOval( canvas.getWidth()/4,
                        canvas.getHeight() - canvas.getWidth()/4,
                        canvas.getWidth()/2,
                        canvas.getWidth()/2, canvas );

        instructions = new Text( "Drag the mouse up or down",
                            0, 0, canvas );
        instructions.moveTo( ( canvas.getWidth()-
                            instructions.getWidth() )/2, 20 );
    }

    // Move the sun to follow the mouse's vertical motion
    public void onMouseDrag( Location mousePosition ) {
        sun.moveTo( canvas.getWidth()/4, mousePosition.getY() );
        instructions.hide();
    }

    // Move the sun back to its starting position and redisplay
    // the instructions
    public void onMouseExit( Location point ) {
        sun.moveTo( canvas.getWidth()/4, canvas.getHeight() -
                canvas.getWidth()/4 );
        instructions.show();
    }
}
```

Figure 3.4   Program to make the sun scroll with the mouse

"2 times the width of the canvas" one would write

```
2 * canvas.getWidth()
```

The values being operated upon are called *operands*. In the example above of multiplication, the operands are 2 and `canvas.getWidth()`.

The behavior of the division operator frequently surprises beginners. When both operands of a division are integers, Java returns the integer value of the quotient and simply discards any remainder. Thus, when asked to compute 9/5, Java determines that the answer is 1 with a remainder of 4, discards the remainder, and returns 1 as the answer rather than 1.8. We will examine the logic behind this behavior in Chapter 5.

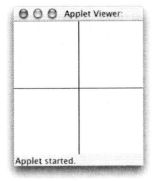

Figure 3.5 Drawing desired for Exercise 3.4.1

The following table summarizes the most commonly used arithmetic operators in Java.

+	addition
−	subtraction
*	multiplication
/	division

EXERCISE 3.4.1

Write the `begin` *method for a program that draws two lines that form a cross (consisting of a horizontal line and a vertical line as shown in Figure 3.5) on the canvas with the intersection of the two lines in the center of the canvas.* ❖

3.4.1 Ordering of Arithmetic Operations

Two of the arithmetic expressions used in the `ScrollingSun` program shown in Figure 3.4 illustrate an issue a programmer must be aware of when writing such expressions: the rules used to determine the order in which operations are performed. The first of these is the expression

```
( canvas.getWidth() - instructions.getWidth() )/2
```

which is used in the `begin` method to position the instructions. The second determines the initial *y* coordinate for the top of the sun:

```
canvas.getHeight() - canvas.getWidth()/4
```

Both involve a subtraction and a division. The first, however, uses parentheses to make it clear that the subtraction should be performed first and that the result of the subtraction should be divided by 2. The correct interpretation of the second expression is not as clear. In fact, Java will first divide the width of the canvas by 4 and then subtract the result of this division from the height of the canvas. In the absence of parentheses that dictate otherwise, Java always performs divisions in an expression before subtractions. Thus, the second formula is equivalent to the formula:

```
canvas.getHeight() - ( canvas.getWidth()/4 )
```

The rule that division is performed before subtraction is an example of a *precedence rule*. When evaluating simple arithmetic expressions, Java follows two basic precedence rules:

* Perform divisions and multiplications before additions and subtractions. We therefore say that division has higher precedence than addition but that division and multiplication are of equal precedence.
* When performing operations of equal precedence (i.e., additions and subtractions or divisions and multiplications), perform the operations in order from left to right as written.

Parentheses can be used to override these precedence rules, as seen in the first example above. Any part of a formula enclosed in parentheses will be evaluated before its result can be used to perform operations outside the parentheses.

➡ EXERCISE 3.4.2

What are the values of the following expressions?

a. 4 + 3 * 8 / 2 - 3
b. (4 + 3) * 8 / 2 - 3
c. 4 + (3 * 8) / 2 - 3
d. 4 + 3 * 8 / (2 - 3)
e. (4 + 3) * 8 / (2 - 3)
f. (4 + 3 * 8) / 2 - 3

3.5 Numeric Instance Variables

In the previous chapter, we saw that it is sometimes necessary to associate instance variable names with Locations or other objects to enable one method to communicate information to commands in another method. Unsurprisingly, it is often useful to associate names with numeric values in a similar way. We can illustrate this by adding yet another feature to our RisingSun program.

As the real sun rises, the sky becomes brighter and brighter. Suppose we wanted to try to simulate this in our program. For this example we will return to the original interface where the user clicks repeatedly to make the sun rise. Now, when the sun is near the bottom of the screen, we would like the background to be filled with a dark shade of gray. We can do this by constructing a FilledRect as big as the canvas and setting its color to an appropriate shade of gray. As the user clicks, we can make the background become lighter by using setColor to replace the original shade of gray with lighter and lighter shades until it is eventually white.

We have seen that each color is described by a triple of numbers giving the amounts of red, green, and blue in the color. Shades of gray correspond to triples in which all three values are the same. The bigger the number used, the brighter the shade. So,

    new Color(0, 0, 0)

describes black,

    new Color(50, 50, 50)

describes a dark shade of gray,

    new Color(200, 200, 200)

would be a fairly light shade of gray, and

new Color(255, 255, 255)

is white.

To control the brightness of the background, we would like to associate an instance variable name with the number to be used to generate the shade of gray currently desired. We will use the name brightness for this variable. This name can then be used to construct shades of gray for the background by using the construction:

new Color(brightness, brightness, brightness)

To use such a name, of course, we must first declare the name and then add assignment statements to ensure that it is associated with the correct number at each point in time as the program executes.

In each instance variable declaration, the declared name must be preceded by the name of the type of information with which the declared name will be associated. Java distinguishes between numbers that include fractional components like 3.14 and .95, and integers like 17 and −45. It uses the name double to describe numbers with fractional components and the name int to describe integers. In Chapter 5, we will discuss why Java distinguishes between integers and nonintegers in this way. For now, we merely observe that the values associated with brightness in our program will always be integers. Accordingly, to declare the name brightness we say

private int brightness;

In the begin method, we will associate the name brightness with a number corresponding to a dark shade of gray by including an assignment statement of the form:

brightness = 50;

Each time the user clicks the mouse, we want to associate a larger number with brightness. We can do this by including the assignment statement

brightness = brightness + 1;

in onMouseClick. This statement tells the computer to take the current value associated with the name brightness, add one to it, and then associate the name brightness with the result. The first time the mouse is clicked, brightness will be associated with the value 50 specified in the begin method. The result of adding 1 to 50 is 51. So, after the assignment statement is executed, brightness will be associated with the value 51. The next time the mouse is clicked, Java will add 1 to the new value of brightness, 51, and set it equal to 52. Thus, each time the mouse is clicked, the value of brightness will become 1 greater and the color generated by the contruction

new Color(brightness, brightness, brightness)

will become a little bit brighter.

The action of increasing the value associated with a numerical variable by 1 as described by the assignment

brightness = brightness + 1;

```
//   A program to simulate the brightening of the sky at sunrise
public class LightenUp extends WindowController {

    private FilledRect sky;     // Background rectangle
    private int brightness;     // Brightness of sky's color
    private FilledOval sun;      // Circle that represents the sun

    public void begin() {
        //   Create the sky and make it a dark gray
        brightness = 50;
        sky = new FilledRect( 0, 0, canvas.getWidth(),
                              canvas.getHeight(), canvas );
        sky.setColor( new Color( brightness, brightness, brightness ) );

        // Place the sun and some brief instructions on the screen
        sun = new FilledOval( 50, 150, 100, 100, canvas );
        new Text( "Please click the mouse repeatedly", 20, 20, canvas );
    }


    //   Brighten the sky and move the sun with each click
    public void onMouseClick( Location point ) {
        brightness = brightness + 1;
        sky.setColor( new Color( brightness, brightness, brightness ) );
        sun.move( 0, -5 );
    }
}
```

Figure 3.6   Using a numeric instance variable

is so common that Java provides a special shorthand notation. We can instruct Java to increase
the value associated with a name by 1 by simply following the name by a pair of adjacent plus
signs, as in:

    brightness++;

The notation

    brightness--;

can also be used to tell Java to reduce the value associated with a numeric variable by 1.

With these details we can complete the program. The code is shown in Figure 3.6.

EXERCISE 3.5.1

What would you expect to happen in LightenUp *if you changed the assignment of* brightness
to brightness = 200 *and then changed the first line in the* onMouseClick *method to the
following?*

    brightness = brightness − 1;

3.6 Initializers

We have seen that we must complete two steps before using a variable. We must include a declaration to tell Java that we plan to use the name and to specify the type of information with which the name will be associated. We must also include an assignment statement associating a particular meaning with the name before using it.

Although declaration and assignment are logically separate actions, it is often useful to combine them. When we declare a variable, we often know what value we will assign to it first. Putting a variable's declaration and the assignment of its initial value together (and topping it off with a comment describing the purpose of the variable being declared) can often improve the readability of a program.

To make this possible, Java allows the programmer to include an initial value for a variable in the variable's declaration. The result looks like an assignment statement preceded by private and the name of the type of the variable. It is, however, interpreted as a declaration by Java.

In the example considered in the preceding section, the variable brightness is introduced by the instance variable declaration

    private int brightness;

Then, the initial value of this variable is set to 50 by the assignment statement

    brightness = 50;

in the begin method. Using Java's notation for initialized variable declarations, we could remove this assignment from the begin method and rewrite the variable's declaration as

    private int brightness = 50;   // Brightness of sky's color

When an initial value is included in an instance variable declaration in this way, the variable's value is set before the begin method or any other method is invoked.

Although initialized declarations are most often used with numeric variables, Java will allow you to include an initializer in the declaration of a variable of any type. For example, if we wanted to keep a name associated with the current color of the sky, we might declare this new variable as

    private Color skyShade = new Color(brightness, brightness,
                                        brightness);

As this example suggests, Java will allow you to use expressions of many forms to describe the initial value of a variable. The main restriction is that any names used in the expression must already be declared and associated with a value. For example, the declaration shown for skyShade above would only be valid if preceded by a declaration of brightness. Furthermore, it will only function as desired if brightness is assigned its initial value in its declaration (as shown above) rather than in the begin method (as in the original version of the program).

The predefined name canvas is not initialized until just before your begin method is invoked. Java handles initialization expressions in declarations of instance variables before this happens. Therefore, it is generally not safe to use the name canvas in any initializer within your WindowController class. In particular, you could **not** eliminate the assignments that appear in the begin method of the program in Figure 3.6 by declaring these variables with initializers, because the expressions that are required to initialize the variables correctly reference the canvas.

➡ EXERCISE 3.6.1
_____

How would you initialize the following instance variables:

    a. *an integer called* count *starting with a value of 0*
    b. *a* Location *called* origin *starting at (0,0)*   ❖

3.7   Naming Numeric Constants

In Chapter 1, we introduced the comment. Comments are a rather interesting construct precisely because they have no effect on how the programs that contain them actually behave. As far as the computer is concerned, comments are useless. Nevertheless, a special notation is included in Java (and in almost every other programming language) to enable us to include these "useless" comments in our program. This reflects the fact that it is very important that your programs be made as easy as possible to understand.

Comments are just one mechanism Java provides to help you improve the readability of your programs. Another similar feature is the fact that Java ignores white space (i.e., blanks, tabs and new lines) added to a program. This makes it possible to use blank lines and indentation to structure code so that its physical appearance reflects its logical organization. Such formatting can be an important aid to an individual trying to understand the code.

The appropriate use of comments and good program layout are aspects of good programming style. To the beginner, the importance of good style may be difficult to appreciate. Short example programs can generally be read and understood even if they are not designed to be as readable as possible. As a programmer becomes more experienced and becomes involved in the construction of larger programs, the practice of good programming style becomes more critical. It is very easy to produce a large program that is impossible for any human reader (including its author!) to understand. Accordingly, it is best to develop the habit of always considering how to make the code you write as clear as possible from the very beginning.

Unfortunately, there is one rule of good style that we have been violating in almost all of our example programs. In this section, we will introduce a Java mechanism designed to support this rule of good style, and then we will begin following the rule ourselves.

In nearly all the examples we have presented, we have specified coordinates and dimensions of objects using numbers. We have also used numeric values to specify object colors and to determine how far certain items should move in reaction to a user action.

In most of these examples, we have simply typed numeric literals that specify the desired information into the constructions and method invocations where they were needed. While this approach certainly works, it is considered poor style. To appreciate why, just consider the instruction

```
new FilledOval( 50, 150, 100, 100, canvas );
```

By now, you have seen this instruction often enough that you may recognize it and know what it is for. It is the construction that creates the circle representing the sun in our rising sun example. Suppose, however, that you encountered this construction while reading through a complex Java program composed of thousands of lines of code. How would you guess the purpose of the program's author? How could you understand the significance of the numbers 50, 100, and 150 that appear in the statement?

The preferred alternative to using numbers explicitly in program instructions is to associate variable names with the numeric values and then to use the names in place of the numbers. For example, the above construction might be rewritten as

```
new FilledOval ( sunCornerX, sunCornerY, sunSize, sunSize, canvas );
```

Of course, if we want to use names like this instead of typing the numbers themselves, we will need to declare the names and initialize them. For example, we might say

```
// Values that determine position and size of the sun
private int sunCornerX = 50;
private int sunCornerY = 150;
private int sunSize = 100;
```

There is one flaw with this alternative. If you were reading a large program and found a construction like the one shown above, finding the declarations of the three names used in the construction would not be enough to assure that you knew what the actual values employed by the construction would be. The problem is that there might be some other point in the program where values other than 50, 150, and 100 were assigned to the variables, thus changing their initial values. If the program you were reading was large, it could be time consuming to search the program to make certain such assignments did not occur.

To avoid this problem, Java provides a mechanism through which the programmer can assure the reader that the initial value assigned to a variable in its declaration will not be changed anywhere else in the program. To do this, the programmer simply adds the word "final" to the declaration after the word "private". Using this feature, the declarations above would be rewritten as

```
// Constants that determine position and size of the sun
private final int sunCornerX = 50;
private final int sunCornerY = 150;
private final int sunSize = 100;
```

Including the word "final" in a declaration tells Java not to allow any assignment statement that would change the value of the variable being declared. That is, if the assignment

```
sunSize = 200;
```

was included at some point in a program containing the final declaration shown above, the assignment would be reported as an error to the programmer, and Java would refuse to run the program.

There are two conventions followed by most Java programmers when using final in declarations. First, so that it is easy to identify names with fixed values when reading a program, such names are usually composed of all uppercase letters, with underscores being used to separate the parts of a multiword name. Second, because doing so may in some cases improve program efficiency, it is customary to add the modifier static to declarations that contain the modifier final. Following these conventions, the declarations of our constants would be rewritten as

```
// Constants that determine position and size of the sun
private static final int SUN_CORNER_X = 50;
private static final int SUN_CORNER_Y = 150;
private static final int SUN_SIZE = 100;
```

Of course, the same use of uppercase letters would have to appear in uses of these names like

```
new FilledOval ( SUN_CORNER_X, SUN_CORNER_Y, SUN_SIZE, SUN_SIZE,
                 canvas );
```

EXERCISE 3.7.1

How would you convert the following initialized declaration into a constant declaration?

```
private int initialSize = 50;
```
❖

EXERCISE 3.7.2

Revisit DrawGrid *from Section 1.4 and add declarations of appropriate constants for this class.*
❖

3.8 Displaying Numeric Information

We have seen how we can use the computer's ability to work with numbers to produce better drawings on the computer's screen. Sometimes, however, it is the numbers themselves rather than any drawing that we really want to see. The main purpose of many computer programs is to perform numerical calculations. Examples include programs that determine your taxes, determine your GPA, and estimate the time required to travel from one point to another. Such programs often simply display the numbers they compute rather than drawing a graph of some sort on the screen. Even programs that are not primarily focused on numerical computations often need to display numerical information. For example, a word processor might need to display the current page number. In this section we will describe two mechanisms in Java that can be used to display numerical information.

3.8.1 Displaying Numbers as Text

As a very simple first example, let's make the computer count. You probably don't remember it, but at some point in your early childhood you most likely impressed some adult by demonstrating your remarkable ability to count to 10 or 20 or maybe even higher. To enable the computer to produce an equally impressive demonstration of its counting abilities, we will construct a program that will count. It will start at 1 and move on to the next number each time the mouse is clicked. The current value will be displayed on the computer's screen.

We have already introduced one mechanism that can be used to display numbers on the screen. We just didn't mention at the time that it could be used with numbers. In the very first program in Chapter 1, we used a construction of the form:

    new Text("I'm Touched", 40, 50, canvas);

and explained that the Text construction requires four parameters:

* the information to be displayed,
* *x*- and *y*-coordinate values specifying the upper left corner of the region in which the information should be displayed, and
* the canvas.

In all the examples of Text constructions we have seen thus far, the first parameter has been a sequence of characters surrounded by quotes. In fact, Java will accept many different types of information for the first parameter of a Text construction and will display whatever information is provided in textual form. "Text" in Java is not just letters, but any information that can be encoded using the symbols on a typical keyboard.

In particular, if we define a variable

    private int theCount = 1;

with the intent of using it to count up from 1, and then we execute a construction of the form:

    new Text(theCount, 100, 100, canvas);

Java will display the current value of the variable theCount, 1, at the point (100,100) in the program's window as shown in Figure 3.7.

Of course, displaying the number 1 isn't counting. The program we want to construct should start by displaying 1, but the first time the user clicks the mouse, we want to replace 1 by 2. On the next click, we want to replace 2 by 3, and so on.

In case you didn't notice, one of the examples considered in this chapter already demonstrates how to teach a computer to count. In the version of the rising sun program in which the background became brighter as the sun rose, the operations we performed on the variable named brightness

Figure 3.7 A computer counting program takes its first step

essentially told the computer to count upward starting at 50. The instruction that we used to progress through the different values of brightness was

```
brightness = brightness + 1;
```

A very similar assignment statement involving the variable theCount:

```
theCount = theCount + 1;
```

is what we need to complete the counting program described above.

Such a counting program is shown in Figure 3.8. The body of the onMouseClick method uses the assignment statement shown above to associate the next counting number with theCount each time the mouse is clicked. Note that changing the value associated with the variable theCount does not cause the value displayed by the Text object named countDisplay to change. To change the Text displayed, we use a method named setText. This is a mutator method that can be used to change the information displayed by a Text object. It expects a single parameter, the new information to be displayed. Like the first parameter expected in a Text construction, this information can be a quoted sequence of characters, or a numeric value, or just about any other form of information we might want to display in textual form. The statement

```
countDisplay.setText( theCount );
```

in the onMouseClick method tells Java to change the information displayed by the Text object named countDisplay that was created in the begin method.

An alternative to using setText would be to clear the canvas and then construct a new Text object displaying the new value of theCount. Construction of a new object, however, is a fairly time-consuming process for the computer. When possible, it is better to reuse an existing object rather than create a new one. Accordingly, in an example like this it is preferable to use setText.

3.8.2   Using System.out.println

In a program that mixes graphical output with numerical or other textual information, Text objects and the setText method are the most appropriate tools for displaying textual information. In programs that only display textual information, there is another tool that is often simpler and more appropriate, System.out.println.

All the output displayed by the Java programs we have considered so far appears in the window associated with the name canvas. These programs can, however, display output in another window

---

There are several other mutator methods that can be applied to Text objects. In Chapter 2 we already showed that show and hide could be used with Text objects. In addition, the move and moveTo methods can be used to reposition Text objects, just as they can be used with rectangles and ovals. Finally, there are several special mutator methods for use with Text objects. For example, the setFontSize method can be used to change the size of displayed text. It expects a single integer as a parameter, which it interprets as a font size. Thus,

```
countDisplay.setFontSize( 24 );
```

could be added to the end of our program's begin method if we wanted to increase the size of the numbers displayed.

```
// A program to count as high as you can click.
public class ICanCount extends WindowController {

    // Location where count should be displayed
    private static final Location COUNT_POS = new Location( 100, 100 );

    private int theCount = 1;      // How high we have counted
    private Text countDisplay;     // Current screen display of count

    // Create the Text to display the current count
    public void begin() {
        countDisplay = new Text( theCount, COUNT_POS, canvas );
    }

    // Increase the count with each click
    public void onMouseClick( Location point ) {
        theCount = theCount + 1;
        countDisplay.setText( theCount );
    }
}
```

Figure 3.8 A simple counting program

provided by the Java system. There is no special name that can be used to refer to this window from within your program. It is simply known as the *console window*.

The console window is more limited than the canvas in that it can only be used for text. On the other hand, it is more convenient for the display of text than is the canvas.

To display information in the console you use either a method named System.out.println or a similar method named System.out.print. Both of these methods take a single parameter specifying the information to be displayed. Anything that could be used as a parameter to the setText method or as the first parameter of a Text construction can be used as a parameter to System.out.println or System.out.print. In particular, you can certainly use either a quoted sequence of characters or a numeric value.

A revised version of our counting program that uses the Java console to display values as it counts is shown in Figure 3.9. The only text this version displays on the canvas is a message telling the user to click in order to make the program count. This will be displayed instead of the number 1 when the program first starts. The first time the user clicks, 1 is placed in the Java console by the System.out.println in the onMouseClick method. Each succeeding click will place another value in the console window.

When System.out.println or System.out.print is used, you do not have to provide coordinates to specify where the text should be displayed. The Java console window displays the information you provide to these methods, much as text might be displayed in a word processor's window. Each time your program executes a System.out.println or System.out.print, the text specified is placed in the Java console window following any text placed there by previous uses of System.out.println and System.out.print. The only difference between these two methods is that if the preceding output was placed in the console window using

```
// A program to count as high as you can click.
public class ICanCount extends WindowController {

    // Where to display the instructions
    private static final Location INSTR_POS = new Location( 20, 100 );

    private int theCount = 0;        // How high we have counted

    // Create the Text to display the instructions
    public void begin() {
        new Text( "Click to make me count", INSTR_POS, canvas );
    }

    // Increase the count with each click
    public void onMouseClick( Location point ) {
        theCount = theCount + 1;
        System.out.println( theCount );
    }
}
```

Figure 3.9   Counting in the Java console

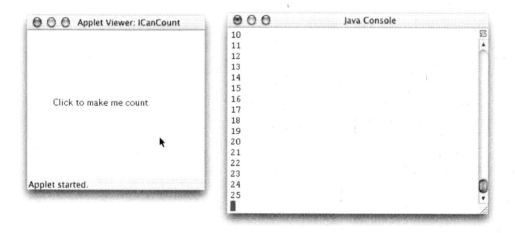

Figure 3.10   Counting using the Java console

System.out.print, then the new output will be placed on the same line as the previous output. If System.out.println was used last, then new output will begin on the next line in the console window. Once the console window fills up, the older text scrolls off the top of the window, leaving the newer lines visible. A scroll bar is provided so that a person running your program can look at the older items if desired. Figure 3.10 shows how both the canvas and the Java console window might look after this program is run and its user clicks 25 times.

3.8.3 Mixing Text and Numbers

Often, a number displayed all by itself has little meaning. The difference between just displaying "3" and displaying "Strike 3" or "3 P.M." or "Line 3" can be quite significant. Accordingly, in many programs, rather than just displaying a number on the screen it is desirable to display a number combined with additional text that clarifies its meaning. Luckily, this can be done easily in Java with both Text objects and System.out.println.

When specifying the information to be displayed in a Text object or on the Java console, we can use the + operator to combine quoted text with numeric information. Suppose, for example, that we wanted our counting programs to display a message like "You have clicked 3 times" instead of just displaying 3. For the version that uses Text objects to place the information on the screen, we could accomplish this by replacing the command

```
countDisplay.setText( theCount );
```

shown in Figure 3.8 with the command

```
countDisplay.setText( "You have clicked " + theCount + " times" );
```

Similarly, for the println version shown in Figure 3.9 we could replace the command

```
System.out.println( theCount );
```

with the command

```
System.out.println( "You have clicked " + theCount + " times" );
```

You have to be a bit careful when using this feature. Basically, Java has two different ways of interpreting the + operator. When the operands to + are both numbers, Java performs normal, arithmetic addition. If, however, either of the operands to a + is textual rather than numeric, Java instead just sticks together the textual representations of both operands. This operation of sticking text together is called *concatenation*.

When Java sticks together bits of text, it doesn't think about things like words. It just sticks the letters and digits it is given together. This means you have to include all the characters you want displayed, including any spaces. If you look carefully at the setText command shown above, you will notice that there is a space after the word clicked and before the quotation symbol that follows it and another space between the word times and the quote that precedes it. If these were not included, Java would display the text

```
You have clicked3times
```

instead of displaying

```
You have clicked 3 times
```

as desired.

It is also important to be aware of how Java decides when a + means addition and when it simply means to stick pieces of text together. For example, if the value of theCount is 10, then the command

```
countDisplay.setText( "You have clicked " + ( theCount + 1 ) +
                      " times" );
```

will display the message

```
You have clicked 11 times
```

on the screen, while the command

```
countDisplay.setText( "You have clicked " + theCount + 1 +
                      " times" );
```

will produce the message

```
You have clicked 101 times
```

This is because, in the version with parentheses around "theCount + 1", Java has to do the + operation within these parentheses first. Both operands of this + operator are numbers, so Java does addition yielding the number 11. Without the parentheses, Java processes the + operators in order from left to right. The first operand to the first + is a quoted string, so Java performs concatenation sticking the textual representation of the value of theCount, "10", together with the quoted text. The result of this first operation is then treated as the first operand of the next + operation. Since this first operand is text, Java now interprets the second + as another concatenation operator and just sticks a "1" on the end of the text rather than performing a numeric addition.

EXERCISE 3.8.1

What output would you expect from the following statements? Assume count *is 34.*

```
a. System.out.println( "The count is: + count - 3" );
b. System.out.println( "The count is: " + ( count + 2 ) );
c. System.out.println( "The count is:" + count + 4 );
```

EXERCISE 3.8.2

Suppose you are trying to write a simple program to help someone practice the multiplication tables. The program repeatedly displays a message of the form:

```
What is 5 x 9?
```

in a Text *object named* question *that is created in the program's* begin *method. The program uses two variables named* factor1 *and* factor2 *that are assigned randomly generated numbers between 0 and 9 to determine which question to display. For example, the question shown above would be displayed if* factor1 *equaled 5 and* factor2 *equaled 9.*

Write the statement needed to update the message displayed by question *after new values for* factor1 *and* factor2 *are chosen. (Don't worry about how the numbers are chosen or how the user tells the program the correct answer.)*

"Pick a number. Any number."

You might expect to hear this phrase from the hawker at a carnival game table. You might not expect it to be a useful instruction to give a computer within a Java program, but just the opposite is true. There are many programming contexts in which it is handy to be able to ask the computer to pick a random number for you. Obvious examples are game programs. Programs that deal cards, simulate the tossing of dice, or simulate the spinning of a roulette wheel all need ways of picking items randomly. Many programs that simulate the behavior of real systems for practical purposes need ways to incorporate the randomness of the real world in their calculations. With this in mind, Java and most other programming systems include what are called random number generators.

In our library, we have incorporated two classes designed to make it quite easy to obtain a sequence of random values in a program. One of our classes is designed for situations where you need random integers and the other for random real numbers.

Suppose that you wanted to write a program to simulate some board game in which at each turn the player rolls two dice. Our class for generating random integers can be used to create a Java object that behaves just like a single die.[1] To illustrate the use of this class, we will construct a simple program that simulates the rolling of a pair of dice each time the mouse is clicked.

In our library, the class of random integer generators is named `RandomIntGenerator`. Like other objects, the first step in using one of our `RandomIntGenerator`s is to define a variable name that will refer to the object. We might define a variable like

```
private RandomIntGenerator die;
```

to refer to the random number generator in a program that simulated dice.

When we construct a new `RandomIntGenerator` we must provide two `int` values as parameters. These values determine the range of values that might be produced by the `RandomIntGenerator` created. Since a single die must show a number between 1 and 6 and we want our random number generator to simulate a single die, we would say

```
new RandomIntGenerator( 1, 6 );
```

In general, the first parameter value determines the smallest value that should ever be produced by the random number generator, while the second number specifies the largest value. We could include this construction in our program's `begin` method or as an initializer in the variable declaration. As a matter of good style, we would define a constant

```
private static final int NUM_SIDES = 6;
```

so that we could replace the literal 6 with a name that suggests its significance. The declaration that creates our random number generator would therefore look like

```
private RandomIntGenerator die = new RandomIntGenerator( 1,
                                                    NUM_SIDES );
```

---

[1] The English word for the little cubes you roll while playing many board games has an irregular plural form. If you have several of these cubes, you call them dice. If you have just one, then it is a die.

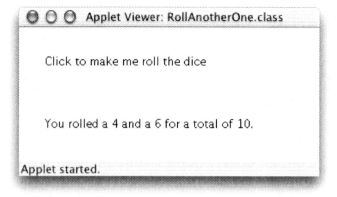

Figure 3.11   Sample message drawn by dice simulation program

Now, when the user clicks the mouse, we need to tell the object named die to pick a random number for us. In fact, if we want to simulate the rolling of a pair of dice we will have to do this twice. We can ask a RandomIntGenerator to pick a number by invoking its nextValue method. That is, an expression like

```
die.nextValue()
```

will produce a (possibly different) random number each time it is evaluated.

The complete code of a simple program to simulate rolling two dice is shown in Figure 3.12. A sample of the program's output is shown in Figure 3.11. Note that even though the program simulates the rolling of two dice, it only uses a single random number generator named die. As long as we have created a single random number generator that generates values in the desired range, we can (and should) use it over and over again whenever we need a random number selected from that range. In the example, we therefore use the nextValue method of die to determine the values seen on the first die (roll1) and the second die (roll2).

▨➡ EXERCISE 3.9.1

Write a program that draws a rectangle named box *at the* Location *(50,50). The box should be 50 pixels wide and its height should be determined by a* RandomIntGenerator *that generates values for the height between 10 and 100 pixels. The height of* box *should change each time the mouse is clicked.* ❖

3.10   Summary

Early applications of computers involved scientific and engineering problems that required large amounts of numerical computation. The first computers clearly earned the name "computer". When using a word processor, reading your email or browsing the Web, it is easy to forget that computers perform arithmetic computations. Even in programs that do not appear to involve

```java
// A program to simulate the rolling of a pair of dice.
public class RollAnotherOne extends WindowController {

    // Coordinates to determine positions of text displayed
    private static final int TEXT_X = 30;
    private static final int PROMPT_Y = 30;
    private static final int RESULT_Y = 100;

    // How many sides our dice have
    private static final int NUM_SIDES = 6;

    // The object that represents a single die
    private RandomIntGenerator die =
                        new RandomIntGenerator( 1, NUM_SIDES );

    // A Text message updated to describe each simulated roll
    private Text result;

    // Value of each die on a given roll
    private int roll1;
    private int roll2;

    // Display a prompt and create the Text used to display the results
    public void begin() {
        new Text( "Click to make me roll the dice",
                    TEXT_X, PROMPT_Y, canvas );
        result = new Text( "", TEXT_X, RESULT_Y, canvas );
    }

    // Roll the dice with each click
    public void onMouseClick( Location point ) {
        roll1 = die.nextValue();
        roll2 = die.nextValue();

        result.setText( "You rolled a " + roll1 + " and a " + roll2 +
                    " for a total of " + ( roll1 + roll2 ) );
    }
}
```

Figure 3.12   Simulating the rolling of a pair of dice

numbers, however, numerical computations continue to play a role. For example, a word processor has to do arithmetic just to determine how many words will fit on a line.

In this chapter, we have explored a few of the mechanisms Java provides to perform numerical computations. At this point, we have only seen how to work with integer values in a program. We will introduce the use of Java's version of real numbers, doubles, in Chapter 5.

We explored the differences between statements and expressions in Java programs. Statements are phrases in a program that instruct the computer to perform an action that will change the visible state of the computer or change the value associated with some variable name. Expressions are phrases that describe a value or object to be used in the program. We have seen that Java recognizes several forms of expressions: literals like "12", variable names, constructions, invocations of accessor methods, and arithmetic formulae involving the operations of addition, subtraction, multiplication and division.

We showed how to instruct Java to produce textual output that included numerical information using both `Text` objects and the `System.out.println` method. `Text` objects are used when such information is to be included in the display of a program that also produces graphical output. `System.out.println` provides a simpler mechanism for producing text output that is appropriate for programs that only produce textual output.

3.11 Chapter Review Problems

➡ EXERCISE 3.11.1

What is the difference between an accessor method and a mutator method? Give an example of each from the Location *class.*   ❖

➡ EXERCISE 3.11.2

   a. *Write the instructions for creating and positioning a 50-by-50-pixel* FramedRect *so that it is centered in any window.*

   b. *Write the instructions for creating a* Text *object, that says "I am centered" and positions it so that it is centered in any window.*   ❖

➡ EXERCISE 3.11.3

Why is the following a bad instance variable declaration?

```
private Line edge = new Line ( 0, 0, 100, 100, canvas );
```
                                                                                                 ❖

➡ EXERCISE 3.11.4

Write a program called RisingMoon *which is similar to* RisingSun *except that we have a crescent moon instead of a sun and the sky is now black. Each time the user clicks, the crescent moon rises slightly.*

Hint: *a crescent can be created by displaying an oval with the same color as the background over another oval.*   ❖

➡ EXERCISE 3.11.5

Assume these variables are at your disposal:

```
private int myCounter = 17;
private int yourCounter = 12;
```

What is the output of the following statements?

a. System.out.println ("The count is" + myCounter + "clicks");
b. System.out.println ("The count is + yourCounter + clicks");
c. System.out.println ("The count is " + myCounter + yourCounter +
                         " clicks");
d. System.out.println ("The count is " + (myCounter − yourCounter)
                         + " clicks");

➡ EXERCISE 3.11.6

Why is the following code inefficient? How would you improve it?

```
public void onMouseClick( Location point ) {
    // Increase the count and display it with each click
    counter++;
    canvas.clear();
    new Text ( "The count is: " + counter, DISPLAY_LOCATION,
            canvas );
}
```

➡ EXERCISE 3.11.7

What modifications would you have to make to RollAnotherOne so that you are now using a twelve-sided die instead of a boring six-sided one and the text is indented another 15 pixels to the right?

(3.12) Programming Problems

➡ EXERCISE 3.12.1

Take the ICanCount program one step further by writing a program called ICanCountALot. It will keep track of the number of mouse clicks, mouse exits and button presses. The display of the program should look similar to the one in Figure 3.13. Don't forget to use constants!

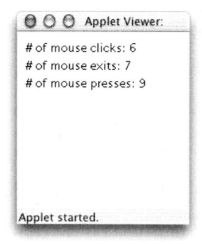

Figure 3.13 Display for ICanCountALot

⟹ EXERCISE 3.12.2

Write a program called GrowMan *which initially draws a little man as shown in Figure 3.14. Each time the user clicks, the man grows by a set amount. After ten more clicks, the display should look like that in Figure 3.15. The following constants and instance variable declarations are given to you.*

```java
public class GrowMan extends WindowController {

    // Amount each body part grows by (should be even)
    private static final int GROW = 2;

    // Initial size of head
    private static final int HEAD_SIZE = 6;

    private static final int LIMB_SIZE = 5; // Initial displacement
                                            // of ends of limbs from
                                            // body, both horizontally
                                            // and vertically

    private static final int HEAD_START = 50; // x and y coordinate of
                                               // initial starting point

    // Coordinates of body parts
    private static final int BODY_X = HEAD_START + HEAD_SIZE / 2;
    private static final int NECK_Y = HEAD_START + HEAD_SIZE;
    private static final int ARMPIT_Y = HEAD_START + 2 * HEAD_SIZE;
    private static final int BODY_END = HEAD_START + 3 * HEAD_SIZE;
    private static final int FEET_Y = BODY_END + LIMB_SIZE;
```

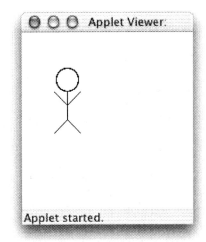

Figure 3.14   Initial display for GrowMan   **Figure 3.15**   Display for GrowMan after ten clicks

```
private static final int ARMS_Y = ARMPIT_Y - LIMB_SIZE;
private static final int LEFT_X = BODY_X - LIMB_SIZE;
private static final int RIGHT_X = BODY_X + LIMB_SIZE;

// Instance variables
private FramedOval head;
private Line      body,
                  leftArm,
                  rightArm,
                  leftLeg,
                  rightLeg;
```

⟹ EXERCISE 3.12.3

a. *Create a program called* RandomBox *with the following features:*

  * *When the program begins, it creates a filled rectangle of random size (make your limits 20–120 pixels) centered on the screen*
  * *When the mouse is clicked, the console reports the dimensions and location of the box*
  * *When the mouse exits the window, the box disappears*
  * *When the mouse re-enters the window, it generates a new size for the box and recenters it on the screen*

b. *Modify the above code so that it generates a random color in addition to the random size for the box. Add code so that the red, green, and blue color components are reported in the console as well. Make sure your box has a frame so that it can easily be seen even if it is given a very light color.*

Hint: *The* Color *class has accessor methods that you may find useful.*

CHAPTER 4

Making Choices

To write interesting programs we must have a way to make choices in Java. For example, we might need to perform different instructions depending on whether a user has clicked inside a particular rectangle. In this chapter we show how to make choices in Java using the `if` statement.

Conditional statements like the `if` statement are programming constructs capable of choosing between blocks of code to execute. These statements provide enormous expressive power to programmers, and yet are very easy to use and understand because they mimic the way we think. For instance, the following forms a conditional statement in English:

```
"If it's sunny outside then we will play frisbee,
    otherwise we will play cards."
```

An example of a conditional statement a bit more relevant to our concerns with programming might be:

```
"If the mouse location is contained in the rectangle then
        display message "success".
    Otherwise display message "missed"."
```

In Java, the `if` statement is the most commonly used conditional statement. It comes in a variety of forms that we will explore, each useful for certain situations. With the help of conditionals we will write programs to determine a win or loss in the game of craps and to figure out what to do on a weekend based on the weather and your finances.

After presenting a brief example illustrating the use of the `if` statement, we formally introduce several of its variations that will allow us to handle more complex situations. We also introduce the `boolean` data type for expressions that can be either `true` or `false`. Finally, we provide some advice on how to use conditionals clearly and effectively so that your programs can be understood correctly by the Java compiler and, more importantly, by other programmers.

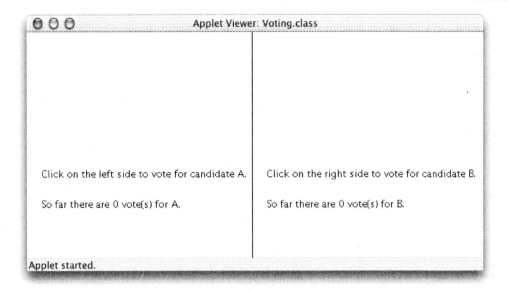

Figure 4.1 Screen shot of Voting program

4.1 A Brief Example: Using the if Statement to Count Votes

We illustrate the use of conditionals with a simple program to count votes in an election. To accomplish this we will divide the program's canvas in half vertically so that the left and right sides represent candidates A and B respectively (see Figure 4.1). A mouse click on either side will be treated as a vote for that half's candidate.

Recall the program ICanCount in Figure 3.8, which keeps track of the number of times the user has clicked the mouse. The code for its onMouseClick method is given below:

```
public void onMouseClick( Location point ) {
    theCount = theCount + 1;
    countDisplay.setText( theCount );
}
```

Whereas this method simply counts *all* mouse clicks on the canvas, by using the if statement our voting program's onMouseClick method will be able to discriminate between votes for candidates A and B.

The code for class Voting is given in Figure 4.2. The constructs used in the begin method should be familiar by now. It creates four new Text objects, of which the top two display voting instructions and the bottom two the current tally for each candidate. The last line of the method draws the vertical line dividing the canvas.

The onMouseClick method, on the other hand, contains a new programming construct. The if statement is used to determine which candidate gets each vote and then updates the appropriate Text object to display the new total. To decide who receives each vote, the program compares

```
public class Voting extends WindowController {
    // Coordinates of canvas, including x-coord of middle
    private static final int MID_X = 300;
    private static final int TOP = 0;
    private static final int BOTTOM = 400;

    // x coordinates of A and B text messages
    private static final int TEXT_A_X = 20;
    private static final int TEXT_B_X = MID_X + 20;

    // y coordinates of instructions and vote count info
    private static final int INSTRUCTION_Y = 180;
    private static final int DISPLAY_Y = 220;

    private int countA = 0;        // Number of votes for A
    private int countB = 0;        // Number of votes for B

    private Text infoA;            // Display of votes for A
    private Text infoB;            // Display of votes for B

    // Create displays with instructions on how to vote
    public void begin() {
        new Text( "Click on the left side to vote for candidate A.",
                TEXT_A_X, INSTRUCTION_Y, canvas );
        new Text( "Click on the right side to vote for candidate B.",
                TEXT_B_X, INSTRUCTION_Y, canvas );
        infoA = new Text( "So far there are " + countA +
                    " vote(s) for A.", TEXT_A_X, DISPLAY_Y, canvas );
        infoB = new Text( "So far there are " + countB +
                    " vote(s) for B.", TEXT_B_X, DISPLAY_Y, canvas );
        new Line( MID_X, TOP, MID_X, BOTTOM, canvas );
    }

    // Update votes and display vote counts
    public void onMouseClick( Location point ) {
        if ( point.getX() < MID_X ) {
            countA++;
            infoA.setText( "So far there are " + countA +
                        " vote(s) for A." );
        }
        else {
            countB++;
            infoB.setText( "So far there are " + countB +
                        " vote(s)  for B." );
        }
    }
}
```

Figure 4.2   Code for Voting class

the *x* coordinate of the location of the mouse click to the middle of the canvas. Note that we have defined the constant MID_X to refer to the *x* coordinate of the middle of the canvas.

The if statement allows the programmer to make choices about which statements are executed in a program based on a *condition*, an expression whose value is either true or false. In the sample program, when the mouse is clicked the program must determine whether to give a vote to candidate A or B. The condition is whether the *x* coordinate of the mouse click, obtained by evaluating point.getx(), is less than MID_X. The condition is written in Java as point.getX() < MID_X. If the condition is *not* satisfied (i.e., if point.getX() is greater than or equal to MID_X) then the code after the else keyword is executed.

The two lines of code following the line containing the if are grouped together by a pair of matching curly braces. A sequence of statements surrounded by curly braces in this manner is called a *block*. Similarly, the two statements immediately following the else also form a block. If the *condition* of an if statement is true, the block of statements immediately after the condition is executed. Otherwise, the block immediately after the else is executed. Recall that the statement x++ indicates that the value of variable x should be increased by 1.

➡ EXERCISE 4.1.1

What are the conditions in the following statements? For example, in the statement, "When it is cold outside, I wear a hat," the condition is "it is cold outside".

a. *When it is Tuesday, I have piano lessons.*
b. *Since today is Halloween, it must be October.*
c. *If Bobby says yes, we will go to the prom.*
d. *Yesterday's game determined the wild card, so if the Red Sox won, they made it to the playoffs.* ❖

4.2 The if Statement

Now that we have seen the if statement in action, let's carefully examine its syntax and meaning.

The code in the Voting class example given in Figure 4.2 contains a form of conditional statement called the if-else statement. Its syntax is:

```
if ( condition ) {
    if-part     // Statements to be executed when condition is true
}
else {
    else-part   // Statements to be executed when condition is false
}
```

The text *condition* in the syntax template represents an expression whose value is true or false. The phrases if-part and else-part represent sequences of Java statements. We've included comments to make it clear when each of these sequences of statements is executed, even though these comments are not part of the formal syntax.

When an if-else statement is executed, the computer first determines whether *condition* is true. If so, it executes the statements in the block of code surrounded by the first pair of curly

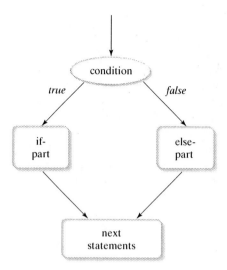

Figure 4.3 Semantics of the if-else statement

```
// Update votes and display vote counts
public void onMouseClick( Location point ) {
    if ( point.getX() < MID_X ) {
        countA++;
        infoA.setText( "So far there are " + countA + " votes for A." );
    }
    else {
        countB++;
        infoB.setText( "So far there are " + countB + " votes for B." );
    }

    infoTotal.setText( "Votes so far: " + ( countA + countB ) );
}
```

Figure 4.4 Code to display individual and total vote counts

braces, "{" and "}", called the if-part, and then skips over the rest of the statement. Otherwise (i.e., if *condition* is false), it skips over the if-part and will instead execute the block of statements after the else keyword, called the else-part. Exactly one of the two blocks of code is processed when the if-else statement is executed. When that block is completed, execution resumes immediately after the if-else statement. This execution sequence is illustrated in Figure 4.3.

The following example shows how execution resumes with the statements that follow an if-else statement. Suppose we want to modify our Voting program so that it always displays the total number of votes. Let infoTotal be a variable of type Text that has been initialized in the begin method. Figure 4.4 shows a revised version of onMouseClick that displays the current vote total. Each time the user clicks on the canvas, the line sending the setText message to infoTotal will be executed regardless of which half of the screen the mouse was clicked on.

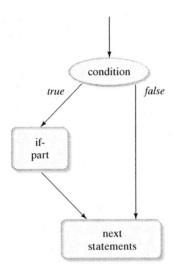

Figure 4.5   Semantics of the if with no else

There are many situations in which we don't need an else-part. Fortunately, there is a simple variant of the if-else statement, the if statement, which does not have the else keyword or the else-part.

```
if ( condition ) {
    if-part  // Statements executed when condition is true
}
```

If *condition* is true, then the if-part is executed as before. If it is false, however, the program simply moves on to the *next statement* after the if-part because there is no else-part to execute. The execution sequence is illustrated in Figure 4.5.

➡ EXERCISE 4.2.1

Write the following statements as if-else *or* if *statements. For example, the statement, "On Mondays I ride my bike to class. On other days, I walk." can be rewritten as "If it is Monday, I ride my bike to class. Else, I walk."*

   a. *On Sunday I eat pancakes. On other days, I eat cereal.*
   b. *I go to class on weekdays, but on weekends, I watch movies.*
   c. *In the summer I always wear sandals, but during the other seasons, I wear sneakers.*
   d. *If it is raining, I bring an umbrella.*

4.2.1   Example: Using the if Statement with 2-D Objects

Suppose we want to write a program that begins by displaying a square on the canvas. If the user clicks inside the square, then the computer moves the square 50 pixels to the right. If the click is not inside the square, nothing happens.

How can we determine if a point is inside a square? We could compare the coordinates of the point to the locations of the left, right, top, and bottom edges of the square. However, such tests are so common that all of the two-dimensional geometric objects (e.g., FramedRect, FilledRect, FramedOval, FilledOval) provide the accessor method contains that does this for us.

For example, let square be a variable of type FramedRect, and let point be a variable of type Location. Then the expression square.contains(point) evaluates to true if the object held in square *contains* the point, and false otherwise.

For the sake of brevity we will only write out the onMouseClick method of this program. We assume that square has been declared elsewhere to be a variable of type FramedRect and that it has been initialized in the begin method.

```
public void onMouseClick( Location point ) {
    if ( square.contains( point ) ) {
        square.move( X_OFFSET, 0 );
    }
}
```

An English translation of the above method would read: "If the square contains the point where the mouse was clicked *then* tell the square to move to the right by X_OFFSET pixels. Otherwise do nothing." (Of course, the computer code doesn't say, "Do nothing." Instead it simply omits the else-part.)

We will present further variations of if statements later in this chapter, but first we will explore the kinds of expressions that can be used to form the *condition* part of these statements.

➡ EXERCISE 4.2.2

a. *What would happen if you clicked the mouse inside* square *given the* onMouseClick *method shown below? Assume* X_OFFSET *is 60.*

```
public void onMouseClick( Location point ) {
    if ( square.contains( point ) ) {
        square.move( X_OFFSET, 0 );
    }
    square.move( -X_OFFSET/2, 0 );
}
```

b. *What would happen if you now clicked the mouse outside of* square *and* onMouseClick *was changed to the following?*

```
public void onMouseClick( Location point ) {
    if ( square.contains( point ) ) {
        square.move( X_OFFSET, 0 );
    }
    else {
        square.move( -X_OFFSET/2, 0 );
    }
}
```

4.3 Understanding Conditions

Comparison operators like < are used in expressions that evaluate to either true or false, called boolean expressions. Java contains several comparison operators. They include:

    < , > , ==, <=, >=, !=

We must use == to test for equality because = has already been used as the assignment operator. Because ≠ isn't available on all keyboards, the symbol != (read as "does not equal") stands for inequality. Because keyboards also do not always include the symbols ≤ or ≥, Java uses the combinations <= and >= in their places.

Be very careful not to confuse = and ==. The first is only used in assignment statements, while the second is used only for comparisons.

Using these comparison operators, we can write x > 4, y != z+17, and x+2 <= y. Depending on the values of the variables, each of these expressions will evaluate to either true or false. Arithmetic operators have higher precedence than comparison operators. Thus in the last example above, x+2 is evaluated before the result is compared with y.

Suppose the current value of x is 3, y is 6, and z is −10. Here are the results of evaluating the above expressions:

* x > 4 is false because 3 is not greater than 4.
* y != z+17 is true because 6 is different from −10 + 7.
* x+2 <= y is true because 3+2 is less than or equal to 6.

⇒ EXERCISE 4.3.1

Suppose the current value of x *is 2,* y *is 4, and* z *is 15. Determine whether each of the following conditions evaluates to* true *or* false.

    a. x + 2 < y.
    b. z − 3 * x != y + 5.
    c. x * y == z − 9.
    d. z >= 3 * y.

4.3.1 The boolean Data Type

Java contains a data type called boolean. Unlike the int type, which has a large number of elements, the boolean type has only two values: true and false. Just as one can write down integer values directly as 17, −158, or 47, we can write down boolean values directly in Java as true or false. We can also declare variables of type boolean.

There are a large number of expressions in Java that return values of type boolean. As we have just seen, combining two integer-valued expressions with one of the comparison operators, <, >, <=, >=, ==, and !=, results in a value of type boolean. We have also seen the method contains that returns a value of type boolean.

If ok is a variable of type boolean and x has type int, then the following are valid statements:

```
ok = true;
ok = (x >= 3);
```

```
public class WhatADrag extends WindowController {
    ...    // Constant declarations omitted

    private FilledRect box;        // Box to be dragged

    private Location lastPoint;    // Point where mouse was last seen

    // Whether the box has been grabbed by the mouse
    private boolean boxGrabbed;

    // Make the box
    public void begin() {
        box = new FilledRect( START_LEFT, START_TOP,
                              BOX_WIDTH, BOX_HEIGHT, canvas );
    }

    // Save starting point and whether point was in box
    public void onMousePress( Location point ) {
        lastPoint = point;
        boxGrabbed = box.contains( point );
    }

    // If mouse is in box, then drag the box
    public void onMouseDrag( Location point ) {
        if ( boxGrabbed ) {
            box.move( point.getX() - lastPoint.getX(),
                      point.getY() - lastPoint.getY() );
            lastPoint = point;
        }
    }
}
```

Figure 4.6   Code for dragging a box

In each case the expression of the right-hand side evaluates to a boolean value and hence can be assigned to a variable of type boolean.

We will use both the contains method and boolean variables in the implementation of a new class WhatADrag. The complete code listing for this program is given in Figure 4.6. The program begins by displaying a box on the screen. If the user presses the mouse down while it is pointing inside of the box, and then drags the mouse, the box will follow the mouse on the canvas. If the mouse is not pointing in the box when the mouse button is pressed, then dragging the mouse should have no effect, even if the mouse happens to cross the box at some point during the drag.

Let's look at the code in the mouse-handling methods to see how we can program this behavior. As soon as the mouse button is pressed, the onMousePress method is executed. The first

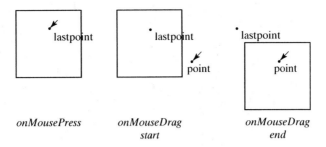

Figure 4.7 Three stages of dragging a rectangle

assignment in onMousePress,

```
lastPoint = point;
```

results in saving the current location of the mouse (as held in parameter point) as the value of variable lastPoint. The location is saved so that it can be used when onMouseDrag is executed later.

The second assignment in onMousePress,

```
boxGrabbed = box.contains( point );
```

determines and then remembers whether the box contained the point where the mouse was initially pressed. Because the result of evaluating box.contains(point) is a value of type boolean, it can be stored in boxGrabbed, a variable of type boolean. The value of boxGrabbed, which reflects whether the user actually pressed the mouse down inside box, will be used in onMouseDrag to determine whether the box should be moved.

As usual, the onMouseDrag method will be executed when the user drags the mouse. At that time the values of the variables boxGrabbed and lastPoint become relevant.

If the value of boxGrabbed is true, box will be moved by the distance between the last location of the mouse, saved in lastPoint, and the current position, held in point. The distance in each of the horizontal and vertical directions is needed to actually perform the move. The horizontal and vertical distances are obtained by evaluating point.getX() - lastPoint.getX() and point.getY() - lastPoint.getY(), respectively.

Figure 4.7 illustrates three stages of dragging a box in class WhatADrag. In the leftmost picture, the mouse button has been pressed with the mouse inside the rectangle. After the execution of onMousePress, the location of the mouse is stored in the instance variable lastPoint. In the middle picture, the mouse has been dragged down and to the right, and onMouseDrag has just begun execution. The current location of the mouse is held in the parameter point, but the if statement has not yet been executed. The rightmost picture shows what has happened immediately after the move message has been sent to box in the if statement during the execution of onMouseDrag. The rectangle has been dragged to the right and down by the difference between the x coordinates and by the difference between the y coordinates of point and lastPoint. The update of the value of lastPoint to the location held in point is not shown.

Rather than using a `boolean` *variable, we might have written a condition that tested to see if* `box` *contained* `point` *each time the mouse was dragged, as shown below.*

```
public void onMouseDrag( Location point ) {
    if ( box.contains( point ) ) {
        box.move( point.getX() – lastPoint.getX(),
                point.getY() – lastPoint.getY() );
        lastPoint = point;
    }
}
```

This would not quite work as desired. On the other hand, replacing the condition in the `if` *statement with* `box.contains( lastPoint )` *would produce a program with exactly the same behavior as the version that used the* `boolean` *variable* `boxGrabbed`*. Explain why the version using* `point` *as a parameter to* `contains` *would not work. In what circumstances and how does the other one behave differently?* ❖

Suppose we replace the method `onMouseDrag` *in class* `WhatADrag` *by the following code:*

```
// If mouse is in box, then drag the box
public void onMouseDrag( Location point ) {
    if ( boxGrabbed ) {
        box.moveTo( point );
    }
}
```

This is simpler than the code in Figure 4.6. For example, we no longer need to keep track of `lastPoint`*. However, it does not result in as nice behavior. Explain why.* ❖

Suppose the statement `lastPoint = point;` *inside of method* `onMouseDrag` *in Figure 4.6 was placed after the end of the* `if` *statement rather than inside the* `if`*-part. How would this change the appearance on the screen during execution?* ❖

4.4   Selecting Among Many Alternatives

The `if-else` statements discussed earlier in this section are particularly suitable when we have to choose between executing two different blocks of statements at some point in a program. However, sometimes more than two alternatives have to be considered.

As a simple example, consider how to assign letter grades based on numeric scores on an examination. Scores greater than or equal to 90 are assigned an "A", scores from 80 to 89 are assigned a "B", scores from 70 to 79 are assigned a "C", and those below 70 are assigned "no credit". Suppose that a variable `score` of type `int` contains the numeric score of a particular examination. We would like to display the appropriate letter grade in a `Text` item, `gradeDisplay`. In this situation we have not just two, but *four* different possibilities to worry about, so it is clear that a simple `if-else` statement is insufficient.

Java allows us to extend the `if-else` statement for more than two possibilities by including one or more `else if` clauses in an `if` statement. Thus we can display the appropriate grade using the following statement:

```
if ( score >= 90 ) {
    gradeDisplay.setText( "The grade is A" );
}
else if ( score >= 80 ) {
    gradeDisplay.setText( "The grade is B" );
}
else if ( score >= 70 ) {
    gradeDisplay.setText( "The grade is C" );
}
else {
    gradeDisplay.setText( "No credit is given" );
}
```

When we execute this `if` statement, the computer first evaluates the `boolean` expression `score >= 90`. If that is `true`, an "A" will be displayed and execution will continue after the last `else`-part of the statement. However, if it is `false`, the program will evaluate the next `boolean` expression, `score >= 80`. If that is `true`, a grade of "B" will be displayed and execution will continue after the last `else`-part. If not, the expression `score >= 70` will be evaluated. If that is `true`, then a grade of "C" will be displayed and execution will continue after the `else`-part. Otherwise, the statement in the `else`-part will be executed and a grade of "no credit" will be displayed.

When checking to see if the student should be given a "B," why didn't we also have to check whether `score < 90`? The reason is that to get to the condition `score >= 80`, the previous test, `score >= 90`, must have already *failed*. That is, we *only* execute the `else` clauses if `score` is less than 90. The same reasoning shows that we do not need to check if `score < 80` when we determine whether to give a "C" as the grade. We can always count on the fact that the conditions within the `if-else` statements are evaluated sequentially, and therefore that all previous tests in the `if` statement have failed, before determining whether to execute the next block.

We can summarize the execution of an `if` statement including `else if`'s as follows:

※ Evaluate the conditions after the `if`'s in order until one is found to be `true`.
※ Execute the statements in the block following that `if` and then resume execution with the first statement after the entire `if` statement.

* If none of the conditions is true and there is an else-part, then execute the statements in the else-part. If there is no else-part, don't execute any of the statements in the if statement.
* Finally, continue execution with the first statement after the if statement.

If there is an else clause in an if statement, then it must be the very last part of the if. That is, no further else if's are allowed after a plain else clause.

We will see later that this more complex if statement is actually a special case of a more general way of *nesting* if statements. However, it is convenient for the moment to consider it by itself.

EXERCISE 4.4.1

What is the output when the following pieces of code are executed? Why does the output of the three pieces of code differ? Assume hamburgerPrice *is 7.*

a.
```
if ( hamburgerPrice < 2 ) {
    System.out.println( "This hamburger is super cheap!" );
} else if ( hamburgerPrice < 4 ) {
    System.out.println( "This hamburger is cheap." );
} else if ( hamburgerPrice < 6 ) {
    System.out.println( "This hamburger is fairly cheap." );
} else if ( hamburgerPrice < 8 ) {
    System.out.println( "This hamburger is moderate." );
} else if ( hamburgerPrice < 10 ) {
    System.out.println( "This hamburger is pricey!" );
} else {
    System.out.println( "This hamburger is super expensive!" );
}
```

b.
```
if ( hamburgerPrice >= 10 ) {
    System.out.println( "This hamburger is super expensive!" );
} else if ( hamburgerPrice < 10 ) {
    System.out.println( "This hamburger is pricey!" );
} else if ( hamburgerPrice < 8 ) {
    System.out.println( "This hamburger is moderate." );
} else if ( hamburgerPrice < 6 ) {
    System.out.println( "This hamburger is fairly cheap." );
} else if ( hamburgerPrice < 4 ) {
    System.out.println( "This hamburger is cheap." );
} else {
    System.out.println( "This hamburger is super cheap!" );
}
```

c.

```java
if ( hamburgerPrice < 2 ) {
    System.out.println ( "This hamburger is super cheap!" );
}
if ( hamburgerPrice < 4 ) {
    System.out.println ( "This hamburger is cheap." );
}
if ( hamburgerPrice < 6 ) {
    System.out.println ( "This hamburger is fairly cheap." );
}
if ( hamburgerPrice < 8 ) {
    System.out.println ( "This hamburger is moderate." );
}
if ( hamburgerPrice < 10 ) {
    System.out.println ( "This hamburger is pricey!" );
}
if ( hamburgerPrice >= 10 ) {
    System.out.println ( "This hamburger is super expensive!" );
}
```

4.5   More on Boolean Expressions

The if-else statement in the Voting class at the beginning of this chapter was sufficient because there were only two candidates to consider when assigning a new vote. However, for more than two candidates the else if clause introduced in the last section becomes necessary.

In the next example our program must choose among three candidates, A, B, and C, of whom each has been allotted a vertical third of the canvas. We will not rewrite the entire program here, but will instead focus on the onMouseClick method.

Let LEFT_SEPARATOR and RIGHT_SEPARATOR be constants representing the *x* coordinates of the vertical lines that divide the canvas into the three pieces. The int variables countA, countB, and countC will keep track of the number of votes for the three candidates. Here is the code:

```java
// Update votes and display vote counts for three candidates
public void onMouseClick( Location point ) {
    if ( point.getX() < LEFT_SEPARATOR ) {    // Clicked in left section
        countA++;
        infoA.setText( "So far there are " + countA + " votes for A." );
    }
    else if ( point.getX() < RIGHT_SEPARATOR ) {    // Clicked in center
        countB++;
        infoB.setText( "So far there are " + countB + " votes for B." );
    }
    else {                                          // Clicked in right section
        countC++;
        infoC.setText( "So far there are " + countC + " votes for C." );
    }
}
```

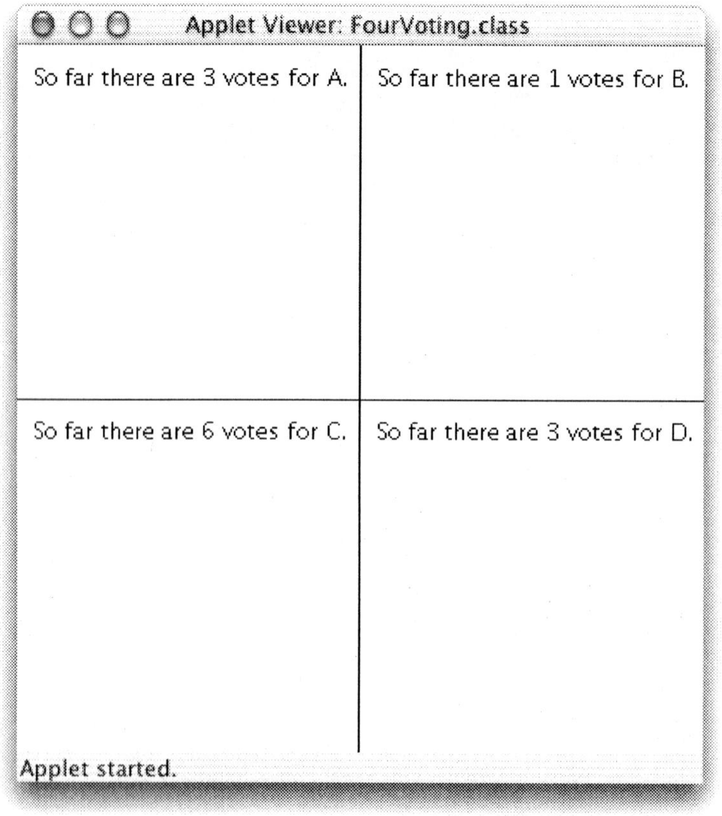

Figure 4.8   Voting for four candidates

When determining whether the click was in the center section, why didn't we have to check that `point.getX()` was to the right of LEFT_SEPARATOR? As with our earlier example, the reason is that to even get to the second condition we *know* that the test `point.getX()` < LEFT_SEPARATOR must have failed (that is, it must have evaluated to *false*).

This same style solution works for determining whether clicks are in four or more vertical strips. However, once we get to four candidates, it might make sense to divide the screen both vertically and horizontally rather than into four narrow, vertical strips, as shown in Figure 4.8. We will count clicks in the upper left-hand corner as votes for A, in the upper right-hand corner as votes for B, lower left for C, and lower right for D. Thus to be a vote for A, the location where the user clicked must be *both* above the horizontal line *and* to the left of the vertical line. How can we write this as a condition?

In Java we use the *and* operator, &&, between two `boolean` expressions to indicate that *both* must be `true` for the entire expression to be `true`. For example, we can ensure that x is positive and y is negative by writing x > 0 && y < 0. While it would be convenient, computer programming languages do not usually allow us to combine two inequalities, as in the expression 1 <= x <= 10. Instead we must write it out as 1 <= x && x <= 10.

The && is an example of a logical, or boolean, operator in Java. Just as the + operator on ints takes two int values and returns an int value, boolean operators take two boolean values and return a boolean value. The && (and) operator returns true exactly when both boolean values are true. Thus x > 0 && y < 0 will be true only if *both* x is greater than 0 *and* y is less than 0.

In order to ensure that point is in the upper left corner of the canvas we would need to write:

```
if ( point.getX() < MID_X && point.getY() < MID_Y ) { // Upper left
    ....
}
```

The if-part is only executed if *both* point.getX() < MID_X *and* point.getY() < MID_Y. If either one of those boolean expressions is false, then the entire condition evaluates to false and the if-part is not executed.

Here is the complete code to assign votes to four candidates:

```
// Update votes and display vote counts
public void onMouseClick( Location point ) {
    if ( point.getX() < MID_X && point.getY() < MID_Y ) {
        // Upper left
        countA++;
        infoA.setText( "So far there are " + countA + " votes for A." );
    }
    else if ( point.getX() >= MID_X && point.getY() < MID_Y ) {
        // Upper right
        countB++;
        infoB.setText( "So far there are " + countB + " votes for B." );
    }
    else if ( point.getX() < MID_X && point.getY() >= MID_Y ) {
        // Lower left
        countC++;
        infoC.setText( "So far there are " + countC + " votes for C." );
    }
    else { // Lower right
        countD++;
        infoD.setText( "So far there are " + countD + " votes for D." );
    }
}
```

Just as Java uses && to represent the logical *and* operator, it uses || to represent the logical *or* operator. Thus x < 5 || y > 20 will be true if x < 5 *or* y > 20. In general, if b_1 and b_2 are boolean expressions, then b_1 || b_2 is true if *one* or *both* of b_1 and b_2 are true.

English contains both an *inclusive* and an *exclusive* "or". The inclusive "or" evaluates to true if either or both operands are true. The exclusive "or" evaluates to true only if exactly one of the operands is true. The || operator represents the inclusive "or". Using the "not" operator, !, defined below, you can get the effect of the exclusive "or" on boolean expressions b_1 and b_2 by writing $(b_1 \ || \ b_2)$ && $!(b_1 \ \&\& \ b_2)$, which states that one of b_1 and b_2 is true, but not both.

A good example illustrating the use of the *or* operation is determining whether someone playing the game of craps has won or lost after his or her first roll of the dice. The "shooter" in craps throws two dice. If the numbers on the faces of the dice add up to 7 or 11, then the shooter wins. A sum of 2, 3, or 12 results in an immediate loss. With any other result, play continues in a way that will be described later.

The `if` statement below has three branches that encode the relevant outcomes of the first roll of the dice. The value of `status` is simply a `Text` object that, as usual, has been created in the `begin` method of the program.

```
if ( roll == 7 || roll == 11 ) {  // 7 or 11 wins on first throw
    status.setText( "You win!" );
}
else if ( roll == 2 || roll == 3 || roll == 12 ) {
                                // 2, 3, or 12 loses
    status.setText( "You lose!" );
}
else {                          // Play must continue
    status.setText( "The game continues" );
}
```

The `if` portion determines whether the player has won by checking if the `roll` was 7 or 11. The `else if` portion determines whether the player has lost by checking if the `roll` was 2, 3, or 12. Finally the `else` portion is executed if further rolls of the dice will be required to determine whether the player wins or loses.

The last `boolean` operator to be introduced here is `!`, which stands for "not". For example, the expression `!box.contains( point )` will be `true` exactly when `box.contains( point )` is `false`, i.e., when `box.contains( point )` is *not* `true`.

Although we can use `!` with equations and inequalities, it is usually clearer to rewrite the statement using a different operator. For instance, `!( x == y )` is more simply written as `x != y`, and `!( x < y )` is simplified to `x >= y`. Similarly, `!( x <= y )` is equivalent to `x > y`, which is much easier to read.

Figure 4.9 summarizes the most common operators in Java that give a `boolean` result.

operator	meaning
&&	*and*
||	*or*
!	*not*
==	*equal*
!=	*not equal*
<	*less than*
<=	*less than or equal*
>	*greater than*
>=	*greater than or equal*

Figure 4.9 A summary of the boolean and comparison operators in Java

➡ EXERCISE 4.5.1

Suppose that the current value of x *is 6,* y *is −2, and* z *is 13. For each of the following conditions, determine whether they evaluate to* true *or* false.

  a. x - 6 < y && z == 2 * x + 1.
  b. !(x - 6 < y && z == 2 * x + 1).
  c. x - 6 < y || z == 2 * x + 1.
  d. !(x - 6 < y || z == 2 * x + 1).

Before we move on, we should note a few last points about && and ||. The first is to be sure and use the double version of each of the symbols & and |, because the single versions represent slightly different operators.

Second, both && and || in Java are implemented as "short-circuit" operations. What this means is that Java will cease evaluating an expression involving one of these operators as soon as it can determine whether the entire expression is true or false.

For example, suppose a program includes a declaration of an int variable, x, and that it contains the expression (x > 10) && (x <= 20). If the computer evaluates that expression when x has value 3, it will only evaluate x > 10 without even considering x <= 20. Because x > 10 is false, the expression will first evaluate to false && (x <= 20). As a result, Java can determine that the final value of the && expression must be false no matter what the value of x <= 20. However, if x > 10 had been true, the rest of the expression would have to be evaluated to determine whether the entire && expression evaluates to true or false.

While you are unlikely to care much in this case whether the second argument is evaluated, there are other cases in which evaluating the second argument may result in an error. For example, if the boolean expression x != 0 && 3/x > 17 were not evaluated in this short-circuit fashion, then if *x* were 0 at run time, a run-time error would result when 3/x was evaluated.

Expressions involving the || operator are also evaluated in a short-circuit fashion. If the left side evaluates to true, then Java knows that the entire || expression *must* evaluate to true, so it does not bother to evaluate the right side. Conversely, if the left side is false, then the right side must be evaluated in order to determine the final value of the entire || expression.

4.6   Nested Conditionals

Occasionally we run into problems that would require complex boolean conditions if they were handled using if or else if statements as we have seen them used so far. Rather than constructing these complex conditions, we will introduce alternative structures for supporting the program logic. Happily, we don't need to introduce any more syntax in order to handle them; we just need to combine if statements in different ways.

Suppose it is a summer weekend and you are trying to figure out what to do. Your choice of recreation will depend on the weather and how much money you have to spend. The following table lists the various options and choices, where the row headings represent your possible financial situation and the column headings represent the weather possibilities.

	sunny	not sunny
rich	outdoor concert	indoor concert
not rich	ultimate frisbee	watch TV

The table entries represent the suggested recreational activity, given the financial situation represented by the row and the weather as represented by the column. Thus if you are feeling rich and it is not sunny, you might want to go to an indoor concert. If you are not feeling rich and it is sunny, you might play some ultimate frisbee.

How can we represent these choices with an if statement? Let rich and sunny be variables of type boolean, and let activityDisplay be a variable of type Text that will display the selected activity. The if statement below uses else if clauses to represent the four choices.

```
if ( sunny && rich ) {
    activityDisplay.setText( "outdoor concert" );
}
else if ( !sunny && rich ) {
    activityDisplay.setText( "indoor concert" );
}
else if ( sunny && !rich ) {
    activityDisplay.setText( "ultimate frisbee" );
}
else  { // !sunny && !rich
    activityDisplay.setText( "watch TV" );
}
```

As we will discuss in more detail in the next chapter, ! has *higher precedence* than &&. This means that the not operator, !, will always be applied before the && operator. Thus the condition !sunny && rich is evaluated by first evaluating !sunny and then using the && operation to determine whether both !sunny and rich are true. Similarly, the && operator has higher precedence than ||.

This code correctly represents all four options, but is rather verbose and loses the nice structure of the table. A related problem is that by the time we arrive at the last case the program has evaluated three fairly complex boolean expressions.

We can write this so that only two evaluations of boolean variables are ever made, and furthermore they are made without the added complication of *negation* or *and* operators. This is accomplished by *nesting* if statements. A nested if statement involves including one or more if statements inside another, as in the example below.

```java
if ( sunny ) {
    if ( rich ) {
        activityDisplay.setText( "outdoor concert" );
    }
    else {  // Not rich
        activityDisplay.setText( "ultimate frisbee" );
    }
}
else {        // Not sunny
    if ( rich ) {
        activityDisplay.setText( "indoor concert" );
    }
    else {  // Not rich
        activityDisplay.setText( "watch TV" );
    }
}
```

The advantage to using these nested if statements is that the organization is quite similar to that of the table. There is an outer if-else statement that determines whether sunny is true. This corresponds to choosing either the first or second column of the table. Inside the outer if-part there is an if-else statement that determines whether rich is true. This corresponds to figuring out which row of the table applies. For example, if rich is false, the outcome should correspond to the first column and second row of the table, and hence the activity should be "play ultimate". The else-part corresponding to its not being sunny is handled in a similar fashion.

➡ EXERCISE 4.6.1

Use nested conditionals to rewrite the onMouseClick method for tabulating votes of four candidates from Section 4.5. ❖

Style Note: The nested if-else statements are indented from the outer ones in order to make the code easier to read and understand. Although Java compilers ignore the layout of code, human readers appreciate the cues of indenting to understand complex code like this. Many Java development environments include an option to "format" the code. Selecting this option usually results in more readable code.

Aside from the indenting, another thing that makes this code easy to understand is the inclusion of comments. In particular, notice how each else clause includes comments indicating under which conditions the else-part is executed. This has the advantage of making it absolutely clear to the reader under what circumstances this code is executed. The more complex the conditional, the more important these comments become. We strongly urge all programmers to include such comments.

While the use of nested if-else statements yields code that is not quite as compact and simple to understand as the table, it is much easier to see its correspondence to the table than the version involving only else if clauses. Notice in particular that no matter what the values of sunny and rich are, only two boolean variables are ever evaluated during the execution of this code, so it is not only clearer, but it is faster as well!

→ EXERCISE 4.6.2

Using the information provided in the table and nested conditionals, write an if *statement that displays which course a student should take based on their interests in math and writing. Let* likesMath *and* likesWriting *be variables of type* boolean, *and let* course *be a variable of type* Text *that will display the recommended course.*

	likes writing	*doesn't like writing*
likes math	Economics	Calculus
doesn't like math	English	Psychology

   In Figure 4.10 we provide another example of complex choices being represented by nested if-else statements. This class provides the code to simulate a complete game of craps. The rules of craps are as follows:

> The shooter rolls a pair of dice. If the shooter rolls a 7 or 11, it is a win. If the shooter rolls a 2, 3, or 12, it is a loss. If the shooter rolls any other number, that number becomes the "point". To win, the shooter then must roll the "point" value again before rolling a 7. Otherwise it is a loss.

   The program simulates a roll of the dice by using a random number generator every time the user clicks the mouse. In order to implement the rules given above, we must organize the game logic in a way that can be represented using if statements. Notice that the rules for winning are quite different depending on whether this is the player's first throw. For instance, if it is the first throw, then rolling a 7 results in a win, but if it is a second or subsequent throw, then 7 results in a loss. Therefore we will organize the first level of conditional to determine whether it is the first throw.
   In order to make such a choice, the Craps class in Figure 4.10 declares a boolean variable, newGame, to remember whether this is the first throw of a new game.
   The outer if statement in the method onMouseClick has the following structure:

```
if ( newGame ) {   // Starting a new game
    ...
}
else {             // Continuing trying to make the point
    ...
}
```

   The if-part of this code is itself a nested if statement with three branches, each of which encodes the relevant actions to be taken based on the first roll of the dice. Recall that we saw a

```
public class Craps extends WindowController {
    ...    // Constant declarations omitted
    private boolean newGame = true;     // True if starting new game
    private Text status,                // Display status of game
                 message;               // Display dice roll value
    private int point;                  // Number to roll for win
    // Generator for roll of a die
    private RandomIntGenerator dieGenerator = new RandomIntGenerator( 1,6 );

    // Create status and message on canvas
    public void begin() {
        status = new Text( " ", TEXT_LEFT, STATUS_TOP ), canvas );
        message = new Text( " ", TEXT_LEFT, MESSAGE_TOP ), canvas );
    }

    // For each click, roll the dice and report the results
    public void onMouseClick( Location pt ) {
        // Get values for both dice and display sum
        int roll = dieGenerator.nextValue() + dieGenerator.nextValue();
        message.setText( "You rolled a " + roll + "!" );

        if ( newGame ) {                  // Start a new game
            if ( roll == 7 || roll == 11 ) {  // 7 or 11 wins on first throw
                status.setText( "You win!" );
            }
            else if ( roll == 2 || roll == 3 || roll == 12 ) {
                                          // 2, 3, or 12 loses
                status.setText( "You lose!" );
            }
            else {                        // Set roll to be the point to be made
                status.setText( "Try for your point!" );
                point = roll;
                newGame = false;          // No longer a new game
            }
        }
        else {                            // Continue trying to make the point
            if ( roll == 7 ) {            // 7 loses when trying for point
                status.setText( "You lose!" );
                newGame = true;           // Set to start new game
            }
            else if ( roll == point ) { // Making the point wins!
                status.setText( "You win!" );
                newGame = true;
            }
            else {                        // Keep trying
                status.setText( "Keep trying for " + point + " ..." );
            }
        }
    }
}
```

Figure 4.10 Craps class illustrating nested conditionals

simplified version of this example earlier in the chapter. The new code is reproduced below:

```
if ( roll == 7 || roll == 11 ) {  // 7 or 11 wins on first throw
    status.setText( "You win!" );
}
else if ( roll == 2 || roll == 3 || roll == 12 ) {
                      // 2, 3, or 12 loses
    status.setText( "You lose!" );
}
else {                   // Set the roll to be the new point to be made
    status.setText( "Try for your point!" );
    point = roll;
    newGame = false;             // No longer a new game
}
```

Rather than having a separate branch for each possible value of the roll of the dice, there are only three. These branches correspond to winning, losing, and establishing a point to be made on subsequent rolls. The variable newGame remains true in the first two branches, so it need not be updated. Only the third branch requires setting newGame to false.

Let us now examine the else-part of the outer if statement. Like the if-part, this nested if statement also has three branches, though the second and third conditions are quite different from those that handle the first roll:

```
if ( roll == 7 ) {               // 7 loses when trying for point
    status.setText( "You lose!" );
    newGame = true;              // Set to start new game
}
else if ( roll == point ) {    // Making the point wins!
    status.setText( "You win!" );
    newGame = true;
}
else {                          // Keep trying
    status.setText( "Keep trying for " + point + " ..." );
}
```

In this statement, both of the first two choices result in setting newGame back to true because they represent the end of a game with either a win or a loss. The third statement merely asks the player to continue rolling, so newGame remains false.

➡ EXERCISE 4.6.3

Try writing out this program using only a single if statement with many else if clauses. It should become painfully clear why nested if statements are useful in situations with complex logic.

4.7   Summary

In this chapter we introduced conditional statements and the boolean data type. The major points discussed were:

* The if-else statement is used when different code is to be executed, depending on the value of a condition.
* if statements without an else clause are used when extra code is to be executed in one case, but nothing extra is needed in the other.
* if statements with else if clauses are used if there are more than two cases to be considered in a choice. if statements with else if clauses may or may not be terminated with an else-part, at the programmer's option.
* Nested if statements can be used to represent complex logic.
* Expressions true and false represent values of type boolean. Comparison operators return boolean values. Boolean expressions can be combined with the boolean operators &&, ||, and !.

4.8   Chapter Review Problems

➡ EXERCISE 4.8.1

Define the following Java terms:

   a. *negation*
   b. *block*
   c. !=
   d. *condition*

➡ EXERCISE 4.8.2

How would you express the following as operators in Java?

   a. *greater than*
   b. *or*
   c. *equal*
   d. *less than or equal*
   e. *not*
   f. *and*
   g. *not less than*

➡ EXERCISE 4.8.3

The database at a doctor's office stores information about each patient. For each piece of information listed below, decide whether or not it would be appropriate to store the information as a boolean.

a. *patient's birthday*
b. *patient's gender*
c. *patient's address*
d. *whether the patient has visited within the last year*
e. *patient's insurance company*
f. *whether the patient's last visit is fully paid*

➠ EXERCISE 4.8.4

Fix the problem(s) in the following code:

```
if ( x = 5 ) {
    message.setText( "You win!" );
}
else if ( x < 5 ) {
    message.setText( "You lose!" );
}
else if ( x > 5 ) {
    message.setText( "Try again!" );
}
```

➠ EXERCISE 4.8.5

What are the values of the following expressions if x = 8, y = −5 *and* z = 2.

a. x + y != z
b. !(2 * x + 3 * y >= z)
c. (x − z) * 2 < z − 2 * y
d. y − z + x >= 0
e. x − 4 * z + 1 == y

➠ EXERCISE 4.8.6

Why is the following code more complex than it needs to be? Simplify it using else if.

```
if ( score <= 100 && score >= 90 ) {
    gradeDisplay.setText( "You got an A" );
}
if ( score < 90 && score >= 80 ) {
    gradeDisplay.setText( "You got a B" );
}
if ( score < 80 && score >= 70 ) {
    gradeDisplay.setText( "You got a C" );
}
if ( score < 70 ) {
    gradeDisplay.setText( "You don't get a grade" );
}
```

➥ EXERCISE 4.8.7

What are the values of the following expressions if x = -2, y = -1 *and* z = 4.

a. x + y < z || (4 * y + z > x && x > y)
b. (x + y < z || 4 * y + z > x) && x > y
c. !(x + y < z) || (4 * y + z > x && x > y)
d. (x + y < z || 4 * y + z > x) && !(x > y)
e. !(x + y < z) || (4 * y + z > x && !(x > y))

➥ EXERCISE 4.8.8

Assume that x = 2, y = -3 *and* z = 5. *What are the values of* x, y *and* z *after the following code has been executed?*

a.
```
if ( 3 * x + y <= z - 1)
    x = y + 2 * z;
else
    y = z - y;
    z = x - 2 * y;
```

b.
```
if ( 3 * x + y <= z - 1) {
    x = y + 2 * z;
}
else {
    y = z - y;
    z = x - 2 * y;
}
```

c.
```
if ( x > y + z )
    y--;
    x++;
```

d.
```
if ( x > y + z ) {
    y--;
    x++;
}
```

➥ EXERCISE 4.8.9

Another variation of the game craps is to play what is called the "No Pass Line". Now rolling a 7 or 11 on the first roll loses and a 2, 3, or 12 wins. After the point is set, rolling a 7 wins, while

Figure 4.11 Display for InvisibleBox

rolling the point again loses. Show how to modify Craps *so that you now are playing the "No Pass Line" instead.*

4.9 Programming Problems

EXERCISE 4.9.1

Create the game InvisibleGame *to master your use of conditionals. The game will have the following features:*

* *When the game begins, it will create three "invisible" boxes. The boxes will all be square but of different sizes. One should be 30 pixels wide, the second one 45 pixels wide, and the third 80 pixels wide. These boxes should be created randomly anywhere on the screen.*
* *The user will click the mouse and try to hit the boxes when doing so.*
* *When the mouse exits the window, the user will be notified of his/her success. The output should look like* Figure 4.11.
* *When the mouse re-enters the window, all variables should be reset and the boxes moved to new random locations.*

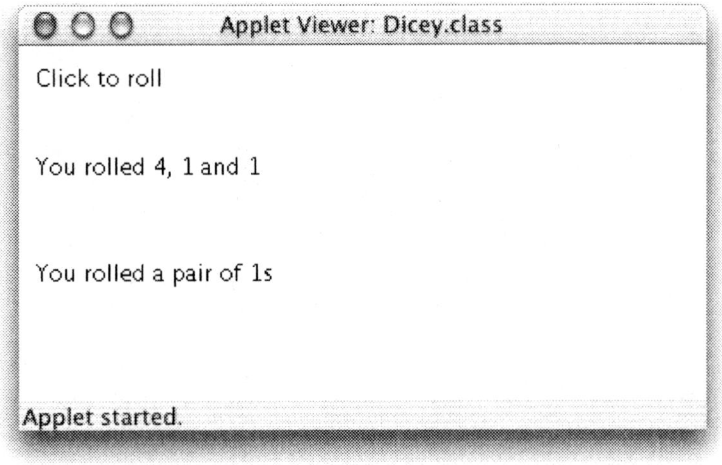

Figure 4.12   Display for Dicey

● *Points are assigned as follows*

    – *200 points: Hitting all three boxes*
    – *150 points: Hitting the small box and the medium box*
    – *125 points: Hitting the small box and the large box*
    – *110 points: Hitting the medium box and the large box*
    – *100 points: Hitting only the small box*
    – *75 points: Hitting only the medium box*
    – *50 points: Hitting only the large box*
    – *−1 point: For each mouse click*

● *If possible, modify the applet settings so that the canvas is 300 pixels wide and 300 pixels high.* ❖

▶ EXERCISE 4.9.2

Write a simple game with three dice called Dicey, *which may remind you of a more popular game with five dice. When the user clicks the mouse, the three dice are "rolled" and the results are displayed on the screen. The display will also include whether the user rolled three of a kind, a pair, or nothing of particular interest. See Figure 4.12.* ❖

CHAPTER 5

Primitive Types, Operators, and Strings

$\mathscr{I}$ n several respects Java treats integers differently from types like FilledRect and Location. One example is the means Java provides to describe a specific piece of information. For most types, we have used constructions. To describe the Color light blue, for example, we might say:

```
new Color( 200, 200, 255 )
```

and to describe the origin of the coordinate system we say:

```
new Location( 0, 0 )
```

For integers, on the other hand, Java provides us with the ability to write literals that directly describe the desired value. A programmer would simply write

```
3
```

rather than

```
new int( 3 )
```

to describe the integer value 3 within a program.

Another distinction between ints and many of the other types is that there are no methods associated with ints. We perform operations on ints using operator symbols like + and *, while we use method invocations when we want to perform operations on Locations or FilledRects.

These differences are partly a matter of convenience. Numbers are used so frequently in programs that it is important to provide convenient mechanisms for manipulating numeric information. At the same time, they represent a more fundamental aspect of the way Java views integers. In Java's view, integers are in some sense less transient than the other kinds of information we have considered. Java doesn't let us say

```
new int( 3 )
```

because 3 already exists before you use it. It would make no sense to talk about making a new 3. How would the new 3 differ from the old 3?

The integers are not the only Java type that has these special properties. The type `boolean` shares these features with the integers. There are no methods to manipulate `boolean`s, and programmers use the literals `true` and `false` rather than constructions to describe specific `boolean` values.

In general, Java refers to pieces of information that we construct using `new` and can manipulate with methods as *objects*, and the types composed of such items are called *object types* or *classes*. Pieces of information that are described using literals and manipulated with operators rather than methods are called *primitive values*, and types composed of primitive values are called *primitive types*.

In this chapter, we will more carefully explore the use of the two primitive types we have already encountered, `int` and `boolean`, and then introduce some additional primitive types. In particular, we will learn about the type `double`, which is used when working with numbers that are not integers.

Finally, we will examine a few aspects of the type `String`. All the examples of quoted text we have seen in the preceding chapters are literals that describe elements of the `String` type. The `String` type is an object type rather than a primitive type. In some ways, however, it resembles a primitive type. Java provides both operators and methods to manipulate `String`s, and it is the only object type in Java whose objects can be described by literals rather than only by constructions.

5.1   Operators vs. Method Invocations

As observed in the introduction, there are no methods associated with primitive types. They can only be manipulated using operators. This reflects the fact that in Java, values of primitive types are permanent and unchanging.

Operators produce new values rather than modifying existing values. Thus, when we evaluate the expression

```
count + 1
```

`count` does not change. Instead, we produce a new value separate from `count`. If we want to change `count`, we could incorporate this expression in an assignment statement such as

```
count = count + 1;
```

but in this case it is the assignment rather than the arithmetic operation that is changing `count`.

Figure 5.1   Pattern constructed by DrawGrid

On the other hand, methods may modify existing objects. If we say

```
box.move( 1, 1 );
```

then box changes. No new object is produced.

To better understand this difference, consider the impact of a small change we might make in the grid drawing program presented in Figure 2.5. Recall that each time the mouse is clicked, this program draws thin vertical and horizontal rectangles. The locations of the corners of the rectangles are changed with each click, so that after several clicks, the pattern drawn forms a grid as shown in Figure 5.1.

The positioning of the rectangles drawn with each click is controlled by two Location variables named verticalCorner and horizontalCorner. In the original version of the program, these variables are initialized by the assignments

```
horizontalCorner = new Location( 0, 0 );
verticalCorner = new Location( 0, 0 );
```

They are then updated with each click by the invocations

```
verticalCorner.translate( 10, 0 );
horizontalCorner.translate( 0, 10 );
```

found in the onMouseClick method.

Each of the two assignment statements that initialize these variables contains a construction that creates a new Location object. In other contexts, we have suggested that, when possible, one should reduce the amount of work required to execute a program by reusing an existing object rather than creating a new object. This suggests that it might be better to replace the assignments used to initialize these variables in the original program with the assignments

```
horizontalCorner = new Location( 0, 0 );
verticalCorner = horizontalCorner;
```

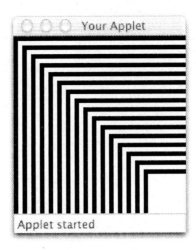

Figure 5.2   Pattern drawn by DrawGrid program after modifications

Surprisingly, making this change would change the behavior of the program considerably. Instead of drawing a grid as shown in Figure 5.1 it would produce the pattern shown in Figure 5.2.

In the original code, the names horizontalCorner and verticalCorner are initialized to refer to two different objects that represent the same point on the canvas. Using the revised code, there would actually only be a *single* Location object created. Both names would refer to the same Location object. This seemingly subtle distinction produces a significant change in the program's behavior, because if the information associated with an object is changed by a mutator method, the change is visible through all names associated with the object.

The names horizontalCorner and verticalCorner still both refer to (0,0) when the revised program first responds to a mouse click, just as they did in the original program. As a result, the first two rectangles drawn are identical to those drawn by the original program. The effect of executing the last two statements found in onMouseClick

```
verticalCorner.translate( 10, 0 );
horizontalCorner.translate( 0, 10 );
```

is, however, quite different in the modified version. In the original program, the intent of these commands is to move the point referred to by verticalCorner a bit to the right and to move the point referred to by horizontalCorner a bit down the screen. After the first execution of these statements in the original program, verticalCorner refers to the point (10,0) and horizontalCorner refers to the point (0,10). In the revised program, both names refer to the same object. When the object named verticalCorner is moved to the right, the object named horizontalCorner must also move to the right. So after the two invocations of translate are complete, both names still refer to the same Location object, and this object describes the point (10,10).

In the original program, the points associated with horizontalCorner and vertical-Corner get farther apart each time the mouse is clicked. In the revised version, they always refer

```java
// A program that draws a grid of thick black lines
// on the canvas
public class DrawGrid extends WindowController {

    // Thickness of FilledRects
    private static final int THICKNESS = 5;

    // Coordinates of the next two rectangles to draw
    private int verticalCornerX, horizontalCornerY;

    // Set coordinates to position first pair of rectangles at upper
    // left corner of the canvas
    public void begin() {
        horizontalCornerY = 0;
        verticalCornerX = 0;
    }

    // Draw a pair of rectangles and move coordinates so that the next
    // pair of rectangles will appear further down and to the right
    public void onMouseClick( Location point ) {
        new FilledRect( verticalCornerX, 0, THICKNESS,
                        canvas.getHeight(), canvas );
        new FilledRect( 0, horizontalCornerY, canvas.getWidth(),
                        THICKNESS, canvas );

        verticalCornerX = verticalCornerX + 2*THICKNESS;
        horizontalCornerY = horizontalCornerY + 2*THICKNESS;
    }
}
```

Figure 5.3 Drawing a grid without Locations

to the same point on the screen. This point will move down the diagonal of the canvas as the mouse is clicked repeatedly. As a result, the corners of the rectangles drawn meet along this diagonal, as shown in Figure 5.2.

By contrast, consider what happens if we perform as similar a sequence of operations as possible using int variables instead of Locations. A version of DrawGrid rewritten to use two int variables instead of two Locations is shown in Figure 5.3. The output of this program is identical to the original version of DrawGrid that used two separate Location objects. This version, however, uses one int named verticalCornerX to keep track of the *x* coordinate of the corner of the next vertical rectangle to be drawn and a second variable, horizontalCornerY, to keep track of the *y* coordinate of the horizontal rectangles. The version shown in the figure initializes the two int variables using the assignments

```java
horizontalCornerY = 0;
verticalCornerX = 0;
```

Suppose we try to mimic the change we made in the version that used Locations by replacing these assignments by the statements shown below:

```
horizontalCornerY = 0;
verticalCornerX = horizontalCornerY;
```

Would the program's output remain the same, change to look like the drawing in Figure 5.2, or be different from both of the versions that used Locations?

The answer is that the behavior of the program would be unchanged. The assignment

```
verticalCornerX = horizontalCornerY;
```

makes the two variables refer to the same value, just as the assignment

```
verticalCorner = horizontalCorner;
```

makes the two variables refer to the same object. The difference is that applying a mutator method can change an object, but primitive values do not change.

The "+" operator does not change one number into another. When we execute the assignment statement

```
verticalCornerX = verticalCornerX + 2*THICKNESS;
```

for the first time, the value associated with verticalCornerX changes from 0 to 10. This is not because the addition operator turns 0 into 10. While the translate method may modify the object to which it is applied, the addition operator produces a new value without in any way modifying its operands. The assignment operation then associates the new value produced with the name verticalCornerX.

In general, changes made by an assignment to a numeric variable only affect the variable explicitly mentioned in the assignment. Changes made by applying a mutator method to an object, however, will be visible through all names associated with the object that is modified.

▸ EXERCISE 5.1.1

Suppose the following Location *variables have been declared as instance variables and then initialized with these assignments:*

```
location1 = new Location( 56, 34 );
location2 = new Location( 34, 53 );
location3 = location1;
```

The following statements are then executed.

```
location1.translate( 22, 14 );
location2.translate( -23, 18 );
location3.translate( 15, -22 );
```

What are the values of the following?

   a. location1.getX()
   b. location2.getY()
   c. location3.getY()

The == operator was introduced in Section 4.3 as a means to compare integer values. It actually can be used to compare values of any type. The only problem is that when used with object types it often returns an unexpected result. When applied to objects, == returns true only if both of its operands describe exactly the same object. That is, if two objects are created by separate constructions, then comparing them with the == operator will produce false as a result.

Recall the scenario discussed in the preceding section in which we considered the behavior of the two Location variables verticalCorner and horizontalCorner of the DrawGrid program. If, immediately after these variables were initialized by the assignments

```
horizontalCorner = new Location( 0, 0 );
verticalCorner = horizontalCorner;
```

we evaluated the expression

```
verticalCorner == horizontalCorner
```

the result produced would be true. On the other hand, if the same equality test was evaluated after the pair of assignments used in the original version of the program:

```
horizontalCorner = new Location( 0, 0 );
verticalCorner = new Location( 0, 0 );
```

then the result would be false.

There are situations in which it is useful to test whether two variables refer to exactly the same object. In these situations, == is just what is needed. It is more common, however, to need to determine if two objects currently have the same characteristics. For example, suppose you want to write a simple program to test how steady your hand is as you click the mouse. The program we have in mind will display the word "STEADY" whenever you manage to click on exactly the same point on the screen twice in a row. Otherwise it will leave the screen blank.

Figure 5.4 shows an almost complete implementation of such a program. Each time the mouse is clicked, the onMouseClick method checks to see if the current point is the same as the last point and shows a "STEADY" message if it is. To do this, the program maintains a variable lastPoint that refers to the last point at which the mouse was clicked. This variable is initialized to refer to a point outside the canvas, so that the person running the program will never appear to succeed on the first click.

The if statement in onMouseClick is incomplete in the figure. To complete the program, we need to add a condition that will test to see if the last point and the current point are the same.

The obvious choice might seem to be

```
if ( point == lastPoint )
```

Unfortunately, this will *not* work. Testing using == will only return true if the point objects being compared are actually the same object. Each time onMouseClick is called, the system constructs a new Location to describe the cursor position, even if two clicks occur at the same point. Therefore, testing with == here would always yield false.

To address such situations, Java objects support a method named equals. This method's purpose is to test if two possibly distinct objects have identical characteristics. In particular,

```
// A program to detect when two consecutive mouse clicks
// occur at exactly the same canvas coordinates
public class SteadyTester extends WindowController {

    // Where to display the word "STEADY"
    private static final Location MESSAGE_LOCATION =
                                        new Location( 100, 100 );

    // Text of the message "STEADY"
    private Text steadyMessage;

    // Last position clicked on
    private Location lastPoint = new Location( -1, -1 );

    // Create and hide the "STEADY" message
    public void begin() {
        steadyMessage = new Text( "STEADY", MESSAGE_LOCATION,
                                  canvas );
        steadyMessage.hide();
    }

    // Display "STEADY" if location of click has not changed
    public void onMouseClick( Location point ) {
        if ( . . . ) { // Need to test that the points are the same
            steadyMessage.show();
        } else {
            steadyMessage.hide();
        }

        lastPoint = point;
    }

}
```

Figure 5.4   A program to test for steady clickers

if we construct two distinct Location objects that happen to have the same *x* and *y* coordinates, the equals method will consider them the same and return true. Thus, we can complete the if statement in the onMouseClick method of our SteadyTester by writing

```
if ( point.equals( lastPoint ) )
```

➡ EXERCISE 5.2.1

Rewrite the SteadyTester *program so it also displays text when the mouse is not clicked on exactly the same point. When the user clicks on a different point, the program should display the message* "UNSTEADY".

We have already encountered quite a few operators that can be applied to primitive types. In Chapter 3, we presented the four basic arithmetic operators, $+$, $-$, $*$, and $/$. The list of operators was expanded in Chapter 4 with the addition of the relational and logical operators, $<$, $<=$, $>$, $>=$, $==$, $!=$, $\&\&$, $||$, and $!$.

With this large collection of operators, it is possible to write fairly complex expressions. Therefore, it becomes important to understand the rules Java follows when evaluating such expressions. We introduced two of these rules, Java's basic *precedence* rules, in Section 3.4. We explained that when evaluating expressions involving just addition, subtraction, multiplication, and division, Java does multiplications and divisions before additions and subtractions, and otherwise it works from left to right. Now we need to expand these rules to cover the much larger set of operators available.

Java's approach to ordering arithmetic operations should not be new to you. The same rules are followed in standard mathematics. They are more important when programming, however, because programmers have fewer means to make the intended interpretation of a formula clear. When writing a formula on a sheet of paper or using a good word processor we can spread the formula over several lines to make things clear. For example, when we compare the two formulae

$$\frac{height - width}{2}$$

and

$$height - \frac{width}{2}$$

the order in which the operations are to be performed is clear, even if one forgets the rule that division should be done before subtraction. When we are forced to write all the symbols in a formula on one line, as we are in Java, it is much easier to accidentally write a formula in which the order of evaluation dictated by the precedence rules is different from the order we had in mind.

The rules for determining the order of arithmetic operators in Java (and mathematics) are based on the notion of assigning operators to precedence levels. Division and multiplication are assigned to one precedence level and addition and subtraction to a different level. Furthermore, the level for multiplication and division is ranked higher than that for addition and subtraction. Java performs operations associated with the higher precedence level before those associated with the lower level.

To extend Java's precedence rules to the expanded set of operators we encountered in the last chapter, all we need to know is which operators are assigned to each precedence level and how these levels are ranked. Java assigns the operators we have considered to the seven precedence levels listed below:

1. Arithmetic and logical negation: $-$, and $!$.
2. Multiplication and division: $*$ and $/$.
3. Addition and subtraction: $+$ and $-$.
4. Comparisons: $<$, $<=$, $>$, $>=$.
5. Equality and inequality: $==$, $!=$
6. And: $\&\&$
7. Or: $||$

The earlier an operator appears in this list, the higher its precedence. That is, Java performs unary operators before multiplications and divisions, multiplications and divisions before additions and subtractions, and so on.

The good news is that Java does not mind if you use extra parentheses. Parentheses can be used to override these precedence rules. Any part of a formula enclosed in parentheses will be evaluated before its result can be used to perform operations outside the parentheses. Therefore, while you should do your best to become familiar with the precedence rules given above, whenever it will make an expression's meaning clearer, do not hesitate to use parentheses. For example, Java will treat the expressions

```
canvas.getHeight() - canvas.getWidth()/2
```

and

```
canvas.getHeight() - ( canvas.getWidth()/2 )
```

as equivalent. If you find yourself writing an expression like the first example and are not quite sure which operator will be evaluated first, add parentheses to make your intent clear to the computer and to anyone who reads your code later.

➡ EXERCISE 5.3.1

What is the value of the following boolean *expressions? Assume* x = 3, y = -1, *and* z = 2.

  a. x * y > -z
  b. 3 * x + 4 * y > 2 * z && x * y > -z
  c. !(x + y <= 1) && -y * (x + 1) == 2 * z
  d. 3 * x + 4 * y > 2 * z && x * y > -z || !(x + y <= 1) &&
     -y * (x + 1) == 2 * z

5.4   Double Time

When we first introduced numeric variables, we mentioned that Java distinguishes between integers and numbers that have fractional components. Java's int type corresponds to the integers. A type named double is provided for numbers with fractional parts. In this section we will discuss the reasons Java makes this distinction and the impact the distinction has on a programmer when working with numbers.

5.4.1   Java Needs More Than One Numeric Type

To understand why Java distinguishes integers from other numbers, consider the following two problems. First, suppose you and two companions are stranded in a life boat. Among your supplies, you have 55 gallons of water. You decide that this water should be divided equally among the three of you. How much water does each person get to drink? (Go ahead. Take out your calculator.)

Now, suppose that you are the instructor of a programming course in which 55 students are currently registered and you want to assign the students to three afternoon laboratory sections. How many students should be assigned to each section?

With a bit of luck, your answer to the first question was 18 1/3 gallons. On the other hand, even though the same numbers, 55 and 3, appear in the second problem, "18 1/3 students" would probably not be considered an acceptable answer to the second problem (at least not by the student who had to be chopped in thirds to even things out). A better answer would be that there should be two labs of 18 students and a third lab with 19 students.

The point of this example is that there are problems in which fractional results are acceptable and other problems where we know that only integers can be used. If we use a computer to help us solve such problems, we need a way to inform the computer whether we want an integer result or not.

In Java, we do this by choosing to use `ints` or `doubles`. For example, if we declare three instance variables:

```
private double gallons;
private double survivors;
private double waterRation;
```

and then execute the assignment statements

```
gallons = 55;
survivors = 3;
waterRation = gallons/survivors;
```

the number associated with the name `waterRation` will be 18.33333.... On the other hand, if we declare the variables

```
private int students;
private int labs;
private int labSize;
```

and then execute the assignments

```
students = 55;
labs = 3;
labSize = students/labs;
```

the number associated with `labSize` will be 18. In the first example, Java can see that we are working with numbers identified as `doubles`, so when asked to do division, it gives the answer as a `double`. In the second case, since Java notices we are using `ints`, it gives us just the integer part of the quotient when asked to do the division.

Of course, the answer we obtain in the second case, 18, isn't quite what we want. If all the labs have exactly 18 students, there will be one student excluded. We would like to do something about such leftovers. Java provides an additional operator with this in mind. When you learned to divide numbers, you probably were at first taught that the result of dividing 55 by 3 was 18 with a remainder of 1. That is, you were taught that the answer to a division problem has two parts, the quotient and the remainder. When working with integers in Java, the / operator produces the quotient. The percent sign can be used as an operator to produce the remainder. Thus, 55 / 3 will yield 18 in Java and 55 % 3 will yield 1. In general, x % y will only equal 0 if x is evenly divisible by y.

Used in this way the percent sign is called the *mod* or *modulus* operator. Java assigns this operator to the same precedence level as division and multiplication. We can use this operator to improve our solution to the problem of computing lab sizes by declaring an extra variable

```
private int extraStudents;
```

and adding the assignment

```
extraStudents = students % labs;
```

➡ EXERCISE 5.4.1

For each numerical value below, decide which values could be stored as ints and which must be stored as doubles.

  a. *the population of Seattle*
  b. *your height in meters*
  c. *the price of a cup of coffee in dollars*
  d. *the inches of rain that have fallen*
  e. *the number of coffee shops in Seattle*
  f. *the number of salmon caught in a month*

5.4.2 Arithmetic with doubles and ints

The distinction between doubles and ints in Java is a feature intended to allow the programmer to control the ways in which arithmetic computations are performed. As a beginning programmer, however, you should be warned that this feature may produce some strange surprises.

Suppose that we want to construct an oval whose width is three-quarters of the width of the canvas and we know that the width of the canvas is 300. According to the rules of normal arithmetic, it should not matter whether we say

```
300*3/4
```

or

```
300*(3/4)
```

In Java, however, the first version will produce the expected result, 225, while the second version will produce the number 0. In the first example, Java begins by multiplying 300 and 3, yielding 900, and then divides by 4 to obtain 225. In the second example, Java first divides 3 by 4. Since both of these numbers look like ints to Java, it decides the correct answer is 0 with a remainder of 3 and returns the quotient, 0, as the result of the division. Then, 300 times the result of this division, 0, yields 0.

To avoid unexpected results like this, one must understand how Java decides when we desire an integer result and when we would prefer to work with numbers with fractional components.

The first rule is simple. When we write numbers out explicitly, Java decides whether the number is an int or a double based on whether it contains a decimal point. Therefore, 3 is an int but 3.0 is a double. This can make a big difference. If we rewrite the second example above as

```
300.0*(3.0/4.0)
```

it will produce 225.0 rather than 0 as its result.

Second, one must understand that while Java distinguishes between `int`s and `double`s, it recognizes that they are related. In particular, in contexts where one should technically have to provide a `double`, Java will allow you to use an `int`. This was already illustrated in the example above where we declared an instance variable

```
private double gallons;
```

and then wrote the assignment

```
gallons = 55;
```

The number 55 is identified by Java as an `int`. The variable is declared to be a `double`. Normally, Java considers an assignment invalid if the type of the value described by the expression to the right of the equal sign is different from the type of the variable on the left side of the equal sign. The assignments

```
gallons = new Location( 33, 100 );
```

and

```
gallons = true;
```

would be considered illegal because `gallons` is a `double` rather than a `Location` or a `boolean`. Java will, however, accept the assignment

```
gallons = 55;
```

even though it assigns an `int` to a variable that is supposed to refer to a `double`.

Java is willing to convert `int`s into `double`s because it knows there is only one reasonable way to do the conversion. It simply adds a ".0" to the end of the `int`. On the other hand, Java knows that there are several ways to convert a `double` into an `int`. It could drop the fractional part or it could round. Because it cannot tell the correct technique to use without understanding the context or purpose of the program, Java refuses to convert a `double` into an `int` unless explictly told how to do so, using mechanisms that we will discuss later. Therefore, given the instance variable declaration

```
private int students;
```

Java would reject the assignment

```
students = 18.333;
```

as erroneous. It would also reject the assignment

```
students = 55.0;
```

Even if the only digit that appears after the decimal point in a numeric literal is 0, the presence of the decimal point still makes Java think of the number as a `double`.

Java's willingness to convert `int`s to `double`s is a factor in understanding how it decides whether the result of an arithmetic operation should be an `int` or a `double`. If both operands of an arithmetic operator are of the same numeric type, then Java will produce a result of this type. Thus, adding two `int`s produces an `int` and dividing a `double` by another `double` yields a double. The interesting question is: What does Java do if one operand is an int and the other a double, as in

    3/4.0

The answer is that when Java sees an operator with two operands of different types, it tries to convert one of the operands to the other type. Since it will convert ints to doubles but not the other way around, if an operation involves one int and one double, Java converts the int into a double (by adding .0) and then performs the operation, yielding a result that is also a double. Accordingly, 3/4.0 would evaluate to 0.75.

The following table summarizes Java's procedure for determining the type of result an operator should produce, given the types of its two operands. The types of the operands determine the row and column of the table that applies. The contents of the selected cell specify the type of the result. Note that the result produced is an int only when both operands are integers.

	int	double
int	int result	double result
double	double result	double result

This means that once you introduce a number which is a double into a computation, you are likely to end up with a result that is a double. Even if the result has a fractional part that is 0, Java will not automatically convert this double into an int. This can lead to unexpected errors in your program. For example, several of the accessor methods associated with graphical objects including getX, getY, getWidth, and getHeight return values that are doubles. Accordingly, the expression in the assignment statement

    midPointX = (currentPosition.getX() +
                    previousPosition.getX()) / 2

which might be used to compute the x coordinate of the midpoint of the line between two points on the canvas, would produce a double. This means that if you had defined the variable to hold the result as

    private int midPointX;

Java would reject the assignment as an error. Instead, the variable would have to be declared as

    private double midPointX;

EXERCISE 5.4.2

What is the value of each of the following expressions?

a. 12 / 5
b. 35 / 7
c. 15.0 / 2.0;
d. 65.0 / 4;
e. 79 % 12;

▶ EXERCISE 5.4.3

Given that the variable `ratio` *is of type* `double`, *what value will be associated with* `ratio`
by each of the following assignments?

a. `ratio = 12.0 / 4;`
b. `ratio = 32 / 6;`
c. `ratio = 48.0 / 5;`
d. `ratio = 22 % 8;`   ❖

5.4.3 Displaying doubles

Text constructions and `System.out.println`, the two mechanisms we have used to display
information on a computer's screen, are flexible enough to display information of many types. In
this section, we will discuss the results that are produced when they are used with `double` values.

For small numbers, the only difference between displaying an `int` and displaying a `double`
is that Java always includes a decimal point when printing a `double`. If we declare

```
private int anInt;
private double aDouble;
```

and then associate these names with equivalent values by executing the assignments

```
anInt = 1000;
aDouble = anInt;
```

executing the command

```
System.out.println( anInt + " = " + aDouble );
```

would produce the output

```
1000 = 1000.0
```

Things get a bit more interesting when large values of type `double` are displayed. Suppose
that rather than initializing the two variables above to 1000, we instead executed the assignments

```
anInt = 1000000000;
aDouble = anInt;
```

so that both variables had a value of one billion. In this case, the output produced would be

```
1000000000 = 1.0E9
```

The strange item "1.0E9" is an example of Java's version of scientific notation. Where Java
displays 1.0E9, you probably would have expected to see 1000000000.0. This value is one billion
or 10^9. The "E9" in the output Java produces is short for "times ten raised to the power 9". The
"E" stands for "exponent". In general, to interpret a number output in this form you should raise
10 to the power found after the E and multiply the number before the E by the result. The table
below shows some examples of numbers written in this notation and the standard forms of the
same values.

E-notation	Standard Representation	Standard Scientific Notation
1.0E8	100,000,000	1×10^8
1.86E5	186,000	1.86×10^5
4.9E-6	.0000049	4.9×10^{-6}

Not only does Java display large numbers using this notation when you use `System.out.println` or `Text` objects, it also recognizes numbers typed in this format as part of a program. So, if you really like scientific notation, you can include a statement like

```
avogadro = 6.022E26;
```

in a Java program.

5.4.4 Why Are Rational Numbers Called double?

As a final topic in this section, we feel obliged to try to explain why Java chooses to call nonintegers `doubles` rather than something like `real` or `rational`. The explanation involves a bit of history and electronics.

To allow us to manipulate numbers in a program, a computer's hardware must encode the numbers we use in some electronic device. In fact, for each digit of a number there must be a tiny memory device to hold it. Each of these tiny memory devices costs some money and, not long ago, they cost quite a bit more than they do now. So, if a program is only working with small numbers, the programmer can reduce the hardware cost by telling the computer to set aside a small number of memory devices for each number. On the other hand, when working with larger numbers, more memory devices should be used.

On many machines, the programmer is not free to pick any number of memory devices per number. Instead only two options are available: the "standard" one, and another that provides **double** the number of memory devices per number. The name of the Java type `double` derives from such machines.

While the cost of memory has decreased to the point where we rarely need to worry that using `doubles` might increase the amount of hardware memory our program uses, the name does reflect an important aspect of computer arithmetic. Since each number represented in a computer is stored in physical devices, the total number of digits stored is always limited.

In the computer's memory, numbers are stored in binary, or base 2. Thirty-one binary digits are used to store the numeric value of each `int`. Just as the number of digits included in a car's odometer limits the range of mileage values that can be displayed before the odometer flips back to "000000", the number of binary digits used to represent a number limits the range of numbers that can be stored. As a result, the values that can be processed by Java as `ints` range from $-2,147,483,648 (= -2^{31})$ to $2,147,483,647 (= 2^{31} - 1)$. If you try to assign a number outside this range to an `int` variable, Java is likely to throw away some of the digits, yielding an incorrect result. If you need to write a program that works with very large integers, there is another type that is limited to integer values but that can handle numbers with twice as many digits. This type is called `long`. There is also a type named `short` that uses half as much memory as `int` to represent a number. For numbers that are not integers, there is also a type named `float` that is like `double` but uses half as many bits to represent numeric values. The examples in this text will not use `long`, `float`, or `short`.

The range of numbers that can be stored as double values is significantly larger than even the long type. The largest double value is approximately 1.8×10^{308} and the smallest double is approximately -1.8×10^{308}. This is because Java stores double values as you might write numbers in scientific notation. It rewrites each number as a value, the mantissa, times 10 raised to an appropriate exponent. For example, the number

$$32,953,923,804,836,184,926,273,582,140,929.584,289$$

might be written in scientific notation as

$$3.295392380483618492627358214092958428 9 \times 10^{31}$$

Java, however, does not always encode all the digits of the mantissa of a number stored as a double. The amount of memory used to store a double enables Java to record approximately 15 significant digits of each number. Thus, Java might actually record the number used as an example above as

$$3.295392380483618 \times 10^{31}$$

This means that if you use numbers with long or repeating sequences of digits, Java will actually be working with approximations of the numbers you specified. The results produced will therefore be slightly inaccurate. Luckily, for most purposes, the accuracy provided by 15 digits of precision is sufficient.

There is one final aspect of the range of double values that is limited. First, the smallest number greater than 0 that can be represented as a double is approximately 5×10^{-324}. Similarly, the largest number less than 0 that can be represented as a double is approximately -5×10^{-324}.

5.4.5   Selecting a Numeric Type

The examples and rules above suggest that a reasonable guideline for dealing with the difference between ints and doubles is to use doubles whenever possible. Most of the surprising examples you are likely to encounter involve integer division. Furthermore, Java will sometimes refuse to accept an assignment of a value to a variable declared as an int, but will always allow you to assign any numeric value to a variable declared as a double, even if it has to turn an int into a double to make the assignment possible.

Of course, there are contexts where you will have to use ints. First, as suggested in the introduction to this section, there are programming problems where the only acceptable results are integers. You will have to use ints in such programs. Finally, there are certain contexts where Java will demand an int. The three numbers provided in a Color construction, for example, must be ints. In such situations, it is possible to convert a double into an int, as discussed in Section 5.5.2.

5.5   Handy Sources of Numeric Information

Java provides a number of methods in its libraries that can be used to generate useful numerical information. Several of these features are described in this section.

5.5.1 What Time Is It?

There are many signs that computers keep track of the time. Most likely, the computer you use displays the current time of day somewhere on your screen as you work. Your computer can tell you when each of your files was created and last modified. While your web browser downloads large files, it probably displays an estimate of how much longer it will take before the process is complete.

To support all the ways in which time is used in programs, Java provides a sophisticated collection of primitives that allow your program to determine the hour, the year, the day of the week, or just about anything else you might imagine that is related to measuring time. These mechanisms provide more than you need at this point, but we would like to introduce you to one of them, a method named `System.currentTimeMillis`.

The `System.currentTimeMillis` method returns a single number telling you what time it is. For example, if you run a program containing the instruction

```
System.out.println( "The time is now " +
                    System.currentTimeMillis() );
```

Java might produce the following mysterious answer:

```
The time is now 1057070809463
```

Apparently, Java uses a different system for telling time than most of us!

Whenever we use a number to answer the question "What time is it?" we are using the number to describe how long it has been since some fixed reference time. If you asked when this book was written and we answered 1422, our answer would appear to be nonsense if you assumed we were using the Gregorian calendar, in which times are measured relative to the year in which Christ was born (at least approximately). In fact, however, the number 1422 describes when our book was written based on the Islamic calendar, which measures time from the migration of the Prophet and his followers from Mecca to Medina.

Java isn't very religious about time, so it measures time from midnight on January 1, 1970. Also, since Java sometimes needs to be very precise about what time it is, Java measures time in milliseconds (i.e., thousandths of a second). The number shown above, 1057070809463, tells you exactly how many milliseconds passed between midnight, January 1, 1970, and the moment at which the Java instruction shown above produced the output

```
The time is now 1057070809463
```

The `System.currentTimeMillis` operation would be very awkward to use if you wanted to display the current time of day in a form a human could understand. Fortunately, it is a very appropriate tool for measuring short intervals of time within a program. This is an ability we will need in many programs in the following chapters. To use `System.currentTimeMillis` to measure an interval, we simply ask Java for the time at the beginning of the interval we need to measure and then again at the end. The length of the interval can then be determined by subtracting the starting time from the ending time.

As an example of how to do such timing, a program that will measure the duration of a click of the mouse button is shown in Figure 5.5. The program first uses `System.currentTimeMillis`

```
// A program to measure the duration of mouse clicks.
public class ClickTimer extends WindowController {

    // Location where messages should be displayed
    private final static Location TEXT_POS = new Location( 30, 50 );

    // When the mouse button was depressed
    private double startingTime;
    // Used to display length of click
    private Text message;

    // Create the Text to display the duration of a click
    public void begin() {
        message = new Text( "Please depress and release the mouse",
                            TEXT_POS, canvas );
    }

    // Record the time that the button is pressed
    public void onMousePress( Location point ) {
        startingTime = System.currentTimeMillis();
    }

    // Display the duration of the latest click
    public void onMouseRelease( Location point ) {
        message.setText( "You held the button down for " +
                        ( System.currentTimeMillis() -
                        startingTime )/1000 +
                        " seconds"      );
    }
}
```

Figure 5.5 Java program to measure mouse click duration

in the onMousePress method. It assigns the time returned to the variable startingTime so that it can access the value after the mouse has been released. In onMouseRelease, the program computes the difference between the time at which the mouse was pressed and released. Then, in order to display the result in units of seconds rather than milliseconds, it divides by 1000. A sample of what the program's output might look like is shown in Figure 5.6.

In this program, the variable used to hold the result of invoking System.currentTimeMillis is declared as a double. In reality, the System.currentTimeMillis method does not return its result as a double. System.currentTimeMillis always returns an integer value as its result, but because these values can become quite large, it uses the type long rather than the type int. Just as Java is willing to convert an int into a double, it will convert a long into a double. It will not, however, convert a long into an int. Therefore, we must use double or long variables to hold time values. We suggest using double as the type for such variables.

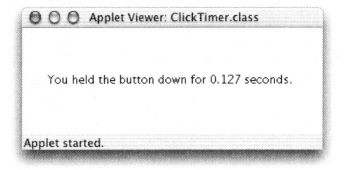

Figure 5.6 Sample output of the ClickTimer program

➡ EXERCISE 5.5.1

Executing the statement:

```
System.out.println( "The time is now " +
                    System.currentTimeMillis() );
```

will produce an output that is difficult to interpret, such as

```
The time is now 1057070809463
```

Show how to write a program using `System.currentTimeMillis` *that will output the time in a more conventional form. Your program's output should look like:*

```
The time is now 9 minutes after 3.
```

You will have to use the modulus operator described in Section 5.4.1. Also, remember that the value returned by `System.currentTimeMillis` *may be too big to associated with an* `int` *variable. If you need a variable to hold the value returned by the method, declare it as* `long` *rather than* `int`. ❖

5.5.2 Sines and Wonders

If you review all the things you have learned to do with numbers in Java, you should be unimpressed at best. Think about it. For just $10 you could go to almost any store that sells office or school supplies and buy a pocket calculator that can compute trigonometric functions, take logarithms, raise any number to any power, and do many other complex operations. On the other hand, with Java and a computer that probably costs 100 times as much as a calculator, all you have learned to do so far is add, subtract, divide, and multiply. In this section we will improve this situation by introducing a collection of methods that provide the means to perform more advanced mathematical calculations.

Roots, Logs, and Powers

A common arithmetic operation available on most calculators is the taking of a square root. In Java, this is done using a method named `Math.sqrt`. `Math` is a class in which many interesting mathematical methods have been collected. `Math.sqrt` is a method that takes any numeric value as a parameter and returns a `double` approximating the number's square root. Thus, if we created a `Text` object named `message` and later executed the instruction

```
message.setText( "The square root of 2 is " + Math.sqrt( 2 ) );
```

the message

```
The square root of 2 is 1.4142135623730951
```

would appear on the canvas.

Of course, the parameter to a method like `Math.sqrt` can be described using any expression that produces a numeric result, and the invocation of `Math.sqrt` can be used as a subpart of a larger arithmetic expression. For example, if the variable names a, b, and c were associated with the coefficients of a quadratic equation

$$ax^2 + bx + c = 0$$

we could compute a solution to the equation by translating the quadratic formula (simplified to produce only the largest answer):

$$\frac{-b + \sqrt{b^2 - 4ac}}{2a}$$

into Java. The result would look like:

```
( -b + Math.sqrt( b*b - 4*a*c ) ) / ( 2 * a )
```

Note that all the parentheses included in this Java fragment are required to ensure that the operations specified are performed in the desired sequence.

Java provides several other methods for performing operations related to raising values to powers:

`Math.pow( a, b )` raises the number a to the power b and returns the result,
`Math.exp( b )` raises the constant e ($\approx$ 2.718) to the power b,
`Math.ln( a )` returns the natural logarithm (i.e., the logarithm base e) of the number a.

In addition, if you need to work with the number e and don't feel like looking it up and typing in enough digits to approximate it accurately, the name `Math.E` is already associated with a very accurate approximation to e.

Trigonometric Functions

Another important set of functions provided in Java through the `Math` class are the standard trigonometric functions: sine, cosine, and tangent and their inverses. The Java names for these functions are shown in the table below:

Java	Function
Math.sin(x)	returns the sine of x
Math.cos(x)	returns the cosine of x
Math.tan(x)	returns the tangent of x
Math.asin(x)	returns the arc sine of x
Math.acos(x)	returns the arc cosine of x
Math.atan(x)	returns the arc tangent of x

For all of these methods, Java assumes that the angles involved are measured in radians rather than degrees. The `Math` class contains features to make it a bit easier for those who prefer to work with degrees rather than radians. There are two methods named `Math.toRadians` and `Math.toDegrees` that can be used to convert from one set of units to the other. Also, the name `Math.PI` is associated with a very accurate approximation of the mathematical constant π. Thus, the cosine of a right angle would be computed by saying:

```
Math.cos( Math.toRadians( 90 ) )
```

or

```
Math.cos( Math.PI / 2 )
```

Converting doubles into ints

There are situations where you need to convert a `double` into an `int`. In such situations, there are two main techniques you can use. If you have a `double` and you want the integer value nearest this double, then you should provide the `double` as a parameter to the method `Math.round`. The result produced will be the `int` obtained by rounding the `double` to the nearest integer value. Thus, given the declarations

```
private double aDouble;
private int anInt;
```

the assignments

```
aDouble = 4.7;
anInt = Math.round( aDouble );
```

will set `anInt` equal to 5.

If instead you just want to discard any fractional component of the `double`, you can convert the `double` into an `int` using an operation called a *type cast*. A type cast is formed by placing the name of the desired type of the result, `int` in our case, in parentheses before an expression that describes the value to be converted. Given the declarations of `anInt` and `aDouble` shown above, the assignments

```
aDouble = 4.7;
anInt = (int) aDouble;
```

will set `anInt` equal to 4.

Absolute Values

The method `Math.abs` can be used to compute the absolute value of a number. This method accepts `int` or `double` values and produces a result that is the same type as its parameter. The expressions

```
Math.abs( 17 )
```

and

```
Math.abs( −17 )
```

both yield the `int` value 17, while the expressions

```
Math.abs( -34.2 )
```

and

```
Math.abs( 34.2 )
```

both yield the `double` value 34.2.

The `Math.abs` method is sometimes used to test whether `double` values are nearly equal. If you test to see whether two `double` values are exactly equal using `==`, the test may yield `false` even when the values being compared should be equal. This occurs because the computer only records about 15 digits of any `double` value. For example, although by definition

$$a = \sqrt{a} \times \sqrt{a}$$

the Java expression

```
3 == Math.sqrt( 3.0 )*Math.sqrt( 3.0 )
```

will evaluate to `false`. Since `Math.sqrt( 3.0 )` produces a value that only approximates $\sqrt{3}$, the product `Math.sqrt( 3.0 )*Math.sqrt( 3.0 )` evaluates to 2.9999999999999996.

To deal with such inaccuracies, it is often better to test whether two values are approximately equal rather than exactly equal. If a and b are two double values, then a test of the form

```
if ( Math.abs( a - b ) < EPSILON )
```

where `EPSILON` is a constant with an appropriately small value, is a simple way to test for approximate equality.

▶ EXERCISE 5.5.2

Below, you will find examples of several well-known mathematical equalities and inequalities. Using the methods discussed in this section, translate each of these mathematical statements into a Java expression. Each expression you write should produce a `boolean` as a result. Given that the mathematical statements are facts, all these expressions should evaluate to `true`. In fact, however, as a result of the limited precision with which computers represent `double` values, some of the formulas you produce may evaluate to `false`. You do not need to make any effort to address these potential "mistakes" in your answers.

For example, if the question asked you to convert the "triangle inequality":

$$|x + y| \le |x| + |y|$$

the correct answer would be the Java expression:

```
Math.abs( x + y ) <= Math.abs( x ) + Math.abs( y )
```

Convert each of the following mathematical statements into a Java expression:

a. *The reverse triangle inequality:*

$$|x - y| \ge ||x| - |y||$$

b. *the formula for the total return t received when p dollars are invested for y years at an annual rate r with interest compounded monthly:*

$$t = p(1 + r/12)^{12y}$$

c. *The triple angle identity for the cosine function:*

$$\cos 3t = 4\cos^3 t - 3\cos t$$

d. *A version of the half-angle identity for the sine function:*

$$\left| \sin \frac{t}{2} \right| = \sqrt{\frac{1 - \cos t}{2}}$$

e. *The exponentiation formula for the log function (use the natural log):*

$$\log x^p = p \log x$$

5.6   Strings

By now it should be clear that Java programs can manipulate many kinds of data and that the language classifies the different kinds of data it can manipulate into types. Also, it is undeniably clear that one of the most important types of data that computers process is text. Text-based programs such as word processors and e-mail applications are among the most important and widely used applications on personal computers. Therefore, it should not be a surprise that Java has a type for manipulating textual data. This type is named String.

We have been using String values since our very first example program in Figure 1.3. Quoted pieces of text like the message

    "I'm Touched"

which appeared in that first program are literals describing values of the String type.

We have also seen that Java provides an operator for manipulating Strings. The operator is the plus sign. When used with Strings it denotes concatenation, the operation of joining two sequences of symbols together, rather than addition. Thus, in examples like

    curDisplay.setText("You have clicked " + theCount + " times.");

we are instructing Java to concatenate the digits of the value of theCount onto the end of the text "You have clicked " and then to tack the text " times." onto the end of the result of this first concatenation.

The fact that Java considers String a type implies that we can do several things with Strings that Java allows us to do with any type. We can use Strings as parameters. We have done this in both Text constructions and invocations of the System.out.println method. We can also define instance variables of String type and use assignment statements to associate values with these variables.

To illustrate the potential value of using String variables, consider the program shown in Figure 5.7. This program implements a simple interface one might use to practice encoding information in Morse code.

```
// A program to display Morse code entered by pressing
// the mouse as dots and dashes on the canvas.
public class MorseCode extends WindowController {

    // Location where code entered is displayed
    private static final Location DISPLAY_POS = new Location( 30, 30 );
    // Minimum time (in milliseconds) for a dash
    private static final double DASH_TIME = 200;

    // String to hold sequence entered so far
    private String currentCode = "Code = ";
    // Text used to display sequence on canvas
    private Text display;

    // Time when mouse was last depressed
    private double pressTime;

    // Create display
    public void begin() {
        display = new Text( "Code = ", DISPLAY_POS, canvas );
    }

    // Record time at which mouse was depressed
    public void onMousePress ( Location point ) {
        pressTime = System.currentTimeMillis();
    }

    // Add a dot or dash depending on click length
    public void onMouseRelease( Location point ) {
        if ( System.currentTimeMillis() - pressTime > DASH_TIME ) {
            currentCode = currentCode + " -";
        } else {
            currentCode = currentCode + " .";
        }
        display.setText( currentCode );
    }
}
```

Figure 5.7 A program to display Morse code as dots and dashes

In Morse code, each letter of the alphabet is encoded using a sequence of long and short signals. These signals are called dashes and dots because a standard way to represent the signals on paper is to draw a dash for a long signal and a dot for a short signal. Thus,

. . . - - - . . .

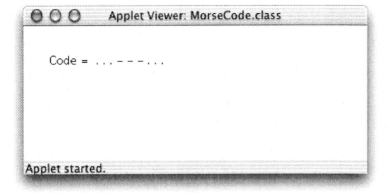

Figure 5.8   Sample of Morse code program display

represents a message composed of three short signals followed by three long signals followed by three short signals. This happens to be the Morse code for the distress signal "SOS".

The program in Figure 5.7 translates short and long presses of the computer's mouse button into a sequence of dots and dashes. If someone running the program used the mouse to enter the sequence discussed above, the program would display the output shown in Figure 5.8. The idea is that a person trying to learn Morse code could use the mouse to practice signaling and then look at the sequence of dots and dashes the program displays on the screen to see if she got it right. This means that we don't need to worry about which sequences of dots and dashes go with which letters of the alphabet to write the program. All we need to know about Morse code is that a short signal is a dot and a long signal is a dash.

The program uses a `String` variable named `currentCode` to keep track of the message it should display on the screen. Initially, the display will simply be

```
Code =
```

Then, each time the user clicks the mouse, the program will add a dot or a dash to the message. If the first thing the user does is a short click, the message will become

```
Code = .
```

If this is followed by two long clicks, the message will become

```
Code = . - -
```

and so on.

To add a dash to the value of the variable `currentCode`, the program uses an assignment statement of the form

```
currentCode = currentCode + " -";
```

which can be found in `onMouseRelease`. This statement looks like and acts a great deal like the similar assignment we have used to increment integer variables

```
count = count + 1;
```

It takes the existing text associated with `currentCode`, adds a dash to it, and then tells Java to make this the new value of `currentCode`.

The program uses the `System.currentTimeMillis` method described in Section 5.5.1 to access the current time when the mouse is pressed and released. It compares the time that elapses between these two events to a value, DASH_TIME. If the elapsed time is greater than this, it executes the assignment shown above to add a dash. Otherwise it uses a similar assignment to add a dot. Either way, after the mouse is released, it uses `setText` to update the `Text` object named `display` to hold the extended sequence of dots and dashes.

Everything we have told you about the `String` type so far would suggest it is a primitive type. Java provides literals for describing its values and allows us to use the + operator to manipulate `String` values. In fact, however, `String` is actually a class rather than a primitive type. It is a very special class. It is the only class with which Java provides literals.

One way to tell that `String` is a class is that Java also provides methods for manipulating `String` values. For now, the most important of these is the `equals` method. As with other objects, when we want to compare two `Strings` to see if they are the same, it is usually not appropriate to use ==. Instead, the `equals` method should be used. For example, if we wanted to check that the code entered in our program was the sequence for SOS, we might say

```
if ( currentCode.equals("Code = . . . - - - . . .") ) {
    . . .
```

Java provides many other accessor methods to operate on `Strings`. For example,

```
currentCode.length()
```

will produce an `int` value telling how many characters long a `String` is, and

```
if (currentCode.endsWith( ". . . - - - . . ." ) ) {
    . . .
```

can be used to check to see if someone using our program entered a sequence that ended with the SOS signal. We will consider these functions and other aspects of using `Strings` in more detail in Chapter 16.

5.7   Chapter Review Problems

EXERCISE 5.7.1

Define the following terms:

  a. *primitive values*
  b. *primitive types*
  c. `long`
  d. *modulus*

EXERCISE 5.7.2

Assuming a program contained the two declarations:

```
private Location myLocation = new Location( 10, 10 );
private Location yourLocation = new Location( 10, 10 );
```

a. *What result would be produced by the expression*

```
myLocation == yourLocation
```

b. *What result would be produced by the expression*

```
myLocation.equals(yourLocation)
```

c. *What coordinates would describe the* Locations *associated with the two variable names after the following statements had been executed?*

```
myLocation.translate( 15, 15 );
yourLocation.translate( -5, -5 );
```

EXERCISE 5.7.3

Assuming a program contained the two declarations:

```
private Location myLocation = new Location( 10, 10 );
private Location yourLocation = myLocation;
```

a. *What result would be produced by the expression*

```
myLocation == yourLocation
```

b. *What result would be produced by the expression*

```
myLocation.equals(yourLocation)
```

c. *What coordinates would describe the* Locations *associated with the two variable names after the following statements had been executed?*

```
myLocation.translate( 15, 15 );
yourLocation.translate( -5, -5 );
```

EXERCISE 5.7.4

Write the code necessary to declare an int *called* number, *initialized to 5, and a* Location *called* point, *initialized to (50,50). What are the differences in the declarations?*

EXERCISE 5.7.5

Let's revisit a classic in the world of mathematics, the Pythagorean theorem. The Pythagorean theorem states that for a right-angle triangle like that in Figure 5.9, $a^2 + b^2 = c^2$. Assume that

Figure 5.9   A right-angle triangle

a, b, *and* c *have been declared as variables of type* double. *Which one of the following expressions accurately describes the length of side* a*? What do the other two expressions represent?*

   a. `Math.sqrt( c * c ) - Math.sqrt( b * b )`
   b. `Math.sqrt( Math.pow( c, 2 ) ) + Math.sqrt( Math.pow( b, 2 ) )`
   c. `Math.sqrt( c * c - b * b )`

EXERCISE 5.7.6

Given that the variable books *is of type* int *and the variable* length *is of type* double, *what value will be associated with the variable given the following assignments?*

   a. `books = 250 * (4 / 5);`
   b. `length = 660 / 22.0;`
   c. `books = 660 / 22.0;`
   d. `length = 485.5 / 7.3;`
   e. `books = 250.0 * (4.0 / 5.0);`
   f. `books = 660 / 22;`
   g. `length = 21 * 7;`
   h. `length = 443 / 17;`

EXERCISE 5.7.7

Fill in the condition for the following code. myNumber *has been declared as an* int.

```
if ( // myNumber is evenly divisible by either 3 or 4 ) {
    // do something
}
```

EXERCISE 5.7.8

Assuming lastTime *has been declared to be of type* double *and then been assigned a value previously using* System.currentTimeMillis, *what is wrong with the following line of code? How would you fix it?*

```
System.out.println( "It has been " + ( System.currentTimeMillis()
                    - lastTime )
                + " seconds since last time" );
```

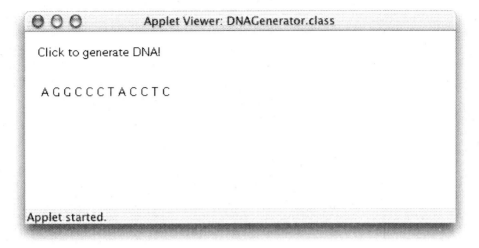

Figure 5.10 Display for DNAGenerator

5.8 Programming Problems

EXERCISE 5.8.1

Write a program called ElapsedTime *that displays the number of seconds that have elapsed between two clicks of the mouse. The program should not display a value after the first mouse click, but should display a value after every subsequent click of the mouse.*

EXERCISE 5.8.2

a. *DNA stands for* deoxyribonucleic acid, *which is a very long polymer of four different types of nucleotide bases. These four bases are guanine (G), adenine (A), thymine (T), and cytosine (C). It is the sequence of these bases that uniquely determines DNA. Write a simple program called* DNAGenerator *that may impress any friends of yours with interests in biology. This program will generate a strand of DNA by randomly adding one of the the four letters "G", "A", "T", or "C" each time the mouse is clicked. It also displays the generated DNA strand, as shown in Figure 5.10.*

b. *Modify your program so that no more than 20 bases are added to the DNA strand.*

EXERCISE 5.8.3

In Morse code, a single dot is used to represent the letter "E", a single dash represents a "T", and the letter "D" is represented by a dash followed by two dots. This means that the sequence

– · ·

has two possible interpretations. It could be a single letter "D" or it could be the word "TEE".

The lengths of the pauses between dots and dashes are used to resolve such ambiguities. If the pause between a pair of dots is short, then the two signals are treated as part of a single letter. If the pause is long, the signals are treated as parts of separate letters. To make it possible to represent such long and short pauses in our graphical representation of sequences of dots and dashes we might represent the sequence for "D" as

        −   ·   ·

and the sequence for "TEE" as

        −   ·   ·

That is, we would put more spaces between pairs of symbols if the pause between them was longer. Thus, the signal for "TED" would look like

        −   ·   − · ·

Modify `MorseCode` *so that it adds extra spaces for long pauses. Assume a pause is long if its duration equals (or exceeds) that of a dash.*

CHAPTER 6

Classes

o far when we have written a program, it has been by defining a single class that extends `WindowController`. The program's behavior results from defining methods with fixed names like `begin`, `onMousePress`, `onMouseClick`, and so on. In this chapter we will be designing very different classes that generate objects that can work together in programs.

All the geometric objects that we have been using have been generated from classes that have been provided for you. The classes include, for example, `Location`, `FilledRect`, `FramedRect`, `FilledOval`, `Line`, etc. The first classes we will be designing will provide methods and constructors similar to those used in the geometric classes. The Java code that we will write to support these will be similar to that which we have already written in earlier programs. We will be declaring constants and instance variables and defining methods in order to provide objects with the desired behavior.

This chapter focuses on how to avoid complexity by using classes. Classes allow programmers to design programs as the interaction of objects, each of which is capable of certain behaviors. While each behavior may be simple, the interactions of the objects allow relatively complicated tasks to be handled simply. In particular, each object will take responsibility for a collection of actions that contribute to the program. This can make testing the objects, assembling the final program, and removing any remaining errors it contains much easier. As a result, the design of classes is one of the most important aspects of object-oriented programming.

6.1   An Example Without Classes

While the focus of this chapter is on designing and writing classes to generate objects, we will begin with a simple example in which we do not create a new class. We will later contrast this approach with one where we define a new class to handle some of the more complex aspects of the program. Our goal is to convince you that the creation of new classes makes the programming process easier.

Recall the program `WhatADrag` from Figure 4.6. This program allowed the user to drag a rectangle around the screen. Only minor changes would be required to replace the rectangle by an oval. The name of the instance variable `box` would likely be replaced by a name like `circle` and its type would be changed from `FilledRect` to `FilledOval`. Then the assignment statement in the `begin` method would include the construction of a `FilledOval` rather than a `FilledRect`. However, aside from these minor changes of names, the structure of the program would remain essentially the same.

These minor changes work fine as long as we use a geometric object supported by our libraries, but suppose we want to drag around a triangle, which is not supported by our library. Now we have to work harder. We have to determine how to build the triangle from three straight lines, and we have to write code to determine whether a point is contained in a triangle.

We could have had the library support a triangle, but then we would still be missing classes to support a pentagon, hexagon, or some other polygon that might be needed for some particular problem. The point here is that we will often not be lucky enough to have exactly the classes we need. In those cases we will have to figure out a way of handling this ourselves.

In this chapter we will illustrate the use and implementation of classes with a fanciful example of a funny face, as shown in Figure 6.1. The program in Figure 6.2 displays a funny face and allows the user to drag it around the screen, very much like the program `WhatADrag`. Because the funny face has several geometric components, the main differences with `WhatADrag` are that several objects need to be moved with each drag of the mouse. The `head`, `leftEye`, `rightEye`, and `mouth` are declared as instance variables and are created in the `begin` method. As in `WhatADrag`, `lastPoint` will be an instance variable that keeps track of where the mouse was after the last mouse press or drag.

When we move the face in `onMouseDrag`, all four pieces must be moved. Imagine how much longer the method would be if the face had many more pieces. Worse yet, suppose we wanted to have two or more faces on the canvas at a time. It would rapidly become hard to keep track of the various pieces without forgetting one of them. This complexity arises because we do not have a class to create and manipulate funny faces in our library.

For the moment, suppose that we were provided with such a class. Assume that the construction of a `FunnyFace` object results in the execution of code to initialize the object including the construction of the geometric shapes that make up the face. Further, assume that the class provides methods `move` and `contains` that can be used to move the funny face and determine if a `Location` is inside the face, respectively. We could use this class exactly as we did the filled rectangle in the program `WhatADrag` in Figure 4.6.

The code for a class that uses `FunnyFace` is given in Figure 6.3. It is named RevFaceDrag. Its details are nearly identical to that of the original `WhatADrag` and is considerably simpler than

Figure 6.1   Funny face generated by FaceDrag

```
// Class to drag a funny face around
public class FaceDrag extends WindowController {
    ...    // Constant declarations omitted
    private FramedOval head;        // Parts of the face
    private FramedOval mouth;
    private FramedOval leftEye, rightEye;
    private Location lastPoint;     // Point where mouse was last seen

    // Whether the face has been grabbed by the mouse
    private boolean faceGrabbed = false;

    // Make the face
    public void begin() {
        head = new FramedOval( FACE_LEFT, FACE_TOP, FACE_WIDTH,
                            FACE_HEIGHT, canvas );
        mouth = new FramedOval( MOUTH_LEFT, MOUTH_TOP, MOUTH_WIDTH,
                            MOUTH_HEIGHT, canvas );
        leftEye = new FramedOval( FACE_LEFT+EYE_OFFSET-EYE_RADIUS/2,
                            FACE_TOP+EYE_OFFSET, EYE_RADIUS,
                            EYE_RADIUS, canvas );
        rightEye = new FramedOval( FACE_LEFT+FACE_WIDTH-EYE_OFFSET-
                            EYE_RADIUS/2, FACE_TOP+EYE_OFFSET,
                            EYE_RADIUS, EYE_RADIUS, canvas );
    }

    // Save point where mouse pressed and whether point was in face
    public void onMousePress( Location point ) {
        lastPoint = point;
        faceGrabbed = head.contains( point );
    }

    // If mouse is in face, then drag the face
    public void onMouseDrag( Location point ) {
        if ( faceGrabbed ) {
            head.move( point.getX() - lastPoint.getX(),
                    point.getY() - lastPoint.getY() );
            leftEye.move( point.getX() - lastPoint.getX(),
                    point.getY() - lastPoint.getY() );
            rightEye.move( point.getX() - lastPoint.getX(),
                    point.getY() - lastPoint.getY() );
            mouth.move( point.getX() - lastPoint.getX(),
                    point.getY() - lastPoint.getY() );
            lastPoint = point;
        }
    }
}
```

Figure 6.2   Code for dragging a funny face

```
// Class to drag a funny face around - uses FunnyFace class
public class RevFaceDrag extends WindowController {
    ...    // Constant declarations omitted

    private FunnyFace happy;        // FunnyFace to be dragged

    private Location lastPoint;    // Point where mouse was last seen

    // Whether happy has been grabbed by the mouse
    private boolean happyGrabbed = false;

    // Make the FunnyFace
    public void begin() {
        happy = new FunnyFace( FACE_LEFT, FACE_TOP, canvas );
    }

    // Save starting point and whether point was in happy
    public void onMousePress( Location point ) {
        lastPoint = point;
        happyGrabbed = happy.contains( point );
    }

    // If mouse is in happy, then drag happy
    public void onMouseDrag( Location point ) {
        if ( happyGrabbed ) {
            happy.move( point.getX() - lastPoint.getX(),
                        point.getY() - lastPoint.getY() );
            lastPoint = point;
        }
    }
}
```

Figure 6.3   Revised code for dragging a funny face

that for FaceDrag, because we don't have to worry about handling all of the different pieces of the funny face. We can treat the face as a single object.

The only differences from WhatADrag are that the variable box of class FilledRect has been replaced uniformly by the variable happy of class FunnyFace, variable boxGrabbed has been renamed as happyGrabbed, and the begin method now creates and names a FunnyFace rather than a FilledRect. Otherwise they are identical.

This "divide-and-conquer" approach makes developing programs much simpler. You can first write and test the class FunnyFace and then use it in other contexts that are now simpler.

In the next section we will discuss the design and implementation of classes, using the FunnyFace class as a first example. Later in the chapter we will reuse the FunnyFace class in yet another program, illustrating the advantages of designing classes to represent objects that may be used in many different situations.

EXERCISE 6.1.1

What are the advantages of creating several classes versus trying to place all of the code within one class?   ❖

6.2   Writing Classes: FunnyFace

A class is a template that can be used to create new objects, called *instances* of the class. So far we have written a number of classes that handle mouse events. These class definitions have included constant and instance variable declarations and method definitions. All classes contain features like this, as well as *constructors*, which determine what actions are to be performed when an object is constructed.

We say that a class *encapsulates* all of the features associated with the class. This is an important property of classes, because it means that we can find all relevant features in one place.

Each class used in a program contains methods that can be executed in order to perform certain behaviors. The methods of a class are said to specify the *behavior* of objects generated from the class. For example the FramedRect class has methods including move, moveTo, contains, and setColor. These methods can be invoked or executed by sending a *message* to a FramedRect object. A message consists of the name of a method supported by the object, and parameters that provide information to be used in executing the method. You can think of sending a message to an object as being analogous to asking or telling a person to do something (perform a particular behavior) for you.

Instance variables of a class are used to maintain the *state* of an object of the class. That is, they are used to store values that the object can use in executing the methods associated with the class. For example, a FramedRect object's state consists of information that allows the methods to determine the object's location, color, width, height, etc.

The constructors defined in a class are used to create new objects with the instance variables and methods specified in the class definition. When a constructor is executed, a new object is constructed with new copies of all of the instance variables specified by the class and with all of the methods.

We begin the study of classes by implementing the class FunnyFace, which was introduced in the last section. It should generate funny faces that can be dragged around on the canvas. In order for this to be possible, we would like each funny face to have methods like those of the geometric objects we have already been using. The class RevFaceDrag has code that sends messages move and contains to a funny face, so we will certainly need to include those. Normally we would add more methods, but these will be sufficient to demonstrate the structure of a class for now.

6.2.1   Instance Variables

First we consider what instance variables might be needed to write the code for the methods move and contains. Luckily the code in the original FaceDrag class in Figure 6.2 gives a clear indication of what is needed. The onMouseDrag method of that class included the following code:

```
if ( faceGrabbed ) {
    head.move( point.getX() - lastPoint.getX(),
               point.getY() - lastPoint.getY() );
    leftEye.move( point.getX() - lastPoint.getX(),
                  point.getY() - lastPoint.getY() );
    rightEye.move( point.getX() - lastPoint.getX(),
                   point.getY() - lastPoint.getY() );
    mouth.move( point.getX() - lastPoint.getX(),
                point.getY() - lastPoint.getY() );
    lastPoint = point;
}
```

This suggests that having instance variables with names like head, leftEye, rightEye, and mouth will be necessary in order to represent a FunnyFace object. These will all be declared as instance variables of FunnyFace, just as they originally were in FaceDrag.

```
private FramedOval head;                    // Parts of the face
private FramedOval mouth;
private FramedOval leftEye, rightEye;
```

6.2.2   Methods and Parameters

Now that we have determined the instance variables, let's write the move method for FunnyFace.

```
// Move funny face by (dx,dy)
public void move( double dx, double dy ) {
    head.move( dx, dy );
    leftEye.move( dx, dy );
    rightEye.move( dx, dy );
    mouth.move( dx, dy );
}
```

To move a funny face by dx in the horizontal direction and dy vertically, we simply tell each of its four parts to move by that much.

The only things really new in this method definition are the *formal parameter* declarations of dx and dy in the method header. (The parameter names dx and dy suggest that they stand for *differences* between the old and new coordinates.) While the methods we have written so far have had at most one formal parameter, the method move takes two parameters to determine the distance to move in the horizontal and vertical directions. When there is more than one formal parameter in a method, we separate the declarations by commas. Unfortunately, unlike instance variable declarations, you may not combine two formal parameter declarations that have the same type. Thus you may *not* write move(double dx, dy) in the declaration of move.

We use the move method in the same way we used the methods for geometric objects. In RevFaceDrag, the onMouseDrag method includes the code

```
happy.move( point.getX() - lastPoint.getX(),
            point.getY() - lastPoint.getY() );
```

where happy is a variable of class FunnyFace. This method invocation has two (somewhat complex) *actual parameters*, point.getX() - lastPoint.getX() and point.getY() - lastPoint.getY(), which are separated by a comma.

The idea is that when happy.move(...) is executed, the formal parameters dx and dy are associated with the values of the actual parameters. Thus when the body of move in FunnyFace is executed as a result of this call, the values of dx and dy represent the differences in the *x* and *y* coordinates of point and lastPoint.

The actual parameters are matched up with the formal parameters in the same order they are written. Formal parameters are declared (with their types) in method headers and are used in method bodies. Actual parameters are used in sending messages to objects (or equivalently, invoking methods of objects). When a method begins execution, the values of actual parameters (which may be given as quite complex expressions) are associated with the formal parameters. Thus in the call of happy.move above, the first actual parameter, point.getX() - lastPoint.getX(), is associated with the first formal parameter, dx. Similarly the second actual parameter is associated with dy.

For example, if point represented (12,33) and lastPoint represented (10,40), then the actual parameters associated with the invocation of happy.move would be 2 and −7. At run time these values would be associated with the formal parameters dx and dy, respectively, so all of the components would be moved by 2 to the right and 7 up.

EXERCISE 6.2.1

When the computer executes happy.move(point.getX(), 0), *what values are associated with the formal parameters* dx *and* dy *of the* move *method of class* FunnyFace? ❖

EXERCISE 6.2.2

Suppose we added a new instance variable, nose, *of type* FramedOval *to* FunnyFace. *How would the body of the* move *method change?* ❖

EXERCISE 6.2.3

Suppose we want to have a class called PictureFrame *which represents two* FramedRects, *one inside of the other, to form a pair of nested rectangles. Define the instance variables of this class and write the* move *method.* ❖

6.2.3 Writing Accessor Methods

With this understanding of methods and parameters, we are now ready to write the contains method, an accessor method that returns a value of type boolean. Writing methods that return values differs in two ways from the kind of methods we have considered to this point. First, we must write a statement in the body of the method indicating the value to be returned. Second, we must indicate in the method header the type of the value to be returned.

To determine if a location is inside a funny face, we need only determine whether it is inside the head (if a point is inside any part of the face it must be inside the head). We write it as follows:

```
// Determine whether pt is inside funny face
public boolean contains( Location pt ) {
    return head.contains( pt );
}
```

Because `contains` is to return a boolean value, we must write the type `boolean` before the method name. In all mutator method definitions we have written, including, for example, `onMousePress` and `onMouseDrag`, that slot has been filled with the type `void`, which is used in Java to indicate that the method performs an action but does not return a value.

A type different from `void` written before the method name in a method declaration indicates that the method returns a value of that type. For example, if `FunnyFace` had a method returning the x coordinate of the left edge of the face, the header of its declaration might look like

```
public double getLeftEdge()
```

From the declaration we can see that this method has no formal parameters but returns a value of type `double`. Similarly, a declaration

```
public FramedOval getBoundary()
```

would indicate that `getBoundary` has no formal parameters and returns a value of type `FramedOval`.

Let's go back to the body of `contains`. The body of a method that returns a value may include several lines of code, but the last statement executed must be of the form `return` *expn*, where *expn* represents an expression whose type is the return type of the method. When the method is invoked, the method body is executed and the value of *expn* is returned as the value of the method invocation. The method `contains` happens to include only a single line, a `return` statement that returns the value of `head.contains( pt )`.

The `contains` method of `FunnyFace` is used in the `onMousePress` method of `RevFaceDrag` in an assignment statement:

```
happyGrabbed = happy.contains( point );
```

Let's trace the execution of this assignment statement to make sure that we understand how the method invocation works. When the expression `happy.contains( point )` is evaluated, the actual parameter `point` is associated with the formal parameter `pt` of the method `contains`. Then the expression `head.contains( pt )` from the `return` statement is evaluated. This will return `true` exactly when the actual parameter `point` is inside of the `FramedOval` associated with `head`. That boolean value is returned as the value of `happy.contains( point )`. After it returns, that boolean value is assigned to `happyGrabbed`.

➡ EXERCISE 6.2.4

Suppose we add two new instance variables, `leftEar` and `rightEar`, of type `FilledOval` to `FunnyFace`, so that the ears stick out of the head. How would the body of the `contains` method change if the method should return `true` if pt is in either the face or one of the ears?   ❖

6.2.4   Constructors

Now that we've discussed the instance variables and the two methods move and contains, we're almost done with the definition of the class FunnyFace. If we look back at our first attempt at this program, FunnyFaceDrag, and compare that with RevFaceDrag and the pieces of FunnyFace we've just discussed, we find that there is only one thing missing.

The begin method of FunnyFaceDrag initialized the instance variables head, leftEye, rightEye, and mouth. The begin method of RevFaceDrag, by contrast, includes only the single line:

```
happy = new FunnyFace( FACE_LEFT, FACE_TOP, canvas );
```

Obviously, the construction new FunnyFace(FACE_LEFT, FACE_TOP, canvas) should create a new object from class FunnyFace, in the process initializing the instance variables of the class. We have used constructions very much like this for geometric objects, but we have not yet seen what the code behind the construction looks like.

To allow this construction we must write a *constructor* definition for FunnyFace. Constructor definitions look very much like method definitions except that there is no return type specified (not even void), and the name of the constructor must be the same as the name of the class. The constructor for class FunnyFace will have three formal parameters: left, top, and canvas, representing the *x* coordinate of the left edge of the face, the *y* coordinate of the top of the face, and the canvas the face will be drawn on. The body of the constructor for FunnyFace, shown below, uses top and left (along with several constants declared in the class) to calculate the locations of each of the components of the funny face, and constructs those components on the canvas.

```java
// Create pieces of funny face
public FunnyFace( double left, double top, DrawingCanvas canvas ) {
    head = new FramedOval( left, top, FACE_WIDTH, FACE_HEIGHT,
                            canvas );

    mouth = new FramedOval( left+(FACE_WIDTH-MOUTH_WIDTH)/2,
                            top+2*FACE_HEIGHT/3, MOUTH_WIDTH,
                            MOUTH_HEIGHT, canvas );

    leftEye = new FramedOval( left+EYE_OFFSET-EYE_RADIUS/2,
                            top+EYE_OFFSET, EYE_RADIUS,
                            EYE_RADIUS, canvas );
    rightEye = new FramedOval( left+FACE_WIDTH-EYE_OFFSET-
                            EYE_RADIUS/2, top+EYE_OFFSET,
                            EYE_RADIUS, EYE_RADIUS, canvas );
}
```

The parameter canvas must be passed to the FunnyFace constructor because only classes that extend WindowController have automatic access to the canvas. If other objects need to use the canvas, then it must be passed to them as a parameter.

The constructor body for FunnyFace is very similar to the code in the begin method of FaceDrag in Figure 6.2. In general, constructors for regular classes play a role similar to that of the begin method in classes that extend WindowController. In this case, the code of the constructor creates the four components of the funny face and associates them with the appropriate instance variables.

The expressions used as parameters in the constructions for the components (e.g., mouth) in the FunnyFace constructor are more complex than they were in the begin method of FaceDrag, because the locations of the components must be computed relative to the parameters left and top.

When a programmer wishes to create a new FunnyFace, as in the begin method of class RevFaceDrag in Figure 6.3, she writes a construction like the following:

    new FunnyFace(leftSide, topSide, canvas)

As with methods, the three actual parameters of the construction are associated with the formal parameters of the constructor in the order they are written. Thus the actual parameter leftSide is associated with the formal parameter left, topSide is associated with top, and the actual parameter canvas, from the RevFaceDrag class, is associated with the formal parameter canvas of the FunnyFace constructor.

The last association might seem strange, as canvas is being associated with canvas. The reason that it is necessary to explicitly make this association is that the canvas from RevFunnyFace has nothing to do with the formal parameter canvas of the constructor. The fact that they have the same name is essentially an "accident".[1] The only reason the two are associated when the constructor is called is that each is the third in the list of parameters for the constructor—one as an actual parameter and the other as a formal parameter.

If the constructor is called several times with different values for left and top, it will result in several funny faces being constructed in different locations on the canvas. Thus if we write

    happyLeft = new FunnyFace(40, 100, canvas);
    happyRight = new FunnyFace(90, 100, canvas);

the program will place two funny faces, happyLeft and happyRight, next to each other on canvas.

It is important to remember that each instance of a class has its own distinct collection of instance variables. Thus happyLeft will have instance variables face, eyeLeft, eyeRight, and mouth. The object named by happyRight will have its own private and distinct copies of each of these variables. Thus the oval representing the face of happyLeft will be 50 pixels to the left of the oval representing the face of happyRight.

⫸ EXERCISE 6.2.5

Write the constructor for the PictureFrame class from Exercise 6.2.3. Assume the class uses two FramedRect instance variables to hold the parts of the picture frame. The parameters to the constructor should determine the upper left corner of the frame, its width and height, and the separation between the two FramedRects. You are free to select the exact parameters expected and their order.

[1] We chose the same name for the two different variables on purpose, as we wished to suggest that they should be associated—it is just that the computer doesn't know to make that association unless we tell it to by passing the actual parameter canvas to be associated with the formal parameter canvas.

➡ EXERCISE 6.2.6

Write a class extending WindowController *that creates two objects of type* FunnyFace. *If the user presses the mouse on one of the two faces, then dragging the mouse will result in dragging that face. The code will be similar to that in Figure 6.3, but the* onMousePress *method will need to keep track of what face was selected so that the* onMouseDrag *method will move the correct face.*   ❖

6.2.5   Putting It All Together

The complete definition of the class FunnyFace can be found in Figure 6.4. As usual, the first line of the class definition specifies the name of the class, in this case, FunnyFace. This class does *not* extend WindowController, as it has nothing to do with reacting to mouse actions on the canvas. The definitions of the features of FunnyFace are enclosed in braces that begin after the class name. The features include constant definitions, instance variable declarations, the constructor definition, and the method definitions.

Class definitions in Java are written as follows:

```
public class Name {

    constant definitions

    variable declarations

    constructor(s)

    methods
}
```

While Java does not insist that the order be exactly that specified above, we will find that ordering convenient for all of the examples in this text.

An important restriction in most development environments for Java is that the name of the file containing a class must correspond to the class name. For example, the name of the file containing class FunnyFace would have to be FunnyFace.java. Similarly, when the class is compiled, the name of the file holding the compiled class will be FunnyFace.class.

It is useful to have a graphical way of presenting important information about a class. We will use a picture like the following to represent classes:

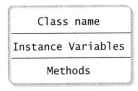

Notice that all of the important features of the class except for the constructors are represented in this diagram.

```
public class FunnyFace {

    private static final int FACE_HEIGHT = 60, // Dimensions of
                                 FACE_WIDTH = 60,  // the face

                                 EYE_OFFSET = 20,  // Eye location and size
                                 EYE_RADIUS = 8,

                                 MOUTH_HEIGHT = 10,       // Dimensions of
                                 MOUTH_WIDTH = FACE_WIDTH/2; // the mouth

    private FramedOval head,                     // Parts of the face
                       leftEye,
                       rightEye,
                       mouth;

    // Create pieces of funny face
    public FunnyFace( double left, double top, DrawingCanvas canvas ) {
        head = new FramedOval( left, top, FACE_WIDTH,
                            FACE_HEIGHT, canvas );
        mouth = new FramedOval( left+(FACE_WIDTH-MOUTH_WIDTH)/2,
                            top+2*FACE_HEIGHT/3, MOUTH_WIDTH,
                            MOUTH_HEIGHT, canvas );
        leftEye = new FramedOval( left+EYE_OFFSET-EYE_RADIUS/2,
                            top+EYE_OFFSET, EYE_RADIUS,
                            EYE_RADIUS, canvas );
        rightEye = new FramedOval( left+FACE_WIDTH-EYE_OFFSET-
                            EYE_RADIUS/2, top+EYE_OFFSET,
                            EYE_RADIUS, EYE_RADIUS, canvas );
    }

    // Move funny face by (dx, dy)
    public void move( double dx, double dy ) {
        head.move( dx, dy );
        leftEye.move( dx, dy );
        rightEye.move( dx, dy );
        mouth.move( dx, dy );
    }

    // Determine whether pt is inside funny face
    public boolean contains( Location pt ) {
        return head.contains( pt );
    }
}
```

Figure 6.4   FunnyFace class

For example, we can represent the FunnyFace class as:

FunnyFace
FramedOval Head FramedOval leftEye FramedOval rightEye FramedOval mouth
move(double, double) boolean contains(Location)

We include the names and types for instance variables. We also include the names of the methods, the types of their parameters, and their return types if they return a value. If the return type is void, then we omit it from the diagram. We do not bother to record the names of the formal parameters because they are not important in invoking a method. The caller need only make sure that there are the appropriate number of actual parameters and that they have the necessary types.

Now that we have completed the FunnyFace class, let's compare that class and RevFaceDrag with the original FunnyFaceDrag. The class FunnyFaceDrag had five instance variables—the four components of the face and the variable lastPoint to keep track of the last location of the mouse. The four components of the face were moved to the FunnyFace class, while lastPoint was kept with the mouse-handling code of RevFaceDrag because it was more relevant to the mouse movements than to the funny face.

All of this effort to create a FunnyFace class may seem like a lot of work for little benefit. After all, the code of class FaceDrag is shorter than the combination of the code in classes FunnyFace and RevFaceDrag. However, there are several advantages to creating and using the class FunnyFace.

One benefit is that, having created the FunnyFace class, we can use this class in any program now or in the future, rather than having to rewrite the functionality. In particular, this class may be used with a variety of other classes to create more complex programs. (We illustrate this later in the chapter by using FunnyFace in a different program.)

Another benefit is that, because this program supports the same kind of methods as the geometric objects in the objectdraw library, we may use it just like these other objects. In the example above, the difference between a program allowing the user to drag around a rectangle and one allowing the user to drag around a funny face is minimal. We can thus reuse with minimal changes other code that we have already determined works with other kinds of objects. In Chapter 10 we'll introduce a feature of Java, the interface, that will make this reuse of code even easier.

6.3 Adding Methods to FunnyFace

If we were to use objects from class FunnyFace in other programs like those we wrote using geometric objects from the library, we would likely need to include additional methods in the FunnyFace class. Such methods might include hide, show, setColor, and getColor, among others. In this section we discuss how we could write such methods.

6.3.1   Some Methods Are Like Those Already Written

The code for hide is similar to that of move in that it simply forwards hide messages to each of its components.

```
// Hide the funny face
public void hide() {
    face.hide();
    leftEye.hide();
    rightEye.hide();
    mouth.hide();
}
```

The code for show, setColor and getColor should be easy for you to write, as they are similar to move, hide, and contains.

➡ EXERCISE 6.3.1

---

a. *Write the methods* show *and* setColor *for the class* FunnyFace.
b. *Write the code for* getColor. *It is an accessor method and should be similar to* contains.

Hint: *Is there any reason to get the colors of* all *of the components?*   ❖

6.3.2   Defining Methods Indirectly

Because FunnyFace has a move method, an obvious addition would be a moveTo method that would take new *x* and *y* coordinates as its formal parameters and would result in moving the object to those coordinates. Writing the method moveTo will be a bit trickier than move. It is tempting to try to mimic the structure of the move method by placing instructions in the moveTo method's body that tell all four parts of the funny face to move to the coordinates provided as parameters. Unfortunately, if we did this, the eyes and the mouth would end up on top of each other in the upper left hand corner of the face.

We could instead calculate where we want all of the pieces to be after the moveTo, and send a moveTo message with different parameters to each component of the funny face. However, it would be pretty painful to have to calculate all of those locations. (Look at how horrible all the calculations were in the constructor!)

There is an alternative that is both clever and simple—an ideal combination. What we will do is figure out *how far* to move the funny face rather than *where* to move it. Once we calculate the horizontal and vertical distance the funny face is to move, we can pass those as actual parameters to the funny face's move method and take advantage of the fact that we have already written that method:

```
public void moveTo( double x, double y ) {
    this.move( x - head.getX(), y - head.getY() );
}
```

In the code for moveTo we calculate the differences between the *x* and *y* coordinates to which the head should move and its current coordinates. These x and y differences are then used as the actual parameters for an invocation of the method move from this class.

One difference between the invocation in the first line of the moveTo method and others we have seen so far is that we want to execute the move method of the funny face itself, rather than telling the objects associated with the face's instance variables to execute their methods.

We indicate that this is our intention by sending the message to this. Java provides the keyword this for programmers to use in method bodies as a name for the object that is currently executing the method. Thus when we write this.move(...) we are telling Java that we want to invoke the move method for this object, the one currently executing the moveTo method.

Let's think about what happens a bit more concretely. The RevFaceDrag class has a variable of type FunnyFace named happy. Suppose we add an onMouseClick method to RevFaceDrag that causes happy to be moved to wherever the user clicked:

```
// Move happy to where clicked
public void onMouseClick( Location point ) {
    happy.moveTo( point.getX(), point.getY() );
}
```

What happens when the statement happy.moveTo(point) is executed? The code for method moveTo of the FunnyFace class is just the single instruction

```
this.move( x - head.getX(), y - head.getY() );
```

where the values of the formal parameters x and y are the actual parameters point.getX() and point.getY(), respectively.

When the message send is executed, the keyword this will stand for happy, as it is the object executing the moveTo method. Thus the move message is sent to happy, with the same effect as if we had written happy.move(...). The formal parameters dx and dy of the method move will be set to the values of pt.getX() - head.getX() and pt.getY() - head.getY(), respectively.

Because it is fairly common to have one method of an object invoke another method of the same object, Java allows the programmer to abbreviate the message send by omitting the "this." prefix. That is, we could instead write the body of moveTo as

```
public void moveTo( double x, double y ) {
    move( x - head.getX(), y - head.getY() );
}
```

At least initially, we will include the target this in message sends in order to remind the reader that messages are sent to objects—they do not stand alone.

It is also possible to attach the this prefix to an instance variable, but, as with methods, we may omit it (as we have to this point in all of our examples). We will generally continue to omit it in our examples, though we will see in Section 8.3 that prefixing an instance variable with this can sometimes be helpful.

From now on we will assume that the definition of FunnyFace includes the method moveTo defined above. As suggested earlier, that will allow us to use FunnyFace more effectively in other programs.

➡ EXERCISE 6.3.2

Normally we would make the FunnyFace class even more flexible by also including parameters in the constructor to specify the width and height of the funny face being created. We left those off in this version of FunnyFace in order to keep the code simpler. Rewrite the constructor for FunnyFace to take two extra parameters width and height of type double to represent the width and height of the funny face being constructed. ❖

6.3.3   Using this as a Parameter

The keyword this, which refers to the object executing a method, has the same type as the object executing the code. As a result, we can pass this as a parameter of a message, so that the receiver can send messages back to the sender. This is not unlike sending someone your e-mail address so that they can correspond with you.

For example, suppose that we wish to create classes for keys and locks, and that moreover, every time we create a key, we want to associate it with the appropriate lock. We can do that by creating a makeKey method for the lock that will both create the key and tell the key what lock it opens.

Let us assume that we have a constructor for the key that takes as a parameter the lock it is associated with. The constructor might look like:

```
public class Key {
    private Lock myLock;
    ...

    public Key( Lock myLock ) {
        myLock = theLock;
        ...
    }

    public Lock getMyLock() {
        return myLock;
    }
}
```

The Lock class and its method makeKey are shown below:

```
public class Lock {
    ...
    public Key createKey() {
        return new Key( this );
    }

    ...
}
```

The use of this as a parameter to the Key constructor in class Lock results in passing the lock itself as a parameter to the constructor for Key. For example, if bikeLock is a variable of type Lock, then

```
Key bikeKey = bikeLock.createKey();
```

results in bikeKey referring to the key that unlocks bikeLock. In particular, evaluating bikeKey.getMyLock() refers to the same value as bikeLock.

6.4   Another Example: Implementing a Timer Class

In this section we practice what we have learned by designing another program that uses classes. There are two main points that we would like to make with this example. The first is that we can define classes like Location that are useful in programs, but that do not result in anything being displayed on the canvas. The second is that we can reuse previously defined classes to solve new problems.

The application we are interested in is a very simple game in which the user tries to click on an object soon after it moves to a new position. Because success in the game depends on clicking soon after the object has moved, we will create a Timer class that provides facilities to calculate elapsed time. We will reuse the FunnyFace class to create the object to be chased. Unlike the FunnyFace class, the Timer does not result in anything being drawn on the screen.

To calculate elapsed time, the Timer class uses the method System.currentTimeMillis introduced in Chapter 5. Recall that this method returns the number of milliseconds (thousandths of a second) since January 1, 1970. Because we are interested in the length of time intervals, we will obtain starting and ending times and then subtract them.

As we can see from the diagram and code in Figure 6.5, the Timer class is very simple. The class has a single instance variable startTime that is initialized in the constructor with the value of System.currentTimeMillis. It can be reinitialized in the reset method by reevaluating System.currentTimeMillis. The methods elapsedMilliseconds and elapsedSeconds calculate the elapsed time between startTime and the time when the methods are called. As the time values used are all in units of milliseconds, the number of seconds of elapsed time must be calculated by computing the number of milliseconds and then dividing by 1000. The type of the value returned by both of these methods is double; neither takes any parameters.

The class Chase is an extension of WindowController. Using the class FunnyFace, it creates a funny face in the upper part of the canvas, and constructs a Text message, infoText, that tells the user to click to start playing the game. When the user clicks for the first time, the funny face moves to a new position on the canvas. If the user clicks on it within TIME_LIMIT seconds, the user wins. If the user misses the funny face with the click, then a message appears indicating that the user missed, and the funny face moves to a new randomly selected location. If the user clicks on the funny face in time, a message is displayed and the user is instructed to click to start the game again. Finally, if the user clicks on the funny face, but too slowly, then the message "Too slow" appears and the funny face is moved.

The code for the class Chase is given in Figures 6.6 and 6.7. Instance variables are declared for the funny face, timer, and text display. There are two different instance variables representing random number generators to obtain new *x* and *y* coordinates of the funny face, because the ranges for the possible values of the *x* and *y* coordinates are different. Finally there is a boolean instance variable, playing, that keeps track of whether or not the game has actually started.

The begin method initializes stopWatch with the current time, and creates random number generators to be used to select new *x* and *y* coordinates when the funny face is moved. The new FunnyFace, which is constructed a little above the center of the screen, is associated with instance variable funFace. The Text object infoText is created just below the face with a startup message telling the user how to start the game. Finally playing is initialized to be false. This instance variable keeps track of whether the game is in progress and the system is

```
                    ┌─────────────────────────────────────┐
                    │              Timer                   │
                    ├─────────────────────────────────────┤
                    │          double startTime            │
                    ├─────────────────────────────────────┤
                    │    double elapsedMilliseconds()      │
                    │       double elapsedseconds()        │
                    │               reset()               │
                    └─────────────────────────────────────┘
```

```java
// Class allowing calculations of timing between events.

public class Timer {

    private double startTime;    // Time when Timer started or reset

    // Create timer, initializing startTime with current time
    public Timer() {
        startTime = System.currentTimeMillis();
    }

    // Return number of milliseconds since last reset
    public double elapsedMilliseconds() {
        return System.currentTimeMillis() - startTime;
    }

    // Return number of seconds since last reset
    public double elapsedSeconds() {
        return this.elapsedMilliseconds() / 1000;
    }

    // Reset startTime
    public void reset() {
        startTime = System.currentTimeMillis();
    }
}
```

Figure 6.5   Timer class and diagram

waiting for the user to click on the funny face, or the system is simply waiting for the user to click to start the game.

The onMouseClick method of Chase determines how the program reacts to a click. The conditional statement provides cases for when the game has not yet started (playing is false), when the click does not occur in funFace, when the user succeeds (the click does occur in funFace and within the appropriate time interval), and when the elapsed time is too long. The code in each of those cases is straightforward.

```java
// Implementation of a chase-the-face game
public class Chase extends WindowController
{
    private static final double TIME_LIMIT = 1.5;
                                            // Time available to click

    private FunnyFace funFace;              // Funny face to be chased

    private Timer stopWatch;                // Timer to see if click
                                           // fast enough

    private Text infoText;                  // Text item to be displayed
                                           // during game

    private RandomIntGenerator randXGen,    // Generators to get new
                               randYGen;    // x and y coords

    private boolean playing;                // Is player playing or
                                           // waiting to start

    // Set up timer and funny face for game
    public void begin() {
        stopWatch = new Timer();
        randXGen = new RandomIntGenerator( 0, canvas.getWidth() );
        randYGen = new RandomIntGenerator( 0, canvas.getHeight() );
        funFace = new FunnyFace( canvas.getWidth()/2,
                        canvas.getHeight()/3, canvas );
        infoText = new Text( "Click to start chasing the FunnyFace.",
                        canvas.getWidth()/3,
                        canvas.getHeight()/2, canvas );
        playing = false;
    }
}
```

Figure 6.6   Chase class: instance variables and begin method

We will make several improvements to this program in the following sections as we introduce new features of Java that are useful in writing classes.

6.5   Local Variables

So far we have seen how to give names to instance variables and formal parameters. There is another kind of variable that can be named and used in Java classes. They are used to hold information that is only needed during the execution of a method. Variables of this kind are called local variables.

```
// Determine if user won and move funny face if necessary
public void onMouseClick( Location pt ) {
    if ( !playing ) {                               // Start playing
        playing = true;
        infoText.setText( "Click quickly on the FunnyFace to win!" );
        funFace.moveTo( randXGen.nextValue(), randYGen.nextValue() );
        stopWatch.reset();
    }
    else if ( !funFace.contains( pt ) ) {      // Missed the funny face
        infoText.setText( "You missed!" );
        funFace.moveTo( randXGen.nextValue(), randYGen.nextValue() );
        stopWatch.reset();
    }
    else if ( stopWatch.elapsedSeconds() <= TIME_LIMIT ) {
                                                // Got it in time!
        playing = false;
        infoText.setText(
                "You got the face in time.  Click to restart." );
    }
    else {                                      // User was too slow
        infoText.setText( "Too slow!" );
        funFace.moveTo( randXGen.nextValue(), randYGen.nextValue() );
        stopWatch.reset();
    }
    }
}
```

Figure 6.7   Chase class onMouseClick method

In order to better motivate the use of local variables, we make the funny face a bit more elaborate. We modify the picture so that rather than having an oval for the mouth, we have a smile. We can accomplish this by painting a white oval over the top part of the mouth, leaving only the bottom part of the mouth showing. We introduce a new instance variable, mouthCover, with type FilledOval, for this purpose. The revised constructor code is given in Figure 6.8.

The code for this constructor involves a number of complex expressions that calculate the *x* and *y* coordinates of the upper left corners of the components of the funny face. Moreover, several of these expressions are calculated more than once. Thus the code involves both difficult-to-understand expressions and redundant calculations. It would be easier to understand this code if we could pre-compute some of these values and give them understandable names to be used in creating the components of the face.

Figure 6.9 contains the code for a revised version of the constructor. The effect of the constructor is exactly the same as the original, but we have pulled out three expressions from the original and given them names: mouthLeft, mouthTop, and eyeTop. As one would hope, the names suggest what they stand for, the coordinates of the left and top of the mouth, and the top of the eyes.

```
// Create pieces of funny face
public FunnyFace( double left, double top, DrawingCanvas canvas ) {
    head = new FramedOval( left, top, FACE_WIDTH, FACE_HEIGHT, canvas );
    mouth = new FramedOval( left+(FACE_WIDTH-MOUTH_WIDTH)/2,
                            top+2*FACE_HEIGHT/3,
                            MOUTH_WIDTH, MOUTH_HEIGHT, canvas );
    mouthCover = new FilledOval( left+( FACE_WIDTH-MOUTH_WIDTH)/2,
                                 top+2*FACE_HEIGHT/3-EYE_RADIUS/2,
                                 MOUTH_WIDTH, MOUTH_HEIGHT, canvas );
    mouthCover.setColor( Color.WHITE );
    leftEye = new FramedOval( left+EYE_OFFSET-EYE_RADIUS/2,
                              top+EYE_OFFSET, EYE_RADIUS,
                              EYE_RADIUS, canvas );
    rightEye = new FramedOval( left+FACE_WIDTH-EYE_OFFSET-EYE_RADIUS/2,
                               top+EYE_OFFSET, EYE_RADIUS,
                               EYE_RADIUS, canvas );

}
```

Figure 6.8 FunnyFace constructor with a smile

Because we now have names for these expressions, the names can be used in the constructions for `mouth`, `mouthCover`, `leftEye`, and `rightEye`. Moreover the calculations for these values are only made once, with the values available for reuse in multiple places in the code.

New identifiers that are declared in constructor or method bodies are known as *local variables*. Local variables may only be used inside the methods or constructors in which they are defined, and their declarations must occur before their uses. Thus `mouthLeft` is used inside the body of the constructor `FunnyFace`, but is not accessible inside any of the methods of the class `FunnyFace`. This is quite different from the instance variables of the class, which are accessible inside any of the constructors or methods of the class. In general we prefer to declare variables locally, unless they need to be retained between invocations of methods or after the execution of the constructor.

Because local variables are accessible only inside the method or constructor in which they are defined, Java does not require or even allow them to be designated as `private`. Instead, local variables are specified by just giving their types and names.

Local variables, like instance variables, may be initialized in their declarations. Thus we may replace the first four lines of the body of the constructor `FunnyFace` in Figure 6.9 by

```
double mouthLeft = left + (FACE_WIDTH-MOUTH_WIDTH)/2;
double mouthTop = top + 2*FACE_HEIGHT/3;
double eyeTop = top + EYE_OFFSET;
```

Local variables must always be initialized before their use.

We can modify the `onMouseClick` method of the class `Chase` to show another use of a local variable. Suppose we wish to display the elapsed time between when the funny face moved and when the user clicked on it. In that case it might be helpful to calculate the elapsed time at the beginning of the method, using that saved time wherever the elapsed time is needed. In the code

```
// Create pieces of funny face
public FunnyFace( double left, double top, DrawingCanvas canvas ) {
    // Coordinates of mouth and eyes
    double mouthLeft, mouthTop, eyeTop;

    mouthLeft = left+(FACE_WIDTH-MOUTH_WIDTH)/2;
    mouthTop = top+2*FACE_HEIGHT/3;
    eyeTop = top+EYE_OFFSET;

    head = new FramedOval( left, top, FACE_WIDTH, FACE_HEIGHT, canvas );
    mouth = new FramedOval( mouthLeft, mouthTop,
                        MOUTH_WIDTH, MOUTH_HEIGHT, canvas );
    mouthCover = new FilledOval( mouthLeft, mouthTop-EYE_RADIUS/2,
                        MOUTH_WIDTH, MOUTH_HEIGHT, canvas );
    mouthCover.setColor( Color.WHITE );
    leftEye = new FramedOval( left+EYE_OFFSET-EYE_RADIUS/2, eyeTop,
                        EYE_RADIUS, EYE_RADIUS, canvas );
    rightEye = new FramedOval( left+FACE_WIDTH-EYE_OFFSET-EYE_RADIUS/2,
                        eyeTop, EYE_RADIUS, EYE_RADIUS, canvas );
}
```

Figure 6.9   A revised version of the smiling FunnyFace constructor using local variables

in Figure 6.10 it is calculated and saved in the local variable elapsedTime and used twice in the third case of the conditional. It is used to test if the user was fast enough, and also to display a message in infoText.

➡ EXERCISE 6.5.1

a. *How are local variables different from instance variables?*
b. *Explain why* eyeTop *in the revised* FunnyFace *can be a local variable.*   ❖

6.6   Overloaded Methods and Constructors

As we saw earlier, the meaning of arithmetic operators may differ depending on the types of the operands. Thus the result of evaluating 7/3 is the int 2, while the result of evaluating 7.0/3.0 is the double 2.333.... Operators like this, which use the same symbol to represent different operations, are said to be *overloaded*. Java does not allow the programmer to define new overloaded operations, but it does allow programmers to define overloaded methods.

Java allows a class to have two methods with the same name, as long as they can be distinguished by the types of their parameters.[2] Methods such as this are also said to be *overloaded*.

---

[2] Of course we have already seen many examples where different classes have methods with the same name. That is never a problem, because when we send a message to an object, the system obtains the corresponding method from the class of the receiver.

```
// Determine if user won and move funny face if necessary
public void onMouseClick( Location pt ) {
    double elapsedTime = stopWatch.elapsedSeconds();
    if ( !playing ) {                           // Start playing
        playing = true;
        infoText.setText( "Click quickly on the FunnyFace to win!" );
        funFace.moveTo( randXGen.nextValue(), randYGen.nextValue() );
        stopWatch.reset();
    }
    else if ( !funFace.contains( pt ) ) {       // Missed the funny face
        infoText.setText( "You missed!" );
        funFace.moveTo( randXGen.nextValue(), randYGen.nextValue() );
        stopWatch.reset();
    }
    else if ( elapsedTime <= TIME_LIMIT ) {   // Got it in time!
        playing = false;
        infoText.setText( "You got the FunnyFace in "+elapsedTime+
                            " seconds. Click to start over." );
    }
    else {                                    // User was too slow
        infoText.setText( "Too slow!" );
        funFace.moveTo( randXGen.nextValue(), randYGen.nextValue() );
        stopWatch.reset();
    }
}
```

Figure 6.10   Chase class: revised onMouseClick method using local variable

The classes representing geometric objects from the objectdraw library provide two different versions of the moveTo method and two versions of their constructions. These different versions allow the programmer either to use two parameters representing the *x* and *y* coordinates of where the object was to appear or to use a single Location parameter.

Let's see how we can define overloaded methods by going back to the class FunnyFace. That class included a method moveTo with two double parameters representing the *x* and *y* coordinates that we wish to move the object to. We repeat the method below:

```
public void moveTo( double x, double y ) {
    this.move( x - head.getX(), y - head.getY() );
}
```

We have seen that the predefined geometric classes have two versions of moveTo—one taking two parameters of type double and the other taking the single parameter of type Location. Let's add the missing version to FunnyFace:

```
public void moveTo( Location pt ) {
    this.move( pt.getX() - head.getX(), pt.getY() - head.getY() );
}
```

```
public void moveTo( double x, double y ) {
    this.move( x - head.getX(), y - head.getY() );
}

public void moveTo( Location pt ) {
    this.moveTo( pt.getX(), pt.getY() );
}
```

Figure 6.11   Writing overloaded methods in terms of one version

An example where the overloaded moveTo would be helpful would be in the method onMouseClicked in Section 6.3.2. We can now replace the body

```
happy.moveTo( point.getX(), point.getY() );
```

by the simpler

```
happy.moveTo( point );
```

which eliminates the need to extract the *x* and *y* coordinates from the Location.

The code for the new version of moveTo is very similar to that of the earlier version, replacing the parameter x by pt.getX() and the parameter y by pt.getY(). This is no coincidence, as overloaded methods should all have the same effect. This follows from the general principle that code that looks the same should do the same thing. If overloaded methods do very different things, then programmers will be more likely to be confused.

➡ EXERCISE 6.6.1

The overloading of + for both addition and string concatenation is an example of where overloading can be confusing. Evaluate "2" + 3 + 4 versus 2 + 3 + "4", remembering that concatenating an int to a String results in converting the int to a String before concatenating. ❖

One way of ensuring that two versions of an overloaded method do the same things is to have one of them written in terms of the other. Because the first version of moveTo is somewhat simpler than the second, we will use that as the base version, writing the version with the Location parameter in terms of the version with two doubles. See the code in Figure 6.11.

The second version of moveTo is obtained by invoking the first version of moveTo on itself (this.moveTo) with parameters pt.getX() and pt.getY(). It has the great advantage of maintaining consistency if either move or one of the moveTo's is modified.

Remember that an overloaded method definition may only be introduced if it can be distinguished from other definitions with the same name by having different parameter types. Java does not allow overloaded methods to be distinguished only by the return type. Thus a class may not contain both versions of m below because they differ only in their return types:

```
public void m( int x ) { ... }
public Location m( int x ) { ... }
```

For example, if ob is an object from this class, then the system cannot determine what method body should be executed when it evaluates an expression like ob.m(17).

We can also overload constructors in Java. We illustrate this with FunnyFace. The original constructor for FunnyFace (repeated below) takes two doubles and a DrawingCanvas as parameters.

```
// Create pieces of funny face
public FunnyFace( double left, double top,
                  DrawingCanvas canvas ) {
    head = new FramedOval( left, top, FACE_WIDTH,
                           FACE_HEIGHT, canvas );
    mouth = new FramedOval( left+(FACE_WIDTH-MOUTH_WIDTH)/2,
                            top+2*FACE_HEIGHT/3,
                            MOUTH_WIDTH, MOUTH_HEIGHT, canvas );
    leftEye = new FramedOval( left+EYE_OFFSET-EYE_RADIUS/2,
                              top+EYE_OFFSET, EYE_RADIUS,
                              EYE_RADIUS, canvas );
    rightEye = new FramedOval( left+FACE_WIDTH-EYE_OFFSET-
                               EYE_RADIUS/2, top+EYE_OFFSET,
                               EYE_RADIUS, EYE_RADIUS, canvas );
}
```

It might also be helpful to include a constructor that takes a Location rather than the two parameters of type double. Recall that the constructor for a class must have the same name as the class, so we have no freedom in naming the constructor—it must be overloaded. If the new version has the header

```
public FunnyFace( Location upperLeft, DrawingCanvas canvas ) {
```

we could simply copy the code from the first version, replacing all occurrences of left with upperLeft.getX() and all occurrences of top with upperLeft.getY(). However, as with overloaded methods, we can also write the constructor so that it executes the code of the original constructor, but with the parameters replaced as above and no copying of code. It would be written:

```
public FunnyFace( Location upperLeft, DrawingCanvas canvas ) {
    this( upperLeft.getX(), upperLeft.getY(), canvas );
}
```

From our example above with overloaded methods, you might have expected the body of the new FunnyFace constructor to begin with this.FunnyFace(...) or even new this.FunnyFace(...), but Java has a different syntax for calling existing constructors from a new constructor. One simply writes this(...). That syntax tells Java to look for another constructor for the class (they all have the same name—FunnyFace in this case) with formal parameters whose types correspond to those in the parentheses after this. Again, the reason for using this notation rather than copying the old method body and editing each line to use the new parameters is that the constructors are more likely to stay consistent if they all execute the same code.

The fact that all constructors for a class have the same name as the class can cause problems in defining overloaded constructors. For example, one of the standard constructors for class `Line` in the objectdraw library takes the *x* and *y* coordinates of the endpoints as well as the canvas it is to be drawn on:

```
public Line( double startx,  double starty,  double endx,
             double endy,  DrawingCanvas c );
```

Suppose now that we wish to add a new constructor that takes the starting point of the line, the length of the line, and the angle of the line from the positive x axis (and of course the canvas). The constructor could be written:

```
public Line( double startx,  double starty,  double length,
             double angle, DrawingCanvas c );
```

Unfortunately Java does not allow both of these constructors, because they both have exactly the same types for the parameters: `double, double, double, double, DrawingCanvas`. The only way we could use both constructors would be to put them in separate classes.[3]

Overloaded methods should be used sparingly in Java. When used, each of the overloaded variants should do the same thing. Overloading should only be used to allow programmers more flexibility in the choice of parameters. Having very different methods with the same names will only confuse programmers (including yourself!). Because all constructors for a class must have the same name (the name of the class itself), if a class has more than one constructor, it must be overloaded.

A common error is updating one version of an overloaded operation to have new behavior, but forgetting to update one or more of the other versions. We urge you to consider guarding against this by having variants call one of the other versions so that changes to one are necessarily reflected in all. While this may result in slightly slower execution time than making duplicate copies of the code, you are more likely to stay out of trouble this way.

➡ EXERCISE 6.6.2

In Exercise 6.3.2 we asked you to write a more flexible constructor for FunnyFace *that would enable the programmer to specify the width and height of the desired drawing. The header for such a constructor would look like:*

```
public FunnyFace( double left, double top, double width,
                  double height, DrawingCanvas canvas )
```

Assuming that such a constructor had been defined, show how to redefine the original constructor shown in Figure 6.4 in terms of the more flexible version. ❖

---

[3] We created another line class, AngLine, in objectdraw solely so we could use the second constructor. See the on-line documentation for more details.

6.7   Summary

In this section we showed how to design new classes in Java. We can design classes to represent interesting collections of objects with similar behaviors. We illustrated these ideas by building classes FunnyFace and Timer. The use of these classes made it much simpler to define programs to drag around a funny face on the screen and a game in which the user is to click on the funny face within a small time interval.

Classes are composed of

* Constant definitions to be used in the class.
* Instance variables representing the state of the objects of the class.
* Contructors to create new objects from the class.
* Methods representing the possible behavior of the objects of the class.

We showed how a method could call another method, m, of the same class by writing this.m(...) or just m(...). We also showed how one constructor could use an expression of the form this(...) to invoke another constructor in the same class.

We introduced local variables in order to hold values that need only be saved temporarily during the execution of a constructor or method.

Finally, we discussed overloaded methods and constructors, and the circumstances in which it makes sense to provide overloaded features.

6.8   Chapter Review Problems

⇒ EXERCISE 6.8.1

Define the following Java terms:

   a. instance *of a class*
   b. *constructor*
   c. *return type*
   d. *local variable*

⇒ EXERCISE 6.8.2

What is meant by formal parameters and actual parameters and how do they relate to each other?

⇒ EXERCISE 6.8.3

Write the following methods for FunnyFace.

   a. removeFromCanvas
   b. getX
   c. setEyeColor

➡️ EXERCISE 6.8.4

Why does the following moveTo *method not do what is expected?*

```
public void moveTo( double x, double y ) {
   head.moveTo( x, y );
   mouth.moveTo( x, y );
   leftEye.moveTo( x, y );
   rightEye.moveTo( x, y );
}
```

❖

➡️ EXERCISE 6.8.5

What would you have to do to Chase *if you wanted to have the console display how long the game has been running when the mouse exits the window? Write the* onMouseExit *method and explain any other changes required.*
❖

(**6.9**)   **Programming Problems**

➡️ EXERCISE 6.9.1

Create a class called Man *which looks like the stick-man in Figure 6.12. A* Man *should have the following methods in addition to a constructor:* move, moveTo, setColor, getColor, removeFromCanvas, *and* contains.
❖

Figure 6.12   A small stick-man

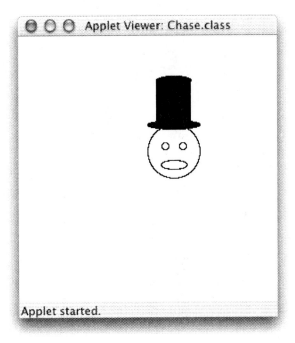

Figure 6.13   FunnyFace with a TopHat

⊪➡ EXERCISE 6.9.2

Write a class called TopHat *which will be a hat like that in Figure 6.13 for a* FunnyFace. *Modify the* Chase *class so that there is also a* TopHat *on the* FunnyFace. *If the user clicks on the face or the hat in time, it will generate the normal correct response. However, if the user is too slow or misses the hat and face, then the hat will change color. The hat should switch color either from red to black or from black to red.*

Hint: *You may want to add additional accessor methods to* FunnyFace.

CHAPTER 7

Control Structures

his chapter discusses *control structures*. These are mechanisms that allow a programmer to control the order in which program statements are executed.

You have already learned a bit about control structures. For example, blocks of code in braces indicate that sequential execution of those statments will take place. You also learned about the conditional statement in Chapter 4. In fact, you saw a variety of different forms of the conditional statement. All of the variants of the conditional statement allow the programmer to specify a choice of statements to be executed, depending upon conditions that arise during the running of a program. This chapter expands on what you learned earlier, providing advice for writing clear conditional statements even in cases that are complex.

This chapter also introduces the `while` statement. This is one of several ways to express the idea of executing code repeatedly in Java. Learning about the `while` statement will serve as a foundation for Chapter 9, in which you will generate simple animations.

7.1 Repetition and while Loops

Many of the programs we have written have involved repetition. The craps game from Chapter 4, for example, involved repeatedly rolling two dice. The grid shown in Figure 2.8 involved repeatedly drawing rectangles to form a grid pattern. These examples, and many of the others we have shown you, have something in common—their repetitive behavior is controlled by a user through the mouse. But what if we want to draw a complex pattern with just a single click (or with no click at all!)? This requires a mechanism for telling Java to perform an action repeatedly. In this section we introduce the `while` statement, which is one of several ways to express the notion of executing code repeatedly in Java.

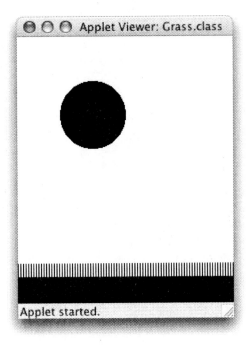

Figure 7.1   Grass

Let's begin our discussion of repetition with a simple example. Consider the drawing of a grassy field shown in Figure 7.1. It is easy to imagine how this scene might be created. The sun is a FilledOval, the base of the grass is a FilledRect, and each blade of grass is a Line. The only problem is that, with the tools you have so far, the process of creating so many blades of grass would be horribly tedious. The code would be extremely repetitive, as illustrated in Figure 7.2. For each individual blade of grass drawn on the canvas, there is one construction in the begin method of the program.

Even with the ability to cut and paste, each line of code that draws a blade of grass must be modified to be different from the line before it. Naturally, it would be nice to think about how we could make this a bit less tedious. One thing we might notice is that the only difference from one line to the next is that the *x* coordinate of each line is four more than the *x* coordinate of the line before it. So we might think about how we can say something like, "Draw a line with an *x* coordinate 4 more than the previous one." We can accomplish this by declaring a local variable to hold the *x* coordinate of a line to be drawn. We will call that variable bladePosition. We can set bladePosition to 0 initially, and then draw the first line as follows:

```
new Line( bladePosition, GRASS_TOP, bladePosition,
          GROUND_LINE, canvas );
```

We can then add 4 to bladePosition before constructing the next new line. The code that draws the grass can now be expressed as in Figure 7.3.

This is better than the previous approach in at least one respect. The process of creating the multiple blades of grass involves cutting and pasting without modification of any of the individual lines. Unfortunately, this is still painfully tedious.

```
// Class that draws a grassy scene
public class Grass extends WindowController {

    ... // Constant declarations omitted

    public void begin() {
        // Draw solid ground and sun
        new FilledRect( 0, GROUND_LINE, canvas.getWidth(),
                        canvas.getHeight()-GROUND_LINE, canvas );
        new FilledOval( SUN_INSET, SUN_INSET, SUN_SIZE, SUN_SIZE,
                        canvas);

        // Add the blades of grass
        new Line( 0, GRASS_TOP, 0, GROUND_LINE, canvas );
        new Line( 4, GRASS_TOP, 4, GROUND_LINE, canvas );
        new Line( 8, GRASS_TOP, 8, GROUND_LINE, canvas );
        new Line( 12, GRASS_TOP, 12, GROUND_LINE, canvas );
        new Line( 16, GRASS_TOP, 16, GROUND_LINE, canvas );
            .
            .
            .

    }
}
```

Figure 7.2 Code for drawing the grass scene

An alternative would be to have the user of this class draw each blade of grass with a mouse click, as shown in Figure 7.4. Again, bladePosition holds the *x* coordinate of the blade of grass to be drawn. As each line is drawn, the *x* coordinate is advanced a bit to the right. The only difference here is that we check whether the *x* coordinate is within the bounds of the canvas, so that a line is only drawn if it will be visible. While this is fairly straightforward to write, it would be terribly dull for the user.

Fortunately, Java provides several constructs for expressing repetition concisely. One of these is the while statement or while loop. Figure 7.5 defines a class that draws the entire grass scene. The important change from the earlier programs is that drawing of the grass is now expressed as a while loop within the begin method. Notice that all of the important elements of the drawing algorithm were already in place in Figure 7.4: drawing a single line, changing the value of bladePosition, and deciding whether more should be drawn. All that was required to write a while loop was modifying the syntax a bit.

Let's look at the structure of a while statement in general first, so that we can better analyze how the example loop draws grass. The syntax of the while statement is as follows:

```
while ( condition ) {
    statements to be repeated
}
```

The *condition* specifies the circumstances under which the body of the loop is to be executed. It must be an expression that describes a boolean value. If *condition* is false, the body

```
// Add the blades of grass
bladePosition = 0;

new Line( bladePosition, GRASS_TOP, bladePosition, GROUND_LINE,
        canvas );
bladePosition = bladePosition + GRASS_SPACING;

new Line( bladePosition, GRASS_TOP, bladePosition, GROUND_LINE,
        canvas );
bladePosition = bladePosition + GRASS_SPACING;

new Line( bladePosition, GRASS_TOP, bladePosition, GROUND_LINE,
        canvas );
bladePosition = bladePosition + GRASS_SPACING;

new Line( bladePosition, GRASS_TOP, bladePosition, GROUND_LINE,
        canvas );
bladePosition = bladePosition + GRASS_SPACING;

new Line( bladePosition, GRASS_TOP, bladePosition, GROUND_LINE,
        canvas );
    .
    .
    .
    .
```

Figure 7.3   Alternate code for drawing grass. Note the pattern that has emerged in the code

of the loop is skipped, and control moves to the statement immediately following the while loop.

If *condition* is true, the body of the loop is executed. Once this is done, *condition* is tested again. If *condition* is false, execution of the loop is terminated, and control moves to the statement following the loop. Otherwise, the statements in the body of the loop are executed again, and so on.

Braces mark the beginning and end of the block of statements to be repeated. If only one statement is to be repeated, the braces can be omitted. We recommend always including them, however.

Now we can look at the structure of our grass-drawing while statement in detail:

```
double bladePosition = 0;
while ( bladePosition < canvas.getWidth() ) {
    new Line( bladePosition, GRASS_TOP, bladePosition,
            GROUND_LINE, canvas );
    bladePosition = bladePosition + GRASS_SPACING;
}
```

We use the integer variable bladePosition to hold the *x* coordinate of the next blade of grass to be drawn, just as we did before. Drawing begins at the extreme left-hand side of the canvas.

```
// Class that allows a user to draw a grassy scene
public class Grass extends WindowController {

    ... // Constant declarations omitted

    double bladePosition; // x coordinate of next blade of grass

    public void begin() {
        // Draw solid ground and sun
        new FilledRect( 0, GROUND_LINE, canvas.getWidth(),
                        canvas.getHeight()-GROUND_LINE, canvas );
        new FilledOval( SUN_INSET, SUN_INSET, SUN_SIZE, SUN_SIZE,
                        canvas );
        bladePosition = 0;
    }

    public void onMouseClick( Location point ) {
        // Grow a blade of grass with each mouse click
        if ( bladePosition < canvas.getWidth() ) {
        new Line( bladePosition, GRASS_TOP, bladePosition, GROUND_LINE,
                canvas );
            bladePosition = bladePosition + GRASS_SPACING;
        }
    }
}
```

Figure 7.4 Code that allows a user to draw the grass in the grass scene

Before drawing each blade of grass, we check whether bladePosition is within the bounds of the canvas. If so, we draw a line and advance the *x* coordinate, bladePosition, and then return to the top of the while to test the condition again. If the newly updated *x* coordinate is still within the bounds of the canvas, we draw a line, advance bladePosition, and again go back to test the condition. If the condition evaluates to false, we skip the body of the loop. We can express this construct in words as follows: as long as bladePosition is within the canvas, draw a new line and advance bladePosition to the next drawing spot.

We can be certain that the while loop will terminate. If bladePosition is initially set to zero and then incremented each time through the loop, it will eventually exceed canvas.getWidth(), terminating the loop.

Notice the similarity between this version of grass drawing and the version in Figure 7.4. In the new version, we have been able to make the declaration of the variable bladePosition local. Other than that, the only difference is that we replaced if with while.

EXERCISE 7.1.1

What is the difference between the function of a while *loop and an* if *statement with no* else *part?*

```
// Class that draws a grassy scene
public class Grass extends WindowController {

    ... // Constant declarations omitted

    public void begin() {

        // Code to draw ground and sun omitted

        // Add the blades of grass
        double bladePosition = 0; // Where to draw next blade of grass
        while ( bladePosition < canvas.getWidth() ) {
            new Line( bladePosition, GRASS_TOP, bladePosition,
                    GROUND_LINE, canvas );
            bladePosition = bladePosition + GRASS_SPACING;
        }
    }
}
```

Figure 7.5   Using a while loop to draw blades of grass

➡ EXERCISE 7.1.2

Assume gameOver *is a* boolean *that is initialized to* false. *What is the difference between the output of the following two control structures?*

a. if (!gameOver) {
```
        System.out.println ( "Roll again." );
}
```
b. while (!gameOver) {
```
        System.out.println ( "Roll again." );
}
```

7.2   More Examples Using while Loops

We now move from the country to the city and consider the scene in Figure 7.6. In the picture we see a moon over a city rooftop. Again, we see a pattern in the picture—the row of bricks that form the top of the roof. A loop is an appropriate construct to use to help us draw the bricks, as shown in the code in Figure 7.7.

Let's consider in some detail the while loop in Figure 7.7. Each brick is a filled rectangle of a specified width and height. The only difference between any two bricks is their location on the canvas. More specifically, the difference is in the *x* coordinate that specifies the left edge of each brick. The *y* coordinates are all the same, as the tops of the bricks line up with each other. Since the top, width, and height of a brick are all fixed, we define constants for each of these.

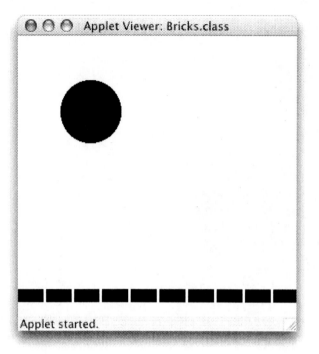

Figure 7.6   Bricks

```
// Class that draws bricks and a moon
public class Bricks extends WindowController {

    ... // Constant declarations omitted

    public void begin() {
        // Draw the moon
        new FilledOval( MOON_INSET, MOON_INSET, MOON_SIZE,
                        MOON_SIZE, canvas );

        // Draw bricks along the bottom of the canvas
        double brickPosition = 0;   // x coordinate of the next brick
        while ( brickPosition < canvas.getWidth() ) {
            new FilledRect( brickPosition, BRICK_TOP, BRICK_WIDTH,
                            BRICK_HEIGHT, canvas );
            brickPosition = brickPosition + BRICK_WIDTH + BRICK_SPACING;
        }
    }
}
```

Figure 7.7   A while loop to draw a row of bricks

The *x* coordinate of the upper left corner of each brick will change, however. We use the variable `brickPosition` to hold this information.

We start with `brickPosition` set to 0, so that the first brick is drawn at the left of the canvas. To draw a single brick, we construct a new `FilledRect`,

```
new FilledRect( brickPosition, BRICK_TOP, BRICK_WIDTH,
                BRICK_HEIGHT, canvas );
```

This is what we want to do over and over in our loop, but each time a new brick is created, we need to be sure that `brickPosition` has been changed. We move `brickPosition` to its next *x* coordinate by adding to it the width of a brick and also a small amount to account for the spacing between bricks. These two lines, the construction of a brick and the movement of `brickPosition`, form the body of the loop.

Of course, we don't want an infinite number of bricks to be drawn. We only want to construct new bricks if they will be visible on the canvas. This helps us to formulate the expression that describes the condition under which our loop is to continue executing:

```
while ( brickPosition < canvas.width() )
```

That is, the loop should be executed as long as the *x* coordinate of the next brick is less than the width of the canvas.

As a slightly more complex example, consider the drawing in Figure 7.8, which should be familiar to you from Chapter 2. The grid has a clear pattern, so it is a good candidate for a while loop. The way the grid was drawn in Chapter 2 is a good starting point for thinking about how to write the `while` loop here. There, with each click of the mouse, two long, thin rectangles were drawn. The location of the vertical rectangle was held in a variable `verticalCorner` and the location of the horizontal rectangle was in `horizontalCorner`. With each mouse click,

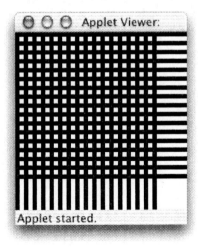

Figure 7.8 Grid

```
while ( verticalCorner.getX() < canvas.getWidth() ||
        horizontalCorner.getY() < canvas.getHeight() ) {
    new FilledRect( verticalCorner, 5, canvas.getHeight(), canvas );
    new FilledRect( horizontalCorner, canvas.getWidth(), 5,
                    canvas );

    verticalCorner.translate( 10, 0 );
    horizontalCorner.translate( 0, 10 );
}
```

Figure 7.9 A while loop to draw the grid

the two rectangles were drawn, and then the vertical and horizontal corners were translated. These statements will form the body of our loop, as shown in Figure 7.9.

We also need to specify a condition for the while statement. Let's draw grid lines (i.e., rectangles) as long as they are at least partially visible on the canvas. Since vertical rectangles are drawn from left to right on the canvas, we need to be sure that the x coordinate of the vertical corner is within the width of the canvas. Analogously, since horizontal rectangles are drawn from the top of the canvas to the bottom, we need to check that the y coordinate of the horizontal corner is within the height of the canvas. As long as either of these is true, that is, as long as either rectangle is visible, we execute the body of the loop.

EXERCISE 7.2.1

Write a program called AlmostBullseye *that draws a variation of a bullseye on the canvas. The biggest circle should be 100 pixels wide and 100 pixels tall, while the smallest circle should be 20 pixels wide and 20 pixels tall. Each circle should be 20 pixels smaller than the circle surrounding it in both width and height. The circles should all have their upper left corner at the* Location *(10,10). Your drawing should resemble the picture in Figure 7.10.*

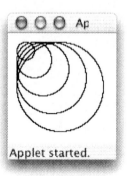

Figure 7.10 The picture for the AlmostBullseye exercise

```
// Draws ten bricks
public class Bricks extends WindowController {

    private static final int BRICKS_TOTAL = 10;

    ... // Other constants omitted

    public void begin() {
    ... // Code to draw moon omitted

        // Draw bricks along the bottom of the canvas
        double brickPosition = 0;   // x coordinate of the next brick
        double brickCount = 0;      // Number of bricks drawn so far
        while ( brickCount < BRICKS_TOTAL ) {
            new FilledRect( brickPosition, BRICK_TOP, BRICK_WIDTH,
                        BRICK_HEIGHT, canvas );
            brickPosition = brickPosition + BRICK_WIDTH + BRICK_SPACING;
            brickCount++;
        }
    }
}
```

Figure 7.11 A while loop to draw a row of exactly ten bricks

7.3 Loops that Count

Let's now go back to our example in which we drew bricks across a canvas. In Figure 7.7 we drew bricks, starting at the left edge of the canvas and continuing until we passed the right edge of the canvas. But what if we, instead, wanted to draw precisely ten bricks, starting at the same initial position?

A while loop can certainly help us accomplish this task. In fact, much of our work is already done. The main difference between the loop in Figure 7.7 and the one we want to write will be the condition on the while loop. In the earlier version, we drew bricks while the x position of the next brick was within the visible canvas. This time we will draw bricks as long as the number we have drawn so far is less than ten.

Figure 7.11 shows the code to draw precisely ten bricks of the sort pictured in Figure 7.6. As just discussed, the while loop is to be executed as long as the number of bricks drawn so far, brickCount, is less than the total number desired. We initialize the counter variable brickCount to 0 before the loop. Then, each time through the loop, i.e., each time we draw a brick, we increment the counter. As you will see in Chapters 9 and 13, the loop shown in Figure 7.11 follows a general pattern of counting loops using while. The pattern is as follows:

```
int counter = initialValue;
while (counter < stopValue) {
    // do stuff
    counter++;
}
```

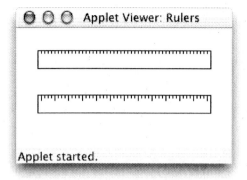

Figure 7.12   Pictures of rulers for Exercises 7.3.1 and 7.3.2

■▶ EXERCISE 7.3.1

Write a program that uses a while *loop to draw a ruler on the canvas. The ruler should show 12 inches and include tick marks for each quarter of an inch. The result should look similar to the ruler shown on top in Figure 7.12.* ❖

■▶ EXERCISE 7.3.2

Modify your program from Exercise 7.3.1 so that the tick marks for each inch are longer than those for the fractions of an inch. The result should look similar to the ruler shown on the bottom in Figure 7.12. ❖

7.4   Nested Loops

The statements that make up the body of a while loop may be any legal Java statements. In fact, a loop body might contain another loop. To understand this notion of *nested loops*, consider the brick wall shown in Figure 7.13. By this point, you can pretty comfortably imagine how you would draw a single row of bricks. To draw the entire wall, we simply need to draw rows of bricks repeatedly, starting at a new location each time. The complete code to draw the brick wall is given in Figure 7.14.

The two variables brickX and brickY are the *x* and *y* coordinates of the next brick to be drawn. The variables level and bricksInLevel are counter variables. The first counts the number of levels drawn so far; the second counts the number of bricks drawn in the current level. Both of these are initialized to 0.

The inner loop is responsible for drawing a single row of bricks. This time, we draw each brick as a black-filled rectangle with a lighter frame. After a brick is drawn, brickX is modified to indicate the position of the next brick on the current level. The counter bricksInLevel is incremented as well. The inner loop draws bricks as long as the desired width has not yet been reached.

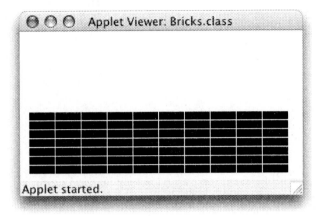

Figure 7.13   A simple brick wall

The outer loop is responsible for drawing several rows of bricks. Each time the loop executes, a new row is drawn. Once it is drawn, brickY is modified to indicate the y position of the next row. (Note that we've chosen to draw the wall from the bottom up.) In addition, the counter variable level is incremented to indicated that another level of the wall is complete.

Note that before each level is drawn by the inner loop, we reset bricksInLevel and brickX to their initial values.

▶ EXERCISE 7.4.1

What would happen if we forgot to include the first two lines of the outer while *loop, i.e., the lines:*

```
bricksInLevel = 0;
brickX = WALL_X;
```

A modification of the code in Figure 7.14 would allow us to draw a picture like that in Figure 7.16. The key here is to note that odd levels (i.e., the first from the bottom, the third from the bottom, etc.) are exactly like the rows of bricks drawn in Figure 7.13. The alternating levels are slightly different. Therefore, before drawing a row, we first determine whether it should be drawn as before or not. We do this by checking whether the value of level is evenly divisible by 2. If so, i.e., if we have drawn 0, 2, etc. rows so far, then we are currently on an odd level of the wall. If not, we are on an even level. If we are on an even level, then we draw two half-size bricks at the left and right ends of the wall. We then set bricksInLevel to 1, since the two half-size bricks make up one full brick. We also set the value of brickX so that we can begin drawing the remainder of the bricks at that level in the right location. Everything else is as before. The code for drawing the better brick wall is shown in Figure 7.15.

▶ EXERCISE 7.4.2

Modify your program from Exercise 7.3.2 so that your solution makes use of nested loops.

```
// Class to draw a brick wall
public class Bricks extends WindowController {

    ... // Constant declarations omitted

    public void begin() {
      // Initial x and y positions for drawing a brick
      double brickX = WALL_X;
      double brickY = WALL_Y;

        int level = 0;          // Number of levels drawn so far
        int bricksInLevel = 0;  // Number of bricks drawn in
                                // the current level

      while ( level < WALL_HEIGHT) {
          bricksInLevel = 0;
          brickX = WALL_X;
          // Draw one row of bricks
          while ( bricksInLevel < WALL_WIDTH ) {
              new FilledRect( brickX, brickY, BRICK_WIDTH,
                              BRICK_HEIGHT, canvas );
              new FramedRect( brickX, brickY, BRICK_WIDTH, BRICK_HEIGHT,
                              canvas ).setColor( Color.YELLOW );
              brickX = brickX + BRICK_WIDTH;
              bricksInLevel++;
          }
          brickY = brickY - BRICK_HEIGHT;
          level++;
      }
    }
}
```

Figure 7.14   Nested loops to draw a brick wall

7.5   Style Guidelines for Control Structures

In this section we provide some style guidelines for writing control structures. As we have seen in this chapter and in Chapter 4, while loops and if statements can be quite complex. Our aim is to benefit from the power we gain from these statements, while keeping our programs as simple and understandable as possible.

It is extremely important to write clear and concise code not only for the sake of others who might read it (including your teachers!), but also for *yourself*. Programmers sometimes waste a great deal of time trying to understand code that they wrote themselves months, weeks, or even days earlier, because they did not pay much attention to clarity and style. As a result we consider it essential to learn and use good coding style.

```
// Class to draw a nice brick wall
public class Bricks extends WindowController {

    ... // Constant declarations omitted

    public void begin() {

        // Initial x and y positions for drawing a brick
        double brickX = WALL_LEFT;
        double brickY = WALL_Y;

        int level = 0;            // Number of levels drawn so far
        int bricksInLevel = 0;    // Number of bricks drawn in
                                  // the current level

        while ( level < WALL_HEIGHT ) {
            if ( level % 2 != 0 ) {
                // Draw two half-bricks
                new FilledRect( WALL_LEFT, brickY,
                            BRICK_WIDTH / 2, BRICK_HEIGHT, canvas );
                new FramedRect( WALL_LEFT, brickY,
                            BRICK_WIDTH / 2, BRICK_HEIGHT,
                            canvas ).setColor( Color.YELLOW );
                new FilledRect( WALL_RIGHT-BRICK_WIDTH / 2, brickY,
                            BRICK_WIDTH / 2, BRICK_HEIGHT, canvas );
                new FramedRect( WALL_RIGHT-BRICK_WIDTH / 2, brickY,
                            BRICK_WIDTH / 2, BRICK_HEIGHT,
                            canvas ).setColor( Color.YELLOW );
                brickX = WALL_LEFT + BRICK_WIDTH / 2;
                bricksInLevel = 1; // Already placed two half-bricks
            } else {
                brickX = WALL_LEFT;
                bricksInLevel = 0;
            }
            while ( bricksInLevel < WALL_WIDTH ) {
                new FilledRect( brickX, brickY, BRICK_WIDTH,
                            BRICK_HEIGHT, canvas );
                new FramedRect( brickX, brickY, BRICK_WIDTH, BRICK_HEIGHT,
                            canvas ).setColor( Color.YELLOW );
                brickX = brickX + BRICK_WIDTH;
                bricksInLevel++;
            }
            brickY = brickY - BRICK_HEIGHT;
            level++;
        }
    }
}
```

Figure 7.15 Nested loops to draw a better brick wall

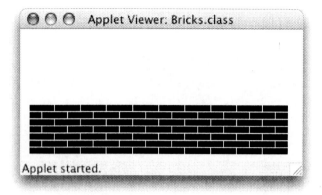

Figure 7.16   A better brick wall

The "bad" examples we illustrate here are legal Java code. However, they can be replaced by code that is much simpler and easier to understand.

Avoid empty if-parts

We mentioned in Chapter 4 that an `if` statement can omit the `else`-part if it is not needed. However, what if we need the `else`-part, but not the `if`-part of an `if` statement? For example, suppose we want to increment a variable named `counter` exactly when `point` is not contained in a rectangle called `box`, but do nothing otherwise. We could write:

```
if ( box.contains( point ) ) {
    // do nothing here
}
else {
    counter++;
}
```

However, writing it that way is considered very bad style. We should instead rewrite it as:

```
if ( !box.contains( point ) ) {
    counter++;
}
```

Here we have used `!` to negate the value of the condition so that the statement we wish to execute now belongs in the `if`-part. Notice that this version of the statement is much shorter and simpler. In general, we will be looking for short, clear ways of writing code in order to make it more understandable to a reader.

Don't be afraid to use boolean expressions in assignments

Recall the class `WhatADrag` contained in Figure 4.6. In that program, `box` was a `FilledRect`, `point` was a `Location`, and `boxGrabbed` was a `boolean` variable.

Many beginning programmers are more comfortable writing

```
if ( box.contains( point ) ) {
    boxGrabbed = true;
}
else {
    boxGrabbed = false;
}
```

rather than the code we actually wrote in that program

```
boxGrabbed = box.contains( point );
```

However, you should become comfortable enough with `boolean` variables that this kind of assignment makes sense to you. The assignment is simpler and easier to understand than the `if-else` statement for an experienced Java programmer.

Don't use true or false in conditions

Again, let `boxGrabbed` be a `boolean` variable. Suppose you want a program to do something exactly when `boxGrabbed` is `true`. Look at the following code excerpt:

```
if ( boxGrabbed == true ) {
    ...
}
```

Can you determine why this code is considered bad style? The code can, and should, be written more simply as:

```
if ( boxGrabbed ) {
    ...
}
```

Both code segments do exactly the same thing. However, the first is unnecessarily verbose. It is like the difference between saying "If it is `true` that it is raining then I will stay home" and "If it is raining then I will stay home." The second version is clearly preferable.

Similarly, rather than writing

```
while ( done == false ) {
    ...
}
```

or

```
while ( done != true ) {
    ...
}
```

we prefer

```
while ( !done ) {
    ...
}
```

A good general rule is to avoid using either `true` or `false` in a condition, as their presence represents verbose and redundant code. The literals `true` and `false` are most commonly used in assignment statements to initialize `boolean` variables, and never in conditional expressions.

Warning about == versus =

One of the most common errors made by beginning Java programmers (and even many experienced programmers) is to use =, the assignment operator, in a condition where ==, the equality operator, is intended. Most of the time Java will produce a compile-time error message warning that the condition is invalid. There is one case, however, where Java will not find your error! That is when you are comparing two `boolean` expressions. For example, if you write:

```
if ( boxGrabbed = true ) { ... }
```

Java will not give you an error message.

The root of the problem is that Java allows assignment statements in the middle of expressions. The value obtained from an assignment statement used in an expression is the value of the variable *after* the assignment. Thus, in the example above, the value used as the condition in the `if` statement is the value of `boxGrabbed` after the assignment, `true`. As a result, the computer will always execute the `then`-part of the `if` statement. Similarly, if you write

```
if ( boxGrabbed = false ) { ... }
```

Java will always execute the `else`-part. This is surely not what was intended.

Fortunately, if you follow the rule we suggested by never including `true` or `false` in a condition, then it is highly unlikely that you will ever need to test `boolean` expressions for equality!

EXERCISE 7.5.1

Simplify the following statements so they use good style. Assume `hungry` *is a* `boolean` *and* `eat()` *is a method.*

a.
```
if ( hungry == true ) {
     eat();
}
```
b.
```
if ( hungry == true ) {

}
else {
     sleep();
}
```

EXERCISE 7.5.2

In the following statement, will `clapHands()` *be executed if* `happy` *is* `true`? *Will* `clapHands()` *be executed if* `happy` *is* `false`? *Why does this statement produce unwanted behavior? Write a conditional statement that executes* `clapHands()` *only when* `happy` *is* `true`.

```
if ( happy = true ) {
     clapHands();
}
```

As you write more complex programs, the conditions in your if and while statements will likely become fairly complicated. In order to ensure that the conditions in your statements mean what you want, it is worth taking a small excursion into propositional logic to study DeMorgan's laws. DeMorgan's laws are rules for understanding complicated boolean expressions by identifying logically equivalent expressions. Of particular interest will be DeMorgan's laws involving negations, &&, and ||.

Recall that if A and B are boolean expressions, then the expression A && B will be true exactly when both A and B are true. We can illustrate this with a diagram called a truth table:

A	B	A && B
true	true	true
true	false	false
false	true	false
false	false	false

A truth table is similar to an addition or multiplication table in that it indicates the results of an operation for given values of the operands.

The first column of the table shows possible values of A, the second column shows possible values of B, while the third column shows the corresponding value of A && B for those values of A and B. Thus the first row shows that if A and B are true then A && B is also true. The second row shows that if A is true and B is false then A && B is false.

We can make a similar truth table for the boolean operator ||:

A	B	A || B
true	true	true
true	false	true
false	true	true
false	false	false

This table show that A || B is only false if both A and B are false.

The truth table for the boolean operator ! is shorter:

A	!A
true	false
false	true

It simply shows that the negation of an expression is always the opposite of the original value.

The table for !A only has two rows because ! is a unary operator. That is, it only takes a single operand. Because the single operand has only two possible values, true and false, only two rows are necessary. The tables for binary operations && and || have four rows because each operation has two operands and there are a total of four distinct combinations of boolean values for those two operands.

We can build more complicated truth tables by adding extra columns to the tables. The following table is formed by starting with the table for A && B and adding an extra column for the negation, !(A && B)

A	B	A && B	!(A && B)
true	true	true	false
true	false	false	true
false	true	false	true
false	false	false	true

The values for the last column are obtained by negating the values in the previous column—the values of A && B.

Next we build the table for !A || !B. To build this table, we will need to compute the values of !A and !B before we compute the *or*.

A	B	!A	!B	!A || !B
true	true	false	false	false
true	false	false	true	true
false	true	true	false	true
false	false	true	true	true

The columns for !A and !B are obtained by negating the values in the corresponding positions in columns A and B. The values for column !A || !B are obtained from the values in the columns for !A and !B. Because an *or* only fails when both operands are false, only the first row results in a value of false for !A || !B.

It is interesting to observe that the column for !A || !B is exactly the same as for !(A && B). This shows that for all possible combinations of values of A and B, those two boolean expressions have exactly the same resulting value. In other words, they are equivalent. This equivalence is one of DeMorgan's laws of logic.

This should make sense intuitively. Here is a simple example in English that is roughly equivalent. Suppose I say that I had wanted to learn to both sing and dance, but I failed. Then I either didn't learn to sing or I didn't learn to dance.

Below we write the truth tables for the expressions !(A || B) and !A && !B.

A	B	A || B	!(A || B)
true	true	true	false
true	false	true	false
false	true	true	false
false	false	false	true

A	B	!A	!B	!A && !B
true	true	false	false	false
true	false	false	true	false
false	true	true	false	false
false	false	true	true	true

Because the final columns for each of these tables are the same, we know that the `boolean` expressions `!(A || B)` and `!A && !B` are equivalent. This is another of DeMorgan's laws.

Whenever possible we will use DeMorgan's laws and the rules for simplifying the negations of comparison operators to simplify complex `boolean` expressions.

➡ EXERCISE 7.6.1

Use the truth table for negation to show that `!!A` *is equivalent to* `A`. *That is, for each* `boolean` *value for* `A`, *the value of* `!!A` *is exactly the same.*   ❖

➡ EXERCISE 7.6.2

Give an intuitive argument for the equivalence of `!(A || B)` *and* `!A && !B`.   ❖

➡ EXERCISE 7.6.3

Convince yourself of the equivalence of `!(x > 0 && x <= 10)` *and* `x <= 0 || x > 10`. *Draw a number line and shade in the regions represented by* `x > 0 && x <= 10` *and* `x <= 0 || x > 10`. *The two regions do not overlap and contain the entire number line between them. Hence* `!(x > 0 && x <= 10)` *is equivalent to* `x <= 0 || x > 10`.   ❖

➡ EXERCISE 7.6.4

Use DeMorgan's laws and the rules for simplifying the negations of comparison operators to simplify the following `boolean` *expression:*

```
!(x == 0 || x >= 100)
```
  ❖

7.7   Simplifying Syntax in Conditionals

You have probably noticed that many lines of code in this chapter have been taken up by curly braces, which simply indicate the beginning and end of code blocks. This was particularly apparent in the complex `if` statements we introduced in Chapter 4.

Java allows the programmer to drop braces when a block includes only a single statement. For example, recall from Section 4.6 the decision table for choosing activities on a summer afternoon. The code corresponding to the table is repeated in Figure 7.17.

The first attempt at coding the decision table for activities can be simplified as follows:

```java
if ( sunny && rich )
    activityDisplay.setText( "outdoor concert" );
else if ( !sunny && rich )
    activityDisplay.setText( "indoor concert" );
else if ( sunny && !rich )
    activityDisplay.setText( "ultimate frisbee" );
else // !sunny && !rich
    activityDisplay.setText( "watch TV" );
```

```
if ( sunny && rich ) {
    activityDisplay.setText( "outdoor concert" );
}
else if ( !sunny && rich ) {
    activityDisplay.setText( "indoor concert" );
}
else if ( sunny && !rich ) {
    activityDisplay.setText( "ultimate frisbee" );
}
else  { // !sunny && !rich
    activityDisplay.setText( "watch TV" );
}
```

Figure 7.17   Choosing an activity on a summer afternoon

Because each of the blocks contains only a single line of code, all of the curly braces can be dropped.

Similarly, the code for the same problem using nested if statements, repeated in Figure 7.18, can be simplified to:

```
if ( sunny )
    if ( rich )
        activityDisplay.setText( "outdoor concert" );
    else    // Not rich
        activityDisplay.setText( "ultimate frisbee" );
else // Not sunny
    if ( rich )
        activityDisplay.setText( "indoor concert" );
    else    // Not rich
        activityDisplay.setText( "watch TV" );
```

While it is easy to see why we can drop the curly braces around all of the invocations of activityDisplay.setText(...), it may not be clear why we can drop the curly braces in the second case. The reason we can drop them is that the if-part is a single nested if statement:

```
if ( rich )
    activityDisplay.setText( "outdoor concert" );
else    // Not rich
    activityDisplay.setText( "ultimate frisbee" );
```

While this statement looks complex, Java treats it as a *single statement*. As a result, the curly braces around it may be dropped. The same reasoning holds true for the lack of curly braces around the else-part.

While dropping curly braces can result in more *compact* code, it does not always result in more *readable* code, and the latter is certainly more important to anyone who might look at the code, including the programmer! To see how removing curly braces can hurt readability, compare the

```
if ( sunny ) {
    if ( rich ) {
        activityDisplay.setText( "outdoor concert" );
    }
    else {  // Not rich
        activityDisplay.setText( "ultimate frisbee" );
    }
}
else {     // Not sunny
    if ( rich ) {
        activityDisplay.setText( "indoor concert" );
    }
    else {  // Not rich
        activityDisplay.setText( "watch TV" );
    }
}
```

Figure 7.18 Nested conditionals to choose an activity on a summer afternoon

original nested if example and the more compact code above. The original has more white space, making its structure more apparent.

Warning!

Aside from hurting readability, dropping curly braces makes it easier for errors to creep in when revising code. Suppose we begin with the following code:

```
if ( score >= 60 )
    gradeDisplay.setText( "Pass" );
else
    gradeDisplay.setText( "Fail" );
```

In this case it is fine and convenient to leave off the curly braces. However, suppose we now want to add a new statement to the else clause to warn the student to work harder:

```
if ( score >= 60 )
    gradeDisplay.setText( "Pass" );
else
    gradeDisplay.setText( "Fail" );
    message.setText( "You are now on academic probation!" );
```

Although this *looks* perfectly fine, when it is executed the user is told that he or she is on academic probation no matter what the score is!

The problem is that the Java compiler ignores the indenting of the program and instead merely examines the code. According to the rules stated above, if curly braces are not used, the blocks of code associated with the if-part and else-part are taken to consist of only one statement.

Thus the above code is equivalent to:

```
if ( score >= 60 ) {
    gradeDisplay.setText( "Pass" );
}
else {
    gradeDisplay.setText( "Fail" );
}
message.setText( "You are now on academic probation!" );
```

rather than the intended code below:

```
if ( score >= 60 ) {
    gradeDisplay.setText( "Pass" );
}
else {
    gradeDisplay.setText( "Fail" );
    message.setText( "You are now on academic probation!" );
}
```

This mistake would be less likely to occur if the original version included the curly braces. While this kind of error is easy to correct once it is discovered, detecting why your program does not function properly is often very, very difficult in the first place. The time lost trying to track down such an error is usually significantly greater than any time saved by not inserting the curly braces.

Yet another problem associated with leaving out curly braces arises when using nested if statements. Suppose we write the following code:

```
if ( sunny )
    if ( rich )
        message.setText( "Go to outdoor concert" );
else
    message.setText( "Try something else" );
```

From the indenting, it appears that the message "Try something else" should be displayed when sunny is false. However, recall that Java compilers ignore indenting and all white space. Thus, to the Java compiler, the above code is exactly the same as:

```
if ( sunny )
    if ( rich )
        message.setText( "Go to outdoor concert" );
    else
        message.setText( "Try something else" );
```

In this case, the indenting seems to indicate that the message "Try something else" is displayed when sunny is true but rich is false.

Which of these is the correct interpretation? This problem is so common and confusing that it has even been given a name, the *dangling-else* problem. It occurs when there are two if clauses in a row, followed by a single else clause.

The second indenting above represents the way Java will interpret the nested if statement. The rule Java uses is that else-parts are always associated with the nearest possible if statement unless, of course, curly braces indicate otherwise. Thus in this example the else is associated with the second if.

Should you memorize this rule? We don't think it is necessary. Instead, if you always use curly braces to ensure that the code is interpreted the way that you want it, you will never experience the *dangling-else* problem. Thus to ensure the interpretation associated with the first indenting above, you should write:

```java
if ( sunny ) {
    if ( rich ) {
        message.setText( "Go to outdoor concert" );
    }
}
else {
    message.setText( "Try something else" );
}
```

To ensure the second interpretation, you should write:

```java
if ( sunny ) {
    if ( rich ) {
        message.setText( "Go to outdoor concert" );
    }
    else {      // Not rich
        message.setText( "Try something else" );
    }
}
```

When you use curly braces, you are forced to write the statement in an unambiguous fashion that the computer cannot misinterpret.

There is one time when it is very helpful to drop the curly braces. Suppose we have an if statement nested within the else-part of another if statement as follows:

```java
if ( temperature >= 100 ) {
    display.setText( "Water is in a gaseous phase" );
}
else {
    if ( temperature >= 0 ) {
        display.setText( "Water is in a liquid phase" );
    }
    else {    // temperature < 0
        display.setText( "Water is in a solid phase" );
    }
}
```

If the temperature is above 100 degrees Celsius, water is in a gaseous phase. Otherwise another
if statement is used to determine whether the temperature is above 0 degrees to decide whether
water is liquid or solid.

With this structure we have an if-else nested in an else-part. Even the indenting gets
complex as each successive else-part is moved farther and farther to the right. Because the first
else-part consists of a single, albeit complex, if statement, we may drop the curly braces around
it as follows:

```java
if ( temperature >= 100 ) {
    display.setText( "Water is in a gaseous phase" );
}
else
    if ( temperature >= 0 ) {
        display.setText( "Water is in a liquid phase" );
    }
    else {    // temperature < 0
        display.setText( "Water is in a solid phase" );
    }
```

If we now move the if statement immediately following the else keyword up to be next to
the else and fix the indentations, we get:

```java
if ( temperature >= 100 ) {
    display.setText( "Water is in a gaseous phase" );
}
else if ( temperature >= 0 ) {
    display.setText( "Water is in a liquid phase" );
}
else {    // temperature < 0
    display.setText( "Water is in a solid phase" );
}
```

These simplifications have given us the same else if structure that we saw in Section 4.4!

We see that there is really nothing special about the else if clause. It is simply obtained by
dropping the curly braces around a nested if statement that happens to be the only statement in
an else-part.

This is the only instance in which we recommend dropping the curly braces around an if or
else-part, as it is equivalent to creating a clearer, more concise else if clause. Otherwise we
strongly recommend that curly braces be used with all other if-parts and else-parts, as it is far
too easy to make errors when they are omitted.

Mismatched braces can also be very hard to find in Java. So when typing program text, always
include a closing brace immediately after typing an opening brace. Then fill in the body of the
block.

▦➡ EXERCISE 7.7.1

Write a nested if *statement that displays the snack of choice based on the table below using* System.out.println. *Use the booleans* sweet *and* warm *to control the statement.*

	sweet	not sweet
warm	brownie	hot pretzel
not warm	ice cream	potato chips

▦➡ EXERCISE 7.7.2

Translate the following English statements into a nested if *statement that prints out the weather.* *"If it is winter, then in New England there is snow, but in Florida there is sun. If it is summer, there is sun in New England and Florida." Use the booleans* winter, summer, florida, *and* newEngland *to control the statement.* ❖

▦➡ EXERCISE 7.7.3

Assume that x = 6, y = 8, *and* z = -5. *What are the values of* x, y *and* z *after the following code has been executed?*

a.
```
if ( x - (3 + y) <= z - 1 )
    x = y + 2 * z;
else if ( x - 2 * y >  2 * z )
    y = z + y;
    z = z + y;
```

b.
```
if ( 1 - z >=  2 * x - y )
    y++;
    x = x + y + z;
```

c. *Add curly braces to the code fragments above to ensure that the code is interpreted in the same way as is suggested by the indenting.* ❖

> **7.8** The switch Statement*

The switch statement is useful in situations where different actions are to be taken based on the value of an expression. Figure 7.19 shows a simple example that uses a RandomIntGenerator to select a color from several options. You should assume that colorChoice is a variable of type Color and colorSelector is a RandomIntGenerator initialized as follows:

RandomIntGenerator colorSelector = new RandomIntGenerator(0, 5);

```
switch ( colorSelector.nextValue() ) {
    case  0:
        colorChoice = Color.RED;
        break ;
    case  1 :
        colorChoice = Color.ORANGE;
        break ;
    case  2 :
        colorChoice = Color.YELLOW;
        break ;
    case  3 :
        colorChoice = Color.GREEN;
        break ;
    case  4 :
        colorChoice = Color.BLUE;
        break ;
    case  5 :
        colorChoice = Color.CYAN;
        break ;
}
```

Figure 7.19   Using a switch statement to randomly select a color

When the statement in Figure 7.19 is executed, the value of `colorSelector.nextValue()` is obtained. If its value is one of the values listed after the `case` keyword, then the statements after the corresponding `case` up until the following `break` statement are executed. When the `break` statement is executed, execution jumps to immediately after the closing brace for the `switch` statement. In our example, since `colorSelector` will only generate values in the range 0 to 5, a color will be selected for `colorChoice`.

A `switch` statement is often used in a context where an `if-else if` compound statement could also be used. If the decision on which block of statements to execute is based on equality comparisons with constants, then a `switch` statement may be the best choice, both from the point of view of readability and efficiency.

The rules for writing a `switch` statement are as follows. First, make sure that the expression immediately after the `switch` keyword has type `int`.[1]

The second rule is that the values after the `case` keywords must be constants. That is, they either must be literals like 17 or they must be declared constants of type `int` (e.g., `static final int ...`). In particular, you may never put a relation in a `case` clause. Thus a clause like `case x > 10` will generate a compile-time error.

Finally, there may only be one value provided after each occurrence of `case` (and there may not be any duplicates). If you wish to do the same thing with several distinct values of the switch expression, you may stack up several case clauses. We included the following code in our initial discussion of the craps example in Section 4.5

---

[1] A few other primitive types not discussed yet in this text are also allowed, such as the type `char`, representing characters, and some variants of `int`.

```
if ( roll == 7 || roll == 11 ) {   // 7 or 11 wins on first throw
    status.setText( "You win!" );
}
else if ( roll == 2 || roll == 3 || roll == 12 ) {
                                   // 2, 3, or 12 loses
    status.setText( "You lose!" );
}
else {                             // Play must continue
    status.setText( "The game continues" );
}
```

We can rewrite this with a switch statement as follows:

```
switch (roll) {
    case  7:
    case  11:                      // 7 or 11 wins on first throw
        status.setText( "You win!" );
        break ;
    case  2:
    case  3:
    case  12:                      // 2, 3, or 12 loses
        status.setText( "You lose!" );
        break ;
    default :                      // Play must continue
        status.setText( "The game continues" );
        break ;
}
```

Because there is no break between case 7 and case 11, if the value of roll is 7, execution will begin immediately after the case 7 and continue until it hits the first break, which is also the break for case 11.

Note that in this example we included a default case. The default clause indicates what should be done if the value of roll does not correspond to any of the values given after the case keywords. Any switch statement may include a default case.

It is often useful to include a default case to catch potential errors. For example, we could modify our switch statement for color selection as shown in Figure 7.20. With the new version, if a programmer decided to modify colorSelector to generate numbers in the range 1 to 6, rather than 0 to 5, without making the appropriate modifications to the switch, he would receive a warning whenever a problematic number was generated.

We caution students about using switch statements, because it is easy to make errors in writing them. The most common error is to omit the break statement at the end of a case. As illustrated in the dice example above, omitting the break is sometimes desirable. However, if a break was omitted after the case for 0 in our first example, the computer would choose the color red, but then continue and choose orange. Experience shows that this omission is very easy to make, so programmers must be on guard against this. Another common error is to omit the default statement when it might catch an error.

```
switch (colorSelector.nextValue()) {
    case  0:
        colorChoice = Color.RED;
        break ;
    case  1 :
        colorChoice = Color.ORANGE;
        break ;
    case  2 :
        colorChoice = Color.YELLOW;
        break ;
    case  3 :
        colorChoice = Color.GREEN;
        break ;
    case  4 :
        colorChoice = Color.BLUE;
        break ;
    case  5 :
        colorChoice = Color.CYAN;
        break ;
    default :
        System.out.println( "Color choice is out of range." );
        break ;
}
```

Figure 7.20   Generating an error message for unexpected cases

The idea of the switch statement is a good one, and other languages have similar constructs that avoid the syntactic pitfalls of Java's switch. However, we feel that the possibility of inadvertently omitting the break without receiving an error message should make programmers very cautious when using this construct.

▶ EXERCISE 7.8.1

Using the table below, write a switch *statement controlled by an* int *variable* channel *that sets the* String *variable* network *to the correct station based on the channel. If the* channel *is not found, the program should display "Channel is out of range."*

channel	network
2	CBS
4	NBC
5	FOX
7	ABC
9	UPN
10	TBS
11	WB

7.9 Summary

In this chapter we discussed control structures. We expanded on conditional statements, which were introduced in Chapter 4. We also discussed the notion of repetition. Java provides a number of constructs for specifying repetition. In this chapter we focused on the `while` statement, particularly in the context of complex drawings.

We also introduced the `switch` statement. The `switch` statement can be useful in certain contexts where an `if-else if` compound statement could also be used. If the decision on which block of statements to execute is based on equality comparisons with constants, then a `switch` statement may be the best choice, both from the point of view of readability and efficiency. However, we also cautioned the reader about potential pitfalls of the `switch` syntax.

It is important to remember that, although these constructs provide immense power and flexibility to programmers, unless used intelligently they can produce confusing, unreadable code. If you follow our suggestions, however, you can avoid this. Here are our tips summarized for your convenience:

* Always indent blocks to make it easier for the reader to understand the structure of your code.
* Use DeMorgan's laws to simplify complex `boolean` expressions.
* Never use the `boolean` literals `true` or `false` in a condition.
* Never omit the `if`-part of a conditional. Negate the condition so what used to be in the `else`-part now belongs in the `if`-part.

7.10 Chapter Review Problems

EXERCISE 7.10.1

Rewrite the body of the following method in a single line of code.

```java
public void onMouseClick ( Location point ) {
    if ( box.contains( point ) == false ) {
        outside = true;
    } else {
        outside = false;
    }
}
```

EXERCISE 7.10.2

Can the following conditions be written more concisely? If so, rewrite them. Assume that the variables a, b, c, *and* d *are* `boolean`s *and that the variables* x, y, *and* z *are* `int`s.

a. (!a && !b)
b. ((x > 7) == true)
c. (a && !b) || (a && c) || (a && !d)
d. !(x < y)
e. (b != c)
f. (x != y) && (x > z)
g. !(a == b)

7.11　Programming Problems

➡ EXERCISE 7.11.1

Write a program that draws a knit scarf by drawing tiny overlapping circles. The circles (or stitches) should be circles that are 12 pixels by 12 pixels and should overlap each other by 4 pixels. The scarf should contain 40 rows, each 12 stitches across. The upper left corner of the scarf should be at coordinates (50,10). Your scarf should resemble the scarf in Figure 7.21.

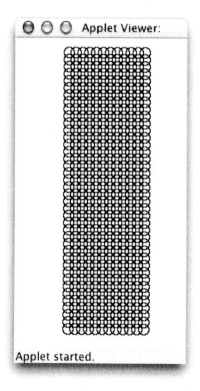

Figure 7.21　Example of scarf for Exercise 7.11.1

➤ EXERCISE 7.11.2

Write a program that simulates the two-player game Rock, Paper, Scissors. Use a RandomIntGenerator *to determine whether each player picks rock, paper, or scissors. The program should play five rounds of the game. For each round, the program should first determine if the players tied (the players tie when they pick the same item). If the players tied, the round should not count and the program should do that round over again. If the players did not tie, the program should display (using* System.out.println*) each player's choice and the winner of the round. After all five rounds have been played, the program should display the number of times each player has won. Base the winner of each round on the table below, where W = win, L = loss, T = tie.*

	Rock	Paper	Scissors
Rock	T	L	W
Paper	W	T	L
Scissors	L	W	T

➤ EXERCISE 7.11.3

Using your program called AlmostBullseye *from Exercise 7.2.1, write a program called* Bullseye *that draws a real bullseye like the one in Figure 7.22. The program should draw six concentric circles, with the color alternating between gray and black. The biggest circle should be 120 pixels in diameter, with each subsequent circle decreasing 20 pixels in diameter.*

➤ EXERCISE 7.11.4

Write a program called PicketFence *that draws a picket fence on the canvas. The fence should look like the picture in Figure 7.23.*

Figure 7.22 Bullseye for Exercise 7.11.3

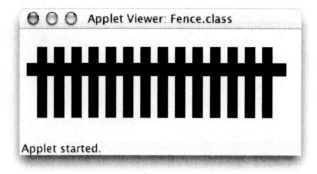

Figure 7.23   Fence for Exercise 7.11.4

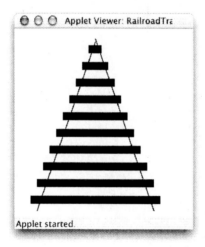

Figure 7.24   Railroad tracks for Exercise 7.11.5

➡ EXERCISE 7.11.5

Write a program called Railroad that draws railroad tracks. The railroad tracks should lead to the horizon and get smaller as they get farther away from the bottom of the canvas, as in Figure 7.24.

8

Declarations and Scope

*I*n this chapter we discuss Java's rules that govern the visibility of variables and methods declared in classes. We begin by giving a more detailed description of what the access modifiers `public` and `private` mean and introduce the notion of `private` methods. We next review the notions of instance variables, parameters, and local variables, reviewing when each of these is the most appropriate to use.

Another important aspect of visibility has to do with the notion of *scope*. As we shall see, the notion of scope determines where an identifier is visible in a program. An important difference between the different kinds of variables and parameters has to do with scope.

Finally we give a brief overview of the use of the `static` keyword in declarations.

The point of this chapter is not to introduce new programming language features, but instead to help you better understand the features that have already been introduced. This better understanding is the key to becoming a good programmer.

8.1 Access Control: public vs. private

Earlier we wrote that instance variables must be declared as `private` and methods should be declared as `public`. In this section we explain what those words actually mean, and discuss how to decide whether methods should be `public` or `private`. The short explanation of these access modifiers is that any feature declared as `public` is accessible anywhere in a program, while a feature declared as `private` is accessible only inside of the class in which it is declared. A good general rule is that an item should be declared to be `private` unless there is a reason that it needs to be accessible from outside of its class.

In order to have an example to refer to, we include in Figure 8.1 condensed forms of the class FunnyFace from Figure 6.4 and RevFaceDrag from Figure 6.3.

If a method or instance variable of a class is declared to be public, then it will be available in other classes. Because FunnyFace declared the method move to be public, the onMouseDrag method of RevFaceDrag can invoke move on happy. Similarly, happy.contains(point) may occur in the method onMousePress because contains is a public method of FunnyFace. If contains had been declared to be private, then that expression would not have been legal in Java.

Similarly, if ear were to be defined as a new public instance variable of FunnyFace, then a programmer could write happy.ear in a method of RevFaceDrag in order to get access to the current value of happy's instance variable, ear. However, because the instance variable head of FunnyFace was declared to be private, it may not be used outside of the class definition of FunnyFace. In particular, writing happy.head anywhere inside of RevFaceDrag would result in an error message. In summary, features declared to be private are accessible anywhere in the class in which they are defined, but not elsewhere.

In this text we will never declare instance variables to be public. It is generally considered bad programming practice to allow other objects access to an object's instance variables by declaring them public. While it is easier to justify this after you have gained more programming experience, the general principle is that an object should be responsible for maintaining its own state. It can provide access to portions of the state by providing accessor methods to return those values and can allow changes by providing mutator methods to update those values. However, by not allowing unfettered access to instance variables, we can prevent other objects from making the instance variables hold inconsistent data. Keeping instance variables private also makes it easier if we later change our mind about how to represent the state of an object by changing the collection of instance variables. If the instance variables were declared private, then we do not have to worry about the impact of this change on code using objects from the class.

While we feel that instance variables should never be public, there are situations where declaring a method to be private is useful. Let us now reexamine the onMouseClick method of the class Chase given in Figures 6.6 and 6.7 to see how a private method may be of help. We repeat the method in Figure 8.2 for convenience. Recall that this class was used in a game in which the user attempted to click on the funny face within a certain time limit.

Notice that there are two lines in the onMouseClick method that are repeated in three different cases of the conditional statement. They are

```
funFace.moveTo( randXGen.nextValue(), randYGen.nextValue() );
stopWatch.reset();
```

If they had been repeated in all four cases in the conditional, we could have just moved them to occur immediately after the conditional. However, this code need not be executed in the case that the user clicked on the funny face in time, so moving it to the end is not a good strategy.

When we have repeated code like this, it is best to determine whether the repeated statements perform some logical operation and to build a method that represents this operation. This particular repeated set of statements resets the game so that it can be played again. Because it is conceptually a single task, we can name this block of code and make it into a method, resetGame. Java code including this method and the revised code for onMouseClick that uses the new method

```
public class FunnyFace {
    ...

    private FramedOval head, leftEye, rightEye, mouth;

    public FunnyFace( double left, double top, DrawingCanvas
                      canvas ) { ... }

    public void move( double dx, double dy ) { ... }

    public boolean contains( Location pt ) { ... }
}

public class RevFaceDrag extends WindowController {
    ...

    private FunnyFace happy;       // FunnyFace to be dragged

    private Location lastPoint;    // Point where mouse was last seen

    // Whether happy has been grabbed by the mouse
    private boolean happyGrabbed = false;

    // Make the FunnyFace
    public void begin() {
        happy = new FunnyFace( FACE_LEFT, FACE_TOP, canvas );
    }

    // Save starting point and whether point was in happy
    public void onMousePress( Location point ) {
        lastPoint = point;
        happyGrabbed = happy.contains( point );
    }

    // If mouse is in happy, then drag happy
    public void onMouseDrag( Location point ) {
        if ( happyGrabbed ) {
            happy.move( point.getX() - lastPoint.getX(),
                        point.getY() - lastPoint.getY() );
            lastPoint = point;
        }
    }
}
```

Figure 8.1   FunnyFace and RevFaceDrag classes

```
public class Chase extends WindowController {
    ...

    // Determine if user won and move funny face if necessary
    public void onMouseClick( Location pt ) {
        if ( !playing ) {                         // Start playing
            playing = true;
            infoText.setText( "Click quickly on the FunnyFace to win!" );
            funFace.moveTo( randXGen.nextValue(), randYGen.nextValue() );
            stopWatch.reset();
        }
        else if ( !funFace.contains( pt ) ) {  // Missed the funny face
            infoText.setText( "You missed!" );
            funFace.moveTo( randXGen.nextValue(), randYGen.nextValue() );
            stopWatch.reset();
        }
        else if ( stopWatch.elapsedSeconds() <= TIME_LIMIT ) {
                                                  // Got it in time!
            playing = false;
            infoText.setText(
                    "You got the face in time.  Click to restart." );
        }
        else {                                    // User was too slow
            infoText.setText( "Too slow!" );
            funFace.moveTo( randXGen.nextValue(), randYGen.nextValue() );
            stopWatch.reset();
        }
    }
}
```

Figure 8.2   Chase class: onMouseClick method

is given in Figure 8.3. Notice how using this new method makes onMouseClick somewhat easier to understand, because the reader need not be concerned about the details of resetting the game.

We have declared resetGame to be a private method because we do not need or want any other object to invoke it. It is only to be used inside the class. Private methods, like private instance variables, are only available inside the classes in which they are declared.

There are two other access modes supported by Java, "default" and protected. We will discuss the protected qualifier in Chapter 17 in connection with inheritance. Classes, methods, and instance variables declared without an access qualifier are assigned "default" mode. Because this mode is most relevant to the design of packages, a topic we do not discuss here, we will not use this mode. Among classes not declared to be part of a package, the "default" access mode results in access similar to public. Thus you should always be careful to include the access

```
// Move funFace to new randomly selected coordinates & reset timer
private void resetGame() {
    funFace.moveTo( randXGen.nextValue(), randYGen.nextValue() );
    stopWatch.reset();
}

// Determine if user won and move funny face if necessary
public void onMouseClick( Location pt ) {
    if ( !playing ) {                          // Start playing
        playing = true;
        infoText.setText( "Click quickly on the FunnyFace to win!" );
        resetGame();
    }
    else if ( !funFace.contains( pt ) ) {   // Missed the funny face
        infoText.setText( "You missed!" );
        resetGame();
    }
    else if ( stopWatch.elapsedSeconds() <= TIME_LIMIT ) {
                                            // Got it in time!
        playing = false;
        infoText.setText(
                "You got the face in time.  Click to  restart." );
    }
    else {                                     // User was too slow
        infoText.setText( "Too slow!" );
        resetGame();
    }
}
```

Figure 8.3   Chase class: revised onMouseClick method using private method resetGame

qualifier private with all instance variable declarations, and use either public or private with all method declarations.

EXERCISE 8.1.1

Why is resetGame *in the revised* Chase *class* private *rather than* public?

8.2   Using Instance Variables, Parameters and Local Variables

So far in this text we have introduced three different kinds of identifiers, i.e., names, that represent values. They are instance variables, local variables, and formal parameters. In the rest of this section we compare and contrast their use, providing advice to help you decide when each is the most appropriate.

Instance variables are visible inside all constructors and methods of the class in which they are declared. They should always be declared as `private`. Local variables and parameters are defined and visible only in the constructors and methods in which they are declared. They may *not* be declared as `private` or `public`, as a compile-time error would result.

If instance variables are not initialized in their declarations, they are automatically provided with *default* values—`null` in the case of objects (see the discussion of `null` below), 0 in the case of numeric instance variables, and `false` in the case of `boolean` instance variables. Instance variables are typically initialized in the constructor of the class, as was the case in class `FunnyFace` in Figure 6.4. Their initial values may depend on the values of the formal parameters of the constructor. Instance variables retain their values between method invocations and can be updated inside of methods of the class. Thus they are used to hold information that must be retained to be used in later invocations of methods.

The special value `null` is a member of every class type. It is most often used as an initial value of instance variables, as indicated above. The programmer can test to see if the value of an instance variable is different from `null` in order to determine if the variable has been assigned a meaningful value. If you send a message to the value `null` it will result in generating a run-time error message in your program.

Formal parameters become associated with actual parameters during a method invocation. Parameters are typically used to transmit information needed into a method body or constructor body. A formal parameter goes out of existence when the execution of the method or constructor in which it is contained finishes. If that information is needed after the method terminates, then it should be associated with an instance variable by a statement in the method body.

Sending a message to an object referred to by a formal parameter may result in changes to the state of the corresponding actual parameter. Look at the following example:

```
public void makeYellow( FilledRect aRect ) {
    aRect.setColor( Color.YELLOW );
}
```

The result of executing the method invocation `someObj.makeYellow( myRect )` will be to change the color of `myRect` to yellow. Notice that we have not replaced `myRect` with a different object; we have instructed the filled rectangle associated with `myRect` to change its state by sending it the `setColor` message.

While a formal parameter may be assigned a new value inside the method or constructor in which it appears, the assignment has no impact on the actual parameter. As a result, assigning to formal parameters is unusual. Suppose we (foolishly) write the following method:

```
public void makeYellowRect( FilledRect aRect ) {
    aRect = new FilledRect( 50, 30, 20, 40, canvas );
    aRect.setColor( Color.YELLOW );
}
```

You might expect that executing the method invocation

```
someObj.makeYellowRect( myRect )
```

would result in `myRect` holding a new 20-by-40-pixel yellow rectangle, but that is incorrect. The assignment in the method body causes the name `aRect` to be associated with a new filled rectangle, but this has no impact on the actual parameter `myRect`. Thus `myRect` still refers to exactly the same rectangle as before the method invocation (and it stays the same color as before the invocation). Exactly the same effect would be obtained if `makeYellowRect` took no parameters and used `aRect` as a local variable. Either way, the new yellow rectangle appears on the canvas, but the version above may confuse the reader into thinking that this will have an impact on the value of the actual parameter to the method.

Local variables may be initialized in their declarations or by assignment statements inside the method or constructor in which they are declared. They are *never* provided with default values. Local variables go out of existence when the method or constructor in which they are declared finishes executing. Hence a local variable must be reinitialized each time the method or constructor containing it is executed. Local variables are thus used to refer to temporary values needed only in a local computation.

Here are general guidelines to determine when each of these three kinds of identifiers should be used.

1. If a value is to be retained after a constructor has been called or is needed by the object after the execution of one of its methods, then it should be associated with an instance variable.
2. If a value must be obtained from the context where a constructor or method is invoked, then it should be passed as a parameter.
3. If a value is only needed temporarily during the execution of a constructor or method, can be initialized locally, and need not be retained for later method calls, then it should be declared as a local variable.

Novices often use instance variables where it makes more sense to be using local variables. Why does it matter? A first reason for preferring local variables to instance variables is that they make it easier to read and understand your classes. When a programmer is looking at a class definition, the instance variables provide information on what state information is retained between invocations of methods. If superfluous variables are declared as instance variables, it makes it harder for the reader to understand the state of objects from the class.

Programmers also find it easiest to understand variables if they are declared close to where they are used. This makes it easier for a reader to find the definitions and hence read the comments explaining what the identifier is standing for. Because instance variables are clustered at the head of a class, local variables are likely to be much closer to their uses.

Another reason to prefer local variables to instance variables is that objects with excess instance variables also take up more space in memory, a problem that may be important for large programs.

For each instance variable declaration in a class, consider why it is there and whether it really needs to be retained for use by later methods. Parameters provide the primary mechanism for passing data between different objects. If a method or constructor needs information that is not held in its own instance variables, it typically needs to obtain that data via a parameter.

If a value is obtained from elsewhere, but needs to be retained for use in later method executions, then it can be passed in as a parameter and saved to an instance variable. However, there is no reason to save parameter values as instance variables if they are not needed later. Just use the parameters directly in the body of the method into which they are passed.

➡ EXERCISE 8.2.1

Why is playing *an instance variable of the class* Chase *(shown in Figure 6.6) rather than a local variable?*   ❖

8.3 Scope of Identifiers

In the last section we compared the uses of instance variables, local variables, and parameters. One important difference between these has to do with where each is visible in a class. It is important to understand these differences in general, but it is especially important when a single name is declared in different ways within a single class. In that circumstance it is very easy to get confused as to which entity is being referred to by a name. We can make sense of this by considering the notion of scope.

The *scope* of an identifier declaration is that section of code in which the feature named in the declaration can be referred to by that simple name. If all of the identifier names in a class are unique, then the scope is easy to explain.

For example, the scope of a method or instance variable is the entire class in which it is declared, while the scope of a parameter declaration is the entire body of the method in which it is declared. However, the definition of the scope of a local variable is a bit more complex. The scope is confined to the block in which the declaration occurs.

Recall that a block of code is a series of statements enclosed by curly braces. For example, the entire body of a method is a block because it is surrounded by curly braces. Similarly blocks occur in if-else statements to indicate the statements to be executed depending on whether the condition evaluates to true or false.

The scope of a local variable declaration includes all of the statements from its point of declaration to the end of the most tightly enclosing block.

As an example, consider the code in Figure 8.4. The declaration of the instance variable v has as its scope the entire class. The parameter w has as its scope the entire method body of m. That is, it can be accessed anywhere in m's method body. The local variable x is declared inside of the block composing the entire method body of m. Thus its scope is the entire method body after its declaration. The local variable y is declared inside of the block corresponding to the if-part of the conditional. As a result, its scope includes only that block. It may not be referred to in the else-part or anywhere else in the method body. Similarly, the scope of the declaration of z is the else-part of the conditional. Neither y nor z can be accessed outside of the blocks corresponding to the if-part or else-part, respectively.

Method n reuses the identifier names y and w in parameter and local variable declarations. Because the scopes of the previous declarations of y and w are restricted to the method body of m, the duplication of names causes no difficulties, and each declaration has scope consisting of the method body of n.

However, things get more complicated when two declarations introducing the same identifier have overlapping scopes. For example, the declaration of instance variable v includes the method body n, while the local variable declaration of v inside n also includes the rest of the method body.

In the case where a new declaration of a name is inside the scope of another declaration of the same name, the new declaration *shadows* the old declaration within the scope of the new

```
public class ScopeTest {
    private int v = -3;
    ...

    public void m( int w ) {    // Block for m
        ...
        int x = 0;
        if (...) {              // Block for if
            int y = 17;         // Only visible in the if block
            ... v + x + y ...   // Local vbles y & x, inst vble v
        } else {                // Block for else
            int z = -5;         // Only visible in the else block
            ... v + x + z ...   // Local vbles v & x, inst vble v
        }
        ... v + x ...           // Inst vble v & local vble x
    }

    public void n( int y ) {
        int w = 12 + v;         // v refers to instance variable
        double v = 1.72;
        ... v ...               // v refers to local variable
    }

    public void p() {
        ... v ...               // v refers to instance variable
    }
}
```

Figure 8.4 Scope example

declaration. In this region references to the name only refer to the most recent declaration. In the example in the figure, the local variable declaration of v shadows its earlier declaration as an instance variable. Inside the scope of the local variable declaration, v refers only to the local variable. We sometimes say that the new declaration creates a *hole* in the scope of the old declaration, because the scope of the old declaration no longer includes the block of code in the scope of the local variable declaration.

Because the new declaration of v in the example is a local variable, it shadows the declaration of the corresponding instance variable from the point of the local variable declaration to the end of the body of method n. Notice however, that the occurrence of v in the declaration of w in the first line of n refers to the instance variable v, as does the occurrence of v inside method p, because neither of these occurrences is within the scope of the local variable declaration of v.

One should generally try to avoid having declarations with the same name which result in overlapping scopes, as the reader of the program will often get confused. Java does not allow declaring two local variables in the same method with the same name, nor does it allow declaring a local variable with the same name as a parameter of the method. However, if a method has a parameter or local variable with the same name as an instance variable, Java provides a way to get access to the shadowed instance variable. This is done by prefixing the parameter with `this`, indicating that it refers to a feature of the object rather than a local variable or parameter, as in the following example.

```
public class C {
    private String address;

    public C( String address ) {
        this.address = address;
    }
    ...
}
```

The class C has a constructor which takes a `String` parameter with the same identifier name, `address`, as the instance variable. By the Java scoping rules, the parameter declaration shadows the instance variable declaration, so occurrences of `address` within the constructor body refer to the parameter. However, prefixing an identifier with `this` indicates that it is the name of an instance variable or method of the class. Thus the occurrence of `this.address` on the left side of the assignment statement refers to the instance variable.

Some programmers like to use duplicate names in this way when a parameter provides a value for an instance variable. Once you are used to this convention, it is not hard to understand the associated code, though it can be very confusing the first time you see this style of writing code. Of course, it is not difficult to come up with unique names and avoid any danger of confusion. For example, the parameter in the above example could have been named `anAddress` and still conveyed the correspondence between the parameter and instance variable without any danger of confusion.

So far we have confined our attention to the scope of a declaration from within the class containing the declaration. However, as you know, features declared to be `public` are also accessible outside of the class. They are accessible anywhere the class name is accessible.

In this section, we saw how Java scope rules allowed us to determine what features were being referred to by an occurrence of an identifier. In general, a new declaration of an identifier within the scope of a previous declaration with the same identifier results in the new declaration shadowing the earlier one, resulting in a loss of access to the feature from the earlier declaration. However, prefixing an instance variable name with `this` can be used to get access to an instance variable even when it is shadowed by another declaration.

A common error made by beginning programmers is to insert a new local variable declaration when an instance variable is needed. For example, suppose we write:

```
public class C {
    private int value;

    public C( int initialValue ) {
        int value;
        value = initialValue;
    }
    ...
}
```

Here the programmer seems to be worried that he or she won't be able to access the instance variable unless it is declared within the constructor. Because the local variable value shadows the instance variable value in the constructor, the assignment only initializes the local variable, not the instance variable with the same name. As a result, value would have only the default initial value of 0.

8.4   The Use of static

Features that are declared to be static are associated with the classes in which they are defined rather than the objects created from the class. In this section we discuss briefly the use of static in the declaration of class features.

We have already seen that constants in Java are declared as static final. The final keyword is used to indicate that the feature may not be modified after it has been initialized. Thus it makes sense that constants should be declared to be final. We generally also include the static keyword with constants if there is no reason to create a different copy of the constant for each object. There can just be a single copy of the constant that is associated with the class.

If you use a constant inside the class in which it is declared, you simply write down the name of the constant to use it. However, unlike instance variables, it is occasionally useful to declare constants to be public. They can then be used outside of the class in which they are defined, by prefixing the constant name with the name of the class in which it is defined. For example, MAX_SIZE is a public constant defined in class D in Figure 8.5. It can be referred to as D.MAX_SIZE in other classes. Because the constant is associated with the class, it can be accessed even when no instances of class D have been created.

We have already seen this usage in some of our earlier examples using constants from standard Java libraries. For example, RED and BLUE are public constants declared in the Color class, and are referred to by writing Color.RED and Color.BLUE.

Class D in Figure 8.5 includes a declaration of a static variable numObjects that is intended to keep track of the number of objects generated from the class. Because it is declared to be static,

```
public class D {
    // Counter for number of objects
    private static int numObjects = 0;
    public static final int MAX_SIZE = 50;
        ...

    public D(...) {
        numObjects++;
        ...
    }
    ...
}
```

Figure 8.5   Example using a static variable

only one copy of the variable exists. It is associated with the class, and the single copy is shared by all objects generated by the class. Because it is defined in the class, it is accessible within the constructor and methods of the class. Thus the constructor code ensures that each time a new object is created, the value of the shared numObjects variable is incremented by 1.

Methods can also be declared to be static, and hence associated with the class rather than with objects generated by the class. For example, the methods sqrt and abs are declared to be static in class Math, and hence are referred to outside of Math as Math.sqrt and Math.abs.

Because static methods are associated with the class rather than with instances (objects) of the class, their bodies may not refer to instance variables, non-static methods, or this. Thus static methods can only be used when no instance variables are needed in the method definition. This is the case for the static methods defined in class Math of the standard Java library.

8.5   Summary

In this chapter we took a closer look at declarations and scope. We began by discussing access control for features of Java by using the keywords public and private. Private features are only available to constructors and methods of the class in which they are defined, while public features are available outside of the class. We will continue to declare all instance variables as private, but we must decide for each method whether or not we want it to be accessible outside of the class.

We also compared the use of instance variables, local variables, and parameters. Instance variables are to be used when information must be retained between calls to constructors and methods. Parameters provide values to be used within the bodies of methods. Formal parameters become associated with the values of corresponding actual parameters during each method invocation. These associations are not retained after the execution of the method body. Local variables are used for values that need only be saved temporarily during the execution of a constructor or method.

We discussed the scope of declarations and how to use this as a prefix to an instance variable name in order to get access to it when it is shadowed by another declaration. Finally we presented a brief discussion of the meaning of the Java keyword static.

8.6   Chapter Review Problems

⇒ EXERCISE 8.6.1

What does each of the following Java terms mean?

   a. private
   b. public
   c. *local variable*
   d. null
   e. *shadow*

➠ EXERCISE 8.6.2

A beginning programmer has written the program below without fully understanding declarations and scope. What problems does the following code have?

```
public class C {
    private int number;

    public C( int aNumber ) {
        int myNumber = aNumber;
        int number = 10;
    }
    ...
    private m() {
        ...
        if ( myNumber > number ) { ... }
    }
    ...
}
```

➠ EXERCISE 8.6.3

Why should a programmer try to use local variables rather than simply declaring all the variables in a class as instance variables?

CHAPTER 9

Active Objects

In Chapter 7 you learned about Java control constructs to perform repetition. So far, the examples that you have seen have largely involved repeated patterns in drawings—blades of grass, bricks, and grid lines. We now consider another type of application in which repetition plays a major role: animation.

In this chapter, we introduce *active objects*, which, together with the while statement, can be used to create simple animations.

9.1 Animation

If you ever owned a "flip book" as a child, you certainly know how animation works. A series of pictures is drawn, each slightly different from the one before it. The illusion of movement is created by quickly flipping through the series of pictures. As an example, consider the snapshots of a ball in Figure 9.1. These are just a few pictures from a series of drawings that illustrate the action of a ball being dropped and falling to the ground. Each image shows the ball at a slightly different (i.e., lower) position than the one before it. If we were to flip through these images quickly, it would appear to us that the ball was actually falling.

You might already be imagining how to write a program to display the falling-ball animation. To display the ball, all you need to do is construct a FilledOval. Once you have constructed the ball, you can create the illusion of movement down the screen by repeatedly moving the FilledOval in the downward direction. If ballGraphic is the name of a variable of type FilledOval, then movement can be achieved by repeatedly doing the following:

```
ballGraphic.move( 0, Y_DISPLACEMENT );
```

where Y_DISPLACEMENT is a small value. A while loop can be used to achieve the repeated movement. Although these ideas are important components of creating moving images, you need to know one more thing before you can begin to create animations of your own.

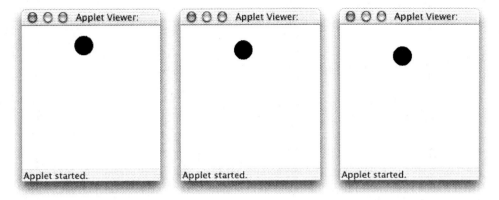

Figure 9.1   A falling ball in motion

9.2   Active Objects

Ultimately we will want to create fairly complex animations. For example, we might want to create a rain animation, where each raindrop is a like a ball falling from the the top of the canvas to the bottom. How can we construct many balls that all have to fall at the same time? It would clearly be very difficult to write a method that needed to be responsible for keeping track of and moving so many objects simultaneously. This task would certainly be easier if we could create an object that represented a ball that knew how to move itself to the bottom of the screen. Fortunately, we can do so by defining a class of *active objects*.

Before looking in detail at a complete animation of rain, let's consider how we can define a FallingBall class. By doing so, you will see that a rain animation can be achieved largely by implementing a class of objects (i.e., droplets) that behave like falling balls. The animation will ultimately appear to be quite complex, because there will be many objects falling. But the implementation of each individual raindrop is fairly simple.

An object of a FallingBall class should look like a round ball and should know how to move itself from the top of the canvas to the bottom. Saying something like new FallingBall(...); should not only draw a picture, but should set it in motion down the canvas.

If we had such a class, we could define a FallingBallController class like that shown in Figure 9.2. In it we display some simple instructions in the begin method. In addition, in onMouseClick we construct a new FallingBall, using information about the location of the mouse click.

When we look at the class FallingBall, shown in Figure 9.3, we see that it is somewhat different from the classes we wrote earlier. First, rather than extending WindowController, this class extends ActiveObject. Whenever we want to create an animation, we will define a class that extends ActiveObject.

Another difference between this class and those we have defined previously is that at the end of the constructor, we have included the line

    start();

The constructor sets up the falling ball by constructing a FilledOval at the location passed in as a parameter. Once the drawing of the ball is created, we need to set it in motion. The start

```
public class FallingBallController extends WindowController {

    ... // Constant declarations omitted...

    public void begin() {
        // Display instructions
        new Text( "Click to make a falling ball...",
                INSTR_LOCATION, canvas );
    }

    public void onMouseClick( Location point ) {
        // Make a new ball when the player clicks
        new FallingBall( point, canvas );
    }
}
```

Figure 9.2   Class that creates a falling ball with each mouse click

statement tells Java that we are ready to initiate the method `run`, which is defined below the constructor. Every `ActiveObject` must have a `run` method. This specifies the behavior that the object will have.

The `run` method of our `FallingBall` class is made up primarily of a single `while` statement. The loop executes as long as the *y* coordinate of the upper left corner of the ball is less than the screen height. That is, it will execute as long as the ball is actually visible on the canvas. The body of the loop moves the ball slightly down, then rests briefly. As long as the ball is visible, these lines will be executed: a slight movement downward, a brief rest, a slight movement downward, a brief rest, and so on. Once the `while` statement terminates, the ball is removed from the canvas, and the `run` method ends.

The line that allows the falling ball to rest is

```
pause( DELAY_TIME );
```

where we have defined the constant to have the value 33. This specifies that we want the ball to rest at least 33 milliseconds before moving again. The `pause` serves an important purpose. It allows us to see the movement of the ball. The computer works at such high speed that if we didn't explicitly pause between movements of the ball, it would zip down the canvas so quickly that we would hardly see it.

To create an animated object like our falling ball, you need to do the following:

- define a class that `extends ActiveObject`,
- include `start();` as the last statement in the constructor.
- make sure the class includes a `run` method,
- be sure to `pause` occasionally within the `run` method,

The constructor will likely have the same general form as our constructor in Figure 9.3. That is, it will do all the setup of the object you are creating, and will then include the `start();` statement to activate `run`.

```java
// Class for an animated ball that falls down the canvas
public class FallingBall extends ActiveObject {

    // The size of the ball
    private static final int SIZE = 10;

    // The delay between successive moves of the ball
    private static final int DELAY_TIME = 33;
    // Number of pixels ball falls in a single move
    private static final double Y_STEP = 4;

    // The image of the ball
    private FilledOval ballGraphic;
    // The canvas
    private DrawingCanvas canvas;

    public FallingBall( Location initialLocation, DrawingCanvas
                        aCanvas ) {
        canvas = aCanvas;
        ballGraphic = new FilledOval( initialLocation, SIZE, SIZE,
                                      canvas );
        start();
    }

    public void run() {
        while ( ballGraphic.getY() < canvas.getHeight() ) {
            ballGraphic.move( 0, Y_STEP );
            pause( DELAY_TIME );
        }
        ballGraphic.removeFromCanvas();
    }
}
```

Figure 9.3   Code for a FallingBall class

It may at first seem odd that you have to define a method named run but never actually invoke this method. Instead of calling run, you initiate its execution by invoking start. While this might seem strange, you have seen something similar to this before. When you write a program that extends WindowController, you write a begin method but never invoke it explicitly. Instead, it is invoked by the Java system, which first makes some preparations that are essential to your program's execution (like creating the window in which it will execute). Invoking start is very much like this. It tells the Java system first to perform the steps necessary to prepare to execute the run method independently of other activities performed by your program and then to invoke the run method.

Figure 9.4   A drawing of a raindrop

ActiveObjects make it simple to write programs that produce animations. Alas, if you have Disney or Pixar in mind when we say "animations", moving `FilledOvals` or `FilledRects` around the screen may not quite live up to your expectations. We can make things a bit better by using features of Java and objectdraw that make it easy to display graphics from image files on your program's canvas. This will allow us to animate images instead of simple geometric objects.

Support for displaying the contents of an image file on the canvas is provided by two classes named `Image` and `VisibleImage`. Within a Java program, an `Image` is used to hold a description of a picture that might be drawn on the canvas. Typically, the description of the image comes from an image file that is either stored on the computer running your program or accessed through the web. To access such a file from your program you will use the `getImage` method. Suppose that we had a drawing of a raindrop like the one shown in Figure 9.4 stored in a file named "raindrop.gif." We could use `Images` and `VisibleImages` to place this drawing on the canvas and animate its motion down the screen. We would first declare an `Image` variable to refer to the picture's description as

```
private Image rainPicture;
```

Then, we could associate this variable with the picture by executing the assignment

```
rainPicture = getImage( "raindrop.gif" );
```

The `getImage` method expects a `String` parameter specifying where the image file can be found. If the file is stored on your machine, this will usually just be the name of the file. If you wish to access a file from another machine on the web, the file-name argument would be replaced by a complete URL for the image such as:

```
rainPicture =
getImage( "http://eventfuljava.cs.williams.edu/images/raindrop.gif" );
```

The relationship between the `Image` and `VisibleImage` classes is similar to the relationship between `Strings` and `Text` objects. If we have a variable declared as

```
private String greeting;
```

and we execute the assignment

```
greeting = "Howdy"
```

the word "Howdy" will not immediately appear on the screen. The `String` certainly describes a message that could be displayed on the screen, but If we actually want it to appear, we have

```
public class FallingRainPicController extends WindowController {

    ... // Constant declarations omitted...

    private Image rainPicture;

    public void begin() {
        // Display instructions
        new Text( "Click to make a falling raindrop...",
                INSTR_LOCATION, canvas );

        rainPicture = getImage( "raindrop.gif" );
    }

    public void onMouseClick( Location point ) {
        // Make a new raindrop when the player clicks
        new FallingRainDrop( rainPicture, point, canvas );
    }
}
```

Figure 9.5   Class that creates a falling raindrop picture with each mouse click

to construct a Text object using a construction like:

```
new Text( greeting, xPos, yPos, canvas );
```

Similarly, an Image object describes a picture, but we have to construct a VisibleImage using the Image to make the picture appear on the screen. For example, to place a copy of our raindrop at the center of the top of the canvas we might say

```
new VisibleImage( rainPicture, 0, canvas.getWidth()/2, canvas );
```

The first parameter to the VisibleImage constructor must be an Image describing the picture to be displayed. Next, we either provide two numbers or a Location specifying the coordinates where the upper left corner of the VisibleImage should be placed. Finally, as with other graphical objects, we must provide the canvas. If we associate a name with a VisibleImage, we can manipulate it with the same methods we use with FilledRects and FramedOvals, including move, moveTo, hide, contains, and others.

The getImage method is associated with the WindowController class. Therefore, it can only be used within your program's controller class. In particular, it cannot be accessed from within an ActiveObject. If we want to use an image in an animation, we will typically use getImage to access the image file in our begin method and then pass the Image as a parameter to the constructor of some class that extends ActiveObject. As an example, in Figures 9.5 and 9.6 we show how to revise the code we provided to animate the motion of a ball down the screen, so that it instead draws our raindrop picture. Note how similar the code for the FallingRainDrop is to the code of the FallingBall class shown in Figure 9.3.

Separating the object that describes an image from the object that actually causes it to appear on the screen is very helpful when you want to display multiple copies of a picture at the same

```
public class FallingRainDrop extends ActiveObject {

    // The delay between successive moves
    private static final int DELAY_TIME = 33;

    // Number of pixels drop falls in a single move
    private static final double Y_SPEED = 4;

    // The image of the raindrop
    private VisibleImage ballGraphic;

    // The canvas
    private DrawingCanvas canvas;

    public FallingRainDrop( Image rainPic, Location initialLocation,
                            DrawingCanvas aCanvas ) {
        canvas = aCanvas;
        rainGraphic = new VisibleImage( rainPic, initialLocation,
                                        canvas );
        start();
    }

    public void run() {
        while ( rainGraphic.getY() < canvas.getHeight() ) {
            rainGraphic.move( 0, Y_SPEED );
            pause( DELAY_TIME );
        }
        rainGraphic.removeFromCanvas();
    }
}
```

Figure 9.6   Code for a FallingRainDrop class

time. For example, if we wanted to simulate a rain shower, we could display several rain drops by creating multiple FallingRainDrops from the single Image named rainPicture. We would only have to invoke getImage once.

9.4   Interacting with Active Objects

We have emphasized that classes that extend ActiveObject must have a run method. In fact, our first example only had a run method. Like other classes, those that extend ActiveObject can have as many methods as needed.

Say that we want to allow a user to create a falling ball with a click of the mouse. In addition, say that we want the ball to have the ability to change its color. We can do this by adding the

```
public class ColorBallController extends WindowController {

    ... // Constant declarations omitted

    private FallingBall droppedBall; // The falling ball

    public void begin() {
        // Display instructions
        new Text( "Click to make a falling ball...",
                INSTR_LOCATION, canvas );
    }

    public void onMouseClick( Location point ) {
        // Make a new ball when the player clicks
        droppedBall = new FallingBall( point, canvas );
    }
        // Falling ball turns gray when mouse exits canvas
    public void onMouseExit( Location point ) {
        if ( droppedBall != null ) {
            droppedBall.setColor( Color.GRAY );
        }
    }
        // Falling ball turns black when mouse enters canvas
    public void onMouseEnter( Location point ) {
        if ( droppedBall != null ) {
            droppedBall.setColor( Color.BLACK );
        }
    }
}
```

Figure 9.7   Defining a class that allows a user to drop a ball that changes color

following method to the FallingBall class:

```
public void setColor( Color aColor ) {
    ballGraphic.setColor( aColor );
}
```

We can now modify our FallingBallController so that the ball turns gray when the user moves the mouse outside the canvas and then turns black again when the user moves the mouse inside the canvas. The new class, called ColorBallController, is shown in Figure 9.4. It has two additional methods to handle mouse events. We have also added a variable droppedBall of type FallingBall, so that when a ball is dropped, we have a way to refer to it in order to change its color.

You will note that both onMouseExit and onMouseEnter check whether droppedBall is null before changing its color. It only makes sense to change the ball's color if there actually is a ball, i.e., if droppedBall is not null. (Remember that instance variables that refer to objects are initialized to null.) For example, say that the user moves the mouse out of the canvas before ever clicking the mouse. If we simply had the line

```
droppedBall.setColor( Color.GRAY );
```

in the onMouseExit method, Java would attempt to send the setColor message to the ball, but there is no ball at this point! Our program would stop, and a message would tell us that we had a null pointer error. This is why we need to check that the ball exists before doing anything else.

➡ EXERCISE 9.4.1

What happens if the user clicks twice, creating two falling balls, and then moves the mouse outside the canvas? ❖

Changing the color of the falling ball while it is dropping is arguably quite dull. What might be more interesting would be to allow the user to stop the ball during its fall. Say that we wanted to modify ColorBallController in such a way that the falling ball would stop and disappear when the mouse exited the canvas. The modified onMouseExit might then look like this:

```
public void onMouseExit( Location point ) {
    if ( droppedBall != null ) {
        droppedBall.stopFalling();
    }
}
```

It is clear that we need to add a method to the FallingBall class to allow a ball to stop itself. What might not be clear yet is how that method can affect what happens in the run method. That is, how can the invocation of the method stopFalling affect the loop in the run method that is making the ball fall?

We solve this mystery by adding an instance variable to the class FallingBall, as shown in Figure 9.8. This is a boolean variable with the name moving. This variable will store information about the state of the ball. That is, its value will tell us whether the ball is currently moving or has been stopped. We initialize the variable in the constructor to have the value true. When a user creates a new falling ball, we assume that it is to move by default.

In the run method, we modify the condition of the while statement. As long as the ball is visible on the canvas *and is moving*, i.e., has not been stopped, it falls. The method stopFalling affects the state of the ball. If this message is sent to a falling ball, the boolean variable moving is set to false. This means that the next time the condition of the while is reached, the condition will evaluate to false. The loop body will not be executed and the ball will be removed.

9.5   Making Active Objects Affect Other Objects

So far we have seen how to define a class of ActiveObjects, and we have explored ways to affect them through mutator methods. To this point, however, our active objects have been fairly isolated, in that they don't affect other objects. In this section we explore a number of different ways in which active objects can affect others.

```
public class FallingBall extends ActiveObject {

    ... // Constant declarations omitted

    // The image of the ball
    private FilledOval ballGraphic;
    // Whether the ball is currently moving
    private boolean moving;
    // The canvas
    private DrawingCanvas canvas;

    public FallingBall( Location initialLocation,
                        DrawingCanvas aCanvas ) {
        canvas = aCanvas;
        ballGraphic = new FilledOval( initialLocation, SIZE, SIZE,
                                      canvas );
        moving = true;
        start();
    }

    public void run() {
        while ( moving && ballGraphic.getY() < canvas.getHeight() ) {
            ballGraphic.move( 0, Y_STEP );
            pause( DELAY_TIME );
        }
        ballGraphic.removeFromCanvas();
    }

    public void stopFalling() {
        moving = false;
    }
}
```

Figure 9.8 Adding stopping functionality to a falling ball

9.5.1 Interacting with a Nonactive Object

Let's imagine that our falling balls don't simply disappear when they reach the bottom of the canvas. Instead, they are collected in a box which becomes ever more full with each ball that falls. You might imagine that the falling balls are raindrops that collect in a pool of water. Figure 9.9 shows how such a pool might look before any drops have fallen and how it might look after many drops have fallen.

Creating the first image in Figure 9.9 is easy. The controller will simply construct a collector, i.e., a FilledRect, at the bottom of the canvas. We then need to make several changes to the FallingBall class. We'll call this new class FallingDroplet, and the first modification we will make is to change the instance variable name ballGraphic to dropletGraphic.

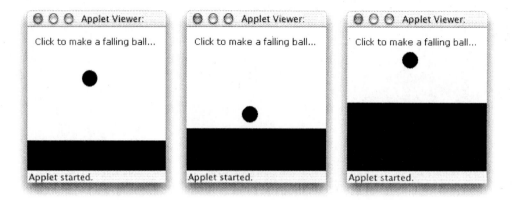

Figure 9.9   A pool filling with rain

We want every falling droplet to know about the collector. The reason is that each droplet will check whether it has reached the collector's surface, and then send a message to the collector telling it to raise its level a bit. Therefore, the next change we need to make is to add an instance variable, `collector`, as in Figure 9.11. As before, the constructor creates the actual droplet, but before it is set in motion, the falling droplet needs to remember the collector for later. Recall from Chapter 8 that parameters to the constructor are not visible outside the constructor. Therefore, we need to remember the collector by assigning the formal parameter `aCollector` to our instance variable `collector`.

We have made some significant changes to the `run` method. The droplet should only continue to move down the screen as long as it is visible. Therefore we modify the condition in the `while` statement so that the droplet will stop moving as soon as it falls below the top of the collector.

Once the loop terminates, we need to remove the droplet as we did before, but we need to do additional work as well. If the collector is not yet full, we need to fill it a bit. In this case we have decided to increase its height by a quarter of the droplet size. To make the collector more full, we change the height of the rectangle and move it up on the canvas so that we can see the new size.

Figure 9.10 shows a modified controller that creates a drop every time the user clicks. An instance variable, `collector`, of type `FilledRect`, represents the pool. It is constructed in the `begin` method. (Note that the constant `COLLECTOR_RATIO` is a fraction that specifies the initial size of the collector relative to the entire canvas.) In order to allow our falling droplets to affect the pool, we need to pass `collector` as a parameter to the `FallingDroplet` constructor. In this way, each falling drop will know about the pool, so that it can effectively change it. Note that we have removed the `onMouseExit` method so that we can focus on the interaction between the drops and the pool.

In general, if we want an active object to have the ability to affect other objects, we can do so by making sure the active object knows about the others. One way to do so is to pass that information in as a parameter to the constructor as we did above. As long as the active object remembers that information for later, it can communicate with the other object as much as it needs to.

In the example above, you might have wondered why the droplets were responsible for modifying the collector. Clearly there has to be some communication between the droplets and the collector. The way we have shown you is just one option. Another possibility is to have the

```
public class DropCollector extends WindowController {

    ... // Constant declarations omitted

    private FilledRect collector;  // Collects falling drops

    public void begin() {
        // Display instructions
        new Text( "Click to make a falling raindrop...",
                INSTR_LOCATION, canvas );

        // Construct a collector for the falling drops
        collector =
            new FilledRect( 0, canvas.getHeight()-
                            canvas.getHeight()*COLLECTOR_RATIO,
                            canvas.getWidth(), canvas.getHeight()*
                            COLLECTOR_RATIO, canvas );
    }

    public void onMouseClick( Location point ) {
        // Make a new droplet when the player clicks
        new FallingDroplet( point, canvas, collector );
    }
}
```

Figure 9.10 Adding a collector to collect raindrops

controller manage the collector. After completing a fall, a droplet could send a message to the controller, telling it to increase the collector size. Note that it would not be a good idea for the collector to know about the droplets, as it would then be responsible for keeping track of potentially many at once.

9.5.2 Active Objects that Construct Other Active Objects

We just saw that active objects can affect nonactive objects. They can also interact with other active objects. In particular, they can create active objects.

We have begun to think about our falling balls as raindrops that can fall into a collector. Naturally, raindrops should fall from a cloud. Rather than having each drop fall with the click of the mouse, let's construct a cloud that knows how to drop its own raindrops. If we want a RainCloud to be created with the click of the mouse, the body of the method onMouseClick will be:

```
new RainCloud( canvas, collector );
```

assuming that we want to catch the rain in a pool.

```
public class FallingDroplet extends ActiveObject {
    ... // Constant declarations omitted

    private FilledOval dropletGraphic; // The droplet

    // Collector into which droplet falls
    private FilledRect collector;

    public FallingDroplet( Location initialLocation, DrawingCanvas
                           canvas, FilledRect aCollector ) {

        // Draw the droplet
        dropletGraphic = new FilledOval( initialLocation, SIZE, SIZE,
                                         canvas );

        // Remember the collector for later
        collector = aCollector;

        // Start the motion of the droplet
        start();
    }

    public void run() {

        while ( dropletGraphic.getY() < collector.getY() ) {
            dropletGraphic.move( 0, Y_STEP );
            pause( DELAY_TIME );
        }

        dropletGraphic.removeFromCanvas();
        if ( collector.getY() > 0 ) {
            collector.setHeight( collector.getHeight() + SIZE/4 );
            collector.move( 0, -SIZE/4 );
        }
    }
}
```

Figure 9.11 Making a droplet fill a collector

The RainCloud class is shown in Figure 9.12. The class header specifies that this class extends ActiveObject. So far we have seen that a class that extends ActiveObject has a constructor that sets up some sort of animation and that the constructor ends with the start statement, which initiates the run method. The run method performs the actual animation. Though ActiveObjects are very useful for creating animations, they are not limited to this activity. In this case, we want the run method to generate raindrops.

```
public class RainCloud extends ActiveObject {

    ... // Constant declarations omitted

    // The canvas on which drops will be drawn
    private DrawingCanvas canvas;
    // Pool in which drops will be collected
    private FilledRect collector;

    public RainCloud( DrawingCanvas aCanvas, FilledRect aCollector ) {

        // Remember the canvas for dropping rain later
        canvas = aCanvas;
        // Remember the collector
        collector = aCollector;

        // Start the rain
        start();
    }

    public void run() {

        // Used to generate random drop locations for rain
        RandomIntGenerator xGenerator =
                    new RandomIntGenerator( 0, canvas.getWidth() );
        int dropCount = 0;
        // Generate specified number of raindrops
        while ( dropCount < MAX_DROPS ) {
            new FallingDroplet( new Location( xGenerator.nextValue(), 0 ),
                            canvas, collector );
            pause( DELAY_TIME );
            dropCount++;
        }
    }
}
```

Figure 9.12 A rain cloud class

We will treat objects of the class FallingDroplet, as in Figure 9.11, as our raindrops. To construct one of these, we need to pass three pieces of information to the contructor: a Location from which to drop it, the canvas on which it is to be drawn, and a collector. Since the FallingDroplet constructor requires these pieces of information, we need to be certain that run knows about locations, about the canvas, and about the collector.

We consider each of these separately. First, let's think about the locations of raindrops. In order to simulate real rain, we should probably have each drop fall from a different location in the sky (in our case, the top of the canvas). What mechanism do we have for generating a variety of *x* coordinates for drop locations? The answer is RandomIntGenerator. In the run method of the RainCloud class, we declare a variable xGenerator that will be used to generate random *x* coordinates as drop locations.

Now we need to consider the canvas and how we can pass information about the canvas to the FallingDroplet constructor. We handle this by having the RainCloud constructor take the canvas as a parameter. The canvas is then remembered as an instance variable, which we have called canvas. This variable is then known in the run method and can be passed on to the FallingDroplet constructor. The collector is handled similarly.

In order to limit the amount of rain to fall, we define a constant MAX_DROPS that gives us the maximum number of droplets to be dropped. In order to count droplets, we declare a local variable, dropCount, in the run method that will keep track of the number dropped so far. This is initialized to 0. The condition of the while statement specifies that the body of the loop should execute as long as the count of drops is less than the maximum allowed. The statements in the body construct a new FallingDroplet, passing a location, the canvas, and collector as parameters. After a raindrop is created, the cloud pauses briefly, and the number of drops so far is incremented. Each time through the loop, a cloud object will create an entirely new active object that is a single raindrop, i.e., a FallingDroplet.

Note that we did not have to limit the number of raindrops. We could have had a RainCloud generate raindrops indefinitely by replacing the while loop as follows:

```
while ( true ) {
    new FallingDroplet( new Location(xGenerator.nextValue(), 0 ),
                        canvas, collector );
    pause( DELAY_TIME );
}
```

Here, as long as the condition evaluates to true, which it does for each iteration, raindrops will be generated.

EXERCISE 9.5.1

a. What would happen if we omitted the statement

dropCount++;

from the run method of RainCloud shown in Figure 9.12?
b. What if we omitted the pause?

9.6 Active Objects without Loops

In this chapter, every class of ActiveObjects has had a run method in which a while loop controlled the main behavior. At this point you might be wondering whether the run method *must*

```
public class CreditScroller extends ActiveObject {

    ... // Miscellaneous declarations omitted

    public CreditScroller( DrawingCanvas aCanvas ) {
        canvas = aCanvas;
        start();
    }

    public void run() {
        new Credit( "Producer . . . Martha Washington", canvas );
        pause(DELAY_TIME);
        new Credit( "Director . . . George Washington", canvas );
        pause( DELAY_TIME );
        new Credit( "Script . . . Thomas Jefferson", canvas );
        pause( DELAY_TIME );
        new Credit( "Costumes . . . Betsy Ross", canvas );
    }
}
```

Figure 9.13   A class to generate movie credits

contain a while loop. The answer is no. There is no requirement that there be a while loop in run.

As an example, consider the way that movie credits scroll on the screen at the end of a film. Typically they rise from the bottom of the screen, float to the top, and then disappear. We can think of each line of the credits as an ActiveObject. Its behavior is similar to that of our falling ball, except that it moves up, rather than down. We might imagine individual lines being generated by a credit generator, similar to our rain cloud. It could generate a line, wait a bit, then generate another line, and so on. But there is a big difference between raindrops and film credits. Each line in the credits is different from any other. The textual information it conveys is unique. With the tools you have learned so far, the best way to generate a series of movie credits would be with the CreditScroller class shown in Figure 9.13, where the Credit class is as shown in Figure 9.14. Note that the CreditScroller does not have a while loop controlling its behavior. The run method in CreditScroller simply generates a series of movie credits, pausing briefly between lines. It passes two parameters to the Credit constructor: the actual information to be displayed and the canvas.

The Credit constructor takes a String and a canvas and constructs a Text object. Of course, we want each line of the credits to be centered on the canvas. To do this, we begin by constructing the line so that it is just below the visible canvas. We then determine where it should be moved so that it is centered. Once the line has been positioned, we start its motion up the canvas, just as we moved a falling ball down the canvas. We move the line only while some piece of it is visible. Once it has moved completely off the canvas, we stop moving it and remove it. The line has moved completely off the canvas when the bottom of the Text is at y coordinate 0. When this is the case, the y coordinate of the top of the Text is a negative value, specifically at $-height$, where *height* is the Text's height.

```
public class Credit extends ActiveObject {

    ... // Constant declarations omitted

    private Text roleAndName; // Information to be displayed

    public Credit( String scrollingLine, DrawingCanvas canvas ) {
        // Create the line to be displayed
        roleAndName = new Text( scrollingLine, 0, canvas.getHeight(),
                                canvas );
        // Center it on the canvas
        roleAndName.move( (canvas.getWidth() -
                        roleAndName.getWidth())/2, 0 );
        // start the movement
        start();
    }

    public void run() {
        // Move up while any part of the credit line is visible
        while ( roleAndName.getY() > -roleAndName.getHeight() ) {
            roleAndName.move( 0, -Y_STEP );
            pause( DELAY_TIME );
        }
        roleAndName.removeFromCanvas();
    }
}
```

Figure 9.14   A class of individual movie credit lines

9.7   Making Animations Smooth

If you were to run the movie credit generator, you would see the four lines of movie credits scrolling up the screen, each line slightly below the one before it. It is also likely that the movement would occasionally appear "jumpy". That is, the movement up the canvas might not be completely smooth. In this section, we consider the cause of such behavior and introduce a way of coping with it.

Consider the while loop in the run method of the Credit class. The line of text is moved a bit, then we pause briefly, then we move a bit, pause briefly, and so on. In a perfect world the line of text would move at exactly the same speed all the way up the canvas. Ideally, the line would move exactly Y_STEP pixels up every DELAY_TIME milliseconds. The problem here is with the statement

```
pause( DELAY_TIME );
```

```
public void run() {
    double lastTime, currentTime, elapsedTime;
    // Remember the time
    lastTime = System.currentTimeMillis();
    while ( roleAndName.getY() > -roleAndName.getHeight() ) {
        // Determine how much time has passed
        currentTime = System.currentTimeMillis();
        elapsedTime = currentTime - lastTime;
        // Restart timing
        lastTime = currentTime;
        roleAndName.move( 0, -SPEED_PER_MILLI * elapsedTime );
        pause( DELAY_TIME );
    }
    roleAndName.removeFromCanvas();
}
```

Figure 9.15 Making movement smoother

pause allows us to pause for *at least* DELAY_TIME milliseconds. It does not say that we will pause for *exactly* that many milliseconds. If the value of DELAY_TIME is 33, we might find that a pause lasts 33 milliseconds, 34 milliseconds, or more. If the pauses are longer than 33, our credit will move more slowly than expected.

Fortunately, we can handle this problem. To do so, we begin by calculating the number of pixels to move per millisecond, as follows:

SPEED_PER_MILLI = Y_STEP / DELAY_TIME;

Then, before we move, we determine how much time has actually passed since the last time we moved. Say that we have this information in a variable elapsedTime. We can now calculate the number of pixels that we really want to move. To do this, we multiply the speed per millisecond, SPEED_PER_MILLI, by the elapsed time. This is illustrated in Figure 9.15, which shows how we have modified the run method of the Credit class.

We declare three local variables in the run method, all of type double. The first two, lastTime and currentTime, will hold snapshots of the time. The third, elapsedTime will be used to hold the result of our calculation of how much time has passed between moves. We begin timing before we reach the while statement. If the condition of the while is true and we enter the loop, we then calculate the amount of time that has passed so that we can move appropriately. We do this by calculating the difference between the current time and the starting time. Before moving the text, we start timing again. In this way, if the condition is true and we re-execute the statements in the body of the while, we can recalculate the time that has elapsed since the last move. This technique can be applied to make the rate at which an animated object moves more uniform.

■➡ EXERCISE 9.7.1

Modify the FallingBall class to make the motion of the falling ball more uniform. ❖

9.8 More Hints about Timing

Even if you were to run the movie credits with the improved, smoother motion of each Credit, you would likely see some odd behavior. While there would be space between the individual credits, the space might not be completely even. In fact, some of the credits might overlap each other slightly. As in the previous section, this is a result of our inability to have complete control over the timing in our program.

Consider the following scenario. A single movie credit is constructed, and then our CreditScroller pauses. We hope that this pause is long enough to allow the movie credit to move upward and out of the way before the next is generated. But suppose that it only moves a little bit before the CreditScroller constructs another line. How can we modify the CreditScroller class to assure that each line of the credits will be a reasonable distance from the one before it?

There are several parts to the solution. First, before we generate a new line of the movie credits, we can ask the previous one how far it has traveled upward. If the distance traveled is over a certain threshold, we can construct the new line. If not, we pause and then try again.

In order to ask a Credit how far it has traveled, we need to add a method to the definition of the Credit class. We will call that method distanceTraveled and write it as follows:

```
public double distanceTraveled() {
    return ( canvas.getHeight() - roleAndName.getY() );
}
```

Since we initially positioned the movie credit so that its top was at the bottom edge of the canvas, we simply calculate the difference between the bottom of the canvas and the current y coordinate of the credit. This additional method requires that we add canvas as an instance variable.

Once we have this method, we can modify the run method of the CreditScroller class as we described above. We put off constructing a new Credit as long as the one before it is still too close. Our modifications are shown in Figure 9.16. We begin by declaring a local variable, lastCredit. We then construct the first movie credit. After doing so, we invoke a method that waits for the credit to get out of the way of the subsequent credit. The method consists of a while loop that pauses as long as the last movie credit is too close.

In order to help us to keep our code clearer, we have written a private boolean method tooClose that determines whether the last movie credit is too close. There we simply ask the last credit how far it has traveled and then determine whether that is less than the desired distance. This is slightly more complex than you might have imagined. The reason is that we want to assure that there is a certain gap between the *bottom* of one credit and the *top* of the next. To do this, we add to the desired gap size the height of the last credit. This requires the addition of another method to the Credit class:

```
public double getHeight() {
    return roleAndName.getHeight();
}
```

```
public void run() {
   Credit lastCredit;
   lastCredit = new Credit( "Director . . . George Washington",
                            canvas );
   waitToScroll( lastCredit );
   lastCredit = new Credit( "Script . . . Thomas Jefferson",
                            canvas );
   waitToScroll( lastCredit );
   lastCredit = new Credit( "Producer . . . Martha Washington",
                            canvas );
   waitToScroll( lastCredit );
   lastCredit = new Credit( "Costumes . . . Betsy Ross", canvas );
}

private boolean tooClose ( Credit lastCredit, int desiredGap ) {
   return lastCredit.distanceTraveled () <
                            desiredGap + lastCredit.getHeight();
}

private void waitToScroll( Credit aCredit ) {
   while ( tooClose( aCredit, GAP_SIZE ) ) {
      pause( DELAY_TIME );
   }
}
}
```

Figure 9.16 Guaranteeing minimum spacing between moving objects

➡ EXERCISE 9.8.1

Given the last modifications for CreditScroller, *do you still expect the credits to be evenly spaced? Why or why not?*   ❖

9.9   Summary

This chapter has focused on ActiveObjects. The main points that you should take from this chapter are:

* Animation is a context in which while statements are used often.
* To define a class of animated objects we extend ActiveObject.
  - Every class that extends ActiveObject must have a run method.
  - The run method is started by invoking start. This will typically happen as the last item in the constructor.
  - The code that guides the animation should include pauses.

9.10 Chapter Review Problems

EXERCISE 9.10.1

Consider the definition of a class, SlidingBox *of* ActiveObjects. *A* SlidingBox *is a rectangle that moves across the canvas from left to right. It should be removed when it goes across the right edge of the canvas. Unfortunately, the class definition below has two errors. Please fix them.*

```java
public class SlidingBox extends ActiveObject {

    ... // Constant declarations omitted

    private FilledRect box;

    private DrawingCanvas canvas;

    public SlidingBox( Location boxLocation, DrawingCanvas aCanvas ) {
        canvas = aCanvas;
        box = new FilledRect( boxLocation, BOXSIZE, BOXSIZE, canvas );
        run();
    }

    public void run() {
        if (box.getX() < canvas.getWidth() ) {
            box.move( X_SPEED, 0 );
            pause( DELAY_TIME );
        }
        box.removeFromCanvas();
    }
}
```

EXERCISE 9.10.2

What are the four key steps when creating an ActiveObject?

EXERCISE 9.10.3

Suppose that FallingDroplet *for* RainCloud *had the line*

```java
    dropletGraphic.hide();
```

instead of

```java
    dropletGraphic.removeFromCanvas();
```

What this difference does this make? Why is it better to use removeFromCanvas?

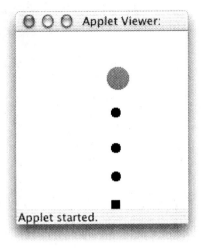

Figure 9.17 Run of HitTheTarget

9.11 Programming Problems

EXERCISE 9.11.1

a. *Revisit* LightenUp *from Chapter 2 and modify it so that now the sun rises slowly and the sky brightens as it rises. The sun should begin rising as soon as the program starts. The sun should stop rising before it begins to exit the window.*

b. *Add methods so that the sun also stops rising if the mouse exits the window.*

EXERCISE 9.11.2

Write a program that creates a ResizableBall *centered around the point where the mouse is clicked. A* ResizableBall *is an animated ball that grows up to twice its original size and then shrinks down to half its size before beginning to grow again. It continues to grow and shrink until the program is stopped. The center of the* ResizeableBall *should never move.*

EXERCISE 9.11.3

Write a program called HitTheTarget *with the following attributes (refer to Figure 9.17):*

* *When the program begins, there should a be a target moving back and forth horizontally between the left and right edges of the canvas. This is depicted as the large oval in Figure 9.17.*
* *When the user clicks the mouse, a ball shooter is created at the bottom of the window and aligned with the mouse. The ball shooter will shoot three balls that move up the screen, one after another.*
* *If the user hits the target with a ball, the console should indicate this.*

CHAPTER 10

Interfaces

ccasionally we wish to have a variable in a program that can refer to objects from several different classes. For example, we might have a drawing program in which a variable can refer sometimes to a framed square and at other times to a framed circle. In those circumstances, we cannot declare the variable to have both types `FramedRect` and `FramedOval`. Instead, we will need to declare the type of the variable to be something that includes objects from both of these classes.

There are several ways of providing such general types in Java. One of the most important involves the use of **interfaces**. A Java interface provides a description of the `public` methods that objects of that type need to provide. In this chapter we will focus on the use of interfaces to specify a contract that several classes may satisfy. In the following chapter we introduce the use of Java's Graphical User Interface components, such as buttons and menus, and examine the role that interfaces play in their use.

10.1 Interfaces for Flexibility

Interfaces allow the programmer to describe exactly what features are needed in a particular programming context and to declare variables and parameters that can refer to values from more than one class. We will introduce the use of interfaces through a simple example in this section.

10.1.1 A First Example

To develop a first example using interfaces, let's go back to the `RevFaceDrag` program in Figure 6.3 and its associated `FunnyFace` class from Figure 6.4. This program allowed the user to drag around a `FunnyFace` object in the window.

Suppose our goal is to generalize this program to allow the user to drag around different kinds of objects. In that case, it will be useful to specify the methods needed by objects in order to be dragged. While we eventually added `show`, `hide`, `setColor`, and `moveTo` methods to the

FunnyFace class, the only methods of FunnyFace actually used in the RevFaceDrag class are the contains and move methods. Thus we will construct an interface, Movable, with only those two methods.

```
public interface Movable {
    // Move receiver by dx in x direction and dy in y direction
    public void move( double dx, double dy );

    // Determine whether point is contained in receiver
    public boolean contains( Location point );
}
```

In an interface we provide only the headers for the methods listed—never the method bodies. That is, we include the method name, return type, and parameters, but we leave out the actual code for the method—i.e., the portion that is surrounded by curly braces—and instead we insert a semicolon, ";".

Our main reason for using interfaces will be to provide a specification of methods that an object must support. That is, we can think of it as a kind of contract that an object must satisfy. For example, if we have a declaration,

```
Movable geometricObject;
```

then any object referred to by geometricObject must have methods move and contains with the same parameter and return types as specified by the interface. While this sounds restrictive, an object satisfying the interface may have many more methods than those specified by the interface.

⟹ EXERCISE 10.1.1

Define an interface called VisualInterface *that contains methods* show, hide, *and* setColor.   ❖

10.1.2 Associating Objects and Classes With Interfaces

As we have seen, all objects are associated with classes. Thus the objects actually referred to by variables must themselves be associated with classes. If we wish objects of a given class to be associated with an interface as well, then we must specify that in the class header. We must also ensure that all methods promised in the interface are actually contained in the class definition.

We associate an interface with a class by adding an implements clause to the class header:

```
public class C implements SomeInterface { ... }
```

This class header indicates that objects of the class C can be associated with the interface SomeInterface. For example, if we had wanted class FunnyFace associated with interface Movable, we would have to replace the header of the class definition by

```
public class FunnyFace implements Movable {
```

while the rest of the class definition would remain exactly the same as given in Figure 6.4.

It is not sufficient to simply declare that a class is associated with an interface; the class must contain corresponding method definitions (both header and body) for all of the method headers contained in the interface. It is easy to see that class FunnyFace does indeed supply method definitions for all of the method headers contained in interface Movable. If it did not, when we compiled the class, the compiler would issue an error message complaining that a method in the interface was not included in the class.

A class implementing an interface may contain more methods than are specified by the interface. The declaration that a class implements an interface represents a promise that the class contains at least those methods specified in the interface. We illustrate this by writing a new version of class FunnyFace in Figure 10.1. It contains the required methods move and contains, but also has an additional moveTo method. Thus it keeps the promise of implementing all methods mentioned in Movable. The additional method has no impact on whether or not the class implements Movable.

While Java compilers do not enforce it, methods of a class implementing an interface should also satisfy the comments associated with those methods in the interface. For example, the comment associated with method move in interface Movable specifies that execution of the method should result in moving the receiver by dx in the *x* direction and by dy in the *y* direction. The method move in class FunnyFace does indeed move the object as desired, so it satisfies the comments associated with move in the interface. Similarly, the contains method of FunnyFace satisfies the comments associated with contains in Movable. Thus class FunnyFace satisfies the contract required to implement Movable.

Now let's write another class, StraightFace, that also implements the interface Movable. It appears in Figure 10.2, and it generates faces in which the eyes, mouth, and nose are straight lines. Like FunnyFace it can claim to implement Movable, because it includes definitions of methods move and contains that are compatible with those of the interface.

The class TwoFaceDrag, in Figure 10.3, is an example of how to use interfaces. The begin method of the class constructs a new FunnyFace, referred to with variable happy, and a new StraightFace, referred to with variable straight. The types of the variables are FunnyFace and StraightFace, respectively.

When the user presses the mouse button, the onMousePress method determines which, if any, face the mouse is on. If a face has been selected, then it is assigned to variable dragged, and boolean variable dragging is set to be true. Otherwise, dragging is set to be false. If the mouse is dragged and dragging is true, the face referred to by dragged is moved in the window.

This program is not that different from other programs that you have already seen. In fact, the only point of interest is the type of the variable dragged. Sometimes it will hold an object from class FunnyFace, while at other times it will hold an object of class StraightFace. If we were to use either FunnyFace or StraightFace as the type of the variable, dragged would not be able to refer to values from the other class. However, because both FunnyFace and StraightFace classes implement Movable, objects from both of those classes can be referred to by a variable of type Movable.

There is an important thing to point out here. The move methods of FunnyFace and StraightFace are different. The move method of FunnyFace itself sends move messages to four instance variables that are all FramedOvals, while the move method of StraightFace sends move messages to five instance variables, four of which are Lines. How can we know

```
public class FunnyFace implements Movable {

    private static final int FACE_HEIGHT = 60,   // Dimensions of the face
                             FACE_WIDTH = 60,

                             EYE_OFFSET = 20,    // Eye location and size
                             EYE_RADIUS = 8,

                             MOUTH_HEIGHT = 10, // Dimensions of the mouth
                             MOUTH_WIDTH = FACE_WIDTH/2;

    private FramedOval head,        // Parts of the face
                      leftEye,
                      rightEye,
                      mouth;

    // Create pieces of funny face
    public FunnyFace( double left, double top, DrawingCanvas canvas ) {
        head = new FramedOval( left, top, FACE_WIDTH, FACE_HEIGHT, canvas );
        mouth = new FramedOval( left+(FACE_WIDTH-MOUTH_WIDTH)/2,
                        top + 2*FACE_HEIGHT/3,
                        MOUTH_WIDTH, MOUTH_HEIGHT, canvas );
        leftEye = new FramedOval( left+EYE_OFFSET-EYE_RADIUS/2, top+EYE_OFFSET,
                        EYE_RADIUS, EYE_RADIUS, canvas );
        rightEye = new FramedOval( left+FACE_WIDTH-EYE_OFFSET-EYE_RADIUS/2,
                        top+EYE_OFFSET, EYE_RADIUS, EYE_RADIUS,
                        canvas );
    }

    // Move funny face by (dx,dy)
    public void move( double dx, double dy ) {
        head.move( dx, dy );
        leftEye.move( dx, dy );
        rightEye.move( dx, dy );
        mouth.move( dx, dy );
    }

    // Move funny face to pt
    public void moveTo( Location pt ) {
        this.move( pt.getX() - head.getX(), pt.getY() - head.getY() );
    }

    // Determine whether pt is inside funny face
    public boolean contains( Location pt ) {
        return head.contains( pt );
    }
}
```

Figure 10.1 FunnyFace class

```
public class StraightFace implements Movable {
    ... // Constant declarations omitted

    private FramedOval head;       // oval for head

    private Line leftEye,          // Parts of the face
                 rightEye,
                 nose,
                 mouth;

    // Create pieces of straight face
    public StraightFace( double left, double top, DrawingCanvas canvas ) {
        head = new FramedOval( left, top, FACE_WIDTH, FACE_HEIGHT, canvas );
        mouth = new Line( left+(FACE_WIDTH-MOUTH_WIDTH)/2, top + 2*FACE_HEIGHT/3,
                          left+(FACE_WIDTH+MOUTH_WIDTH)/2,
                          top + 2*FACE_HEIGHT/3, canvas );

        nose = new Line( left+FACE_WIDTH/2, top+EYE_OFFSET,
                         left+FACE_WIDTH/2, top + FACE_HEIGHT/2, canvas );

        leftEye = new Line( left+EYE_OFFSET-EYE_RADIUS/2, top+EYE_OFFSET,
                            left+EYE_OFFSET+EYE_RADIUS/2, top+EYE_OFFSET,
                            canvas );
        rightEye = new Line( left+FACE_WIDTH-EYE_OFFSET-EYE_RADIUS/2,
                             top+EYE_OFFSET,
                             left+FACE_WIDTH-EYE_OFFSET+EYE_RADIUS/2,
                             top+EYE_OFFSET, canvas );
    }

    // Move straight face by (dx,dy)
    public void move( double dx, double dy ) {
        head.move( dx, dy );
        leftEye.move( dx, dy );
        rightEye.move( dx, dy );
        mouth.move( dx, dy );
        nose.move( dx, dy );
    }

    // Move straight face to pt
    public void moveTo( Location pt ) {
        this.move( pt.getX() - head.getX(), pt.getY() - head.getY() );
    }

    // Determine whether pt is inside straight face
    public boolean contains( Location pt ) {
        return head.contains( pt );
    }
}
```

Figure 10.2   StraightFace class

```
public class TwoFaceDrag extends WindowController {
    ... // Constant declarations omitted

    private FunnyFace happy;        // Funny face in window

    private StraightFace straight;  // Straight face in window

    private Movable dragged;        // Face chosen to be dragged

    private Location lastPoint;     // Point where mouse was last seen

    private boolean dragging;       // Whether should be dragging face

    // Make the faces
    public void begin() {
        happy = new FunnyFace( FACE_LEFT, FACE_TOP, canvas );
        straight = new StraightFace( FACE_GAP+FACE_LEFT, FACE_TOP,
                                    canvas );
    }

    // Save starting point and whether point was in one of faces --
    // and which one.
    public void onMousePress( Location point ) {
        lastPoint = point;

        if (happy.contains( point )) {
                dragged = happy;
                dragging = true;
        } else if (straight.contains ( point )) {
                dragged = straight;
                dragging = true;
        } else {
                dragging = false;
        }
    }

    // If mouse is in a face, then drag it with the mouse
    public void onMouseDrag( Location point ) {
        if ( dragging ) {
            dragged.move( point.getX() - lastPoint.getX(),
                        point.getY() - lastPoint.getY() );
            lastPoint = point;
        }
    }
}
```

Figure 10.3 TwoFaceDrag class

which version of the move method will be executed when the move message is sent to the object associated with dragged?

The obvious (and, luckily, correct) answer is that the code executed is determined by the object associated with dragged when the message is sent. If the associated object is an instance of FunnyFace at run time, then the move method from class FunnyFace will be executed, while if the object is from StraightFace, then the StraightFace method will be executed.

Because the code to be executed is determined at run time, the process of selecting the code to be executed is called *dynamic method invocation*. It is one of the most important distinguishing features of object-oriented programming.

Thus when the type of a variable is an interface, we can send any message listed in the interface to it, but the actual code executed will be determined at run time based on the class of the object associated with the variable at that time. Because the receiver's class implements the interface, the class is guaranteed to have an appropriate method to execute when the message is sent.

EXERCISE 10.1.2

Use the definition of the Resizable *interface to complete the exercises below and on the following pages.*

```
public interface Resizable {
    public void resize ( double size );
    public boolean contains ( Location point );
}
```

a. *Write the class header for a class called* Square *that implements the* Resizable *interface.*
b. *What methods must the* Square *class define to legally implement the* Resizable *interface?*
c. *Finish the* Square *class. The constructor should take three parameters: a* Location, *a* double *for size, and the canvas. It should draw a* FilledRect *at the* Location, *with each side having length specified by the size parameter. The* resize *method should set the height and width of the* FilledRect *to the size determined by the* double *parameter. The* contains *method should return* true *if the* FilledRect *contains the* Location *that was passed as a parameter. Otherwise, it should return* false.

EXERCISE 10.1.3

Now define a second class called Circle *that resembles* Square *except that the instance variable for the* Circle *class is a* FilledOval.

10.1.3   Using Interfaces

Before seeing how we can use variables whose types are specified as interfaces, let's summarize what we have just discussed:

* An interface declaration looks a lot like a class declaration except that it only includes public methods, and the bodies of the methods are omitted. Constructors may not appear in an interface.
* A class can be declared to implement an interface as long as the class provides public methods for all methods declared in the interface. The methods should have the same return

and parameter types as specified in the interface, and should satisfy the comments associated with the methods in the interface. That is, the class should satisfy the contract represented by the interface.

* A variable whose type is an interface may refer to objects from any class that implements that interface. When a message is sent to that variable, it will execute the code for the corresponding method from the class of the object associated with the variable at run time.

As a consequence, any object held in a variable whose type is an interface will have `public` methods for all methods declared in the interface. Thus in the `TwoFaceDrag` class, we can safely send `move` and `contains` messages to the object referred to by variable `dragged`.

On the other hand, because the method `moveTo` is not included in `Movable` and the variable `dragged` has type `Movable`, we may *not* send the message `moveTo` to `dragged`, even though classes `FunnyFace` and `StraightFace` have this method. This will generate a compile-time error message, because Java cannot guarantee that all objects that could be associated with `dragged` will support a `moveTo` method. This error message will appear even if the programmer knows that only objects supporting the `moveTo` message will ever be associated with the variable.

Thus we can only send a message to a variable of an interface type if the message corresponds to one of the methods of the interface. Of course, if we added `moveTo` to the interface `Movable`, then we could send that message to `dragged`.

While we can assign objects from the class to a variable whose type is an interface that the class implements, we may not make an assignment in the opposite direction. For example, in the `TwoFaceDrag` class, the assignment

```
happy = grabbed;
```

would be illegal. The reason is that the object referred to by `grabbed` may be either from the class `FunnyFace` or from `StraightFace`. Because we cannot guarantee that it will always be from `FunnyFace`, we may not assign it to a variable type `FunnyFace`.

We say that a class is *assignment compatible* with an interface if an object of that class can be assigned to a variable whose type is given by the interface. From above, we see that a class is assignment compatible with an interface if the class implements the interface. When we discuss the meaning of `extends` later in this chapter and in Chapter 17, we will see that more types are assignment compatible.

The same compatibility rules that are used to determine if an object can be assigned to a variable are used to determine whether an actual parameter is compatible with the type of the corresponding formal parameter. For example, suppose that we added a method with the following header to the `StraightFace` class:

```
public void placeNextTo( Movable otherFace )
```

Then, within the `FunnyFace` class, both of the invocations

```
straight.placeNextTo( grabbed );
```

and

```
straight.placeNextTo( happy );
```

would be allowed since the types of the actual parameters shown, Movable and FunnyFace, both guarantee that the objects to which they refer will implement the Movable interface. These rules are also used to determine whether the type of an expression included in a return statement is compatible with the return type specified in the method's header.

EXERCISE 10.1.4

Using the Resizable *interface from Exercise 10.1.2 and the classes* Square *and* Circle, *write a program called* ShapeSizer. *When the mouse is pressed, the program should randomly decide to draw either a* Circle *or a* Square *at the point of press. When the shape is drawn, it should have size 100. When the mouse is released, the shape should shrink to half its original size.*

EXERCISE 10.1.5

Below are three class skeletons that claim to implement Resizable. *For each class below, determine if the class legally implements the* Resizable *interface.*

a. public class Shape implements Resizable {
```
    ...
    public Shape(...) {
        ...
    }
    public void resize( double size ) {
        ...
    }
    public String label() {
        ...
    }
    public boolean contains( Location point ) {
        ...
    }
}
```
b. public class Octagon implements Resizable {
```
    ...
    public Octagon(...) {
        ...
    }
    public void resize( int size ) {
        ...
    }
    public boolean contains( Location point ) {
        ...
    }
}
```

c. ```public class``` Triangle ```implements``` Resizable {
    ...
    ```public``` Triangle(...) {
      ...
    }
    ```public void``` resize(```double``` size) {
      ...
    }
}

EXERCISE 10.1.6

Define two instance variables of type Resizable. *One should be a 50 by 50 pixel* Square *at the origin called* box *and the other should be a 75 by 75 pixel* Circle *at (100, 100) called* ball.

10.1.4 Other Features of Interfaces

Constants can also be declared in an interface. For example, we can write

```
public interface IntExample {
    // Some sample constant definitions
    public static final int DAYS_IN_YEAR = 365;
    public static final Location ORIGIN = new Location ( 0, 0 );
    ...
}
```

Constant definitions do *not* have to be repeated in classes that implement the interface. Instead they may be used freely in any class that implements the interface.

It is also possible for a class to implement multiple interfaces. We can write this by separating the interfaces with commas as follows:

```
public class C implements I1, I2, ..., Ik { ...
```

This can be handy if at different times we want to treat a class as playing different roles reflecting the different interfaces.

Finally, we note that interfaces may only contain public features. As a result, we may omit the qualifier "public" from each of the headers in the interface without having any impact on the meaning of the interface definition. Similarly, because constants are the only fields that may be declared in interfaces, the qualifiers "static" and "final" may also be omitted.

10.1.5 Summary

If we wish to have a variable that can refer to objects from several different classes, we can define an interface. The interface should include all of the public methods that we wish to be able to call on objects referred to by the variable. Each class implementing the interface must include definitions (including method bodies) for each method named by the interface. The name, return type, and parameter types must match those of the interface exactly, though the names of the parameters need not match. The header of the class definition must explicitly declare that it implements the interface. The class may also include other methods not mentioned in the interface, as well as constructors and instance variables.

⟹ EXERCISE 10.1.7

> **a.** *Design and implement a Java interface,* Reshapable, *that supports three methods that allow the user to change the width, height, and color of the receiver object.*
>
> **b.** *Design and implement a Java class representing a picture frame (a filled colored rectangle with slightly smaller filled white rectangle centered inside that presents an image of a thick colored border). The class should implement interface* Reshapable.
>
> **c.** *Modify the definition of the* FunnyFace *class so that it implements both the* Movable *and* Reshapable *interfaces.*   ❖

10.2   Using Interfaces in the objectdraw Library

Suppose we wish to write a program to play the following simple game. The program should randomly draw shapes that are either filled rectangles or ovals on the screen. If the user clicks on the most recently created shape, then it is removed from the screen. Each time the user successfully clicks on three shapes, the program speeds up. The program continues running forever (i.e., until the user quits the window controller).

Programming most of this is straightforward, given what you already know. However, like the last example, it will be handy to use an interface to declare a variable that can refer to objects from either class FilledRect or FilledOval.

The objectdraw library uses interfaces to classify the graphics objects that can be drawn on the screen. For example, the library includes an interface called DrawableInterface. It includes familiar methods like move, moveTo, hide, show, contains, setColor, getColor, sendToFront, etc. All of the geometric classes from the objectdraw library, including FramedRect, FilledRect, FramedOval, FilledOval, Line, and Text, implement this interface.

As a result, we can declare a variable shape to have type DrawableInterface and have it refer to both filled ovals and filled rectangles. The code for doing this is in the class ShapeGenerator in Figures 10.4 and 10.5. The if statement in the run method of Figure 10.5 is the place where we use the fact that the instance variable shape has type DrawableInterface. The class ShapeController in Figure 10.6 controls the user interaction with the shapes.

The objectdraw library uses several different interfaces to specify aspects of the behavior of different collections of geometric objects. For example, Drawable2DInterface includes all of the methods of DrawableInterface as well as getWidth and getHeight. All of the geometric objects of the objectdraw library aside from Line satisfy this interface. The notions of width and height don't make much sense for one-dimensional objects like lines, so the getWidth and getHeight methods were not implemented in that class.

Another interface supported by the library is Resizable2DInterface. It includes all of the methods of Drawable2DInterface as well as methods setWidth and setHeight. Neither Text nor Line implements Resizable2DInterface because neither includes the methods setWidth or setSize.

```
public class ShapeGenerator extends ActiveObject {
    private static final int MIN_SIZE = 10; // Minimum dimension of new object
    private int maxX, maxY;                  // Largest x, y values in window
    private DrawingCanvas canvas;            // Canvas on which to draw objects
    private int delay = 4000;                // Pause time between
                                             // drawing objects

    // Random number generators for size and location of next graphic object
    private RandomIntGenerator widthGenerator, heightGenerator,
                               xGenerator, yGenerator;

    // Random number generator to choose whether to draw oval or rectangle
    private RandomIntGenerator shapeSelector;

    // Random number generator to choose color of new graphic object
    private RandomIntGenerator colorGenerator;

    // Last shape generated in window
    private DrawableInterface lastShape;

    // Create a new shape generator.  The dimensions of the shapes generated
    // are bounded by the parameters.  The shapes are drawn on theCanvas
    public ShapeGenerator ( int maxWidth, int maxHeight, int maxX, int maxY,
                            DrawingCanvas a Canvas ) {
        this.maxX = maxX;
        this.maxY = maxY;
        canvas = theCanvas;

        shapeSelector = new RandomIntGenerator( 1, 2 );
        colorGenerator = new RandomIntGenerator( 0, 255 );

        widthGenerator = new RandomIntGenerator( MIN_SIZE, maxWidth );
        heightGenerator = new RandomIntGenerator( MIN_SIZE, maxHeight );
        xGenerator = new RandomIntGenerator( 0, maxX - MIN_SIZE );
        yGenerator = new RandomIntGenerator( 0, maxY - MIN_SIZE );

        start();
    }

    // Return last shape generated
    public DrawableInterface getLastShape () {
        return lastShape;
    }

    // Cut the pause time in half
    public void goFaster () {
        delay = delay / 2;
    }
```

Figure 10.4 ShapeGenerator class, part 1

```
/* Generate new ovals and rectangles in random places and colors,
 * pausing by delay between generation of new objects.
 */
public void run() {
    // Dimensions and location of new object
    int nextWidth, nextHeight, nextX, nextY;

    // Components of the color of new object
    int redness, greenness, blueness;

    while ( true ) {
        // Generate new object's width & height
        nextWidth = widthGenerator.nextValue();
        nextHeight = heightGenerator.nextValue();

        // Generate x and y coordinates of object
        nextX = xGenerator.nextValue();
        nextY = yGenerator.nextValue();

        // Determine whether rectangle or oval
        if ( shapeSelector.nextValue () == 1) {
            lastShape = new FilledRect( nextX, nextY, nextWidth,
                                        nextHeight, canvas );
        }
        else {
            lastShape = new FilledOval( nextX, nextY, nextWidth,
                                        nextHeight, canvas );
        }

        redness = colorGenerator.nextValue(); // Generate color components
        greenness = colorGenerator.nextValue();
        blueness = colorGenerator.nextValue();
        lastShape.setColor( new Color ( redness, greenness, blueness ) );
        pause( delay );        // Give the user a chance to click on object
    }
}
}
```

Figure 10.5 ShapeGenerator class, part 2

10.3 Extending Interfaces

As mentioned in the previous section, the interface `Drawable2DInterface` from the objectdraw library contains all of the methods in `DrawableInterface`. Because it is not uncommon for one interface to include all of the methods of a previously defined interface and then provide more, Java gives us a convenient shorthand notation to define the extending interface.

```
public class ShapeController extends WindowController {

    private static final int CANVAS_WIDTH = 400;   // Width & height of
    private static final int CANVAS_HEIGHT = 400;  // canvas

    private ShapeGenerator generator;        // Generator of new shapes
    private int numRight = 0;                // Number of clicks that
                                             // erased shapes

    // Create a shape generator of the desired size
    public void begin () {
        generator = new ShapeGenerator ( CANVAS_WIDTH / 5,
                                         CANVAS_HEIGHT / 5,
                                         CANVAS_WIDTH, CANVAS_HEIGHT,
                                         canvas );
    }

    /* If user presses the mouse button on the last shape drawn,
     * remove it from the canvas.  For every third time the user
     * removes a shape, speed up the drawing of new shapes.
     */
    public void onMousePress( Location point ) {
        DrawableInterface lastShape = generator.getLastShape();
            if (lastShape.contains( point )) {
                numRight = numRight + 1;
                lastShape.removeFromCanvas();
                if (numRight % 3 == 0) { // Speed up if numRight
                                         // is multiple of 3
                    generator.goFaster ();
                }
            }
    }

}
```

Figure 10.6   ShapeController class controls user interaction

To define a new interface ExtI that contains all of the methods in interface I we begin the definition of ExtI with

```
public interface ExtI extends I { ... }
```

The phrase ExtI extends I indicates that all of the methods declared in I are considered to also be part of ExtI. We say that ExtI *inherits* all of the methods of I. When ExtI extends I, we say that ExtI is a *subinterface* of I. Similarly, we say that I is a *superinterface* of ExtI.

As an example of the use of `extends`, the declaration of the interface `Drawable2DInterface` in the objectdraw library begins with

```
public interface Drawable2DInterface extends DrawableInterface {

    /*
     * Gets the width of the object's bounding rectangle
     */
    public double getWidth();

    /*
     * Gets the height of the object's bounding rectangle
     */
    public double getHeight();

    ...

}
```

This indicates that `Drawable2DInterface` contains all of the methods declared in `DrawableInterface`, as well as the methods listed after the header, including both `getWidth` and `getHeight`.

The extends relation on interfaces is *transitive*. That is, if interface K extends J and J extends I, then K extends I. In particular, K is a subinterface of I, I is a superinterface of K, and K contains all of the methods of I.

Just as it is possible to have a class implement multiple interfaces, an interface may extend more than one interface. As with classes implementing multiple interfaces, the interfaces being extended are separated by commas:

```
public interface I extends I1, I2, ..., Ik { ... }
```

For this to be legal, the methods included in the various interfaces must not give rise to conflicts. For example, if there is more than one method with the same name and parameter types, then all occurrences must have the same return type. This is related to the restriction on overloaded methods in a single class that was discussed in Section 6.6.

As well as providing the convenience of not having to copy over method headers from the superinterface, declaring an interface to extend another indicates to the Java compiler that an expression with the type given by the subinterface can safely be used in a context that expects an expression with the type given by a superinterface. In particular, if `ExtI` is a subinterface of `I`:

1. Any message that can be sent to an object of type `I` can be sent to an object of type `ExtI`.
2. An object of type `ExtI` can be assigned to a variable of type `I`.
3. An object of type `ExtI` can be used as an actual parameter to a method whose corresponding formal parameter has type `I`.

In each of these cases, an object of type `ExtI` can be used in a context that expects an element of type `I`, because objects of type `ExtI` have all of the capabilities (methods) that objects of type `I` have.

Polymorphic methods are those that can take arguments of different types. Suppose I is an interface and C and D are classes that implement I. Then we have already seen that if m is a method that takes an argument of type I, then an expression of type C or D may be used as a parameter with m. Thus m is a polymorphic method.

We have just seen that if interface ExtI extends I, then any expression of type ExtI can be used as a parameter to a method m whose formal parameter type is I. Thus interface extension is another source of polymorphism in Java.

In the objectdraw library Drawable2DInterface extends DrawableInterface, class Line implements DrawableInterface, and FramedRect implements Drawable2DInterface. Class Line does not implement Drawable2DInterface because it does not have a getWidth method. Also, move(dx, dy) is a method of DrawableInterface. Suppose there is also a class C with a method m taking a parameter of type DrawableInterface and a method n taking a parameter of type Drawable2DInterface. Then all but the last two lines of the following code are legal in Java.

```
Drawable2DInterface draw2d = new FramedRect(...);
draw2d.move( 3, 4 );              // Case 1
DrawableInterface draw = draw2d;  // Case 2
draw.move( 2, 5 );
C cObj = new C();
cObj.m( draw2d );                 // Case 3
draw2d = draw;                    // Compile-time error!
cObj.n( draw );                   // Compile-time error!
```

The lines labeled Case 1, 2, and 3 are justified by the numbered items in the list above. On the other hand, the last two lines above will generate an error at compile time, even though the object associated with draw at run time implements the interface Drawable2DInterface. Because not all objects implementing a superinterface also implement a subinterface, Java always flags as incorrect an assignment from an expression with type given by a superinterface to a variable whose type is a subinterface.

10.4 Summary

In this chapter we introduced Java interfaces. Like classes, interfaces can be used as the types of variables and parameters. Interfaces include only the definitions of public constants and the headers of public methods. They never include variable definitions, constructors, or any class feature that is not public.

Classes may implement one or more interfaces. If a class implements an interface, then it must provide a public method definition for every method listed in the interface. An interface may be defined to extend one or more interfaces. In that case, it includes all of the features explicitly included in the interface definition as well as all of the features in the extended interfaces.

A variable whose type is an interface may refer to objects from any class that implements that interface or any extension of that interface. Interfaces are commonly used as types for variables (and parameters) when the variable might refer to objects from different classes at run time. For example, if a variable has type DrawableInterface from the objectdraw library, then at run time it might refer to objects from classes FramedRect, FilledOval, Line, etc., each of which implements DrawableInterface.

10.5) Chapter Review Problems

⟹ EXERCISE 10.5.1

Given the interface Alphabet *below, which of the following classes could implement* Alphabet?

```
public interface Alphabet {
    public void x( Color aColor );
    public double y( int number );
    public boolean z( Location point );
}
```

   a. *Class:* A
      Methods: public void x(Color newColor)
                public int y(int number)
                public boolean z(Location point)
   b. *Class:* B
      Methods: public void w()
                public void x(Color someColor)
                public double y(int number)
                public boolean z(Location point)
   c. *Class:* C
      Methods: public void w()
                public void x(Color aColor)
                public double y(int number)
   d. *Class:* D
      Methods: public void x(Color newColor)
                public int z(int number)
                public boolean y(Location point)
   e. *Class:* E
      Methods: public double y(int number)
                public boolean z(Location point)
                public void x(Color aColor)

⟹ EXERCISE 10.5.2

Given the Alphabet *interface above and the two classes below that implement the* Alphabet *interface, which statements are legal? Assume that each class has a constructor that takes no parameters.*

Class: A
Methods: public void x(Color aColor)
         public double y(int number)
         public boolean z(Location point)
         public String w()

Class: B
Methods: public String w()
         public void x(Color aColor)
         public double y(int number)
         public boolean z(Location point)
         public void v(boolean aBoolean)

a. private Alphabet letter = new A();
b. private A letter = new A();
c. private A letter = new Alphabet();
d. private Alphabet letter = new B();
e. B letter = new B();
   letter.v(true);
f. Alphabet letter = new B();
   letter.v(true);
g. Alphabet letter = new A();
   letter.w();
h. A letter = new A();
   letter.w();
i. Alphabet letter = new A();
   letter.x(Color.RED);

10.6 Programming Problems

EXERCISE 10.6.1

a. *Write an interface called* Breakable *that includes the* void *and parameterless methods* break, fix, *and* removeFromCanvas *as well as the* boolean, *parameterless methods* isBroken *and* contains.
b. *Write two classes that implement the* Breakable *interface. The first, called* IceCubes, *should be four square* FramedRects. *In the unbroken state, these squares should be assembled into one larger square. In the broken state, they should be separated slightly. The second class, called* Plate, *should be two concentric, circular* FilledOvals *of different colors of your choice. A* FramedOval *should form the edge of the plate. When the* Plate *is in the unbroken state, this should be all that is visible. In the broken state, cracks (composed of* Lines) *should appear in the plate. (The* break *method should not have any effect on a broken* Breakable, *nor should the* fix *method have any effect on an unbroken* Breakable.)*

c. *Next, write a class* `Breaker` *that extends* `ActiveObject`. *This class should take a* `Location`, *a* `RandomIntGenerator` *(assume it will return either 0 or 1), and a* `DrawingCanvas` *as parameters. It should then put a random unbroken* `Breakable` *object at the specified point on the canvas. After a certain amount of time, the object should break. After a little more time, the object should disappear.*

d. *Now write a class called* `BreakTime` *that extends* `WindowController`. *When the user clicks the mouse on the canvas, a random unbroken* `Breakable` *object should appear at the point of the click, break after a little while, and then disappear.*

e. *Feel free to add any additional features you choose.*

CHAPTER 11

Graphical User Interfaces in Java

sers typically interact with computers via *graphical user interfaces*. Because that is a mouthful, they are typically referred to as *GUI*'s, where GUI is pronounced as "gooey". These user interfaces provide the user with multiple windows on the screen and support the use of a mouse to click on buttons, drag items around, pull down and select items from menus, select text fields in which to type responses, scroll through windows, and perform many other operations. GUI components are items like buttons and menus that can be added to the user interface to provide a way for users to interact with a program.

So far we have not been able to write programs that use these components. We can draw geometric objects on a canvas and interact with programs using mouse actions, but we haven't yet seen how to construct and interact with GUI components in the way that one does with most programs running on personal computers. In this chapter we will introduce you to techniques for programming a graphical user interface with your Java programs.

Java provides two libraries to assist in the programming of GUI interfaces: AWT, standing for Abstract Windowing Toolkit, and Swing. Swing is intended to supplement and replace AWT, Java's original windowing toolkit. In this chapter we will focus on Swing. However, many aspects of GUI programming still depend on AWT classes, so we will use classes from both of these libraries as well as libraries providing support for event handling.

A thorough discussion of the Swing package and how to use it could fill an entire book. In this chapter we will introduce some of the basic features of the package. More detailed information on the package should be available on your local computer system or on-line at the Java web site: http://java.sun.com/apis.html.

11.1 Text Fields

As our first example of using GUI components we introduce the class JTextField from Java's Swing package. An object from the class JTextField displays a single line of user-updatable text.

JTextField differs from objectdraw's Text class in two important ways. First, while only the programmer can change the contents of a Text object, a user may change the contents of a JTextField object by clicking in the field and typing new text. Thus JTextFields are very useful for obtaining user input.

Another important difference between the two is the way objects are placed in a window. A Text object can be placed at any location desired on a canvas. A JTextField can be added to a window, but we cannot specify its exact location in the window.

Figure 11.2 contains the code for a class that displays a window with a text field at the top of the window and a canvas filling the rest of the window. Each time the user clicks on the canvas, the program generates a Text object with the contents of the text field. Figure 11.1 displays a window that shows the operation of this program.

11.1.1 Constructing a Text Field

Text fields are constructed using the built-in JTextField class that is part of Java's Swing package. You can use the JTextField class like any other class. For example, the

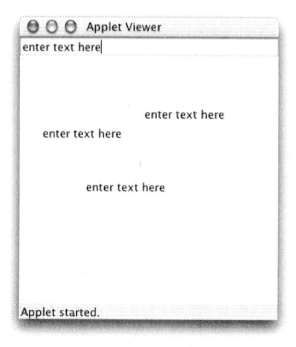

Figure 11.1 JTextField in window

```
import objectdraw.*;
import java.awt.*;
import javax.swing.*;

// Display text field and copy contents to canvas when clicked
public class TextController extends WindowController {
    private JTextField input;

    public void begin() {
        // Construct text field
        input = new JTextField( "Enter text here" );

        // Add text field to content pane of window
        Container contentPane = getContentPane();
        contentPane.add( input, BorderLayout.NORTH );
        contentPane.validate();
    }

    // Add new text item where clicked
    // Get contents from text field
    public void onMouseClick( Location point ){
        new Text( input.getText(), point, canvas );
    }
}
```

Figure 11.2   TextController class using JTextField

TextController class in Figure 11.2 contains the instance variable declaration:

```
private JTextField input;
```

The constructor for JTextField that we will use takes a String parameter specifying the initial contents appearing in the text field. In our example, the component is constructed in the begin method with the construction:

```
input = new JTextField( "Enter text here" );
```

If you do not want the text field to contain any text initially, you may also use a parameterless constructor, as in:

```
input = new JTextField();
```

To use the JTextField class, you must *import* it from the Swing package into any classes that use it. Importing information from a package makes the names in the package accessible to the class to which it is being imported.

We have two choices in importing classes from a package. We may import only the names of the classes we need, or we may import all of the names defined in that package. We import a single name in an import declaration by listing the name with the package's name prefixed to it.

For example, we import the name of the `JTextField` class from the Swing package by writing:

```
import javax.swing.JTextField;
```

Notice that the full name of the Swing package is `javax.swing`. Alternatively, we can import all of the names in the package by simply writing:

```
import javax.swing.*;
```

The "*" at the end indicates that all names from the package `javax.swing` should be imported. The advantage of this shorthand is that many classes can be imported by a single import statement. The disadvantage is that it is no longer as easy to figure out which package a class came from.

Import statements for a class or interface definition should be placed before the first line of the `class` or `interface` declaration, in the same place we write `import objectdraw.*`. The relative ordering of import statements does not matter in Java.

While we normally omit import statements in our code examples, we have included them in Figure 11.2 and many of the other examples in this chapter in order to make it clear where they belong. In the example, we have imported all of the names in packages `objectdraw`, `java.awt`, and `javax.swing`.

11.1.2 Adding a Text Field to a Window

While the construction of a `Text` object makes it appear immediately on the `canvas`, creating a `JTextField` object does not make it appear in the window. To make a component appear in a window, we must add it to the "content pane" of the window. The content pane represents the interior of the window.

We can obtain the content pane of a class extending `WindowController` by evaluating the built-in method `getContentPane`. The statement

```
Container contentPane = getContentPane();
```

in the `begin` method of Figure 11.2 associates the content pane of the window with the variable `contentPane`, which has type `Container`. A `Container` object can hold GUI components like text fields, buttons, and menus. The class `Container` comes from Java's AWT package. To use it we must import `java.awt.Container` or `java.awt.*`, as we did above.

Every `Container` object constructed comes with a *layout manager*. The layout manager arranges components in the window according to the instructions of the programmer. Content panes associated with classes extending `WindowController` come with a `BorderLayout` layout manager as the default.

Figure 11.3 shows how components can fit into the different parts of a window using `BorderLayout`. Components may be added in the center, north, south, east, or west position in a `Container` with this layout manager. Normally, we will avoid adding to the center of the content pane of a window associated with an extension of `WindowController` because the `canvas` is already there.

If you wish to construct an applet that does not have the `canvas` already in the center position, you may define your class to extend `Controller`, rather than `WindowController`. The class `Controller` was included in the objectdraw library precisely for those situations where the

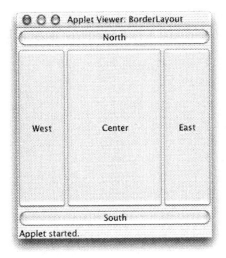

Figure 11.3   Layout of a window using BorderLayout layout manager

canvas was not needed. Of course, classes that extend `Controller` no longer suppose the mouse-handling methods like `onMouseClick`, because those methods were called in response to mouse actions on the `canvas`.

The method for adding a component to a container that uses `BorderLayout` is

```
someContainer.add( aComponent, position );
```

where `someContainer` has type `Container`, and `position` is one of the following five constants:

* `BorderLayout.NORTH,`
* `BorderLayout.EAST,`
* `BorderLayout.SOUTH,`
* `BorderLayout.WEST,` or
* `BorderLayout.CENTER.`

For example, the `input` text field is added to the top edge of the window in the `begin` method when the following statement is executed:

```
contentPane.add( input, BorderLayout.NORTH );
```

When a text field is added in the north or south positions in a `Container` that uses the `BorderLayout` layout manager, the text field will be stretched to fill the entire width of the window. If it is added to the east or west, it will be stretched vertically to reach from the top of the south item to the bottom of the north item. Items added to the center stretch to fill all space between the north, east, south, and west components. We will learn later how to use panels in Java to provide more control over the display of GUI components, but we postpone that discussion for now.

The last thing you should do after adding components to a container is to send the message `validate()` to that container. While most of the time this will have no effect, many times it is necessary to get the system to recompute the size and layout of all of the components in the container. If you leave this off, components might not be displayed properly.

11.1.3 Getting Information from a Text Field

The class `TextController` constructs a new `Text` object on the canvas every time the user clicks the mouse on the canvas. The string displayed in the new `Text` object is obtained from `input`, an object of type `JTextField`. The current contents of a text field are obtained by sending it a `getText` message, as is shown in the `onMouseClick` method. It is also possible to send a text field a `setText` message to reset the contents of the field.

In summary, a text field can be a useful way of getting text input from a user into a program. To use a text field you must construct it and then add it to the desired location in the window. The `getText` method can be used to retrieve the contents of a text field.

▧ EXERCISE 11.1.1

Write a class called `TextMimic` that places a text field at the bottom of the window and another at the top. When the mouse is clicked on the top half of the canvas, the program should display the contents of the text field at the top of the window as a `Text` object at the location the mouse was clicked. Similarly, if the user clicks on the bottom half of the screen, the program should display the contents of the text field at the bottom of the window as a `Text` object at the location the mouse was clicked. For example, if the canvas was over 200 pixels tall, the text field at the top showed "Hello world." and the mouse was clicked at the location (100,100), then the program would display a `Text` object at the location (100,100) that read "Hello world." ❖

11.2 Buttons and Events in Java

In the previous section we showed how to construct, add, and get the contents of a `JTextField`. In this section, we show how to use buttons in Java. Buttons require slightly more programming effort than text fields, because we want clicks on buttons to trigger program actions. We explain how to accomplish this using Java events and event-handling methods.

As a simple example of the use of a button in a Java program, we will modify the `TextController` class from the previous section so that the canvas is erased whenever a button is pressed. The new `TextButtonController` class is shown in Figure 11.4.

11.2.1 Creating and Adding Buttons

Buttons are represented in the Swing package by the class `JButton`. Buttons may be constructed and added in the same way as text fields. Because the button is only referenced in the `begin` method of Figure 11.4, it can be declared as a local variable:

```
JButton clearButton = new JButton( "Clear Canvas" );
```

```
import objectdraw.*;
import java.awt.*;
import java.awt.event.*;
import javax.swing.*;

// Display text field and copy contents to canvas when clicked
// Clear screen when click on "clear" button
public class TextButtonController extends WindowController
                                  implements ActionListener {
    private JTextField input;

    public void begin() {
        // Construct text field and button
        input = new JTextField( "Enter text here" );
        JButton clearButton = new JButton( "Clear Canvas" );

        // Add text field and button to content pane of window
        Container contentPane = getContentPane();
        contentPane.add( input, BorderLayout.NORTH );
        contentPane.add( clearButton, BorderLayout.SOUTH );
        contentPane.validate();

        // Set this class to respond to button clicks
        clearButton.addActionListener( this );
    }

    // Add new text item where clicked.
    // Get contents from text field
    public void onMouseClick( Location point ) {
        new Text( input.getText(), point, canvas ) ;
    }

    public void actionPerformed( ActionEvent evt ) {
        canvas.clear();
    }
}
```

Figure 11.4 TextButtonController class using JTextField

The constructor takes a String parameter representing the label that appears on the button. As with a text field, the button must also be added to the content pane of the window. This time we add it to the south part of the window:

```
contentPane.add( clearButton, BorderLayout.SOUTH );
```

11.2.2   Handling Events

We already know that when the user clicks on the canvas, the code in the onMouseClick method is executed. When a user clicks on a button constructed from the class JButton, however, the onMouseClick method is not executed. Instead, the operating system begins executing a method, actionPerformed, that is designed to handle button clicks.

To understand how this works, let's back up for a minute to get a better understanding of how Java programs respond to user actions. Java supports a style of programming known as *event-driven programming*. We have been programming in this style with our programs that react to mouse actions. For example, whenever the user clicks the mouse button, it generates an event that results in the onMouseClick method being executed by the computer.

A button generates an event of type ActionEvent whenever the user clicks on it. This in turn results in the execution of an actionPerformed method. For example, the method actionPerformed in TextButtonController is executed each time the button is pressed. In this example it simply erases the canvas.

Just as the onMouseClick method is provided with a parameter representing the location where the mouse was clicked, the actionPerformed method is provided with a parameter of type ActionEvent that contains information about the object that triggered the event. For example, evt.getSource() returns the GUI component that triggered an event, evt. While we don't need that information for this example, we will present examples later that do use that information.

There is one extra step that must be taken when handling events in standard Java. In order for a program to respond to an event generated by a GUI component, we must designate one or more objects to be notified when an event is generated by that component.

An object that is to be informed when an event is generated by a component is said to be an event *listener*. Different kinds of events require different types of listeners. The only requirement for an object to be a listener for a particular kind of event is that it promise to provide an appropriate method to be triggered when the event occurs.

Pressing on a button triggers the execution of an actionPerformed method. Thus any listener for a button must implement the method:

```
public void actionPerformed( ActionEvent evt );
```

We associate a listener with a button by sending the button an addActionListener message, such as:

```
clearButton.addActionListener( actionListenerObject );
```

After this code has been executed, actionListenerObject is registered as a listener for clearButton, and its actionPerformed method is executed each time the button is pressed.

What is the type of the parameter of addActionListener? As we have seen, we only require that it provide an actionPerformed method. The Java AWT package contains an interface ActionListener whose only method declaration is the actionPerformed method. Thus ny object that implements the ActionListener interface can be used as a parameter for ldActionListener.

While we could design a class that constructs objects that are only used as listeners, for simplicity we will generally handle interaction with GUI components similarly to the way in which we have been handling mouse actions. That is, we will have the window class itself contain the method that responds when the user interacts with a GUI object. Thus we write

```
clearButton.addActionListener( this );
```

in the begin method of TextButtonController. That indicates that the TextButton-Controller object will do the listening. In order for this to be legal, the class TextButtonController must implement the interface ActionListener and include a method actionPerformed. As described earlier, the actionPerformed method in Figure 11.4 erases the canvas.

Both ActionEvent and ActionListener are in the java.awt.event package; any program using them must include the following import statement:

```
import java.awt.event.*;
```

Warning!

Do not make the mistake of trying to handle a button click by writing an onMouseClick *method. That method is only executed when the user clicks on the canvas, not on a GUI component. The* onMouseClick *method handles clicks on the canvas, while* actionPerformed *handles clicks on a button.*

Also don't forget to add a listener to buttons in your program. If you leave that line out of your class, the system won't complain but will just ignore all clicks on the button.

11.3 Checklist for Using GUI Components in a Program

We have now seen examples using both text fields and buttons. With that background, we can now summarize the actions necessary to construct and use a GUI component in a class extending WindowController, where that class also serves as the listener for the component.

1. **Construct the GUI component**:

```
input = new JTextField( "enter text here" );
clearButton = new JButton( "Clear Canvas" );
```

2. **Add the component to the content pane of the WindowController extension and validate it**:

```
Container contentPane = getContentPane();
contentPane.add( input, BorderLayout.NORTH );
contentPane.add( clearButton, BorderLayout.SOUTH );
contentPane.validate();
```

3. **If a `WindowController` extension is to respond to events generated by the component,**
   (a) **Add `this` as a listener for the component**:

   ```
   clearButton.addActionListener( this );
   ```

   (b) **Add a declaration that the `WindowController` extension implements the appropriate listener interface**:

   ```
   public class TextButtonController extends WindowController
                                     implements ActionListener {
   ```

   (c) **Add to the `WindowController` extension the event-handling method promised by the listener interface**:

   ```
   public void actionPerformed( ActionEvent evt ) {
       . . .
   }
   ```

While different kinds of GUI components generate different kinds of events requiring different event-handling methods and listener types, the checklist above summarizes the steps a programmer must take in order to add and use any kind of GUI component. Always make sure that you have taken care of each of these requirements when using GUI components.

EXERCISE 11.3.1

Write a class called `ClickMe` that places a button on the bottom of the window. The button should be labeled "Click Me". When the button is clicked, a `Text` object should display the number of times the user has clicked. For example, after the user has clicked twice, the canvas should read, "You have clicked 2 times." Be sure to follow steps 1 through 3 to add the button.

EXERCISE 11.3.2

Write a class called `RandomCircles` that places a button on the top of the window. The button should be labeled "Draw a circle." When the button is clicked, the program should draw a circle of a random size (between 10 and 100 pixels in diameter) at a random location on the canvas. Be sure to follow steps 1 through 3 to add the button.

11.4   Combo Boxes

A popular GUI component used in Java programs is a pop-up menu, called a *combo box* in Java's Swing package. In this section, we will introduce the use of such menus by showing how to make a menu that controls the speed of an animation.

In Figure 11.5 we introduce a slight variant of the `FallingBall` class from Figure 9.3 in Chapter 9. In this new version we have added a new method `setSpeed` that allows us to change how far the ball falls between pauses. Using a large value for the integer parameter makes the ball appear to move more quickly, while a small value makes it appear to move more slowly.

```java
// Animate a falling ball
public class FallingBall extends ActiveObject {
    ... // Constant declarations omitted
    private DrawingCanvas canvas; // Canvas to draw on
    private FilledOval ball;      // Image of ball as circle
    private int speed;            // Current speed of ball

    // Draw ball at location and w/speed given in parameters
    public FallingBall( Location ballLocation, int initSpeed,
                        DrawingCanvas aCanvas ) {
        canvas = aCanvas;
        ball = new FilledOval( ballLocation, BALLSIZE, BALLSIZE,
                               canvas );
        speed = initSpeed;
        start();
    }

    // Move ball down until off canvas
    public void run() {
        while ( ball.getY() < canvas.getHeight() ) {
            ball.move( 0, speed );
            pause( DELAY_TIME );
        }
        ball.removeFromCanvas();
    }

    // reset speed of ball
    public void setSpeed( int newSpeed ) {
        speed = newSpeed;
    }
}
```

Figure 11.5 FallingBall class

We will write a class extending WindowController to handle user interactions with the ball. As with the previous case, when the user clicks on the canvas, the program will construct a ball that will begin falling. However, we will also introduce a combo box (menu) to allow the user to change the speed at which the ball will fall. This will be accomplished in the class MenuBallController in Figure 11.7. The combo box will include three alternatives, "Slow", "Medium", and "Fast". A picture showing the window with the combo box at the bottom is given in Figure 11.6.

Let's follow through the checklist from the previous section to make sure that we do everything necessary to properly add and use a combo box GUI component generated from the class JComboBox. As we do this, we will also highlight those places where combo boxes are handled differently from buttons or text fields.

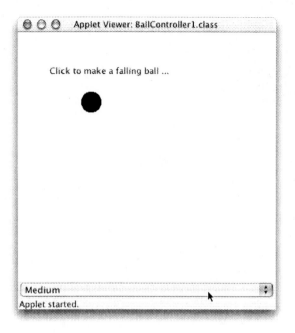

Figure 11.6   Menu constructed by MenuBallController

1. **Construct the combo box**: Combo boxes are a bit more complicated than buttons, in that we must add the selection options to the combo box once it has been constructed. The relevant code in the class is:

```
speedChoice = new JComboBox();

speedChoice.addItem( "Slow" );
speedChoice.addItem( "Medium" );
speedChoice.addItem( "Fast" );

speedChoice.setSelectedItem( "Medium" );
```

The first line constructs the combo box and associates it with variable speedChoice. The next three lines use the addItem method to add the items "Slow", "Medium", and "Fast" to the combo box.

Items appear on the pop-up menu of the combo box in the order that they are added, with the first item added showing when the combo box is first displayed. Thus "Slow" will normally be displayed when the combo box first appears. If we want to have a different item showing initially, we can send either a setSelectedIndex or a setSelectedItem message to the combo box.

With setSelectedIndex, we must provide an int parameter that specifies the index (i.e., the number) of the item that is to be displayed. Indices in Java always start with 0, so in our

```
import objectdraw.*;
import java.awt.*;
import java.awt.event.*;
import javax.swing.*;

// Menu controls speed of falling ball
public class MenuBallController extends WindowController
                                implements ActionListener {
    ... // Constant declarations omitted
    private FallingBall droppedBall; // The falling ball
    private JComboBox speedChoice;   // Combo box to select ball speed
    private int speed;               // Current speed setting

    // Display instructions and combo box
    public void begin() {
        new Text( "Click to make a falling ball...", INSTR_LOCATION, canvas );
        speed = SLOW_SPEED;

        speedChoice = new JComboBox();            // Construct combo box
        speedChoice.addItem( "Slow" );            // Add 3 entries
        speedChoice.addItem( "Medium" );
        speedChoice.addItem( "Fast" );
        speedChoice.setSelectedItem( "Medium" );  // Display "Medium"
                                                  // initially

        speedChoice.addActionListener( this );    // This class is listener

        Container contentPane = getContentPane(); // Add combo box to south
        contentPane.add( speedChoice, BorderLayout.SOUTH );
        contentPane.validate();
    }

    // Make a new ball when the player clicks
    public void onMouseClick( Location point ) {
        droppedBall = new FallingBall( point, speed, canvas );
    }

    // Reset ball speed from combo box setting
    public void actionPerformed( ActionEvent evt ) {
        Object newLevel = speedChoice.getSelectedItem();
        if ( newLevel.equals( "Slow" ) ) {
            speed = SLOW_SPEED;
        } else if ( newLevel.equals( "Medium" ) ) {
            speed = MEDIUM_SPEED;
        } else if ( newLevel.equals( "Fast" ) ) {
            speed = FAST_SPEED;
        }
        if ( droppedBall != null ) {
            droppedBall.setSpeed( speed );
        }
    }
}
```

Figure 11.7   MenuBallController class

speedChoice example, adding the statement

```
speedChoice.setSelectedIndex( 1 );
```

would result in the item "Medium" being displayed, as in Figure 11.6.

If, as in the actual code, the setSelectedItem method is used, then the parameter should be the actual item to be selected. Thus executing the statement

```
speedChoice.setSelectedItem( "Medium" );
```

also results in the item "Medium" being displayed.

2. **Add the combo box to the content pane of the WindowController extension and validate it**:

```
Container contentPane = getContentPane();
contentPane.add( speedChoice, BorderLayout.SOUTH );
contentPane.validate();
```

3. **Because we need a listener**:

(a) **Add this as a listener for the combo box**: Like buttons, combo boxes require a class that implements the ActionListener interface to handle the events generated. The method addActionListener is used to add a listener

```
speedChoice.addActionListener( this );
```

(b) **Add a declaration that the WindowController extension implements the appropriate listener interface**: ActionListener is the appropriate interface for a combo box:

```
public class MenuBallController extends WindowController
                              implements ActionListener {
```

(c) **Add to the WindowController extension the event-handling method promised by the listener interface**: The ActionListener interface includes the method actionPerformed, which takes a parameter of type ActionEvent:

```
public void actionPerformed( ActionEvent evt ) {
    ...
}
```

There is little difference between adding and using a combo box and a button. The body of the actionPerformed method resets the speed of the last ball dropped as well as balls to be dropped in the future. To make these changes to the speed, it needs a way to determine the current setting of a combo box. The class JComboBox provides two methods that return the combo box's current setting. The first is getSelectedItem, which returns the object that the user chose from the combo box. The other is getSelectedIndex, which returns the index of the item chosen (starting from 0 as usual).

In this case, it is reasonable to use getSelectedItem to return the item selected by the user from the combo box, storing the value in the variable, newLevel. The method getSelectedItem has return type `Object`. Thus the local variable `newLevel` in `actionPerformed` must have type `Object`.

`Object` is used as the return type of `getSelectedItem`, because any type of object may be inserted as an item in a combo box. That is, the parameter in method `addItem` is of type `Object`. The actual text displayed for that item in the combo box is the string obtained by sending a `toString` message to that object.

Even though we don't know what kind of object will be returned from `getSelectedItem`, we can still use the `equals` method to compare the value returned from the invocation of `getSelectedItem` with the items inserted into the combo box. In our example these are all strings and the comparisons work as expected.

⟹ EXERCISE 11.4.1

Under what circumstances might `droppedBall` *have the value* `null` *in the execution of the method* `actionPerformed`?   ❖

⟹ EXERCISE 11.4.2

If you click the mouse in the window several times in rapid succession, multiple balls will be constructed and will fall toward the bottom of the window. If you use the combo box to change the speed, only the last ball constructed will change speed. Explain why.   ❖

⟹ EXERCISE 11.4.3

This exercise builds on the previous one. Suppose you wish to use the combo box to change the speed of all of the balls still falling. How would you change the `MenuBallController` *and* `FallingBall` *classes so that this will happen?*

Hint: *The ball must be able to know the speed setting at all times.*   ❖

`Object` is a built-in Java class that represents all objects. It includes all values aside from those belonging to primitive types like `int`, `double`, and `boolean`, and supports the methods:

    public boolean equals(Object other);

    public String toString();

If not redefined in a class, the method `equals` returns `true` if the receiver and the parameter are the *same* object. That is, it behaves like `==`. However, it is a good idea for classes to provide different behavior where appropriate. For example, the `String` class has redefined `equals` so that it returns true if `other` is a `String` with the same sequence of characters as the receiver.

The method `toString` returns a `String` representing the object. If not redefined in a class, it simply returns the name of the type along with an integer. For example, an object from class `Letters` might return `Letters@858610` when sent the `toString` message. It is, again, a good idea to redefine this method in classes so that you get back a reasonable `String` representation of an object. For example, if you send a `toString` message to `Color.RED`, it will return "java.awt.Color[r=255,g=0,b=0]". Sending `toString` to a `FramedRect` will return a string that provides information about its location, dimensions, and color. Not surprisingly, sending a `toString` method to an object of type `String` returns a copy of the receiver, as it is already a string.

➡ EXERCISE 11.4.4

Add a new speed setting, "Very Slow", as the first entry in the combo box. Also, make the initial speed setting be "slow" and have the "Slow" item showing initially on the combo box. ❖

➡ EXERCISE 11.4.5

Write a class called BoxColor *that initially draws a black* FilledRect *on the canvas. Add a combo box to the bottom of the window. The combo box should include the items "red", "yellow", "green", "blue", and "black". When a color is chosen from the combo box, the color of the* FilledRect *should change appropriately.* ❖

11.5   Panels and Layout Managers

We now know how to add a text field, a button, or a combo box to a window. However, the buttons and combo boxes may not look as expected, because they are distorted to fill the entire width of the window.

Another problem is that we often want to insert two or more components in the same part of the window. For example, it may be easier for the user if all of the components provided to control a program are adjacent. However, if we insert two GUI components, say a combo box and a button, to the same part of the window (e.g., the south side), the second one will simply, and unfortunately, appear in place of the first.

In this section we will learn how to solve these problems and make more attractive user interfaces by using panels and by introducing several different layout managers.

11.5.1   Panels

We begin by solving the following simple problem. Rather than using a combo box to set the speed of the falling ball, as in the MenuBallController class, we would like to have three buttons to set the speed to three values.

We could add each button to a different part of the window. For example, we could put one each on the east, north, and west sides of the window. However, this would both look strange and be inconvenient for the user. We would rather place all three buttons on the south side of the window, as shown in Figure 11.8, but, as we just remarked, only one component can be placed in each of the four available positions in the window.

To help solve problems like this, Swing provides a component called a JPanel. A panel can contain GUI components just like a window does, but can also serve as a component in the same way as a button or combo box. Panels are typically used to organize the window into collections of subcomponents. In particular, if we wish to put more than one GUI item in the same part of a window, we can construct a panel, add the GUI components to the panel, and then add the panel to the window.

We illustrate this in Figure 11.9. In the begin method of the ButtonsBallController class we construct a panel with three buttons that will be inserted at the bottom (i.e., south side) of the window. Figure 11.8 shows the resulting window with three buttons at the bottom.

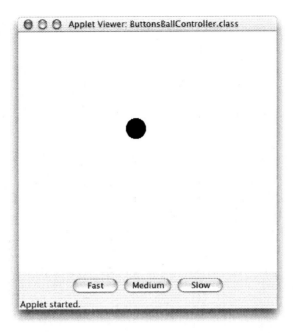

Figure 11.8 Using a panel to group GUI components

A panel uses a different layout manager, FlowLayout, than classes that extend WindowController. The FlowLayout manager lays out its components from left to right across the panel. If there is insufficient space to fit all of the components in a single row, new rows are added as necessary. Notice that each of the buttons in Figure 11.8 is just large enough to display its label, rather than being stretched to fill up all of the available space. Unlike the BorderLayout manager a FlowLayout manager does not stretch the components it manages.

In Figure 11.9, the second line of the begin method declares and initializes a local variable, southPanel, to be a JPanel. It is created with a parameterless constructor. The statements,

```
southPanel.add( fastButton );
southPanel.add( mediumButton );
southPanel.add( slowButton );
```

add the three buttons to southPanel. Because the buttons are displayed from left to right in the order they are added, there is no parameter specifying where the button goes in the panel.

Finally, the code:

```
Container contentPane = getContentPane();
contentPane.add( southPanel, BorderLayout.SOUTH );
contentPane.validate();
```

adds southPanel to the content pane of the window and then validates the content pane. Because the window uses BorderLayout, the method call includes the constant BorderLayout.SOUTH, specifying in which part of the window the panel is inserted.

```
import objectdraw.*;
import java.awt.*;
import java.awt.event.*;
import javax.swing.*;

// Control speed of falling ball with buttons
public class ButtonsBallController extends WindowController
                                implements ActionListener {
    ... // Constant declarations omitted

    private FallingBall droppedBall;  // The falling ball

    private JButton fastButton,        // Buttons to control speed
                    mediumButton,
                    slowButton;

    private int speed;                 // Current speed setting

    // Display buttons
    public void begin() {
        speed = SLOW_SPEED;

        JPanel southPanel = new JPanel();

        fastButton = new JButton( "Fast" );
        mediumButton = new JButton( "Medium" );
        slowButton = new JButton( "Slow" );

        fastButton.addActionListener( this );
        mediumButton.addActionListener( this );
        slowButton.addActionListener( this );

        southPanel.add( fastButton );
        southPanel.add( mediumButton );
        southPanel.add( slowButton );

        Container contentPane = getContentPane();
        contentPane.add( southPanel, BorderLayout.SOUTH );
        contentPane.validate();
    }

    // Make a new ball when the player clicks
    public void onMouseClick( Location point ) {
        droppedBall = new FallingBall( point, speed, canvas );
    }
```

Figure 11.9 ButtonsBallController with multiple buttons in a panel: Part 1

```
// Set new speed when the player clicks a button
public void actionPerformed( ActionEvent evt ) {
    if ( evt.getSource() == slowButton ) {
        speed = SLOW_SPEED;
    } else if ( evt.getSource() == mediumButton ) {
        speed = MEDIUM_SPEED;
    } else {
        speed = FAST_SPEED;
    }

    if ( droppedBall != null ) {
        droppedBall.setSpeed( speed );
    }

}
}
```

Figure 11.10 ButtonsBallController with multiple buttons in a panel: Part 2

There is still one problem we must solve. When the user clicks on one of the buttons, the actionPerformed method of the class is executed because this was declared to be a listener for each of the three buttons. Inside the method we need to know which button was pressed so that we can set the speed appropriately. The actionPerformed method is given in Figure 11.10.

We can find the source of an event by sending a getSource message to the event parameter. We can then compare the source of the event with each of the three buttons to see which was responsible for the event. The if-else statement in Figure 11.10 compares the source of the event with the buttons to determine which button was pressed. Once this has been determined, the ball's speed can be updated.

Each of Java's event types supports a getSource method. Thus if you have multiple components in a program that call the same method to handle events, you can send a getSource message to the event parameter to determine which component generated the event.

As with the earlier getSelectedItem method, the getSource method returns a value of type Object. Thus if we save the results of evaluating evt.getSource() in a temporary variable, that variable must have type Object in order to pass the type checker. As before, there is no difficulty in comparing the returned value with other objects, in this case the buttons in the window.

In the same way that we added a panel to the south side of the window, we could add panels to the north, east, and west sides. With more complex collections of GUI components, one can even add panels which themselves contain other panels. Because our focus here is on programming rather than on the layout of GUI components, we will not explore these possibilities further. However, we will discuss layout managers briefly in the next section.

➥ EXERCISE 11.5.1

Suppose we only added one button to southPanel. *How would the appearance of the window differ from that that obtained if we just inserted the button directly in the south of the window?*   ❖

➡ EXERCISE 11.5.2

Variable southPanel *is declared to be a local variable of the* begin *method rather than an instance variable. Why?*   ❖

➡ EXERCISE 11.5.3

Revise ButtonsBallController *to add a combo box to change the color of the ball. Put the combo box in a new panel in order to have the combo box look better (try it both with and without the panel to see the difference). Place the panel on the north of the window.*   ❖

11.5.2 More on Layout Managers

You may be wondering why we don't just specify the size and location of components in the window, as we did with graphics objects on the canvas, rather than depending on layout managers and panels to arrange them. One reason is that the user can resize the window at any time. It would be very inconvenient to have the user resize the window so that some of the components were no longer visible. Of course, if the user makes the window too small, it is possible that there really is not room for all of the components. However, the window managers do their best to display all of the components if that is at all possible. Play around with some of the example programs using GUI components to see that this is indeed the behavior.

Layout managers determine how GUI components are displayed in a window or panel. Container classes like panels and the content panes of windows have default layout managers, but the programmer can change them before adding components by sending the container a setLayout message.

The BorderLayout manager, the default layout manager for the content pane of classes extending WindowController, enables a program to add new components (including panels) to the north, south, east, or west portions of a container with that layout manager. As stated earlier, the canvas has already been added to the center of extensions of WindowController, so it is important not to add a component in the center. If you wish to insert a component in the center, you should extend Controller instead.

The FlowLayout manager, which is the default for panels, enables a program to add an unlimited number of components to a container with that layout manager. These components are laid out from left to right in the order in which they are added, in the same way that you add new text with a word processor. If there is not enough room for all of the components, new rows are added, which are also filled from left to right.

The layout manager of a container can be changed by sending it a setLayout message. For example, the layout manager for a content pane, contentPane, of a window can be changed to be FlowLayout by invoking:

```
contentPane.setLayout( new FlowLayout() );
```

Similarly, the layout manager of somePanel can be set to be BorderLayout by invoking:

```
somePanel.setLayout( new BorderLayout() );
```

The GridLayout manager can be used to divide a container into equally sized parts. A container with this layout manager is divided into a group of equally sized cells arranged in a grid. Like the FlowLayout manager, components are displayed from left to right across each row in the order in which they are added. The GridLayout manager differs from the FlowLayout manager by forcing each component to take the same amount of space and by being limited to a predetermined number of rows and columns.

Suppose southPanel is a panel that we wish to divide into a grid with numRows rows and numCols columns. This can be accomplished by executing:

```
southPanel.setLayout( new GridLayout( numRows, numCols ) );
```

Suppose we modify the ButtonsBallController class in Figure 11.9 by adding the statement:

```
southPanel.setLayout( new GridLayout( 1, 3 ) );
```

after the panel has been constructed, but before any buttons have been added. As before, the three buttons will be added in order, but this time they are stretched so that each takes up one-third of the space in the panel. See the picture in Figure 11.11.

There are other layout managers available for Java, but we do not cover them here. Instead we turn our attention to other GUI components.

➡ EXERCISE 11.5.4

How would you change the statement

```
southPanel.setLayout( new GridLayout( 1, 3 ) );
```

used to make the three-button display in Figure 11.11 to make it display three buttons stacked vertically instead of side by side?   ❖

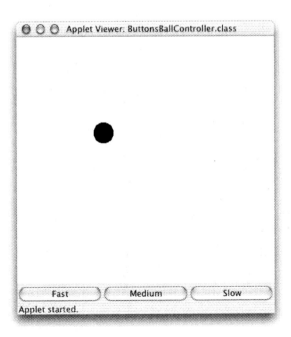

Figure 11.11   A panel with GridLayout manager to group buttons

▶ EXERCISE 11.5.5

Write a class called ColorBox *that initially draws a black* FilledRect *on the canvas. Add four buttons to the bottom of the window using a panel and* GridLayout. *The buttons should be labeled "Black", "Red", "Yellow", and "Blue". When a button is clicked, the color of the* FilledRect *should change appropriately.*   ❖

11.6   Other GUI Components

In this section we look at some of the other GUI components that you may find useful. We do not attempt to list all of them, but instead include a representative sample.

11.6.1   Sliders

Sliders can be used to graphically select values in a range. A slider, constructed from class JSlider, consists of a horizontal or vertical line with a marker that can be dragged to indicate a value between the maximum and minimum values represented by the slider. Figure 11.12 shows the window for a program that uses a slider to determine the speed of a falling ball.

Using buttons or a combo box to select speeds can be inconvenient, because they only allow us to choose from a very limited selection of speeds. While we could certainly add more choices to the combo box, it makes more sense to use a slider to allow the user to smoothly choose from a range of values. The code for the class SliderBallController can be found in Figure 11.13.

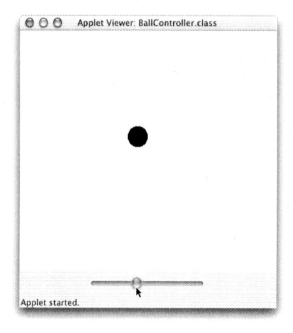

Figure 11.12   A window with a Slider to set the speed

```
import objectdraw.*;
import java.awt.*;
import java.awt.event.*;
import javax.swing.*;
import javax.swing.event.*;

// Control speed of falling ball with slider
public class SliderBallController extends WindowController
                                    implements ChangeListener {
    ... // Constant declarations omitted
    private FallingBall droppedBall; // The falling ball

    private JSlider speedSlider;     // Slider to set speed

    private int speed = SLOW_SPEED;  // Speed of ball

    // Construct and add slider to control ball speed
    public void begin() {
        speedSlider = new JSlider( JSlider.HORIZONTAL, SLOW_SPEED,
                                   FAST_SPEED, SLOW_SPEED );
        speedSlider.addChangeListener( this );

        Container contentPane = getContentPane();
        contentPane.add( speedSlider, BorderLayout.SOUTH );
        contentPane.validate();
    }

    // Make a new ball when the player clicks
    public void onMouseClick( Location point ) {
        droppedBall = new FallingBall( point, speed, canvas );
    }

    // Get new speed from slider
    public void stateChanged( ChangeEvent evt ) {
        speed = speedSlider.getValue();
        if ( droppedBall != null ) {
            droppedBall.setSpeed( speed );
        }
    }
}
```

Figure 11.13   SliderBallController class with slider

For the most part, the steps in constructing and using a slider are very similar to those required to construct and use combo boxes and buttons. The only real differences are in the actual constructor for the slider, the listener name, and the method used to get the value represented by the slider.

The steps are as follows:

1. **Construct the slider**: This is taken care of in the first line of the begin method. The constructor takes four parameters.

   * The first parameter is a constant that determines whether the slider is oriented horizontally or vertically. The possible values are JSlider.HORIZONTAL and JSlider.VERTICAL.
   * The second and third parameters are used to indicate the minimum and maximum integer values that can be represented by the slider.
   * The fourth parameter sets the initial value of the slider.

   The slider in SliderBallController is initialized to be horizontal, representing the range of values between SLOW_SPEED and FAST_SPEED, and with initial value set to SLOW_SPEED by the following call of the constructor.

   ```
   speedSlider = JSlider( JSlider.HORIZONTAL, SLOW_SPEED,
                          FAST_SPEED, SLOW_SPEED );
   ```

2. Add the slider to the content pane of the WindowController extension and validate it.

   ```
   Container contentPane = getContentPane();
   contentPane.add( speedSlider, BorderLayout.SOUTH );
   contentPane.validate();
   ```

3. **Because a listener is required**:
   (a) **Add this as a listener for the slider**: Sliders require change listeners, so we write:

   ```
   speedSlider.addChangeListener( this );
   ```

   (b) **Add a declaration that the WindowController extension implements the appropriate listener interface**.

   ```
   public class SliderBallController extends WindowController
                             implements ChangeListener {
   ```

   (c) **Add to the WindowController extension the event-handling method promised by the listener interface**. The event-handling method for sliders is stateChanged. The method can obtain the value represented by the slider by sending a getValue message. In the example, the stateChanged method uses that value to reset the speed of the ball most recently dropped and to remember that speed for balls constructed subsequently.

   ```
   public void stateChanged( ChangeEvent evt ) {
       speed = speedSlider.getValue ();
       if ( droppedBall != null ) {
           droppedBall.setSpeed( speed );
       }
   }
   ```

Because the ChangeEvent class is new to Swing, it must be imported from the javax.swing.event package.

⇒ EXERCISE 11.6.1

Write a class called SquareSizer *that uses a slider to determine the size of a square* FilledRect. *The* FilledRect *should initially be 100 pixels by 100 pixels. The slider should allow the user to change the size of the box to any size between 10 and 300 pixels.* ❖

⇒ EXERCISE 11.6.2

Write a class called RectangleSizer *that uses two sliders to determine the size of a* FilledRect. *One slider should control the length of the box and the other the height of the box. Both sliders should have an upper bound of 300 pixels and a lower bound of 10 pixels. The box should start as a 100-by-100-pixel square.* ❖

11.6.2 Labels

One problem with the program above is that it is not at all clear to the user what the slider is for. We should label it to make it clear to the user what it controls. We might be tempted to use an object of the class Text to handle this, but Text items may only be put on the canvas. Instead we would like to have the label next to the slider in the window, but not on the canvas.

We can add a label to the left of the slider in our example by adding a panel to the bottom of the window with both the label and the slider. We want the label to show the current speed once the slider has been adjusted. Figure 11.14 shows the window with this label.

The Java Swing package includes a JLabel class that does exactly what we want. It is a GUI component that contains a single line of read-only text. It is a passive component and is

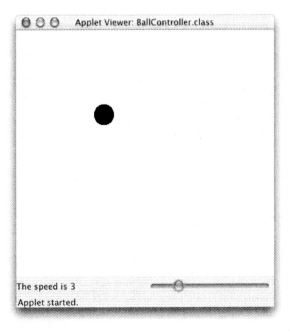

Figure 11.14 JSlider with JLabel in JPanel

not designed to respond to user interactions, so no event listener is required. Instead we simply construct the label and add it to the window or panel where we want it to be.

The code for the class `LabelBallController` is shown in Figure 11.15. The `begin` method constructs the label, while the `stateChanged` method changes the label as well as the speed.

There are several constructors for labels. The simplest constructor just takes the string to be displayed as a parameter.

```
new JLabel( labelString )
```

An alternative version allows the user to specify whether the label is left or right justified or centered:

```
new JLabel( labelString, justification )
```

where `justification` is one of the following constants: `JLabel.LEFT`, `JLabel.RIGHT`, or `JLabel.CENTER`.

We can change the text on the label by sending it a `setText` message. In the class `LabelBallController`, `setText` is used to update the text in `speedLabel` with the new value of the speed every time the user changes the slider. Though we do not need it for this example, the `JLabel` class also supports a `getText` method.

➡ EXERCISE 11.6.3

Revise your `RectangleSizer` *class from Exercise 11.6.2 so that each slider has a corresponding label. The labels should display the height and width of the box and should change as the dimensions of the box change.* ❖

11.6.3   JTextField and JTextArea

The first example of this chapter used text fields to hold user input. Text input can be supported with both the `JTextField` and `JTextArea` classes. An object from the class `JTextField` displays a single line of user-updatable text, while a `JTextArea` can display multiple lines of user-updatable text. Both `JTextField` and `JTextArea` components differ from `JLabel` components by allowing the user to directly edit the information displayed.

JTextField

The most common constructor for `JTextField` is invoked as follows:

```
new JTextField( initialContents, numberOfColumns )
```

where `initialContents` is a string representing the text shown when the `JTextField` is first displayed and `numberOfColumns` is an `int` representing the desired width of the text field in terms of the number of characters of text to be displayed. You should be aware that the specification of `numberOfColumns` is an approximation, as the width of characters differs unless you are using a monospaced font. Moreover, if a text field is inserted in a container using the `BorderLayout` manager (as it was in the first example of this chapter), the `numberOfColumns` parameter is generally ignored, as the text field is stretched or shrunk to fit the space provided.

```java
import objectdraw.*;
import java.awt.*;
import java.awt.event.*;
import javax.swing.*;
import javax.swing.event.*;

// Control speed of falling ball with labeled slider
public class LabelBallController extends WindowController
                                 implements ChangeListener {
    ... // Miscellaneous declarations omitted
    private JLabel speedLabel;

    // Construct and add GUI items
    public void begin() {
        JPanel southPanel = new JPanel();

        // Construct label and slider, and add to southPanel
        speedLabel = new JLabel(
                    "Use the slider to adjust the speed" );
        speedSlider = new JSlider( JSlider.HORIZONTAL, SLOW_SPEED,
                                   FAST_SPEED, SLOW_SPEED );
        southPanel.add( speedLabel );
        southPanel.add( speedSlider );

        // Add the panel to south of window
        Container contentPane = getContentPane();
        contentPane.add( southPanel, BorderLayout.SOUTH );
        contentPane.validate();

        // Add listener only for slider
        speedSlider.addChangeListener( this  );
    }

    // Make a new ball when the user clicks
    public void onMouseClick( Location point ) {
        droppedBall = new FallingBall( point, speed, canvas );
    }

    // Update speed from slider
    public void stateChanged( ChangeEvent evt ) {
        speed = speedSlider.getValue();
        if ( droppedBall != null ) {
            droppedBall.setSpeed( speed );
        }
        speedLabel.setText( "The speed is " + speed );
    }
}
```

Figure 11.15   LabelBallController class with label showing speed

It is also possible to use one of two other constructors if you do not wish to specify the number of columns or the initial contents of the text field:

```
new JTextField( initialContents )
new JTextField( numberOfColumns )
```

There are two main ways of associating events with changes to text fields. The simplest is to display a button next to the text field and have the user click on the button when finished editing the field. Alternatively, interacting with the text field can generate events.

The user triggers an event from a text field by hitting the enter or return key. For example, the user might type in a response to a question, hitting the return key at the end of the response. This generates an `ActionEvent` just like a button. To use a text field in this way, the programmer must add an `ActionListener` to the field, have the listener implement the `ActionListener` interface, and provide an `actionPerformed` method in the listener.

As noted earlier in the chapter, the actual text displayed in an object of class `JTextField` can be obtained by sending it a `getText` message, which will return the `String` displayed in the field. Similarly, the program can display new text in the text field by sending the object a `setText` message with the `String` to be displayed as a parameter.

JTextArea

The `JTextArea` class is similar to `JTextField`, but objects of this class can display multiple lines of text. A window with a `JTextArea` is displayed in Figure 11.16.

The most common constructor for this class is invoked as:

```
new JTextArea( initialContents, numRows, numCols )
```

where `initialContents` is a `String` representing the text shown when the text area is first displayed, and `numRows` and `numCols` are `ints` representing the desired number of rows and

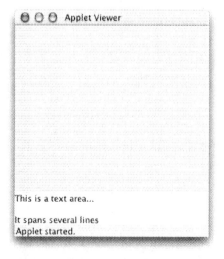

Figure 11.16   JTextArea in window

columns of text shown in the text area. Because a JTextArea contains multiple lines of data, hitting the return key will not generate an event. Instead, events triggered by other components may result in executing code that includes message sends to the text area, thus obtaining the current contents. Objects from the class JTextArea support methods getText and setText that behave the same way as those for JTextField. An append message can also be used to add a string to the end of whatever is currently displayed in the text area.

Often we cannot predict in advance how much information will be displayed in a JTextArea. If more information is displayed than will fit in the given space, then some information may not be displayed. So that all of the information can be seen, scrollbars may be associated with a text area by wrapping the text area with a JScrollPane. The following example illustrates this, where we have used a constructor for JTextArea that only provides the desired number of rows and columns:

```
simpleTextArea = new JTextArea( 30, 20 );
JScrollPane scrollableTextArea = new JScrollPane( simpleTextArea );
somePanel.add( scrollableTextArea );
```

where simpleTextArea is an instance variable and somePanel has been declared elsewhere as a JPanel. As before, messages are sent to the text area, not the scroll pane.

This way of wrapping one component with another is a common Java idiom. We will see similar uses of this in Chapter 19, "Streams."

Figure 11.17 shows the window generated by the class TextApplet shown in Figure 11.18. The class creates a text field at the top of the screen, a text area in the center, and a button at the bottom. Each time the user types a line of text in the text field and then hits the return key, the contents of the text field will be added to the end of the text in the text area. When the user clicks on the button at the bottom of the screen, the contents of the text area will be erased. Notice that the text field supports scrolling, because it is placed in a ScrollPane.

The command output.setEditable(false); in the begin method restricts the user from being able to change the contents of the output text area by typing. By default both text fields and text areas are editable by the user, but they can be restricted with this command.

11.7 Handling Keystroke and Mouse Events

Keystrokes and mouse actions generate events that can be handled by the appropriate kind of listener. In this section we discuss how to handle these events and discuss how the objectdraw package has so far provided support for handling mouse actions.

11.7.1 Keystroke Events

We can write Java programs so that every keystroke made by the user generates an event that can be handled by the program. This can be useful in processing input one character at a time or in using keyboard input to control actions in games. For example, in a game that controls a rocket ship one could use the arrow keys on the keyboard to change the direction of movement of the ship or use the space bar to trigger an action such as shooting a missile or putting up defense shields.

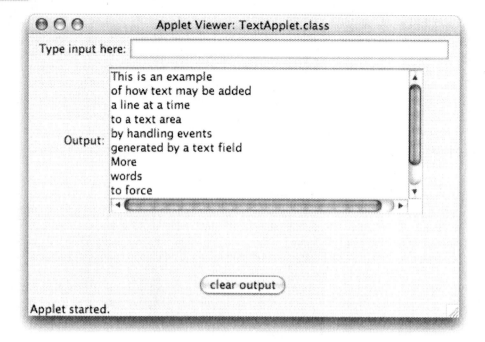

Figure 11.17   JTextArea in window

Keyboard events are generally associated with whichever window is topmost on the screen.[1] Because the window already exists, we can skip the usual steps of creating and adding a component. Instead, all we need to do is associate a listener with the keyboard events, and make sure the listener has the appropriate methods to handle key events.

If, as usual, we let the WindowController extension be the listener, then we need to include the following statement in the begin method:

```
this .addKeyListener( this );
```

While we have normally omitted occurrences of this as the receiver of a message, we include it here to emphasize that the key events are coming via the active window.

Because of problems and inconsistencies between some applet viewers and web browsers, you may also have to add a key listener to the canvas:

```
canvas.addKeyListener( this );
```

Finally, we need to inform the system that we wish our applet to gain the "focus". When a component has the "focus", the key events are directed to it. We can request the focus by executing:

```
setFocusable( true );
```

---

[1] Keyboard events can also be associated with other components, such as JTextFields and JTextAreas, but we will not deal with that here.

```java
// Typing in the text field and hitting return adds text to text area.
// Clicking on button erases the text area.
public class TextApplet extends Controller implements ActionListener {
    private static final int ROWS = 10; // Rows in TextArea
    private static final int COLS = 30; // Cols in text field & area

    private JTextField inField;        // Input field
    private JTextArea output;          // Output area
    private JButton clear;             // Button to clear output

    public void begin() {
        Container contentPane = getContentPane();
        JPanel topPanel = new JPanel();        // Prepare text field & label
        JLabel inLabel = new JLabel( "Type input here:" );
        inField = new JTextField( COLS );
        inField.addActionListener( this );

        topPanel.add( inLabel );
        topPanel.add( inField );
        contentPane.add( topPanel, BorderLayout.NORTH );

        JPanel centerPanel = new JPanel();     // Prepare text area & label
        JLabel outLabel = new JLabel( "Output:" );
        output = new JTextArea( ROWS, COLS );
        output.setEditable( false );           // Prevent user from writing
                                               // in output
        centerPanel.add( outLabel );
        centerPanel.add( new JScrollPane( output ) );
        contentPane.add( centerPanel, BorderLayout.CENTER );

        JPanel bottomPanel = new JPanel();     // Create button
        clear = new JButton( "clear output" );
        clear.addActionListener( this );
        bottomPanel.add( clear );
        contentPane.add( bottomPanel, BorderLayout.SOUTH );
        validate();
    }

    // Add text to area if user hits return, else erase text area
    public void actionPerformed( ActionEvent evt ) {
        if ( evt.getSource() == inField ){
            output.append( inField.getText() + "\n" );
            inField.setText( "" );
        } else {    // Clear button pressed
            output.setText( "" );
        }
    }
}
```

Figure 11.18 Window with text field, text area, and button

Including all three of these statements in a `begin` method should ensure that key events are picked up properly and passed to the listener, once the user clicks on the canvas to make sure the applet's window has the focus.

The next step is to declare that the class implements the `KeyListener` interface:

```
class KeyBallController ... implements KeyListener { ... }
```

The `KeyListener` interface contains three methods:

```
public void keyPressed( KeyEvent evt )
public void keyReleased( KeyEvent evt )
public void keyTyped( KeyEvent evt )
```

These three methods behave similarly to `onMouseClick`, `onMousePress`, and `onMouseRelease`. The first is invoked when a key is pressed, the second is invoked when the key is released, and the third is invoked when a key is pressed and then released.

For simple applications only one of the three may be needed. However, the listener object must support all three methods. If only one is really needed, then the other two may be included with empty bodies. Thus if they are invoked, the method finishes immediately without performing any actions.

The two most useful methods available on objects of type `KeyEvent` are `getKeyChar()` and `getKeyCode()`. The first of these returns the character that was typed, while the second returns a code of type `int` representing the character.[2] The second often turns out to be the most useful, in that not all keys (e.g., the arrow keys) return distinct characters.

The class `KeyEvent` contains integer constants, called virtual key codes, for each of the keys on the keyboard. For example, keys corresponding to letters on the keyboard are associated with constants `VK_A` through `VK_Z`, digits are associated with `VK_0` to `VK_9`, and the arrow keys are associated with `VK_UP`, `VK_DOWN`, `VK_LEFT`, and `VK_RIGHT`. Constants associated with other keys can be found in the on-line documentation for the class `KeyEvent`, which is in the package `java.awt.event`.

Sample code that uses arrow keys to change the speed of a falling ball is shown in Figure 11.19. When the up arrow key is pressed, the ball's speed increases, while the down arrow key reduces the speed (and can even make it negative). The methods `keyTyped` and `keyReleased` must be included, even though their bodies are empty. They must appear because the listener must implement all of the methods of `KeyListener`, even though we only want to associate an action with `keyPressed` events.

11.7.2 Mouse Events

You have been reading and writing code to handle events generated by mouse actions from the beginning of this text, but you have been using features of the objectdraw package to simplify the code to be written. Not surprisingly, Java also provides a way to handle mouse events.

Fundamentally, mouse events are handled very similarly to keyboard events. You associate an appropriate mouse listener with the canvas and then write appropriate methods to handle the mouse events.

---

[2] The first method, getKeyChar, returns a value of type char. Characters and their integer codes are introduced in Chapter 16.

```
import objectdraw.*;
import java.awt.*;
import java.awt.event.*;
import javax.swing.*;

// Control speed of falling ball with up and down arrow keys
public class KeyBallController extends WindowController
                            implements KeyListener {
    ... // Constant declarations omitted
    private FallingBall droppedBall; // The falling ball
    private int speed = SLOW_SPEED;  // Speed of ball
    private JLabel speedLabel;       // Label showing speed

    // Construct and add GUI items
    public void begin() {
        JPanel southPanel = new JPanel();
        speedLabel = new JLabel( "The speed is "+speed, JLabel.CENTER );
        southPanel.add( speedLabel );
        Container contentPane = getContentPane();
        contentPane.add( southPanel, BorderLayout.SOUTH );
        contentPane.validate();

        canvas.addKeyListener( this );
        this .addKeyListener( this );
        setFocusable( true );
    }

    // Make a new ball when the player clicks
    public void onMouseClick( Location point ) {
        droppedBall = new FallingBall( point, speed, canvas );
    }

    // Required by KeyListener Interface but not used here.
    public void keyTyped( KeyEvent e ) { }

    // Required by KeyListener Interface but not used here.
    public void keyReleased( KeyEvent e ) { }

    // Change speed with up and down arrow keys
    public void keyPressed( KeyEvent e ) {
        if ( e.getKeyCode() == KeyEvent.VK_UP ) {
            speed++;
        } else if ( e.getKeyCode() == KeyEvent.VK_DOWN ) {
            speed--;
        }
        if ( droppedBall != null ) {
            droppedBall.setSpeed( speed );
        }
        speedLabel.setText( "The speed is "+speed );
    }
}
```

Figure 11.19 Controlling ball speed with the keyboard

Mouse events can be generated by mouse clicks, presses, and releases, by having the mouse enter or leave a window, and by moving or dragging the mouse. The methods `mouseClicked`, `mousePressed`, `mouseReleased`, `mouseEntered`, and `mouseExited`, which handle the first five kinds of events, are part of the interface `MouseListener`, while the methods `mouseMoved` and `mouseDragged` for handling moving and dragging events are part of the interface `MouseMotionListener`. As with classes implementing `KeyListener`, if a class implements one of the mouse listener interfaces, then it must provide all of the associated methods, even if they are not needed in the class.

All of the mouse-event-handling methods take a parameter of type `MouseEvent` that contains information about where the event occurred. If `evt` is a `MouseEvent`, then `evt.getX()` and `evt.getY()` return the *x* and *y* coordinates of where the mouse was when the event occurred.

Classes extending `WindowController` support methods with similar, but slightly different, names corresponding to each of these methods. Our methods also differ by taking a `Location` as a parameter rather than an event. That was done in order to make it simpler for you to get the information you needed about each kind of mouse event. Appendix D.2 discusses how to use the standard Java mouse-event-handling methods when a class extends `JApplet` rather than `WindowController`. You should avoid using standard Java mouse-event-handling code with a class that extends `WindowController`.

11.8 Summary

In this chapter we introduced the standard Java event model and a number of GUI components. While a lot more can be learned about the design of graphic user interfaces, the information provided here should be enough to get you started in writing programs using simple GUI components.

The tasks to be performed in creating and using GUI components include the following:

1. Construct the GUI component.
2. Add the GUI component to a container (either a panel or the content pane of a window) and validate it.
3. If a listener is needed,
   (a) Add `this` as a listener for the GUI component.
   (b) Add a declaration that the `WindowController` or `Controller` extension implements the appropriate listener interface.
   (c) Add the event-handling methods promised by the listener interface.

Tables 11.1 and 11.2 summarize the information needed to use GUI components and handle the associated events. Listeners for particular events are associated by sending a message of the form `addSomeListener` to the GUI component generating the event, where `SomeListener` should be replaced by the name of the listener. For example, to associate a listener with a button, send an `addActionListener` message to the button, because the listener associated with buttons is `ActionListener`.

A `getSource` message can be sent to any event to obtain the object that generated the event. Events from the class `KeyEvent` support methods `getKeyCode` and `getKeyChar`, while events from `MouseEvent` support methods `getX` and `getY` that return integer *x* and *y* coordinates of

Table 11.1 Constructors and methods associated with GUI components

Component	Constructors	Associated Methods
JButton	new JButton(String label)	String getText() void setText(String newText)
JComboBox	new JComboBox()	void addItem(Object item) void setSelectedItem(Object item) Object getSelectedItem() void setSelectedIndex(int itemNum) int getSelectedIndex()

JSlider	new JSlider(int orientation,
	    int lowVal, int highVal,
	    int startValue)
		int getValue()

JLabel	new JLabel(String text)	String getText() void setText(String newText)

JTextField	new JTextField(
	    String initialContents,
	    int numCols)
	new JTextField(
	    String initialContents)
	new JTextField(int numCols)
		String getText()
		void setText(String newText)

JTextArea	new JTextArea(
	    String initialContents,
	    int numRows, int numCols)
		String getText()
		void setText(String newText)
		void append(String newText)

Table 11.2 Events, GUI components generating them, and associated interfaces and methods handling the events. Parameter evt always has the associated event type.

Event type	Generated by	Listener Interface	Method invoked
ActionEvent	JButton, JTextField, JComboBox	ActionListener	void actionPerformed(evt)
ChangeEvent	JSlider	ChangeListener	void stateChanged(evt)
KeyEvent	Keyboard	KeyListener	void keyTyped(evt) void keyPressed(evt) void keyReleased(evt)
MouseEvent	Mouse	MouseListener	void mouseClicked(evt) void mousePressed(evt) void mouseReleased(evt) void mouseEntered(evt) void mouseExited(evt)
MouseEvent	Mouse	MouseMotionListener	void mouseDragged(evt) void mouseMoved(evt)

where the mouse was when the event was generated. There are many more methods available that we have not listed. See the JavaDoc on-line documentation of Java library classes for more details.

We discussed three Java layout managers for container classes like windows and panels. The FlowLayout manager inserts GUI components in the container from left to right, starting a new row when there is no more space available. It is the default layout for panels. GridLayout divides the container into a rectangular grid, where each cell has the same size. It inserts components from left to right, starting with the top row, proceeding to the next row after each row is filled. BorderLayout is the default for content panes of extensions of WindowController and Controller. That layout manager allows items to be inserted in the center, north, south, east, and west of the container. The layout manager for a container may be changed by sending it the message setLayout(manager) where manager is a new object generated from one of the layout managers.

The add message is sent to a container in order to add a new component. With FlowLayout and GridLayout only the component to be added is sent as a parameter. However, with BorderLayout the location must also be specified. Thus a second parameter, one of BorderLayout.NORTH, BorderLayout.SOUTH, BorderLayout.EAST, BorderLayout.WEST, or BorderLayout.CENTER, must be included.

You will discover that it often takes a fair amount of experimentation to make graphical user interfaces look good. Further information on Java GUI components from either the AWT or Swing package should be available on-line either locally or from http://java.sun.com/apis.html. See Appendix C for instructions on how to use the JavaDoc web pages.

Many books are also available on effective graphical user design. Our goal in this chapter was not to make you an expert on GUI design, but instead to introduce you to the standard GUI components and the use of standard Java event-driven programming.

11.9   Chapter Review Problems

➡ EXERCISE 11.9.1

Write a program called SunriseSunset *that draws a sun near the bottom of the canvas. Create a button on the bottom of the screen that is labeled "Rise". When the button is clicked, the sun should rise by moving up 5 pixels. Once the top of the sun reaches the top of the canvas, the label of the button should change to "Set" and clicking the button should cause the sun to move down 5 pixels. When the sun reaches the bottom of the canvas, the button should be relabeled "Rise."*   ❖

➡ EXERCISE 11.9.2

Modify your SunriseSunset *program so that the rising and setting is controlled by a slider instead of buttons. The slider should be on the right side of the screen and the level of the slider should correspond to the level of the sun.*   ❖

➡ EXERCISE 11.9.3

Modify your SunriseSunset *program again so that the rising and setting is controlled by the arrow keys on the keyboard instead of buttons or a slider. When the user presses the up arrow, the sun should move up 5 pixels (unless it is already at the top of the screen). When the user presses the down arrow, the sun should move down 5 pixels (unless it is already at the bottom of the screen).* ❖

EXERCISE 11.9.4

Write a class called Bubbles *that places a combo box on the bottom of the screen and a button at the top of the screen. The combo box should include as items the numbers 0 to 10. When a number is selected, the program should draw that number of* FramedOvals *on the screen. The size and location of each* FramedOval *should be determined randomly. Be sure to use the* getSelectedIndex() *method of the* JComboBox *class to access the selected number. The button should be labeled "Erase". When the button is pressed, all the bubbles on the screen should disappear.* ❖

EXERCISE 11.9.5

Write a class called SizableColorfulBox *that initially draws a black* FilledRect *on the canvas. Add two buttons and a combo box to the top of the screen using a panel. The buttons should be labeled "bigger" and "smaller". The "bigger" button should increase the size of the* FilledRect *by 10 pixels in each dimension and the "smaller" button should decrease the size of the* FilledRect *by 10 pixels in each dimension. The combo box should include items "black", "red", "yellow", "green", and "blue" and should change the color of the box appropriately.* ❖

11.10 Programming Problems

EXERCISE 11.10.1

Write a class called VotingBooth *that simulates voting. Use three different buttons labeled "Candidate 1", "Candidate 2", and "Candidate 3" to collect the votes. Above each button, the program should display the number of votes the candidate has received.* ❖

EXERCISE 11.10.2

Write a class called IceCreamStand *that allows the user to "purchase" ice cream. On the top of the window there should be three buttons and a combo box. The buttons should be labeled "Small", "Medium", and "Large". The combo box should include five different ice cream flavors. Below each button there should be a label that displays the price of that particular size of ice cream. When the user clicks a button, the bill should be displayed in the middle of the window as a* TextArea. *(As a result, the class should extend* Controller, *not* WindowController.) *The bill should include the size, flavor, and price of the ice cream and should grow as the user orders more ice cream. Also, the bill should display the total cost of all the ice creams on the bill. On the bottom of the window, there should be a "New Order" button that resets the bill so that it is blank.* ❖

12

Recursion

key idea in designing a program to solve a complex problem is to break it into simpler problems, solve the simpler problems, and then assemble the final answer from these simpler pieces. Sometimes it is possible to fashion a solution to a problem by solving one or more simpler versions of the *same* problem, and then using those to complete the solution to the original version of the problem. This technique is called *recursion*.

In this chapter we explain how to write programs using recursion in Java. Programming with recursion does not require the introduction of new features. Instead it represents an important new way of approaching problems.

For a simple example, let's look at Russian nesting dolls. You have probably encountered these in gift shops. They consist of a collection of hollow wooden dolls of decreasing sizes that nest inside each other. Each can be opened by twisting the upper body, revealing a hollow cavity inside. Typically the smallest doll is solid wood, though it can be hollow so that small items can be stored inside. The sizes of the dolls are chosen so that each doll can hold the nested collection of smaller dolls inside it.

In particular, the second smallest doll can hold the smallest inside. The third can hold the second (which has the smallest inside). In fact each doll can hold the next largest doll with all smaller dolls nested inside.

Let's look at the problem of providing directions on how to make a collection of nested dolls. To make the problem more interesting, suppose that we wish to provide instructions that, given the size of the largest doll, will always result in the largest number of nested dolls in a collection.

Let MIN_SIZE represent the smallest doll that can fit other dolls inside. Clearly if the size of the largest doll is smaller than MIN_SIZE, our collection will only have a single doll.

On the other hand, if we start with a doll with size startSize $\geq$ MIN_SIZE, then we can build the outer doll with space inside for the other nested dolls. Suppose that to fit inside another doll, the gap between the sizes of the dolls must be at least GAP_SIZE.

A procedure for building a collection of nested dolls where the outermost doll has size `startSize` is the following:

* If `startSize` < `MIN_SIZE`, build a doll of that size and you are done.
* If `startSize` ≥ `MIN_SIZE`, then do the following:

  1. Build the hollow outer doll with size `startSize`.
  2. Build a collection of smaller nested dolls whose outer doll has size `startSize` - `GAP_SIZE`. When finished, you are done.

What instructions should be used in the second case to build the collection of smaller dolls? Exactly the same set of instructions can be used, because they are general instructions to build collections of nested dolls of any size.

For example, suppose there is a production line with several workers, where the first worker is given a slip of paper with the value of `startSize` for the outer doll. Each of the workers is told to follow the instructions given above. If the starting size is less than `MIN_SIZE`, then the first worker builds a doll of that size, and the order is complete. If the starting size is greater than or equal to `MIN_SIZE`, then the first worker builds a hollow doll of that size and hands a slip of paper to the next worker with the value `startSize` - `GAP_SIZE`. If the number is greater than or equal to `MIN_SIZE`, that worker will build a doll of that size, handing a slip of paper with an even smaller value to the next worker. This continues until the last doll is built.

This collection of nested dolls is an example of a recursively defined structure. Recursive structures consist of a base structure (the smallest doll in this example) as well as a way of describing more complex structures in terms of simpler ones of the same sort (a set of nested dolls consists of the largest hollow doll plus a smaller collection of nested dolls that fit inside it). Methods can be defined based on this recursive structure.

We will begin by first examining recursive structures, those structures that contain one or more subcomponents from the same class as the entire structure. Later we investigate recursive methods, whose execution involves further invocations of the methods themselves to solve slightly simpler problems.

12.1 Recursive Structures

A *recursive structure* is one in which a piece of the structure is similar to the entire structure. Usually this is represented by defining a class that includes one or more instance variables that may refer to objects of the same type as those being defined by the class. In this section we will create different recursive structures that create and manipulate pictures of nested rectangles, create and search collections of strings, and create and manipulate drawings that resemble broccoli.

12.1.1 Nested Rectangles

Our first example of a recursive structure will be quite simple. We will design a class that will draw nested rectangles of the sort shown in Figure 12.1. Eventually we would like to make these have as many capabilities as the `FramedRect` or `FilledRect` objects from the objectdraw library. For example we would like them to have `move` and `moveTo` methods. For now, however, we'll just be content in being able to draw them.

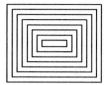

Figure 12.1   Nested rectangles

In order to motivate our final solution, we will present three versions of classes to build and
draw nested rectangles. The first will use *iteration* or loops of the sort that you have already seen,
while the last two will involve recursion.

An Iterative Solution

Because you are used to thinking in terms of loops, you can probably figure out a nice iterative way
of drawing a non-empty collection of nested rectangles using a `while` loop. Here is an example
of a constructor for the class `NestedRects` that uses a `while` loop.

```
// Draw nested rectangles at the given x and y coordinates and
// with the given height and width (both of which must be
// non-negative)
public NestedRects( double x, double y, double width,
                    double height, DrawingCanvas canvas ) {
    new FramedRect( x, y, width, height, canvas );
    while ( width >= 8 && height >= 8) {
        width = width - 8;
        height = height - 8;
        x = x + 4;
        y = y + 4;
        new FramedRect( x, y, width, height, canvas );
    }
}
```

The idea of the constructor is quite simple. It first draws a framed rectangle at the given *x*
and *y* coordinates with the given dimensions. Then, while the width and height of the rectangle
it has just drawn are both greater than or equal to eight, it adjusts the width, height, and *x* and *y*
coordinates in order to draw a new, smaller, framed rectangle centered inside the one just drawn.

Suppose, however, that we want to write a `moveTo` method that moves the nested rectangles
to a given location on the canvas. In order to do this we will need to associate names with the
individual framed rectangles drawn as part of the nested rectangles. Unfortunately, when we write
the program we do not know how many framed rectangles will be needed, as the number will
vary depending on what parameters are sent to the constructor. At this point we don't know any
way in Java to introduce a variable number of names to be used in a program if we do not know
the maximum number that might be required. As we will see, the recursive solution given in the
next section does not have that problem.

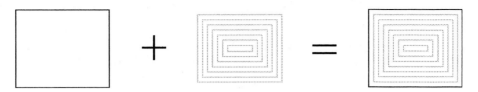

A Recursive Solution

The iterative NestedRects class above is not a recursive definition. To represent a collection of nested rectangles as a recursive structure, we need to change the way we understand nested rectangles. Instead of thinking of them as a series of FramedRects, we instead think of them as having an outer FramedRect and then, if there is enough space, a smaller collection of nested rectangles inside. In Figure 12.2 we demonstrate how a collection of nested rectangles can be formed from an outer framed rectangle and a smaller collection of nested rectangles. In general, when we look at pictures as being recursive, we try to find a smaller copy in the whole picture that we are looking at.

Figure 12.3 contains a recursive version of the class NestedRects that corresponds to this description. It contains an instance variable outerRect with type FramedRect corresponding to the outer framed rectangle and rest with type NestedRects corresponding to the smaller collection of nested rectangles. The class NestedRects is a recursive structure, because the instance variable rest has the same type as the class.

In the constructor of this recursive version of the class, we first construct the framed rectangle just as before, but then, if the width and height are both at least eight, we go ahead and construct a new nested rectangle in a position four to the right and down from the first one, and with width and height both reduced by eight pixels. If the width or height is less than eight, then rest is assigned null, and nothing more is drawn. The assignment of null isn't really needed, as instance variables with object types are initialized by the system to null, but we include the else clause to remind the reader that rest is null and that no more framed rectangles are constructed when the width or height becomes less than eight.

Thus we have created a collection of nested rectangles by first creating the outermost framed rectangle and then, if it is large enough, calling the constructor recursively to draw a smaller and therefore slightly simpler collection of nested rectangles inside.

The new constructor is a bit shorter than the iterative version, but that is not really very important. What is important is that we have a simple description of a collection of nested rectangles as an outer rectangle with a slightly smaller collection of nested rectangles centered inside. This is actually easier to grasp than a description that forces the programmer to think about executing a while loop some unknown, but possibly large, number of times.

In the iterative version of the constructor for a nested rectangle, the while loop terminated when either the width or height was reduced to a value below eight. We need a similar way to stop a recursive algorithm. In this case, when the width or height passed in as parameters gets to be less than eight, only the outer rectangle is drawn. If we initially start with positive values of width and height, then each call of the constructor for NestedRects inside the if statement will use smaller and smaller values for width and height—to be exact, each is eight units smaller than the previous. Eventually either the length or width will get to a value smaller than eight, the condition in the if statement will be false, and no more nested rectangles will be drawn.

```
// Class to draw and manipulate a collection of nested rectangles
public class NestedRects {
    private FramedRect outerRect;     // Outermost rectangle in
                                      // nested rectangles
    private NestedRects rest;         // Inner nested rect

    // Draw nested rectangles at the given x and y coordinates and
    // with the given height and width (both of which must be
    // non-negative)
    public NestedRects( double x, double y, double width,
                        double height, DrawingCanvas canvas ) {
        outerRect = new FramedRect( x, y, width, height, canvas );
        if ( width >= 8 && height >= 8) {
            rest = new NestedRects( x+4, y+4, width-8,
                                    height-8, canvas );
        } else {                // Nothing more to construct
            rest = null;
        }
    }

    // Move nested rects to (x,y)
    public void moveTo( double x, double y ) {
        outerRect.moveTo( x, y );
        if ( rest != null ) {
            rest.moveTo( x+4, y+4 );
        }
    }

    // Remove the nested rects from the canvas
    public void removeFromCanvas() {
        outerRect.removeFromCanvas();
        if ( rest != null ) {
            rest.removeFromCanvas();
        }
    }
}
```

Figure 12.3   Recursive version of NestedRects class

We will next illustrate exactly what happens when we call this constructor. The trace of its execution will be relatively long and detailed but should help us understand better what actually happens during recursion.

Suppose we evaluate

```
new NestedRects( 50, 50, 19, 21, canvas )
```

This will result in the execution of

```
outerRect = new FramedRect( 50, 50, 19, 21, canvas );
```

Thus the value of `outerRect` for this collection of nested rectangles will be a 19-by-21 rectangle with upper left corner at (50,50).

Next the `if` statement is evaluated. Because `width` is 19 and `height` is 21, the condition is `true`. Thus we execute:

```
rest = new NestedRects( 54, 54, 11, 13, canvas );
```

where the new parameters are calculated according to the expressions given in the constructor call.

How do we construct this set of nested rectangles? We execute the same constructor code as last time, but this time we have different parameters. We begin by evaluating

```
outerRect = new FramedRect( 54, 54, 11, 13, canvas );
```

Thus the value of `outerRect` for this new smaller collection of nested rectangles will be an 11-by-13 rectangle with upper left corner at (54,54). The `if` statement is again evaluated. Because `width` is 11 and `height` is 13, the condition is again `true`. Thus we execute:

```
rest = new NestedRects( 58, 58, 3, 5, canvas );
```

where the new parameters are calculated according to the expressions given in the constructor call. Thus the value of `rest` for the set of nested rectangles at (54,54) is yet another set of nested rectangles, this time located at (58,58).

To construct these rectangles we once more execute the constructor code, but with yet another set of parameters. Thus we execute

```
outerRect = new FramedRect( 58, 58, 3, 5, canvas );
```

But now when we evaluate the condition for the `if` statement, it will be `false`, because the new width, 3, is not 8 or larger. As a result, the `rest` instance variable of this object will be set to `null` and the constructor will terminate. This will return control to the constructor that called it, namely the call of `new NestedRects( 54, 54, 11, 13, canvas )`. The value of `NestedRects` just constructed (the simple 3-by-5 pixel framed rectangle) will get assigned to the instance variable `rest` of this instance of `NestedRects`, completing the execution of that constructor. The resulting object consists of an outer 11-by-13-pixel framed rectangle and an inner object of type `NestedRects` that consists of a single 3-by-5-pixel framed rectangle.

Control now returns to the original constructor call, `new NestedRects( 50, 50, 19, 21, canvas )`. The object just constructed (the two nested rectangles) is assigned to this object's `rest` instance variable, and the execution of that constructor now terminates. This final object has an outer rectangle that is a 19-by-21-pixel framed rectangle and `rest` consisting of two nested rectangles.

The final picture will look as shown in Figure 12.4.

In summary, the net result of the original call of the constructor is that the constructor is executed three times, which results in the construction of three framed rectangles. Because the constructor ends up being executed three times, three objects of the class `NestedRects` are constructed, each having different values for its `outerRect` and `rest` instance variables. For example, the value of `outerRect` for the initial `NestedRects` object is a framed

rectangle at (50,50), while that for the last `NestedRects` object is a framed rectangle
at (58,58).

Suppose next that we want to write a method that moves the nested rectangles to a fixed
location on the canvas. As we saw above, we were not able to do that in the iterative version
of the algorithm because we did not have names for all of the framed rectangles created by
the constructor. However, the recursive version of the class only needed two instance
variables—`outerRect` to refer to the outer framed rectangle and `rest` to refer to the smaller
collection of nested rectangles to be drawn inside of `outerRect`.

According to the code for `moveTo` in Figure 12.3, to move a `NestedRects` object to a new
location, we simply move `outerRect` to the new location by executing `outerRect.moveTo
(x, y)` and then, if there are any nested rectangles inside (i.e., if the value of `rest` is different
from `null`), we move those to a location that will again place them inside the outer rectangle. In
this case, that will be four pixels to the right and below the location of the outer rectangle. We
accomplish this move by sending a `moveTo` method to `rest` with these coordinates. This is said
to be a *recursive* invocation of `moveTo` because the message we are sending has the same name
as the method that we are defining, and it is being sent to an object of the same type as the objects
generated by the class. Because `rest` holds a simpler collection of nested rectangles, we claim
the message send will work correctly.

If we trace through sending the message `moveTo( 80, 100 )` to the nested rectangles we
created earlier by the evaluation of `new NestedRects( 50, 50, 19, 21, canvas )`, then
we can see that all of the framed rectangles will be moved appropriately. Because the value of
`outerRect` for this object is the framed rectangle at (50,50), that will be moved to (80,100) by the
first line of the `moveTo` method's code. Next the message `moveTo( 84, 104 )` will be sent to
the `rest` instance variable, which holds the nested rectangles at (54,54) that we saw constructed
in the example above.

If you trace the execution of the `moveTo( 84, 104 )` message on the second collection of
nested rectangles, you will see that its framed rectangle, `outerRect`, gets moved to (84,104).
Because its `rest` instance variable is a collection of nested rectangles at (58,58) (and hence
different from `null`), the message `moveTo( 88, 108 )` will be sent to `rest`.

As we saw when tracing the execution of the constructor, the collection of nested rectangles
at (58,58) has width three, which is less than eight. As a result, the value of its `rest` instance
variable is `null`. Hence the evaluation of the message `moveTo( 88, 108 )` on that object will
move the framed rectangle in its `outerRect` instance variable to (88,108) and then will not
execute the body of the `if` statement. As a result, the method finishes execution, having moved
all three framed rectangles.

We include the conditional statement in the code for `moveTo` in order to terminate the method
when there is nothing else to move. Of course the program would crash if we tried to send a
message to `rest` when its value was `null`, but the real reason for that check is to stop executing
the method when it has completed its task. Because of the way we wrote the constructor for
`NestedRects`, every construction will eventually terminate with the construction of an object

for which the value of the `rest` instance variable is `null`. Hence the `moveTo` method will always terminate when it reaches that object.

From this example we see that the methods of `NestedRects` can have a structure which is based on the recursive structure of objects from the class. That is, they do what is necessary to `outerRect` and then, if there is more to do and `rest` is not `null`, they call the method recursively on `rest` (though possibly with slightly different parameters).

The method `removeFromCanvas` included in `NestedRects` is another example of this structure. It operates by removing `outerRect` from the canvas, and then, if `rest` is non-`null`, removing `rest` from the canvas.

Not all methods need to have this recursive structure. For example, if we were to add a `contains` method for `NestedRects`, we would simply check to see if the `Location` parameter were contained in `outerRect`, as any point contained in the nested rectangles is contained in `outerRect`. However, most methods will follow the recursive structure of the objects.

EXERCISE 12.1.1

a. *Add methods* `setColor` *and* `move` *to the recursive version of* `NestedRects`. *If we were to add a method* `getColor`, *why wouldn't it have to be recursive as well?*

b. *Use the existence of the* `move` *method from part (a) to simplify the* `moveTo` *method of* `NestedRects` *in the same way we did with the class* `FunnyFace` *in Section 6.2.*

c. *Write a class extending* `WindowController` *that draws a* `NestedRects` *object when the mouse button is pressed, drags it around the screen when the mouse is dragged, and removes it from the screen when the mouse button is released.* ❖

A Better Recursive Solution

With a little more work, we can make our recursive class definition even easier to understand and program. While this new solution involves more classes and interfaces, it scales well to more complicated problems and reflects a uniform way of building recursive structures.

If you look again at the definition of `NestedRects` in Figure 12.3, you will notice that each method requires a check that `rest` is different from `null` before executing recursive calls. Unfortunately, omitting this check is one of the most common mistakes programmers make in writing recursive methods. If the check is omitted, the program will crash when it attempts to send a message to `null`.

There is an alternative style of writing recursive classes that allows the programmer to avoid checking for `null`. In this style of solution we always write two kinds of classes for each recursive structure. One is similar to the recursive `NestedRects` class we just wrote. It corresponds to the *recursive* case where there is at least one instance variable with the same type as the class being defined.

The other kind of class corresponds to a *base* case where we have objects that are simple enough that the constructors and methods can be written without recursion. In the case of the nested rectangles example, we will define a new base class, `BaseRects`, that represents an empty collection of nested rectangles.

It might seem odd to you to have a class that represents an empty collection of nested rectangles. However, being able to represent empty collections is extremely important. The invention of "0" was a major accomplishment in mathematics, as was the invention of "∅" to represent the empty set. As we shall see, objects from classes like BaseRects will play a similarly important role in making it easier for us to represent recursive structures.

The new classes, NestedRects and BaseRects, both implement the interface, NestedRectsInterface, which includes methods moveTo and removeFromCanvas. Thus a variable with type NestedRectsInterface can be associated with either NestedRects or BaseRects. The code for the interface and two classes can be found in Figure 12.5.

The constructor for NestedRects differs from the previous recursive version by assigning rest a non-null value no matter what the values of width and height. If both width and height are eight or greater, then rest is associated with a new object created from the class NestedRects. Otherwise it is assigned a new object from the class BaseRects.

Because rest is always assigned a non-null object that implements the NestedRectsInterface interface, we can send moveTo and removeFromCanvas messages to whatever object is associated with rest. Thus the moveTo and removeFromCanvas methods no longer need to check to see whether rest is null before sending messages to it. Each just sends the appropriate moveTo or removeFromCanvas messages to both outerRect and rest.

Now let us look at the design for BaseRects. In the constructor for NestedRects, the instance variable rest is only set to an object from BaseRects if at least one of the values of width and height is less than eight. When that is the case, reducing the width and height by eight would result in at least one of them being negative. Because it makes no sense to draw a rectangle with negative height or width, constructing an object of the class BaseRects should not result in anything being drawn on the screen. Similarly, because no rectangles will be associated with BaseRects, neither moveTo nor removeFromCanvas has anything to do.

As a result, neither the constructor nor the two methods of BaseRects include any code.[1] This may seem strange, but BaseRects objects do provide a way for us to detect the end of a collection of NestedRects.

Let's see what happens this time when we call the constructor for NestedRects. For simplicity, we will start with the second nested-rectangles object that we constructed last time. To make the evaluation of this constructor a bit clearer, let's give names to the objects of the class NestedRects as we construct them. See Figure 12.6 for a diagram showing the objects that will be constructed.

Suppose we evaluate

```
new NestedRects( 54, 54, 11, 13, canvas );
```

and call the resulting object *nest1*. As before, evaluating the constructor will result in the execution of

```
outerRect = new FramedRect( 54, 54, 11, 13, canvas );
```

which assigns to the outerRect instance variable of *nest1* an 11-by-13 rectangle with upper left corner at (54,54). Next the if statement is evaluated. Because width is 11 and height is 13, the condition is true. Thus we execute:

```
rest = new NestedRects( 58, 58, 3, 5, canvas );
```

where the new parameters are calculated according to the expressions given in the constructor call. This new object, which we'll call *nest2*, is assigned to *nest1*'s rest instance variable.

---

[1] Java allows you to omit the constructor in this case. We include it for clarity.

```
// Interface for base and recursive classes for nested rectangles
public interface NestedRectsInterface {
    // Move nested rectangles to (x,y)
    void moveTo( double x, double y );
    // Remove nested rectangles from canvas
    void removeFromCanvas();
}


// Recursive structure for collection of nested rectangles
public class NestedRects implements NestedRectsInterface {
    private FramedRect outerRect;         // Outermost rectangle in picture
    private NestedRectsInterface rest;    // Remaining nested rectangles

    public NestedRects( double x, double y, double width, double height,
                        DrawingCanvas canvas ) {
        outerRect = new FramedRect( x, y, width, height, canvas );
        if ( width >= 8 && height >= 8 ) {
            rest = new NestedRects( x + 4, y + 4, width - 8,
                                    height - 8, canvas );
        } else {        // Construct a base object
            rest = new BaseRects();
        }
    }

    // Move nested rectangles to (x,y)
    public void moveTo( double x, double y ) {
        outerRect.moveTo( x, y );
        rest.moveTo( x + 4, y + 4 );
    }

    // Remove the nested rectangles from the canvas
    public void removeFromCanvas() {
        outerRect.removeFromCanvas();
        rest.removeFromCanvas();
    }
}


// Class representing empty collection of nested rectangles
public class BaseRects implements NestedRectsInterface {
    // Constructor has nothing to initialize
    public BaseRects() { }

    // Move nested rectangles to (x,y)
    public void moveTo( double x, double y ) { }

    // Remove nested rectangles from canvas
    public void removeFromCanvas() { }
}
```

Figure 12.5 Recursive version of NestedRects classes with interface

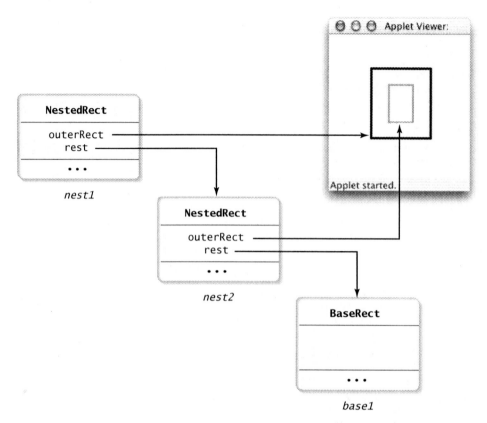

Figure 12.6 Objects constructed by evaluating new NestedRects(54, 54, 11, 13, canvas)

We start executing the constructor with the new parameters, and hence evaluate

```
outerRect = new FramedRect( 58, 58, 3, 5, canvas );
```

which assigns to *nest2*'s outerRect instance variable a new 3-by-5 rectangle with upper left corner at (58,58). But now when we evaluate the condition of the if statement, it will be false, because the new width, 3, is not greater than or equal to 8. As a result we evaluate the else-part of the if statement, setting *nest2*'s rest instance variable to a new object, *base1*, from class BaseRects, and the constructor terminates.

If we compare this with the previous recursive algorithm, we see that we end up constructing exactly the same two FramedRects, but at the end we create a BaseRects object rather than just leaving the value of rest to be null in the last NestedRects object created.

The main difference between this recursive definition of NestedRects and the earlier one is that we have eliminated all of the tests for null in the methods of the class in exchange for creating two classes that each implement the same interface. While the amount of code written is greater with this new definition, the methods of the class are less cluttered with tests. This will be an even larger advantage in more complex examples, so from now on we will define recursive structures in this way.

➡ EXERCISE 12.1.2
_____

Trace the execution of the sending the message moveTo(80, 100) *to the object nest1 to make sure you understand how it moves all of the rectangles and then terminates.* ❖

12.1.2 Building and Searching Data Collections with Recursive Structures

Many modern web browsers make it easy for you to type in the URL (universal resource locator) for a web page by offering automatic address completion. For example, if I start typing "http://www.a" my browser first suggests "http://www.aol.com" as a completion. If that is the address that I want, I press the tab key to accept it, and then press the return key to go to that address. On the other hand, if that is not the address I have in mind, then I keep typing. For example, if I next type a "p", my browser suggests "http://www.apple.com" as the completion. In order to do this the browser must keep a collection of URLs typed in by users, and then must be able to provide a sublist that includes all of the strings that match a given prefix.

We can model this collection using recursive structures. We will start with an empty list of Strings. Then, every time the user enters a new String (say in a JTextField), we will construct a new list that consists of the existing list of Strings plus the new one. We won't bother to add another copy of a String that is already in the list. To avoid entering duplicates we will need a method, contains, that will allow us to check if a String is already in the list.

When the user starts typing a new URL, we will display (say in a JTextArea) the existing URLs that match the portion of the URL typed so far. Thus we will need a method getMatches that returns a list of URLs that match. In order to convert a list of URLs into a String that can be displayed, we will also need a method toString.

The class constructor will take care of building new lists out of old ones. Therefore the only methods that we will need are contains, getMatches, and toString. The interface UrlListInterface is given in Figure 12.7.

Implementing a class representing an empty URL list is easy, as nothing needs to be remembered for an empty list. The class EmptyUrlList is given in Figure 12.8. The constructor does nothing, as there are no instance variables to initialize. The method getMatches always

```
// Interface for classes representing lists of URLs
public interface UrlListInterface {
    // Returns a list of all entries starting with prefix
    public UrlListInterface getMatches( String prefix );

    // Determines whether the collection contains url
    public boolean contains( String url );

    // Convert list to a string with entries separated by new lines
    public String toString();
}
```

Figure 12.7 UrlListInterface interface

```java
// Class representing empty lists of URLs
public class EmptyUrlList implements UrlListInterface {

    // Constructor has nothing to initialize
    public EmptyUrlList() { }

    // Returns a list of all entries starting with prefix
    public UrlListInterface getMatches( String prefix ) {
        return new EmptyUrlList();
    }


    // Determines whether the collection contains url
    public boolean contains( String url ) {
        return false;
    }

    // Convert list to a string with entries separated by new lines
    public String toString() {
        return "";
    }
}
```

Figure 12.8 EmptyUrlList class

returns an empty URL list, `contains` is always `false`, and `toString` always returns an empty string.

➠ EXERCISE 12.1.3

Are the methods for `EmptyUrlList` *correct?*

The class `NonemptyUrlList` in Figure 12.9 is more interesting. The constructor takes a new URL and an existing `UrlListInterface` and builds a new list by associating the new URL with the instance variable `firstURL`, and the old list with `rest`. This structure is very similar to the one we used with `NestedRects`. A trivial difference is that the first instance variable is called `firstURL` rather than `outerRect` and the types of these variables are different. However, these instance variables play essentially the same roles in `NonemptyUrlList` as they did in `NestedRects`.

A more significant difference between the constructors in these two classes is that the constructor in `NonemptyUrlList` is not recursive. That is, there is no invocation of new `NonemptyUrlList(...)` inside the body of the constructor. Instead the constructor takes a parameter of type `UrlListInterface` and builds a new, more complicated `NonemptyUrlList` that includes the list passed in as well as a new URL. This is fairly common when building new recursive structures out of existing structures, rather than building the entire structure at once (as we did with nested rectangles).

```java
// Class representing non-empty lists of URLs
public class NonemptyUrlList implements UrlListInterface {
    private String firstUrl;          // The first URL in the list
    private UrlListInterface rest;     // The rest of the list of URLs

    // Create a new list
    public NonemptyUrlList( String newURL,
                            UrlListInterface existingList ) {
        firstUrl = newURL;
        rest = existingList;
    }

    // Returns a list of all entries starting with prefix
    public UrlListInterface getMatches( String prefix ) {
        if ( firstUrl.startsWith( prefix ) ) {
            return new NonemptyUrlList( firstUrl,
                                        rest.getMatches( prefix ) );
        }
        else {
            return rest.getMatches( prefix );
        }
    }

    // Determines whether the collection contains url
    public boolean contains( String url ) {
        return firstUrl.equals( url ) || rest.contains( url );
    }

    // Convert list to a string with entries separated by new lines
    public String toString() {
        return firstUrl + "\n" + rest.toString();
    }
}
```

Figure 12.9 NonemptyUrlList class

The methods of NonemptyUrlList are written in the same style as those of NestedRects. Let's start by looking at the contains method, as it is one of the simplest. The NonemptyUrlList contains url if it is either the first element of the list or it is in the rest of the list.

When trying to understand a recursive method, we are allowed to assume that simpler recursive calls of the method work correctly. In this case, that means we can assume that the result of evaluating rest.contains(url) is true exactly when url is contained in the rest of the list. (We already saw that contains returns the correct answer—false—in the case of the empty list in class EmptyUrlList.) Hence the method will return true exactly when url equals firstURL or is contained in the rest of the list.

The method `toString` is very similar. The method concatenates the `String` in `firstUrl` with `"\n"` and then the result of converting `rest` into a `String`. If `"\n"` appears in a string, then when the string is printed, it is transformed into a "new line" character. That is, it forces the rest of the string to be printed on a new line.

If we assume `toString` works correctly on the smaller list in `rest`, then the result of the concatenation gives us a string representing all of the elements in the list, where consecutive elements will be printed on separate lines.

The `getMatches` method uses a built-in `String` method, `startsWith`, that we have not yet used. The invocation `someString.startsWith( otherString )` returns `true` exactly when `otherString` is a prefix of `someString`. That is, it returns `true` when a sequence of letters at the start of `someString` corresponds exactly to the sequence of letters in `otherString`.

The `getMatches` method should return a `UrlListInterface` of all strings in the list that start with the value of the parameter `prefix`. Suppose `rest.getMatches( prefix )` returns a list of all the strings in `rest` that start with `prefix`. If the first element of the list, `firstUrl`, starts with `prefix`, then it should be an element of the list to be returned, so we build a new list out of `firstUrl` and the list of matches from the rest of the list. Otherwise we simply return the set of matches from the rest of the list.

▮➡ EXERCISE 12.1.4

Check your understanding of what the methods of these classes do by determining the results of sending the messages `contains("abcd")`, `toString()`, *and* `getMatches("abc")` *to each of* w, x, y, *and* z *if they have been initialized as follows:*

```
w = new EmptyUrlList();
x = new NonemptyUrlList( "abcd", w );
y = new NonemptyUrlList( "bca", x );
z = new NonemptyUrlList( "abce", y );
```

▮➡ EXERCISE 12.1.5

We could replace the body of the `getMatches` *method of the class* `EmptyUrlList` *by the simpler:*

```
return this;
```

Does this change make any difference to a program using these classes? Why might it be an improvement over the old body?

12.1.3   Designing Recursive Structures

We have now presented the design of two recursive structures, one representing a collection of nested rectangles and the other a list of URLs. The final recursive implementation of nested rectangles and the implementation of the list of URLs were very similar. In each case we wrote two classes and an interface, where each of the classes implemented the interface.

In each of these examples, one class was designed to represent an empty collection. In each case, the class for the empty collection of objects was not recursive. That is, it included no instance variables with the same type. Similarly the methods and constructor for empty objects were non-recursive. It was easy to verify that they they did what they were supposed to—i.e., that they were correct.

In each example, one class was designed to represent a non-empty collection. Each class included two instance variables. One represented one of the objects of the collection, with the other representing the rest. The type of the second variable is the same as the type of the collection. Thus these classes were recursive. The methods in these cases were also recursive. The constructor for `NestedRects` was recursive, calling the constructor recursively to build a simpler collection, while the constructor for `NonemptyUrlList` took a simpler collection as a parameter.

Let's step back and see if we can extract from these two examples some principles that we can use to design other recursive structures:

* Recursive structures are built by defining classes for base and recursive cases, both of which implements the same interface.
* A class represents a *base* case if it has no instance variable whose type is the defined interface or one of the other classes. As we have seen, the base case is generally easy to write and verify.
* A class represents a *recursive* case if it has one or more instance variables whose type is the interface or one of the classes being defined. Designing the constructors and methods of a class representing a recursive structure requires a bit more care. The idea is that we must make sure that the constructors and methods always terminate (don't run forever), and convince ourselves that the constructors and methods work properly.

In our final recursive solution for nested rectangles the class `BaseRects` represents the base case, `NestedRects` represents the recursive case, and `NestedRectsInterface` is the interface that both implement. In the URL list example, the class `EmptyUrlList` represents the base case, `NonemptyUrlList` represents the recursive case, and `UrlListInterface` is the interface that both implement.

We write the classes and interface representing a recursive structure as follows:

1. Define an interface with all of the methods that both base case and recursive case classes must implement.
2. Define one or more classes representing base cases. Make sure that all methods from the interface are implemented. Convince yourself that the constructors and methods work correctly.
3. Define the constructors for recursive classes. Recursive calls of the constructor should only create objects that are simpler than the one being built by the constructor. Similarly, instance variables whose types are either the interface or class should only refer to objects simpler than the one being constructed. In particular, the construction of simpler objects in the constructor body should eventually end up at a base case. Convince yourself that the constructor will be correct under the assumption that the construction of simpler objects is correct.
4. Write each method under the assumption that it works correctly on all simpler objects. Convince yourself that the methods will be correct under the assumption that instance variables hold simpler objects.

Following the first two points in defining the interface and base classes is generally very straightforward. The third point ensures that eventually the constructor will finish and that instance variables only hold simpler objects than the one being defined. If it does not hold, then the constructor will never terminate, and the computer will run out of memory.[2] This is used in the fourth point when reasoning about the correctness of methods.

---

[2] The error reported will be something like `StackOverflow error`, indicating that there is no more room on the "run-time stack" to create new objects.

We brushed over one key item in the instructions above: What does it mean to be simpler? This depends on the recursive structure. With a collection of nested rectangles, for example, the complexity of the collection could either be defined by the number of nested rectangles in the collection or by the width and height of the outer rectangle. In our case it will be most straightforward to say that one collection of nested rectangles is simpler than another if the width and height of the first are both smaller than the width and height of the second (though we could also have used the number of rectangles). We will say that an object from a base class like BaseRects is always simpler than an object from a recursive class like NestedRects.

For the list of Strings, the easiest measure of complexity is the number of Strings in the list. Again an object from EmptyUrlList is always simpler than an object from NonemptyUrlList.

Let's examine the four steps as applied to the collection of nested rectangles. As expected, the definitions of the interface and BaseRects are straightforward, so points one and two are easily accomplished.

The third point has to do with the constructor of NestedRects. If the width and height are at least eight when the constructor is executed, then the construction in the if statement results in a new object from NestedRects that has smaller width and height, and hence is simpler. If either the width or height is less than eight, then only an object of class BaseRects is created, and that is, by definition, simpler than the object of class NestedRects being constructed. Thus it doesn't matter which branch of the if-else statement is executed; the object constructed and associated with rest is simpler than the full collection of nested rectangles.

Now let us worry about the correctness of the constructor. First we create an outer FramedRect with the same dimensions and location as the entire collection of nested rectangles. Next, if the width and height are both at least eight, the constructor creates a new NestedRects object four units to the right and below, and with width and height eight units less than the original. That object is simpler than the original one we are trying to create. As a result, we are allowed to assume that it really does create a collection of nested rectangles with the given dimensions and location. Under that assumption, the framed rectangle associated with outerRect will be drawn in just the right place to symmetrically surround the collection of nested rectangles.

On the other hand, if either the width or height is less than eight, the constructor creates an object from BaseRects, which does not result in anything being drawn aside from the outer rectangle. Hence only a single framed rectangle is drawn at the given position, which is correct.

Thus, in either case, if we assume that the simpler recursive calls of the constructor do what they are supposed to do, then the general case will work properly.

The fourth point has to do with writing and convincing yourself of the correctness of methods. According to that point, when attempting to argue that a constructor or method is correct for an object, we are allowed to assume that it works correctly on all simpler structures.

Let's use that to investigate the design of the moveTo method. We've already determined that the moveTo method does the right thing (i.e., nothing) when we send a moveTo message to an object from the class BaseRects. Now we need to show that an object from the class NestedRects is moved correctly when a moveTo message is sent to it.

When a message of the form moveTo(u, v) is sent to an object from the class NestedRects, first the framed rectangle associated with outerRect is moved to location (u, v). Then the object associated with rest is sent the message moveTo(u+4, v+4). Because the value of rest is simpler than the whole object, we can assume that the message send to rest works correctly. In particular it moves the simpler collection of nested rectangles to a point four pixels to the right and below where the framed rectangle was sent. This results in the rectangles represented by rest being centered in the newly moved framed rectangle represented by outerRect, because the inner nested rectangles were originally located four pixels to the right and below the original location of the framed rectangle. Hence the entire collection is moved correctly to the new location.

Similar arguments can be used to show that removeFromCanvas correctly removes all of the rectangles from the canvas.

12.1.4 Why Does This Work?

Reasoning according to the third and fourth points in the previous section is sufficient to ensure that the constructors and methods of a recursive class will work correctly. A proof of this could be given using mathematical induction. But since not all readers may have encountered mathematical induction yet, we will instead give a more intuitive argument for why this suffices.

Rather than giving an argument in general, let's give the justification for the specific case of the constructor for NestedRects. A similar justification works for other cases of recursive constructors and methods.

We will start from the smallest collections of NestedRects and work our way up. Let's consider evaluating new NestedRects(x, y, width, height, canvas), where the smallest of width and height is less than eight pixels, but both are greater than or equal to zero. Then the constructor will construct exactly one FramedRect of the desired size at (x,y), and will construct one object from BaseRects, which does not result in any drawing on the canvas. The recursive call of the constructor is not executed, because the condition in the if statement is false. Clearly, drawing the one FramedRect is what should happen, so everything works fine when the smallest side is less than eight pixels.

Now suppose the smallest of width and height is less than sixteen pixels, but greater than or equal to eight pixels. Then when new NestedRects(x, y, width, height, canvas) is called, a FramedRect is drawn with the specified dimensions at (x,y). The condition on the if statement is now true, so the recursive call of new NestedRects(x+4, y+4, width-8, height-8, canvas) is executed. Because the original smallest side was less than sixteen pixels, and the recursive call involves parameters for width and height that are reduced by eight each, the smallest side for the recursive call is less than eight pixels. It is also drawn four pixels to the right and below the original call.

We know the call of the constructor is correct when the smallest side is less than eight pixels, so we know that the recursive call does the right thing—that is, it draws a single FramedRect at (x+4,y+4). Because the original call resulted in drawing a FramedRect which is eight pixels larger on each side, we know that the combination of drawing the FramedRect and the recursive call result in drawing two nested rectangles, as desired.

Now suppose the smallest of width and height is less than twenty-four pixels, but greater than or equal to sixteen pixels. Examining the evaluation of new NestedRects(x, y, width, height, canvas) we see that it draws a FramedRect with the specified dimensions at (x,y), and then calls the constructor recursively with new NestedRects(x+4, y+4, width-8, height-8, canvas). The recursive call now has smallest side less than sixteen pixels, but greater than or equal to eight pixels. However, we already know that a call of the constructor with smallest side of this size draws a collection of two nested rectangles correctly. Thus it is easy to convince ourselves by looking at where each of these is drawn that a call with smallest side less than twenty-four pixels, but greater than or equal to sixteen pixels, works correctly and draws three nested framed rectangles.

We could continue in this way as far as we like, but you should be able to recognize the pattern now. Each time we draw a new framed rectangle and rely on the fact that we already know that the recursive call of the constructor does what it is supposed to. This is exactly what our instructions told us to do in order to write and verify a recursive constructor or method.

Very similar arguments can be used to show that the moveTo and removeFromCanvas methods for NestedRects are correct. The rules for checking constructors and methods tell us exactly what must be verified in order to have confidence that our recursive constructors and methods will be correct.

⇒ EXERCISE 12.1.6

What would go wrong if the constructor for NestedRects *resulted in a recursive call creating an object of type* NestedRects *with larger width and height as the value of the* rest *instance variable?*   ❖

⇒ EXERCISE 12.1.7

Apply the four points above to the design of the classes and the interface for the list of URLs.   ❖

⇒ EXERCISE 12.1.8

Suppose we made a mistake in the definition of the moveTo *method in* NestedRects *by leaving out the statement* outerRect.moveTo(x, y)*. What would go wrong? Show where the correctness argument for that method would break down.*   ❖

⇒ EXERCISE 12.1.9

Suppose we made a mistake in the definition of the method moveTo *in* NestedRects *by writing* rest.moveTo(x, y) *rather than* rest.moveTo(x+4, y+4)*. What would go wrong? Show where the correctness argument for that method would break down.*   ❖

12.1.5 Broccoli

Recursion can be used to create other interesting pictures. A drawing of broccoli is shown in Figure 12.10. If you examine the drawing carefully, you will notice the recursive structure of the plant. At the base is a stem that is about one-fourth of the height of the plant. At the upper end, the stem branches off three ways—one to the left, one straight up, and one to the right. If we look at what grows out of the upper end of the stem, we see that those structures themselves look exactly like smaller broccoli plants. We will take advantage of this structure by drawing broccoli as a stem with three smaller broccoli plants attached to the ends of the stem. Thus it can be represented as a recursive structure.

We draw broccoli by following the approach in the previous section. We will define a class Flower to handle the base case of drawing the flowering end of broccoli, while Broccoli will handle the recursive case. As in our previous recursive designs, we will define an interface,

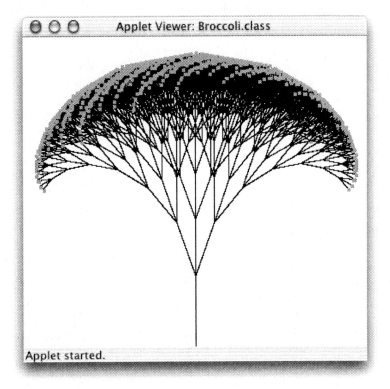

Figure 12.10 A broccoli plant

BroccoliPart, that both Flower and Broccoli must implement. We will keep track of the
size of the broccoli by keeping track of the size of the stem. This will help us decide whether we
are in the base case where we construct a flower or in the recursive case where we construct a full
broccoli plant.

If the stem is more than MIN_SIZE pixels long then we will attach three smaller broccoli plants
to the end of the stem. Each of these will have a stem which is 80% of the size of the one just
drawn. Otherwise, if the stem is at most MIN_SIZE pixels long, then we will attach three flowers
to the end of the stem. Thus the base case occurs when the stem length is at most MIN_SIZE pixels
and the recursive case when it is larger than MIN_SIZE pixels.

In order to draw broccoli, we will need to draw lines at a variety of angles. While the first stem
will be drawn vertically, successive stems will be drawn at other angles (in particular, the leftmost
and rightmost branches will be drawn at angles of $\pi/9$ radians (or $20°$) from that of the base stem.
The Line class in the objectdraw library has a constructor that takes end points of a line, but
if we were only given a starting point and an angle, then we would have to use trigonometry to
calculate the end point of the line. It would be more convenient to have a constructor that took
the starting point, angle, and length of a line.

The objectdraw library contains a class AngLine that has the same methods as Line, but has
a constructor with parameters that are more convenient for drawing lines at an angle. We show

```
// BroccoliPart is an interface for parts of broccoli.
public interface BroccoliPart {
    // Move the broccoli part by dx in the horizontal direction and
    // dy in the vertical direction
    public void move( double dx, double dy );


    // Whether a point is contained in the broccoli part
    public boolean contains( Location point );
}
```

Figure 12.11   Broccoli interface

the constructor declaration below:

```
public AngLine( Location start, double length, double radianAngle,
                DrawingCanvas canvas )
```

All we will require of our broccoli is that we can drag it around the screen. Thus, we need it to support move and contains methods. The rather trivial definition of the interface BroccoliPart is given in Figure 12.11. This completes step 1 in the definition of a recursive structure.

The base case, the Flower class, is shown in Figure 12.12. The constructor for Flower takes as parameters the starting location startCoords, the length of the stem, size, the angle that the stem makes with the *x* axis, direction, and the canvas that it will be drawn on. An instance of Flower is composed of an AngLine, stem, which is colored green, connected to a FilledOval, bud, which is colored yellow. The method getEnd of AngLine makes it easy to find the end of the stem in order to draw the bud. The move method for Flower is straightforward, as it simply moves the stem and bud the appropriate distance. The contains method simply returns whether stem or bud contains point. This completes step 2 of our guidelines.

Figure 12.13 contains the code for the recursive Broccoli class. The constructor takes the same parameters as Flower. It draws the stem and then, depending on size, adds either three Broccolis or three Flowers to the end of the stem. The instance variables, left, center, and right, all have type BroccoliPart, so they can hold values from either the Broccoli or Flower classes. The object associated with center (whether flower or broccoli) will face the same direction as the stem, while the the objects associated with left and right are tipped at angles of $\pi°/9$ or $20°$ to the left and right of the stem.

If we start with a stem length of greater than MIN_SIZE pixels in the constructor, then, after creating new objects of class Broccoli with the stem length reduced to 80% of its value over and over, we will eventually get a stem length which is MIN_SIZE pixels or smaller. Thus each invocation of the constructor creates a simpler structure (i.e., with shorter stem length), and these simpler structures will eventually terminate with the construction of a flower.

Now we must verify that the constructor does the right thing if we assume that all simpler calls of the constructor do the right thing. In this case, it is clear that the constructor does the right

```
// Flower represents the flower of a broccoli plant
public class Flower implements BroccoliPart {
    ... // Constant declarations omitted

    private AngLine stem;                    // Stem of broccoli

    private FilledOval bud;                  // Flower of broccoli plant

    // Construct stem with flower at end
    public Flower( Location startCoords, double size,
                   double direction, DrawingCanvas canvas ) {
        // Draw stem and color green
        stem = new AngLine( startCoords, size, direction, canvas );
        stem.setColor( Color.GREEN );

        Location destCoords = stem.getEnd();     // End of stem

        bud = new FilledOval( destCoords, BUD_SIZE, BUD_SIZE, canvas );
        bud.setColor( Color.YELLOW );
    }

    // Move the broccoli part by dx in the horizontal direction and
    // dy in the vertical direction
    public void move( double dx, double dy) {
        stem.move(dx,dy);                        // Move stem
        bud.move(dx,dy);                         // Move bud
    }

    // Return whether a point is contained in the flower
    public boolean contains( Location point ) {
        return stem.contains( point ) || bud.contains( point );
    }
}
```

Figure 12.12 Flower class implementing BroccoliPart

thing, as it is easy to see from the picture that a nontrivial Broccoli consists of a stem with three Broccoli objects or flowers attached to the end of the stem. Thus we have satisfied the third point for the definition of recursive structures.

Now let us take a look at the move method for Broccoli. To move Broccoli we just move the stem and the left, center, and right BroccoliParts. Because the left, center, and right pieces are simpler than the entire broccoli, we are allowed to assume the recursive invocations of move work correctly. Under this assumption, it is easy to see that the complete method works correctly: the stem is moved the appropriate amount and each of the three broccoli parts is moved the same amount. Verifying the contains method is similarly easy.

```
// Class to recursively draw broccoli
public class Broccoli implements BroccoliPart {
    ... // Constant declarations omitted
    private BroccoliPart left, center, right;    // Branches of broccoli
    private AngLine stem;                          // Stem of broccoli

    // Draw broccoli by recursively drawing branches (and flowers)
    public Broccoli( Location startCoords, double size,
                     double direction, DrawingCanvas canvas ) {
        // Draw stem and color green
        stem = new AngLine( startCoords, size, direction, canvas );
        stem.setColor(Color.GREEN);
        Location destCoords = stem.getEnd();     // End of stem

        if ( size > MIN_SIZE ) {                  // Big enough to keep growing
            left = new Broccoli( destCoords, SHRINK_PERCENT*size,
                                 direction + Math.PI/9.0, canvas);
            center = new Broccoli( destCoords, SHRINK_PERCENT*size,
                                   direction, canvas );
            right = new Broccoli( destCoords, SHRINK_PERCENT*size,
                                  direction - Math.PI/9.0, canvas );
        } else {                                  // Draw flowers
            left = new Flower( destCoords, SHRINK_PERCENT*size,
                               direction + Math.PI/9.0, canvas );
            center = new Flower( destCoords, SHRINK_PERCENT*size,
                                 direction, canvas );
            right = new Flower( destCoords, SHRINK_PERCENT*size,
                                direction - Math.PI/9.0, canvas );
        }
    }

    // Move the broccoli part by dx in the horizontal direction and
    // dy in the vertical direction
    public void move( double dx, double dy ) {
        stem.move( dx, dy );                      // Move stem

        left.move( dx, dy );                      // Move other parts
        center.move( dx, dy );
        right.move( dx, dy );
    }

    // Whether a point is contained in the broccoli
    public boolean contains( Location point ) {
        return stem.contains( point ) || left.contains( point ) ||
               center.contains( point ) || right.contains( point );
    }
}
```

Figure 12.13   Broccoli class

```
// Draws broccoli on screen and allows user to drag it around
public class BroccoliDrag extends WindowController {

    ... // Constant declarations omitted

    private Location lastCoords;        // Where mouse was before last move

    private BroccoliPart plant;         // Broccoli object to be
                                        // drawn & moved

    private boolean broccoliPressed;    // Whether the broccoli
                                        // has been pressed

    // Create the broccoli
    public void begin() {
        plant = new Broccoli( ROOT_LOCN, START_STEM, Math.PI/2.0, canvas );
    }

    // Get ready to move broccoli
    public void onMousePress( Location pt ) {
        lastCoords = pt;
        broccoliPressed = plant.contains( pt );
    }

    // Drag the broccoli around
    public void onMouseDrag( Location pt ) {
        if ( broccoliPressed ) {
            plant.move( pt.getX()-lastCoords.getX(),
                        pt.getY()-lastCoords.getY() );
            lastCoords = pt;
        }
    }

}
```

Figure 12.14 BroccoliDrag class

We have now satisfied all four conditions for the definition of a recursive structure, so we can have confidence that our classes and interface support the creation and manipulation of broccoli.

Figure 12.14 contains the code for a class BroccoliDrag that extends WindowController. It creates a broccoli and allows the user to drag it around the screen.

➡ EXERCISE 12.1.10

Add new methods moveTo *and* removeFromCanvas *to the* Broccoli *and* Flower *classes.* ❖

➠ EXERCISE 12.1.11

If you were to run the `BroccoliDrag` *program, you would discover that it takes a while to respond to a mouse drag, and the motion is somewhat jerky. To understand why this is so, calculate the number of lines that are included in the broccoli created in* `BroccoliDraw`*. You should assume that* START_STEM *has the value 95, that* MIN_SIZE *is 25, and that* SHRINK_PERCENT *is 80. You may find it easiest to do this by first counting lines for a broccoli whose stem length is 25, then, moving up to 31.25 (25 is 80% of 31.25), 39, 48.8, 61, 76, and finally 95.* ❖

➠ EXERCISE 12.1.12

To make the `Broccoli` *drawing more interesting, animate its growth by making the class into an* `ActiveObject`*. The constructor should draw the stem and then call* `start()`*. The* run *method should pause for 500 milliseconds and then create the three branches.* ❖

➠ EXERCISE 12.1.13

The first class we designed for drawing nested rectangles used a loop in the constructor to create the framed rectangles. One might imagine that one could do something similar for drawing broccoli. What is it about broccoli that makes it hard to draw it using a `while` *loop and no recursive invocations of the constructor?* ❖

12.2 Recursive Methods

In this section we develop recursive methods that are not part of recursive structures. Instead we write recursive methods where the complexity is controlled by an integer parameter. As before, we will ensure that recursive invocations are simpler, though in this case that will be done by making recursive invocations with smaller, but non-negative, integer parameters.

Recursive methods differ from the methods in classes supporting recursive structures in that the methods must include at least one base case in which there are no recursive invocations of the method. These base *cases* replace the base *classes* that we needed to support recursive structures. Recursive methods typically contain a conditional statement in which at least one of the cases is a base case and at least one involves recursive invocations. In this way these recursive methods are similar to those included in our first attempt at writing a recursive class for a collection of nested rectangles.

After we present the first example, we will provide a slightly different set of guidelines to write and verify recursive methods where the recursion is based on parameter values rather than recursive structures.

We present two different problems in this section. The first example involves a fast algorithm for raising a number to a non-negative integer power, while the second involves the solution to an interesting puzzle.

12.2.1 Fast Exponentiation

Fast algorithms for raising large numbers to large integer powers are important to the RSA algorithm for public key cryptography. We won't discuss cryptography here, but we will investigate a recursive algorithm that is substantially faster than the usual way of raising numbers to powers.

As a warm-up, we describe a simple recursive method to raise a number to a non-negative power that is no more (or less) efficient than the obvious iterative algorithm. As usual, the basic idea is to describe how you would complete the solution to the problem if there were solutions to simpler problems. In this case, if we want to raise a number to the nth power, we presume the algorithm for raising the number to the $(n-1)$st power works correctly.

```java
// Returns base raised to exponent power as long as exponent >= 0
public double simpleRecPower( double base, int exponent ) {
    if ( exponent == 0) {                  // Base case
        return 1;
    } else {                               // Recursive case
        return base * simpleRecPower( base, exponent-1 );
    }
}
```

Notice that the method includes a conditional statement which has both a base case and a recursive case. A simpler case is one with a smaller value of `exponent`.

The following are the rules for writing recursive methods:

1. Write the base case. This is the case where there is no recursive call. Convince yourself that this works correctly.
2. Write the recursive case.

   * Make sure all recursive calls go to simpler cases than the one you are writing. Make sure that the simpler cases will eventually get to a base case.
   * Make sure that the general case will work properly if all of the recursive calls work properly.

Let's apply these rules to `simpleRecPower`:

1. The base case is where `exponent == 0`. It returns 1, which is the correct answer for raising `base` to the 0th power. It is the base case because there is no recursive invocation of `simpleRecPower`.
2. The recursive case uses the `else` clause.

   * The recursive call is to `simpleRecPower( base, exponent-1 )`. It involves a smaller value for the second argument. Because the value of `exponent` is greater than 0 (*why?*), and the exponent always goes down by one, the recursive calls will eventually get down to the base case of 0.
   * Assuming that evaluating `simpleRecPower( base, exponent-1 )` results in $\text{base}^{(\text{exponent}-1)}$, the `else` clause returns

$$\text{base*simpleRecPower(base, exponent-1)} = \text{base} * \text{base}^{(\text{exponent}-1)}$$
$$= \text{base}^{\text{exponent}}.$$

Thus we can be confident that the above algorithm calculates $base^{exponent}$. It is also easy to see that the evaluation of `simpleRecPower( base, n )` results in exactly n multiplications, because there is exactly one multiplication associated with each recursive call.

Using a simple modification of the above recursive program, we can get a much more efficient algorithm for calculating very large powers. In particular, if we use the above program (or the equivalent simple iterative program), it will take 1024 multiplications to calculate b^{1024}, for some number b, while the program we are about to present cuts this down to only 11 multiplications!

The algorithm above takes advantage of the following simple rules of exponents:

* $base^0 = 1$
* $base^{exp+1} = base * base^{exp}$

The new algorithm that we present below takes advantage of one more rule of exponents:

* $base^{m*n} = (base^m)^n$

In the program we use this rule where m is 2 and n is exponent / 2.

The key is that by using this rule as often as possible, we can cut down the amount of work considerably, by reducing the size of the exponents in recursive calls faster. See the code below:

```
// Returns base raised to exponent power as long as exponent >= 0
public double fastRecPower( double base, int exponent ) {
    if ( exponent == 0 ) {                    // Base case
        return 1;
    } else if ( exponent%2 == 1 ) {           // exponent is odd
        return base * fastRecPower( base, exponent-1 );
    } else {                                   // exponent is even
        return fastRecPower( base * base, exponent / 2 );
    }
}
```

The `fastRecPower` method performs exactly the same computation as the previous one when the exponent is 0 or an odd integer. However, it works very differently when the exponent is even. In that case, it squares the base and divides the exponent in half.

Before analyzing exactly why this method works, let's first look at an example of the use of this algorithm and count the number of multiplications.

```
fastRecPower( 3, 16 ) = fastRecPower( 9, 8 )
                      = fastRecPower( 81, 4 )
                      = fastRecPower( 6561, 2 )
                      = fastRecPower( 43046721, 1 )
                      = 43046721 * fastRecPower( 43046721, 0 )
                      = 43046721 * 1
                      = 43046721
```

The computation only takes five multiplications using `fastRecPower`, whereas it would have taken 16 multiplications the other way. Division by 2 can be done as easily in binary as divisions by 10 can be done with numbers in decimal notation. Thus we will not bother to count division by 2 or using the % operation with 2 as worth worrying about in terms of the time complexity of the algorithm.

In general it takes somewhere between $\log_2(\text{exponent}) + 1$ (for exponents that are exact powers of 2) and $2 * \log_2(\text{exponent})$ multiplications to compute a power this way. While the difference between $2 * \log_2(\text{exponent})$ and `exponent` is not great for small values of `exponent`, it does make quite a difference when `exponent` is large. For example, as noted above, computing `fastRecPower( b, 1024 )` would only take 11 multiplications, while computing it the other way would take 1024 multiplications.

Let's once again use the standard rules for understanding recursion to see why this algorithm is correct.

1. The base case is again where `exponent == 0`. It returns 1, which is the correct answer for raising `base` to the 0th power.
2. The recursive case is in the `else` clause, but this time it divides into two cases, depending on whether `exponent` is odd or even.

   * When `exponent` is odd, the recursive call is with `exponent - 1`, while, when `exponent` is even, the recursive call is with `exponent / 2`. In either case, each of these calls is for a smaller integer power, because `exponent` is greater than zero. Thus, no matter which case is selected at each call, eventually the power will decrease to the base case, 0.
   * We have already given the correctness argument for the code in the odd case in our earlier analysis of the `simpleRecPower` method. Let's convince ourselves that it also is correct for the even case.

     Let `exponent` be an even positive integer. Then the method returns the value of

     ```
     fastRecPower( base * base, exponent / 2 )
     ```

     That is simpler than the original call, because `exponent/2` is less than `exponent`. Thus we can assume that it returns the correct answer. However,

     $$(\text{base} * \text{base})^{\text{exponent}/2} = (\text{base}^2)^{\text{exponent}/2}$$
     $$= \text{base}^{2 \ * \ (\text{exponent}/2)}$$
     $$= \text{base}^{\text{exponent}}$$

     Thus the result of `fastRecPower( base * base, exponent / 2 )` is the correct answer.
     Note that $2 * (\text{exponent}/2) = \text{exponent}$ only because `exponent` is even. If `exponent` were odd, the truncation in integer division would cause the product to evaluate to `exponent` -1.

Thus we see that the `fastRecPower` algorithm is correct.

While this algorithm can be rewritten in an iterative style, the recursive algorithm makes it clear where the rules of exponents are coming into play in the algorithm.

⇒ EXERCISE 12.2.1

   a. *Rewrite the* `simpleRecPower` *algorithm with a loop.*

   b. *Write the iterative equivalent of the* `fastRecPower` *algorithm. Do you find the iterative or recursive version easier to understand?* ❖

12.2.2 Towers of Hanoi

An amusing use of recursion comes up in the solution of the Towers of Hanoi puzzle. The puzzle is based on a story about a group of Buddhist monks in the Tower of Brahma. The monastery contains a large table in which are embedded 3 diamond-tipped needles. There are also 64 golden disks, each with a different radius. Each disk has a hole in the center so that it can be placed on one of the needles. At the start, the 64 golden disks are placed on the first diamond-tipped needle, arranged in order of size, with the largest on the bottom.

The monks are supposed to move the 64 golden disks from the first to the third golden-tipped needle. This sounds easy, but there are restrictions on how disks can be moved. First, only one disk at a time can be moved from one needle to another. Second, it is strictly forbidden to put a large disk on top of a smaller one. As we shall see, there is a rather simple recursive strategy for solving this puzzle, though we shall also see that completing this task will take quite a bit of work.

One can buy a children's puzzle based on this story, though these puzzles are typically made of plastic or wood, and only come with 8 or fewer disks (for reasons that will become apparent later). See the picture in Figure 12.15.

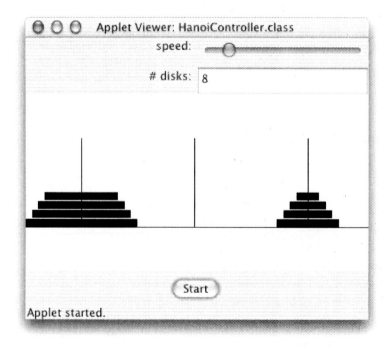

Figure 12.15   Towers of Hanoi puzzle with 8 disks

The key to solving the puzzle is to consider how you could move the biggest disk from the bottom of the first needle to the bottom of the third needle. Then think recursively!

A little thought should convince you that to move the biggest disk from the first to last needle, you must first move all of the smaller disks to the middle needle in order to get the smaller disks out of the way. If any of the smaller disks are left on the first needle, then the biggest disk cannot be moved. Similarly, if any of the smaller disks are on the third needle, then we could not possibly move the biggest disk onto that needle, as that would be an illegal move.

Hence, all but the largest disk must be moved to the middle needle. Then the biggest disk must be moved to the third needle. Finally the remaining $(n - 1)$ smaller disks must be moved from the middle needle to the last needle. We can write down this procedure more carefully as follows:

To move n disks from the start needle to the target needle using a helper needle:

1. If there is only one disk to move, just move it from the start to the target needle, and you are done.
2. Otherwise move the top $(n - 1)$ disks from the start needle to the helper needle (following the rules, of course).
3. Then move the bottom disk from the start to the target needle.
4. Then move the top $(n - 1)$ disks from the helper to the target needle (following the rules, of course).

Here is a method to do this, written in Java. It assumes that the method moveDisk, which moves a single disk from one needle to another, has been written elsewhere.

```java
public void recHanoi( int numDisks, int start, int target,
                      int helper ) {
    if ( numDisks == 1 ) {      // Base case
        moveDisk( numDisks, start, target ); // Move the only disk
    } else {                    // Recursive case
        recHanoi( numDisks - 1, start, helper, target );
        moveDisk( numDisks, start, target ); // Move the bottom
                                             // disk
        recHanoi( numDisks - 1, helper, target, start );
    }
}
```

We can understand this method a little better by looking at a specific example where we call recHanoi with 3 disks, where we wish to move the 3 disks from needle A to needle C while using needle B as a helper needle.

$$
\text{recHanoi}(3, A, C, B) \begin{cases} \text{recHanoi}(2, A, B, C) \Rightarrow \begin{cases} \text{recHanoi}(1, A, C, B) \Rightarrow \text{moveDisk}(1, A, C) \\ \text{moveDisk}(2, A, B) \\ \text{recHanoi}(1, C, B, A) \Rightarrow \text{moveDisk}(1, C, B) \end{cases} \\ \text{moveDisk}(3, A, C) \\ \text{recHanoi}(2, B, C, A) \Rightarrow \begin{cases} \text{recHanoi}(1, B, A, C) \Rightarrow \text{moveDisk}(1, B, A) \\ \text{moveDisk}(2, B, C) \\ \text{recHanoi}(1, A, C, B) \Rightarrow \text{moveDisk}(1, A, C) \end{cases} \end{cases}
$$

That is, a call to recHanoi(3, A, C, B) results in calls to recHanoi(2, A, B, C), moveDisk(3, A, C), and recHanoi(2, B, C, A). Each of the recursive calls of method recHanoi gets expanded. For example, the call to recHanoi(2, A, B, C) results in calls to recHanoi(1, A, C, B), moveDisk(2, A, B), and recHanoi(1, C, B, A). If we look at the order in which the moveDisk methods are executed, we see that the order of moves is:

```
moveDisk( 1, A, C )
moveDisk( 2, A, B )
moveDisk( 1, C, B )
moveDisk( 3, A, C )
moveDisk( 1, B, A )
moveDisk( 2, B, C )
moveDisk( 1, A, C )
```

This sequence of moves results in legally moving all 3 disks from needle A to needle C.

How do we know this method will work properly? Once more, we go back to our standard check list.

1. The base case of a single disk just moves it where it is supposed to go, and hence is correct.
2. The recursive case:

   * If you start with a positive number of disks, then the recursive calls to recHanoi will be with one fewer disk. Hence recursive calls will eventually get down to 1 disk, the base case.
   * If we assume that the method works for ($n - 1$) disks, then it will work for n disks. (*Can you give a convincing argument?*)

➡ EXERCISE 12.2.2

a. *We have not shown the code for the method* moveDisk. *It could either just print out a message (using* System.out.println) *describing which disk is moved from where to where, or it could result in altering a picture of needles and disks. Write out the code for the text-only version of* moveDisk.

b. *(The following program requires arrays, covered in Chapter 14) Write the code for an animated graphic version of Towers of Hanoi where there is a delay between each move of a disk. That is, let an* ActiveObject *control the animation of the algorithm. Interestingly, the code for the graphics is several times as long as the actual code for determining which disk should be moved next.* ❖

➡ EXERCISE 12.2.3

Determine how many calls of moveDisk *are required to run* recHanoi(n, A, B, C) *to completion.*

Hint: *first make a table of the number of moves for n ranging from 1 to 10. From the table, guess a formula involving n for the number of calls of* moveDisk. *Use an inductive argument similar to that given for the correctness of recursive programs to give a convincing argument that your formula is correct. If a robotic arm could move 1 disk per second, how long would it take to* *move all 64 disks from the start needle to the target needle using this algorithm? Do you now understand why the commercial version of the game only includes 8 disks?* ❖

➠ EXERCISE 12.2.4

The recursive algorithm given in the method is the most efficient solution in terms of the number of disks moved. Try to find a convincing argument for this.

Hint: *Think about what has to be the configuration in order to move the biggest disk.* ❖

12.3 Summary

In this chapter we introduced problem solving using recursion. In the first part of the chapter we described how to create recursive structures, classes that have instance variables of the same type as the entire class. Examples included collections of nested rectangles, lists of strings, and a broccoli plant. We presented the following set of rules for designing recursive structures and ensuring that the constructors and methods did what they were supposed to:

1. Define an interface with all of the methods that both base case and recursive case classes must implement.
2. Define one or more classes representing base cases. Make sure that all methods from the interface are implemented. Convince yourself that the constructors and methods work correctly.
3. Define the constructors for recursive classes. Recursive calls of the constructor should only create objects that are simpler than the one being built by the constructor. Similarly, instance variables whose types are either the interface or class should only refer to objects simpler than the one being constructed. In particular, the construction of simpler objects in the constructor body should eventually end up at a base case. Convince yourself that the constructor will be correct under the assumption that the construction of simpler objects is correct.
4. Write each method under the assumption that it works correctly on all simpler objects. Convince yourself that the methods will be correct under the assumption that instance variables hold simpler objects.

In the second part of the chapter we looked at examples of recursive methods where the complexity was measured by an integer parameter. Examples included methods for raising numbers to powers and a solution to the Towers of Hanoi problem. A slightly different set of rules was presented to help in writing and ensuring correctness of these recursive methods:

1. Write the base case. This is the case where there is no recursive call. Convince yourself that this works correctly.
2. Write the recursive case.

   ❋ Make sure all recursive calls go to simpler cases than the one you are writing. Make sure that the simpler cases will eventually get to a base case.
   ❋ Make sure that the general case will work properly if all of the recursive calls work properly.

Recursive structures and methods are extremely important in computer science. We will encounter them again when we discuss algorithms for searching and sorting in Chapter 20.

Figure 12.16   Parsley

They also play a very important role in the study of data structures and algorithms in computer science.

12.4   Chapter Review Problems

⟹   EXERCISE 12.4.1

What is wrong with the following proof by induction that in any group, all people are the same height?

Base case: If the group only has 1 person in it, then clearly every person in the group is the same height.

Induction case: Suppose that in every group with n people in it, all of the people are of the same height. Show the same is true for all groups with (n + 1) people. Let G be a group of (n + 1) people. Remove 1 person, P, from the group. Let G' denote the group still remaining. By the induction hypothesis, because G' is now a group of n people, all of the people that remain in the group are of the same height. Put person P back in the group and remove a different person, P'. Let G' denote the new group still remaining. Because there are n people in G'', by induction all of them are the same height. Thus P is the same height as everyone else in that group. Meanwhile, we already determined that P' was the same height as everyone else in G'. Thus P and P' are the same height and everyone in the original group G is the same height.

12.5 Programming Problems

EXERCISE 12.5.1

a. Write an interface and two classes that can be used to construct and drag around a bullseye target. The constructors should take as parameters the center of the circle, the radius, and a DrawingCanvas. The interface and classes should support move, moveTo, contains, and removeFromCanvas methods. If the radius is less than 5 pixels, just draw a FilledOval as the bullseye. If the radius is greater, then draw a circle and then inside of it draw a target whose radius is 4 pixels smaller.

b. Write a class extending WindowController defined so that when the user clicks on the canvas, it should draw a target with a radius of 18 pixels that is centered at the place the user clicked.

EXERCISE 12.5.2

Parsley, like broccoli, can be drawn recursively. Write a program to draw parsley as shown in Figure 12.16. New parsley branches are drawn at distances of one-third and two-thirds of the length of the stem and at its end. The lowest branch is three-fourths of the size of the main branch and is drawn at an angle of $\pi/6$ radians from that of the main branch. The next branch is drawn at two-thirds of the size of the main branch and is drawn at an angle of $-\pi/5$ to the main. The topmost branch is half of the size of the original and is at an angle of $\pi/4$ from the original.

CHAPTER (13)

General Loops in Java

In this chapter, we will take another look at loops in Java. We will begin by identifying some patterns in the use of loops in examples we have already presented. Then we will introduce a new kind of loop, the for loop, that is useful in circumstances in which you know or can calculate in advance the number of times that the loop should be executed. We next discuss a minor variant of the while loop in which the exit test for the loop is placed after the loop body rather than at the beginning. Finally, we will discuss common errors associated with loops and provide guidance on when to use each kind of loop.

13.1 Recognizing Patterns with Loops

A very important part of programming is recognizing patterns. Suppose you recognize a pattern of code usage and the context in which it is useful. Then when you recognize that you have a similar context, you can go back and reuse the pattern. For example, here is a pattern that you have seen many times:

```java
public void onMousePress( Location point ) {
    lastPoint = point;
    dragging = someShape.contains( point );
}

public void onMouseDrag( Location point ) {
    if ( dragging ) {
        ... // Do something with point and lastPoint
        lastPoint = point;
    }
}
```

We used this pattern when we were dragging things around (in that case the "Do something" involved moving some object by the difference between point and lastPoint). We saw a similar pattern when we were scribbling on the screen. In that case we drew a line between lastPoint and point, but did not need the if statement.

Here is a very similar type of pattern that you have also seen:

```
lastTime = System.currentTimeMillis();
while (...) {
    ...
    elapsedTime = System.currentTimeMillis() - lastTime;
    screenObj.move( elapsedTime*xspeed, elapsedTime*yspeed );
    ...
    lastTime = System.currentTimeMillis();
    pause(...);
}
```

This pattern showed up with active objects when we wanted to make sure that we moved each item a distance proportional to the amount of time since it was last moved.

Actually, these two patterns are really the same. They involve remembering a value before a change happens, then doing something that involves both the new and old values after the change, and then remembering the current value so it can be used after the next change occurs. The main difference between the two examples is that in the first example the initialization takes place when the mouse is pressed, while the updates take place in repeated calls to onMouseDrag. In the second example, by contrast, the initialization takes place just before entering the loop, while the updates all take place within the loop.

This notion of having to set a value before repeatedly performing an action is so common that it has even been given a name. Performing the initialization before the loop and then at the end of the loop is sometimes said to be "priming" the loop. The name has nothing to do with prime numbers; instead it has to do with the old notion of "priming a pump". The dictionary definition of "priming" includes the notion of "making ready, preparing". In the examples above, we prepare for the execution of the code that will be repeated by assigning values to lastPoint and lastTime. These values will be used during the first iteration of the repeated code. All subsequent iterations depend on the value assigned at the end of the preceding iteration. As a result the needed value is always available at the beginning of each iteration of the loop.

If you learn to recognize these patterns in code, you will be able to apply them to your own programming. The idea is that most of the time, you can use familiar techniques to accomplish whatever it is you want to do. That way you can save your time and energy for the new hard problems when you encounter them. In many of the problems in this book, the first exercises attempt to get you to recognize and apply a pattern that has just been presented, while later problems attempt to stretch your creativity and problem-solving skills to accomplish something newer and more interesting.

13.2 Counting and for Loops

In this section we introduce Java for loops. The for loop is included in Java because it captures a very common pattern found in while loops.

The conditions of loops are often based on counting. Let's look at some examples. In our falling raindrops example in Figure 9.12, we had code:

```
int dropCount = 0;
// Generate specified number of raindrops
while ( dropCount < MAX_DROPS ) {
   new FallingDroplet(
            new Location( xGenerator.nextValue(), 0 ), canvas );
   pause( DELAY_TIME );
   dropCount++;
}
```

If we carefully examine the loop in the falling raindrop example above, we can see that it has the following structure:

```
int counter = initialValue;       // Initialize
while ( counter < stopVal ) {      // Test for termination
      ...                          // Do stuff
   counter++;                      // Increment
}
```

There are many, many examples that have very similar structure. In fact, this pattern is so common that most programming languages introduce a special loop construct to make it easier to express the pattern. In Java this construct is called a for loop. It can be used for counting by writing the following:

```
for ( int counter = initialValue; counter < stopVal; counter++ ) {
   ... // Do stuff - but omit counter++ at end
}
```

The code in the parentheses consists of three parts, which are separated by semicolons:

* The first part is executed only when we first reach the for loop. It is used to initialize the counter and, in most cases, to declare the counter variable.
* The second part is a condition, just as in while statements. It is evaluated just before we execute the loop body and before each subsequent iteration of the loop. It defines the continuation condition for the loop, in this case by comparing the counter to the upper limit.
* The third part performs an update. It is executed at the *end* of each iteration of the for loop, just before testing the condition again. It is used to update the counter before the test.

It is easy to rewrite the falling raindrop example to use a for loop:

```
// Generate specified number of raindrops
for ( int dropCount = 0; dropCount < MAX_DROPS; dropCount++ ) {
   new FallingDroplet( new Location( xGenerator.nextValue(), 0 ),
                                     canvas );
   pause( DELAY_TIME );
}
```

Essentially we have taken three lines from the above while loop version and combined them into one line of the for loop version. Because we included the declaration of the counter inside the loop (the code `int dropCount` in the initialization section), `dropCount` is only available inside the loop. If you try to use `dropCount` outside of the loop, Java will claim to have never heard of a variable with that name.

Notice how the `for` construct localizes the use of the counter. This has two benefits. First, it simplifies the body of the loop so that it is somewhat easier to understand the body. More importantly, it becomes evident, in one line of code, that this is a counting loop. Once you get used to this more compact notation, you will find that its use makes it harder to forget the three key steps in writing a counting loop: initializing the counter, testing for loop exit, and incrementing the counter.

As we will see later, the variable used in the `for` loop need not be used to count the number of times through a loop. Hence we will tend to refer to the variable used in the `for` loop more generally as the loop *index*.

13.2.1 Examples of Using for Loops

Let's look at another example of a `for` loop. Suppose that we wanted to determine how much money we would have if we invested it for 10 years, gaining 5% interest each year (compounded annually). Let `amount` represent the amount of money we have invested. After one year, we would have a total of:

```
amount + amount * 5/100.0;
```

We can use a `for` loop to repeat this computation 10 times, each time updating the value of `amount` to reflect the total amount of money including the interest. Here is a method that calculates the final value of the investment for any starting value, interest rate, and number of years to invest:

```java
// Return the value of startInvestment when invested at rate
// (specified as a percentage) for the given number of years.
public double investmentValue( double startInvestment, int rate,
                               int years ) {
    double amount = startInvestment;
    for ( int yearNum = 1; yearNum <= years; yearNum++ ) {
        amount = amount + amount * rate/100.0;
    }
    return amount;
}
```

➤ EXERCISE 13.2.1

Suppose we divided by 100 rather than 100.0 above. Would it make a difference in the final answer?

➤ EXERCISE 13.2.2

Suppose the interest for the investment is compounded quarterly (four times per year) rather than annually. Rewrite the method to calculate the final amount. Assume the interest rate provided is the annual rate (e.g., it will need to be divided by four to obtain the quarterly rate).

Hint: *The index in the* `for` *loop should represent the number of quarters rather than years, and the upper bound will be an expression written in terms of* `years`.

Next, suppose we are considering different types of investments that have different interest rates associated with them. We want to determine what effect the different interest rates would have in the final value of the investment. We can write a new method that will take as parameters a lower and an upper bound on interest rates rather than a single interest rate. This new method will use the `investmentValue` method defined above to calculate the value of the investment for a series of interest rates starting at `startRate` and going up to `endRate`. The method will use `println` to display each value calculated.

```java
public void printValues( double startInvestment, int years,
                         int startRate, int endRate ) {
   for ( int rate = startRate; rate <= endRate; rate++ ) {
      System.out.println( "At "+rate+"%, the amount is: " +
            investmentValue( startInvestment, rate, years ) );
   }
}
```

Each time through the loop, we calculate and print out the value of the investment using the current value of `rate`, then increment the rate, and continue until the rate exceeds `endRate`.

Note that `rate` in the above example does not start at 0 or 1, like all of our previous loop indices did. Instead it starts at `startRate`. This is fine. We can initialize the loop index any way that we like in the first part of the `for` loop.

If we had not already written the method `investmentValue`, we might instead insert the `for` loop to calculate the value of the investment inside of the `for` loop that iterates through the possible interest rates:

```java
public void printValues( double startInvestment, int years,
                         int startRate, int endRate ) {
   for ( int rate = startRate; rate <= endRate; rate++ ) {
      double amount = startInvestment;
      for ( int yearNum = 1; yearNum <= years; yearNum++ ) {
         amount = amount + amount * rate/100.0;
      }
      System.out.println( "At "+rate+"%, the amount is: "+amount );
   }
}
```

Note that the inner `for` loop is executed all the way through each time the outer loop goes through one iteration. Thus, when the initial rate is `startRate`, the inner `for` loop is executed a total of `years` times in order to calculate an amount, which is then printed. Next, `rate` is incremented by 1, the inner loop is executed `years` times again, and the new value is printed. Notice that we would get the wrong answer if we did not reset `amount` to `startInvestment` each time we begin the outer loop, because we would start with the wrong value for `amount` with all interest rates after the first.

The example above illustrates the use of *nested* `for` loops. The notion of nesting loops should be familiar to you from Chapter 7, in which we introduced nested `while` loops. Indeed, any kind of loops may be nested. For example, we can have a `for` loop nested inside of a `while` loop or vice versa.

⇒ EXERCISE 13.2.3

With a little work some of the examples of while *loops given in Chapter 7 can be written using* for *loops. Rewrite either the* Grass *class from Figure 7.5 or the* Bricks *class from Figure 7.7 to use a simple counting* for *loop rather than a* while *loop. In each case the program will need to calculate the number of objects to be drawn.* ❖

The previous example incremented the index rate each time through the outer loop, but it was not like our other counting loops because it didn't start at 0 or 1. Here is a simple code fragment to draw a checkerboard on the screen that is an example of nested for loops that is more similar to our other counting loops:

```
for ( int row = 0; row < 8; row++ ) {
    for ( int col = 0; col < 8; col++ )  {
        FilledRect square = new FilledRect( LEFT + col*SIZE,
                                    TOP + row*SIZE, SIZE,
                                    SIZE, canvas );
        if ((row+col) % 2 == 0) {
            square.setColor( Color.RED );
        }
    }
}
```

A black-and-white picture of the output is shown in Figure 13.1.

As the outer loop iterates through successive values of row, each time the inner loop runs to completion the computer will draw an entire row of cells. For example, when row is equal to 0, the inner for loop will draw the 8 squares of row 0. Each time the inner for loop body is executed, a new FilledRect is drawn, and then possibly colored red.

The key idea that allows us to decide which squares should be red has to do with the *parity* of the sum of the loop indices. Recalling that both the row and column numbers start at 0, note that when the sum of the row and column numbers is even, the squares are red, while when the sum

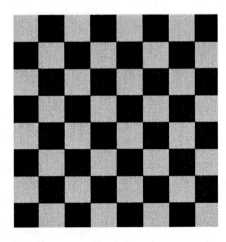

Figure 13.1 Checkerboard program output

is odd, the squares remain black. We determine whether a value is odd or even by looking at the remainder when we divide by 2, which is easily done with the % operator on integers.

Let us now examine how we compute the location of the squares. According to the program code, the location of the square in a particular row and column is (LEFT + col*SIZE, TOP + row*SIZE). Thus, when row and col are both 0, the location of the square is given by (LEFT,TOP). As we move across a row, the values of col increase by 1 for each new square. Thus the value of the *x* coordinate increases by SIZE for each successive square. Because the side of the square is SIZE units wide, successive squares will be adjacent from left to right. Similarly, when moving to the next row, the value of row will increase by 1, resulting in a *y* coordinate that also increases by SIZE. Because the height of each square is SIZE, again successive rows will be adjacent.

13.2.2   Other Variations on for Loops

The for loop in the interest example incremented the index by 1 each time through the loop, but didn't start at 0 or 1. Other variations are also possible. For example, we might want to write a counting loop that could *count down* instead of up. To do this, we would initialize the counting variable with the largest value desired, decrease the loop variable at each step, and use a condition that checks for the smallest value desired rather than the largest. To illustrate this, the loop shown below prints out the numbers 10, 9, 8, ..., 1 on successive lines and then prints "Blast off!":

```
for ( int countdown = 10; countdown >= 1; countdown-- ) {
    System.out.println( countdown );
}
System.out.println( "Blast off!" );
```

Recall that index-- results in decreasing the value of index by 1.

We can also increment the loop index by other values. For example, Exercise 13.2.3 above asked you to rewrite the Grass class from Figure 7.5 using for loops. We suggested that you start by calculating the number of blades of grass to be drawn. There is, however, another alternative. If we can increase or decrease the loop index by values different from 1, then we no longer need to calculate the number of blades of grass to draw. Here is the code fragment to draw the class using a for loop, where each time through the loop, the loop index, bladePosition, is increased by GRASS_SPACING:

```
for ( int bladePosition = 0;
        bladePosition < canvas.getWidth();
        bladePosition = bladePosition + GRASS_SPACING ) {
    new Line( bladePosition, GRASS_TOP,
            bladePosition, GROUND_LINE, canvas );
}
```

In the code above, we spread out the for loop header into three separate lines for readability—recall that Java does not care about line breaks. The initialization code for bladePosition and the test are as usual. However, in the third position we now have a regular assignment statement. This is perfectly legal, as the third slot in a for loop header may be any simple statement (e.g., increment or decrement statement, assignment statement, method invocation, or new object creation).

Though we will not provide examples here, it is also possible to have more complex conditions in the second position in the for loop header. The for loop is an exceptionally flexible statement, but you are better off using it in relatively simple ways so as not to confuse the reader. If your for loop header is becoming too complex, consider replacing it by a while loop.

In summary, the general syntax of the for loop is:

```
for ( initialization; condition; update ) {
    statements to be repeated
}
```

where initialization is executed at the beginning of the loop only, update is a simple statement that is executed at the end of each iteration of the loop, and condition is a boolean-valued expression that is executed before each iteration of the loop, just as in the following generalized while loop:

```
initialization
while ( condition ) {
    statements to be repeated
    update
}
```

Note that if condition is false after the initialization code is executed, then the body of the loop will never be executed. Instead program execution will begin with the next executable statement after the loop.

13.3   The do-while Loop

Both the while and for loops always check the condition expression before executing the body of the loop. However, there are times when we want to execute the body of a loop at least once, no matter what. In those circumstances, the check of the termination condition before executing the loop body is at best a waste of time, and at worst may result in incorrect early termination if the loop condition fails inadvertantly when evaluated before executing the loop body for the first time.

To help the programmer avoid such errors, Java includes a do-while statement. The general syntax is:

```
do {
    statements to be repeated
} while ( condition )
```

The do-while statement differs from the while statement by moving the while (condition) clause after the loop body, signalling that the condition is only evaluated *after* the body of the loop has been executed.

Recall the program to play the game of craps from Figure 4.10. That particular program depended on the user to click each time he or she wanted to roll the dice. This could be quite

```
// Class that allows a user to play the game of craps
public class Craps extends WindowController {
    // Locations for textual displays
    private static final Location STATUS_POS = new Location( 10, 70 );
    private static final Location MESSAGE_POS = new Location( 10, 50 );
    // Generator for roll of a die
    private RandomIntGenerator dieGenerator = new RandomIntGenerator( 1, 6 );
    private Text status,        // Display status of game
                 message;       // Display dice roll value
    private int point;          // Number to roll for win

    // Create status message on canvas
    public void begin() {
        status = new Text( " ", STATUS_POS, canvas );
        message = new Text( " ", MESSAGE_POS, canvas );
    }

    // For each click, roll the dice until the game is over and report the results
    public void onMouseClick( Location pt ) {
        // Get values for both dice and display sum
        int roll = dieGenerator.nextValue() + dieGenerator.nextValue();
        message.setText( "You rolled a " + roll + "!" );

        // Starting a new game
        if ( roll == 7 || roll == 11 ) {  // 7 or 11 wins on first throw
            status.setText( "You win!" );
        } else if ( roll == 2 || roll == 3 || roll == 12 ) {  // 2, 3, or 12 loses
            status.setText( "You lose!" );
        } else {                      // Set the roll to be the new point to be made
            status.setText( "Try for your point!" );
            point = roll;
            int rollNum = 1;
            do {
                roll = dieGenerator.nextValue() + dieGenerator.nextValue();
                rollNum++;
            } while ( roll != point && roll != 7 );
            if ( roll == point ) {
                status.setText( "You win after "+rollNum+" rolls!" );
            } else {
                status.setText( "You lose after "+rollNum+" rolls!" );
            }
        }
    }
}
```

Figure 13.2   Craps class illustrating do-while loops

fatiguing to the user. It might make more sense to have the user click to initiate the game, but then have the computer continue to "roll the dice" until the player wins or loses. The code for the revised class can be found in Figure 13.2. This version of the program uses a do-while loop, because it makes no sense to check to see if the player won until after the program generates a value of roll.

Suppose the inner do-while loop were replaced with a while loop with exactly the same condition and the same loop body. Explain why the program would not work correctly. ❖

13.4   Avoiding Loop Errors

When a loop is executed, a block of code is generally executed multiple times without user intervention. As a result, it is easy to make errors that are hard to track down. In this section we enumerate some of the most common errors associated with loops.

Off-by-one errors

The counting for loops used as examples in this chapter all have the following structure:

```
for ( int counter = 0; counter < MAX_COUNT; counter++ ) { ... }
```

The body of such a loop is executed exactly MAX_COUNT times. It is easy to write a minor variation of this and end up with the count off by one. For example, if counter is initialized to 1 rather than 0, the loop will only be executed MAX_COUNT - 1 times. On the other hand if the condition is written as counter <= MAX_COUNT rather than counter < MAX_COUNT, then the loop will be executed MAX_COUNT + 1 times.

However, if the loop is written as:

```
for ( int counter = 1; counter <= MAX_COUNT; counter++ ) { ... }
```

then it will again be executed exactly MAX_COUNT times. While both forms execute the loop body the appropriate number of times, many Java programmers prefer the first form. The reasons will become most clear when using for loops with arrays. The main thing is to develop a consistent style for writing for loops, as then errors are less likely to result.

Infinite loops

While loop bodies are designed to be executed repeatedly, it is usually not desirable to have them execute without termination. Unfortunately, it is easy to make mistakes that result in a loop's never terminating properly.

One simple mistake is to change an increasing index to be decreasing, but to forget to change the termination condition. For instance, the first example in this section might be changed to:

```
for ( int counter = MAX_COUNT - 1; counter < MAX_COUNT;
      counter-- ) { ... }
```

Because the programmer forgot to change the exit condition to counter >= 0, the condition will never become false, and the loop will continue until the user quits the program.

Another simple mistake is to forget to update variables after the execution of a loop. For example, suppose we tried writing one of the earlier loops in this chapter, but forgot to update a critical variable:

```
int dropCount = 0;
// Generate specified number of raindrops
while ( dropCount < MAX_DROPS ) {
    new FallingDroplet( new Location( xGenerator.nextValue(), 0 ),
                        canvas );
    pause( DELAY_TIME );
}
```

Because we omitted the statement dropCount++ from the end of the loop body, the condition never becomes false. Errors like these are quite hard to track down, so always examine your loop constructions carefully before running your programs. Of course, using a for loop in this example makes it harder to forget to update the critical variable.

Several tricky errors can arise as a result of accidental misuse of semicolons and braces. It is our practice to always include braces around the statements controlled by a loop or if statement. As a result, you may have come to think of the braces as part of the loop or if statement. In fact, according to the technical rules of Java's grammar, braces do not need to be included in loops or if statements. In Java, a while or for loop header is applied to the first logical statement that follows the header. When writing loops that require multiple steps, placing braces around a group of statements tells Java to treat those statements as a block, which functions as a single logical statement. Very confusing errors can result if such braces are omitted or misplaced.

Consider the following incorrect version of the loop to create FallingDroplets:

```
int dropCount = 0;
// Generate specified number of raindrops
while ( dropCount < MAX_DROPS )
    new FallingDroplet( new Location( xGenerator.nextValue(), 0 ),
                        canvas );
    pause( DELAY_TIME );
    dropCount++;
```

This time, we have included the statement dropCount++ but omitted the pair of braces that should be placed before the FallingDroplet construction and after the statement to increment dropCount. Even though we have indented these statements to suggest that they are intended to be the body of the loop, without any braces, Java will assume that we only want to consider the first statement, the FallingDroplet construction, as part of the loop. As a result, this loop will never pause or increment dropCount. Since dropCount never changes, the loop will never end. Of course, omitting the braces is just the most extreme mistake one can make when placing the braces that should surround a loop's body. Any misplacement of these braces is almost certain to lead to a serious error.

Another difficult error to track down results if the programmer accidentally adds a semicolon after the header of a `while` or `for` loop. Look at the following code:

```
int dropCount = 0;
// Generate specified number of raindrops
while ( dropCount < MAX_DROPS ); {
    new FallingDroplet( new Location( xGenerator.nextValue(), 0 ),
                        canvas );
    pause( DELAY_TIME );
    dropCount++;
}
```

In this case, the statements intended to form the loop body will never be executed at all. Java interprets that semicolon as indicating the end of the `while` loop. Technically it inserts an empty statement before the semicolon—a statement that has no effect. As a result, the `while` loop executes that empty statement as the loop body. Executing this empty statement repeatedly never changes the value of `dropCount`. Therefore, the loop will never stop.

If you accidentally place a semicolon after the header of a `for` loop, you get slightly different erroneous behavior. Look at the following code:

```
for ( int counter = 0; counter < MAX_COUNT; counter++ ) ;
{ some code }
```

In this case the empty statement before the semicolon will be executed exactly MAX_COUNT times. At that point the loop will finish, and the statements in "some code" will be executed exactly once. No infinite loop results, but the resulting behavior is certainly not what was desired.

Using doubles in termination conditions

We indicated earlier that it is dangerous to use `doubles` in comparisons because of round-off errors. This warning is especially important in the use of comparisons involving doubles as the condition in loops. Consider the following code:

```
for ( double index = 1.0; index < 5.0; index = index + 1./3. ) {
    System.out.println( "Index is " + index );
}
```

This is a pretty trivial loop that starts with `index` having value 1.0. The value of `index` is increased by the value of `1./3.` each time through the loop as long as `index` is less than 5.0. You would expect that the last value of `index` printed out would be something like 4.6666666..., but you would be wrong. Here is what was printed out during the execution of this loop:

```
Index is 1.0
Index is 1.3333333333333333
Index is 1.6666666666666665
Index is 1.999999999999998
Index is 2.333333333333333
Index is 2.6666666666666665
```

```
Index is 3.0
Index is 3.3333333333333335
Index is 3.666666666666667
Index is 4.0
Index is 4.333333333333333
Index is 4.666666666666666
Index is 4.99999999999999
```

One can see that the last significant digit of `index` is not always what might have been expected. However, even more importantly, the last value printed was a number incredibly close to 5.0, not 4 2/3. Because the last value of `index` was a tiny fraction less than 5.0, the loop executed one more time than was expected.

What is the solution? First, try to avoid having the condition of a loop depend on the value of a `double`. If that must be the case, avoid using `==` (using that in the above example would have resulted in an infinite loop!), and instead use a comparison in which you have built in a "fudge factor" that will compensate for any round-off errors due to the representation of `double`s in computer memory. For example, the condition of the `for` loop above could have been changed to `index < 4.9`, because the expected last value will certainly be less than `4.9`, yet the difference between the last expected value (4 2/3) and the test bound is much greater than any round-off error.

13.5   Summary

In this chapter we covered Java's three general loop structures. They are the `while` loop, which was also introduced in Chapter 7, the `do-while` loop, and the `for` loop.

The general structure of the `while` loop is:

```
while ( condition ) {
   statements to be repeated
}
```

The *condition* is checked each time *before* executing the loop body. When it is `false`, execution of the loop terminates and the statement after the loop is executed. Thus if the condition is `false` the first time that it is checked, then the loop body will not be executed at all.

The general structure of the `do-while` loop is:

```
do {
    statements to be repeated
} while ( condition )
```

The *condition* is checked each time *after* executing the loop body. When it is `false`, execution of the loop terminates, and the statement after the loop is executed. If the condition is `false` the first time that it is checked, then the loop body will have been executed exactly once.

The general structure of a `for` statement is the following:

```
for ( initialization; condition; update ) {
   statements to be repeated
}
```

* The *initialization* part is executed only once, when we first reach the for loop.
* The *condition* is checked before each iteration, including the first one.
* The *update* part is executed after each iteration, before testing the condition.

While any one of the loop constructs can be used to emulate any of the others, some general guidelines can be helpful in determining which type of loop to use. A for loop should be used instead of a while loop when

* The number of times that the loop body should be executed can be determined before beginning execution of the loop
* The initialization, condition, and update all are expressed in terms of the same variable.
* The variable is not modified elsewhere in the loop.
* It is correct to do the update command as the last step in executing the body of the loop.

While these conditions may seem very restrictive, there are many cases in which they all hold and a for loop is the most appropriate loop construct.

In most other cases, the while loop is to be preferred. The one exception is when the loop body should always be executed at least once. In that case a do-while loop should generally be used.

13.6 Chapter Review Problems

⟹ EXERCISE 13.6.1

The following method is meant to determine whether a given number, passed in as a parameter, is prime (i.e., divisible only by itself and 1).

```
// Determines whether an integer greater than 1 is prime
public boolean isPrime( int n ) {
    int divisor = n;
    boolean evenlyDivisible = false;
    while ( divisor > 1 && !evenlyDivisible ) {
        evenlyDivisible = ((n % divisor) == 0);
        divisor--;
    }
    return !evenlyDivisible;
}
```

The main idea behind the method is to determine whether the number is evenly divisible by any number less than itself. Unfortunately, it doesn't quite accomplish what it is meant to do.

a. *Simulate the method to see what happens when the value passed in is 7.*
b. *Identify and correct the error in the method.*

⟳➡ EXERCISE 13.6.2

The following method is meant to calculate n! (n factorial), which is defined as follows: if n is 0, then n! is 1. For all integers greater than 0, n! = n(n − 1)(n − 2)...(1).

```java
// Returns n! for n >= 0
public int factorial( int n ) {
    int result = 1;
    for ( int counter = 1; counter < n; counter++ ) {
        result = result * counter;
    }
    return result;
}
```

Unfortunately, the method doesn't quite accomplish what it is meant to do.

a. Simulate the method to see what happens when the value passed in is 4. The result returned by the method should be 24.

b. What went wrong? Identify and correct the error in the method.

⟳➡ EXERCISE 13.6.3

Write a **for** loop that will print the two-times table, from 2 × 1 through 2 × 10.

⟳➡ EXERCISE 13.6.4

Write a pair of nested **for** loops that print the multiplication tables for 1 through 10.

⟳➡ EXERCISE 13.6.5

Write a pair of nested **for** loops that will print the following triangular pattern:

```
1
2 2
3 3 3
4 4 4 4
5 5 5 5 5
6 6 6 6 6 6
7 7 7 7 7 7 7
```

13.7 Programming Problems

⟳➡ EXERCISE 13.7.1

Rewrite the program that draws a simple brick wall that is given in Figure 7.14. This time use nested **for** loops, rather than nested **while** loops.

⟁➡ EXERCISE 13.7.2

If you were asked to calculate the natural logarithm (ln) of a number greater than 0 and less than or equal to 2, you would undoubtedly press the ln button on your calculator. An alternative would be to find its value as follows.

$$ln(n) = (n - 1) - 1/2(n - 1)^2 + 1/3(n - 3)^3 - 1/4(n - 1)^4 + 1/5(n - 1)^5 \ldots$$

The more terms you include in your calculation, the more precise your answer will be. Write a method that will return ln(n) to a specified precision. That is, your method should take two parameters, n and a positive integer that gives the number of terms to be included in the calculation.

⟁➡ EXERCISE 13.7.3

Write a program that will simulate the roll of a die to determine which of two players goes first in a game. When the user clicks the mouse, the program should print a message on the canvas saying whether player 1 or player 2 is to go first. Since it is possible that both players will roll the die and get the same value, the process might have to be repeated before there is a clear winner. Use a do ... while *loop here.*

CHAPTER 14

Arrays

I f you look down at the bottom of the page you are reading, you will find a number. Page numbers are very handy. We don't think about them much, but without them, it would be harder to use a text book like this one. You wouldn't be able to look things up in the index. The table of contents would be much less useful as well.

Pages aren't the only things that it is helpful to number. Obviously, in this text we also number the chapters and sections. If this were a really important book (like the Bible or a play by Shakespeare), then individual lines or verses would be numbered. If someone asked you what year it was or what time it was, the answers would involve numbers. If you were asked what day it was, on the other hand, you might answer "the 25th" or you might answer "Tuesday". Your answer would depend on whether you thought you were being asked about the day of the week or the day of the month. This reveals a little bit more about how we use numbers to identify things. When we are dealing with small collections, like the seven days of the week, we use a distinct name for each member of the collection. For larger collections, like the days of the month or the pages in this book, numbering seems much handier.

The same turns out to be true in computer programs. When writing programs that manipulate relatively small collections of data, we can associate each item with a distinct instance variable. On the other hand, when writing a program that manipulates a large collection of similar data items, it is often useful to be able to simply number the items instead of using a distinct name for each item. In Java, and many other programming languages, this is accomplished using the feature we will describe in this chapter, the *array*.

An array is a collection of primitive values or objects. Each member of the collection is associated with a number called its *index*. To use a member of an array in a program, the index value associated with the desired member must be provided. This can be done by explicitly writing the number in the program or by using a formula involving variables, constants, and arithmetic operations. We can vary which elements of an array are accessed as the program is running by varying the values of the expressions that specify array index values. This makes arrays a powerful programming tool.

In this chapter, we will explain how to declare names that refer to arrays, how to create arrays, and how to make associations between index values and members of an array. Then we will look at a variety of common techniques for processing the information kept in an array.

14.1 Declaring Array Names

When we use numbers to identify members of a collection, we usually have to specify the collection we have in mind. For example, if we told you to read 12 of this book, you would not know what we were talking about. We would have to be more specific and tell you to read page 12 or Chapter 12 (or even Section 12 of a particular chapter). Similarly, in Java, to use an array we need a name that will refer to the entire collection of elements in the array. To access an element of an array, the programmer places the number of the desired element after the name of the array itself surrounded by square brackets. Thus if page were the name of an array used to hold String values corresponding to the pages of a book, one could say

```
page[12]
```

to access the 12th element of the collection of pages.

Like other names in Java programs, array names must be declared before they can be used. An array name can be declared as an instance variable, as a parameter, or as a local variable. The notation used to declare an array name combines the square brackets used to refer to elements of the array with the element type of the array. For example, to declare page as the name of an array of String values, one could say

```
private String [ ] page;
```

The name page could then be used to refer to an entire collection of strings.[1] By contrast, the declaration

```
private String firstPage;
```

would declare firstPage as a name that could only be used to refer to a single string.

Note that choosing a good name for an array is a bit tricky. The declaration shown makes the name page refer to a whole collection of pages, suggesting that pages might be a better choice. When referring to a single element of the collection, however, you have to use the name of the collection together with an index value. In this context, saying page[12] makes more sense than saying pages[12].

The fact that the name String appears in these declarations raises an important point. In Java, all the elements of a single array must be of the same type. You cannot have an array whose

---

[1] To be flexible, Java allows you to place the square brackets that appear in the declaration of an array name either after the type or after the name being declared. Thus, the declaration shown above could have been written as

```
private String page[ ];
```

Throughout this text, we will use the first form, placing the square brackets immediately after the type in array declaration. The spaces before and between the square braces are also optional. That is, Java will also accept a declaration of the form

```
private String[] page;
```

first element is a number, whose second element is a `String`, and whose third element is a `FilledRect`. On the other hand, you can work with arrays of any type you need. Thus, in a program that drew checkers on a checkerboard you might declare an array

```
private FilledOval [ ] piece;
```

to refer to a collection of ovals that represent the pieces on the board.

14.2 Creating an Array

The declaration of the array `piece` shown above introduces a name that can be used to refer to a collection of `FilledOval`s. This declaration alone, however, does not create the collection or any of the ovals that represent the checker pieces. Instead, we must create the array using a construction and assign this new object as the meaning of the name `piece`. Then, in addition, we will need to construct the individual ovals that represent the checkers and use assignments to add these ovals to the collection represented by the array. In general, the construction of an array is a separate step from the declaration of an array name, and the construction of an array is separate from the construction of the members of the collection it represents.

The construction of an array is simple. All that Java needs to know is the type of items that will be members of the array and the total size of the collection the array will represent. In the case of our checkers example, the elements of the array will be `FilledOval`s and the size of the collection will be 24, the number of pieces placed on the board when a game of checkers begins. The construction for our checkers example would therefore be

```
new FilledOval[24]
```

As in other constructions, an array construction starts with the word `new`. Next, we specify the type of the items that will be placed in the array. Finally, we must provide the size of the collection surrounded by square brackets.

Typically, such a construction would be used to associate an array with an array name. This can be done in an assignment statement such as

```
piece = new FilledOval[24];
```

It is also common to use array constructions as initial values in array name declarations. For example, an array of `String`s intended to hold the text of the pages of a book might be defined as

```
private String [ ] page = new String[723];
```

assuming the book had 723 pages.

Remember that the construction of an array does not create the elements of the collection. It only creates the array itself. Thus, after the assignment

```
piece = new FilledOval[24];
```

we will have an array, but no `FilledOval`s. At this point, we have not told Java what `FilledOval` to associate with `piece[3]` or any of the other possible index values. When the `piece` array is first constructed, `piece[3]` and all the other elements of the array are associated with the special value `null`. Trying to execute a statement such as

```
piece[3].setColor( Color.RED );
```

at this point would produce a null pointer exception.

Assignment statements are used to associate members of an array with index values just as they are used to associate values with simple variables. Thus, if the construction

```
new FilledOval( checkerLeft, checkerTop,
                SIZE, SIZE, canvas )
```

created an oval appropriate to represent a checker on the board, the assignment

```
piece[3] = new FilledOval( checkerLeft, checkerTop,
                           SIZE, SIZE, canvas );
```

could be used to add this element to the `piece` array and associate it with the index value 3. Once such an assignment had been executed, an instruction such as

```
piece[3].setColor( Color.RED );
```

could be used successfully to make that particular checker red.

This simple example illustrates a fact that is key to understanding how to use arrays. In every assignment statement we have seen up to this point, the item to the left of the equal sign has been a variable. In this example, we have instead used the phrase `piece[3]`, a combination composed of an array name and an index value. In fact, an array name followed by an index value is called an *indexed variable* and can be used in any context where a variable of the array's element type could be used. When discussing a program we will "pronounce" `piece[3]` as "piece indexed by 3".[2]

All Java arrays use 0 as the first index value, and the last usable index is always one less than the size of the array. So `piece[3]`, in fact, refers to the fourth array element.

Thus far, our examples of array names and constructions have all involved arrays whose elements were objects. It is possible to use arrays to hold collections of values like `int`s and `double`s that are not objects of any class. For example, to create an array that could hold a collection of 24 integers rather than 24 `FilledOval`s, we would say

```
new int[24]
```

Arrays composed of `int`s or other primitive types are initialized somewhat differently from arrays whose elements are objects of a class. The special value `null` is not the default value for the elements of a new `int` array. Instead, all the elements of an `int` array are initially associated with 0, the same value that is associated by default with an uninitialized instance variable of type `int`.

---

[2] It is also common to use the term *subscripted variables* for what we will call indexed variables, since the array mechanisms in Java and other programming languages are rooted in the use of subscripted variables, like a_0, in mathematical notation. As a result, many programmers read `piece[3]` as "piece sub 3".

14.2.1   Array Initializers

There is a way to combine the creation of an array and the association of values with its elements into a single step. This is done by including an *array initializer* in the declaration of the array's name. An array initializer is a list of the values to be associated with the array's elements separated from one another by commas and surrounded by the curly braces "{" and "}". An array initializer constructs an array containing exactly the number of values specified in the initializer list.

For example, in a program that worked with calendar dates, it might be handy to have a list of the number of days in each month of the year. We could declare an array name for such an array, create the array and initialize its elements with the single line

```
private int [ ] monthLength = {31, 28, 31, 30, 31, 30, 31, 31,
                               30, 31, 30, 31};
```

Given this declaration, `monthLength[0]` would equal 31, the number of days in January, `monthLength[1]` would equal 28, the number of days in a non-leap-year February, and so on. A reference to `monthLength[12]` or any other element with a larger index value than 12 would lead to a program error.

The use of array initializers is not limited to `int` arrays. For example, if we wanted to create an array to hold a list of the names of the months we could use the declaration

```
private String [ ] monthName =  { "January", "February", "March",
                                  "April", "May", "June", "July",
                                  "August", "September", "October",
                                  "November", "December" };
```

➠ EXERCISE 14.2.1

Provide an instance variable declaration for each of the names suggested in the following list. Include an initial value specification that associates the name with an appropriately constructed array. For example, if asked to declare `dailyTemp` *as a name that could refer to a list of the high temperature readings for every day of a given year, an appropriate answer would be:*

```
private double [ ] dailyTemp = new double[365];
```

a. *Provide a declaration for* `cityPopulation`, *an array used to hold the current populations of each of the 20 most populous cities in the world.*
b. *Provide a declaration for* `scenes`, *an array used to hold the text of each of the scenes in Shakespeare's play The Comedy of Errors.*
   Hint: *The play has eleven scenes.*
c. *Provide a declaration for* `star`, *an array used to refer to 10 line segments drawn to make a 5-pointed star on the screen.*
d. *Provide a declaration for* `planets`, *an array used to refer to nine* `FilledOvals` *drawn on the screen to represent the nine planets in the solar system.*
e. *Provide a declaration for* `planetName`, *an array used to refer to the names of the nine planets in the solar system. Include in the declaration an array initializer to associate the name with an array containing* `Strings` *equal to the names of the planets.*

⟶ EXERCISE 14.2.2

Consider the drawing of a diamond shown below:

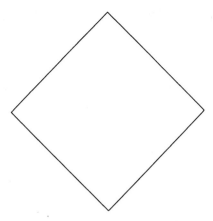

a. *Provide a declaration for* diamond, *a name that could be used to refer to an array including the four* Lines *needed to make this drawing. In your declaration, include an array construction that initializes the name* diamond *to refer to an appropriate array object.*

b. *Write the four assignment statements needed to create the diamond drawing and to associate the four lines drawn with the names* diamond[0], diamond[1], diamond[2], *and* diamond[3]. *Assume that the diamond is drawn to just fit within a 200-by-200-pixel window.*

c. *Suppose that we wanted to make the drawing a bit more colorful by making the top two* Lines *of the diamond red. Show the two invocations that would be required to make this color change, assuming the* diamond *array has been initialized by the assignments you provided for part (b).* ❖

14.3 Using Arrays: A Triangle Class

In the preceding sections, we have explained how to declare an array name, how to construct an array, how to associate a newly constructed array with an array name, and how to refer to a single element of an array. This is really all there is to learn about arrays in Java. At this point, however, you probably have little or no idea how to actually use an array in a program. To develop this ability, you need to become familiar with the patterns and strategies an experienced programmer employs when using arrays. In this and the remaining sections of this chapter, we will examine three extended examples of class definitions using arrays that illustrate important techniques frequently used when programming with arrays.

As a first example, suppose you wanted to write a program that involved drawing triangles on the screen. There are no classes included in objectdraw or the standard Java libraries designed to draw triangles. We could simply draw triangles by creating three Lines for the edges of each triangle, but if triangles play a significant role in a program, it would make good sense to define a new class that makes it as convenient to work with a triangle as it is to work with a FilledRect or FramedOval.

Within such a Triangle class, we would need instance variables to refer to the three Lines that make up the triangle. We could define three independent variables with names like edge1, edge2, and edge3. It would be better, however, to define an array of three Lines to keep track of the edges. The following declaration could be used to introduce such an array:

```
private Line [ ] edge = new Line[3];
```

This declaration states that we plan to use the name edge to refer to a collection of 3 Lines. The indexed variables edge[0], edge[1], and edge[2] can be used to refer to the Lines in the collection. Note that the first indexed variable is edge[0] rather than edge[1]. Remember that all Java arrays use 0 as the first index value, and the last usable index value is always one less than the size of the array.

The above declaration of edge does not actually create the Lines that make up the triangle. Initially, edge[0], edge[1], and edge[2] will all have null as their values. Code will be included in the constructor for the Triangle class to create three Lines and associate them with elements of the array.

The simplest way to describe a triangle is to provide the coordinates of its three vertices. We will therefore define the constructor for our Triangle class to expect four parameters: three Locations describing the vertices together with the canvas. These parameters will be used within the constructor to create the Lines that make up the triangle and associate them with elements of the edge array. A fragment of the complete Triangle class including such a constructor is shown in Figure 14.1. Figure 14.2 shows the triangle that would be drawn if this constructor were invoked with the Locations (100,50), (50,150), and (250,50) as parameters. The figure also shows the relationship between the array edge and the Lines displayed on the screen. Arrows are included to indicate which of the Lines would be associated with each array entry.

```
public class Triangle {

    private Line [ ] edge = new Line[3];

    public Triangle( Location vert1, Location vert2, Location vert3,
                     DrawingCanvas canvas ) {
        edge[0] = new Line( vert1, vert2, canvas );
        edge[1] = new Line( vert2, vert3, canvas );
        edge[2] = new Line( vert3, vert1, canvas );
    }

    // additional method declarations
    ...
}
```

Figure 14.1   Constructor for the Triangle class

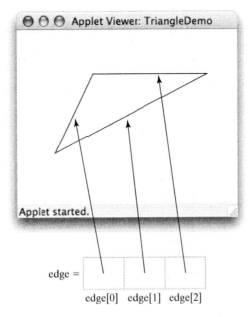

edge =

edge[0]   edge[1]   edge[2]

Figure 14.2   Elements of the edge array refer to components of a Triangle

```
public void hide() {
    edge[0].hide();
    edge[1].hide();
    edge[2].hide();
}
```

Figure 14.3   A straightforward implementation of the hide method for Triangles

The Triangle class should include implementations of methods like move, setColor, and hide that are associated with the graphics classes included in the objectdraw library. One of the easiest of these methods to implement is hide. We can implement hide by simply using the three indexed variables edge[0], edge[1], and edge[2], much as we might have used three simple variables that refer to the edges of the triangle. The definition of hide we would produce in this way is shown in Figure 14.3.

The value we include in an indexed variable does not have to be an integer constant. We can instead use a variable or any other expression that describes an int that identifies the desired element of the array. For example, if edgeNum is an int variable, then we can say

```
edge[edgeNum].hide();
```

We can use this to help us write an alternate version of hide that takes advantage of the fact that the edges are gathered together in an array. If we include the statement

```
edge[edgeNum].hide();
```

```
public void hide() {
    for ( int edgeNum = 0; edgeNum < edge.length; edgeNum++ ) {
        edge[edgeNum].hide( );
    }
}
```

Figure 14.4   Using a loop to implement the hide method for Triangles

in a loop that varies the value of edgeNum from 0 to 2, execution of the loop will hide all three edges. A version of hide implemented using this approach is shown in Figure 14.4.

The condition that determines when the for loop in Figure 14.4 terminates takes advantage of a feature of arrays we have not previously discussed. The name of an array variable followed by .length produces the number of elements in the array. Therefore, in this code edgeNum < edge.length is equivalent to edgeNum < 3. This ensures that the loop is executed once for each edge of the triangle.

Comparing the versions of hide in Figures 14.3 and 14.4, it may not be immediately obvious that using a loop to write hide is desirable. The code that uses the loop is initially harder to understand than the first version of hide. Using a loop, however, makes the code more flexible. Suppose that instead of defining a triangle class, we had decided to define a class that drew hexagons. The name edge would have to be associated with an array of six Lines instead of three. The code in the constructor of the Hexagon class would create six Lines and associate them with the elements of the array. The definition of the hide method shown in Figure 14.4, however, could be used in the Hexagon class without any changes. Futhermore, of course, the same loop could also be used for octagons or figures with even more edges. This illustrates the advantage of using arrays. Loops that are quite short and simple can describe the processing of large collections of objects.

The loop in Figure 14.4 is a simple representative of a very common form of array-processing loop, a loop designed to apply some operation to every element of an array. The general form of such loops is

```
for ( int elementPosition = 0; elementPosition < array.length;
        elementPosition++ ) {
    // perform desired operation on array[ elementPosition ]
    ...
}
```

To provide additional examples of the use of such loops, we have included definitions of the move and show methods for our Triangle class in Figure 14.5. Like the definition of the hide method, the loops in these methods use edge.length to determine how often the loop body should be repeated. As a result, like the hide method, identical code could be used to define these methods in a Hexagon or Octagon class.

The graphic classes in the objectdraw library provide methods through which one can obtain information about the position and dimensions of an object. For example, methods like getLocation, getWidth, and getHeight allow one to obtain a complete description of a FilledRect. To provide a similar feature for our Triangle class, we would like to define a method named getVertices that will return the Locations of all three vertices of

```
public void move( double dx, double dy ) {
    for ( int edgeNum = 0; edgeNum < edge.length; edgeNum++ ) {
        edge[edgeNum].move( dx, dy );
    }
}

public void show() {
    for ( int edgeNum = 0; edgeNum < edge.length; edgeNum++ ) {
        edge[edgeNum].show();
    }
}
```

Figure 14.5 Methods to move and show Triangles

```
public Location [ ] getVertices() {
    Location [ ] result = new Location[edge.length];

    for ( int edgeNum = 0; edgeNum < edge.length; edgeNum++ ) {
        result[edgeNum] = edge[edgeNum].getStart();
    }
    return result;
}
```

Figure 14.6 Definition of the getVertices method

a Triangle. A method, however, can only return a single result. Therefore, rather than returning the Locations themselves, our method will return an array containing the Locations of the three vertices.

The code for getVertices is shown in Figure 14.6. This method is yet another example in which we use a loop to perform a simple operation on every element of an array. In this case, the operation is to use the getStart method of the Line class to extract one of the triangle's vertices from each of the Lines that are its edges.

A more interesting aspect of this method is that it returns an array as its result. The getVertices method is the first example we have seen that uses this ability. In Java, arrays are objects. There are certain operations one can perform with objects of any class in Java. You can define names and associate them with objects of any type. You can write methods that return objects of any type. Finally, it is also possible to pass any object, including an entire array, as a parameter to a method.

➡ EXERCISE 14.3.1

Provide a definition for a setColor *method for the* Triangle *class discussed in this section. Use a loop as shown in the implementations of the* move *and* show *methods in Figure 14.5.*

EXERCISE 14.3.2

In the preceding section, we suggested that many of the methods written for our Triangle *class could be used without change in classes that drew other kinds of polygons. The only difference between these classes and our* Triangle *class would be the way in which the* edge *array was initialized and the definition of the constructor.*

Next to a triangle, the simplest form of polygon is a rectangle. There already are rectangle classes included in objectdraw, but for this problem we would like you to consider how you could define a rectangle class of your own named MyownFramedRect. *In particular:*

a. *Show how to declare and initialize the* edge *array variable.*
b. *Show the code for the constructor. Assume that the parameters to the constructor will be identical to those used by the common* FramedRect *constructor: the x and y coordinates of the corner, the width and height, and the canvas.*

EXERCISE 14.3.3

We were able to implement all the methods in the Triangle *class using loops. In the constructor, however, it was not possible to use a loop, because we passed the vertices of the triangle to the constructor as three separate* Location *parameters. An alternate way to define the constructor is to have the vertices passed as a single array of* Locations. *The header for this new constructor would then be*

```
public Triangle( Location [ ] vertex, DrawingCanvas canvas )
```

This would make it possible to write the constructor's body using a loop. Show how to complete the definition of the constructor in this way.

Hint: *You may find it handy to use the modulo operator, %.*

14.4 Enhanced for loop in Java 1.5

Java 1.5 includes an *enhanced for loop* that will make it easier to iterate through collections of objects, including arrays.

For example, consider the hide method of the Triangle class that is presented in Figure 14.4. The code given there is:

```
public void hide() {
    for ( int edgeNum = 0; edgeNum < edge.length; edgeNum++ ) {
        edge[edgeNum].hide( );
    }
}
```

where edge is an array of Line with size 3.

Java 1.5's enhanced `for` loop will allow programmers to write this in a more compact form where they will not need to deal with the indices of the array:

```
public void hide() {
    for ( Line nextLine: edge ) {
        nextLine.hide( );
    }
}
```

This code results in exactly the same actions as the one given earlier, but allows the user to write the code more compactly. The line:

```
for ( Line nextLine: edge ) {
```

declares `nextLine` as a variable representing the individual elements of `edge`. We would read this new version of the complete `for` loop as "for each `Line`, `nextLine`, in `edge`, hide that line."

In this new `for` loop, the variable `nextLine` is initialized to the value of `edge[0]`. Each time through the loop, `nextLine` is associated with the next value of `edge`. The `for` loop terminates after the last element of the array has been processed. Thus this new, more compact syntax behaves exactly like the original code above.

Notice that we could not have used the enhanced `for` loop if we had only wanted to iterate through some of the elements of `edge`, e.g., the first two. It is only useful when you want to iterate through all the elements of the array.

Be sure to check with your instructor to see if your compiler supports Java 1.5 before using this new `for` loop. You will get a compilation error if you try to use it with an earlier version of Java.

14.5 Gathering Information from an Array

In many situations it is useful to gather information about the entire collection of elements in an array rather than processing the members of the collection independently. Suppose, for example, that we wanted to determine the perimeter of a triangle represented using our `Triangle` class. We could not accomplish this by applying an operation independently to each element, as we did in the `hide` method. Instead we would have to write a loop which added together the lengths of all the edges. In this section we will examine several examples of loops that gather information from a collection of array elements.

As a context for examining such loops, we will consider the construction of Java code needed to control the device shown in Figure 14.7. The picture shown in this figure comes from a web site maintained by the town of Vernon Hills, Illinois.[3] The device shown is called a traffic radar trailer.

The Vernon Hills web page contains the following helpful description of the device's purpose:

> The S.M.A.R.T. (Speed Monitoring Awareness Radar Trailer) can be used in neighborhoods, school zones, construction sites, dangerous areas, or any other appropriate location to help promote compliance with the speed limit. The S.M.A.R.T. trailer is a portable, self-contained

---

[3] http://www.vernonhills.org/police/programs/SMART.htm.

Figure 14.7   Vernon Hills S.M.A.R.T.

speed display unit that is towed to the desired location. It is left on the roadway to display speeds of oncoming vehicles on a highly visible LED (light emitting diode) display. A speed limit sign mounted on the unit reminds drivers what the actual speed limit is on the road that they are on.

These radar trailers have become very popular with local police forces. Our town purchased one recently, and we get to test its accuracy regularly as we drive around town. We suspect, however, that many drivers who pass such radar trailers underestimate the sophistication of these devices. The trailer shown can be purchased with the "StatPak" option that includes a traffic statistics computer that provides traffic counts and an analysis of speed categories. Basically, there is a computer in the radar cart running a program that keeps statistical summaries of the traffic that passes by.

It isn't hard to imagine how the statistics collected by such a radar unit could assist police efforts to enforce speed limits. If it simply kept a count of the number of speeders detected, the radar trailer could be used to identify those roads on which speeding is a problem. This information could be used to determine where to assign police officers to monitor traffic.

Let's consider how we might collect more specific information about the pattern of speeding violations. In particular, we will consider how to write a program that determines the number of speeders that pass the trailer during each of the 24 hours of a single day.

The 24 numbers used to count speeders will be kept in an array. The necessary array can be declared and initialized by the instance variable declaration

```
private int [ ] speedersAt = new int[24];
```

The indexed variable

speedersAt[hour]

will be used to access the number of speeders detected during a given "hour". Thus,

speedersAt[9]

will refer to the number of speeders detected at 9 o'clock (i.e., between 9:00 and 9:59). We will use a 24-hour clock so that a unique index value is associated with each hour. This will enable us to avoid using "a.m." and "p.m." to distinguish morning from evening. Instead, we will add 12 to the hour of any "p.m." time. Rather than saying 3 p.m., we will say 15, and for 10 p.m., we will use 22. Of course, 2 a.m. will still be 2, and 5 a.m. will still be 5.

One special case is worth noting. In a 24-hour clock, midnight is 0:00, one minute after midnight is 0:01 and so on. Thus midnight is hour 0 and

speedersAt[0]

will be the element of the array used to keep track of the number of speeders seen between midnight and 12:59 a.m. Obviously, this is convenient, given that Java starts numbering the elements of all arrays with 0 rather than 1.

While we don't actually know any details about the organization of the software sold with these radar trailers, it is not difficult to imagine a possible structure for such a program. There would be (at least) two classes. One class would act as the "controller". We will assume it is named RadarController. Just as our WindowController classes defined event-handling methods to respond to mouse or keyboard events, the RadarController would define an event-handling method that would be invoked whenever a vehicle was detected. This method would include code to use the trailer's radar system to determine the vehicle's speed.

The other class would be responsible for recording statistics. We will assume it is called RadarStats. The RadarController would invoke an appropriate method on an object of the RadarStats class each time it detected a vehicle and measured its speed. Within the code of this method, we would need to update the array when a new speeder was detected. Accordingly, the declaration of the speedersAt array would be included as an instance variable declaration in the RadarStats class. The class would also have to provide methods to enable someone to access the statistics that had been collected. There might be methods to draw a graph showing the number of speeders detected at each hour of the day or to report the hour during which the highest number of speeders had been detected.

14.5.1   Counting Speeders

Let's start by seeing how we might write the method of the RadarStats class that the RadarController will invoke to handle the detection of a new vehicle. We will assume that this method is named vehicleReport and that it takes three parameters: a double giving the vehicle's speed and two integers reporting the time of day. The first integer will be the hour (encoded using a 24-hour clock as described above). The second integer will be the minute within the hour. Thus the header for this method might be:

```
public void vehicleReport( double speed, int hour, int minute )
```

```
public void vehicleReport( double speed, int hour, int minute ) {

    if ( speed > speedLimit ) {
        speedersAt[hour]++;
    }
}
```

Figure 14.8   The vehicleReport method

Figure 14.8 shows a version of the vehicleReport method designed to add one to the appropriate element of the speedersAt array each time a speeder is detected. The if statement included in the method determines whether or not the detected vehicle is speeding. It does so by comparing the vehicle's speed to speedLimit, which we assume was set in the RadarStats constructor. Like the loops in the methods of the Triangle class, this method depends upon the fact that an array index can be specified using a variable or parameter name. Since the parameter hour contains the hour at which the speeder was detected,

        speedersAt[hour]

will refer to the array element that should be incremented. The body of the if statement increments this indexed variable.

⟹ EXERCISE 14.5.1

Suppose that we want to determine the fraction of the cars that pass by the radar trailer that are speeding during each hour of the day. To do this, we have to count both the total number of cars that pass by during each hour and the number of speeders and then divide the second number by the first to determine the fraction of the cars that are speeding.

Assuming that the RadarStats class includes the following instance variable declarations:

```
private int [ ] speedersAt = new int[24];
private double [ ] driversAt = new double[24];
private double [ ] speedingFraction = new double[24];
```

show how to rewrite the vehicleReport method so that driversAt[h] refers to the total number of drivers seen at hour h and speedingFraction[h] refers to the fraction of cars that were speeding at hour h. Your code should update these arrays appropriately each time vehicleReport is invoked.   ❖

14.5.2   Drawing a Histogram

Of course, to be useful, our program has to display or report the data it has collected. One way to do this would be to draw a histogram or bar graph like the one shown in Figure 14.9, showing how many speeders were seen during each hour of the day. The code to draw such a graph will provide yet another example of a loop that performs some operation on each element of an array. In this case, the operation will be to draw a bar corresponding to each value found in the speedersAt array. In addition, however, drawing a histogram will also require the use of a loop that gathers information about all the elements in the array.

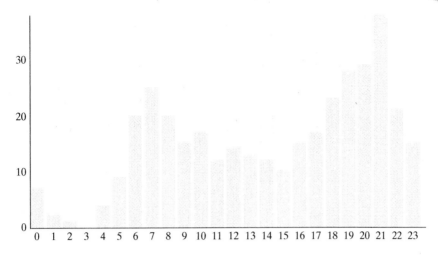

Figure 14.9 A graph displaying numbers of speeders detected at different times of the day

One decision we must make before drawing a bar graph is what scale to use on the *y* axis. If the radar trailer is placed on a busy highway, the number of speeders detected might be in the thousands. To ensure that all the bars drawn fit on the screen, we would have to make each pixel on the display correspond to 10 or more speeders. Unfortunately, using the same scale when the trailer is placed on a quiet road would lead to a graph where all the bars were too short to see. Somehow, we have to look at the data collected to pick an appropriate scale before drawing the graph.

We will consider two ways to set the scale based on the data collected. The first is to graph the percentage of speeders seen in each hour rather than the actual number of speeders seen. If 20% of the speeders were seen at 7 a.m., we would draw a bar whose height was equal to 20% of the vertical space available for the graph. If only 10% of the speeders were seen at some hour, the bar drawn for that hour would be one-tenth of the maximum. In general, to determine the size of the bar to be drawn for a given hour we would multiply the maximum bar size by the result of dividing the number of speeders seen in that hour by the total number of speeders seen. To do this, we need to compute the total number of speeders seen.

Summing the Values in a Numeric Array

We can compute the total number of speeders by adding up all the values in the `speedersAt` array. The method in Figure 14.10 shows the code required. This method would be added to the `RadarStats` class. The loop in the method adds the number of speeders associated with each hour of the day to a variable named `total`. Before the loop is executed, `total` is initialized to the value 0.

The body of the loop in the `speedersSeen` method depends on two simple variables, `total` and `hour`. The variable `hour` serves the same function as the variable `edgeNum` used in the triangle examples. The variable `total` is used in a new way. It summarizes the information collected in the previous steps. After each repetition of the loop, `total` will equal the sum of all of the entries in the `speedersAt` array, up to and including the entry at position `hour`. Therefore, when all the iterations are complete, `total` will be equal to the sum of all the entries.

```
private int speedersSeen() {
  int total = 0;

  for ( int hour = 0; hour < speedersAt.length; hour++ ) {
    total = total + speedersAt[hour];
  }

  return total;
}
```

Figure 14.10   The speedersSeen method

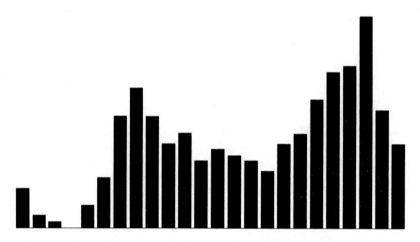

Figure 14.11   A drawing of the essence of a histogram

Drawing a Simple Histogram

With this private method available, we can write a method to draw the desired graph. To keep things simple, we will just worry about drawing the bars without adding any labels. That is, the code we write will draw something that looks more like Figure 14.11 than Figure 14.9.

The loop that draws the histogram is structurally similar to the loops used in the Triangle class. The body of the loop will contain code to independently process each of the elements of the array. This time, the operation performed will be to draw the bar in the graph that corresponds to a particular hour.

We will assume that a number of instance variables describing the dimensions of the graph are declared in the RadarStats class and initialized by its constructor. In particular, we assume that:

graphHeight is the height of the area in which the graph is to be drawn,
graphLeft is the x coordinate of the left edge of the graph, and
graphBottom is the y coordinate of the bottom edge of the graph.
barWidth is the width of a single bar.

```
public void drawHistogram() {
    double barHeight;
    double totalSpeeders = speedersSeen();

    for ( int hour = 0; hour < speedersAt.length; hour++ ) {

        barHeight = (speedersAt[hour]/totalSpeeders)*graphHeight;

        new FilledRect( graphLeft + hour*barWidth,
                        graphBottom - barHeight,
                        barWidth-1,
                        barHeight,
                        canvas
                      );

    }
}
```

Figure 14.12 Method that draws histograms

In addition, we use the speedersSeen method described above to set the variable totalSpeeders equal to the total number of speeders detected.

The method that draws the bars of the histogram is shown in Figure 14.12. The header of the loop that draws the bars is identical to the header of the loop in speedersSeen. The body of this loop contains two statements. The first:

    barHeight = (speedersAt[hour]/totalSpeeders)*graphHeight;

computes the correct height for the bar representing the speeders seen during hour. It does this by dividing speedersAt[hour], the number of speeders seen in the hour being processed, by the total number of speeders seen. The result is then multipled by the height of the longest possible bar to determine the height of the bar that should be drawn.

Finding the Largest Value in a Numeric Array

Unfortunately, if we use this method to draw a histogram of the speeder data collected, the result is likely to look like the image shown in Figure 14.13. The bars in this graph are all rather short. The problem is that the number of speeders seen at any hour will on average be 1/24th of the total number of speeders seen. Therefore, the average bar our program draws will be 1/24th of the total vertical space available for the graph.

Figure 14.13 A bar graph with rather short bars

To make the bars taller, we should make the bar for the hour with the largest number of speeders as tall as space allows and then adjust the sizes for all the other bars accordingly. To do this, we have to determine how many speeders were counted during the hour at which the largest number of speeders were seen. This involves writing another simple loop that gathers information as it processes all of the elements of the speedersAt array.

To understand how this loop will function, it helps to think carefully about the array-processing loop in speedersSeen.

```
int total = 0;

for ( int hour = 0; hour < speedersAt.length; hour++ ) {
    total = total + speedersAt[hour];
}
```

In particular, recall how the variable total is used. Each time an iteration of the loop is completed, the value of this variable has a simple connection to the elements of the array. The value of total is always the sum of all of the array elements that the loop has processed so far.

Similarly, to find the largest value in the array, we will need a loop that manipulates a variable that keeps track of the largest array element processed by the loop so far. The loop in the method shown in Figure 14.14 uses such a variable named max to find the largest element in the array and return its value. We begin by setting max equal to the value of the first element in the array. Each of the other elements in the array is then compared to max as the loop executes. The loop uses another variable, hour, to sequentially select and process each element in the array. max will always be associated with the largest element found in the array before the entry currently being processed by the loop, speedersAt[hour]. If speedersAt[hour] is greater than the value of max, then the value of max is changed to make it equal to this element.

If the maxSpeeders method is added to our RadarStats class, it is quite easy to modify the method shown earlier to draw histograms like those shown in Figure 14.11. The modified version of drawHistogram is presented in Figure 14.15. The only change is that the variable totalSpeeders used in the original version has been replaced by a variable named mostSpeeders, which is set using the maxSpeeders method.

```
private int maxSpeeders() {
    int max = speedersAt[0];

    for ( int hour = 1; hour < speedersAt.length; hour++ ) {

        if ( speedersAt[hour] > max ) {
            max = speedersAt[hour];
        }
    }
    return max;
}
```

Figure 14.14 Method to find largest value in speedersAt array

```
public void drawHistogram()    {
   double barHeight;
   double mostSpeeders = maxSpeeders();

   for ( int hour = 0; hour < speedersAt.length; hour++ )    {
      barHeight = (speedersAt[hour]/mostSpeeders)*graphHeight;

      new FilledRect( graphLeft + hour*barWidth,
                      graphBottom - barHeight,
                      barWidth-1,
                      barHeight,
                      canvas  );
   }
}
```

Figure 14.15 Method that draws well-scaled histograms

➡ EXERCISE 14.5.2

a. Write a minSpeeders *method that will return the number of speeders detected during the hour in which the fewest speeders were detected.*

b. Write a minSpeederHour *method that returns the hour during which the smallest number of speeders was seen. If there is a tie, your method can return any hour during which the smallest number of speeders was seen.* ❖

➡ EXERCISE 14.5.3

A histogram or bar graph is just one of many ways we could display the counts of speeders stored in the RadarStats *class. A simple alternative would be to draw lines connecting the points with coordinates* (hour,speedersAt[hour]) *for all the values of* hour *from 0 to 23. A picture of what we have in mind is shown in Figure 14.16.*

Write a method drawLineGraph *that would draw a graph like that shown in the figure. Assume that your method is included within the* RadarStats *class and can therefore access the names* graphLeft, graphBottom, barWidth, *and* graphHeight. *Although you aren't drawing any bars, you should use the value of* barWidth *to determine how to space the points you connect horizontally.* ❖

14.6 Collections with Variable Sizes

Let's consider a new set of examples using arrays while sticking with the theme of speed.

Over the last few years, one of the authors has had the pleasure of spending a lot of time watching and sometimes helping to run long-distance races involving teams from our local high school. In the fall, there is cross country running. Then, in the winter, the sneakers get replaced by skis and poles as the cross country skiing season starts. The examples we will discuss in this section are based on the process of timing and scoring a cross country race.

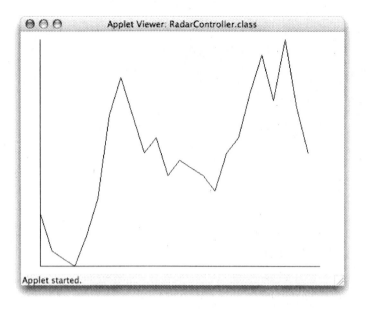

Figure 14.16   Sample of output expected from the drawLineGraph method

Place	Bib No.	Elapsed Time
1	81	20:16
2	71	21:32
3	170	22:34
4	31	23:06
5	200	23:08
6	41	23:10
7	73	23:16
8	83	23:29
9	189	23:53
10	20	23:54
11	9	23:56
12	21	24:00
13	259	24:07
14	60	24:20
15	111	24:33

Figure 14.17   List of finishing times for racers

The timing part is pretty simple. When the race starts, several volunteer timers start their stop watches. Each racer is assigned a number and wears a bib displaying that number. As the racers cross the finish line, the timers write down each racer's bib number and the elapsed time when the racer finished. At the end of the race, the timers have a list that looks something like the example shown in Figure 14.17.

From this list, it is easy to determine where each racer placed. A bit more work is required, however, to determine a team's score. A team's score is determined by adding together the placements of that team's four fastest racers. The team with the smallest score wins the race.

To make it easy to determine which runners are from which teams, our local high school league assigns bib numbers in such a way that the last digit on each runner's bib is the number of that runner's team. (Obviously, our county league has less than 11 teams.) Looking at the sample results in Figure 14.17, the bib numbers for the first two runners, 81 and 71, indicate that they belong to team number 1. The fourth- and sixth-place finishers, numbers 31 and 41, also ran for team 1. Accordingly, team one's score for the race is $1 + 2 + 4 + 6$ for a total of 13. Team zero's runners took third place (bib number 170), fifth place (bib number 200), tenth place (bib number 20), and fourteenth place (bib number 60). Their team score is $3 + 5 + 10 + 14$ for a total of 32.

To explore more ways of manipulating arrays, we will consider how we might write a program to assist in the process of compiling race results when given a list of finishing times, as shown in Figure 14.17. We assume that the program will consist of two classes, a `RaceController` class and a `RaceStatistics` class. The `RaceController` will be an extension of `WindowController` that provides a user interface designed to enable race officials to enter the data collected by the timers. The `RaceStatistics` class uses an array to keep track of the data entered and provides methods to perform operations like determining a particular team's score.

We will describe the implementation of the `RaceStatistics` class in some detail, but we will not explore the implementation of the associated `RaceController`.

Our motivation for largely ignoring the contents of the `RaceController` class is the desire to focus attention on the subject of this chapter, arrays. Our ability to do this, however, illustrates a more general design principle. When writing a program, it is desirable to separate those components of the code that determine the interface presented to the user from those that organize and process the underlying data. User interfaces change frequently. If the league purchased an electronic timing system, manual entry of finishing times might be eliminated entirely. The rules for determining which team won, however, would likely remain the same. Separating the implementation of the user interface from the code that manipulates the data collected makes it easier to change the interface without having to revise the entire program.

While we will not describe the details of the user interface provided by the `RaceController`, we must discuss its functionality in order to understand the methods that will be required in the `RaceStatistics` class. The idea is that as soon as the race ended, the lists of finishing times would be entered into the program. To make this possible, the `RaceController` might provide two text fields, where the user could type a bib number and a time, along with an "Enter" button to press after each racer's time is entered. The `RaceStatistics` class would provide an `addRacer` method that would take a bib number and time as parameters and add the information to the collection maintained by the `RaceStatistics` object.

Once all the data have been entered, the user should be able to press a button to request race results, including a list of all the finishing times and bib numbers and a list of team scores. Since there might be situations where one of these reports was desired without the other, the `RaceStatistics` class should probably include one method to list individual finishing times and another to list team scores. Also, it might be useful to be able to ask how a particular racer did. That is, there should be a method which would take a bib number as a parameter and return the place that runner finished.

14.6.1 Parallel Arrays vs. Arrays of Objects

To start, we must consider how to represent the data found in the list of finishing times. In the `RadarStats` class, each element we wanted to keep track of was a simple integer, so an array of `int`s was sufficient. Now the list of items we want to manipulate is not a list of integers but a list of pairs. Each item includes both a bib number and a finishing time.

We could use two arrays to represent the list of finishers. One array would be used to hold the bib numbers. The other array would be used to hold finishing times. The arrays might be declared as:

```
private int [ ] bibNumber;
private String [ ] elapsedTime;
```

with the understanding that `bibNumber[i]` and `elapsedTime[i]` would hold the bib number and finishing time for a single racer. We have two potentially independent arrays, but the code that manipulates these arrays is designed to ensure that the item associated with a given index in one array is associated with the same index in the other array. When used in this way, we say that the arrays are *parallel arrays*.

An alternate approach is to define a new class whose objects will represent the complete state of a single item in the list and then to create an array whose elements belong to this new class. Taking this approach, we would define a `RacerInfo` class to represent racers and make an array of `RacerInfo`s.

The code to define such a `RacerInfo` class is shown in Figure 14.18. The class provides a constructor that takes a racer's bib number and finishing time. These values are associated with instance variables in the object constructed. The class provides two accessor methods, `getBib` and `getTime`, that simply return these values. In addition, there is a `getTeam` method which determines a racer's team by extracting the last digit of the racer's bib number.

Given this class definition, we can then include in our `RaceStatisitcs` class an array name declaration of the form

```
private RacerInfo [ ] racer;
```

to refer to an array in which descriptions of all the racers' finishes are maintained.

The `RacerInfo` class provides a way to combine the two pieces of information that describe a racer's finish into a single object so that a list of such objects can be placed in a single array. In addition, it incorporates in our program's design a concrete specification of the aspects of a racer that are significant. This would be an appropriate design decision even if the new class did not also facilitate the collection of information about many racers into a single array. In situations like this, it is much better to define a new class and use a single array than to use parallel arrays.

14.6.2 Keeping Track of a Collection's Size

In order to construct the `racer` array, we need to specify its size. Unfortunately, we can't predict exactly how many racers there will be while writing the program. Each race may involve a different number of racers. Even if we somehow knew that the same number of racers would start each race, we couldn't say for sure how many would finish. Ankles do occasionally get sprained during these events.

While we can't say exactly how many racers there will be, we can confidently predict an upper limit on the number of racers. If we multiply the number of racers on the largest team in the league

```
public class RacerInfo {
  private int bibNumber;
  private String time;

  public RacerInfo( int number, String finishingTime )   {
    bibNumber = number;
    time = finishingTime;
  }

  public int getBib()  {
    return bibNumber;
  }

  public String getTime()  {
    return time;
  }

  public int getTeam()  {
    // The last digit on a runner's bib
    // determines the team
    return bibNumber % 10;
  }
}
```

Figure 14.18 Definition of RacerInfo class

by the largest number of teams that ever participates in a single meet, we will obtain a safe upper limit. We can then use this upper limit as the size when we create our array. The declarations might look like this:

```
private static final int TEAMSIZE = 100;
private static final int TEAMSINMEET = 3;

private RacerInfo[ ] racer = new RacerInfo[TEAMSIZE*TEAMSINMEET];
```

The resulting array will have more than enough room to hold information about all the runners that actually finish. Our program will be able to associate information about each finisher with a distinct index value and still leave some index values unused.

To make this approach work, we need to keep track of which indices have been associated with values and which indices are unused. A simple way to do this is to use the smallest index values first, leaving the larger index values unused. Then, if we keep a count of the number of array indices that are being used in an integer variable, we will always be able to tell exactly which array entries are in use and which are idle.

For example, we might declare an instance variable

```
private int racerCount;
```

racerCount = 10

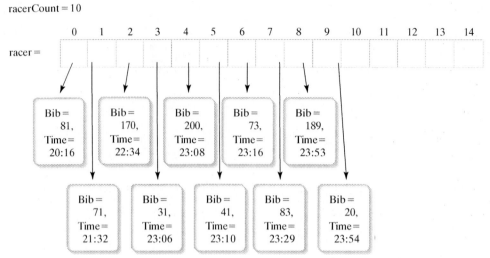

Figure 14.19   State of racer array and racerCount after adding 10 racers

and include instructions in the methods of the class to ensure that this variable's value always equals the number of racers for whom finishing times have been recorded in the array.

Figure 14.19 depicts the relationship that should exist between `racerCount` and the `racer` array. The diagram corresponds to a point in the execution of the program when information has been entered describing the first 10 racers to finish using the bib numbers and times shown in Figure 14.17. The value of the `racerCount` variable is equal to the number of `RacerInfo` objects created, 10. Each of the 10 `RacerInfo` objects describes one racer and each is associated with an index of the `racer` array. These objects are associated with the first 10 index values, the numbers 0 through 9. Index values 10, 11, 12, and all higher index values have no objects associated with them at this point.

As we have seen, all arrays in Java start with index value 0 rather than 1. Therefore, even though we normally say that the racer to complete the course most quickly comes in first place, in Java this runner is identified as the zeroth runner. In fact, the index values associated with all the `racerInfo` objects are one smaller than the "place" in which they finished the race. `racer[1]` refers to the racer who came in second place, `racer[2]` refers to the racer who came in third place and so on.

14.6.3   Adding an Entry to the Array

With this scheme in mind, we can now show how to write a method named `addRacer` that will take a bib number and a time, create a `RacerInfo` object to hold this information, and associate this new object with the appropriate array index. In doing so, this method will both use and change the value of the `racerCount` variable. As one can see by re-examining Figure 14.19, when `racerCount` has the value of 10, indices 0 through 9 are already in use and 10 is the next index that should be associated with a racer. That is, the value of `racerCount` and the next index that should be used are the same. This will be true in all cases. So, the method should use `racerCount` as the index when assigning the new object to the array and then increment `racerCount` to reflect the fact that the collection has grown.

```
public void addRacer( int bib, String time ) {

   if ( racerCount < racer.length )  {
      racer[racerCount] = new RacerInfo( bib, time );
      racerCount++;
   }
}
```

Figure 14.20   The addRacer method

The complete code for this method is shown in Figure 14.20. The steps just described are performed within the body of the `if` statement. The first line constructs the new `RacerInfo` object and associates it with the index equal to the current value of `racerCount`. The second line increments `racerCount` by 1.

The `if` statement surrounding these lines checks for a situation our program is not designed to handle. We said earlier that we would choose a size for the `racer` array based on an estimate of the largest number of racers that could ever participate in a race. What if someone gives a copy of this program to a different league with larger teams but does not realize that the size of the array is based on the size of the teams? In this case, when the program is run, the user may enter more finishing times than will fit in the array. The `if` statement checks for this situation. It uses `.length` to access the actual size of the array. So this `if` statement ensures that we never try to add more racers to the array when the array has no unused elements.

Unfortunately, as written, the program does not give its user any feedback if too many finishing times are entered. It just ignores any extra finishing times. This is the best we can do in this example, however, if we want to continue to ignore the details of the program's user interface while focusing on the implementation of `RaceStatistics`. In addition, the best feature of Java to address the detection of an error like this, exceptions, will not be discussed until later in the text. Despite this weakness, we include the `if` statement in our code to highlight the need for such checking in a well designed program.

▪▶ EXERCISE 14.6.1

Suppose that we reversed the order of the statements within the body of the `if` *statement in our* addRacer *method so that they appeared as*

```
      racerCount++;
      racer[racerCount] = new RacerInfo( bib, time );
```

Draw a diagram similar to the picture in Figure 14.19 showing what the array would look like after addRacer *had been invoked 3 times to add the first 3 entries used in our example.*   ❖

▪▶ EXERCISE 14.6.2

The code in the following sections assumes that the entries in the racer *array are added in the order that the racers finished. Show how to modify the* addRacer *method to ensure that this is true. You should assume that the* RacerInfo *class includes a method named* getTimeInSeconds *that converts the* String *used to represent the finishing time when a* RacerInfo *object is created into an* `int` *that expresses the finishing time in seconds. As we did in the version of* `addRacer` *shown in Figure 14.20, your version should not bother to display an error message if an attempt is made to add a racer out of order. Instead, your method should simply return without actually adding information about the new racer.*   ❖

14.6.4   Displaying the Results

We described three ways in which the `RaceStatistics` class should be able to provide information about race results: by listing all the runners in the order that they finished, by returning the placement for a particular runner given that runner's bib number, and by listing team scores. We will show methods that perform each of these functions.

Listing the Elements in an Array

We would like the method that lists all the runners to produce a display that looks something like:

```
1. Racer 81 20:16
2. Racer 71 21:32
3. Racer 170 22:34
4. Racer 31 23:06
5. Racer 200 23:08
6. Racer 41 23:10
7. Racer 73 23:16
   .
   .
   .
```

There are several ways that the program might present this information. It might simply use `System.out.println` to write the text on the system output, or it might want to include a `JTextArea` component in the program's GUI and present the text there. To provide a method flexible enough to support either of these approaches, we will write code that creates a string holding the entire display and then returns this string.

The code for such a method named `individualResults` is shown in Figure 14.21. The body of the method contains a loop that resembles the loops we used earlier in this chapter in several ways. As in those loops, we want to apply the instructions in the body of the loop to each piece of information in the array. The difference here is that the number of pieces of information in the array is not equal to the size of the array as specified in its construction. Instead, the number of pieces of information in the array can be determined from the value of the `racerCount` variable. Therefore, the condition to specify when the loop should terminate uses this variable.

Before the loop, we declare and initialize the variable `results` to be an empty string. The body of the loop consists of a single assignment statement that adds the text of one line of the list of results to the string associated with the name `results`. Each time the loop is executed, the loop variable `place` refers to an index identifying the entry in the array `racer` that should be added to the list. The code that describes the text that is added to `result` on each iteration is

```
public String individualResults() {

    String results = "";

    for ( int place = 0; place < racerCount; place++ ) {

        results = results +
                    (place+1) + ". " +
                    "Racer " + racer[place].getBib() + "   " +
                    racer[place].getTime() +
                    "\n";
    }
    return results;
}
```

Figure 14.21   The individualResults method

divided into four lines to highlight how each piece of the text is obtained:

* (place+1) + ". " +

adds the number of the current racer's placement followed by a period to the result string.

As discussed above, while its name suggests that place will equal a racer's placement in the results, it will actually be off by one. When place equals 0, racer[place] will refer to the racer who took first place. In general, (place+1) will equal the "place" that racer[place] finished.

Note that the parentheses around place+1 are essential. If they were omitted, Java would interpret the plus sign as concatenation rather than addition, and the place values displayed would be 01, 11, 21, ... rather than 1, 2, 3, ...

* "Racer " + racer[place].getBib() + " " +

adds the word "Racer" followed by the racer's bib number to result.

This and the following line are where the array becomes essential to the loop. Array item racer[place] refers to the object describing the racer being processed by this iteration of the loop. We use this object's getBib method to add the bib number to the result.

* racer[place].getTime() +

uses one of the methods associated with a RacerInfo object found in the array to obtain the current racer's finishing time.

* "\n"

places a new line after the text that describes each racer.

The most important thing to understand about this loop is the degree of similarity between it and the array-processing loops seen earlier in this chapter. The bodies of these loops are all designed to perform some operation on one element of an array. The loop header ensures that the loop body is executed once for each relevant entry in the array.

Finding a Single Element in the Array

We would also like to provide a method to determine where a particular racer placed without displaying the entire list. This method will take a bib number as a parameter and return that

```
public int getPlacement( int bib ) {

    int result = -1;

    for ( int place = 0;
          place < racerCount && result == -1 ;
          place++
        ) {

      if ( racer[place].getBib() == bib ) {
        result = (place+1);
      }
    }
    return result;
}
```

Figure 14.22   A version of the getPlacement method

racer's placement in the race. To do this, we will write a loop that searches through the elements of the array until it finds the entry with the desired bib number. This loop will be a bit different from the others we have considered. It doesn't always have to process every element of the array. It can stop as soon as the requested bib number is found.

There is one unexpected possibility which we have to account for when writing this loop. The person using the program might make a mistake when typing in the bib number and therefore ask our code to search for something it will never find. We have to decide what value our method should return in this case. We should return a value that will make it clear that something went wrong. The method is supposed to return a racer's place. Accordingly, if we can't find the racer, returning something that couldn't possibly be someone's placement is an effective way to signal that a problem occurred. Returning 0, -1 or any other negative value would do. We will use -1.

We will name this method getPlacement. We will compare two versions of this method. (The first is in Figure 14.22.) It mimics several of the loops we saw earlier in that it uses a variable to hold a form of summary of what the iterations of the loop have seen. We use result to keep track of the answer we would have to return if the last array entry we had processed was also the last entry in the array. This means that the variable's value will be -1 until we see the bib number we are looking for. Once we find the desired bib number, result will be set to that racer's placement. Eventually the final value of the variable result will be returned by the method.

The code for this method is shown in Figure 14.22. Note that the value of result is used in the header of the for loop. This loop stops either when it reaches the end of the array or as soon as the value of result becomes something other than -1 because the desired bib number was found.

A second version of getPlacement is shown in Figure 14.23. This version takes advantage of the fact that one can include several return statements in a single method. As soon as any of these return statements is executed, the method is completed and a result is returned. Accordingly, when the if statement within the body of the for loop finds the desired entry in the array, it immediately executes a return that specifies the appropriate value for that racer's placement.

```
public int getPlacement( int bib ) {

   for ( int place = 0; place < racerCount; place++ ) {
      if ( racer[place].getBib() == bib ) {
          return place+1;
      }
   }
   return -1;
}
```

Figure 14.23   Alternate version of getPlacement

This second version is likely to be a bit more efficient than the first. Each time around the loop, only two tests are made: the test that place is less than racerCount and the test for a matching bib number. The version in Figure 14.22 also had to test whether result was still equal to −1. However, the approach taken in the more efficient version works in this context only because this method's role is simply to return the position of a specified entry in an array. If the method needed to do additional computation after finding the desired entry, then the method could not simply return once the entry was found.

➡ EXERCISE 14.6.3

How would the behavior of the getPlacement *method shown in Figure 14.22 change if the condition in the* for *loop were simplified to*

```
place < racerCount
```

Computing Team Scores

We will consider how to write two methods dealing with team scores. First, we will work on a method named teamScore. It will take a parameter named teamNo that identifies a particular team and return that team's score. Next, we will construct a teamStandings method that will compute the scores of all the teams that participated in a meet.

In our local high school cross country meets, a team's score is determined by adding together the places of the team's top four finishers. With this in mind, we will assume that the constant

```
private static final int LASTSCORER = 4;
```

has been declared. The exact number of finishers counted actually varies from sport to sport. The value associated with LASTSCORER could easily be changed to make our program work correctly for another sport.

Computing a team's score requires a loop that combines aspects of several of the loops we have considered. We will be adding together place values, just as we added together numbers of speeders in Section 14.5.2. We will be looking for specific entries, just as we did when looking for a bib number in the getPlacement method. Finally, like the loop in getPlacement, this loop does not have to examine every element in the array. It can stop as soon as it has found four racers for the team specified.

```
public int teamScore( int teamNo ) {

    int racersCounted = 0;      // Number of finishers found so far
    int score = 0;              // Sum of finishing places

    // Find the first four racers for the specified team
    for ( int place = 0;
          place < racerCount && racersCounted < LASTSCORER;
          place++ ) {

        if ( racer[place].getTeam() == teamNo )    {
            racersCounted++;
            score = score + (place + 1);
        }
    }

    // Make sure that at least four racers were found
    if ( racersCounted < LASTSCORER ) {
        score = -1;
    }

    return score;

}
```

Figure 14.24   The teamScore method computes the score for one team

We will again use variables to hold information determined by previous iterations of the processing loop. One variable, racersCounted, will keep track of how many racers from the specified team have been found so far. The other variable, score, will hold the sum of the place values for those racers.

A complete version of teamScore is shown in Figure 14.24. The header of the for loop ensures that the loop will terminate if either four runners from the specified team are found or the end of the list of racers is reached. The if statement that forms the body of the loop ensures that only racers associated with the specified team are processed. For each racer that is processed, we add 1 to racersCounted and add the racer's place to score.

The if statement after the loop addresses the possibility that the user of the program asks it to compute a team score for a team that did not have enough of its racers finish the race. In this situation, the method returns −1, a value that can be recognized as an error indicator, since it could not possibly be an actual team's score.

Our next task is to write a method named teamStandings that will determine the scores for all the teams that competed. Obviously, this method cannot return a single score as its result. Instead, we will design it to return an array of integers containing one element for each of the ten possible teams. The element of the array associated with the team number will refer to that team's score.

We could use teamScore to write the teamStandings method. We would simply write a loop that would call teamScore once for each team number from 0 to 9. If you think about it for a moment, you will realize that this would make the computer do a lot of unnecessary work. First, we would call teamScore to determine the score for team 0. This would involve checking the team number of all of the racers up to the fourth racer from team 0. Next, we would do the same thing for team 1. Unless the first four racers for team 1 came in before all the racers from team 0, the computer would again check some of the team 0 racers to see if they were from team 1.

The source of inefficiency here is the fact that such code would instruct the computer to make 10 passes through the entries at the beginning of the racer array. This is unnecessary. All of the team scores can be computed at the same time during one pass through the list. To do this, we need to keep track of how many racers we have found from each of the 10 teams and the accumulated score for each team. That is, we need a collection of team scores and "racers counted" variables. We can do this easily by replacing each of these simple variables used in teamScore with arrays containing 10 elements. First, we would define a constant in the class to refer to the number of elements stored in these arrays:

```
private static final int MAXTEAMS = 10;
```

Then, the declarations found in teamScore:

```
int racersCounted = 0;
int score = 0;
```

can be replaced by the declarations

```
int [ ] racersCounted = new int[MAXTEAMS];
int [ ] score = new int[MAXTEAMS];
```

in the teamStandings method.

The definition of the teamStandings method is shown in Figure 14.25. The method has two loops. The first looks through the list of finishers and tries to compute scores for all the teams that competed. Three statements in the body of this loop do the bulk of the work. The assignment

```
teamNo = racer[place].getTeam();
```

extracts the team number for the current racer. The two statements

```
racersCounted[teamNo]++;
score[teamNo] = score[teamNo] + (place+1);
```

increase the count of the number of racers from this team that have been seen and add this racer's placement to the team score. These two statements are placed in an if statement to ensure that at most four racers from each team are considered when determining the team's score.

The final loop then checks the elements of the racersCounted array looking for any teams that did not have at least LASTSCORER racers finish. Such teams receive a score of −1. Finally, the array containing the scores is returned as the method's result.

➡ EXERCISE 14.6.4

The version of the teamStandings *method shown in Figure 14.25 may do a bit more work than necessary. The* for *loop in this method looks at every single entry in the* racer *array. Typically,*

```
public int [ ] teamStandings() {

    // How many racers have been found from each team
    int [ ] racersCounted = new int[MAXTEAMS];

    // Sum of places of each team's racers
    int [ ] score = new int[MAXTEAMS];

    // Look for four finishers from each team
    for ( int place = 0; place < racerCount; place++ ) {

        int teamNo = racer[place].getTeam();

        if ( racersCounted[teamNo] < LASTSCORER ) {
            racersCounted[teamNo]++;
            score[teamNo] = score[teamNo] + (place+1);
        }
    }

    // Identify teams that had less than four finishers
    for ( int teamNo = 0; teamNo < MAXTEAMS; teamNo++ ) {
        if ( racersCounted[teamNo] < LASTSCORER ) {
            score[teamNo] = -1;
        }
    }

    return score;
}
```

Figure 14.25   The teamStandings method

there will be many racers who finish after the slowest racer who scores. That is, once the loop has found enough racers from each of the teams to compute a score for every team, it can stop without looking at the remaining entries in the array.

Show how to modify our definition of teamStandings to take advantage of this observation. Your new version of this method should expect an int parameter, teamCount, which will tell it how many teams were actually competing in the meet. You will have to change the first loop so that it keeps track of how many team scores have been determined and stops when this number equals teamCount.   ❖

14.7   Adding and Removing Elements

In the preceding section, we assumed that the finishing times and bib numbers were supplied to our program in the desired order and that they were entered correctly. It is not always possible to make such assumptions about the data processed by a program that uses arrays. In fact, it is not at all clear that it is reasonable to make this assumption about our finishing-time data.

Having been a volunteer timer, I know that mistakes get made at races. At the end of one race, for example, someone noticed that one racer somehow finished twice! (i.e., that someone's bib number was misread and written down incorrectly so that it was actually the number of another racer). To preserve faith in the system, the coaches do what they can in the back room to repair such recording errors. Therefore, if we want a program that really assists in the process of compiling race results, it should facilitate making corrections to deal with errors made by the timers and errors made while entering the data they recorded. In the context of learning about arrays, the most interesting types of corrections to consider are adding a new racer to the list and deleting an incorrect entry from the list.

14.7.1 Adding an Element to an Ordered Array

Suppose that a person using our program gets distracted while entering the finishing times and skips one of the racers listed. Such mistakes are almost certain to happen, so we should think about how our program could provide the ability to add an omitted entry at the correct position in the array.

We will not worry about the user interface we would have to implement to make such insertions possible. Instead, we will focus on the implementation of a new method of the RaceStatistics class designed to support the addition of entries to the array. Let us assume this method is named addRacerAtPosition to highlight how it differs from the addRacer method already included in the class (see Figure 14.20).

It will help to think about the steps required to perform a specific insertion before trying to construct the code for this method. Suppose that while entering the times shown in Figure 14.17, a person using our program skips the fifth finisher and does not notice the mistake until six more finishing times have been entered. Figure 14.26 depicts the information that would be recorded in the array and the racerCount variable in this event. This figure is very similar to Figure 14.19, which depicts the state of the array after the first 10 finishing times are entered correctly. If one compares the two diagrams closely, however, it becomes clear that the racerInfo objects associated with array elements 4, 5, 6, 7, 8, and 9 are all wrong! We can't fix the problem by just adding the correct entry at position 4. We have to fix all the incorrect entries. The racer associated with the fourth position (i.e., index) of the array should be associated with the fifth position in the array, the racer associated with the fifth position should be associated with the sixth position, and so on.

The task of inserting the new element can be broken into two subtasks. First, we have to move all the entries associated with array indices greater than or equal to 4 over one position. The diagram shown in Figure 14.27 suggests the state of the array after this step is complete. Next, we would create a new RacerInfo object describing the omitted racer and associate it with index value 4. At this point, we would also have to increase racerCount by 1 to reflect the addition. Figure 14.28 describes the desired state of the array and variable after the insertion is complete.

Moving all the misplaced racers over one position in the array is the hard part. There is no special Java instruction to move a whole collection of array entries at once. Instead, the RacerInfo objects will have to be associated with new array indices one by one using assignment statements.

racerCount = 10

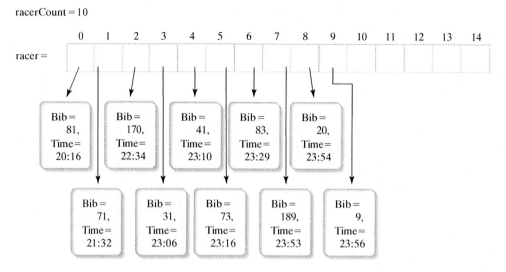

Figure 14.26   racer array with a missing element

racerCount = 10

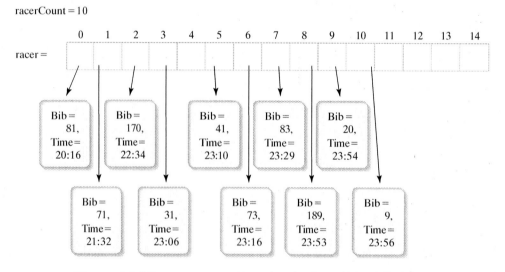

Figure 14.27   racer array with entries after the omission shifted right

Let's start by seeing how we can use an assignment statement to move the last element in the array, the `RacerInfo` object for the racer with bib number 9, from its initial position in the array, position 9, to the next position to the right, position 10. To do this, we would use the assignment

```
racer[10] = racer[9];
```

This assignment tells Java to make the tenth position of the array refer to the racer already associated with the ninth position of the array. As a result, after this assignment, both the ninth

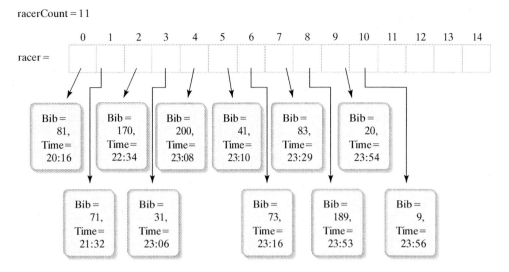

Figure 14.28 racer array after insertion is complete

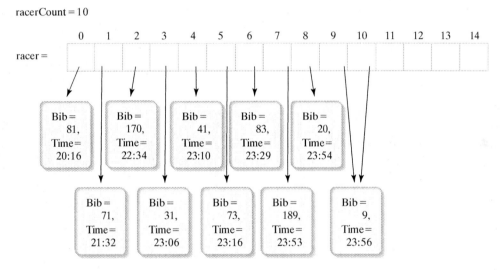

Figure 14.29 racer array after moving element 9

and tenth positions of the array would refer to the same racer. The diagram in Figure 14.29 depicts the state of the array after this assignment.

This situation, shown in Figure 14.29, is probably not quite what you thought we had in mind when we said we wanted to move the entry from position 9 to position 10. You probably were expecting only the entry in position 10 to refer to the racer when we were done.

To see how we reach the expected state, consider the next step in the process. The assignment

```
racer[9] = racer[8];
```

racerCount = 10

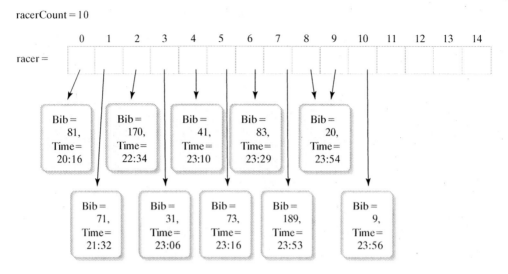

Figure 14.30   racer array after moving elements 8 and 9

would be used to move the object describing the racer wearing bib 20 from entry 8 to entry 9. At the same time, this assignment would have the effect of ensuring that the racer with bib number 9 is referred to only by array entry 10. After executing this assignment, the array will look like the picture in Figure 14.30. While only array element 10 refers to the racer with bib number 9, racer 20 is temporarily associated with two array index values, 8 and 9. The association of racer 20 with array element 8 is undesired, but the next step,

```
racer[8] = racer[7];
```

will eliminate this unwanted association.

The complete set of assignment statements needed to move the last six racers over one position is

```
racer[10] = racer[9];
racer[9]  = racer[8];
racer[8]  = racer[7];
racer[7]  = racer[6];
racer[6]  = racer[5];
racer[5]  = racer[4];
```

Executing these assignments would move all the necessary elements of the array over by one position, as shown in Figure 14.31. Note that this figure is slightly different from the goal depicted in Figure 14.27. Entry 4 still refers to the racer that has been moved to entry 5. This reference must be replaced by a reference to a new RacerInfo object for the added racer to complete the insertion process.

The assignments shown in the list above are quite similar to one another. They are all of the form

```
racer[position] = racer[position-1];
```

racerCount = 10

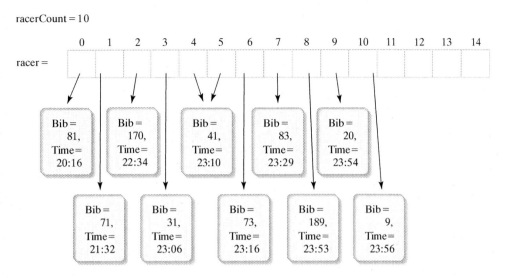

Figure 14.31 racer array after moving six elements over by one

This makes it easy to write a loop to perform the assignments rather than actually writing the assignments out in our code. The loop will simply execute the assignment statement shown above for all values of the variable `position` from the current value of `racerCount` down to but not including the index of the position where the new element will be inserted. The index where the new element is to be inserted will be provided as a parameter to the `addRacerAtPosition` method. Assuming we name that parameter `insertionPos`, the loop needed to move the required elements over by one position would be:

```
for ( int position = racerCount; position > insertionPos;
      position-- ) {
    racer[position] = racer[position-1];
}
```

This loop is different from the other array loops we have seen in this chapter. It goes backward. The other loops have all started with the smallest index and worked toward the largest by increasing the loop variable by 1 with each iteration. This loops starts at the largest index and decreases the loop variable by 1 with each iteration.

Consider what would happen if we performed the assignments with the array indices in increasing order. We would first execute the assignment

```
racer[5] = racer[4];
```

This would make the two array indices, 4 and 5, refer to the same `RacerInfo` object. Assuming we started with the array in the configuration shown in Figure 14.26, the diagram in Figure 14.32 shows the result of starting with this assignment. The array indices 4 and 5 are both associated with racer 41.

This isn't too surprising. When we started with the assignment

```
racer[10] = racer[9];
```

racerCount = 10

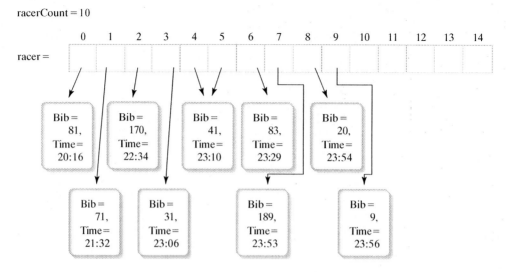

Figure 14.32 racer array after executing racer[5] = racer[4];

we also ended up with two array entries associated with a single racer, but a surprising thing has happened. The racer object that entry 5 referred to before the assignment, the object for racer 73, is lost. No array entry refers to this object.

Things get worse if we continue to execute the assignment statement for the next larger pair of index values:

```
racer[6] = racer[5];
```

This makes array entry 6 refer to the same object as entry 5, as shown in Figure 14.33. Now three entries refer to the same object and two racers have been lost!

If we continue executing the assignments in increasing order of index values, we will end up leaving the array in the state shown in Figure 14.34. All of the entries after the insertion point now refer to the element initially found at the insertion point, and all of the objects after this point have been lost. Clearly, we have to use a loop that works from the largest subscript to the smallest.

To complete the addRacerAtPosition method, we need to combine the loop that moves each of the elements after the insertion point with code to add the new entry and to increment racerCount. Adding this code yields a complete implementation for addRacerAtPosition, as shown in Figure 14.35. The code to insert the new element is identical to that seen in addRacer except that the parameter insertionPos is used as the index for the new element's position. In particular, note that we include the test to make sure that there is still room for an extra element in the array. We also make sure that the new racer's position is contiguous to the existing racers.

14.7.2 Removing an Element from an Array

Programs that manipulate data in arrays often need to update the collection by removing a specific item. It is not hard to imagine such a need arising in the context of our race results program. An error might be made in which the information for a single racer was entered twice, or, after the results were entered, a racer might be disqualified for some infraction reported after the finish. To

racerCount = 10

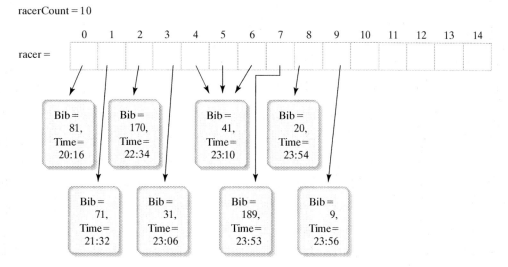

Figure 14.33 Array after executing racer[6] = racer[5];

racerCount = 10

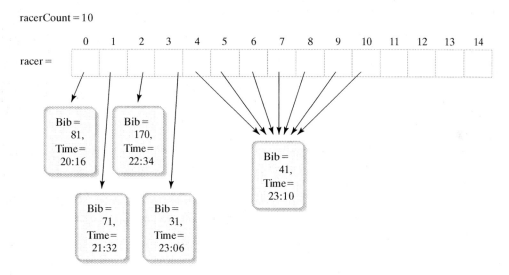

Figure 14.34 Where did all the racers go?

address these situations, we will consider how to implement a removeRacerAt method which will remove the racer at a particular position from the array.

Like the process of adding an element, the task of removing an element requires the ability to shift a sequence of elements over one position. In Figure 14.19, we showed a diagram of the state of the array after the first 10 recorded finishing times from Figure 14.17 were correctly entered. Suppose, starting from that configuration, we wanted to delete the entry in position 6.

```
public void addRacerAtPosition( int bib, String time,
                                int insertionPos ) {
  if ( racerCount < racer.length && insertionPos <= racerCount) {

    for ( int position = racerCount;
          position > insertionPos;
          position-- ) {
      racer[position] = racer[position-1];
    }
    racer[insertionPos] = new RacerInfo( bib, time );
    racerCount++;
  }
}
```

Figure 14.35   The addRacerAtPosition method

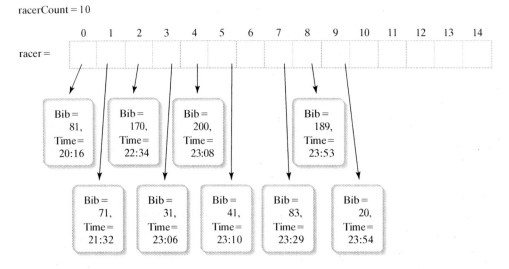

Figure 14.36   Array after executing racer[6] = null

Simply executing the statement

```
racer[6] = null;
```

would be insufficient. The assignment would remove the association between the sixth element of the array and the racer with bib number 73. This would leave the array in the state shown in Figure 14.36. The code we have written thus far, however, depends on the assumption that all of the elements of the array that refer to racers will be contiguous. Leaving element 6 null violates this assumption. So, to complete the removal, we have to shift all of the entries after position 6 to the left one place.

racerCount = 10

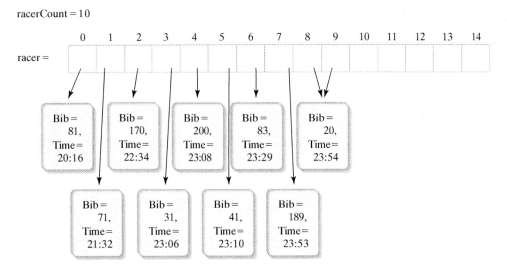

Figure 14.37   racer array with last element duplicated

In this case, the required shift can be performed by the statements

```
racer[6] = racer[7];
racer[7] = racer[8];
racer[8] = racer[9];
racer[9] = null;
```

together with a statement to decrement the `racerCount` variable. Note that the first assignment associates a new value with element 6. This would just undo the effect of the statement

```
racer[6] = null;
```

Therefore, it is not necessary to start by explicitly setting element 6 to null.

On the other hand, the last assignment in the list above sets element 9 to null. This is to avoid leaving two array entries referring to the same element. If this last assignment were omitted from the list above, then the diagram in Figure 14.37 would depict the final state of the array. Both elements 8 and 9 refer to the same entry. In most cases, this would not affect the correctness of our program. Since `racerCount` will be decremented as part of the process of removing an element, none of the other loops we have written would ever get to element 9 unless extra entries were added. As soon as a single new element is added, `racer[9]` will be associated with this new element, eliminating the duplicate reference. Nevertheless, we prefer to eliminate the unwanted reference to the last `RacerInfo` object because it seems logically appropriate to do so.

As in the method to add a racer, we will want to create a loop to execute the sequence of assignments necessary to shift the appropriate elements over by one when an entry is deleted from an array. The actual index values used in the assignment statements will depend on the number of elements in the array and the size of the array. In particular, the array element set by the first assignment should be the element associated with the index of the element being deleted, and the index of the last element set should be equal to the value of `racerCount` after it is

```
public void removeRacerAtPosition( int position ) {

  if ( position < racerCount ) {
    racerCount--;

    for ( int place = position; place < racerCount; place++ ) {
      racer[place] = racer[place + 1];
    }

    racer[racerCount] = null;
  }
}
```

Figure 14.38   The removeRacerAtPosition method

decremented. Just as in the code that shifted elements during an addition, the order in which these assignments is executed is critical. The loop must first execute the assignment with the smallest subscript values and then increase the values used by one on each iteration.

The complete code for removeRacerAtPosition is shown in Figure 14.38. The entire body of this method is included within an if statement that tests to make sure the operation requested is possible. In this case, the test made is that the position provided as a parameter actually refers to one of the elements in the array.

Note that racerCount is decremented before the loop. Therefore, the largest value associated with the loop variable place is one smaller than the index used to hold the last element of the array before the deletion process.

EXERCISE 14.7.1

In Section 14.7.1, we explained that it was important that the loop in the addRacerAtPosition method start at the end of the array and work its way down to the point of insertion. In the removeRacerAtPosition method, however, we have used a loop that steps through the elements to be moved in the opposite direction. To appreciate why this is necessary, draw a diagram like the one in Figure 14.19, showing how the array would look if we invoked removeRacerAtPosition with parameter value 7 after redefining removeRacerAtPosition as shown in Figure 14.39.

14.8 Summary

Arrays provide a convenient and efficient mechanism for manipulating collections of related data items. The features of the Java language that support arrays are actually fairly simple. We can 'eclare array variables and parameters, create arrays using array constructors or array initializers, sociate arrays with names through assignments or parameter passing, write methods that return ays, and, finally and most importantly, access individual members of an array using indexed

```
public void removeRacerAtPosition( int position ) {

  if ( position < racerCount ) {
    racerCount--;

    for ( int place = racerCount-1;  position <= place;  place-- ) {
      racer[place] = racer[place + 1];
    }

    racer[racerCount] = null;
  }
}
```

Figure 14.39 The removeRacerAtPosition method with the loop reversed

variables. These simple features, however, can be used to organize collections of data in ways that range from simple to quite complex.

The challenge for the beginner is to learn to use Java's array features effectively. In this chapter, we have introduced several common and important techniques for using arrays to organize data. We have seen how to write loops that process all the elements of an array independently and examples of loops that instead gather information about the collection as a whole. We also showed how to search an array to find a particular element of the collection. We showed that in some cases, an array can be constructed that has exactly as many elements as there are data values to process. We also saw how the use of a counter variable made it possible to use arrays in situations where the number of data values was somewhat unpredictable. We learned how to add and remove elements from such collections.

Our exploration of arrays continues in the next chapter where we discuss arrays whose elements are themselves arrays.

14.9   Chapter Review Problems

EXERCISE 14.9.1

The following table shows the percentage of the total land area of the Earth located in each of the seven continents.

Continent	Percent of Total Land Area
Africa	20.3
Antarctica	8.9
Asia	30.0
Australia	5.2
Europe	6.7
North America	16.3
South America	8.9

a. *Provide declarations for two parallel arrays named* `continentalArea` *and* `continentName` *designed to hold the information in this table. Include array initializers in each declaration so that the elements of the array are associated with the data provided in the table.*

b. *Write a loop which will print a table of the actual area of each continent, given an estimate of the total land area of the Earth. Assume that the total land area is associated with a constant named* TOTAL_AREA. *Don't bother to format your output as a table with a heading or to deal with the fairly ugly way Java displays* `double` *values. For example, using a fairly accurate value of 57 million square miles for* TOTAL_AREA, *your loop's output might look like:*

```
Africa   1.1571E7
Antarctica   5073000.000000001
Asia   1.71E7
Australia   2964000.0000000005
Europe   3819000.0
North America   9291000.0
South America   5073000.000000001
```

c. *Assuming that the class named* `Continent` *is defined as shown in Figure 14.40, provide a declaration for an array of continents to hold the information in the table above. Include an array initializer in the declaration to associate the elements of the array with appropriate* `Continent` *objects.*

d. *Write a loop to print the estimated areas of each of the continents using the array of* `Continent` *objects rather than the two parallel arrays defined for part (a).*

```java
public class Continent {

    private String name;
    private double area;

    public Continent( String aName, double theArea ) {
        name = aName;
        area = theArea;
    }

    public String getName() {
        return name;
    }

    public double getArea() {
        return area;
    }
}
```

Figure 14.40   A class to represent continents

```
private void mystery() {

    int [ ] report = {5, 4, 10, 4, 6, 3, 4};

    int turn = 0;
    int shot = 0;
    int lastTotal = 0;

    while ( shot < report.length && turn < 10 ) {

        int increment = report[shot] + report[shot+1];

        if ( increment >= 10 ) {
            increment = increment + report[shot+2];
        }

        if ( report[shot] < 10 ) {
            shot++;
        }

        lastTotal = lastTotal + increment;
        shot++;
        turn++;

        System.out.println( shot + " : " + lastTotal);

    }

}
```

Figure 14.41 Method mystery for Exercise 14.9.2

EXERCISE 14.9.2

Show the output that would be produced when the method mystery *shown in Figure 14.41 is invoked.*

EXERCISE 14.9.3

Consider how one might represent a polynomial like

$$4x^3 + 2.3x^2 + x + 7$$

by placing its coefficients in an array of doubles. *A natural approach is to place the coefficient of the term including* x^i *in the ith element of the array. For example, the polynomial above could be represented by an array declared as*

```
private double [ ] coef = { 7, 1, 2.3, 4 };
```

The skeleton of a class named `Polynomial` designed to represent polynomials using this scheme is shown in Figure 14.42. The constructor for this class takes the degree of the polynomial, i.e., the highest power of x included in the terms of the polynomial, as a parameter. The `setCoef` method can be used to specify the coefficients of each term. For example, to create and initialize a `Polynomial` object representing the polynomial used as an example above we would declare

```
private Polynomial sample = new Polynomial(3);
```

and then execute the invocations

```
sample.setCoef( 7, 0 );
sample.setCoef( 1, 1 );
sample.setCoef( 2.3, 2 );
sample.setCoef( 4, 3 );
```

One method that should be included in the definition of such a polynomial class is a method to evaluate the polynomial at a given value of x. Four possible definitions of such a method are provided below. Some of them function correctly, while others contain errors. Identify the correct method(s) and indicate how the others would fail.

```java
public class Polynomial {

    // coef[i] is the coefficent of x to the ith power
    private double [ ] coef;

    public Polynomial( int degree ) {
        coef = new double[degree+1];
    }

    // Set the value of the coefficient of x to the ith
    public void setCoef( double value, int i ) {
        if ( i >= 0 && i < coef.length ) {
            coef[i] = value;
        }
    }

    //  Other methods would be included below

    . . .
}
```

Figure 14.42 Skeleton of a Polynomial class for Exercise 14.9.3

a.
```
public double eval( double x ) {
   double result = coef[0];
   double power = x;

   for ( int i = 1; i < coef.length; i++ ) {
     result = result + power * coef[i];
     power = power * x;
   }
   return result;
}
```
b.
```
public double eval( double x ) {
   double result = 0;
   double power = x;

   for ( int i = 0; i < coef.length; i++ ) {
     result = result + power * coef[i];
     power = power * x;
   }
   return result;
}
```
c.
```
public double eval( double x ) {
   double result = 0;
   double power = 1;

   for ( int i = 1; i <= coef.length; i++ ) {
     result = result + power * coef[i-1];
     power = power * x;
   }
   return result;
}
```
d.
```
public double eval( double x ) {
   double result = 0;

   for ( int i = coef.length-1; i >= 0; i-- ) {
     result = result*x + coef[i];
   }
   return result;
}
```

EXERCISE 14.9.4

Our addRacer *method handles the situation where the array becomes full by simply ignoring the request to add a new element. An alternative would be to simply make more room when the array became full.*

To make more room, the program would have to first create a new, larger array of racers. Then, it would have to copy the racers associated with the elements of the original array into the new array. Finally, it would associate the new array with the name racer.

a. *Write a method named* `growRacerArray` *that would perform these steps. Assume that the method would be included within the* `RaceStatistics` *class so that it could access the existing* `racer` *array as an instance variable. Your method should take one parameter, an* `int` *specifying how much bigger the new array should be than the exisiting* `racer` *array.*

b. *Rewrite* `addRacer` *so that it invokes* `growRacerArray` *when the* `racer` *array becomes full so that it never has to ignore an attempt to add a racer, as we did in the original version of the method. Each time you invoke* `growRacerArray`, *add* `TEAMSIZE` *entries to the array.*   ❖

EXERCISE 14.9.5

a. *Write a method,* `sum`, *that takes an array of* `doubles` *as a parameter and returns the sum of all elements in the array. Do not use the enhanced* `for` *loop.*

b. *Rewrite the* `sum` *method to use the enhanced* `for` *loop.*   ❖

14.10   Programming Problems

EXERCISE 14.10.1

In Exercise 14.9.3 we described parts of a `Polynomial` *class. In that exercise we provided code for a constructor, a method to set its coefficients, and a method to evaluate a polynomial at a particular value.*

Complete the `Polynomial` class by implementing the methods described below. For the purpose of presenting examples to illustrate how the methods should behave, assume that we have declared two `Polynomial` variables p and q and executed the code

```
p = new Polynomial(2);   // Create a second-degree polynomial
q = new Polynomial(3);   // Create a third-degree polynomial

p.setCoef( 3, 0 );
p.setCoef( 1, 2 );

q.setCoef( 4, 3 );
q.setCoef( 2.5, 2 );
q.setCoef( 1, 1 );
q.setCoef( 7, 0 );
```

so that p *represents the polyomial* $x^2 + 3$ *and* q *represents*

$$4x^3 + 2.5x^2 + x + 7$$

The methods you should define are

• `public String toString()`
This method should return a `String` *representing the polynomial in a form suitable for human consumption. Since superscripts are not available, use the character "^" to denote*

exponentiation. Thus, invoking the `toString` *method on the* `Polynomial` `q` *should produce a string like*

```
4.0x^3 + 2.5x^2 + 1.0x^1 + 7.0x^0
```

When possible, simplify the string returned by eliminating unnecessary terms. For example, it would be best if `q.toString()` *returned*

```
4.0x^3 + 2.5x^2 + x + 7.0
```

and `p.toString()` *returned*

```
x^2 + 3.0
```

⁕ `public Polynomial plus( Polynomial addend )`
This method should return the `Polynomial` *which is the sum of the polynomial represented by the* `Polynomial` *object on which it is invoked and the* `Polynomial` *passed as a parameter to the method. For example,*

```
Polynomial r = p.plus(q);
System.out.println( r.toString() );
```

should display

```
4.0x^3 + 3.5x^2 + x + 10.0
```

⁕ `public Polynomial times( Polynomial multiplicand )`
This method should return the `Polynomial` *which is the product of the polynomial represented by the* `Polynomial` *object on which it is invoked and the* `Polynomial` *passed as a parameter to the method. For example,*

```
Polynomial r = p.times(q);
System.out.println( r.toString() );
```

should display

```
4.0x^5 + 2.5x^4 + 13.0x^3 + 14.5x^2 + 3.0x + 21.0
```

❖

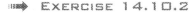 EXERCISE 14.10.2

Write a program that implements the following puzzle-like test of a user's visual acuity. The program should display an eight-by-eight grid of rectangles of different shades of gray, as shown in Figure 14.43. (If you want to make it look prettier than our version, you can use different colors instead of shades of gray.) Each shade that appears in your grid should appear exactly twice. Each rectangle in your grid should be surrounded by a black `FramedRect` *so that the gray patches are clearly separated from one another.*

The goal of this puzzle is to identify the pairs of rectangles that are the same color. The user of your program will do this by using the mouse to identify rectangles that appear to match. When the user clicks on a rectangle to identify it as the first member of a matching pair, your program should highlight the selected rectangle by turning the `FrameRect` *that surrounds it red. In Figure 14.43, the rectangle containing the mouse cursor has just been selected and the frame has been painted red (making it appear light gray in the figure).*

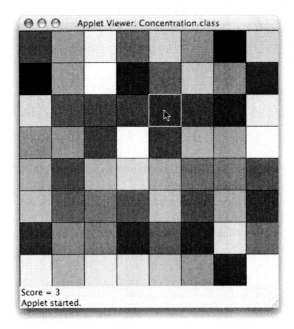

Figure 14.43   Matching patches program after one patch is selected

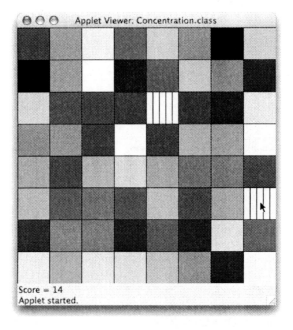

Figure 14.44   Matching patches program after one pair has been identified

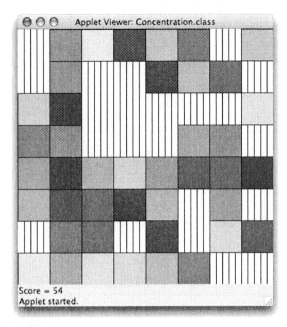

Figure 14.45 Matching patches program after many pairs have been identified

If the next rectangle the user clicks on is exactly the same shade as the first, they should both be removed from the display, revealing a pattern drawn underneath the rectangles, as shown in Figure 14.44. The pattern we have drawn is simply a set of vertical lines. You could use any pattern you want or even place an image in the background. If the second rectangle the user selects does not exactly match the first, the frame around the first rectangle selected should be set back to black and the user should be allowed to try again.

Each time the user clicks, the program should add one to the user's "score" and display this score at the bottom of the window. Figure 14.45 shows the state of the display after many matches have been found. The goal is to find all the matching pairs, revealing the entire background, with as few clicks as possible. ❖

CHAPTER 15

Multidimensional Arrays

*n Chapter 14 you learned that an array is a collection of values or objects, where each member of the collection is numbered by an index value. Arrays give us a natural way to represent collections of objects or values in the real world—for example, pages in a text book, speeders per hour in a day, or the order of racers completing a race.

In this chapter, we explore *arrays of arrays*—i.e., *two-dimensional arrays*. You already know that an array can represent a collection of any type of value or object. So, naturally, an array can represent a collection of arrays. The world is filled with examples of collections such as these. Consider, for instance, a monthly magazine. We number the monthly editions as well as the pages of each. Now consider a calendar. We number the months as well as the days of each month. Because two-dimensional arrays are used so frequently in programming, Java provides convenient notation for constructing two-dimensional arrays and for accessing the values in them.

In the next section, we introduce a calendar program for which a two-dimensional array is a natural data structure. In the context of this example, we discuss the declaration and construction of two-dimensional arrays, and how to make associations between index values and members of a two-dimensional array. We then go over common algorithms for traversing, i.e., walking through, a two-dimensional array in order to process the information contained there.

We then turn our attention to *matrices*. In a two-dimensional array, the arrays in the collection need not be of the same size. In some situations, however, all arrays in the collection do have the same size. A chess board is a good example. If you think of each row of a chess board as an array of eight elements, then the entire board can be represented by an array of these rows. This type of array is called a *matrix*. While matrices are really just two-dimensional arrays, they are conceptually a bit different and deserve separate treatment.

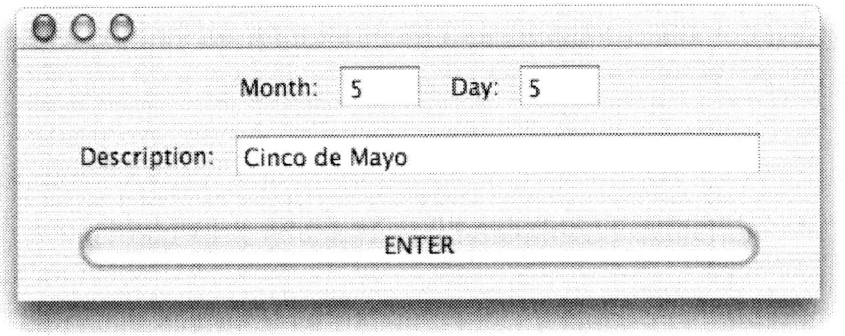

Figure 15.1   Interface used to enter new calendar events

15.1   General Two-Dimensional Arrays

We will explore two-dimensional arrays through an example of an interactive calendar manager. You have probably seen or used one of these. A sample user interface for such a calendar manager is shown in Figure 15.1. This program allows the user to enter the description of an event that will occur on a given date.

If our calendar is meant to represent a full year of days, then we need the ability to represent up to 365 strings that describe daily events. You might imagine using a 365-element array to do so. But is this conceptually the best choice? While it is true that a year is made up of 365 days, we tend not to describe any individual date as "day 364" or "day 32". Instead, we describe a date by giving the month and then the day within that month, as in 12/30 or 2/1. So let's develop a data structure that serves as a better representation of this idea. Let's think of each month as an array of strings that represent daily events. A year then is a 12-element collection of months. That is, a year is an array of months, each of which is an array of Strings.

15.1.1   Declaring an Array of Arrays

In writing our calendar program, we will define a class YearlyCalendar that will describe a full year of daily events. As we just discussed, we will think of a year as a 12-element array of months, each of which is an array of Strings that describe the daily events. To declare dailyEvent as the name of this array of arrays of Strings, we say:

```
private String[ ][ ] dailyEvent;
```

The square brackets should already be familiar to you, as they are used both to surround numeric index values and in declarations of arrays. Since dailyEvent is meant to be an array of String arrays, you simply write one extra pair of brackets in the declaration.

15.1.2   Creating an Array of Arrays

As you already know, the declaration of an array introduces its name, but it does not actually create a new array. To construct our array of arrays, we will proceed in two steps.

dailyEvent

Figure 15.2   A 12-element array. Each element in the array has the potential to refer to an array of strings

We know that there are 12 months in a year, so dailyEvent should represent 12 months (i.e., arrays of Strings). To construct this 12-element array we say:

```
dailyEvent = new String[12][ ];
```

After this construction, we have a 12-element array as in Figure 15.2. At this point each element of the array is null. Each element has the potential to refer to an array of Strings, but none does yet, as we haven't explicitly created any String arrays.

Next we can create the 12 String arrays. Let's begin simply, by looking at the construction of just one of these arrays. We know that January has 31 days, so our String array for January will need to be 31 elements long. Since array indexing begins at 0, dailyEvent[0] refers to January's daily events. So we construct the String array for January as follows:

```
dailyEvent[0] = new String[31];
```

his says that the first element (with index 0) in the array dailyEvent is a 31-element array Strings.

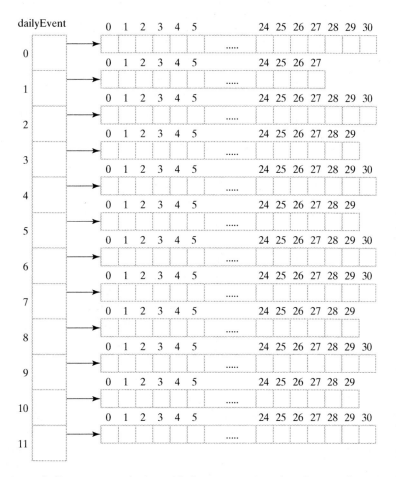

Since the String array for each month will be created similarly, it is natural to use a loop. To create all 12 String arrays, we would write:

```
for (int month = 0; month < 12; month++) {
    int numDays = getDays( month+1 );
    dailyEvent[month] = new String[numDays];
}
```

Here you can imagine that getDays is a private method that returns the number of days in each month. For now, let's not worry about leap years. We'll assume that February has 28 days.

After this loop has been executed, we have a data structure like the one in Figure 15.3. Notice that there are 12 rows in the figure, and each row has from 28 to 31 elements, representing the number of days in each month. While there are no strings in this data structure yet, we are now at a point where we can begin to remember daily event descriptions.

15.1.3 Indexing an Array of Arrays

Say that a user of our calendar program enters the following information

```
1/28 Spring semester starts
```

That is, the month entered is 1; the day entered is 28; and the event description is "Spring semester starts". We want to record this information in the two-dimensional array, dailyEvent. Specifically, we want the twenty-seventh entry in the first row of dailyEvent refer to the string "Spring semester starts".

Remember that array indexing begins at 0, so we want to reference the row called 0. Within that row, we want to refer to the element called 27. So we say

```
dailyEvent[0][27] = "Spring semester starts";
```

Figure 15.4 shows dailyEvent after two assignments have been made to array elements—the one above, as well as

```
dailyEvent[4][30] = "Mom's birthday";
```

This assignment indicates that May 31 is "Mom's birthday".

More generally, the YearlyCalendar class should have a method setEvent that takes three parameters—a month, a day, and an event description—and should set that entry appropriately. The method is as follows:

```
// Set the event description for a given month and day
public void setEvent( int month, int day, String description ) {
    dailyEvent[month-1][day-1] = description;
}
```

Note that we subtract one from both the month and the day. Since we count actual dates beginning with 1 and array indices beginning with 0, it is necessary to make this adjustment.

A similar method can be written to retrieve the event associated with a particular date. Given a month and a day, the method simply returns the corresponding entry in dailyEvent:

```
// Returns the event associated with a given date
public String getEvent( int month, int day ) {
    return dailyEvent[month-1][day-1];
}
```

Now let's take another look at the dailyEvent array. A different view is shown in Figure 15.5. In this figure we have "squashed" the rows together so that the array of arrays looks more like a table with rows and columns. When you think of the data structure in this way—i.e., as a *two-dimensional array*—it is then natural to think of the indices in brackets as specifying a row and a column in a table. Therefore, if someArray is a two-dimensional array, then

```
someArray[rowNum][colNum]
```

refers to the element in the row numbered rowNum and the column numbered colNum.

EXERCISE 15.1.1

rite the assignment statement that records that July 4 is Independence Day.

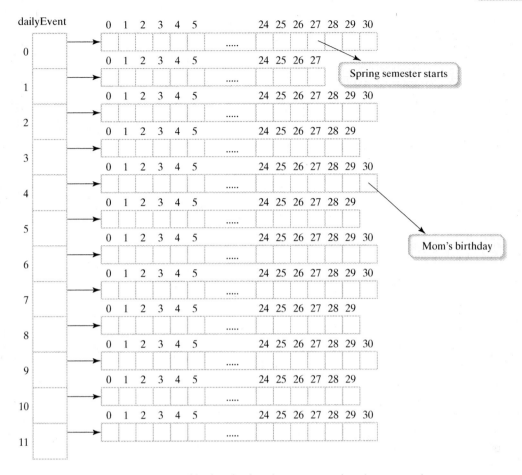

Figure 15.4 Yearly calendar after two events have been entered

15.1.4 Traversing a Two-Dimensional Array

As you saw in Chapter 14, we often want to do something with every element in an array. If so, we use a loop to iterate through the elements, performing on each one the specific action desired. We will continue to follow this basic pattern even with two-dimensional arrays, but with a little extra work to handle the extra dimension.

Say that in our calendar program, we want to initialize each entry to the description "No event today". Let's first think about how we would initialize each entry for just one month. If month is an int variable that refers to a specific month, then we initialize the entries for that month with a simple loop:

```
// Fill all entries for one month with "No event today"
for (int day = 0; day < dailyEvent[month].length; day++) {
    dailyEvent[month][day] = "No event today";
}
```

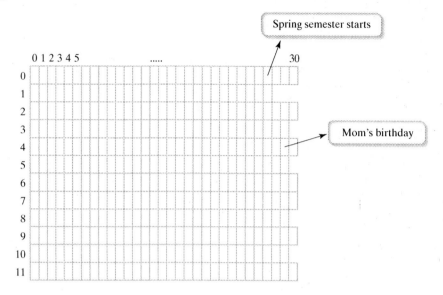

Figure 15.5   Another view of daily events as a jagged table

The row to be traversed is the row corresponding to month. We go through each of the elements in that month, beginning with day 0. We stop as soon as day is equal to the length of that row. Recall that we can get the length of an array by following the array name with .length. Note that this loop is similar to the array-traversal loops you saw in Chapter 14.

What we really want, however, is to do this sort of initialization for each of the 12 months of the year, as follows:

```
// Fill all entries in each month with "No event today"
for (month = 0; month < 12; month++) {
    // Fill all entries for one month with "No event today"
    ...
}
```

Like the for loop above, this one simply steps through the array element by element. Putting these together, we get:

```
// Fill all entries in each month with "No event today"
for (int month = 0; month < 12; month++) {
    // Fill all entries for one month with "No event today"
    for (int day = 0; day < dailyEvent[month].length; day++) {
        dailyEvent[month][day] = "No event today";
    }
}
```

In general, traversal of a two-dimensional array is accomplished with nested for loops, one of which handles the rows and the other the columns. Figure 15.6 outlines this idea.

Figure 15.7 shows the definition of the YearlyCalendar class that we have been discussing. This class has two instance variables, dailyEvent, the two-dimensional array, and

```
for (row = 0; row < myArray.length; row++) {
    for (col = 0; col < myArray[row].length; col++) {
        // Do something with array element myArray[row][col]
        ...
    }
}
```

Figure 15.6   General structure of nested for loops to traverse a two-dimensional array

an integer-valued year. This variable can be used to determine leap years, so that February has the appropriate number of days. The constructor takes a single parameter that is the year of the calendar to be constructed. It then constructs the two-dimensional array and initializes each daily event to "No event today". The method setEvent allows a user to add an event to the calendar; the method getEvent returns the event description associated with a particular date.

➡ EXERCISE 15.1.2

Add a method to the YearlyCalendar *class called* printYear, *with the following header:*

   public void printYear()

This method should print the entire year's activities. That is, for each day of the year it should print the date followed by the activity for that day. The format of each printed line should be as follows:

   month/day: activity

Nothing should be printed for a day whose entry is "No event today". ❖

15.1.5   Beyond Two Dimensions: Extending the Calendar Program

The class YearlyCalendar that we have been discussing is admittedly quite limited. Any good calendar manager should allow a user to enter more than one event for any given date. In this section, we briefly examine ways in which the YearlyCalendar class can be extended.

Any given date in your calendar has the potential to be fairly complex. As Figure 15.8 shows, you might have general event descriptions for a day as well as hourly appointments or meetings. Since any single day is filled with a variety of information, let's define a new class, CalendarDay, that can be used to describe the events in any single day.

As illustrated in Figure 15.8, there are at least two different kinds of event descriptions you might find on a single date. These include descriptions for the day as a whole and a listing of appointments. In order to represent these two related, but distinct, types of information, we'll define two arrays in the CalendarDay class. One of these will be the collection of full-day events, and the other will be the collection of hourly appointments. Both arrays will be collections of type String. The declarations are as follows:

   private String[ ] fullDayEvent;
   private String[ ] hourlyEvent;

```java
// Class to represent a yearly calendar of daily events
public class YearlyCalendar {

    // A two-dimensional array of event descriptions.
    // rows are months; columns are days
    private String[][] dailyEvent;

    private int year;        // The year

    // Create a calendar for the given year
    public YearlyCalendar( int aYear ) {
        year = aYear;

        // Set up two-dimensional array of months and days
        dailyEvent = new String[12][];
        for (int month = 0; month < 12; month++) {
            int numDays = getDays( month );
            dailyEvent[month] = new String[numDays];
        }

        // Initialize event descriptions
        for (int month = 0; month < 12; month++) {
            for (int day = 0; day < dailyEvent[month].length; day++) {
                dailyEvent[month][day] = "No event today";
            }
        }
    }

    // Returns number of days in the month
    private int getDays( int monthNumber ) {
        ... // Code omitted here
    }

    // Set the event description for a given month and day
    public void setEvent( int month, int day, String description ) {
        dailyEvent[month-1][day-1] = description;
    }

    // Returns the event associated with a given date
    public String getEvent( int month, int day ) {
        return dailyEvent[month-1][day-1];
    }
}
```

Figure 15.7   The YearlyCalendar class

```
9/8

    Dad's birthday
    Poster sale


    10:00 CS class
    11:00 Calculus
    12:00 Lunch with Bob
    1:00 CS Lab
    5:30 Dinner with Karen
    7:00 Choir practice
    9:00 CS study session
```

Figure 15.8 Calendar entries for one day

Before the arrays can be used, of course, we need to construct them. To do so, we need to specify their respective sizes. Since we intend for hourlyEvent to refer to appointments scheduled "on the hour", we want it to have a capacity of 24. On the other hand, we can't anticipate exactly how many full-day events there will be. Instead, we construct this array with a capacity that we think is reasonable. If NUM_DAILY_EVENTS is a constant that specifies this number, then the two arrays can be constructed as written here:

```
fullDayEvent = new String[NUM_DAILY_EVENTS];
hourlyEvent = new String[24];
```

A partial definition of the class CalendarDay is shown in Figure 15.9. Two of the instance variables, fullDayEvent and hourlyEvent, are as described above. There are two additional instance variables that will refer to the date as described by the month and day. Finally, there is an instance variable numDaily that will be used to remember the actual number of full-day events. The constructor simply creates the two arrays, remembers the values of the parameters, aMonth and aDay, and sets numDaily to 0, since there are initially no events.

There are two methods shown, which add descriptions to the full-day events and hourly events, respectively. Note that before we can add a full-day event, we need to be sure that there is space left in the array. We also need to adjust the number of events currently remembered. The method that adds a description to the hourly events assumes that an hour is passed in as a parameter and that the hour is based on a 24-hour clock.

We can now modify YearlyCalendar to make use of this new class. The first thing we need to do is declare that a year of daily events is a two-dimensional array of CalendarDays, rather than simply Strings:

```
private CalendarDay[ ][ ] dailyEvent;
```

So, in essence, dailyEvent is an array of months, each of which is an array of days, each of which is two arrays of daily and hourly events.

```java
// Class to describe events for a single calendar day
public class CalendarDay {

    // Maximum number of full-day events
    private static final int NUM_DAILY_EVENTS = 5;

    // Descriptions of full-day events
    private String[ ] fullDayEvent;

    // Number of full-day events
    private int currentDaily;

    // Descriptions of hourly events
    private String[ ] hourlyEvent;

    // Month / Day
    private int month, day;

    // Set up an empty calendar for the given month and day
    public CalendarDay( int aMonth, int aDay ) {
        fullDayEvent = new String[NUM_DAILY_EVENTS];
        currentDaily = 0;

        hourlyEvent = new String[24];

        month = aMonth;
        day = aDay;
    }

    // Add description of a full-day event for this day
    public void addFullDayEvent( String description ) {
        if (currentDaily < NUM_DAILY_EVENTS) {
            fullDayEvent[currentDaily] = description;
            currentDaily++;
        }
    }

    // Add event description for a specific hour of the day;
    // time is based on a 24-hour clock
    public void addHourlyEvent( int time, String description ) {
        hourlyEvent[time] = description;
    }
}
```

Figure 15.9   A partial CalendarDay class

We leave the remainder of the implementation of this class as an exercise. The important idea to take from this section is that it can be very useful to construct arrays which have, as their elements, other objects containing arrays.

➡ EXERCISE 15.1.3

Complete the class CalendarDay *by adding the following methods:*

```
// Clear all event entries for this day
// All event entries are set to "---"
public void clearDay()

// Return the event for a specific hour on this day
public String getHourlyEvent( int time )

// Print all hourly events;
// Each hourly event on a separate line in the form
// hour:00 event
public void printHourlyEvents()

// Print all full day events
public void printFullDayEvents()

// Print all events for this day
public void printDay()
```

In addition, modify the constructor so that it calls the method clearDay *to initialize all of the event entries for the day.* ❖

15.2 Matrices

We now turn our attention to *matrices*. As we said in the introduction to this chapter, a *matrix* is simply a two-dimensional array in which all the rows have the same length. If all the months of the year had 31 days, for example, our two-dimensional array, dailyEvent could be called a matrix.

Let's consider several additional examples to illustrate the structure of a matrix. First, consider the image in Figure 15.10. The image is a magnified square region of pixels from a drawing (like one you might create with primitives from the objectdraw library). If you were to consider what data structure might nicely represent this, a two-dimensional array should come to mind. This is a nice conceptual fit, because the image has a two-dimensional structure. Each pixel can be described by its row and column position, as well as its color value.

There are some interesting and important differences between Figure 15.10 and the two-dimensional dailyEvent array we discussed in the preceding sections. First, each row has the same length. More importantly, however, there is no special meaning we can ascribe to any given row or column. Whereas a calendar can be described as an array of months, each of which is

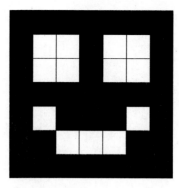

Figure 15.10 Magnified pixels from an image

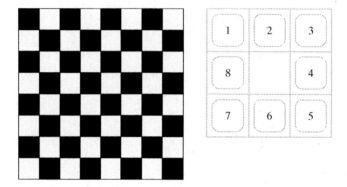

Figure 15.11 A chessboard and sliding block puzzle: examples of objects that can be represented by two-dimensional matrices

an array of days, this is simply a collection of pixels in a particular configuration. Other similar examples include the chessboard and sliding block puzzle shown in Figure 15.11.

We'll begin our discussion of two-dimensional arrays like these, i.e., matrices, with a puzzle not pictured in Figure 15.11, "magic squares". We'll then return to the example of pixels in an image.

15.2.1 Magic Squares

A square of numbers is said to be a *magic square* if all of the rows, columns, and diagonals add up to the same number. Figure 15.12 shows two magic squares. In the first, each row, column, and diagonal adds up to 15. In the second, each row, column, and diagonal adds up to 65. Notice that the first is filled with the integers 1–9 and the second with the integers 1–25. It turns out that as long as n is odd, there is a simple algorithm for creating an n-by-n magic square from the numbers 1 through n^2. We'll get back to the algorithm a bit later. For now, let's focus on the way we would check whether a given n-by-n square is a magic square. Before we can do this, we examine the declaration of a magic square.

$$
\begin{array}{|c|c|c|}
\hline
4 & 9 & 2 \\ \hline
3 & 5 & 7 \\ \hline
8 & 1 & 6 \\ \hline
\end{array}
\qquad
\begin{array}{|c|c|c|c|c|}
\hline
11 & 18 & 25 & 2 & 9 \\ \hline
10 & 12 & 19 & 21 & 3 \\ \hline
4 & 6 & 13 & 20 & 22 \\ \hline
23 & 5 & 7 & 14 & 16 \\ \hline
17 & 24 & 1 & 8 & 15 \\ \hline
\end{array}
$$

Figure 15.12 Magic squares

15.2.2 Declaring and Constructing a Matrix

We have already said that a matrix is simply a two-dimensional array. It should come as no surprise, then, that it will be declared in the same way. To declare a variable name `magicSquare` to be a matrix of integer values, we say

```
private int[ ][ ] magicSquare;
```

Before it can be filled, the matrix must be constructed. Since each row is of the same length, i.e., since the matrix has a rectangular form, we can do this more simply than we could in our calendar example above. We simply say

```
magicSquare = new int[SIZE][SIZE];
```

where `SIZE` is a constant that represents the number of rows and columns in the magic square. In general, we can construct an *n*-row and *m*-column matrix `rectangularArray` as follows

```
rectangularArray = new type[n][m];
```

Here `type` is the name of a data type such as `int`, `boolean`, or `String`.

15.2.3 Traversing a Matrix

In order to determine whether a square is a magic square, we need to find the sum of each row, each column, and each diagonal. We will consider the traversals of the rows, columns, and diagonals separately.

Row-by-Row Traversal

When we are given a square to examine, we don't know at the outset what the sum of any row, column, or diagonal should be. So, before we can confirm that all the sums are the same, we need to find a sum that will be our target. We do this by computing the sum of the elements in the first row of our square:

```
// Compute sum of elements in row 0
int targetSum = 0;
for (int col = 0; col < SIZE; col++) {
    targetSum = targetSum + magicSquare[0][col];
}
```

We declare a variable `targetSum` that will be the sum of the first-row elements. We initialize it to 0, and then add to it the value of each element we examine. In order to index the matrix, we need to specify both a row and a column. Since the first row is being examined here, the row index is always 0. The column index, on the other hand, begins at 0 and goes sequentially through the columns as long as the index is less than `SIZE`.

After `targetSum` is computed, we can examine the rest of the matrix. First, we consider each of the rows. We compute the sum of each row, in turn, and compare it to the target. If the sum of any row is different from the target, we set a boolean variable `isMagicSquare` to false. We go on to check the next row, as long as there is at least one remaining to be checked:

```
// Assume we have a magic square unless a sum is incorrect
boolean isMagicSquare = true;
for (int row = 1; row < SIZE; row++) {
    // Check sum of each row
    int sum = 0;
    for (col = 0; col < SIZE; col++) {
        sum = sum + magicSquare[row][col];
    }
    if (sum != targetSum) {
        isMagicSquare = false;
    }
}
```

The inner loop that traverses each row should look very familiar; it's almost identical to the loop we wrote to compute `targetSum`. Around it is the loop that controls movement through the matrix row by row. Note that the first row index is 1, rather than 0, this time. This is because row 0 was used to compute the initial target sum.

You may have noticed that the row-checking code above is less efficient than it might be. If the sum of any row does not match the target, we set the boolean `isMagicSquare` to `false`, but we continue to check the remaining rows. This is completely unnecessary. Therefore, we modify the loop so that we only continue if there are more rows to check *and if the square still looks like it might be a magic square*:

```
// Assume we have a magic square unless a sum is incorrect
boolean isMagicSquare = true;
for (int row = 1; row < SIZE && isMagicSquare; row++) {
    // Check sum of each row
    int sum = 0;
    for (col = 0; col < SIZE; col++) {
        sum = sum + magicSquare[row][col];
    }
    if (sum != targetSum) {
        isMagicSquare = false;
    }
}
```

EXERCISE 15.2.1

We can further modify the code for checking row sums by replacing the if-then by a single assignment statement

```
isMagicSquare = (sum == targetSum);
```

Can we replace the if-then in the earlier version of the row-checking code, as follows?

```
// Assume we have a magic square unless a sum is incorrect
boolean isMagicSquare = true;
for (int row = 1; row < SIZE; row++) {
    // Check sum of each row
    int sum = 0;
    for (col = 0; col < SIZE; col++) {
        sum = sum + magicSquare[row][col];
    }
    isMagicSquare = (sum == targetSum);
}
```

Why or why not?   ❖

Column-by-Column Traversal

To check that the sum of each column is equal to the target, we again write a pair of nested loops. The loops will be virtually identical to those that check the rows, but we will reverse the order of the nesting. The inner loop will check a complete column by going through all of the rows in a given column, while the outer loop will control movement through the array column by column:

```
// Assume we have a magic square unless a sum is incorrect
boolean isMagicSquare = true;
for (int col = 0; col < SIZE && isMagicSquare; col++) {
    // Check sum of each column
    int sum = 0;
    for (row = 0; row < SIZE; row++) {
        sum = sum + magicSquare[row][col];
    }
    isMagicSquare = (sum == targetSum);
}
```

The works as desired because the inner loop is executed entirely for each iteration of the outer loop. So when the variable col has the value 0, the inner loop goes through each row number in column 0. When the variable col has the value 1, the inner loop goes through each row number in column 1; and so on.

Diagonal Traversal

Once we have checked the rows and columns, we can check each of the diagonals. We'll do this by writing two separate loops. (No nesting of loops within loops is required this time!) In the complete program, the loops would be nested within if statements to ensure the program would not check a diagonal if it had already determined that the matrix did not form a magic square. Below, however, we will focus our attention on the loops themselves.

The key to traversing a diagonal is to recognize that both the row and column indices need to change with each iteration of the loop. Let's consider the major diagonal first. Here, we need to examine the elements in positions [0][0], [1][1], [2][2], etc. The row and column indices certainly change, but each time they remain equal to each other. As a result, we only need a single variable to help us iterate over the elements on the diagonal:

```
// Check sum of major diagonal
int sum = 0;
for (int element = 0; element < SIZE; element++) {
    sum = sum + magicSquare[element][element];
}
isMagicSquare = (sum == targetSum);
```

The minor diagonal, which starts in the upper right corner and moves to the lower left, is a bit more tricky. This time we notice that when the row value is 0, the column value is the maximum column value, SIZE-1. When the row value is 1, the column value is 1 less than the maximum. When the row value is 2, the column value is 2 less than the maximum. That is, if the row value is given to us by the variable row, then the appropriate column is:

```
(SIZE-1) - row
```

We use this information to help us write a for loop to traverse the minor diagonal as follows:

```
// Check sum of minor diagonal
int sum = 0;
for (int row = 0; row < SIZE; row++) {
    sum = sum + magicSquare[row][SIZE-1-row];
}
isMagicSquare = (sum == targetSum);
```

15.2.4   Filling a Magic Square

Now we turn to filling a magic square. As we indicated earlier, as long as *n* is odd, there is a simple algorithm for creating an *n*-by-*n* magic square. The algorithm is as follows:

* Place a 1 in the center of the bottom row. Then fill in the remainder of the square by following these rules:
* Try to place the next integer (one greater than the last one you placed) in the cell one slot below and to the right of the last one placed. If you fall off the bottom of the array, go to the top row of the same column. If you fall off the right edge of the array, go to the leftmost column. If that cell is empty, write the next integer there and continue. If the cell is full, go back to where you wrote the last integer and write the next one in the cell directly above it.

Try this yourself. Consider a small example, like a square with three rows and three columns.

➠ EXERCISE 15.2.2

To ensure that you really see how the magic-square-filling algorithm works, try it on a larger square. This time use the algorithm to fill in a square with five rows and five columns. ❖

Now let's write Java code to implement this algorithm. Let's begin by initializing each cell in the square to 0. This will allow us to determine whether a given cell has been filled or not. If the matrix to be filled is `magicSquare` as above, we initialize it with a pair of nested loops:

```
// Initialize all entries in the square to 0
for (int row = 0; row < SIZE; row++) {
    for (int col = 0; col < SIZE; col++) {
        magicSquare[row][col] = 0;
    }
}
```

Next we'll declare and initialize two integer variables, `currRow` and `currCol`. These will refer to the row and column of the current cell to be filled. Since the first cell to be filled is in the bottom row of `magicSquare`, the initial value of `currRow` will be `SIZE-1`. Since the cell is in the middle of the bottom, our column index needs to refer to the middle element. To find the middle column, we simply divide `SIZE` by 2. So

```
int currRow = SIZE-1;
int currCol = SIZE/2;
```

Remember that `SIZE` is always an odd-valued `int` and that integer division always gives us an integer-valued result. That is, any remainder is lost. So, 3/2 evaluates to 1, which is the middle of the three indices 0, 1, and 2. Similarly, 5/2 evaluates to 2, which is the middle index of 0, 1, 2, 3, and 4; and so on.

Now we can begin to fill the matrix. Since filling `magicSquare` is a matter of repeatedly applying the rules above, we'll place the code in a loop. The loop will control the values placed in the matrix, so we can write it as:

```
for (int nextInt = 1; nextInt <= SIZE*SIZE; nextInt++) {
    // fill a cell
}
```

As we enter the loop, we know the row and column indices of the cell to fill, so we say:

```
magicSquare[currRow][currCol] = nextInt;
```

Now we need to find the next cell to fill, so that the next loop iteration will fill it properly. First we try to move one space to the right and one space down:

```
int nextCol = currCol + 1;
int nextRow = currRow + 1;
```

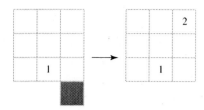

Figure 15.13   Wrapping around after falling off the bottom of the square

But we need to take into account the possibility that we'll fall off the right edge or the bottom edge of the matrix. For instance, if magicSquare is a three-by-three matrix and we just finished filling the first cell (i.e., the cell in the middle of the bottom row), then the next cell to fill would be the one with row index 3 and column index 2. But, as illustrated in Figure 15.13, this is not a valid cell in the matrix. In this case, we need to move to the first row in the same column, i.e., to the row with index 0. We can handle this easily by modifying the lines that update nextRow and nextCol as follows:

```
int nextCol = (currCol + 1) % SIZE;
int nextRow = (currRow + 1) % SIZE;
```

Remember that the % operator gives us the remainder when dividing one integer by another. So if currRow is 2, then next row is (2 + 1) % 3, which evaluates to 0.

We still have to take care of one more thing before we can fill the cell. We need to be sure that it is actually available, i.e., that it hasn't already been filled. For example, Figure 15.14 shows magicSquare after three cells have been filled. The next one to fill would be the center bottom cell, which already has a value. In this case, the algorithm tells us to go back to the cell just filled (the cell with value 3) and move one cell up. We can accomplish the check for availability and possible index adjustment as follows:

```
if (magicSquare[nextRow][nextCol] == 0) {
    // Use the cell if it is available
    currRow = nextRow;
    currCol = nextCol;
} else {  // Move up one cell otherwise
    currRow = (currRow - 1 + SIZE) % SIZE;
}
```

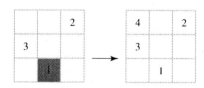

Figure 15.14   Moving up if the next cell to be filled is already full

```
// Place values to make a magic square
public void fillSquare ( ) {

   // Initialize to all 0s
   for (int row = 0; row < SIZE; row++) {
      for (int col = 0; col < SIZE; col++) {
         magicSquare[row][col] = 0;
      }
   }

   // Set the indices for the middle of the bottom row
   int currRow = SIZE - 1;
   int currCol = SIZE / 2;

   // Fill each cell
   for (int nextInt = 1; nextInt <= SIZE*SIZE; nextInt++) {
      magicSquare[currRow][currCol] = nextInt;

      // Try to move down and to the right with wraparound
      int nextRow = (row + 1) % SIZE;
      int nextCol = (col + 1) % SIZE;

      // If the cell is empty, remember those indices for the
      // next assignment
      if (magicSquare[nextRow][nextCol] == 0) {
         currRow = nextRow;
         currCol = nextCol;
      } else {
         // The cell was full – Use the cell above the previous one
         currRow = (currRow - 1 + SIZE) % SIZE;
      }
   }
}
```

Figure 15.15 A method to fill a magic square

The final statement makes an adjustment in the case that moving up moves us out of the matrix. That is, it wraps us around the bottom.

Now that we know the next cell, the next iteration of the loop can fill it. A method called fillSquare with the complete implementation is shown in Figure 15.15.

15.2.5 Digital Image Smoothing

In this section we consider a real application for which matrices provide a useful data structure – digital images and, in particular, digital image smoothing.

Columns

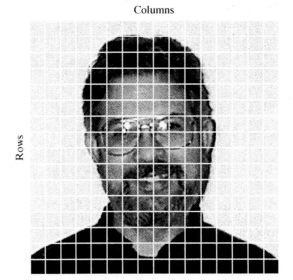

Rows

Figure 15.16   Digitization of an image

Figure 15.17   Magnified region of an image to be digitized. If one value is to represent this region,
information will be lost

Imagine that you have scanned an old black-and-white family photo into your computer. The resulting image is a *digital image*. While the quality of the image may be very good, it is really only an approximate rendering of the original photo, as Figure 15.16 illustrates. Ultimately, the photo will be represented by a two-dimensional grid (i.e., matrix) of pixel values. Small regions of the photo are sampled, and for each one, a pixel value is determined. This process is good, but imperfect. For example, consider Figure 15.17. This represents the region in the next to last row that is on the left edge of the picture in Figure 15.16. If just one value is used to represent this complex region, some information will clearly be lost.

As a result, many *smoothing algorithms* have been developed that adjust the pixel values. The hope is that the resulting digital image, with softer edges between objects in the image, will look better. In this section, we'll examine one very simple smoothing algorithm—an averaging algorithm.

An Image as a Matrix of Brightness Values

We'll assume that we are given a digitized black-and-white image that is represented as a matrix of brightness values. (Recall from Section 3.5 that new Color(brightness, brightness, brightness) creates a shade of gray.) This is, we won't concern ourselves with the initial

Pixel value to be replaced by average

Figure 15.18 A pixel and its immediate neighborhood to be considered by the averaging algorithm

process of digitization. The declaration of the matrix, called `brightness`, is as follows:

```
private int[ ][ ] brightness;
```

We also assume that we know the width and height of the image in pixels, and that these are represented by the constants `WIDTH` and `HEIGHT`, respectively.

A Simple Smoothing Algorithm

The smoothing algorithm that we will implement is a simple averaging algorithm. For each pixel in the image, we'll replace its brightness value with the average of the brightness values in the region immediately surrounding it. If the pixel in the center of Figure 15.18 is the one to be replaced, the region we consider is the single layer of pixels encircling it, as shown.

When we traverse the matrix in order to modify its pixel values, we need to be particularly careful about two issues. First, we need to treat the borders of the image slightly differently from the way we treat the interior. After all, a corner pixel does not have as many neighbors as an interior pixel. We also have to be sure that the averaged image is represented by a new matrix.

If we modified the original image, pixels that had already been replaced by averages would affect averages computed later.

Let's give our second matrix the name `avgBrightness` and declare it as follows:

```
private int[ ][ ] avgBrightness;
```

Don't forget that before we fill `avgBrightness` with average brightness values, we need to construct the matrix:

```
avgBrightness = new int[HEIGHT][WIDTH];
```

We're now ready to implement the part of the algorithm that does the actual averaging. We will do this in stages, focusing first on the central pixels—i.e., all of those that are not on the border of the image. We need to replace each pixel by an average value, so we will use a pair of nested loops to traverse the matrix:

```
for (int row = 1; row < HEIGHT-1; row++) {
    for (int col = 1; col < WIDTH-1; col++) {
        // replace brightness value by average value
        ...
    }
}
```

Now if we look again at Figure 15.18, we will notice that the pixels in the region to be averaged are arranged in a row-column matrixlike pattern. Therefore, we can write another pair of nested loops to take us through those pixels so that we can determine their average:

```
// Calculate average brightness at position specified by row and col;
// position is not on an edge of the image.
int totalBrightness = 0;
for (int r = -1; r <= 1; r++) {
    for (int c = -1; c <= 1; c++) {
        totalBrightness = totalBrightness + brightness[row+r][col+c];
    }
    avgBrightness[row][col] = totalBrightness/9;
}
```

The variables r and c help us to traverse the pixels with respect to the current row and col. Once we have found the sum of all the brightness values in the pixel's neighborhood, including the pixel itself, we compute the average and set the corresponding entry in the average brightness matrix.

Next we can consider the pixels on the border of the image. Here the algorithm is similar; we simply need to be careful to include only legitimate matrix entries in the averaging process. To adjust the pixels on the top border of the image (except for the corners), we can say:

```
// Calculate average brightness at position specified by row and col;
// position is top edge of the image, not in a corner.
int totalBrightness = 0;
for (int r = 0; r <= 1; r++) {
    for (int c = -1; c <= 1; c++) {
        totalBrightness = totalBrightness + brightness[row+r][col+c];
    }
    avgBrightness[row][col] = totalBrightness/6;
}
```

and similarly, for the bottom row (except for the corners), we can say:

```
// Calculate average brightness at position specified by row and col;
// position is bottom edge of the image, not in a corner.
int totalBrightness = 0;
for (int r = -1; r <= 0; r++) {
    for (int c = -1; c <= 1; c++) {
        totalBrightness = totalBrightness + brightness[row+r][col+c];
    }
    avgBrightness[row][col] = totalBrightness/6;
}
```

It turns out that the left and right borders and each of the corners involve similar loops. The only differences are how far to the left the neighbors extend, how far to the right, how far up, and how far down, and, of course, the number of neighbors there are. Since we see this pattern, let's write a private method `adjustPixel` so that we needn't repeat such similar code over and over. This method will take six parameters: the row and column currently under consideration, the distance to look for neighbors to the left, the distance to the right, the distance up and the distance down:

```
// Calculate average brightness at position specified by
// row and col; distLeft, distRight, distUp, and distDown
// specify the neighborhood to be averaged.
private int adjustPixel( int row, int col, int distLeft,
                         int distRight, int distUp, int distDown ) {
    int totalBrightness = 0;
    int neighbors = 0;
    for (int r = distUp; r <= distDown; r++) {
        for (int c = distLeft; c <= distRight; c++) {
            totalBrightness = totalBrightness + brightness[row+r][col+c];
            neighbors++;
        }
    }
    return totalBrightness/neighbors;
}
```

The complete smoothing algorithm is shown in Figure 15.20. Figure 15.19 shows the result of applying the algorithm to an image (the pixels are intentionally magnified so that you can see the detail). Note that the method `smoothImage` returns the averaged copy of the image. Note also that we take care of all of the special cases discussed (positions in the center, on the top row, on the bottom row, etc.) in a single statement. To see how this works, trace through the algorithm in Figure 15.20 for a four-by-four array of brightness values.

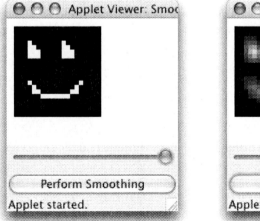

Figure 15.19 An image before and after smoothing

```
// Smooth a digital image by averaging
public int[ ][ ] smoothImage( ) {
    int[][] avgBrightness = new int[HEIGHT][WIDTH];

    for (int row = 0; row < HEIGHT; row++) {
        for (int col = 0; col < WIDTH; col++) {
            avgBrightness[row][col] = adjustPixel(row, col,
                Math.max(-1, -col), Math.min(WIDTH-(col+1), 1),
                Math.max(-1, -row), Math.min(HEIGHT-(row+1), 1));

    return avgBrightness;
}
```

Figure 15.20 A simple smoothing algorithm

15.3 Summary

In this chapter we introduced multidimensional arrays, focusing on two-dimensional arrays. Conceptually, we can consider two distinct types of two-dimensional arrays. In the first case, we can think of the two-dimensional array as an array of arrays. That is, we can view each of the rows as having a significant meaning. In the second form, i.e., the matrix, the structure is simply a two-dimensional grid, with no special significance to the rows or columns. While it is useful to think of these as different conceptually, they really are the same, and, as a result, the mechanisms for declaring them, constructing them, indexing, and traversing them are the same:

* To declare a two-dimensional array, we give the type of element to be represented in the array, followed by two pairs of square brackets, followed by the name of the array:

    ```
    type[ ][ ] arrayName;
    ```

* To construct a two-dimensional array, we need to specify the maximum number of rows in the array, as well as the maximum number of entries in each row. If each row is of the same length, we can say:

    ```
    arrayName = new type[NUM_ROWS][NUM_COLS];
    ```

    Otherwise, we specify the number of rows first:

    ```
    arrayName = new type[NUM_ROWS][ ];
    ```

    and then construct each of the rows separately.

* To refer to an individual element within a two-dimensional array, we give its row and column indices in brackets:

    ```
    arrayName[myRow][myCol];
    ```

* Typically, working with a two-dimensional array involves traversing it row by row, column by column, or along diagonals. To traverse an entire array, we write nested loops.

15.4) Chapter Review Problems

▨➡ EXERCISE 15.4.1

A particular university enrolls 5000 students. In a semester, a student can take up to six classes. The grades assigned at this university are numbers in the range 0.0 to 4.0, where 4.0 corresponds to the letter grade A.

a. *Declare an array of arrays called* `grades` *that can hold all of the grades for a single semester. You can think of each row representing the grades for one of the 5000 students. Remember that some rows will be longer than others, depending on the number of courses taken by each student.*

b. *Write a method* `printAvgs` *that will print the average grade for each of the 5000 students. Remember that each student can take from one to six courses. (You may assume that each student takes at least one course.)* ❖

▨➡ EXERCISE 15.4.2

Company X pays its employees every four weeks. Their payroll system is implemented in Java. This exercise will ask you to help develop one class, `EmployeeTime` *to manage the time worked by an employee during a four-week period.*

a. *Declare an instance variable* `hoursWorked` *that can keep track of the number of hours worked per day in a four-week pay cycle. This should be an array of arrays. You can think of each row as a week. The number of hours worked in a single day should be recorded as a* `double`.

b. *Write the constructor for this class. The constructor should take two parameters: a* `String` *that is the employee ID and a* `double` *that is the employee's hourly wage. The constructor should construct* `hoursWorked`. *Remember that it is good style to define constants for the number of weeks and the number of days (i.e., the number of rows and columns in* `hoursWorked`). *In addition, the constructor should remember the employee ID and hourly wage in instance variables.*

c. *Define constants* SATURDAY *and* SUNDAY, *with values 5 and 6, respectively. These will be the index values for Saturday's hours worked and Sunday's hours worked. What is the index pair used to access the array entry for the third Saturday in the four-week cycle? What is the index pair for the first Tuesday?*

d. *Employees get paid double on Saturdays and Sundays. Write a method that will calculate the pay earned by an employee for regular hours worked, i.e., hours worked Monday through Friday.*

e. *Write a method that will calculate the pay earned by the employee for working on Sundays.* ❖

▨➡ EXERCISE 15.4.3

Your friend has written a tic-tac-toe program. He has declared the game board to be a matrix with three rows and three columns. To represent the players X and 0, he has defined constants with values 1 and 2, respectively. The matrix, then, is a matrix of `int`.

Your friend has written the following method that is meant to return true if the player passed in as a parameter is a winner along the major diagonal (from upper left to lower right). Unfortunately, it doesn't work. Fix the method.

```
// the number of rows and columns
private static final int SIZE = 3;

public boolean diagWin( int player ) {
    for (int i = 0; i <= SIZE; i++) {
        if (board[i][i] != player) {
            return false;
        }
    }
    return true;
}
```

➠ EXERCISE 15.4.4

You are on a team that is developing a game, in which the player must escape from a monster. Both the monster and the player move through a space that looks like a grid. In a single move, the monster can move one space vertically, horizontally, or diagonally. The player can only move vertically or horizontally. This certainly appears to give the advantage to the monster. Fortunately, the player can do something that the monster cannot do. The monster can never move off the grid. If it is at the right edge of the grid, for example, it cannot move to the right. The player, on the other hand, can move to the right, re-entering the grid on the opposite side, as indicated in Figure 15.21. The player can make analogous moves off the left edge of the grid.

a. Write a method `moveRight` that takes an `int` parameter `col` that is the player's current column. The method should return an `int` that is the column into which the player should move if going right. You may assume that a constant `COLS` has been defined that gives the total number of columns in the grid.

b. Now write a method `moveLeft`.

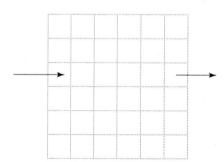

Figure 15.21 Player moving off the right of the game grid re-enters from the left.

15.5 Programming Problems

➡ EXERCISE 15.5.1

Write a program that will allow a user to draw a simple image and then apply the smoothing process described in this chapter to the image. The program should provide the user with a GUI as shown in Figure 15.19. To enable the user to see the details of the smoothing process more clearly, the drawing canvas will be viewed as a grid of small rectangles rather than individuals pixels. When the user clicks on the canvas, the color (actually a shade of gray) of the rectangle that contains the mouse should be changed. The user will determine what color will be used by adjusting the slider shown below the drawing area before clicking. The left end of the slider will correspond to black and the right end to white.

The GUI should also provide a button that the user can click when ready to see the smoothed version of the image. Each time this button is clicked, the smoothing algorithm should be applied and the drawing displayed should be updated accordingly.

Your program should consist of two classes. The controller class sets up the GUI and manages user actions, as described above.

The PixelImage *class represents the image on the canvas. The constructor and method headers for the* PixelImage *class should be as follows:*

```
// Construct empty pixel field
// fieldX - the x coordinate of the upper left corner of the field
// fieldY - the y coordinate of the upper left corner
// size - the width and height of the rectangular field (in
//            actual pixels)
// granularity - the size of each rectangle in the image
// pixelColor - the default color for the image
// Canvas - the canvas
public PixelField( double fieldX, double fieldY, int size,
                   int granularity, Color pixelColor,
                   DrawingCanvas canvas )

// Change the rectangle at the given point to pixelColor
public void adjustPixel( Location point, Color pixelColor )

// Smooth the image
public void smoothImage()
```

When you are done with the above, add two more buttons to the GUI: one to flip the image vertically, and the other to flip it horizontally. Write the corresponding methods flipVertical() *and* flipHorizontal *in the* PixelImage *class.*   ❖

➡ EXERCISE 15.5.2

Write a program that will let a user play with ice blocks on a canvas. Your controller should begin by drawing a wall of rectangular ice blocks on the canvas. Each ice block will consist of a light FilledRect *surrounded by a darker* FramedRect. *When the user clicks on an ice block, it should be removed. When all the ice blocks in a level of the wall have been removed, the layers above it should fall down on top of the remaining levels below.*

     In addition to your controller class, you should implement three classes called IceWall, IceLayer, *and* IceBlock. *The constructors and methods for these classes should be as follows:*

```
// A wall of ice blocks
public class IceWall {

    // Construct an ice wall
    // upperLeft - location of the upper left of the wall
    // width - number of ice blocks on each level
    // height - number of layers
    // iceWidth - width in pixels of a block of ice
    // iceHeight - height in pixels of a block of ice
    // canvas - canvas on which to draw ice wall
    public IceWall( Location upperLeft, int width, int height,
                    double iceWidth, double iceHeight,
                    DrawingCanvas canvas )

    // Hit the ice block at point (if any)
    // If a block is hit, it is removed.
    // If removing this block empties the layer, the layers above
    // it fall into their new positions.
    public void hit( Location point )
}

// A single layer of ice blocks
public class IceLayer {

    // Construct a layer of ice blocks
    // layerX - the x coordinate of the upper left of the layer
    // layerY - the y coordinate of the upper left
    // blockHt - the height of a block of ice
    // blockWidth - the width of a block of ice
    // numBlocks - number of blocks initially
    // canvas - canvas on which to draw the ice layer
    public IceLayer( double layerX, double layerY,
                     double blockHt, double blockWidth,
                     int numBlocks, DrawingCanvas canvas )

    // Returns true if a point is contained in one of the
    // ice blocks in this layer; false otherwise
    public boolean isHit( Location point )

    // Returns true if the layer is empty; false otherwise.
    public boolean isEmpty()

    // Make the layer of ice blocks fall
    public void fall()
}
```

```
// Class to represent a block of ice
public class IceBlock {

    // Construct a block of ice
    // upperLeft - the location of the upper left of the ice block
    // width - the width of the ice block
    // height - the height of the ice block
    // canvas - canvas on which to draw the ice block
    public IceBlock( Location upperLeft, double width,
                     double height, DrawingCanvas canvas )

    // Move the ice block dx horizontally and dy vertically
    public void move( double dx, double dy )

    // Return true if the ice block contains point; false otherwise
    public boolean contains( Location point )

    // Remove the ice block from the canvas
    public void removeFromCanvas()

}
```

CHAPTER (16)

Strings and Characters

$\mathcal{U}$ p to this point, we have focused our attention on programs that manipulate graphical or numeric information. You're undoubtedly aware, of course, that there are also many computer applications that manipulate textual data. These include word processors, on-line dictionaries, web browsers, and so on. In this chapter we explore Java's `String` class, which will allow us to refer to and manipulate textual information.

We briefly introduced the `String` class in Section 5.6. There you learned that strings are, in their simplest form, quoted text. You have seen that you can define variables that refer to strings and that you can use them in various contexts. You have used them often, in fact, as parameters to the `Text` constructor and `System.out.println`.

You have also learned that strings can be manipulated in a variety of ways. You can concatenate strings using the + operator. You can also manipulate them with a variety of methods. For example, you can compare them using `equals`, and you can find their length with the `length` method.

Strings are interesting for a variety of reasons. They are objects. That is, `String` is a class rather than a primitive type, and Java provides many methods for manipulating strings. However, Java also provides `String` literals and the concatenation operator. These special nonobject features are provided in recognition of the fact that strings are used in many programs.

We begin this chapter with a discussion of a small but very useful string—the empty string. We then turn our attention to `String` methods. Java's `String` class provides a vast number of interesting methods. While we do not cover all of the Java `String` methods, we will cover many of them here. A description of the complete set can be found at http://java.sun.com/apis.html.[1] We then turn our attention to the characters from

---

[1] You may find it useful to consult Appendix C for guidance in using the format in which these descriptions of the `String` methods are provided.

which strings are built. We discuss their importance as a separate data type and then discuss their relationship to strings. We show how characters can be used to construct strings and how they can be extracted from strings.

16.1 Little Strings and Big Strings

16.1.1 The Empty String

The smallest possible string is one that is made up of no characters at all. This string of length 0 is called the *empty string*. Expressed as a literal, the empty string is written as two double quotes with nothing between them: ""

Typically, the empty string is used in contexts where we want to build a string "from nothing". As an example, recall the Morse code program from Figure 5.7. That program displays a series of dots and dashes, based on a user's mouse clicks. A long click signifies a dash, while a short click signifies a dot. In that program, the resulting Morse code message is a string named currentCode. We initialize currentCode to "Code = " and then add either a dot or dash to it with each mouse click. But, what if we want currentCode to refer only to the series of dots and dashes entered by the user? That is, what if we don't want the string to have the prefix "Code = "? We can accomplish this by simply initializing currentCode to the empty string, as in Figure 16.1. This initialization says that currentCode is a string that is empty until the first dot or dash is concatenated to it.

The empty string serves a purpose that is in many ways analogous to the purpose of the number 0 in arithmetic. It provides us with a way to begin with nothing so that we can accumulate a "bigger" value over time.

16.1.2 Long Strings

As we have just seen, strings in Java can be extremely short. They can also be arbitrarily long. The text of this chapter, for instance, could be treated as a single string. While long strings don't require any special handling, one practical issue deserves a bit of discussion—readability. We have already said that this chapter could be a single string. What if we wanted to print that very long string using System.out.println? If our string was comprised of just the characters in the chapter, without any special attention given to the line breaks, the resulting printed text would be unreadable.

Often it is useful to place line breaks into a long string by including the special character \n, which is the newline character. Say, for example, that we want to print instructions for the Morse code program described in Section 16.1.1. Sample instructions are given in Figure 16.2.

We could obviously print the instructions in Figure 16.2 with a series of five System.out.println statements. As an alternative, we could define a String constant named INSTRUCTIONS to be all of the instructions, as in Figure 16.3 and then simply print them with the single statement

```
System.out.println( INSTRUCTIONS );
```

Note the use of \n in Figure 16.3 to control the formatting of the instructions by forcing line breaks. You'll also notice that the string INSTRUCTIONS is split over five lines, with the concatenation

```
// A program to display Morse code entered by pressing the mouse as
// dots and dashes on the canvas.
public class MorseCode extends WindowController {

    // Location where code entered is displayed
    private static final Location DISPLAY_POS = new Location( 60, 30 );
    //  Minimum time (in milliseconds) for a dash
    private static final double DASH_TIME = 200;

    //  String to hold sequence entered so far
    private String currentCode = "";
    //  Text used to display sequence on canvas
    private Text display;

    //  Time when mouse was last depressed
    private double pressTime;

    // Set up text display location
    public void begin() {
        display = new Text( currentCode, DISPLAY_POS, canvas );
    }

    // Record time at which mouse was depressed
    public void onMousePress ( Location point ) {
        pressTime = System.currentTimeMillis();
    }

    // Add a dot or dash depending on click length
    public void onMouseRelease( Location point ) {
        if ( System.currentTimeMillis() - pressTime > DASH_TIME ) {
            currentCode = currentCode + " -";
        } else {
            currentCode = currentCode + " .";
        }
        display.setText( currentCode );
    }
}
```

Figure 16.1 A program to display Morse code as dots and dashes

This program will allow you to enter a message in Morse Code.

To enter your message:
Click the mouse quickly to generate a dot;
Depress the mouse longer to generate a dash.

Figure 16.2 Instructions for the Morse code program

```
private static final String INSTRUCTIONS =
    "This program will allow you to enter a message in Morse Code.\n" +
    "\n" +
    "To enter your message:\n" +
    "Click the mouse quickly to generate a dot;\n" +
    "Depress the mouse longer to generate a dash.";
```

Figure 16.3   Using \n to force line breaks

operator (+) at the end of each line to tie the pieces together. The reason for writing the instructions on five lines is to improve readability. This way, the format in the program mimics the format of the actual instructions. This will be useful to anyone reading our program. Finally, it is useful to note that the string "\n" is simply a newline string. While it appears to have length two, it really has length one, since it contains only the newline symbol.

Often it is useful to express a long String literal as the concatenation of two or more short strings. One place where this can be done is in the context of System.out.println. Say that we had implemented a Morse code translator (which we will do later in this chapter), and that a user of our program had entered an inappropriate (i.e., untranslatable) character, and say that we wanted to print a useful one-line error message in response to this. We could do so with the following statement:

```
System.out.println( "The message that you have entered contains " +
                    "characters that cannot be translated." );
```

This would print our error message on a single line as desired, but it also makes our program more readable than it would be if we did not split the string over two lines.

   Java does not allow us to write a single String literal with actual line breaks in it, as in:

```
System.out.println( "The message that you have entered contains
                    characters that cannot be translated." );
```

If you want to split a String literal over several lines, you will need to use the concatenation operator to join substrings of the larger string, as above.

16.2   A Collection of Useful String Methods

Java's String class provides many useful methods. You have already seen some of these. In Section 5.6, we introduced the methods length and endsWith. The invocation

```
someString.length()
```

returns an int that is the number of characters in someString. The invocation

```
someString.endsWith( otherString )
```

returns true if and only if otherString is a suffix of someString. In Section 12.1.2, we introduced the method startsWith. An invocation of this method is similar to endsWith, but it returns true if and only if otherString is a prefix of someString. In this section we introduce several additional useful `String` methods. We begin by discussing a class for maintaining and searching a URL history list, which will serve as an example throughout this section.

16.2.1 Building a String of URLs

In Section 12.1.2 we discussed one implementation of a URL list. Many web browsers make it easy for you to type in the URL (universal resource locator) for a web page by offering automatic address completion. If I type "http://www.a" my browser suggests "http://www.aol.com" as a completion. The browser does this by keeping track of URLs typed in by users. It can then provide a sublist of URLs that includes all of the strings in the list that match a given prefix. In this section, let's imagine a similar type of functionality. We will implement a class that will maintain a URL history. Based on that history, we will add methods to do automatic address completion.

You will notice that the implementation given here is different from that in Section 12.1.2. As discussed in Chapter 21, there are often many possible ways to implement a data structure or a particular type of functionality.

Figure 16.4 shows a class `UrlHistory` that maintains a history of URLs. At this point it is fairly simple. The constructor builds an empty history, and the method `addURL` adds a URL to the list.

This class maintains the URL history as one long string called `urlString`. Thus creating an empty history simply requires initializing `urlString` to the empty string. To add a new URL to the existing string, we simply concatenate it to the front, with a newline character to separate it

```java
// Class to maintain a history of URLs
public class URLHistory {

    // A string of URLs
    private String urlString;

    // Create a new (empty) history
    public URLHistory() {
        urlString = "";
    }

    // Add a new URL to the existing history
    public void addURL( String aURL ) {
        urlString = aURL + "\n" + urlString;
    }

    // Returns the history as a string with URLs separated by newlines
    public String toString() {
        return urlString;
    }
}
```

Figure 16.4 URLHistory class

from the existing history. We choose the newline character as a separator, since we are guaranteed that it will not also appear in a given URL.

16.2.2 Finding the Position of a Substring with indexOf

Say that we want to determine whether a particular URL is in the URL history. To do so easily, we can take advantage of the String method indexOf. In an invocation of this method, such as

```
someString.indexOf( otherString )
```

we can think of otherString as a pattern to be found. The method returns an int giving the first index in someString, where the pattern, otherString, is found. For example, if sentence is

```
"Strings are objects in Java."
```

and if pattern is "in" then

```
sentence.indexOf( pattern )
```

returns the int 3. (Indexing starts at 0.) Note that indexOf returns the start of the first occurrence of "in", even though it appears twice. The value −1 is returned if the pattern is not found within the string to be searched. So if pattern is "primitive type" then

```
sentence.indexOf( pattern )
```

yields the value −1.

Figure 16.5 shows a method of the URLHistory class called contains. It takes a string as a parameter that is a URL to be found in the current URL history. If that URL is found, it returns true. Otherwise, it returns false. It works as follows. First, it invokes the indexOf method on urlString, passing it the URL to be found *terminated by a newline*. The reason for doing this is that we want to be certain that we've found exactly the URL that is desired. If we were looking for

```
"http://www.cs.williams.edu"
```

in a URL history that contained only

```
"http://www.cs.williams.edu/~cs134"
```

for example, we would not want contains to return true, because our URL was not found. Once this is done, we compare the result of the invocation of indexOf to 0. As long as a legitimate index was found (i.e., an index greater than −1), then we know we found the URL.

```
// Return true if and only if the history contains the given URL
public boolean contains( String aURL ) {
    // Look for URL terminated by newline separator
    return urlString.indexOf( aURL + "\n" ) >= 0;
}
```

Figure 16.5 The contains method

There is a second version of the `indexOf` method that we will use later in this chapter. It takes two parameters. An invocation such as:

    someString.indexOf(pattern, startIndex)

searches for `pattern` in `someString`, beginning at the index indicated by `startIndex`. Thus if `someString` is

    "Strings are objects in Java."

and if `pattern` is `"ing"`, then

    sentence.indexOf(pattern, 0)

returns the `int` 3, but

    someString.indexOf(pattern, 5)

returns −1. On the other hand,

    someString.indexOf("in", 5)

returns 20.

It is important to note that `indexOf` is case sensitive. Since the upper- and lower-case characters are distinct from each other, the string `"IN"` is completely different from `"in"`. Thus

    someString.indexOf("IN")

would return −1.

⊪➡ EXERCISE 16.2.1

Modify the method add *so that it only adds a URL to the history if it is not already there.*

16.2.3 Dealing with Lower and Upper Case

While there are certainly contexts in which it is useful to distinguish between lower- and upper-case characters, there are other times when it is unnecessary (or even wrong) to do so. For example, if the URL

    http://www.cs.williams.edu

were in our history, we would surely want to recognize

    HTTP://www.cs.williams.edu

as being the same thing.[2]

In Section 5.6 we discussed using the method `equals` to test for string equality. This determines whether one string is equal to another in the sense of being composed of the same sequence of characters. Sameness is taken to be a strict equality with respect to case. `"A"` is not the same as `"a"`, `"R"` is not the same as `"r"`, and so on. If we want to test for equality but also want

---

[2] The part of a URL following the domain name may, in fact, be case sensitive. For purposes of this example, we will ignore that issue.

to ignore differences in case, we can instead use the String method equalsIgnoreCase. Thus if urlString is

```
"http://www.cs.williams.edu"
```

then

```
urlString.equalsIgnoreCase( "HTTP://www.cs.williams.edu" )
```

returns true.

Two other useful methods for helping us deal with issues of case are toLowerCase and toUpperCase. An invocation such as

```
someString.toLowerCase()
```

returns a *copy* of someString, with all upper-case characters replaced by their lower-case counterparts. An invocation of toUpperCase does the opposite. It is interesting (and important) to note that the expression

```
someString.toLowerCase()
```

does not change someString in any way. Instead, it returns a new string that is a copy of the string associated with someString with all its characters shifted to lower case. toUpperCase and toLowercase are not mutator methods, even though their names suggests that they might be. In fact, the String class *has no mutator methods*. Java Strings are *immutable*.

The methods toLowerCase and toUpperCase are extremely useful in many contexts. For example, in Figure 16.5, we showed a method that used indexOf to determine whether a URL history contained a specific URL. Our method would be improved considerably if we were to make it insensitive to case.

To improve our contains method, we can do the following. Before invoking indexOf, we'll make both the URL history and the URL to be found lower case (or equivalently, we could make them upper case). Our method would then look like this:

```
// Return true if and only if the history contains the given URL
public boolean contains( String aURL ) {
    String lowerUrlString = urlString.toLowerCase();
    // Look for URL terminated by newline separator
    return lowerUrlString.indexOf( aURL.toLowerCase() + "\n" ) >= 0;
}
```

That is, we first make a fully lower-case copy of the URL history. We do this by invoking the method toLowerCase on urlString. We do this in an assignment statement to the variable lowerUrlString. Remember that toLowerCase is not a mutator method. It does not affect urlString at all. Next, we invoke indexOf on lowerUrlString, passing it a fully lower-case copy of aURL.

As an alternative, we could choose to simply maintain the history using lower case only. That is, we could modify our class definition as in Figure 16.6. There we modify the addURL method

```java
// Class to maintain a history of URLs
public class URLHistory {

    // A string of URLs
    private String urlString;

    // Create a new (empty) history
    public URLHistory() {
        urlString = "";
    }

    // Add a new URL to the existing history
    public void addURL( String aURL ) {
        urlString = aURL.toLowerCase() + "\n" + urlString;
    }

    // Returns the history as a string with URLs separated by newlines
    public String toString() {
        return urlString;
    }

    // Return true if and only if the history contains the given URL
    public boolean contains( String aURL ) {
        // Look for URL terminated by newline separator
        return urlString.indexOf( aURL.toLowerCase() + "\n" ) >= 0;
    }
}
```

Figure 16.6   Case-insensitive URLHistory class

so that each time a URL is concatenated to urlString, we concatenate a lower-case copy. Then in contains all we have to do is make the pattern to be found, i.e., aURL, lower case.

⫸ EXERCISE 16.2.2

What is printed by each of the following code fragments if bookTitle *is* "Java: An Eventful Approach":

```java
bookTitle.toUpperCase();
if (bookTitle.indexOf( "JAVA" ) == -1) {
    System.out.println( "No JAVA here!" );
} else {
    System.out.println( "There's JAVA in here!" );
}
System.out.println( bookTitle );
```

```
bookTitle = bookTitle.toUpperCase();
if (bookTitle.indexOf( "JAVA" ) == -1) {
    System.out.println( "No JAVA here!" );
} else {
    System.out.println( "There's JAVA in here!" );
}
System.out.println( bookTitle );
```

16.2.4   Cutting and Pasting Strings

You already know that you can paste strings together with the concatenation operator (+). In this section we will show you how to pull strings apart. In particular, we will show you how to extract a substring of a given string. To do this, you can use the method substring. The invocation

```
someString.substring( startIndex, endIndex )
```

returns the substring of someString beginning at index startIndex and up to, but not including, the character at position endIndex. That is, endIndex should be the position of the first character *after* the desired substring. Thus if urlString is "http://www.cs.williams.edu" then

```
urlString.substring( 7, 10 )
```

returns "www" and

```
urlString.substring( 0, 7 )
```

returns "http://" and

```
urlString.substring( 7, urlString.length() )
```

returns "www.cs.williams.edu".

Let's look at this last example in a bit more detail. Here we gave the value 7 as the index of the first character of our substring. We then gave the value urlString.length() as the position of the first character not to be included in the substring. The length of urlString is 26. Since indexing begins at 0, the index of the final character in urlString is 25. Thus everything from index 7 is included in the substring, because the first index to be excluded is just outside the valid indices. Note that startIndex must be a valid index in the string and that endIndex may not be greater than the length of someString.

Now let's see how we can use substring to help us find possible completions for a partially entered URL. Figure 16.7 shows one way to do this. We begin by making a copy of prefix that is entirely lower case. We do this because we want our URL history methods to be case insensitive, and urlString is all lower case. We then use indexOf to find the first occurrence of prefix in the history. Our aim is to extract the entire URL from this position to the closest following newline character, which is acting as a separator between URLs. To find the newline character, we again use indexOf, this time beginning our search from the position where we just found prefix. We then get the substring from the history, beginning with the first position of our URL and ending with (and including) the position where we found the newline character. We keep the newline character so that it can continue to serve as a separator. We then concatenate this to allCompletions, which is a string of all matching URLs found. Once we have extracted a

```
// Return all URLs in history that have the parameter as a prefix
public String findCompletions( String prefix ) {
    String allCompletions = "";
    // All lower case for case insensitivity
    prefix = prefix.toLowerCase();

    // Find first possible completion
    int urlStart = urlString.indexOf( prefix );

    // Extract possible completions as long as they can be found
    while (urlStart >= 0) {
        // Find the end of this URL
        int urlEnd = urlString.indexOf( "\n", urlStart+1 );
        // Extract URL from history
        String possCompletion = urlString.substring( urlStart,
                                                      urlEnd+1 );
        // Add to all completions
        allCompletions = allCompletions + possCompletion;
        // Look for the next occurrence of the prefix
        urlStart = urlString.indexOf( prefix, urlEnd+1 );
    }
    return allCompletions;
}
```

Figure 16.7 A method to find all possible completions for a partial URL

URL, we begin to look for the next possible completion. Again, we use the method `indexOf`, but this time we begin the search from the point where we just ended. We continue to extract URLs as long as the prefix can be found in the history.

➡ EXERCISE 16.2.3

At this point we assume that each time we find `prefix` *in* `urlString`, *we are finding the prefix of a URL. That is, we assume that the starting index is one that begins a new URL, rather than being in the middle of one. This is quite reasonable if the prefixes we are aiming to find are fairly long. For example, a prefix like* `"http://www.cs"` *is not likely to be found in the middle of some URL in the history. If we wanted to be completely safe, however, we would need to modify the method* `findCompletions`. *Modify* `findCompletions` *so that it checks that each URL completion is indeed a complete URL.* ❖

16.2.5 Trimming Strings

Throughout this chapter we have been making a very important assumption about the strings passed as parameters to our methods. We have assumed that they have no leading or trailing blanks. This is an important and perhaps overly optimistic assumption. What if the string passed to the add method is

   "http://www.cs.williams.edu   "

Do we really want to treat this as being different from

   "http://www.cs.williams.edu"

Of course not. The String method trim is very useful in cases such as this one. The invocation

   someString.trim()

returns a copy of someString with the white space removed from both ends. Like toLowerCase and toUpperCase, this is not a mutator method. In the invocation above, someString is not modified. If we wanted to modify someString to be the string with leading and trailing blanks removed, we would say

   someString = someString.trim();

Figure 16.8 shows a modified version of our URLHistory class. This time, the add method takes care of both trimming new URLs and converting them to lower case. When we send the message trim to aURL, we get a copy with all leading and trailing blanks removed. To this string we send the message toLowerCase, which returns yet another string, this time with all letters converted to lower case. As a result, all the URLs in urlString are remembered as lower case, with no extraneous blanks.

   The contains method does something similar to add. Before checking whether a URL is found in urlString, we trim aURL and then send the message toLowerCase to the new trimmed string.

➡ EXERCISE 16.2.4

Modify the method findCompletions in Figure 16.7 so that the prefix passed in to the method as a parameter is trimmed before any searching is done for completions of that prefix. ❖

16.2.6 Comparing Strings

You already know that you can compare strings for equality with the method equals. You can also compare two strings with the method compareTo. The invocation

   someString.compareTo(anotherString)

returns a positive integer, zero, or a negative integer. If someString and anotherString are equal, i.e., if they look the same, then compareTo returns 0. If someString would appear after anotherString in a lexicographic ordering, then a positive integer is returned. If someString would appear before anotherString in lexicographic ordering, then a negative integer is returned. If the two strings are made up of alphabetic characters and both are either all lower case or all upper case, then lexicographic ordering corresponds to alphabetical ordering. Thus you can use the method compareTo to alphabetize strings.

   As an example of the use of compareTo, say that we would like to maintain our URL history in alphabetical order. If so, we could rewrite the method addURL as in Figure 16.9.

```
// Class to maintain a history of URLs
public class URLHistory {

    // A string of URLs
    private String urlString;

    // Create a new (empty) history
    public URLHistory() {
        urlString = "";
    }

    // Add a new URL to the existing history
    public void addURL( String aURL ) {
        urlString = aURL.trim().toLowerCase() + "\n" + urlString;
    }

    // Returns the history as a string with URLs separated by newlines
    public String toString() {
        return urlString;
    }

    // Return true if and only if the history contains the given URL
    public boolean contains( String aURL ) {
        // Look for URL terminated by newline separator
        return urlString.indexOf( aURL.trim().toLowerCase() + "\n" ) >= 0;
    }
}
```

Figure 16.8 Case-insensitive URLHistory class with trimmed URLs

The method addURL works as follows. First we trim aURL, the URL to be added, and use a copy that is all lower case. Now we need to compare aURL with the other URLs to determine where the new one should be placed. Figure 16.10 helps to illustrate how we'll go about this. The figure shows a list of strings that are names of fruits and nuts. A new string, grape, is to be added to the list. We consider the first string, apple, so that we can compare grape to apple. The invocation

```
"grape".compareTo( "apple" )
```

returns a positive integer, indicating that grape is "bigger" than apple. In other words, if placed in order, grape would come after apple. So we go on to compare grape to the next string, banana. Once again, the integer returned by an invocation of compareTo will be positive. We then compare grape to grapefruit. This time the invocation of compareTo will be negative, meaning that grape is "smaller" than grapefruit, i.e., that grape should appear before grapefruit in alphabetical order. Since this is the first time that compareTo returns a negative integer, we know that this is the correct spot to insert the new string.

```
// Add a new URL to the existing history.
// History is maintained in alphabetical order.
public void addURL( String aURL ) {
    // Trim aURL and make it all lower case
    aURL = aURL.trim().toLowerCase();

    // aURL has not been placed yet
    boolean urlPlaced = false;

    // Start index of first URL to be compared
    int urlStart = 0;
    // End of first URL to be compared
    int urlEnd = urlString.indexOf( "\n" );

    // While there is a URL to compare and no placement has been made
    while (urlEnd >= 0 && !urlPlaced) {
        // get a URL for comparison
        String oneURL = urlString.substring( urlStart, urlEnd );
        if (aURL.compareTo( oneURL ) > 0) {
            // Get next URL for comparison
            urlStart = urlEnd+1;
            urlEnd = urlString.indexOf( "\n", urlStart );
        }
        else {  // Found correct position for new URL
            urlString = urlString.substring( 0, urlStart ) + aURL + "\n" +
                            urlString.substring( urlStart,
                                                    urlString.length() );
            urlPlaced = true;
        }
    }
    // If aURL wasn't placed inside the list of URLs
    if (!urlPlaced) {  // it must belong at the end
        urlString = urlString + aURL + "\n";
    }
}
```

Figure 16.9 Adding a URL to a history of URLs maintained in alphabetical order

apple	←	grape
banana	←	grape
grapefruit	←	grape
mango		
peanut		
pear		

Figure 16.10 Inserting a string into a list in alphabetical order

The `while` loop in Figure 16.9 does exactly this. It extracts a URL for comparison from `urlString`. The variables `urlStart` and `urlEnd` give the starting and ending indices of the URL to be extracted. Initially the values of these variables are 0 and *n*, where *n* is the position of the first newline character. Once the comparison string has been extracted, the method compares `aURL` to the comparison string. If the comparison yields a positive integer, we know that `aURL` should appear later in the list of strings, so we keep searching for the appropriate position. To do this, we update the values of `urlStart` and `urlEnd`. However, if the comparison yields a negative integer or 0, then we know that we have found the right place to insert `aURL`. We construct a new string by concatenating the part of `urlString` up to the position where `aURL` is to be placed, together with `aURL`, a newline to serve as a delimiter, and the rest of `urlString`. We then remember this as the new value of `urlString`.

There is one more thing that the method `addURL` needs to handle. It is possible that `aURL` needs to be inserted as the final string in `urlString`. If so, the `while` loop will complete without placing `aURL` where it belongs. Before the method terminates, we check for this case and, if necessary, concatenate `aURL` to the end of `urlString`.

EXERCISE 16.2.5

The condition that is checked at the end of `addURL` *in Figure 16.9 takes care of the case where* `aURL` *is the first URL to be inserted into* `urlList`. *Trace through the method to convince yourself that this happens correctly.*

Java `String`s are immutable. This means that any time you perform an operation on a string, Java actually gives you a brand new copy of the string with the desired modifications. This can result in inefficiencies in certain cases. As a result, there is a related class, `StringBuffer` that can be used.

A `StringBuffer` is essentially a mutable string. Not all `String` methods are available for `StringBuffer`s. For instance, `toLowerCase` and `toUpperCase` are missing. However, this class can be very useful, especially in programs where you will be appending to the end of a string very frequently.

There are a number of ways to construct a `StringBuffer`. You can, for example, construct an empty one, providing as a parameter an integer that gives the initial capacity of the `StringBuffer`:

        StringBuffer urlStringBuffer = new StringBuffer(1000);

You can also construct a `StringBuffer` from an existing string:

        StringBuffer ulrStringBuffer = new StringBuffer(urlString);

Once you have constructed a `StringBuffer`, there are many ways in which you can modify its contents. In particular, this class provides an append method, which will allow you to add a `String` representation of an element to the end of a `StringBuffer`. Other methods include `replace`, which will replace a substring at a specified position with a new one, and `delete`, which will remove a substring from a specified position. For a complete listing of `StringBuffer` methods, we refer you to http://java.sun.com/apis.html.

16.3 Characters

We have referred numerous times to the fact that strings are sequences of *characters*. It should come as no surprise then, that Java provides a data type called `char`, which represents characters.

This data type is a primitive type, and therefore we use literals to represent values of this type. There are also a number of operators that can be used to manipulate char values.

A char literal in Java is written by putting the character within single quotes. So, for example, the following are chars:

'a', 'A', '?', '&', '7', '\n'

These are not the same as

"a", "A", "?", "&", "7" and "\n"

which are all strings of length one. To declare a variable of type char we say

    char letter;

where letter can be any variable name of our choosing.

A character is represented within the computer's memory as an integer. Various standard codes can be used to represent characters. ASCII (American Standard Code for Information Interchange), for example, can represent 256 characters. Characters in Java follow the Unicode encoding scheme. Unicode can represent many more characters than ASCII. The first 256 of these are the same as ASCII codes, for compatibility.

Because chars in Java are represented internally as integers, they share many properties with ints. For example, you can add chars to each other (or perform other arithmetic operations on them). You can also compare them with operators like < and >. This is useful in many situations. Say, for example, you want to determine whether a char named mysteryChar is one of the characters '0', '1', '2', '3', '4', '5', '6', '7', '8', '9', i.e., a character that represents a digit in the range 0 to 9. You can do this by checking whether mysteryChar has a value in the range '0' to '9':

    if (mysteryChar >= '0' && mysteryChar <= '9')

The reason this comparison works is that the integers representing the characters '0' to '9' are consecutive numbers. Note that you don't need to know what those numbers are; you simply need to know that they are consecutive. Similarly, if you wanted to determine whether mysteryChar was a lower-case alphabetic character, you could say:

    if (mysteryChar >= 'a' && mysteryChar <= 'z')

Again, these comparisons work because the integers representing the characters 'a' to 'z' are consecutive. The same is true for 'A' to 'Z'. We will make use of these properties of characters in later sections of this chapter.

16.3.1 Characters and Strings

Constructing Strings from Characters

We have stated a number of times that strings are objects, i.e., that String is a class in Java. In our examples, however, we have tended to make use of a special feature of strings, the ability to write them as String literals. While Java provides us with this convenient way to define a string, it is also provides several String constructors. You can find the complete list of constructors at http://java.sun.com/apis.html.

0	'J'
1	'a'
2	'v'
3	'a'
4	':'
5	' '
6	'A'
7	'n'
8	' '
9	'E'
10	'v'
11	'e'
12	'n'
13	't'
14	'f'
15	'u'
16	'l'
17	' '
18	'A'
19	'p'
20	'p'
21	'r'
22	'o'
23	'a'
24	'c'
25	'h'

Figure 16.11   Character array containing the sequence of letters in the title of this book

The String constructor we introduce here makes the relationship between chars and Strings very obvious. Specifically, it allows us to build a String from its char components:

```
new String( characterArray )
```

constructs a new String with the sequence of characters in characterArray. Say, for example, that titleChars is the character array shown in Figure 16.11. This array contains the sequence of characters in the title of this book. Then the assignment

```
String title = new String( titleChars );
```

creates the String

```
"Java: an Eventful Approach"
```

and gives it the name title.

It is important to note that this constructor can be tricky. What if, for example, only part of the array is actually filled? What is the string constructed from empty array elements? The best way to avoid this issue to to be sure that you begin with an array that is completely filled. If you're curious about what happens otherwise, try experimenting a bit. Construct a string from an array that is partially empty. Then invoke the length method on the string you constructed.

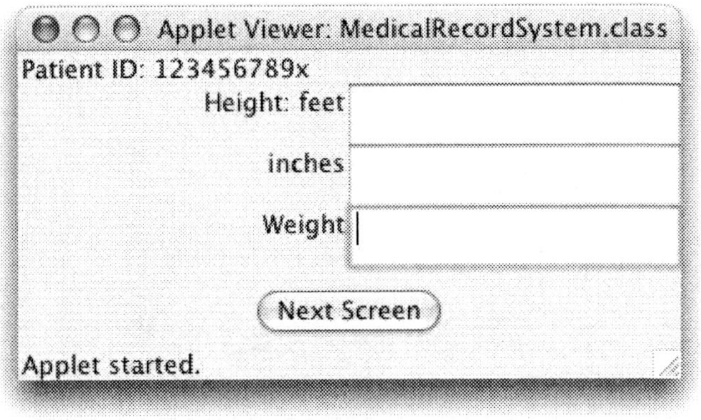

Figure 16.12   User interface for a medical record system

While there are many `String` constructors available, we will find it convenient to continue to use `String` literals.[3]

Extracting Characters from Strings

Just as we can construct strings from arrays of characters, we can also access the characters that make up a string. The Java `String` class includes a method `charAt`, which takes an `int` as an index and returns the `char` at that location. Indexing begins at 0, so the last character in a string of length 10, for example, is at index 9. So if `aString` is `"Coffee"`, then `aString.charAt( 1 )` is 'o'.

One common use for this method is to check whether the characters in a string all have some property, like being numeric or upper case. Consider, for example, a medical record management program that would allow a physician to enter patient information. One screen from such a program might look like that in Figure 16.12. This interface has, among other things, a `TextField` for entering the patient's weight. Say that this information is used in various parts of the program to perform calculations and that we want to be able to treat the patient's weight as an `int`.

We can extract the information from the `TextField` with the method `getText`. So, for example, if the name of the `TextField` is `weightField`, we can say:

```
String weight = weightField.getText();
```

To convert this string into an `int`, we can use the `parseInt` method of the `Integer` class as follows:

```
int weightValue = Integer.parseInt( weight );
```

However, this will only work if the weight that was entered *looks like* an integer value.[4] So `"154"` can be made into an `int`, but `"154lbs"` cannot. Furthermore, even extraneous blanks in a string, as in `" 12"`, cause it to be rejected for conversion. (On the other hand, leading zeros,

---

[3] Interestingly, there is no `String` constructor that takes a single `char` as a parameter. To construct a string from a single character, aChar, simply concatenate the empty string to it as follows: `""` + aChar.

[4] In fact, we attempt to convert a string that is not of the proper form, an exception will be raised.

```
// Returns true if and only if number is a string of
// digits in the range 0-9
public boolean validInt( String number ) {
    for (int i = 0; i < number.length(); i++) {
        char digit = number.charAt( i );
        if (digit < '0' || digit > '9') {
            return false;
        }
    }
    return true;
}
```

Figure 16.13 A method to check whether a string looks like a valid integer

as in "00012", are allowed.) To check whether all of the characters in weight are numeric, we could write a method validInt as in Figure 16.13. In the method validInt, the for loop considers the characters in number, one at a time. If a non-numeric character is encountered, the method returns false. If the for loop terminates after examining all of the characters, then a non-numeric character was not found, and the method returns true.

EXERCISE 16.3.1

Write a method called lowerCase *that returns* true *if and only if all the characters in a string are lower-case letters.*

16.3.2 Performing Operations on Characters

We mentioned above that in Java chars are represented internally as integers. As a result, they share many properties with the ints, including the types of operations that can be performed on them. As you will see in this section, the ability to perform arithmetic operations on characters can be extremely useful.

To illustrate the utility of various character operations, let's consider a Morse code program. This time, rather than simply allowing a user to generate a message of dots and dashes, as in Figure 16.1, our program will translate messages into Morse code. Let's keep things simple for the moment and concentrate on translating only alphabetic messages. That is, we won't allow numbers or punctuation. In fact, let's assume that all letters are upper case.

Each letter in the alphabet is represented by a unique series of dots and dashes, as in Figure 16.14. This means that it is conceptually quite straightforward to translate a message that is a string. All we have to do is consider each of the characters in the message and find its equivalent Morse code representation. So, for example, the message

    I LOVE JAVA

becomes

    ..   .-.. --- ...- .   .--- .- ...- .-

The method in Figure 16.15 does exactly that. For each position in message, it extracts the character at that position. It then determines whether the character is a blank or a letter

A	. -	N	- .
B	- . . .	O	- - -
C	- . - .	P	. - - .
D	- . .	Q	- - . -
E	.	R	. - .
F	. . - .	S	. . .
G	- - .	T	-
H	. . . .	U	. . -
I	. .	V	. . . -
J	. - - -	W	. - -
K	- . -	X	- . . -
L	. - . .	Y	- . - -
M	- -	Z	- - . .

Figure 16.14 A partial Morse code alphabet

```
// Converts an alphabetic string into Morse code
public String toMorseCode( String message ) {
    String morseMessage = "";
    for (int i = 0; i < message.length(); i++) {
        char letter = message.charAt( i );
        if (letter == ' ') {
            morseMessage = morseMessage + WORD_SPACE;
        } else {
            morseMessage = morseMessage + morseCode( letter ) + " ";
        }
    }
    return morseMessage;
}
```

Figure 16.15 A method to translate a message into Morse code

to be translated. If it is a blank, WORDSPACE is concatenated to the translation so far, i.e., to morseMessage. Otherwise, it concatenates the Morse code series of dots and dashes for that letter to the translation so far.

The interesting question here is how the method morseCode determines the sequence of dots and dashes that corresponds to a letter. The method is shown in Figure 16.16. All it does is look up the letter in an array to find the appropriate sequence of dots and dashes. The array, called letterCode, is a 26-element array that includes all of the 26 codes from Figure 16.14 in sequence. That is, the first element of the array, the element at index 0, is the code for the letter A, ".-", the second element, at index 1, is the code for the letter B, "-...", and so on. All we

```
// Returns the sequence of dots and dashes corresponding to
// a letter of the alphabet
public String morseCode( char letter ) {
    return letterCode[letter - 'A'];
}
```

Figure 16.16 A method to translate a single character into Morse code

need to do is figure out how to use character information to help us find its corresponding index in the array.

We have mentioned a number of times that characters are represented as integers, which are exactly what we need for indexing the array. It would certainly be convenient if the integer equivalent of 'A' was 0, with 'B' equivalent to 1, and so on, but this is not the case.[5] However, we can calculate the appropriate index by determining how far away the given letter is from the beginning of the alphabet. We do this by subtracting 'A' from letter as in Figure 16.16. If we subtract the value of 'A' from 'A', we get 0; subtracting 'A' from 'B' yields 1. Subtracting 'A' from 'Z' yields 25, since their integer values are different by a value of 25. Note that this works because the integers representing the characters 'A' to 'Z' are consecutive. (The same is true for the characters 'a' to 'z' and '0' to '9'.)

Just as it is possible to treat a char as an int, you can also get the char value that corresponds to a given int code. To do this, cast the int value as a char. So, if charValue is an int variable, then the expression

```
(char) charValue
```

yields a character.[6] You will see examples using this idea in Chapter 18.

> Our Morse code example assumes that an array, letterCode, refers to 26 strings of dots and dashes that correspond to the letters A through Z. How is this array initialized? Recall from Chapter 14 that Java provides us with a way to initialize an array at the time it is declared. This is done by placing all of the values of the array, in order, within braces. The elements are separated by commas. Therefore, we can declare and initialize letterCode as follows:
>
> ```
> private String[] letterCode = { ".-" , "-...", "-.-.", "-..", ".",
>                    "..-.", "--.", "....", "..", ".---",
>                    "-.-", ".-..", "--", "-.", "---", ".--.",
>                    "--.-", ".-.", "...", "-", "..-", "...-",
>                    ".--", "-..-", "-.--", "--.." };
> ```

➡ EXERCISE 16.3.2

The Morse code alphabet includes numbers and punctuation. Modify the method morseCode *so that it translates numbers as well as the punctuation symbols given in Figure 16.17. For this problem it is useful to note that the Unicode representations of '0' to '9' are one consecutive block of integers, just as the characters 'A' to 'Z' are one block.* ❖

---

[5] The integer value associated with 'A' happens to be 65, but the specific value doesn't matter.

[6] This only works for integer values that have a corresponding character value.

0	- - - - -	5	. . . . .	.	. - . - . -
1	. - - - -	6	-	,	- - . . - -
2	. . - - -	7	- - . . .	?	. . - - . .
3	. . . - -	8	- - - . .		
4	. . . . -	9	- - - - .		

Figure 16.17   Additional Morse code symbols

➡ EXERCISE 16.3.3

Write a method to check whether a string is valid for translation to Morse code. Check whether the characters in the string are upper-case letters, numbers, or the punctuation symbols '.', ',', '?'. You should also allow blanks.   ❖

16.4   Summary

In this chapter we expanded on your earlier understanding of strings. Java provides `String` literals and the concatenation operators, giving strings some of the characteristics of a primitive type. However, strings are objects, and the `String` class provides many useful methods.

We also introduced the primitive type `char`. As strings are sequences of characters, it is particularly useful to understand this data type in relation to strings.

The main points about strings that you should take from this chapter are as follows:

* The empty string, `""`, is a very useful string, particularly in cases where a string is to be built incrementally from nothing.
* Java strings are immutable. There are no mutator methods that modify strings. Instead, all `String` methods that would make changes to a string return a new copy with the appropriate modifications.
* Java's `String` class provides many useful methods, including:

   - equals: `someString.equals( otherString )` returns `true` if and only if `someString` and `otherString` look alike, i.e., they are made up of the same sequence of characters.
   - equalsIgnoreCase: `someString.equalsIgnoreCase( otherString )` returns `true` if and only if `someString` and `otherString` look alike, ignoring differences between lower- and upper-case characters.
   - compareTo: `someString.compareTo( otherString )` returns a positive or negative integer, indicating whether `someString` falls after `otherString` or before `otherString` in lexicographic order. If the two strings are equal, `compareTo` returns 0.
   - toUpperCase: `someString.toUpperCase()` returns a copy of `someString`, where all lower-case letters have been replaced by their upper-case counterparts.
   - toLowerCase: `someString.toLowerCase()` returns a copy of `someString`, where all upper-case letters have been replaced by their lower-case counterparts.

- indexOf: someString.indexOf(patternString) gives the starting index of the first occurrence of patternString in someString. If the pattern is not found, −1 is returned.
someString.indexOf(patternString, startIndex) gives the starting index of the first occurrence of patternString in someString, beginning at the position indicated by startIndex. If the pattern is not found, −1 is returned.
- substring: someString.substring(startIndex, endIndex) returns the substring of someString beginning at index startIndex and up to, but not including, the character at position endIndex.
- trim: someString.trim() returns a copy of someString with any leading or trailing white space removed.
- startsWith: someString.startsWith(otherString) returns true exactly when otherString is a prefix of someString.
- endsWith: someString.endsWith(otherString) returns true exactly when otherString is a suffix of someString.
- charAt: someString.charAt(index) returns the character at index.

The main points about characters that you should take from this chapter are:

- The data type char allows us to manipulate characters in Java.
- char literals are written as individual characters between single quotes.
- chars are represented internally as integers. This allows us to perform many useful operations on them, including comparisons and arithmetic.

16.5   Chapter Review Problems

EXERCISE 16.5.1

What do we mean when we say that strings are immutable?

EXERCISE 16.5.2

What is returned by each of the following method invocations when bigString *is*

"I drank java on the island of Java."

a. bigString.indexOf("java")
b. bigString.indexOf("java", 8)
c. bigString.indexOf("java", 9)
d. bigString.indexOf("an")
e. bigString.indexOf("an", 4)
f. bigString.indexOf("an", 5)

EXERCISE 16.5.3

What is returned by each of the following method invocations when firstString, secondString, *and* thirdString *are initialized as follows?*

```
String firstString = "sunshine";
String secondString = "Sunshine";
String thirdString = " sunshine";
```

   a. firstString.equals(secondString)
   b. firstString.equals(thirdString)
   c. firstString.equalsIgnoreCase(secondString)
   d. firstString.equalsIgnoreCase(thirdString)
   e. firstString.trim().equalsIgnoreCase(thirdString.trim())

EXERCISE 16.5.4

What is returned by bigString.endsWith("Java"), *when* bigString *is*

   "I drank java on the island of Java."

EXERCISE 16.5.5

What is returned by each of the following method invocations when bookTitle *and* isbn *are initialized as follows?*

```
String bookTitle = "Artificial Intelligence: A Modern Approach";
String isbn = "0-13-790395-2";
```

   a. bookTitle.toUpperCase()
   b. isbn.toUpperCase()
   c. isbn.substring(5, 11)
   d. bookTitle.substring(25, bookTitle.length())
   e. bookTitle.substring(25, bookTitle.length()-1)

EXERCISE 16.5.6

What is returned by each of the following method invocations when bigString *is*

   "I drank java on the island of Java."

   a. bigString.charAt(5)
   b. bigString.charAt(bigString.length()-1)
   c. bigString.charAt(bigString.length())

EXERCISE 16.5.7

The following method is meant to return the number of times that pattern *occurs in the string* toSearch. *For example, if* toSearch *is*

   "ATCGGTGGGTTCCAAGGG"

and pattern *is* "GG", *then the method should return 5.*

```
public static int patternCount(String toSearch, String pattern) {
    // Number of times pattern found
    int count = 0;
    // Index of the first occurrence of pattern, if any
    int index = toSearch.indexOf( pattern );
    // Number of characters to skip before looking for next pattern
    int skipDist = pattern.length();
    while (index != -1) {
        count++;
        index = toSearch.indexOf( pattern, index+skipDist );
    }
    return count;
}
```

a. *Unfortunately, the method does not do what it is meant to do. What does the method return when* `pattern` *is* `"GG"`?

b. *Fix the method so that it does what it was intended to do.*

───▶ EXERCISE 16.5.8

The following method is meant to return a boolean, indicating whether `pattern` *can be found in the string* `toSearch`. *It is meant to be case insensitive. For example, if* `toSearch` *is*

  `"ATCGGTGGGTTCCAAGGG"`

and `pattern` *is* `"atcg"`, *the method should still return* `true`.

```
public static boolean find( String toSearch, String pattern ) {
    // Make sure both strings are lower case for comparison purposes
    toSearch.toLowerCase();
    pattern.toLowerCase();
    return toSearch.indexOf( pattern ) != -1;
}
```

The method, however, does not work as expected. Please fix it.

───▶ EXERCISE 16.5.9

Write a method that takes an array of words (i.e., Strings*) as a parameter and returns* true *if and only if the array is in alphabetical order. Mixed case (i.e., both lower and upper case) can be used in the words, so be sure to take that into account. You may assume that the array is completely filled; there are no empty entries in the array.*

───▶ EXERCISE 16.5.10

Write a method that takes a name in the format "First Middle Last" and returns the name in the format "Last, First MiddleInitial". That is, given the name string `"Andrea Pohoreckyj Danyluk"`, *the method should return* `"Danyluk, Andrea P."`

16.6 Programming Problems

➠ EXERCISE 16.6.1

Write a program that allows someone to draw ovals in a window. Each time the user clicks the mouse, a small oval (having width and height of 20) should be drawn at the location of the mouse click. If the user exits the window, the program should print the locations of all the ovals drawn so far, with the following format:

$$(x_1, y_1)$$
$$(x_2, y_2)$$
$$\vdots$$
$$(x_n, y_n)$$

That is, if four ovals have been constructed at Locations (10.0, 20.0), (45.0, 23.0), (22.0, 105.0), and (150.0, 120.0), the following should be printed:

```
(10.0, 20.0)
(45.0, 23.0)
(22.0, 105.0)
(150.0, 120.0)
```

You can keep track of the locations to be printed as a string that becomes longer each time the user clicks the mouse to construct a new oval. ❖

➠ EXERCISE 16.6.2

One strand of DNA can be described by a sequence of bases. Four different bases are found in DNA: adenine (A), guanine (G), cytosine (C), and thymine (T). Two strands are twisted together in the structure of a double helix. Interestingly, if you know the sequence of bases on one strand, you can infer the sequence on the other. A always pairs with T and G always pairs with C. So if one strand of DNA has a partial sequence AGCCTGG, then its complementary strand has the bases TCGGACC.

Write a program that allows a user to type a sequence of bases on one DNA strand. The string of bases should be entered in a JTextField. You should also provide a button that, when pressed, will give the user the complementary sequence, displayed in another JTextField.

Now expand your program in the following ways:

a. The generated complementary sequence should always be displayed in upper case. However, you should allow the user to type their initial sequence in either lower or upper case (or mixed case).

b. Include a method that will check whether the user's sequence is legitimate, i.e., whether it contains only the characters A, G, C, and T. If the sequence to be converted is not entered properly, you should display an error message, rather than the complementary sequence. ❖

CHAPTER 17

Inheritance

*I*n large Java programs, it is common to define collections of classes that share many features. The graphics classes of our library are a good example of such a collection. There are clearly many similarities between the `FilledRect` class and the `FramedRect` class.

When two classes share many common features and behaviors, it is desirable to let them share the code that implements these features. Doing so could certainly save a programmer considerable time. It is also likely to improve the reliability of the code. If a method is only written once, it only needs to be debugged once.

Java supports a mechanism called *inheritance* that provides the means to share code easily when implementing such related classes. We have actually been using this mechanism throughout this text. In almost every program, there has been one class with a header that states that the class `extends WindowController`. You may have noticed that these classes share several common features. For example, within any class that extends `WindowController`, you have been able to access the name `canvas` without declaring it. This is because the variable `canvas` is defined in the class `WindowController`. This one declaration (which you have never actually even seen) is shared by all classes that extend `WindowController`. These classes are said to *inherit* this variable from `WindowController`. They also inherit other features from `WindowController` such as the `getContentPane` method introduced in Section 11.1.2.

While we have been using `extends` throughout the text, we have only extended three classes: `WindowController`, `Controller`, and `ActiveObject`. In this chapter, we will provide a more general explanation of the use of the word `extends`. You will learn that it is not limited to just three classes. The word `extends` can be used to inform Java that we want to define a new class in terms of any previously written class. We will see how this mechanism can provide the means to logically organize the definitions of related classes and to share common code. This will also enable you to better understand how classes that extend `ActiveObject` or one of the controller classes behave.

17.1 Extension as Specialization

Before we delve into the details of Java's interpretation of `extends`, it is useful to discuss the nature of the relationship between two classes, one of which extends the other. In Java, we say that a class that extends another is a *subclass*. A class that is extended in this way is said to be a *superclass*. The term inheritance describes the relationship between a subclass and superclass. A subclass is said to *inherit* features from the superclass it extends. Inheritance in Java, however, is different from the notions of inheritance common in human affairs. A human child inherits some features from one parent and some from the other but never actually inherits all the attributes of just one parent. On the other hand, when a new class extends an existing class in Java, the subclass always inherits *all* of the features of the superclass. By features in this context we mean method definitions and instance variable declarations. As a result, if one class extends another, the subclass will include every method and every instance variable found in the superclass plus whatever new features are described within the body of the subclass.

The consequence of the fact that inheritance in Java is so complete and involves only a single "parent" is that any object that belongs to a subclass can do everything that an object of the superclass could do. A good analogy for this relationship is the inclusion of "option packages" in the marketing of automobiles. Whether you order a base model Volkswagen Beetle or the fully loaded Beetle GLX, you still have a Volkswagen Beetle. The Volkswagen Beetle GLX can do anything a base model Beetle can do. There are some things you can do with the GLX model that you could not do with the base model, like opening the sunroof or turning on the cruise control, but they are both still Beetles.

The idea here is that you don't change what something is by adding features. You just make it more special or specialized. Thus, if you take people and train them to develop special abilities, they are still people. A doctor is still a person, a pilot is still a person, and so on. In Java, an object created from a subclass has all the features of an object of its superclass. Accordingly, the object is also considered to be an object of the superclass. In particular, Java will allow us to assign an object to a variable as long as the type of the variable is a superclass of the type of the object. This behavior is an extension of the notion of assignment compatibility discussed in Section 10.1.3. If the type of a variable or parameter is the name of a class, then Java will allow us to associate the variable or parameter with any object that belongs to that class or one of its subclasses. If the type of a variable or parameter is the name of an interface, then Java will allow us to associate the variable or parameter with any object that belongs to a class that implements the interface.

➠ EXERCISE 17.1.1

Above, we pointed out that the canvas *variable and the* getContentPane *method are examples of features that the classes you have defined inherit from the* WindowController *superclass. What features can you identify that are inherited when you define a class that extends* ActiveObject?

Hint: *Try to identify variables and/or methods that you can use within a class that extends* ActiveObject *without having declared them yourself.*   ❖

17.2 Using extends

To illustrate the use of extends in Java, consider the user interface presented by the computer solitaire card game shown in Figure 17.1. The relevant feature of this game's user interface is that the author of the program apparently liked to use little, framed subregions of the screen to

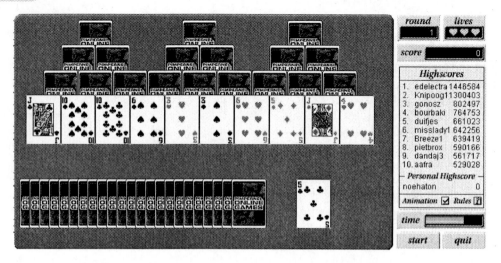

Figure 17.1   The user interface of an interactive card game

display various pieces of information. For example, near the upper right corner of the screen, the program displays the current score in a small frame.

Above the score display, the program indicates how many "lives" the player has left by drawing the appropriate number of hearts within a similar frame.

Toward the bottom of the screen the program uses an animated framed graphic to display the amount of time remaining in a round. It does this by drawing a silver bar that shrinks as time passes.

Such frames could certainly display elements other than those used in this particular game. In fact, this game is just one example of a collection of games implemented in Java that can be found at the site www.pimpernel.com. Many of the games available in this collection use such frames. For example, in the implementation of Euchre found at this site, the interface displays the framed message

on the first screen.

The framed displays seen in these card games provide a good example of a simple collection of classes that share important similarities. If we wanted to implement such game programs, we could define an independent class for each category of framed display used. It would be better, however, to exploit the relationships between these classes by defining a class describing an empty

Figure 17.2 An empty frame

frame and then extending that class to define classes of frames specialized to display information of various forms. In this way, we will only have to specify the details required to create and manipulate the frame itself once.

In this chapter, we will use the construction of such classes as an example to illustrate the use of inheritance in Java. We will start with a simple pair of class definitions to introduce the use of `extends`. We will then introduce the idea of protected features and revise our class definitions to take advantage of this mechanism. Finally, we will explain how to override method definitions.

To begin, we will design and implement a class that implements an empty frame. We will not try to make our frames exhibit the fancy, three-dimensional look of the frames used in the card game we showed to motivate this example. Instead, to keep things simple, we will form frames by overlapping a rounded rectangle[1] with a slightly smaller rounded rectangle of a different color. The result will look like the image shown in Figure 17.2.

We will also keep the interface for this class quite simple. The only methods we include will be named `highlight` and `unHighlight`. The `highlight` method will change the color of the frame from its initial shade of gray to bright red to draw attention to the frame. The `unHighlight` method will restore the original gray border. There are many other useful methods that might be included in this class, such as `moveTo` or `setWidth`. Later in the chapter we will add some of these methods. For now, however, the two methods we have chosen are sufficient for our main purpose, explaining how `extends` works.

The definition of a `FramedDisplay` class that implements such frames is shown in Figure 17.3. The constructor is defined to expect parameters similar to those used to create a rectangle on the screen. For example, a construction of the form

```
new FramedDisplay( 20, 20, 100, 30, canvas );
```

would place a frame like that shown in Figure 17.2 at coordinates (20,20) in the canvas. The frame would be 100 pixels wide and 30 pixels high.

An empty frame isn't very interesting. What we really want is to place some text or graphics within the frame. We could accomplish this by carefully positioning a separate graphical object over the `FramedDisplay`. For example, the pair of constructions:

```
new FramedDisplay( 20, 20, 100, 30, canvas );
new Text( "HELLO", 55, 28, canvas );
```

could be used to display

HELLO

---

[1] For a summary of classes representing filled and framed rounded rectangles, please see Appendix B.

```
// A FramedDisplay is a composite graphic intended to serve
// as a frame in which a program can display various forms
// of information.
public class FramedDisplay {

    private static final double BORDER = 3;     // Border thickness
    private static final double ROUNDNESS = 5; // Corner roundess

    // Colors used for the frame
    private static final Color BORDERCOLOR = Color.GRAY;
    private static final Color HIGHLIGHTCOLOR = Color.RED;

    private FilledRoundedRect body;         // The background
    private FilledRoundedRect border;        // The border

    // Create the display area's background and border and set
    // their colors appropriately
    public FramedDisplay( double x, double y,
                          double width, double height,
                          DrawingCanvas canvas ) {

        border = new FilledRoundedRect( x, y,
                                        width, height,
                                        ROUNDNESS, ROUNDNESS,
                                        canvas );

        body = new FilledRoundedRect( x + BORDER, y + BORDER,
                                      width - 2*BORDER,
                                      height - 2*BORDER,
                                      ROUNDNESS, ROUNDNESS, canvas );

        border.setColor( BORDERCOLOR );
    }

    // Change the border's color to make it stand out
    public void highlight() {
        border.setColor( HIGHLIGHTCOLOR );
    }

    // Restore the standard border color
    public void unHighlight() {
        border.setColor( BORDERCOLOR );
    }

}
```

Figure 17.3 Implementation of an empty framed display class

Of course, it would be better to define a class specialized for the task of displaying framed text so that we could use a single construction of the form

```
new FramedText( "Hello", 20, 20, 100, 30, canvas );
```

If we wrote a definition for a `FramedText` class from scratch, we would have to repeat much of the code from the `FramedDisplay` class. We would still need to define all the instance variables found in `FramedDisplay`. We would just add another instance variable for the `Text` object. We would also still want to define the `highlight` and `unHighlight` methods. In addition, we might want to add methods to modify the appearance of the text.

We can easily avoid repeating the code that would be shared between these two class definitions by defining `FramedText` as an *extension* of `FramedDisplay`. That is, in the header of the definition of `FramedText` we will say

```
public class FramedText extends FramedDisplay
```

Including the phrase `extends FramedDisplay` tells Java to include all the instance variables and methods found in `FramedDisplay` in the new `FramedText` class. This means we can omit definitions for `highlight` and `unHighlight` from the body of the new class. They are inherited from the superclass `FramedDisplay`. The only methods we need to define in the body of the new class will be methods to manipulate the `Text` object displayed within the frame. These methods can be written just as they would have been if `FramedText` had been defined without using extension. In our example, we will include just one such method, `setTextSize`.

The complete specification of `FramedText` as a subclass of `FramedDisplay` is shown in Figure 17.4. The only subtle aspect of using `extends` to define this new class is the specification of its constructor. The methods of the `FramedText` class are either inherited from `FramedDisplay` or defined from scratch in the new class. As a result, there is no interaction between the definitions of the new and old methods. For the constructor, however, we would like to inherit the behavior of the constructor written for `FramedDisplay`, but we can't simply inherit this code. We need to add extra steps to create the desired `Text` object. The new constructor must itself be an extension of the old constructor.

Java allows us to accomplish this by writing a new constructor that begins with an instruction telling Java to invoke the constructor of the superclass. In this context, we do not invoke the constructor of the superclass by writing `new` followed by the name of the superclass. Instead, we write what looks like an invocation of a method with the name `super`. Thus, in the code shown in Figure 17.4, the constructor begins with the line

```
super( x, y, width, height, canvas );
```

Since the superclass of `FramedText` is `FramedDisplay`, this line tells Java to execute the code found in the constructor for a `FramedDisplay` using the parameters provided. The result will be to create the two `FilledRoundedRects` that form the frame for the text. The remainder of the constructor displays the string, `contents`, in the center of this frame. The code that actually centers the text is placed in a separate `positionContents` method, since it is also needed when the text is resized.

```
// A FramedText object displays a specified text message on a
// background framed by a distinct border
public class FramedText extends FramedDisplay {

    // Color used for the text
    private static final Color TEXTCOLOR = Color.WHITE;

    private Text message;          // The message displayed
    private Location frameCenter;  // Where message belongs

    // Create a FramedText object displaying the text 'contents'
    // at the position and with the dimensions specified
    public FramedText( String contents, double x, double y,
                       double width, double height,
                       DrawingCanvas canvas ) {

        // Construct the frame
        super( x, y, width, height, canvas );

        // Construct and appropriately position the message
        frameCenter = new Location( x + width/2, y + height/2 );
        message = new Text ( contents, x, y, canvas );
        message.setColor( TEXTCOLOR );
        positionContents();
    }

    // Position the message to center it in the frame
    private void positionContents() {
        message.moveTo( frameCenter );
        message.move( -message.getWidth()/2, -message.getHeight()/2 );
    }

    // Change the font size used
    public void setTextSize( int size ) {
        message.setFontSize( size );
        positionContents();
    }

}
```

Figure 17.4 Definition of the FramedText subclass

An invocation of "super" can only appear as the first command within a constructor's body. In most classes defined using extension, it is necessary to include such an invocation. If you do not, Java will insert an invocation of the form

```
super();
```

before the first command in your constructor's body. This will result in an error message unless the class you are extending has a constructor that does not expect any parameters.

The class definition shown in Figure 17.4 includes one public method that can be used to change the appearance of the text, setTextSize. When this method is invoked, the text should be repositioned so that it will still be centered within the frame. A private method, positionContents, is included to perform this task. This private method depends on an instance variable, frameCenter, which is initialized in the constructor to refer to the Location of the center of the frame.

The public method setTextSize defined in FramedText can be applied to any object of the class in the usual way. Thus, if we define a variable

```
private FramedText welcome;
```

and execute the assignment

```
welcome = new FramedText( "Hello", 20, 20, 100, 30, canvas );
```

we can then legally execute instructions such as

```
welcome.setTextSize( 24 );
```

In addition, we can invoke public methods defined within FramedDisplay on a FramedText object. For example, we can change the color of the border around the text by saying

```
welcome.highlight();
```

This is the advantage of using inheritance when appropriate. We get to use the code included in the superclass definition without having to rewrite it or even copy and paste it.

EXERCISE 17.2.1

It would be helpful if the FramedText class included a method named setText that could be used to change the text displayed. The method would take a single String as a parameter and replace the text displayed in the frame with the contents of this parameter. Provide a definition for such a setText method that could be added to the definition of the FramedText class shown in Figure 17.4.

EXERCISE 17.2.2

We have only introduced a few of the mechanisms Java provides to support the use of inheritance to define new classes. If we limit ourselves to these mechanisms, then when a new class extends an existing class, it inherits the existing methods of the superclass "as is". This is not always appropriate. To understand why, suppose we had added the following definition for a move method in the FramedDisplay class shown in Figure 17.3.

```
// Move the components of the frame
public void move( double dx, double dy ) {
    border.move( dx, dy );
    body.move( dx, dy );
}
```

Explain what would happen if we then declared a variable

```
private FramedText stopSign;
```

initialized this variable with the assignment

```
stopSign = new FramedText( "STOP", 100, 100, 80, 25, canvas );
```

and executed the statement

```
stopSign.move( 0, 50 );
```

17.3 Protected vs. Public

Associated with each instance variable and method defined in a class is a specification that determines where its name can be accessed. In all the classes we have seen thus far, these specifications have been provided by including either `public` or `private` in the variable or method declaration. Names that are defined as `public` can be accessed in other classes. Names that are defined as `private` can only be accessed within the definition of the class in which they are defined. This restriction still applies even for subclasses. A private name or method defined in a superclass cannot be accessed by code written in the definition of the subclass.

To illustrate this, suppose we wanted to create a class that would extend `FramedDisplay` to implement a display like the one used to show the time remaining as in Figure 17.1. It will draw a bar within the frame in such a way that the fraction of the frame filled is equal to the fraction of the time remaining. The picture below shows what our display would look like when set to indicate that about one fourth of the time had expired.

We will design a version of this class with a very minimal interface. We will name the class `FramedBarMeter`. The constructor for the class will expect all the parameters required when constructing a `FramedDisplay` plus a value between 0 and 1 for the initial fraction to be displayed. Thus, a construction of the form

```
new FramedBarMeter( .75, 350, 50, 80, 20, canvas )
```

would create an 80-by-20-pixel frame positioned at (350,50) on the canvas with a bar that filled three quarters of the frame.

The only method we will include in `FramedBarMeter` is `setFraction`, which will resize the bar based on the parameter value passed to the method (which should again fall between 0 and 1). We will define the class by extending `FramedDisplay`, so it will also be possible to use the `highlight` and `unHighlight` methods with an object of this class.

One aspect of implementing this class that is a bit tricky is positioning the bar within the frame. The bar will simply be a `FilledRect`. We would like to place this `FilledRect` just to the right of the left side of the frame's border and set its width and height so that it almost fills the frame from top to bottom and fills the frame from side to side when the fraction has been set to 1.

To place the `FilledRect` for the bar in the correct position, we will need to determine the x coordinate of the right edge of the left side of the frame and the y coordinate of the bottom edge of the top of the frame. If we look at the constructor of the `FramedDisplay` class (see Figure 17.3), it is clear that the x coordinate we need can be computed by the expression

    x + BORDER

and the y coordinate of the top of the display area can be computed using

    y + BORDER

Unfortunately, if we try to use such expressions within the constructor for our `FramedBarMeter` class, Java will consider our program to be in error. The problem is the reference to the name BORDER. BORDER is defined within the `FramedDisplay` class which `FramedBarMeter` will extend. Within `FramedDisplay`, BORDER is declared to be `private`. This means it can only be accessed by code that appears within the definition of `FramedDisplay`. A reference to BORDER in the constructor of `FramedBarMeter` would be treated as a reference to an undeclared name and would result in an appropriate error message if one tried to compile the code for the class.

This problem could be resolved by changing the modifier in the declaration of BORDER from `private` to `public`. This would enable us to refer to BORDER inside the definition of `FramedBarMeter`. The problem with this solution, however, is that it would make it possible to refer to BORDER in any other class as well. The reason that we normally use the modifier `private` in the declaration of names like BORDER is that doing so limits the ways in which one class can depend upon the details of how we choose to implement another class. Suppose that in the future we decided to revise our `FramedDisplay` class so that it produced a more sophisticated border. If, as a result of this improvement, the thickness of the border varied from side to side, then the variable BORDER might become insufficient. We might need to define separate names like LEFTBORDER and RIGHTBORDER instead. If BORDER had been specified as `private`, we would know that making this change would have no impact outside the `FramedDisplay` class. If it was `public`, however, we might have to modify many classes as a result of this change.

For such situations, where we want to be able to access features of a class when defining subclasses but would rather not make these features `public`, Java provides a third alternative. If we define a variable or method as `protected` rather than `public` or `private`, then Java will allow us to use this name in the bodies of classes that extend the one in which the name was defined.[2] Accordingly, if we revise the definition of BORDER in `FramedDisplay` to read:

    protected static final int BORDER = 3;   // Border thickness

---

[2] The rules for interpreting `protected` are actually a bit more complex than presented here. Java allows a programmer to group classes into larger units called *packages*. In this text, we do not discuss the use of packages. They are intended for larger software projects than are appropriate for a beginning programmer. When applied to classes that belong to different packages, the description of `protected` given here is accurate. A name that is `protected`, however, can be referenced

then it is possible to refer to BORDER from within a subclass. A definition of the FramedBarMeter class that could be used if the variable BORDER was declared to be protected is shown in Figure 17.5.

17.4   Designing for Extension

While changing the declaration of BORDER from public to protected provides a simple illustration of the use of this new access modifier, it is not the best way to solve the problem of positioning the bar.

It is not hard to imagine situations in which implementing subclasses of FramedDisplay will require ways to access information about the dimensions and location of various parts of the frame. We have already seen that the FramedText class needed a way to determine where the center of the frame is located. It was possible for FramedText to compute this location in its constructor, but because it also needed this information in the positionContents method, the class definition included an instance variable that referred to this location. Similarly, in the complete definition of FramedBarMeter, we need to access information about the width of the frame in the setFraction method. This requires the addition of a maxWidth instance variable to this class.

Up to this point, when designing the interface of a class, we have only had to think about what methods would be helpful to those using objects of that class. Now we also should think about what sorts of features might be useful to those *extending* the class. In the case of FramedDisplay, this should include providing the means for subclasses to determine the boundaries of the display area.

We could try to provide the information that subclasses of FramedDisplay might need by defining several protected variables like BORDER. In general, however, just as we have avoided public variables, it is useful to avoid protected variables and instead use protected methods to provide functionality needed for potential subclasses. It is risky to use public or protected with any variable that is not declared final, since modification of such a variable by code outside the defining class could lead to errors that are quite difficult to diagnose. On the other hand, final variables are not very flexible. If we ever added a setWidth method to the FramedDisplay superclass, it would become impossible to describe the location of the right edge of the frame using just final variables.

Accordingly, to make it easier to construct subclasses of FramedDisplay, we will add four protected methods to FramedDisplay. These will return the coordinates of the upper left corner of the display area and its width and height. The complete code for such a revised version of FramedDisplay is shown in Figure 17.6. We have compacted the formatting of some of the original methods in this figure. You should focus on the additions made to the class, the methods to access the dimensions and coordinates of the display area.

---

by any other class included in the same package as the class that defines the name, even if the referencing class is not a subclass. Because we do not include information about how Java should group classes into packages in the examples we present, Java assumes that all of our classes belong to one package. In such programs, public and protected are actually indistinguishable. Nevertheless, we feel it is good for beginners to develop the habit of using protected to identify those features whose use should be restricted to subclasses. It is a habit which will become practical when you move on to larger projects formed from multiple packages.

```
// A FramedBarMeter displays a variable-width rectangle on a
// background framed by a distinct border
public class FramedBarMeter extends FramedDisplay {

    // Space between the frame and the bar
    // BORDER is inherited from FramedDisplay
    private static final double INSET = BORDER + 2;

    // The color of the bar
    private static final Color BARCOLOR = Color.BLUE;

    // The bar itself
    private FilledRect bar;

    // Maximum width bar that will fit
    private double maxWidth;

    // Create frame and bar filling a fraction of the display
    public FramedBarMeter( double fraction,
                           double x, double y,
                           double width, double height,
                           DrawingCanvas canvas ) {

        super( x, y, width, height, canvas );

        maxWidth = width - 2*INSET;
        bar = new FilledRect( x + INSET,  y + INSET,
                        maxWidth*fraction, height - 2*INSET,
                        canvas );
        bar.setColor( BARCOLOR );
    }

    // Change the fraction of the display filled by the bar
    public void setFraction( double fraction ) {
        bar.setWidth( maxWidth*fraction );
    }
}
```

Figure 17.5 A FramedBarMeter class that references a protected superclass member

   A complete version of FramedBarMeter designed to take advantage of these additional methods is shown in Figure 17.7. The phrase "take advantage of" is very appropriate here. The main reason to include methods like displayLeft and displayWidth in a superclass is to make it easier to define subclasses. Since the functionality they provide will clearly be useful to many subclasses, it makes sense to do the work of specifying how to perform these functions just once in the superclass in anticipation of the needs of the subclasses.

```
// A FramedDisplay is a composite graphic intended to serve
// as a frame in which a program can display various forms
// of information.
public class FramedDisplay {

    private static final int BORDER = 3;      // Border thickness
    private static final int ROUNDNESS = 5;   // Corner roundess

    // Colors used for the frame
    private static final Color BORDERCOLOR = Color.GRAY;
    private static final Color HIGHLIGHTCOLOR = Color.RED;

    private FilledRoundedRect body;       // The background
    private FilledRoundedRect border;      // The border

    // Create the display area's background and border
    public FramedDisplay( double x, double y,
                          double width, double height,
                          DrawingCanvas canvas ) {

        border = new FilledRoundedRect( x, y, width, height,
                                        ROUNDNESS, ROUNDNESS,
                                        canvas );
        body = new FilledRoundedRect( x + BORDER, y + BORDER,
                                      width - 2*BORDER, height - 2*BORDER,
                                      ROUNDNESS, ROUNDNESS,
                                      canvas );
        border.setColor( BORDERCOLOR );
    }

    // Change the border's color to make it stand out
    public void highlight() { border.setColor( HIGHLIGHTCOLOR ); }

    // Restore the standard border color
    public void unHighlight() { border.setColor( BORDERCOLOR );  }

    // Return the x coord of the left edge of display area
    protected double displayLeft() {    return body.getX();    }

    // Return the y coord of the top edge of display area
    protected double displayTop() {    return body.getY();    }

    // Return the width of the display area
    protected double displayWidth() { return body.getWidth();  }

    // Return the height of the display area
    protected double displayHeight() { return body.getHeight();  }
```

Figure 17.6   FramedDisplay class with added protected accessors

```
// A FramedBarMeter displays a variable-width rectangle on a
// background framed by a distinct border.
public class FramedBarMeter extends FramedDisplay {

    // Space between the frame and the bar
    private static final double INSET = 2;

    // The color of the bar
    private static final Color BARCOLOR = Color.BLUE;

    // The bar itself
    private FilledRect bar;

    // Create frame and bar filling a fraction of the display
    public FramedBarMeter( double fraction,
                           double x, double y,
                           double width, double height,
                           DrawingCanvas canvas )   {

        super( x, y, width, height, canvas );

        bar = new FilledRect( displayLeft()+INSET,
                       displayTop()+INSET,
                       (displayWidth() - 2*INSET) * fraction,
                       displayHeight() - 2*INSET, canvas );
        bar.setColor( BARCOLOR );
    }

    //  Change the fraction of the display filled by the bar
    public void setFraction( double fraction ) {
        bar.setWidth( (displayWidth() - 2*INSET)*fraction );
    }

}
```

Figure 17.7 Definition of the FramedBarMeter class

Having improved the interface of the FramedDisplay class, we should now revise the FramedText subclass. In particular, while the positionContents method had been written to depend on an instance variable private to FramedText, we can now rewrite it to use the protected accessor methods we added to FramedDisplay and eliminate the instance variable. In addition, we will alter the declarations of the message variable and the positionContents method by replacing the access modifier private with protected. We will take advantage of these changes in the next section. The revised code for this class is shown in Figure 17.8.

```
// A FramedText object displays a specified text message on a
// background framed by a distinct border
public class FramedText extends FramedDisplay {

    // Color used for the text
    private static final Color TEXTCOLOR = Color.WHITE;

    protected Text message;              // The message displayed

    // Create a FramedText object displaying the text 'contents'
    // at the position and with the dimensions specified
    public FramedText( String contents, double x, double y,
                       double width, double height,
                       DrawingCanvas canvas )    {

        // Construct the frame
        super( x, y, width, height, canvas );

        // Construct and appropriately position the message
        message = new Text ( contents, x, y, canvas );
        message.setColor( TEXTCOLOR );
        positionContents();
    }

    // Position the message to center it in the frame
    protected void positionContents() {
        message.moveTo( displayLeft(), displayTop() );
        message.move( (displayWidth() - message.getWidth()) / 2,
                      (displayHeight() - message.getHeight()) / 2 );
    }

    // Change the font size used
    public void setTextSize( int size ) {
        message.setFontSize( size );
        positionContents();
    }

}
```

Figure 17.8   Revision of the FramedText subclass

EXERCISE 17.4.1

The program whose interface is shown in Figure 17.1 included a numeric display that presented the current score within a simple frame:

score [0]

Define a class named FramedCounter *to implement such a display by extending the version of the* FramedDisplay *class presented in Figure 17.6. The main differences between the behavior of the class you define and the* FramedText *class we have considered will be that (a) the score displayed is right justified rather than centered, and (b) the class should include an* increment *method to increase the score by an integer amount provided as a parameter to the method. The initial value displayed should be 0 (i.e., the only parameters the constructor should expect are those passed to the constructor of a* FramedDisplay). ❖

17.5 Inheritance Hierarchies

In Exercise 17.4.1, we suggested implementing a FramedCounter class by extending FramedDisplay. The function of the FramedCounter class is to display the value of a counter within a FramedDisplay. As suggested in the exercise, it should include an increment method that increases the value of the counter displayed by an amount provided as a parameter.

To define this class as an extension of FramedDisplay, you would define a Text instance variable and construct a Text object positioned within the frame to display the value of the counter. While this Text object would be used to display numeric data, it would still be a Text object just like the one placed within a frame by the FramedText class. As a result, an alternative to the approach suggested in the exercise is to define the FramedCounter class as an extension of FramedText. To show how this would be done, we will define such a FramedCounter class. The only functional difference between the class described in the exercise and the one we will define is that our FramedDisplay will center the number displayed within the frame rather than right justifying the value.

Our definition of the FramedCounter class is shown in Figure 17.9. The class is really very simple. The body of its constructor consists of just a single line to invoke the constructor of its superclass, FramedText. It only defines one new instance variable, counter, and one new method, increment. What makes this class interesting is that it is defined by extending a class that was itself defined as an extension of a third class.

When one class is defined by extending another, we know that the new class inherits all the instance variables and methods of the class it extends. To understand the definition of FramedCounter, it is important to recognize that this applies both to features explicitly defined in the class being extended and to features that the extended class inherits from its superclass. For example, the highlight and unhighlight methods that FramedText inherits from FramedDisplay are inherited by FramedCounter from FramedText. In addition, of course, if FramedDisplay had been defined by extending yet another class, FramedCounter would inherit all the features of this fourth class.

To make sense of such complex inheritance relationships, it is often helpful to draw a diagram depicting the connections between groups of classes. We now have a total for four classes in our collection of "framed displays". The diagram in Figure 17.10 captures the inheritance relationships among these four classes. It shows that we have defined two classes that directly extend FramedDisplay and that we have now defined a fourth class, FramedCounter, that extends FramedText. The structure represented by this diagram is called the *inheritance hierarchy* for our collection of framed display classes.

```
// A FramedCounter object displays a numeric counter on
// a background framed by a distinct border
public class FramedCounter extends FramedText {

    private int counter = 0;            // Current value of counter

    // Create a FramedCounter object displaying 0
    // at the position and with the dimensions specified
    public FramedCounter( double x, double y, double width,
                          double height, DrawingCanvas canvas ) {
        super( "0", x, y, width, height, canvas );
    }

    //  Increase the counter's value and update display
    public void increment( int amount ) {
        counter = counter + amount;
        message.setText( counter );
        positionContents();
    }
}
```

Figure 17.9   Definition of FramedCounter as an extension of FramedText

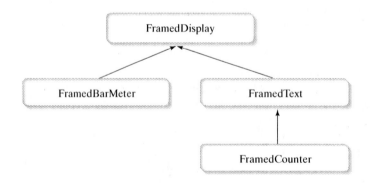

Figure 17.10   Inheritance hierarchy for subclasses of FramedDisplay

Recognizing that it is possible to extend a class that was itself defined as an extension, we must reconsider the meaning of the terms subclass and superclass. FramedCounter is clearly a subclass of FramedText, because it directly extends FramedText. As we discussed in the first section of this chapter, however, the more fundamental reason to describe FramedCounter as a subclass of FramedText is that a FramedCounter object can do anything a FramedText object can do (and more) because it possesses all the features that a FramedText object possesses. In this sense, of course, it is fair to say that FramedCounter is also a subclass of FramedDisplay, since a FramedCounter possesses all the features associated with a FramedDisplay.

In Java, therefore, we say that a class A is a superclass of another class B if B extends A or if B extends some other class C and A is a superclass of C. Similarly, a class B is a subclass of A if B extends A or if B extends some class that is a subclass of A. In terms of the diagram shown in Figure 17.10, one class is a subclass of another if there is a path following the arrows in the diagram from the first class to the second.

17.5.1 Subclass Type Compatibility

This refinement of the notions of superclass and subclass has concrete implications for the interpretation of Java's rules for assignment compatibility. Java will allow us to assign an object to a variable as long as it is certain that the type of the object is either the same as or a subclass of the type of the variable. For example, if we have defined the following variables

```
FramedDisplay someFrame;
FramedText someText;
FramedCounter someCounter;
```

all of the following forms of assignment statement would be considered legal:

```
someFrame = new FramedDisplay( ... );
someFrame = new FramedText( ... );
someFrame = new FramedCounter( ... );
someText = new FramedText( ... );
someText = new FramedCounter( ... );
someCounter = new FramedCounter( ... );
```

In addition, the assignments

```
someFrame = someText;
someFrame = someCounter;
someText = someCounter;
```

are also legal.

Java provides the same flexibility when determining whether the actual parameters provided in a method invocation are acceptable. An actual parameter expression is considered compatible as long as its type is the same as or a subclass of the type specified in the declaration of the corresponding formal parameter. For example, suppose we defined a new class to keep track of a collection of text frames used in some program. To make it possible to add frames to such a collection, we might define a method with the header

```
public void addFrame( FramedText someText ) { ...
```

If scoreDisplays was the name of an object of this collection class, the invocations

```
scoreDisplays.addFrame( someText );
scoreDisplays.addFrame( someCounter );
```

would both be considered valid.

On the other hand, the assignments

```
someCounter = someFrame;
someText = someFrame;
```

and the invocation

```
scoreDisplays.addFrame( someFrame );
```

would all be considered illegal, even if they occurred in a context like

```
someFrame = new FramedCounter( ... );
someCounter = someFrame;
someText = someFrame;
scoreDisplays.addFrame( someFrame );
```

When determining the validity of an invocation or assignment statement, Java only considers the types of the expressions and variables used in the statement or invocation, not the code that precedes the assignment.

In situations like this, where Java will reject a statement even though it is obvious to the programmer that the objects being used will be of an appropriate class, it is possible to tell Java to accept the statement by introducing a type cast. A type cast is formed by placing the name of a type in parentheses before an expression. It instructs Java to treat the value of the expression as if it had the type specified. For example, if we were confident that someFrame was currently associated with a FramedCounter, we could say

```
someCounter = (FramedCounter) someFrame;
```

Java would then accept the assignment as valid. When the program is run, however, Java will actually check that the object associated with the name someFrame belongs to the FramedCounter class or one of its subclasses. If not, the program will terminate with an error message.

Java also provides a mechanism that can be used to determine whether an object can be successfully cast to a particular type. An expression of the form

```
someExpression instanceof   SomeType
```

produces a boolean value depending on whether the current value of someExpression is an object that belongs to SomeType or one of its subclasses. For example, the expression

```
someFrame instanceof  FramedText
```

would produce true if immediately preceded by the assignment

```
someFrame = new FramedCounter( ... );
```

and would produce false if preceded by the assignment

```
someFrame = new FramedDisplay( ... );
```

In particular, we can ensure that the example of a cast shown above will execute without error by placing it within an if statement using instanceof as part of its boolean condition such as

```
if ( someFrame instanceof  FramedCounter ) {
    someCounter = (FramedCounter) someFrame;
}
```

➔ EXERCISE 17.5.1

Suppose that classes named A, B, C, D, *and* E *have been defined with the following class headers:*

```
public class A { ... }

public class B extends D { ... }

public class C extends A { ... }

public class D extends A { ... }

public class E extends D { ... }
```

and that the following variables have been defined:

```
private A someA;
private B someB;
private C someC;
private D someD;
private E someE;
```

a. *Draw a diagram of the inheritance hierarchy relating these five classes similar to the diagram shown in Figure 17.10.*

b. *Indicate which of the following assignment statements would be identified as errors during compilation.*

```
*  someD = someB;
*  someE = someA;
*  someA = someE;
*  someA = new A( ... );
*  someD = someC;
```

c. *Indicate whether each of the following code fragments would always, sometimes, or never result in errors while the program was running (assume that all variables have non-null values):*

```
*  someA = new D( ... );
   someB = (B) someA;

*  someA = new B( ... );
   someD = (D) someA;

*  someA = new C( ... );
   someD = (D) someA;
```

```
    someA = someD;
    someB = (B) someA;

    someA = someD;
    someC = (C) someA;
```

17.6 Overriding Method Definitions

In some situations, when we extend a class, we need to do more than add new instance variables and methods. We also need to change the behavior of some of the existing methods of the superclass so that they function appropriately for the new class. Java makes this possible by allowing us to define a method in the body of a subclass with the same name and parameters as a method in the superclass. In this case, the new method is said to *override* the original method. As this name suggests, this means that the new method in some sense replaces the old method. When one executes a method invocation that uses the name shared by the new and inherited methods, Java will execute the code found in the new method body rather than the inherited code. This makes it possible to define a subclass in which we both add methods and instance variables and specialize some of the existing methods to better fit the purpose of the new class.

As a simple example, recall that when we first defined the FramedDisplay class, we included two methods named highlight and unHighlight. As defined, these methods change the color of the border of the frame. As the name highlight suggests, however, their logical function is not to change the border's color but rather to simply make some change in the appearance of the display that will draw the user's attention.

If we want to draw attention to a FramedText display, it might be more appropriate to change the color of the text than the color of the border. We can specify that we would prefer this behavior by overriding highlight and unHighlight in the definition of FramedText. In particular, if we add a definition for highlight of the form:

```java
public void highlight() {
    message.setColor( HIGHLIGHTCOLOR );
}
```

to the definition of the FramedText class, it will override the definition of highlight included in FramedDisplay. A complete, revised specification of the FramedText class including this definition of highlight and a corresponding definition of unHighlight is shown in Figure 17.11. Given this version of the class, if we define and associate a variable with a FramedText object by saying

```java
FramedText gloat = new FramedText( "You lost!", 20, 20, 80, 30,
                                    canvas );
```

executing the invocation:

```java
gloat.highlight();
```

will change the color of the text "You lost!", but the color of the surrounding frame will be left unchanged. At the same time, if we were to invoke the highlight method on an object belonging

```
// A FramedText object displays a specified text message on a
// background framed by a distinct border
public class FramedText extends FramedDisplay {

    // Colors used for the text
    private static final Color TEXTCOLOR = Color.WHITE;
    private static final Color HIGHLIGHTCOLOR = Color.RED;

    protected Text message;              // The message displayed

    // Create a FramedText object displaying the text 'contents'
    // at the position and with the dimensions specified
    public FramedText( String contents, double x, double y,
                       double width, double height,
                       DrawingCanvas canvas ) {

        // Construct the frame
        super( x, y, width, height, canvas );

        // Construct and appropriately position the message
        message = new Text ( contents, x, y, canvas );
        message.setColor( TEXTCOLOR );
        positionContents();
    }

    // Position the message to center it in the frame
    private void positionContents() {
        message.moveTo( displayLeft(), displayTop() );
        message.move( (displayWidth() - message.getWidth()) / 2,
                      (displayHeight() - message.getHeight()) / 2 );
    }

    // Change the font size used
    public void setTextSize( int size ) {
        message.setFontSize( size );
        positionContents();
    }

    // Highlight the display by changing the text color
    public void highlight() {
        message.setColor( HIGHLIGHTCOLOR );
    }

    // Restore the standard text color
    public void unHighlight() {
        message.setColor( TEXTCOLOR );
    }

}
```

Figure 17.11 Definition of FramedText with specialized highlight method

to a different subclass of FramedDisplay, such as FramedBarMeter, the original version of highlight would be accessed and the color of the border would change.

→ EXERCISE 17.6.1

Define a class named FramedTextLeft *which behaves just like the version of* FramedText *shown in Figure 17.11 except that the text displayed is left justified within the frame rather than centered. Do this by extending* FramedText *and overriding* positionContents. *Note that the declaration of* message *in our latest version of* FramedText *is* protected *rather than* private *to make this possible.*   ❖

17.6.1   The Object class and the equals and toString Methods

Java includes a class called Object that is a superclass of all Java classes. Thus, if you define a class that does not include an extends clause, Java implicitly assumes the new class extends Object. It is rarely useful to actually construct an object of this class, but defining variables and parameters of the Object class can be useful. Java will allow you to assign any object to a variable whose type is Object.

Another important consequence of the fact that all classes are subclasses of Object is that all classes inherit certain methods from Object. We have seen that many classes include a method named equals that can be used to test whether objects of the class are equivalent. In fact, this method is available in all classes because it is defined in the Object class. The version of equals defined in the Object class simply compares two objects using the == operator. We have seen, however, that in other classes, including the String and Location classes, the equals method performs a more appropriate test to see if the properties of objects are equivalent even if the objects are not identical. Classes that provide such improved versions of equals do so by overriding the version they would have otherwise inherited from Object. It is frequently a good idea to include an appropriate definition of equals when defining a new class.

Another feature all classes inherit from Object is a method named toString. toString takes no parameter and returns a String describing the object on which it is invoked. When you pass an object as a parameter to System.out.println or to the setText method of a Text object, the string that will actually appear on the screen is the string returned by invoking toString on the object. As a result, it is also usually a good idea to override toString when defining a new class. Even if you do not expect to use println with objects of the class in the final program, you may find it handy to be able to print a quick description of an object of the class while debugging.

17.6.2   Using super to Access Overridden Methods

In many situations, we do not really want to totally change the steps performed by a method when we override it. Instead, we simply want to extend the steps performed to account for the new instance variables added in the subclass. For example, suppose that we had included a move method in our original definition of FramedDisplay. This method would move the rectangles sed to construct the frame and its background. A subclass like FramedText would need to erride this method, because if it simply inherited the method, telling a FramedText object to move would move the frame but leave the text behind. FramedText needs to override the move method so that it moves both the frame and the text.

The task of overriding a method like move is a bit like the task of defining a constructor for a subclass. In a subclass constructor, we still need to make sure that the actions specified in the superclass constructor are performed, but we want to add additional steps to the initialization process. As we have seen, Java lets us include an invocation of the superclass constructor using the special name super. Java also uses the name super to provide a means of accessing an overridden method from within a subclass.

To see how this mechanism is used, let us consider the details of how we would override a move method in FramedText. First, let us assume that we have added to FramedDisplay a definition of move of the form:

```
// Move the parts of the framed display by offsets
public void move( double xoff, double yoff ) {
    border.move( xoff, yoff );
    body.move( xoff, yoff );
}
```

Now, we need to add a method definition to the FramedText class that will look something like this:

```
// Move the display by specified offsets
public void move( double xoff, double yoff) {
    ... // Code to move the body and border
    positionContents();
}
```

That is, we first need to write instructions to move the frame. Then, we can simply call positionContents to ensure that the text is repositioned appropriately.

The question is what to insert to move the body and border. We cannot simply say

```
border.move( xoff, yoff );
body.move( xoff, yoff );
```

because border and body are declared as private variables in FramedDisplay. What we can do instead is invoke the original move method of the FramedDisplay class. Within FramedText or any class that extends FramedDisplay we can do this by using an invocation of the form

```
super.move( xoff, yoff );
```

In general, we can refer to any nonprivate method of a superclass by typing "super.methodname" in the definition of a subclass.

Thus, the complete definition we should include in FramedText to override move appropriately is:

```
// Move the display by specified offsets
public void move( double xoff, double yoff ) {
    super.move( xoff, yoff );      // Move the body and border
    positionContents();
}
```

Of course, if we add a move method to FramedDisplay, we should modify all the subclasses that extend FramedDisplay, so that move works appropriately for all subclasses.

At this point, the only other subclass of FramedDisplay that we have defined is FramedBarMeter. Just as we did with FramedText, we will add a method to FramedBarMeter that will override the move found in FramedDisplay. The code that should be added to FramedBarMeter is:

```java
public void move( double xoff, double yoff ) {
    super.move( xoff, yoff );
    bar.move( xoff, yoff );
}
```

➡ EXERCISE 17.6.2

In the preceding section we defined versions of highlight *and* unHighlight *for* FramedText *that highlighted the display by changing the color of the text rather than the color of the frame's border. If we wanted to highlight a text display more boldly (even garishly), we could change the colors of both the text and the frame's border. Please show the code that would be used to define such versions of* highlight *and* unHighlight. *The code you provide should work if we used it in place of the copies of* highlight *and* unHighlight *included in the definition of* FramedText *found in Figure 17.11.* ❖

17.6.3   Dynamic Method Invocation

When we invoke a method that has been overridden, Java executes the code for the version of the method associated with the class of the object on which the method is invoked. Sometimes, it is not possible to determine which version of a method should be used until the program is executing. For example, suppose that the move method has been overridden, as described in the preceding sections. Now, assume we declare a variable

```java
private FramedDisplay someFrame;
```

and later execute the invocation

```java
someFrame.move( 100, 50 );
```

Which version of the move method will be executed in this case?

At first, it may seem obvious that the version of move included in the definition of FramedDisplay would be used. Recall, however, that Java considers objects which are members of subclasses of the FramedDisplay class to be members of the FramedDisplay class itself. As a result, since FramedText is a subclass of FramedDisplay, it is legal to assign a value to the someFrame variable by executing the assignment

```java
someFrame = new FramedText( "Follow me", 50, 50, 80, 25, canvas );
```

If the version of move defined in FramedDisplay was used to execute the invocation

> someFrame.move(100, 50);

after someFrame was assigned the FramedText object described by the construction, then the frame would be moved, leaving the text "Follow me" behind. Fortunately, when the value associated with someFrame is a member of FramedText, Java will execute the version of move associated with FramedText.

In general, Java invokes the version of a method associated with an object's class regardless of the type of the name through which the object is accessed. This is exactly the same situation that we saw with interfaces. Recall that the process of identifying the correct method to use is called *dynamic method invocation*. In the case of classes and subclasses, it ensures that invocations of overridden methods behave as expected.

Dynamic method invocation can be very important when one method in a class is defined in terms of another method of the class which is later overridden. For example, consider how we would add a moveTo method to FramedDisplay. One might expect that the process of adding this method to FramedDisplay would be similar to that of adding move. First we would add the method to FramedDisplay and then override it in each subclass. In fact, the way Java handles overridden methods makes implementing moveTo much simpler.

Let's start by thinking about what the definition of moveTo would look like in the FramedDisplay class. Recall that we can move an object to a specified location by moving it by the right offsets from its current location. That is, we can turn a moveTo into a move. A definition of moveTo for FramedDisplay based on this observation is shown below.

```
public void moveTo( double x, double y ) {
    move( x - border.getX(), y - border.getY() );
}
```

It simply moves the entire FramedDisplay by the offsets needed to move the border from its current position to its desired final position.

The invocation

> move(x - border.getX(), y - border.getY());

is just an abbreviation for

> this.move(x - border.getX(), y - border.getY());

It is important to remember this, because it reinforces the fact that the invocation refers to the move method of this, the object whose moveTo method was invoked. Java interprets this dynamically. That is, even though the reference to this appears in the text of the FramedDisplay class, if the object to which moveTo is being applied is actually a member of a class that extends FramedDisplay and overrides move, then Java will invoke the version of move associated with the subclass. So, if we have executed the statement

> FramedText welcomeMessage = new FramedText("Click to begin",...);

and we later say

> welcomeMessage.moveTo(centerX, centerY);

Java will execute the version of moveTo found in FramedDisplay (since we have not overridden this method in FramedText). When it executes the invocation of move within moveTo, it will select the specialized version of move defined in the FramedText class. The version of move defined in FramedText first invokes super.move, which is the version of move defined in FramedDisplay. This moves the border and background. Then, FramedText's version of move calls positionContents, which moves the text itself.

Accordingly, adding a new moveTo method to FramedDisplay does not require further modification to any of its subclasses. All it depends on is that move works appropriately for all these subclasses.

17.6.4   Planned Obsolescence

In certain situations, it is useful to define a method in a superclass with the expectation that it will be overridden by every class that extends the superclass. Such an arrangement can make it possible to define extensions without needing to override many methods of the superclass.

Consider the difference between the processes used in the previous section to define the move and moveTo methods for our framed display classes. The addition of a move method to FramedDisplay adds new functionality to the class but it also increases the work required to define an extension of the class. Almost every class that extends FramedDisplay will have to override move or it will not work correctly. This is not an uncommon situation. Suppose we added a setWidth or setHeight method to FramedDisplay. The FramedText class would have to override these methods to re-center the text. The FramedBarMeter class would also have to override each of these methods to resize the bar it displays.

Adding the moveTo method to FramedDisplay, however, did not make it any more complicated to extend the class. It was not necessary to override moveTo in either of the subclasses we have written. Adding moveTo is simpler, because its implementation relied on move, a method we assumed that all subclasses of FramedDisplay would override appropriately.

Suppose that we assumed that all subclasses of FramedDisplay would define a method similar to the positionContents method defined in FramedText. If this method were also defined in FramedDisplay itself, then we could invoke it as the last step within the definitions of move, setWidth, and setHeight defined within FramedDisplay. If each subclass defined a version of positionContents that did whatever was appropriate to reposition or resize its contents to match the size and position of the frame, it would no longer be necessary for subclasses to override move, setWidth or setHeight.

The definition of positionContents included within FramedDisplay will look like:

```
protected void positionContents(   )  {

}
```

The body of this method is empty because an object of the FramedDisplay class will have no contents. Nothing needs to be done to position them! Defining such a method may seem pointless at first. It is necessary to define the method in this class, however, so that other methods in FramedDisplay can use its name.

In particular, we will want to place calls to positionContents in move, setWidth, and any other method that changes the location or dimensions of the display area. Thus, the revised version of the move method for FramedDisplay will look like:

```
// Move the parts of the framed display by offsets
public void move( double xoff, double yoff ) {
    border.move( xoff, yoff );
    body.move( xoff, yoff );
    positionContents();
}
```

A complete version of FramedDisplay revised to use positionContents is presented in Figure 17.12.

A version of FramedText revised to be compatible with our new version of FramedDisplay is shown in Figure 17.13. The biggest change is that it is no longer necessary to override move in this class. The version defined in the superclass works correctly because it relies on positionContents.

There is also a subtle change in positionContents. Although its body has not changed, it is now declared as a protected method rather than a private method. When a method is overridden, Java insists that the new method be at least as widely accessible as the method that is being overridden. Since positionContents was declared protected in the superclass FramedDisplay, it cannot be declared private in FramedText.

In recognition of this change, we have also made a slight change in the constructor. It no longer invokes positionContents. Instead, it places the text in the correct position explicitly. We make this change because it is, in general, dangerous to invoke any method that might be overridden from within a class's constructor.

The problem is that although FramedText is a subclass of FramedDisplay, the FramedText class itself can be extended so that it serves as the superclass for some other class. If this is done, positionContents might be overridden by the new subclass. The constructor of such a subclass will invoke the constructor for FramedDisplay by using "super" in the first line of its own constructor. If the constructor for FramedDisplay were invoked in this way, any invocation of positionContents in the FramedDisplay constructor would actually invoke the version of positionContents defined within the subclass. This new version of positionContents might reference instance variables defined in the subclass that were initialized by code appearing after the first line of its constructor. In this case, the variables would not yet be initialized when positionContents was invoked.

To complete the revision, we also include a version of FramedBarMeter that is compatible with the version of FramedDisplay shown in Figure 17.12. It can be found in Figure 17.14. In the original version of this class, there was no instance variable to keep track of the fraction currently displayed by the bar. We need to add such a variable in this version, because its value is needed within positionContents.

▪▶ EXERCISE 17.6.3

In this section, we suggested that revising our collection of framed display classes to depend upon the existence of the positionContents method would simplify the definition of methods such as setWidth and setHeight. We did not, however, actually discuss how such methods would be implemented. For this exercise, we would like you to implement one of these methods, setWidth. To help you appreciate the significance of the changes we made to the design of our classes in this

```java
// A FramedDisplay is a composite graphic intended to serve
// as a frame in which a program can display information
public class FramedDisplay {
    private FilledRoundedRect body;        // The background
    private FilledRoundedRect border;      // The border

    // Create the display area's background and border
    public FramedDisplay( double x, double y,
                          double width, double height,
                          DrawingCanvas canvas ) {
        border = new FilledRoundedRect( x, y, width, height,
                                        ROUNDNESS, ROUNDNESS, canvas );
        body = new FilledRoundedRect( x + BORDER, y + BORDER,
                                      width-2*BORDER, height-2*BORDER,
                                      ROUNDNESS, ROUNDNESS, canvas );
        border.setColor( BORDERCOLOR );
    }

    // This method should be overridden by any subclass so
    // it correctly positions the contents of the display
    protected void positionContents( ) {    }

    // Change the border's color to make it stand out
    public void highlight() {  border.setColor( HIGHLIGHTCOLOR ); }

    // Restore the standard border color
    public void unHighlight() { border.setColor( BORDERCOLOR );   }

    // Return the x coord of the left edge of display area
    protected double displayLeft() {     return body.getX();    }

    // Return the y coord of the top edge of display area
    protected double displayTop() {    return body.getY();      }

    // Return the width of the display area
    protected double displayWidth() { return body.getWidth();  }

    // Return the height of the display area
    protected double displayHeight() { return body.getHeight();  }

    // Move the parts of the framed display by offsets
    public void move( double xoff, double yoff ) {
        border.move( xoff, yoff );
        body.move( xoff, yoff );
        positionContents();
    }

    // Move the parts of the frame to a specific location
    public void moveTo( double x, double y ) {
        move( x - border.getX(), y - border.getY() );
    }
}
```

Figure 17.12   Version of FramedDisplay based on positionContents

```java
// A FramedText object displays a specified text message on a
// background framed by a distinct border
public class FramedText extends FramedDisplay {

    // Color used for the text
    private static final Color TEXTCOLOR = Color.WHITE;

    private Text message;            // The message displayed

    // Create a FramedText object displaying the text 'contents'
    // at the position and with the dimensions specified
    public FramedText( String contents, double x, double y,
                       double width, double height,
                       DrawingCanvas canvas ) {

        // Construct the frame
        super( x, y, width, height, canvas );

        // Construct and appropriately position the message
        message = new Text( contents,
                            displayLeft(), displayTop(),
                            canvas );
        message.move( (displayWidth() - message.getWidth()) / 2,
                      (displayHeight() - message.getHeight()) / 2 );
        message.setColor( TEXTCOLOR );
    }

    // Position the message to center it in the frame
    protected void positionContents() {
        message.moveTo( displayLeft(), displayTop() );
        message.move( (displayWidth() - message.getWidth()) / 2,
                      (displayHeight() - message.getHeight()) / 2 );
    }

    // Change the font size used
    public void setTextSize( int size ) {
        message.setFontSize( size );
        positionContents();
    }

}
```

Figure 17.13 FramedText with revised positionContents

```java
// A FramedBarMeter displays a variable-width rectangle on a
// background framed by a distinct border.
public class FramedBarMeter extends FramedDisplay
    // Space between the frame and the bar
    private static final double INSET = 2;

    // The color of the bar
    private static final Color BARCOLOR = Color.BLUE;

    // The bar itself
    private FilledRect bar;

    // Fraction currently being displayed
    private double fraction;

    // Create frame and bar filling a fraction of the display
    public FramedBarMeter( double aFraction,
                           double x, double y,
                           double width, double height,
                           DrawingCanvas canvas ) {

        super( x, y, width, height, canvas );

        fraction = aFraction;

        bar = new FilledRect( displayLeft()+INSET, displayTop()+INSET,
                        (displayWidth()-2*INSET)*fraction,
                        displayHeight()-2*INSET, canvas );
        bar.setColor( BARCOLOR );
    }

    //  Change the fraction of the display filled by the bar
    public void setFraction( double aFraction ) {
        fraction = aFraction;
        positionContents();
    }

    //  Resize and reposition the bar appropriately
    protected void positionContents() {
        bar.moveTo( displayLeft()+INSET, displayTop()+INSET );
        bar.setWidth( (displayWidth()-2*INSET)*fraction );
        bar.setHeight( displayHeight()-2*INSET );
    }
}
```

Figure 17.14   Definition of the FramedBarMeter class

section, we ask that you consider how to implement setWidth *in both the versions of the display classes presented in this section and the earlier versions that did not assume* positionContents *was defined by all classes in the collection.*

a. *Show how to modify the definitions of* FramedDisplay, FramedText, *and* FramedBarMeter *found in Figures 17.6, 17.8, and 17.7 to include a* setWidth *method. When invoked, this method should both change the width of the frame and reposition its contents as necessary.*

b. *Next, show how to modify the definitions of* FramedDisplay, FramedText, *and* FramedBarMeter *found in Figures 17.12, 17.13, and 17.14 to include a* setWidth *method.* ❖

17.6.5 Abstract Classes and Methods

It should seem a bit odd to you that we had to define a version of the positionContents method in the version of FramedDisplay shown in Figure 17.12. A FramedDisplay has no contents. How can we position them? In fact, because there were no contents to position, we defined the method with an empty body. It would be more satisfying, however, if we had not had to define it at all.

The real reason we defined positionContents in FramedDisplay was to ensure that every subclass of FramedDisplay would define a version of the method. Java provides a more explicit way to accomplish this purpose. When we define a class, we can include declarations of *abstract methods*. We do this by adding the word abstract to the method's header and also replacing the message's body by a semicolon. Thus, we could replace the declaration of positionContents with the abstract method declaration:

```
abstract protected void positionContents();
```

If a class declaration contains one or more abstract method declarations, then the class itself must also be declared abstract. Again, this is done by adding the word abstract to the class header as in

```
public abstract class FramedDisplay { . . .
```

An abstract class is designed to provide a base for defining useful subclasses rather than as a useful class by itself. If a class is declared to be abstract, one cannot construct objects of the class. That is, once we state that FramedDisplay is an abstract class, we cannot create FramedDisplay objects. We can, however, extend an abstract class, and, as long as the extension overrides all the abstract methods with actual method declarations, we can create instances of the subclasses. Thus, if we add the word abstract to the header of the FramedDisplay class and make positionContents abstract, all of the examples of subclasses of FramedDisplay we have defined will still be correct and useful.

17.7 Summary

Inheritance is an important tool for advanced programming in Java. Its use can save work by facilitating the sharing of common code. More importantly, it can provide the means to explicitly identify relationships among related classes in a program. Structuring code in a way that makes it easy to grasp the relationships among the parts is critical to producing programs that are understandable and therefore maintainable.

In Java, a new class can be defined to inherit features from an existing class by including an `extends` clause in the header of the new class. In this case, the new class is treated as if it contained declarations of all the methods and instance variables of the class it extends.

We say that a class defined using `extends` is a subclass of the class it extends and that the class it extends is a superclass of the new class. The subclass/superclass relationship is transitive. That is, if class C extends class B and class B extends class A, C is a subclass of both B and A. Similarly, A is a superclass of both B and C in this situation.

Because a class that extends another inherits *all* the features of the superclass, Java allows us to use an object of a given class as if it were an object of any of its superclasses. Suppose that class A is a superclass of class B. Java will allow us to assign a value known to be of type B to a variable declared to refer to objects of type A. We can also pass a value known to be of type B to a method expecting a parameter of type A or return a value of type B from a method declared to return a value of type A.

Java has several mechanisms that provide the programmer with the flexibility to use the valuable features of a superclass while replacing or modifying features that are not quite suited to the purpose of the new class. The `protected` access modifier enables a programmer to give subclasses access to instance variables and methods that are hidden from other classes. If the definition of a given method associated with a superclass is not quite appropriate for use with a subclass, the subclass can override the original definition by including its own definition. At the same time, Java provides the means to access an overridden method within the new class definition. The notation `super.methodname` can be used to access any method as it was defined in a class's immediate superclass.

The opportunity to extend a class imposes additional concerns on the programmer when defining a class. Without inheritance, the issues to be addressed when designing a new class focused on the interface the new class provided to other classes that invoked its methods. With inheritance, we also have to consider whether the mechanisms we include in a class will meet the needs of other classes defined by extending it. In some cases, in fact, classes are designed with the assumption that they will only be used as the basis for designing other classes through inheritance. In such situations, Java allows us to declare that the class defined is `abstract`. Java will not allow us to create objects of such classes, but they can be extended to define other classes that can be instantiated.

17.8 Chapter Review Problems

Exercises 17.8.1 through 17.8.4 are related to the following scenario.

Suppose that we want to define classes to draw balls used in various games. As suggested by the drawing below, if we start with a simple `FilledOval`, we can make it look like a rubber ball by painting it red (use your imagination!) and adding a border. Thus, we might define a class named `RubberBall` by extending the familiar `FilledOval` class. Similarly, we can make a `RubberBall` look like a tennis ball by changing the color to a shade of yellow and adding appropriate curved lines. Then, given a tennis ball, if we change its color to orange and add a vertical and horizontal line, we get a picture that looks like a basketball.

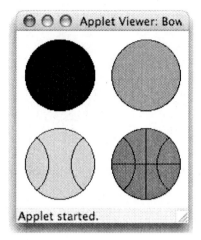

In the questions below, we ask you to consider the relationships between the four classes FilledOval, RubberBall, TennisBall, and BBall corresponding to the four shapes shown in the picture above. Figure 17.15 shows possible implementations of RubberBall and TennisBall. Exercise 17.8.4 asks you to provide an implementation for BBall.

➥ EXERCISE 17.8.1

Draw an inheritance hierarchy diagram for the four classes FilledOval, RubberBall, TennisBall, *and* BBall *described above.* ❖

➥ EXERCISE 17.8.2

Assuming that we have defined four ball drawing classes using inheritance as suggested above and then defined the following variables:

```
FilledOval oval;
RubberBall ball1;
TennisBall ball2;
BBall ball3;
```

and initialized them by executing the following code, which draws a picture like the one shown above:

```
oval = new FilledOval( 10, 10, 80, 80, canvas );
ball1 = new RubberBall( 110, 10, 80, canvas );
ball2 = new TennisBall( 10, 110, 80, canvas );
ball3 = new BBall( 110, 110, 80, canvas );
```

```java
public class RubberBall extends FilledOval {
    // Add black edge to the ball
    private FramedOval border;

    public RubberBall( double x, double y, double size,
                       DrawingCanvas canvas ) {
        super( x, y, size, size, canvas );
        setColor( Color.RED );
        border = new FramedOval( x, y, size, size, canvas );
    }

    public void move( double dx, double dy ) {
        super.move( dx, dy );
        border.move( dx, dy );
    }

    public void moveTo( double x, double y ) {
        move( x-getX(), y-getY() );
    }
}


public class TennisBall extends RubberBall {
    // Size and starting angles for cut arc in degrees
    private static final int CUTSIZE = 100;
    private static final int RIGHTCUTSTART = 90 + (180 - CUTSIZE) / 2;
    private static final int LEFTCUTSTART = 270 + (180 - CUTSIZE) / 2;

    // The two curves on the sides of the ball
    private FramedArc leftCut, rightCut;

    public TennisBall( double x, double y, double size,
                       DrawingCanvas canvas ) {
        super( x, y, size, canvas );
        setColor( Color.YELLOW );

        rightCut = new FramedArc( x + size * 2 / 3, y, size, size,
                                  RIGHTCUTSTART, CUTSIZE,  canvas );
        leftCut =  new FramedArc( x - size * 2 / 3, y, size, size,
                                  LEFTCUTSTART, CUTSIZE,   canvas );
    }

    public void move( double dx, double dy ) {
        super.move( dx, dy );
        rightCut.move( dx, dy );
        leftCut.move( dx, dy );
    }
}
```

Figure 17.15 The RubberBall and TennisBall classes for Exercises 17.8.3 and 17.8.4

indicate whether each of the following code fragments would be (a) identified as an error before the program was even run, (b) cause the program to terminate with an exception when run, or (c) execute without causing any error.

a. ball1 = ball2;
b. oval = ball3;
c. ball2 = ball1;
d. ball1 = ball3;
    ball2 = (TennisBall) ball1;

➡ EXERCISE 17.8.3

In Figure 17.15 we show possible implementations of two of the four ball classes discussed above. Using these definitions and assuming that we have defined the following variables:

```
FilledOval oval;
RubberBall ball1;
TennisBall ball2;
```

and initialized them by executing the following code (which would create the drawings of three of the four balls shown above):

```
oval = new FilledOval( 10, 10, 80, 80, canvas );
ball1 = new RubberBall( 110, 10, 80, canvas );
ball2 = new TennisBall( 10, 110, 80, canvas );
```

indicate what each of the following invocations would do. It is possible that the invocations would be identified as errors either before the program was run or during execution. For each example you should either indicate how the invocation would affect the drawing or explain what type of error would be detected.

a. ball2.move(50, 50);
b. ball1.setColor(Color.BLUE);
c. ball2.moveTo(0, 0);
d. ball2.hide();

➡ EXERCISE 17.8.4

Provide a definition for a class BBall *that could be used to draw basketballs. Your class should extend the* TennisBall *class shown in Figure 17.15.*

Exercises 17.8.5 through 17.8.8 are related to the following scenario.

We can define classes to draw on a canvas objects resembling those ubiquitous sticky notes. The simplest sticky class, SimpleSticky, creates objects consisting of a yellow sticky outlined in black. A slightly more refined sticky class, MessageSticky, creates objects that also contain a line of text in the sticky. Finally the ErasableMessageSticky class generates objects that contain a message, but also contains a small "go away" box in the upper left corner that can be clicked on to make the sticky disappear.

For simplicity we will provide each class with only two methods, contains and react. The first is self-explanatory. The react method will take a Location as a parameter, draw a small red dot at the Location, and change the outline of the sticky to red. If it has a message, it will also change the message to red. However, if the location is in the "go away" box of the ErasableMessageSticky, then the entire sticky will be hidden (though the red dots will remain on the canvas).

For the following problems, assume that we plan to define these three classes using inheritance.

EXERCISE 17.8.5

Draw an inheritance hierarchy diagram for the three classes SimpleSticky, *Message-Sticky, and* ErasableMessageSticky *using inheritance as suggested in the description above.*

EXERCISE 17.8.6

Assuming that we have defined three sticky drawing classes using inheritance as suggested above and then defined the following variables:

```
SimpleSticky simpSticky;
MessageSticky messSticky;
ErasableMessageSticky eraseSticky;
```

and initialized them by executing the following code:

```
simpSticky = new SimpleSticky( 10, 10, 80, 80, canvas );
messSticky = new MessageSticky( 10, 110, 80, 50, "Test", canvas );
eraseSticky = new ErasableMessageSticky( 200, 10, 80, 80,
                                         "Erasable", canvas );
```

indicate whether each of the following code fragments would be (a) identified as an error before the program was even run, (b) cause the program to terminate with an exception when run, or (c) execute without causing any error.

a. simpSticky = messSticky;
b. simpSticky = eraseSticky;
c. messSticky = simpSticky;
d. simpSticky = eraseSticky;
  messSticky = simpSticky;
e. simpSticky = messSticky;
  messSticky = (MessageSticky) simpSticky;
f. simpSticky = eraseSticky;
  messSticky = (MessageSticky) simpSticky;

```
public class SimpleSticky {
    protected FilledRect interior; // Inside of Sticky
    protected FramedRect outline;  // Outline of Sticky
    private DrawingCanvas canvas;

    // Create yellow Sticky
    public SimpleSticky( double left, double top, double width,
        canvas = aCanvas; double height, DrawingCanvas aCanvas ) {
        interior = new FilledRect( left, top, width, height, canvas );
        interior.setColor( Color.YELLOW );
        outline = new FramedRect( left, top, width, height, canvas );
    }

    // Return whether pt is in Sticky
    public boolean contains( Location pt ) {
        return outline.contains( pt );
    }

    // Change color of Sticky to red
    public void react( Location pt ) {
        new FilledOval( pt, 1, 1, canvas ).setColor( Color.RED );
        outline.setColor( Color.RED );
    }
}

public class MessageSticky extends SimpleSticky {
    private static final double GAP = 2;
    protected Text message;  // Message displayed on Sticky
    // Create Sticky with message
    public MessageSticky( double left, double top, double width,
                          double height, String messageString,
                          DrawingCanvas canvas ){
        super( left, top, width, height, canvas );
        message = new Text( messageString, left+GAP, top+height/2-10,
                          canvas );
    }

    // Change color and message of Sticky to red
    public void react( Location pt ) {
        super.react( pt );
        message.setColor( Color.RED );
    }
}
```

Figure 17.16 The SimpleSticky and MessageSticky classes for Exercises 17.8.7 and 17.8.8

EXERCISE 17.8.7

In Figure 17.16 we show possible implementations of two of the three sticky classes discussed above. Using these definitions, provide a definition for a class ErasableMessageSticky *that could be used to draw stickies with a message and "go away" box. Your class should extend the* MessageSticky *class shown in Figure 17.16.*   ❖

The examples used in the two preceding sets of exercises illustrate a danger inherent in the use of inheritance and a way to avoid this danger.

While completing Exercise 17.8.3, you may have noticed that one of the invocations included in that question highlights a form of undesirable behavior that can result when inheritance is used. The problem arises from the fact that RubberBall inherits *all* of the methods associated with the FilledOval class, not just the methods that are appropriate for a RubberBall.

For example, balls should be round. It should not be possible to set the width of a rubber ball without also setting its height to the same value. Therefore, it would not make sense to include a setWidth method in the definition of the RubberBall class. Unfortunately, because the definition of RubberBall shown in Figure 17.15 extends FilledOval, our RubberBall class will inherit a setWidth method. If the inherited setWidth method is used, it will change the width of the interior of the ball without changing the width of the FramedOval that forms its border. Worse yet, this undesired behavior will also be inherited by the TennisBall and BasketBall classes.

When using inheritance, it is important to remember that the subclass always inherits all of the methods of the superclass, not just the methods you want it to inherit. If a potential base class includes methods that should not be associated with the classs you wish to define, you should not use inheritance. Instead, you should include an object of the potential superclass as an instance variable in the class you wish to implement. This is the approach taken in the SimpleSticky class. Rather than defining this class as an extension of FilledRect, we have defined the interior instance variable to refer to a FilledRect.

EXERCISE 17.8.8

What would be output by a program composed of the following class definitions?

```
public class Mail extends Controller {

    private MailItem [ ] delivery = new MailItem[4];

    public void begin() {
        delivery[0] = new Catalog( "L.L.Bean" );
        delivery[1] = new BirthdayCard( "from Mom" );
        delivery[2] = new Magazine( "Time" );
        delivery[3] = new Bill( "Phone company" );

        for ( int i = 0; i < 4; i++ ) {
            delivery[i].process();
        }
    }
}
```

```java
public class MailItem {
   protected  String desc;

   public MailItem( String description ) {   desc = description;   }

   public void open() {             }

   public void examine() {   System.out.println( "Read " + desc );   }

   public void file() {   System.out.println( "Recycle " + desc );   }

   public void process() {
      open();
      examine();
      file();
   }
}

public class Catalog extends MailItem {

   public Catalog( String description ) {   super( description );   }

   public void examine() {System.out.println( "Order goodies from " +
                                     desc );   }
}

public class Magazine extends MailItem {

   public Magazine( String description ) {   super( description +
                                  " magazine" );   }

   public void file() {   System.out.println( "Place " + desc +
                                  " on coffee table" );   }
}

public class Enveloped extends MailItem {

   public Enveloped( String description ) {   super( description );   }

   public void open() {   System.out.println( "Rip open the envelope" );   }

   public void file() {
      fileContents();
      System.out.println( "Throw out the envelope" );
   }

   public void fileContents() {   }
}
```

```
public class Bill extends Enveloped {

    public Bill( String description ) {    super( description );    }

    public void examine() {    System.out.println( "Pay bill from " + desc );    }

    public void fileContents() {    System.out.println( "Save bill " + desc +
                                                    " in drawer" );    }
}

public class BirthdayCard extends Enveloped {

    public BirthdayCard( String description ) {    super( "birthday card " +
                                                        description );    }

    public void fileContents() {    System.out.println( "Stick " + desc +
                                                " on the fridge" );    }
}
```

❖

17.9 Programming Problems

▮▶ EXERCISE 17.9.1

In most of the examples in this text the "main" class extends WindowController*.*
WindowController *is not a standard Java class. It is part of our objectdraw library.*
WindowController *is defined as a subclass of a standard Java class named* JApplet*. The main
difference between* WindowController *and* JApplet *is that* WindowController *is designed
to make it easy for students to handle mouse events in their very first days as Java programmers.*

*You may have noticed that to handle events associated with buttons, scrollbars, other GUI
components, and event keystrokes you have to do a fair amount of work. You have to define a
method with a name like* actionPerformed*, you have to declare that your main class implements
a listener interface, and you have to add the class as a listener to the GUI components you create.
In programs that extend* JApplet*, the work required to handle mouse events is similar. Within
a class that extends* WindowController*, however, all you have to do is define a method like*
onMouseClick*.*

To give you a sense of how WindowController *works, we would like you to define two
classes named* SimpleButton *and* ButtonAndWindowController *that will make it just as
easy to handle events associated with clicking on a button as it is to handle a mouse event in a*
WindowController*.*

*To make our goals concrete, we have included an example of a program that uses the two
classes we have in mind in Figure 17.17. The example we have chosen for this purpose is a
re-implementation of a program used as an example in Section 11.5.1. The code for the original
program can be found in Figures 11.9 and 11.10. In the earlier version, as you would expect, we
defined an* actionPerformed *method, added listeners to the buttons, etc. The new version is
quite a bit simpler.*

```
// Program that lets user drop balls that fall at different
// speeds.  Intended to illustrate use of ButtonAndWindowController
public class ButtonBallController extends ButtonAndWindowController {
    // The speeds the ball can move at
    private static final int SLOW_SPEED = 2;
    private static final int MEDIUM_SPEED = 4;
    private static final int FAST_SPEED = 6;

    // The falling ball
    private FallingBall droppedBall;

    // Buttons to control speed
    private SimpleButton fastButton, mediumButton, slowButton;

    // Current speed setting
    private int speed;

    // Create and display the speed control buttons
    public void begin() {
        speed = SLOW_SPEED;

        fastButton = new SimpleButton( "Fast", this );
        mediumButton = new SimpleButton( "Medium", this );
        slowButton = new SimpleButton( "Slow", this );

        JPanel southPanel = new JPanel();
        southPanel.add( fastButton );
        southPanel.add( mediumButton );
        southPanel.add( slowButton );
        Container contentPane = getContentPane();
        contentPane.add( southPanel, BorderLayout.SOUTH );

        contentPane.validate();
    }

    // Make a new ball when the player clicks
    public void onMouseClick( Location point ) {
        droppedBall = new FallingBall( point, speed, canvas );
    }

    // Set new speed when the player clicks a button
    public void onButtonClick( SimpleButton source ) {
        if ( source == slowButton ) {
            speed = SLOW_SPEED;
        } else if ( source == mediumButton ) {
            speed = MEDIUM_SPEED;
        } else {
            speed = FAST_SPEED;
        }

        if ( droppedBall != null ) {
            droppedBall.setSpeed( speed );
        }
    }
}
```

Figure 17.17 Using the SimpleButton and ButtonAndWindowController classes

There is no `actionPerformed` *method in Figure 17.17. Instead, we define an* `onButton-Click` *method, very much as we might define* `onMouseClick` *to handle mouse events. Unlike* `actionPerformed`, *this method is specialized for handling button events simply. It takes a button as a parameter rather than an* `ActionEvent`. *Also, if you look at the* `begin` *method, you will notice we never invoke a method to add a listener to any of the buttons we create.*

Two facts about the code in Figure 17.17 make these simplifications possible. The class shown is defined as an extension of `ButtonAndWindowController` *rather than* `WindowController`, *and the buttons we create are members of a class named* `SimpleButton` *rather than* `JButton`. *For this problem, we want you to define these two classes.*

The `ButtonAndWindowController` *class you define should be an extension of our* `WindowController`. *It should be an abstract class, because it will contain an abstract method declaration for* `onButtonClick`. *It should implement the* `ActionListener` *interface. To do this, you will need to include an* `actionPerformed` *method. Your* `actionPerformed` *method should invoke* `onButtonClick` *whenever a button causes an event. To keep things simple, it can ignore any other events.*

The `SimpleButton` *class should be defined as an extension of* `JButton`. *Its constructor should expect a* `BallAndWindowController` *as a parameter. The constructor should add this controller as a listener.*

To actually test your classes, combine these two classes with the `ButtonBallController` *in Figure 17.17 and the* `FallingBall` *class found in Figure 11.5.*

CHAPTER 18

Exceptions

$\mathscr{I}$ t is not at all uncommon for a program to do unexpected things when run. In many cases a program behaves so badly that all the computer can do is display an error message. A sample of the type of error message many Java development systems produce in such situations is shown below. Does it look familiar?

```
java.lang.ArrayIndexOutOfBoundsException: 44
    at Calendar.setEvent(Calendar.java:38)
    at CalendarController.actionPerformed(CalendarController.java:52)
    at java.awt.Button.processActionEvent(Button.java:381)
    at java.awt.Button.processEvent(Button.java:350)
    at java.awt.Component.dispatchEventImpl(Component.java:3598)
    at java.awt.Component.dispatchEvent(Component.java:3439)
    at java.awt.EventQueue.dispatchEvent(EventQueue.java:450)
```

Many such errors are the results of mistakes made by the programmer. One might forget to initialize a variable or might specify an incorrect condition in a loop that allows an index to exceed an array's range. In such situations, all you can do is try to understand the error messages the system produces and examine your code carefully to identify the source of the problem.

Sometimes, however, an error occurs in a "correct" program because a situation arises that the program was not designed to handle. For example, if a program uses a value entered in a JTextField to determine which element in an array to access, the program might encounter an indexing error if the user enters an inappropriate value in the JTextField.

In some sense, such problems are the fault of the program's user rather than its author. After all, the problem can be avoided by correcting the user's input without changing the program's text. However, if the only explanation presented to the user is an error message like the one shown above, the user is very likely to blame the programmer. At the very least, the user will have more trouble than necessary determining how to correct the input. Accordingly, a well-written program should anticipate such user errors and include code to validate all input before using it. If user input is invalid, the program itself should display a message that the user will be able to comprehend.

In this chapter, we will learn about *exceptions*, a feature of the Java language that supports the construction of programs that are robust in the face of errors in user input and other unexpected events. An exception is an object that a method can use to signal that it is unable to complete its intended function. Code can be written to respond appropriately when a method generates an exception. Such code is placed in a new control structure presented in this chapter, the `try-catch` statement.

18.1   Exception Handlers

To provide a context that illustrates the use of Java's exception mechanism, we will consider the implementation of a calendar management program. Such a program would include a data structure in which events scheduled for various days could be recorded and would provide an interface through which a user could enter a description of an event to be scheduled on a specific day. In Section 15.1 we showed how a two-dimensional array of `String`s could be used to represent such a calendar of events. We will assume that the same type of array is used to represent the calendar in this chapter.

The array we have in mind would be declared as

```
private String[][] dailyEvent;
```

with the intent that

```
dailyEvent[month - 1][day - 1]
```

refers to a string describing events scheduled on the month and day specified. For example, `dailyEvent[0][0]` might refer to the string "New Year's Day", while `dailyEvent[11][24]` might refer to the string "Christmas Day".

This array would be declared as an instance variable of a `Calendar` class which maintains all events scheduled for a given year. This class would provide methods to manipulate a calendar, including a method to associate an event with a date and a method to get the event description for a date. We will assume the first method is declared with the header:

```
public void setEvent( int month, int day, String description )
```

To enable a user to enter new events, the program might pop up a simple dialog box like that shown in Figure 18.1. The built-in `parseInt` method could be used to convert the `String`s found in the first two `JTextField`s into `int` values, which would then be used as array indices within the `setEvent` method. Assuming that the three `JTextField`s shown in the figure are named `monthField`, `dayField`, and `descriptionField`, then the code executed when the user clicks ENTER would likely include the statement

```
theCalendar.setEvent( Integer.parseInt( monthField.getText() ),
                      Integer.parseInt( dayField.getText() ),
                      descriptionField.getText()
                      );
```

If the user fills in all the `JTextField`s correctly, we may assume that this statement will update the calendar appropriately. There are, however, several ways in which a user error might cause this code to fail.

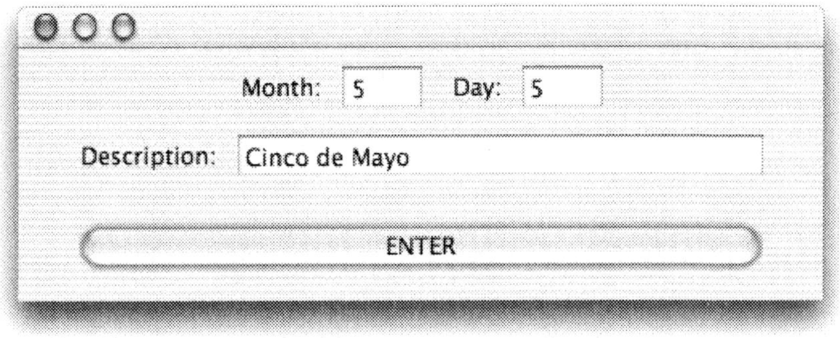

Figure 18.1 Interface used to enter new calendar events

Suppose that the user failed to realize that the program was expecting the month to be entered in numeric form and entered "May" instead of "5" in the JTextField named monthField. The string "May" would then be passed as a parameter to the parseInt method, which is only designed to handle parameter strings that resemble integer literals. Accordingly, the invocation of parseInt would fail, resulting in an error message that looked like:

```
java.lang.NumberFormatException: For input string: "May"
    at java.lang.Integer.parseInt(Integer.java:476)
    at CalendarController.actionPerformed(CalendarController.java:50)
    at java.awt.Button.processActionEvent(Button.java:381)
    at java.awt.Button.processEvent(Button.java:350)
```

The user is unlikely to consider this "user friendly". It would be much better if the program produced a simple, succinct message such as:

```
Date entered is invalid.  Enter numeric values for the month and day.
```

We could accomplish this by writing a method to test that a string is composed only of numeric digits and using an if statement to test the user's entries before attempting to invoke parseInt. Assuming that the method to test whether a String would be a valid input to parseInt is named validInt, then the simple invocation of setEvent shown above might be expanded to look like the code in Figure 18.2.

This approach has several shortcomings. First, the code has become more complex than it was before error checking was added. The simple invocation of setEvent has become part of an if statement with a condition that depends on the validInt method, which is probably even longer and more complicated than the code shown. In total, there will be more lines of code devoted to checking for unexpected input than there are lines of code devoted to handling the expected case. To keep our code as readable as possible, it would be better if we could make it easier to focus on the code for the expected case without immediately worrying about all the special cases that must be addressed.

Second, the checking that the added code performs is in some sense redundant. Within the validInt method there must be a loop to examine each character in the strings entered by the user to make sure that they are digits. The parseInt method, however, must perform a similar check to detect cases where it is asked to process a string that is not valid. When the code shown

```
if ( validInt(monthField.getText()) && validInt( dayField.getText() )) {
    theCalendar.setEvent(
                Integer.parseInt( monthField.getText() ),
                Integer.parseInt( dayField.getText() ),
                descriptionField.getText()
                );
} else {
    System.out.println(
                "Date entered is invalid. " +
                "Enter numeric values for the month and day."
            );
}
```

Figure 18.2 Cautious code to add a calendar entry

in Figure 18.2 is run, the validity of each user entry will be checked twice—once by validInt and then again within parseInt. In this case, it would be much better if we could let Java try to complete the invocation of the parseInt operations and somehow notify our code if the attempt failed. In this way, our code can be written to depend on the correctness checking already included within parseInt.

Java makes it possible to perform error checking in this way using a construct called a try-catch statement. As its name suggests, this construct has two main parts. The try clause specifies the action the programmer would like Java to perform. This is followed by one or more catch clauses that specify various actions to perform in the event that an error occurs while executing the code in the try clause. In this and the following sections we will show a series of examples illustrating the use of the try-catch to provide error handling for our calendar example.

Figure 18.3 shows how the try-catch construct can be used to rewrite the code to add an entry to the calendar. The construct begins with the word try followed by a sequence of statements surrounded by curly braces. This is the try part of the construct. Java will attempt to execute these statements, but if an error occurs during the process, Java will examine the catch that follows to find instructions on how to handle the error.

```
try {
    theCalendar.setEvent(
                Integer.parseInt( monthField.getText() ),
                Integer.parseInt( dayField.getText() ),
                descriptionField.getText()
                );
} catch ( NumberFormatException e ) {
    System.out.println(
                "Date entered is invalid. " +
                "Enter numeric values for the month and day."
            );
}
```

Figure 18.3 Exception handling with a try-catch statement

The line

```
catch ( NumberFormatException e )
```

is the beginning of the catch part of the construct. It is followed by a list of instructions to be executed if a number-format exception occurs while attempting to follow the instructions in the try part. In this case, we say that the parseInt method raises or throws an exception and that the catch phrase handles or catches the exception. If no errors occur while executing the try part, then Java will skip the instructions in the catch part.

Note that in this version, the validInt method is no longer required. This code depends on parseInt to check the validity of the input. Thus, the approach shown in Figure 18.3 is significantly simpler to implement correctly than that used in Figure 18.2.

Also, notice that in this version, the only text before the code for the normal processing of a calendar entry in Figure 18.3 is the word try. Because the if statement and its boolean condition are no longer needed, there is less to distract someone reading the code from the instructions that handle the normal case.

➡ EXERCISE 18.1.1

The code shown in Figure 18.3 uses a single catch to handle two similar but distinct errors. As a result, the error message printed when an error is detected does not make it clear whether the problem was detected in the value entered for the month or in the value entered for the day of the month. Just as we can nest one if statement within another or one while loop within another, we can nest one try-catch within another. Below, we show most of the code required to use a set of nested try-catch statement to distinguish the two errors that might occur. One of the catch clauses should print a message indicating that the month entered was invalid. The other should indicate that the day entered was invalid. In the code we have given below, we have deliberately left the message out of the invocations of println. Please indicate which message should be printed by each of the two printlns.

```
try {
    int monthNum = Integer.parseInt( monthField.getText() );

    try {
        int dayNum = Integer.parseInt( dayField.getText() );

        theCalendar.setEvent( monthNum, dayNum,
                            descriptionField.getText()
                        );
    } catch ( NumberFormatException e ) {
        System.out.println ( "       . . .           " );
    }
} catch ( NumberFormatException e ) {
    System.out.println( "       . . .           " );
}
```

18.2 Exceptions Are Objects

If you look carefully at the first line of the catch clause shown in the last section:

```
catch ( NumberFormatException e )
```

you will notice that we have not completely explained its syntax. What is the role of the text (NumberFormatException e) in this construct?

The name NumberFormatException is used to identify the type of error that this catch will handle. NumberFormatException is the name of a class of objects used in Java to represent information about errors detected by parseInt, parseDouble, and similar methods. Java includes many other exception classes, such as NullPointerException and ArrayIndexOutOfBoundsException, that are used to represent other types of errors.

When parseInt detects an error, it constructs a NumberFormatException object. This object contains information describing the error that can be useful within a catch clause. To make it possible to access this object within the code of the catch clause, Java requires the programmer to declare a name that will refer to this object. In the catch clause, the class name NumberFormatException is followed by the identifier e and surrounded by parentheses. This looks very much like the format used to declare a parameter in a method header. In fact, this phrase is a declaration introducing the name e, which can then be used to refer to the object describing the exception that has occurred.

Objects of the NumberFormatException class and of Java's other exception classes include a method named getMessage, which returns a String that provides information about the cause of the exception. The string returned by getMessage when invoked on an exception object thrown by parseInt consists of the phrase "For input string:" followed by the invalid text that was passed as a parameter to parseInt. Therefore, if we add the statement

```
System.out.println( e.getMessage() );
```

before the statement to print our error message in the catch clause, then the program will display the message

```
For input string: "May"
Date entered is invalid.  Enter numeric values for the month and day.
```

if a user enters the name "May" rather than the number 5 as the month.

18.3 Exception Propagation

Suppose we make a relatively simple change in the design of the Calendar class. Rather than defining the setEvent method to expect two numbers as parameters, let's redefine it to accept two Strings as parameters with the expectation that these will be strings of digits representing the desired month and day. This will enable us to move the invocations of parseInt from the event-handling method in the controller to the setEvent method, providing an opportunity to explore an important aspect of the way exceptions behave in Java.

```
public void setEvent( String month,
                      String day,
                      String description ) {

    dailyEvent[Integer.parseInt(month)-1][Integer.parseInt(day)-1]
                                        = description;
}
```

Figure 18.4   setEvent method that takes String parameters

```
try {
    theCalendar.setEvent(
            monthField.getText() ,
            dayField.getText() ,
            descriptionField.getText()
    );
} catch ( NumberFormatException e ) {
    System.out.println(
            "Date entered is invalid. " +
            "Enter numeric values for the month and day."
            );
}
```

Figure 18.5   Event-handling code that passes Strings to setEvent

A definition for such a version of setEvent is shown in Figure 18.4. The event-handling code revised to reflect the change in setEvent is shown in Figure 18.5. The interesting thing about these versions of the code is that the try-catch construct is no longer in the same method as the invocations of parseInt.

This code still functions correctly because, when an exception occurs, Java looks for a try-catch to handle the exception in each method along the sequence of methods that were invoked to lead to the point where the error was encountered. If there is no appropriate try-catch in the method where the error is detected, Java looks for an appropriate try-catch in the method that invoked the one where the error occurred. If no try-catch is found in the method's invoker, it looks at the invoker's invoker, and so on, until a try-catch is found or the sequence of invocations is exhausted. If no try-catch can be found, then Java displays one of the complex error messages of which we have shown examples in this chapter. We say that an exception propagates up the chain of invocations until it finds a handler or the end of the chain of invocations.

EXERCISE 18.3.1

Figure 18.6 shows the code for three methods containing a number of try-catch *statements. The methods are not intended to perform any useful function. They are merely designed to provide some examples of exception propagation.*

```
public void justTesting( String part1, String part2 ) {
    try {
        firstStep( Integer.parseInt( part1 ), part2 );
    } catch ( ArrayIndexOutOfBoundsException e ) {
        System.out.println( "Error caught by 1st catch" );
    }
}

public void firstStep( int part1, String part2 ) {
    try {
        int partTwo = Integer.parseInt( part2 );

        try {
            secondStep( part1, partTwo );
        } catch ( NullPointerException  e ) {
            System.out.println( "Error caught by 2nd catch" );
        }
    } catch ( NumberFormatException e ) {
        System.out.println( "Error caught by 3rd catch" );
    }
}

public void secondStep( int part1, int part2 ) {
    try {
        if ( ! names[part1 + part2].equals( "george" ) ) {
            System.out.println( names[part1 + part2] );
        }
    } catch ( NumberFormatException e ) {
        System.out.println( "Error caught by 4th catch" );
    }
}
```

Figure 18.6 Methods for Exercise 18.3.1

Assuming that the methods are part of a class that includes an instance variable declared as

```
private String [ ] names = new String[10];
```

and that the only assignments that have been performed to associate values with the elements of the names array are

```
names[2] = "george";
names[5] = "gerard";
names[7] = "geraldine"
```

what would be the result of each of the following method invocations?

a. justTesting("4", "Three");
b. justTesting("3", "3");
c. justTesting("Four", "3");
d. justTesting("7", "7");

18.4 Handling Multiple Exceptions

There are several forms of input errors that an application like our hypothetical calendar manager must address if it is to give users helpful feedback when they make mistakes. Suppose that someone using this program tries to enter the date 3/17 but accidentally hits the "3" key twice, so that the number entered for the month is 33 rather than 3. The parseInt method will have no trouble converting this input into int values, but when we use 33 − 1 to index the dailyEvent array in setEvent, Java will recognize that the array index is out of range and raise an exception.

This type of error produces an ArrayIndexOutOfBounds exception rather than producing a NumberFormatException. Since the catch clauses in our previous examples specify that they are meant to handle only NumberFormatExceptions, Java will find no appropriate try-catch if such an error occurs. Instead, it will resort to displaying one of its difficult-to-decipher error messages.

Java provides a simple way to handle this. A single try-catch statement may include several catch clauses designed to handle different exceptions that might arise while executing the statements in the try part. An example showing how such a collection of catch clauses could be used is shown in Figure 18.7. For this example, we have returned to our original design for setEvent, assuming that the method expects integers as its first two parameters. Note that this

```
try {
    theCalendar.setEvent(
            Integer.parseInt( monthField.getText() ) ,
            Integer.parseInt( dayField.getText() ),
            descriptionField.getText()
        );
} catch ( NumberFormatException e ) {
    System.out.println( e.getMessage() );
    System.out.println(
            "Date entered is invalid." +
            "Enter numeric values for the month and day."
        );
} catch ( ArrayIndexOutOfBoundsException e ) {
    System.out.println( "Date value is out of range." );
    System.out.println( "Month must fall between 1 & 12;" +
                        "date must fall within selected month" );
}
```

Figure 18.7 A try-catch with two catch clauses

```
try {
    try {
        try {
            System.out.println( entries[monthField.getText()].getDesc() );
        } catch ( NumberFormatException e ) {
            System.out.println( "Numeric input required" );
        }
    } catch ( ArrayIndexOutOfBoundsException e ) {
        System.out.println( "Specified entry does not exist" );
    }
} catch ( NullPointerException e ) {
    System.out.println( "No information available for that entry" );
}
```

Figure 18.8 Example of nested try-catch statements for Exercise 18.4.1

use of the `try-catch` keeps the code for the expected case simple while separating it from the code to handle each of the exceptional situations.

➡ EXERCISE 18.4.1

The ability to associate multiple catch *clauses with a single* try *is definitely convenient, but it is not really essential. Any program written to use a* try-catch *with multiple* catch *clauses can be rewritten as a set of nested* try-catch *statements.*

    a. *Rewrite the collection of nested* try-catch *statements shown in Figure 18.8 as a single* try-catch *with three* catch *clauses.*

    b. *Rewrite the code in Figure 18.7 as a pair of directly nested* try-catch *statements.*   ❖

18.5   Exception Subclasses

Within the examples of this chapter, we have encountered two exception classes: `NumberFormatException` and `ArrayIndexOutofBoundsException`. Those of you who read your error messages carefully have probably also encountered the `NullPointerException` when testing your programs. These are just a few of the exception classes provided by Java.

All of these exception classes share several common features. For example, they all support the `getMessage` method introduced earlier. As we saw in Chapter 17, when a collection of classes shares common features, it is sometimes appropriate and beneficial to define them using inheritance. In fact, the Java exception classes are all derived from a common superclass named `Exception`. Any class that is to be used to represent exceptions must be defined as a subclass of `Exception`.

A portion of the inheritance hierarchy that relates `Exception` to all the other predefined exception classes is shown in Figure 18.9. While we have not shown the entire hierarchy in this figure (it would be very hard to fit), we have included enough classes to show the

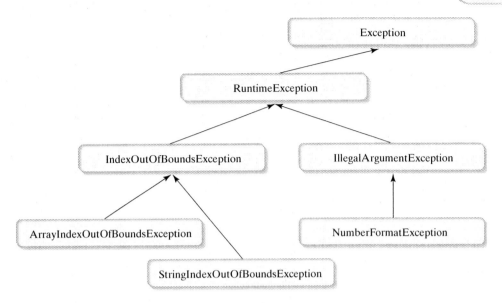

Figure 18.9   A portion of the Exception inheritance hierarchy

relationship between the two exception classes we have used in this chapter and the Exception base class.

The organization of this hierarchy is significant to the Java programmer in several ways. First, Java allows a programmer to define new exception classes to represent conditions that may arise while a program is running. When defining such exception classes, the programmer must use the extends clause to ensure that the new exception class is recognized as a subclass of Exception. We will consider an example of defining such a class in Section 18.7.

Second, the inheritance hierarchy is used to distinguish two major types of exceptions that can be treated differently by the Java programmer. Exceptions that are subclasses of RuntimeException are called *unchecked* exceptions. Exceptions that are not subclasses of RuntimeException are called *checked* exceptions. Writing try-catch statements to handle unchecked exceptions is optional in a Java program. If a checked exception can be raised within a method, a programmer is required either to include a try-catch to handle the exception within the method or to explicitly declare that the exception may propagate to the method's invoker. All the exceptions we have considered thus far are unchecked exceptions. We will examine the handling of checked exceptions in Section 18.6.

Finally, the superclasses in the hierarchy can be used to write catch clauses that handle exceptions of several different types. We have seen that when an exception occurs, Java searches backward through the sequence of currently active method invocations looking for a try-catch statement that contains a catch clause matching the exception. If during this process a try-catch construct with multiple catch clauses is encountered, the clauses are searched in order to find a clause that matches the exception raised. This matching process is based on the inheritance hierarchy of exception classes. A catch clause matches an exception as long as the exception class named in the catch is either the same as the class of exception raised or is a superclass of the class of exception raised.

```
try {
    theCalendar.setEvent(
            Integer.parseInt( monthField.getText() ) ,
            Integer.parseInt( dayField.getText() ),
            descriptionField.getText()
        );
} catch ( RuntimeException e ) {
    System.out.println( e.getMessage() );
    System.out.println(
            "Date entered is invalid." +
            "Enter numbers between 1 & 12 and 1 & 31" );
}
```

Figure 18.10   A try-catch that catches all RuntimeExceptions

For example, suppose that in our calendar example we are willing to display the same message whether the user's error is to make a non-numeric entry or to type a number that is out of range. ArrayIndexOutOfBoundsException and NumberFormatException, the two exceptions that these user errors would produce, are both subclasses of RuntimeException, as shown in Figure 18.9. Accordingly, we can merge the two catch clauses from Figure 18.7 into a single catch clause that handles all exceptions represented by subclasses of RuntimeException. The revised code is shown in Figure 18.10.

The catch clause shown in Figure 18.10 will be used if any exception represented by a subclass of RuntimeException is raised. As desired, this includes ArrayIndexOutOf-BoundsException and NumberFormatException, but it also includes StringIndexOut-OfBoundsException and many other exception classes not included in Figure 18.9. This is not a good feature of our code. If a programming error caused parseInt or setEvent to raise a StringIndexOutOfBoundsException or any other unexpected RuntimeException, the program would react by printing an error message stating that the user had entered invalid information. It would be better, in such situations, to have the program produce an error message that made it clear a flaw existed in the program rather than the input. Accordingly, while it is tempting to write catch clauses that handle exceptions of many types, it is generally best to be as specific as possible when selecting the class of exceptions a catch clause will handle.

➡ EXERCISE 18.5.1

Consider the following two code fragments:

```
a. try {
       someArray[Integer.parseInt( indexEntered )] = null;
   } catch ( Exception e ) {
       System.out.println( "Index is out of range" );
   } catch ( NumberFormatException e ) {
       System.out.println( "Index must be numeric" );
   }
```

b. try {
    someArray[Integer.parseInt(indexEntered)] = null;
} catch (NumberFormatException e) {
    System.out.println("Index must be numeric");
} catch (Exception e) {
    System.out.println("Index is out of range");
}

One of these fragments will always print a message appropriate for any error that occurs. The other will sometimes print inappropriate messages. Identify the fragment that does not work correctly and describe a situation (i.e., a value for indexEntered*) in which it will function incorrectly. Briefly explain why the other fragment functions correctly.*

18.6 Checked vs. Unchecked Exceptions

As mentioned in Section 18.5, Java distinguishes between two groups of exception classes, called *checked* and *unchecked* exceptions. If a Java method contains an operation that might cause a checked exception to be thrown, Java requires the programmer either to include a try-catch to handle the exception or to include a declaration in the method's header that explicitly states that the exception may propagate back to any code that invokes the method. Including code to handle unchecked exceptions, on the other hand, is not required.

All the exceptions we have encountered so far are examples of unchecked exceptions. In the next chapter, we will begin working with Java Streams and encounter many methods that throw checked exceptions. To provide an example of dealing with a checked exception in this section, we will discuss one simple example using a Stream.

In Chapter 3, we introduced the use of System.out.println to display output on the Java console. Just as there is a System.out, there is a System.in that provides a way to read a line of text typed on the computer's keyboard. We did not show you how to use this feature earlier because its use requires handling checked exceptions.

A method named System.in.read can be used to access input from the keyboard. Unlike System.out.println, which makes it quite easy to display a full line of output on the screen, System.in.read does not read a complete line of text from the keyboard. Instead, it reads just one character of typed input each time it is invoked. Worse yet, it does not return this input as a String. Instead, it returns it as an int. Fortunately, if we cast the value returned to the type char, we can then work with it as text data.

For example, to read a date in the form mm/dd/yyyy from the keyboard we might write the private method readDate shown in Figure 18.11. Unfortunately, the Java compiler will reject this method as erroneous. The problem is that if the program encounters some difficulty when trying to read from the keyboard, the read method may raise an IOException. The class IOException is the first example we have discussed of a checked exception. Java will refuse to run any program containing this code until changes are made to handle the exception.

One way to address the problem is to add an appropriate try-catch to the method. Figure 18.12 shows how we might do this. Obviously, this is no different from handling an unchecked exception.

```
private String readDate()  { // JAVA WILL NOT ACCEPT THIS METHOD!
    String date = "";

    for ( int x = 1; x <= 10; x++ )  {
        date = date + (char) System.in.read();
    }
    return date;
}
```

Figure 18.11   Failing to handle a checked exception

```
private String readDate()  {
    String date = "";

    try {
        for ( int x = 1; x <= 10; x++ ) {
            date = date + (char) System.in.read();
        }
        return date;
    } catch ( IOException e ) {
        System.out.println( "Read failed:" + e.getMessage() );
        return null;
    }
}
```

Figure 18.12   Handling a checked exception

The code shown in Figure 18.12 will be accepted by the Java compiler, but it does not represent the best way to handle an exception raised when trying to read a date from System.in. Most likely, any code that invokes readDate will need to take some special action if the method is not able to actually read a date because an exception occurs. If the method shown in Figure 18.12 were used, code that used readDate would have to include a test for null as a return value. It might be better to let the IOException propagate back to the method that invoked readDate and let this method print a more specific error message or respond in some other appropriate way.

If we want to let an *unchecked* exception propagate back to the invoker of a method, we don't have to do anything within the method where the exception first occurs. As long as we don't include a catch that handles the exception, it will propagate back up to the invoker. If we try to do this with a *checked* exception, Java will consider our program as erroneous. Java wants to make sure we take responsibility for handling checked exceptions. Therefore, Java insists that we add code explicitly acknowledging that we want the exception to propagate back to the method's invoker.

To tell Java that we want an exception to propagate back to a method's invoker, we include a throws clause in the method's header. A throws clause consists of the word throws followed by a list of the classes of exceptions that might be raised that are not handled by the method itself. A version of readDate modified to include a throws clause is shown

```
private String readDate() throws IOException {
    String date = "";

    for ( int x = 1; x <= 10; x++ ) {
            date = date + (char) System.in.read();
    }
    return date;
}
```

Figure 18.13 A method with a throws clause

in Figure 18.13. If a method is declared to throw a checked exception, then any code that uses the method must either include a `try-catch` to handle the exception or occur in a method that itself includes a `throws` clause for the same exception or a superclass.

The distinction between checked and unchecked exceptions represents a compromise in the design of Java. In the best case, a well-written program would handle all exceptions that might occur. As a result, one might argue that the language should force programmers to write such code by making all exceptions checked. Unfortunately, this would clutter code with exception handlers. Instead, the Java designers attempted to identify the exceptions that were most critical to handle and make them checked.

➡ EXERCISE 18.6.1

The `ActiveObject` *class introduced in Chapter 9 is defined within our objectdraw library as an extension of a standard Java class named* `Thread`. *One of the differences between* `ActiveObject` *and* `Thread` *is the* `pause` *method used to delay execution of an* `ActiveObject`. *The* `Thread` *class defines a similar method named* `sleep`. *The two differences between* `pause` *and* `sleep` *are that:*

* `pause` *expects a* `double` *value as a parameter while* `sleep` *expects a value of the extended-range integer type* `long`.
* `sleep` *may throw an* `InterruptedException` *while* `pause` *does not.*

`InterruptedException` *is a checked exception.* `pause` *was defined not to throw this exception, since at the point we introduced* `ActiveObjects`, *we had not covered how to handle checked exceptions. All* `pause` *does if an* `InterruptedException` *occurs is ignore it! A possible definition for* `pause` *in terms of* `sleep` *is shown below:*

```
public void pause( double delay ) {
    try {
        sleep( (long) delay );
    } catch( InterruptedException e ) {
    }
}
```

Suppose we wanted to include a new method named `pause2` *in the* `ActiveObject` *class which accepted a* `double` *as a parameter like* `pause`, *but could throw an* `InterruptedException` *like* `sleep`. *Show how to define such a method using* `sleep`.   ❖

18.7 Throwing Exceptions

The code shown in Figure 18.7 exhibits a troubling design flaw. Classes should hide the details of the implementation of the objects they represent. Following this principle, the code that uses a `Calendar` object should not need to know whether the internal implementation of the `Calendar` class depends on an array or some other data structure. Unfortunately, the fact that the code in Figure 18.7 handles `ArrayIndexOutOfBounds` exceptions generated by `setEvent` makes this code dependent on the assumption that the `Calendar` implementation is based on an array.

To ensure that the `Calendar` class encapsulates the details of its implementation, we should redesign the `setEvent` method so that it does not produce an `ArrayIndexOutOfBoundsException` when it is invoked with invalid parameter values. We can't just ignore such invalid parameters, but we can change the method so that it signals that an error has been detected by raising a different type of exception.

We could define a new exception class and use objects of this class to represent errors detected by `setEvent`. We will, in fact, show how to create such a class later in this section. Java, however, already includes an exception class named `IllegalArgumentException` which the Java documentation suggests should be used "to indicate that a method has been passed an illegal or inappropriate argument." This seems to fit our needs nicely. Accordingly, we will show how to rewrite `setEvent` so that it generates an `IllegalArgumentException` when inappropriate values are passed to it rather than generating an `ArrayIndexOutOfBoundsException`.

The first step is to make sure that `setEvent` does not raise an `ArrayIndexOutOfBoundsException`. We will do this by placing a `try-catch` statement around the assignment statement that accesses the `events` array. Within the `catch` clause for `ArrayIndexOutOfBoundsExceptions`, we will then place the code needed to raise an `IllegalArgumentException`. A version of `setEvent` revised in this way is shown in Figure 18.14.

Java provides a special statement type to raise exceptions. It is known as a `throw` statement and consists of the word `throw` followed by an expression that describes the exception object to be raised. In most cases, the expression in the `throw` statement is a construction for an object representing the exceptional condition that has been encountered.

```
public void setEvent( int month, int day, String description ) {
    try {

        dailyEvent[month - 1][day - 1] = description;

    } catch ( ArrayIndexOutOfBoundsException e ) {
        throw
            new IllegalArgumentException(
                "Invalid Date: " + month + "/" + day
            );
    }
}
```

Figure 18.14 setEvent revised to throw an IllegalArgumentException

```
public void setEvent( int month, int day, String description ) {

    if ( month >= 0 && month <= 12 ) {
        try {
            dailyEvent[month - 1][day - 1] = description;

        } catch ( ArrayIndexOutOfBoundsException e ) {
            throw
                new IllegalArgumentException(
                        "Invalid day specified: " + day
                );
        }
    } else {
        throw
            new IllegalArgumentException(
                    "Invalid month specified: " + month
            );
    }
}
```

Figure 18.15 setEvent with two throw statements

The constructors for Java's IllegalArgumentException class and most other exception classes accept a String that describes the error detected as a parameter. This string will be returned if the getMessage method described in Section 18.2 is invoked on the exception object. Accordingly, the parameter to the constructor shown in Figure 18.14 is a string formed by concatenating a brief message together with the date described by the parameter values provided.

A throw statement can appear anywhere within a method. In particular, it does not need to appear within a try-catch. As an example of this, another version of setEvent is shown in Figure 18.15. It provides a message with a more specific description of the error detected. This version of the method contains two throw statements. Both of the throw statements raise IllegalArgumentExceptions, but they use different strings as arguments when constructing the exceptions they throw.

The method first uses an if statement to check that the month entered is valid. The else branch of this if throws an IllegalArgumentException without even attempting to access the array. Therefore, if this branch of the if is taken, no ArrayIndexOutOfBoundsException is ever raised. The then part of the if does attempt to subscript the array, once the month value has been checked. If the value of day is invalid, this will generate an ArrayIndexOutOfBoundsException, which will be handled by the catch clause that contains the method's other throw statement.

While IllegalArgumentException is an appropriate class to represent errors detected by setEvent, it might be desirable to have a specialized class to distinguish the errors that setEvent detects. This can be done easily by defining a new exception class. All that is required is that the new class extend some class that is a subclass of Exception and that its constructor

```
public class DateRangeException extends IllegalArgumentException
{
    public DateRangeException( String message ) {
        super( message );
    }
}
```

Figure 18.16   Definition of an Exception class

pass the String that describes the error detected to the superclass constructor. It does not need to include any method declarations. They can all be inherited from the superclass. This leads to a very simple class definition like the one shown in Figure 18.16. We can then modify the code found in Figure 18.15 by replacing references to IllegalArgumentException with DateRangeException.

18.8   Summary

In this chapter, we have examined Java's mechanisms for handling exceptional conditions that occur during program execution. Java's exception-handling mechanism is based on the use of the Exception class and its subclasses. When a method detects an error condition that it wishes to report using the exception mechanism, it creates an object of the Exception class or one of its subclasses that describes the error that has been detected. The method then uses the throw statement, one of two statement types included in Java to support exception handling, to initiate the error recovery process.

The second statement type that supports exception handling is the try-catch statement. This construct is used to describe how to respond if exceptions are raised while executing a sequence of statements. The try-catch construct has two components. The first, the try part, is just the set of instructions whose exceptional conditions are to be handled by the construct. When asked to execute a try-catch statement, the computer begins by executing the statements in the try part. If these statements execute without raising any exceptions, then the execution of the try-catch is considered complete.

The second component of a try-catch is a list of clauses each identifying a subclass of the Exception class and a sequence of statements that should be executed in the event that one of the statements in the try part throws an exception that belongs to the identified Exception class. When an exception is thrown, the computer abandons the execution of the statements in the try part and examines the list of catch clauses sequentially, searching for the first clause that specifies how to handle the type of exception thrown. If such a catch clause is found, its statements are executed. If an appropriate catch clause cannot be found in the current method, the exception propagates backward along the chain of method invocations searching for an appropriate catch clause.

Java distinguishes between exceptions represented by subclasses of the RuntimeException class and those that are not. The former are known as unchecked exceptions and the latter as checked exceptions. If a checked exception may be raised by the statements within a method, then that method must either contain a try-catch statement to handle the exception or it must include a throws clause in its method header explicitly declaring that invoking the method may cause an exception to be thrown.

In many cases, exceptional conditions are the result of user error. Robust programs should be designed to respond to user errors in appropriate ways that assist users to recognize and correct their mistakes. Java's exception mechanisms are a valuable tool for the construction of such programs. In addition, Java's exception mechanisms are essential to handling unexpected events that occur when a program depends on external sources such as files or network connections for input processing as we will see in the next chapter.

18.9 Chapter Review Problems

EXERCISE 18.9.1

In Exercise 18.1.1 we suggested a way to use nested try-catch statements to provide more detailed feedback about errors. It might seem that a simpler alternative would be to simply use separate try-catch constructs for the two invocations of parseInt as shown below. In fact, Java will not accept this approach. It will report an error when this code is compiled.

Please explain what is wrong with this approach.

```
int monthNum, dayNum;
try {
    monthNum = Integer.parseInt( monthField.getText() );
} catch ( NumberFormatException e ) {
    System.out.println ( "Month entered is invalid" );
}

try {
    dayNum = Integer.parseInt( dayField.getText() );
} catch ( NumberFormatException e ) {
    System.out.println ( "Day entered is invalid" );
}

theCalendar.setEvent( monthNum, dayNum,
                    descriptionField.getText() );
```

EXERCISE 18.9.2

Explain the difference between checked and unchecked exceptions.

EXERCISE 18.9.3

Suppose we wanted to write code to keep track of appointments for a single day. We might define an Appointment class to represent information about a single item on the schedule. This class would provide methods like getDescription, getLocation, *etc. to access various properties of an appointment. We could then define an array*

```
private Appointment [ ] schedule = new Appointment[24];
```

with one element of the array associated with each hour of the day. If something is scheduled at a particular hour, the corresponding array element would be associated with an appropriate Appointment *object. If nothing is scheduled, the array entry would be null.*

If the user requests information from the program about a particular time of the day, and hour *is a* String *variable associated with the hour the user entered, we might use the statement*

```
System.out.println( schedule[Integer.parseInt( hour ) - 1].
                    getDescription() );
```

to display the requested information. This statement could throw three types of exceptions:

- *A* NumberFormatException *if the string* hour *is not numeric,*
- *An* ArrayIndexOutOfBoundsException *if the hour is outside the range 1–24,*
- *A* NullPointerException *if no* Appointment *is associated with the selected array entry.*

Suppose that we want to print "Invalid hour specified" if one of the first two exceptions occurs and that we want to print "No appointment scheduled" in the case of a NullPointerException. *Show how to place the* println *within a* try-catch *statement that will handle all three exception types as desired with only two* catch *clauses.*   ❖

▶ EXERCISE 18.9.4

We have seen that a list of objects can be either associated with the elements of an array or organized into a recursive list. When objects are placed in an array, we can access selected elements by indexing the array. It is possible to include a method to provide similar access to the elements of a recursive list.

Recall the definition of classes to implement recursive lists of URLs presented in Section 12.1.2. Suppose that we add an entry of the form:

```
// Extract a URL from the list by specifying its position
public String selectByIndex( int index );
```

to the URL list interface definition with the intent that selectByIndex(0) *would return the first URL in the list,* selectByIndex(1) *would return the second URL, and so forth. Furthermore, we would like the method to throw an* IndexOutOfBounds *exception if the value provided for* index *is negative or too large.* IndexOutOfBounds *is a standard Java exception type which is unchecked.*

We would have to add definitions of selectByIndex *to both the* EmptyUrlList *and* NonemptyUrlList *classes. Please provide definitions for these methods compatible with the definitions of these classes found in Section 12.1.2. It will be sufficient if the* String *returned by applying* getMessage *to the exceptions thrown simply returns* "Invalid index". *(As a challenge, consider how to include the index provided to the initial invocation in the message associated with the exception.)*   ❖

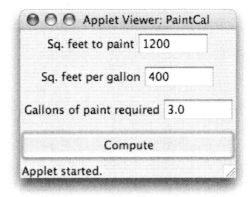

Figure 18.17 Interface for program described in Exercise 18.10.1

18.10 Programming Problems

EXERCISE 18.10.1

Write a program that can be used to calculate information about paint coverage. The program should display a window with a "Compute" button and text fields for the number of gallons of paint, the number of square feet covered by a gallon of paint, and the number of square feet painted. A sample of this interface is shown in Figure 18.17. The user is expected to fill in any two of the three fields. Then, when the Compute button is pressed, the program should place the correct value in whichever field was left empty. Pressing Compute should have no effect unless exactly two of the three fields contain numeric values.

We would like you to experiment with the use of inheritance and exception handling to write this program. First, rather than using JTextFields *directly to build the interface, define a new class* NumericField *that extends* JTextField. *Your new class should provide a* setValue *method that takes a* double *and displays it in the field and a* getValue *method that returns the value in the field as a* double *(or throws a* NumberFormatException*). Alternately, you might consider defining a* LabeledNumericField *class that extends* JPanel *and creates a panel containing both a* JLabel *and a* JTextField. *Using this approach, you would still want to provide the* getValue *and* setValue *methods described above.*

Second, in the ActionPerformed *method of your* Controller *class, you will have to* catch *the* NumberFormatExceptions *that might be thrown by* getValue. *Rather than simply treating these exceptions as errors, we would like you to use them to determine which field, if any, needs to be completed. That is, we will take advantage of the fact that invoking* getValue *on a blank* NumericField *will raise an exception, and we will design the program so that as long as exactly one of the three fields raises an exception, the program will update the contents of that field based on the other two.*

With this in mind, your code should create an array of NumericFields *holding all three fields. Then, you can write a loop that invokes* getValue *on all three. Place a* try-catch *in the loop. Rather than printing an error, as we have in all of our* catch *clauses, the* catch *clause in this loop should count how many exceptions are raised and remember which array entry was the last to raise an exception. When the loop completes, if exactly one exception was counted, then fill in the field corresponding to the last array entry to raise an exception. You can use a sequence of* if *statements or a* switch *to identify the right calculation to perform.*   ❖

➡ EXERCISE 18.10.2

Define two new classes named MyDate *and* DateFormatException. *Define the* DateFormatException *class as an extension of the* IllegalArgumentException *class. The* MyDate *class should be designed to represent a date. It should provide accessor methods named* getMonth, getDay, *and* getYear *that each return an* int *value. It should also implement a* toString *method that will return the date's representation in the "mm/dd/yy" format.*

The constructor for the MyDate *class should take a string as a parameter and interpret this string as a date in the format "mm/dd/yy". If the constructor finds that its parameter value is not in the correct format, it should throw a* DateFormatException, *including a message indicating that an improperly formatted date was encountered and including the contents of the parameter string. The constructor should be forgiving about the use of blank spaces and leading zeroes. That is, both*

    7/1/04

and

    7 / 1 / 4

should be considered valid representations for July 1, 2004. You should use both the exceptions thrown by Integer.parseInt *and appropriate* if *statements to detect errors.*

Write a simple interface to test your class. It should provide one JTextField *in which a user can enter a date, a button to press to request that the date entered be used to create a* MyDate, *and another* JTextField *in which the program will either display the* toString *output of the* MyDate *object created or the message associated with the exception thrown by the constructor.*   ❖

CHAPTER 19

Streams

*I*f you examine the menu bars provided by a variety of computer applications, you will find that they exhibit a bit of diversity. A word processor is likely to have a "Format" menu, while a web browser provides a "History" or "Favorite" menu and a spreadsheet may offer a "Tools" menu. They all, however, are likely to have a "File" menu, and they all are likely to give it a place of honor before most of the other menus in the menu bar. What makes the "File" menu so common and so important?

Files are a computer's long-term memory. You have seen that a program can make a computer "remember" things by associating pieces of information with variable names. Once a program stops executing, however, all such information is forgotten. People who use computers want to be able to work on a project one day and have the computer remember the work that was completed, even if they stop the program, turn the computer off, and don't continue working on the project for several days. Files provide such memory.

Most programs include a "Save" or "Save as" item in their File menus to enable users to save a copy of their current work as a document in a file. There is also usually an "Open" or "Import" item in the File menu that can be used to bring previously saved information back into a program for further work. Of course, to make such menu items work as expected, someone has to write program statements that will instruct the computer to copy information from program variables to a file or vice versa when one of these items is selected. In this chapter, we will study the mechanisms Java provides to enable a programmer to write such code.

You may be wondering why this chapter is named "Streams" if it is really about files. Unlike instance variables, files can exist on their own, independent of the execution of any program. This is the only way they can serve as long-term information storage. Therefore, some mechanism is needed to provide the connection between the variables that are internal to a program and an external file. In Java, *streams* provide this mechanism. Their name reflects the fact that data flows between the program and an external file.

In fact, streams are designed to manage flows of data between programs and any external entity that can provide or receive data. We have already used one stream in this way. System.out is a stream that enables you to send data from your program to a window on your computer's screen. Even though no file is involved, there is certainly a movement of information. In this chapter, we will first concentrate on the use of streams to work with files, then will explore other uses of streams. In particular, we will learn how streams can be used to send data through the Internet to a remote computer and to receive data from other machines in the network. Such applications of streams are essential to the implementation of programs like web browsers, email clients, and file sharing systems.

19.1   Text Streams

The files stored on your computer contain data encoded in many different formats. You may have pictures stored in JPEG files, sounds encoded as MP3 files, Quicktime movies, MPEG movies, Java.class files, and files of many other varieties. Among these are also many files that contain nothing more exotic than simple text. We will focus our examination of Java's stream mechanism on learning how to work with text files.

19.1.1   Bookmark Files: An Example

As discussed in the introduction, most programs can be explicitly instructed to access files by selecting an item in the program's File menu. Many programs also use files in ways users are not explicitly aware of. If you play a game program that tells you the ten highest scores as you start or finish each game, that program is using a file to remember these scores. When you top one of the existing high scores, it saves new information in the file, even though you might not explicitly select a "Save" item from the File menu. When you start the program, it extracts all the previous high scores from this file, even though you never select "Open".

Another, more practical example of a file that is accessed implicitly is the file used to keep track of bookmarks created by the user of a web browser. Like a high-score list, you expect your web browser to remember your bookmarks even if you quit and later restart your browser. To do this, the program must place a copy of your bookmarks in a file rather than merely keeping track of the bookmarks with program variables. If you search your disk hard enough, you will find this file hiding somewhere. It is probably named favorites.htm or bookmarks.html. Whenever you add a bookmark, your browser sends data describing the new bookmark to this file. Whenever you restart your browser, it must examine the contents of the file to build the bookmark list or menu you expect to see.

As our first example of the construction of Java code that uses streams, we will consider the manipulation of a bookmarks file. For each bookmark you create, your browser stores a pair of strings: a web address or URL and a few words that describe the site at the address. Accordingly, storing bookmarks will require nothing more than a simple text file. Of course, we don't want to implement a complete web browser. Instead, we will focus on the design of a class to hold a list of bookmarks, including methods to retrieve old bookmarks from a file and a method to place the complete list in a file.

First we will need a class to keep track of a single bookmark. A simple version of such a class is shown in Figure 19.1. It provides a constructor that takes two `Strings`. One should be a short description of a web site that could be used as an entry in a bookmarks menu. The other should be the address for the site. The class provides two methods to access these strings—`getDescr`

```
// Class to hold a pair of strings corresponding to a web URL
// and the description that should be associated with the URL.
public class Bookmark {

    private String description;  // words describing web site
    private String address;      // URL for the web site

    // Save web site description and address in new object
    public Bookmark( String aDescription, String anAddress )  {
        description = aDescription;
        address = anAddress;
    }

    // Return the web site's description
    public String getDescr()  {
        return description;
    }

    // Return the web site's URL or address
    public String getAddr() {
        return address;
    }

    // Return a string showing contents of the bookmark
    public String toString() {
        return description + " ---> " + address;
    }

}
```

Figure 19.1 A class of objects designed to represent single bookmarks

and getAddr. It also includes a toString method that returns a single string that shows the complete contents of the bookmark by concatenating the short description with the address while sticking an arrow between them. For example, toString might return

```
Google home page ---> http://www.google.com
```

if applied to a Bookmark object representing a bookmark for the Google web site.

We also need a class to keep track of an entire list of bookmarks. We will not show the code for this entire class. You have seen how to construct such a class in earlier chapters, and we don't want to distract attention from our main topic, streams. We will, however, have to make certain assumptions about methods that this class includes, and we will sketch the code for several methods that provide support for saving bookmarks to a file.

In particular, we will assume that the class is named BookmarkList and that it has a method add which will take a Bookmark and add it to the end of the list. We will also assume that the class provides a size method that will return the total number of bookmarks currently in the

```
//  Print all bookmark entries
public void printBookmarks() {

    for ( int i = 0; i < size(); i++ ) {
        System.out.println( getSelectedItem(i).toString() );
    }
}
```

Figure 19.2 Method to display all bookmarks on the screen

list and a `getSelectedItem` method which will take an integer parameter between 0 and the value produced by `size() - 1` and return the bookmark found at that position in the list. To provide the full functionality needed to implement bookmarks in an actual web browser, this class would also need a method to remove bookmarks and possibly methods to manipulate subfolders of bookmarks. For the purpose of our examples, however, we will ignore these complexities.

The first method we want to consider is a method named `saveBookmarksFile` which transfers descriptions of all the bookmarks currently in the list to a file. Before we learn how to do this, however, let us consider how to write a method that would simply display all the current bookmarks on the screen using `System.out.println`. This would not be of much use in a functioning browser, but it might be helpful while debugging a browser's implementation of the bookmarks menu. It is also very simple to write. All we need is a `for` loop that iterates from 0 to `size() - 1`. The complete code is shown in Figure 19.2.

The reason this simple method is interesting is that, as mentioned earlier, `System.out` is itself a stream that supports the flow of data from a program to a window on the screen. If we construct an appropriate stream to connect our program to a file instead of to a window on the screen, we can use almost exactly the same `for` loop found in `printBookmarks` to place the bookmarks in a file. Our goal in the next section will be to learn to create such a stream.

19.1.2 Creating a Writer

Even though we have been promising to teach you how to use streams in Java, the truth is that there is no class actually named `Stream`. Instead, Java has a large collection of classes with rather imposing names like `BufferedInputStream` and `OutputStreamWriter` that are all considered streams, because each provides the mechanisms required to transfer data between your program and a file or some other external entity. The different names assigned to these classes reflect differences in the details of the functionality they provide.

One characteristic that distinguishes different stream classes in Java is the direction in which the data flows. If data flows from the variables of your program through a stream to a file or other data repository the stream is called an *output* stream. If information flows from some external source through a stream to program variables, then the stream is called an *input* stream. Note that the direction of data flow is described from the point of view of the program. Placing data *in* a file is described as an *out*put operation because the data comes *out* from the program. The term input/output, sometimes abbreviated I/O, is often used in Java and other languages to refer to the process of transferring data between programs and files.

Another important distinction is made between streams that are specialized to handle text versus those streams that can handle other forms of data such as audio and movie files. Input streams specialized to handle text are called Readers, and output streams specialized to handle text are called Writers. In addition, Java distinguishes streams designed to work with files from steams that can be used for other functions such as sending data through the network. As a result, the stream classes through which Java provides access to text files are called FileReader and FileWriter.

The FileWriter and FileReader classes provide constructors that take a string that is the name of a file and create streams that can be used to access that file. Thus, the declaration

```
FileWriter bookmarksFile = new FileWriter( "bookmarks.html" );
```

would create a FileWriter stream that could be used to place data in a file named "bookmarks.html".

The actual interpretation of the string provided is somewhat dependent on the operating system under which the program is run. On some systems, slashes or backslashes may be included in the name to specify that the desired file belongs in a particular subfolder. For now, we will use simple names containing no slashes. Such a name is interpreted as the name of a file in the directory or folder that is current when the program is run. If a file with the name provided does not already exist, a new file with that name is created when we construct a FileWriter. If a file with that name already exists, then its current contents are erased to be replaced by the data sent through the stream as the program runs.

Constructing a FileWriter or FileReader establishes a connection between your program and a file. While such a connection exists, your computer is likely to restrict other actions that would affect the file. You may, for example, have tried at some time to remove a file from your computer and been told by the system that this was impossible because the file was "in use." So that such restrictions can be lifted once you are finished using a file, your program should explicitly destroy the connection between your program and the file when it is no longer needed. To make this possible, all stream classes in Java include a close method. This method expects no parameters. Therefore, to terminate the connection created by the construction shown above, your program would execute the instruction

```
bookmarksFile.close();
```

Operations involving streams and files are capable of failing in many ways. For example, an attempt to create a FileWriter may fail if there is no room left on your disk or if there is already another file with the same name that cannot be overwritten because it is in use or protected by security restrictions. In some cases, even a request to close a stream may fail. Accordingly, many of these operations raise exceptions that must be handled using a try-catch construct. There are several classes used to represent the errors that cause such failures, but they are all subclasses of the IOException class. In simple applications using files, it is common to include the construction of a stream, the code that uses it, and the instruction to close the stream in a try-catch as suggested by the skeleton shown in Figure 19.3. If more precise control over the handling of errors is required, separate try-catch constructs should be placed around individual operations that involve streams.

19.1.3 Sending Data Through a Writer

The FileWriter class is a subclass of the Writer class that includes all output streams designed to handle textual data. All Writer classes include a write method, which takes a String

```
try {
    FileWriter bookmarksFile = new FileWriter( "bookmarks.html" );
    // Code to place data in file
    ...
    bookmarksFile.close();
} catch ( IOException ex ) { ... }   // Code to report failure
```

Figure 19.3   Skeleton of code to handle I/O exceptions associated with streams

```
// Place all bookmark entries in bookmarks.html
public void saveBookmarksFile() {

    try {
        FileWriter bookmarksFile = new FileWriter( "bookmarks.html" );

        for ( int i = 0; i < size(); i++ ) {
            bookmarksFile.write( getSelectedItem(i).toString() );
        }

        bookmarksFile.close();
    } catch ( IOException e ) {
        System.out.println( "Unable to access bookmarks file - "
                          + e.getMessage() );
    }
}
```

Figure 19.4   Definition of the saveBookmarksFile method

parameter and sends it through the `Writer`. Combining the code to create a `FileWriter` shown in the previous section with a loop using the `write` method, we obtain the complete definition for a `saveBookmarksFile` method shown in Figure 19.4.

The loop used in the `saveBookmarksFile` method is identical to the loop shown earlier in Figure 19.2, except that the new loop uses `bookmarksFile.write` where the old loop used `System.out.println`. We must make this change because a simple `FileWriter` does not support the `println` method. Fortunately, the `write` method and the `println` methods are similar. They both send data through a stream. The `println` method is, however, more flexible. In addition to accepting a string as a parameter, it can take `int` values, `doubles`, or just about any value at all as a parameter. Whatever parameter we give it, the `println` method simply produces a textual representation of that value and sends it to the screen. Unlike `write`, the `println` method also separates the text it sends through a stream into separate lines. All the bookmarks written by our `saveBookmarksFile` method will, by contrast, be written as a single line. Eventually, we will see that we can arrange to use `println` with a `FileWriter`. First, however, it is worth noting that, even with just the `write` method, we have considerable flexibility when we place data in a file.

The file produced by our program has a name that ends in ".html", one of the standard suffixes used for text files that contain web pages. We can, in fact, open this file with a web browser to see

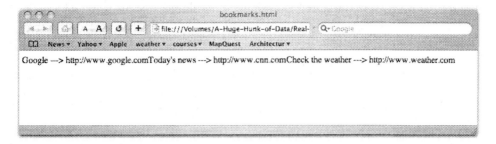

Figure 19.5   Browser display of file produced by saveBookmarksFile

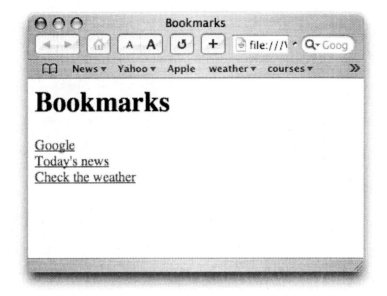

Figure 19.6   Browser display of an actual bookmarks.html file

what it contains. Figure 19.5 shows what we might see if we were to do this. The BookmarkList used to produce the file viewed in this figure contained three bookmarks referring to the web sites of The Weather Channel, CNN, and Google. We can see that the descriptions and addresses of the bookmarks have been recorded in the file. Unfortunately, if we configure a real browser's bookmark menu to contain the same three bookmarks and then view the bookmarks file produced by the browser, the display will look a bit different, as shown in Figure 19.6. Not only does the real bookmarks file look different from our file when viewed using a browser, it also behaves differently. The phrases "Google", "Today's news," and "Check the weather" actually function as links. If we click on one of them, we are taken to the associated web site.

The difference between real bookmark files and what we have produced so far is a matter of encoding. The real bookmarks file contains text that uses a language called HTML (or Hypertext Markup Language) to describe what we should see when we view the bookmarks. This is the standard language used to describe the layout and behavior of web pages. Fortunately, we don't

```
<!DOCTYPE NETSCAPE-Bookmark-file-1>
<!-- This is an automatically generated file.
It will be read and overwritten.
Do Not Edit! -->
<TITLE>Bookmarks</TITLE>
<H1>Bookmarks</H1>

<DL><p>
    <DT><A HREF="http://www.google.com" >Google</A>
    <DT><A HREF="http://www.cnn.com" >Today's news</A>
    <DT><A HREF="http://www.weather.com" >Check the weather</A>
</DL><p>
```

Figure 19.7   Source view of HTML for web page shown in Figure 19.6

have to fully understand this language to make our code produce a file that imitates the behavior of a real bookmarks file.

The HTML text that produces the browser display shown in Figure 19.6 is shown in Figure 19.7.[1] The first seven non-empty lines and the last line must appear as shown in any standard bookmarks file. We don't really need to understand what they mean. They are just the standard prologue and epilogue that many browsers, including Netscape Navigator and Internet Explorer, expect to find when they open a bookmarks file. We have to make sure that our program includes them verbatim in each bookmarks file it produces.

This leaves the three lines that start with <DT> to actually encode the bookmarks that we want displayed. If we look at these lines carefully, we can see that each line contains five parts:

1. the text

        <DT><A HREF="

2. the address portion of a bookmark
3. the text

        " >

4. the short description of the bookmarked site
5. the text

        </A>

While these lines may look complicated, all one has to do to produce them is concatenate the appropriate substrings together. It really is no more complicated than the `toString` method included in the `Bookmark` class shown in Figure 19.1. A method named `toBookmarkFileEntry` is shown in Figure 19.8. This method, which would be included in the definition of the `Bookmark` class, will return a string describing a single bookmark using the HTML notation expected in a

---

[1] In most browsers, there is a menu item that allows one to view the actual HTML text describing the page being viewed.

```
//  Return a string encoding the bookmark in the standard
//  form browsers expect to find in bookmark files
public String toBookmarkFileEntry() {
    return "<DT><A HREF=\"" + address + "\" >" + description + "</A>";
}
```

Figure 19.8   Definition of the toBookmarkFileEntry method

standard bookmarks file. If we simply change the line

```
bookmarksFile.write( getSelectedItem(i).toString() );
```

from the `saveBookmarksFile` method shown in Figure 19.4 to

```
bookmarksFile.write( getSelectedItem(i).toBookmarkFileEntry() );
```

then invoking the `saveBookmarksFile` method will produce lines describing all the bookmarks in a `BookmarkList` in the appropriate format. Thus we can see that, in many cases, placing the data we want in a text file has more to do with manipulating strings than with the details of streams or `Writer`s.

➡ EXERCISE 19.1.1

Write a method named `saveHighScores` *that could be used in a game program to write the latest list of high scores to a file. Assume that the method will be passed an array of* `scoresDescs` *as a parameter where a* `scoresDesc` *is an object that implements at least the two methods:*

```
// Returns the numerical score
public int getScore();

// Returns name of player who earned the score
public String playerName();
```

Assume that the array is full. That is, assume that you can use the length of the array to determine how many scores to place in the file. Each line of the file should consist of the value of a single score followed by a space and the player's name. The file created should be named `highscore.txt`. ❖

19.1.4   PrintWriters

To finish the task of producing a bookmarks file in the standard form, all we have to do is add the lines of the preamble and epilogue to the file. To ensure that this text is broken up into separate lines as shown in Figure 19.7, we could include explicit newline indicators using `"\n"` in the arguments to the `write` method. It would be nice, however, if we could simply produce separate lines using the `println` method instead of being limited to using `write`. Fortunately, we can make it possible to use `println` by making a modification in the declaration of the variable named `bookmarksFile`.

In the version of `saveBookmarksFile` in Figure 19.4, we declared the variable `bookmarksFile` to refer to an object of the class `FileWriter`. `FileWriter` is just one of many subclasses of the `Writer` class. While `FileWriter` does not support `println`, there is another subclass of `Writer` named `PrintWriter` which does support `println`. If we change the declaration of `bookmarksFile` so that this variable refers to a `PrintWriter`, then Java will allow us to use either `println` or `write` to send data to the stream `bookmarksFile`.

Unfortunately, while `PrintWriter` and `FileWriter` are both subclasses of `Writer`, `FileWriter` is not a subclass of `PrintWriter`. As a result, if we simply change the type name in the declaration of `bookmarksFile` to yield the line

```
PrintWriter bookmarksFile = new FileWriter( "bookmarks.html" );
```

the Java compiler will generate an error indicating that the initial value assigned in the declaration is not compatible with the type of the variable being declared. In addition, the `PrintWriter` constructor will not accept a file name as a parameter, so we cannot fix the problem by saying

```
PrintWriter bookmarksFile = new PrintWriter( "bookmarks.html" );
```

What the `PrintWriter` constructor does expect as a parameter is an existing `Writer`. It will accept a `FileWriter` or an object belonging to any other subclass of the `Writer` class. Using the `Writer` provided to it as a parameter, the `PrintWriter` constructor produces a new `PrintWriter` that sends data to the same destination as the `Writer` provided as a parameter. The difference is that it has an interface that supports both the `println` and `write` methods. Accordingly, if we want to be able to use `println` in the `saveBookmarksFile` method, we should revise the declaration of `bookmarksFile` to read

```
PrintWriter bookmarksFile =
        new PrintWriter( new FileWriter( "bookmarks.html" ) );
```

A revised `saveBookmarksFile` method that uses a `PrintWriter` to output a bookmarks file in the standard format is shown in Figure 19.9.

EXERCISE 19.1.2

Rewrite the program requested by Exercise 19.1.1 so that it uses a `PrintWriter` *and the* `println` *method in place of a* `FileWriter` *and the* `write` *method.*

19.1.5 Composing Writer classes

While the code in Figure 19.9 works, the first few lines may seem a bit awkward. We have to construct both a `PrintWriter` and a `FileWriter`, even though we are only accessing a single file. This wouldn't be necessary if the Java `FileWriter` class had been designed to support `println` or if `PrintWriter` included a constructor that would accept a file name. Why did the designers of these Java classes choose to limit their functionality in ways that require us to construct objects of two `Writer` classes when we really only need one?

To appreciate the logic behind the design of these classes, we have to recall that Java streams are not just used for files. It is possible to construct `Writer` objects that send data through network connections or, like `System.out`, allow us to display text in a window. If we were to examine the code that implements the constructor of each type of stream, we would find that the details needed to establish communications between a program and a file are significantly different from the steps involved in establishing a network connection. In addition, the implementation of the `write` method will vary from one type of stream to the next.

```
// Place all the bookmarks in the list into the bookmarks.html
// file. Use the standard format employed by most common
// browsers.
public void saveBookmarksFile() {

   try {

      // Access the file through a PrintWriter
      PrintWriter bookmarksFile =
             new PrintWriter( new FileWriter("bookmarks.html" ) ) ;

      // Place prologue in file
      bookmarksFile.println( "<!DOCTYPE NETSCAPE-Bookmark-file-1>" );
      bookmarksFile.println(
                "<!-- This is an automatically generated file." );
      bookmarksFile.println( "It will be read and overwritten." );
      bookmarksFile.println( "Do Not Edit! -->" );
      bookmarksFile.println( "<TITLE>Bookmarks</TITLE>" );
      bookmarksFile.println( "<H1>Bookmarks</H1>" );
      bookmarksFile.println( "" );
      bookmarksFile.println( "<DL><p>" );

      // Add one <DL> line describing each bookmark
      for ( int i = 0; i < size(); i++ )
         bookmarksFile.println( getSelectedItem(i).toBookmarkFileEntry() );

      // Add epilogue and close file
      bookmarksFile.println( "</DL><p>" );
      bookmarksFile.close();

   } catch ( IOException e ) {
      System.out.println( "Unable to save bookmarks file - "
                       + e.getMessage() );
   }
}
```

Figure 19.9 A completed version of the saveBookmarksFile method

The implementation of println, on the other hand, can be made independent of the particular type of stream. The println method provided by the PrintWriter class is overloaded to provide the programmer with the ability to send values of many different types to a stream. Each version of the method defined must convert the argument provided into textual form and then send this text, together with a newline character, to the appropriate stream. Since every PrintWriter is also a Writer, the implementation of println can use the write method to actually send the text to its destination without worrying about whether the destination is a file, a network connection, or some other possibility.

In saveBookmarksFile, we only used the version of println that takes a String parameter. A possible implementation of this version of println is shown in Figure 19.10.

```
public void println( String toDisplay ) {
    write( toDisplay + "\n" );
}
```

Figure 19.10   Possible implementation of println for Strings

The implementation of a version of println to handle a parameter of some other type such as int would not be much different. We would just replace the parameter type in the method header with int.

The relationship between the PrintWriter and FileWriter classes exhibits a deliberately designed division of labor. The FileWriter class takes on the task of dealing with the details required to access data in a file. The PrintWriter class performs functions necessary to provide programmers with the ability to send data of a variety of forms to a stream. It would clearly have been possible for the designers of these classes to add support for println to the FileWriter class. They would just have added several method definitions like the one shown in Figure 19.10 to the FileWriter class body. If they took this approach, however, and also wanted to provide println with Writers designed to send data through network connections, they would have to place another copy of each of the println definitions in the class specification for a network Writer. Such code duplication is undesirable. It would make each of the classes to which the println code was added seem more complicated. It would mean that any attempt to change the way println behaved would require changing many class definitions.

The design of the Java Writer classes makes it easy for a programmer to use println with any type of Writer without requiring duplicate copies of the code that implements println. The only copy of the code for println appears within the PrintWriter class. When we construct a PrintWriter, we provide an existing Writer as a parameter. The println method defined within the PrintWriter uses the write method of the Writer provided to its constructor to actually send data to the stream. Thus, the implementation of the PrintWriter class does not have to address the complexities of how to actually send data to a file or a network connection. Those issues are handled by the implementation of classes like FileWriter. At the same time, classes like FileWriter don't have to worry about how to convert double values into text for display. Those details are addressed in the implementation of the PrintWriter class. We will see similar examples in which classes are designed to be combined to provide the desired mix of features for a particular application as we learn more about Java's stream classes.

19.2   Readers

When a browser first starts executing, it typically reads the contents of a bookmarks file and uses those contents to create a bookmarks menu. In this section we will learn to write the code that would enable a browser to access a bookmarks file in this way.

In the preceding section, we encountered Java classes that enable us to place textual data in a file. These classes are subclasses of the Writer class. It should come as no surprise that Java also includes classes that can be used to extract text from files and that these classes are all subclasses of the Reader class. In fact, the organization of the Reader classes parallels that of the Writer classes in many ways.

The first subclass of Reader that we will need to use is the FileReader class. Like FileWriter, the FileReader class has a constructor that takes a String file name as a parameter. Thus, we could construct a Reader that would provide access to our bookmarks file by including the declaration

```
FileReader bookMarksReader = new FileReader( "bookmarks.html" );
```

The stream object produced by a FileReader constructor can transport data from the file into program variables. FileReader and all other Reader classes include a close method that is used to terminate the connection between a Reader and its source of data, much like the close method for Writers. In addition, all Readers include a method named read that can be used to actually transfer information from the Reader to a program variable. The constructor and both of these methods may raise IOExceptions that must be handled by catch clauses. For example, if the file whose name is provided as a parameter to a FileReader construction does not exist, a FileNotFoundException will be thrown.

Unfortunately, the read method associated with Reader classes provides very limited functionality. Like many text files, the information in our bookmarks file is divided into lines. Each bookmark is described on its own line. Given this organization, we would like a method which would fetch one line from the file and return its contents to our program as a String so that we could process it. This is not what the read method does. Instead, the primitive

```
bookMarksReader.read()
```

returns one character of the file's contents. Each time it is invoked, read returns the next character from the file.[2] Worse yet, the type of the value returned by the read method is int rather than char or String. The number that read returns is the binary encoding of the character read.

Just as it is possible to obtain a more convenient interface to a FileWriter by creating a PrintWriter, we can avoid having to access a Reader through the read primitive by using an existing Reader to create an object of another class called BufferedReader. The BufferedReader constructor accepts a FileReader or any other object that belongs to a subclass of Reader as a parameter. If we wanted to use a BufferedReader to access the bookmarks file, we would therefore replace the declaration shown above by the declaration

```
BufferedReader bookMarksReader =
    new BufferedReader( new FileReader( "bookmarks.html" ) );
```

The object created by such a construction is a Reader and therefore implements the read method. A BufferedReader, however, also supports a method named readLine that will allow us to access the contents of the file in a more convenient way. An invocation of the form

```
bookMarksReader.readLine()
```

retrieves a complete line from the file and returns it as a String. Each time readLine is invoked, the next line from the file is extracted. When there are no more lines remaining, readLine returns a null reference rather than a String.

---

[2] Actually, the read method is overloaded. One version works as described above. The other takes a char array as a parameter and fills it with characters from the Reader. This still isn't what we want. A char array is not as convenient to work with as a String. Furthermore, the characters that read places in this array do not usually correspond to a single line from the file.

The code to process the contents of a file through a `BufferedReader` usually includes a loop that repeatedly extracts a line from the file and then processes that line appropriately. One might expect that such a loop would take the form:

```
while ( ... ) { // while there are more lines to process.

        String curLine = someBufferedReader.readLine();
        // Code to process one line from the file
        ...
}
```

This form of loop, however, cannot be used to process text from a `BufferedReader`. The problem is that, in order to tell whether there are still more lines to be processed, you have to check to see if `readLine` returned `null`. Therefore, a command that reads a line from the file has to be executed just before evaluating the `boolean` expression that checks to see if there are additional lines. As a result, most loops to process data from a `BufferedReader` take the form:

```
String curLine = someBufferedReader.readLine();

while ( curLine != null ) {
        // Code to process one line from the file
        ...

        curLine = someBufferedReader.readLine();
}
```

The body of this loop reverses the order of the main steps. Instead of reading a line and then processing it, the loop processes a line and then extracts the next line from the stream. The code that processes a line is almost always processing the line extracted from the file during the preceding iteration of the loop. The exception is the first iteration of the loop. The line that is processed during the first iteration, the first line from the `BufferedReader`, is retrieved by the invocation of `readLine` that precedes the `while` loop header.

As a concrete example of the use of such a loop, a method to transfer the contents of a bookmarks file into a `BookmarkList` is shown in Figure 19.11. This method would be included within the `BookmarkList` class. The code that processes each line of data is:

```
// Process lines that appear to contain bookmarks
if ( curLine.indexOf( "<A ") >= 0 ) {
    Bookmark entry = extractBookmark( curLine );
    if ( entry != null ){
            add( entry );
    }
}
```

This code uses the add method, which we described in Section 19.1.1, to add `Bookmark` objects to the list. It also assumes the existence of a private `extractBookmark` method, which uses `String` primitives to locate the address and description associated within a line, when possible. We have not included the code for this method, since it involves `String` manipulation rather than

```
// Add all the bookmarks found in the file "bookmarks.html"
// to this list of Bookmarks.
public void retrieveBookmarksFile() {

    try {
        BufferedReader bookmarksFileReader =
            new BufferedReader( new FileReader( "bookmarks.html" ) );

        // Read through all the lines of the file

        String curLine = bookmarksFileReader.readLine();
        while ( curLine != null ) {

            // Process lines that appear to contain bookmarks
            if ( curLine.indexOf( "<A " ) >= 0 ) {

                Bookmark entry = extractBookmark( curLine );
                if ( entry != null ){
                    add( entry );
                }
            }

            // Move on to the next line
            curLine = bookmarksFileReader.readLine();

        }

        bookmarksFileReader.close();

    } catch ( IOException e ) {
        System.out.println( "Unable to retrieve bookmarks - "
                            + e.getMessage() );
    }
}
```

Figure 19.11 The retrieveBookmarksFile method

the use of streams. If extractBookmark is unable to extract a bookmark, it will return null. The if statements ensure that we ignore any lines in the input file that do not appear to contain bookmark descriptions.

As suggested earlier, the Reader constructors and methods used in this example may raise exceptions. Accordingly, the loop together with the code to create and close the connection to the file are all placed within a try-catch construct.

➤ EXERCISE 19.2.1

When working on a method like saveBookmarksFile, *it is very important to have some way to actually look at the contents of the files produced. Many utilities are available to examine the contents of a text file. In Figure 19.12, we show an attempt to write a simple Java program that*

```
import java.awt.*;
import java.awt.event.*;
import javax.swing.*;
import java.io.*;
import objectdraw.*;

public class DisplayFile extends Controller implements ActionListener {

    JTextField fileNameField = new JTextField( "Enter File Name" );

    // Create and install needed GUI components
    public void begin() {
        JButton displayTheFile = new JButton( "Display File" );
        displayTheFile.addActionListener( this );

        Container pane = getContentPane();
        pane.add( displayTheFile, BorderLayout.SOUTH );
        pane.add( fileNameField, BorderLayout.NORTH );

        validate();
    }

    // Display the file when the button is pressed
    public void actionPerformed( ActionEvent event ) {
        try {
            BufferedReader source =
                new BufferedReader( new FileReader(
                                    fileNameField.getText() ) );

            while ( source.readLine() != null ) {
                System.out.println( source.readLine() );
            }
        } catch ( IOException e ) {
            System.out.println( "Error accessing file - "
                                + e.getMessage() );
        }
    }
}
```

Figure 19.12 DisplayFile program for Exercise 19.2.1

would serve this purpose. The program is supposed to display a window containing a JTextField and a JButton, as shown in Figure 19.13. When the button is pressed, the program should read the file whose name was entered in the JTextField and show its contents in the console window. Unfortunately, the code in the actionPerformed method is incorrect. Explain what the program shown will do, and show how to fix the problem.

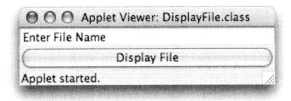

Figure 19.13   User interface of program for Exercise 19.2.1

➤ EXERCISE 19.2.2

Sometimes it is useful to know just how large a file is. With this in mind, write a method named countLines *that takes the name of a file as a* String *parameter and returns the number of lines in the file as a result. Your method should return* −1 *if any sort of* IOException *occurs while you are trying to access the file.*   ❖

19.3 Writing an Application

Because the files we store on our machines may contain sensitive data, most systems provide mechanisms that enable us to restrict access to these files. This is a particularly significant concern when writing Java programs. Java was designed to make it easy to include interactive programs as parts of web pages. When you view a web page that contains such a Java program, you allow someone else's program to run on your machine. It is clear that you would not want such a program to have unlimited access to all your files.

To provide adequate security, Java distinguishes programs designed to be downloaded through a web browser from programs designed to be installed locally. The former are called *applets* while the latter are called *applications*. To ensure that the applets you download while browsing the web do not harm your system or infringe on your privacy, they are restricted in many ways. In particular, web browsers typically do not let applets access any of the files on your machine.

Unfortunately, programs written by extending the WindowController and Controller classes are designed to run as applets. This means that such programs will normally not be able to create FileReaders or FileWriters as described in the preceding sections. To enable you to effectively use these classes, we must show you how to write programs designed to function as applications. Fortunately, this is not at all difficult.

The rules Java uses to determine whether a program is an applet or an application are quite simple. All programs are collections of class definitions. In each program, there must be some class that functions as the starting point of execution. To be an applet, this class must be an extension of the Applet class, JApplet class, or of some class that extends one of these. The WindowController and Controller classes provided in our library extend JApplet. Accordingly, programs constructed by extending one of these classes can function as applets.

To be an application, a program must include a class that defines a static method named main that expects a String array as a parameter and returns no value. The header for this function will look something like:

```
public static void main( String arguments[ ] )
```

If such a program is initiated using a command-line interface, the arguments typed on the command line are passed to the program as elements of the `String` array passed to `main`.

When a Java application is executed, the first thing that happens is the invocation of the `main` method. In some sense, this is like the invocation of `begin` in a `Controller`, but there is an important difference. When Java initiates the execution of a program defined by extending `Controller`, it first creates an object of the class and invokes `begin` on that object. When an application begins executing, on the other hand, the system merely invokes `main` without creating any object first. That is why `main` has to be a static method. It must be possible to invoke it without referring to any object, because no object will have been constructed yet when it is invoked.

Typically, one of the actions of the `main` method of an application is to create one or more objects of the classes that make up the program. In very simple programs, it is not unusual for the `main` method to simply construct an object of the class in which it is defined. If the program is to provide a graphical interface, one of the objects it will need to create is a window in which GUI components can be displayed. Therefore, if we want to write a simple program that provides a graphical interface, a reasonable approach is to define a class that contains a `main` method and that extends Swing's basic window class, `JFrame`.

To illustrate how this is done, the code for a simple application that illustrates everything you need to do to create a window is shown in Figure 19.14. The program consists of a single class named `JustAWindow` that defines just one method, the static `main` method required of an application. The first step performed in the `main` method is the construction of an object of the `JustAWindow` class. Since the class is defined to extends Swing's `JFrame`, this construction creates a window. The construction of this window is included in an assignment that associates it

```java
import javax.swing.JFrame;

public class JustAWindow extends JFrame {

    // Dimensions of the window to create
    private static final int WINDOW_WIDTH = 300;
    private static final int WINDOW_HEIGHT = 300;

    // Create an empty window on the screen
    public static void main ( String args[] ) {
        JFrame self = new JustAWindow();

        self.setSize( WINDOW_WIDTH, WINDOW_HEIGHT );
        self.setTitle( "Just an empty window" );

        self.setDefaultCloseOperation( JFrame.EXIT_ON_CLOSE );
        self.setVisible( true );
    }
}
```

Figure 19.14   A minimal application to create a window

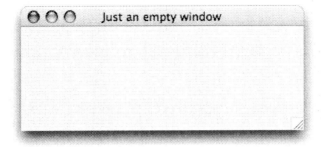

Figure 19.15 Window displayed by JustAWindow program

with the name se1f. This is essential, because we need to apply several methods to this window to make it appear as we would like.

When first constructed, a JFrame does not actually appear on the display. To make it appear, we must invoke its setVisible method. This is the last step performed by the main method shown. Before this is done, the method also uses the JFrame's setSize and setTitle methods to adjust its size and ensure that the window displayed will have an appropriate title. As a result, when the window does appear, it will look like the example shown in Figure 19.15. Finally, executing the command

```
self.setDefaultCloseOperation( JFrame.EXIT_ON_CLOSE );
```

specifies that if the user closes the window in which the program is executing, the execution of the program should terminate.

Of course, if we want our program to be more useful, it will need to use the window to hold some GUI component through which communication can occur with the program's user. To illustrate how this is done, we will implement a simple application that will enable a user to get the current date and time by just clicking on a button in the program's window.

The interface we have in mind is shown in Figure 19.16. The program's window holds two components. Most of the window is occupied by a JTextArea. The second component is a

Figure 19.16 Interface provided by TimeClock application

JButton placed at the bottom of the window and labeled "Display Current Time". Each time this button is clicked, the program should add a line to the JTextArea displaying the current date and time.

This application will require two sections of code beyond the simple statements shown in Figure 19.14. We need to write an event-handling method that will show the current date and time in response to clicks. We also need initialization code to create the two GUI components displayed in the program and to register a listener for the JButton.

There are several reasonable places we could place the required initialization code. We will take an approach that mimics the structure of the code you have written for your earlier programs as closely as possible. We will define a begin method in our class and add an invocation of begin to the main method. The complete code for this application is shown in Figure 19.17. The begin method looks very much like the begin method from a program based on the Controller class. It creates the required JTextField and JButton, adds them to the display, and establishes that this object will be the listener for the button. The begin method is called by the last line of main once the program's window has been created. Because this program uses the Java Date class to determine the time to display, we must import java.util.Date.

We will use a similar structure for all applications shown in this text. In particular, in the next section we will show how to write an application that provides the ability to edit simple text files.

⊫➡ EXERCISE 19.3.1

In Figure 3.12, we presented a program to simulate the rolling of a pair of dice. That program was written as an applet, using support for handling mouse events and drawing graphics provided by the objectdraw library. For this problem, we would like you to write a version of the same program that will run as an application and use Swing GUI components for interaction. The program you write should provide a JButton that the user can click on to roll the simulated dice. The results of the roll should be displayed as the contents of a JLabel. A picture of the interface we have in mind can be seen in Figure 19.18. (You may still use the RandomIntGenerator class in your solution, or if you prefer you can use the Random class provided in the standard java.util package and described in Appendix D.) ❖

19.4 Working with the File System

To keep them neatly organized, the files on your disk are grouped into directories or folders, which are themselves organized in a hierarchical structure. In our bookmarks file examples, we avoided the issue of how to deal with such directory structures by assuming that the file "bookmarks.html" was located in the system's current directory. For more realistic examples, we will need to write programs that can access files in multiple directories.

In this section, we will describe two classes included in the Java libraries to simplify the process of accessing files within a directory hierarchy. The first of these classes is named File. The name is a bit misleading. An object of the File class isn't really a file. It is more appropriate to think of it as a complete file name, often called a *path name*. That is, a File object encapsulates a pair composed of a simple file name, like "bookmarks.html", and a description of the directory

```java
import java.awt.*;
import java.awt.event.*;
import javax.swing.*;
import java.util.Date;

// An application that displays the date and time on request
public class TimeClock extends JFrame implements ActionListener {

    JTextArea timeStamps = new JTextArea();

    // Create and install needed GUI components
    public void begin() {
        JButton getTheTime = new JButton( "Display Current Time" );
        getTheTime.addActionListener( this );

        Container pane = getContentPane();
        pane.add( getTheTime, BorderLayout.SOUTH );
        pane.add( new JScrollPane( timeStamps ), BorderLayout.CENTER );

        validate();
    }

    // Display the time when the button is pressed
    public void actionPerformed( ActionEvent event ) {
        timeStamps.append( new Date() + "\n" );
    }

    // Create window and initiate application execution
    public static void main ( String args[] ) {
        TimeClock self = new TimeClock() ;

        self.setSize( 250, 200 );
        self.setTitle( "Time Clock" );

        self.setDefaultCloseOperation( JFrame.EXIT_ON_CLOSE );
        self.setVisible( true );

        self.begin();
    }
}
```

Figure 19.17 Definition of a TimeClock application

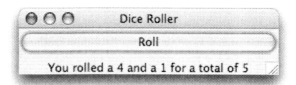

Figure 19.18   Interface for the program described in Exercise 19.3.1

containing the file. In fact, a `File` object can be used in place of a string to specify the name of the file to access when constructing a `FileReader` or a `FileWriter`.

The second class is `JFileChooser`. This class is part of the Swing collection of graphical user interface classes. A `JFileChooser` enables a Java program to display a dialog box through which a program's user can specify a file to retrieve or create. Selecting a file using the dialog box displayed by a `JFileChooser` does not actually create a stream through which the file can be accessed. Instead, the `JFileChooser` class provides a `getSelectedFile` method which returns a `File` object describing the file the user has chosen. This `File` object can then be used to create an appropriate stream to access the file.

To illustrate the use of these two classes, we will define a class named `SimpleEdit` that implements a text editing application. To avoid some complexity, we won't equip this program with all the usual `File` menu entries for accessing and saving files. Instead, when the program begins execution, it will assume that its user wants to open a file to edit and will display a dialog box through which the user can select the desired file. The program will then display the contents of the file in an editable text area, so that the user can modify it as desired. The program's window will also include a Save button. When the user presses this button, the program will display another dialog box through which the user can specify the file name under which the modified text should be saved. An image of the program's main window is shown in Figure 19.19. In this image, the program is shown being used to edit a very important text file, its own definition. The portion of the file currently visible in the program window is the `main` method. This method is nearly identical to the `main` method used in the `TimeClock` example. It simply creates an instance of the program's main class and invokes its `begin` method. The `TextField` shown to the left of the button is used to display error messages.

The `begin` method for this class is also similar to that used in `TimeClock`. The code for this method together with several instance variable definitions used in `SimpleEdit` are shown in Figure 19.20.

To place the contents of the file to be edited in the `JTextArea` named `display`, a method named `loadText` is invoked near the end of `begin`. This is a `private` method designed to read the text from a selected file. For the most part, the implementation of `loadText` follows the pattern we used to load bookmarks from a file in our first use of a `Reader`. The method creates a `BufferedReader` and then executes a loop that reads lines from the file until its contents are exhausted. Each line is appended to the contents of the `JTextArea`. The code for the `loadText` method is shown in Figure 19.21. Like other code that accesses files, this method must handle possible `IOExceptions`. In the example, this is done by displaying a short error message in a `JTextField` on the display.

The most interesting part of `loadText` is its use of another `private` method named `openInput`. This method uses a `JFileChooser` to select a file and then creates a

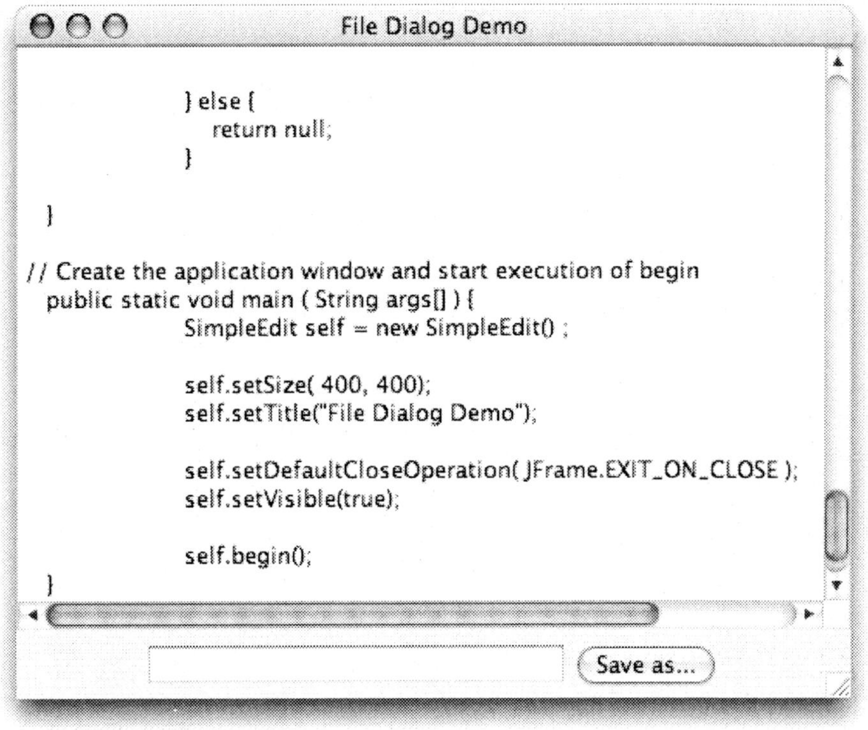

Figure 19.19 Main window of the SimpleEdit program

BufferedReader connected to the selected file. The text of openInput is shown in Figure 19.22. It depends on the fact that the name pickAFile is declared as an instance variable and initialized to refer to a JFileChooser object in the class definition. The first line of the openInput method uses this object to display a dialog box by invoking its showOpenDialog method. When this occurs, a dialog box similar to the one shown in Figure 19.23 will appear on the screen.

The showOpenDialog method requires some Component as a parameter. In this method, we pass it the program window itself. As a result, when the dialog box appears, it will be placed above the program window. The showOpenDialog method does not return the file that was actually selected. Instead, it returns an int whose value indicates whether the user selected a file or pressed the cancel button. If a file was selected, the getSelectedFile method of the JFileChooser can be invoked. It will return a File object describing the selected file's name. In our method, if the return value from showOpenDialog indicates that a file was selected, we use the File object describing the selected file to construct a FileReader and then a BufferedReader connected to the selected file. This is then returned as the method's result.

The process of using a JFileChooser to enable a user to select a destination for an output file is similar to its use with input files. When a user clicks on the Save button in our program, the event-handling method, actionPerformed, invokes a private method named saveText. In turn, this method invokes a second private method, openOutput, which uses a dialog box to determine what output file to use. The code for both of these methods is shown in Figure 19.24. There are

```
// Editable text
JTextArea display = new JTextArea();

// Used to display warning messages
JTextField warnings = new JTextField( 20 );

// Signals when user wants to save text
JButton save = new JButton( "Save as..." );

// Provides file selection dialog boxes
JFileChooser pickAFile = new JFileChooser( );

// Create and install needed GUI components and listeners.
// Then, load the file to be edited.
public void begin() {
    Container pane = this.getContentPane();
    JPanel controls = new JPanel();

    controls.add( warnings );
    controls.add( save );

    pane.add( new JScrollPane( display ), BorderLayout.CENTER );
    pane.add( controls, BorderLayout.SOUTH );
    validate();

    loadText();
    save.addActionListener( this );
}
```

Figure 19.20   Instance variables and begin method for SimpleEdit

only two differences between the openInput and openOutput methods. openOutput uses showSaveDialog rather than showOpenDialog. Also, openOutput uses the File returned by getSelectedFile to construct a PrintWriter rather than constructing a BufferedReader. The saveText method is also very similar to loadText. It is worth noting, however, that saveText is actually a bit simpler. No loop is needed. The entire contents of the TextArea can be transferred to the file using a single write invocation.

EXERCISE 19.4.1

The JFileChooser *class can be used in a program that does not actually access the data in a file at all. As an example of this, write a program that simply displays a* JFileChooser *dialog box as soon as it begins execution, displays the name of the file the user selects, and then does nothing else. To get the name of the file, invoke the* getAbsolutePath *method on the* File *object returned by* getSelectedFile. *The* getAbsolutePath *method returns a* String. *You*

```
// Open a text file and place contents in text area
private void loadText( ) {
    try {
        BufferedReader textFile = openInput();

        if ( textFile != null ) {

            String currentLine = textFile.readLine();

            while ( currentLine != null ) {
                display.append( currentLine + "\n" );
                currentLine = textFile.readLine();
            }
            textFile.close();
        }

    } catch ( IOException e ) {
        warnings.setText( "Unable to read file" );
    }
}
```

Figure 19.21 The loadText method of SimpleEdit

```
// Use dialog box to let user select a file to open
private BufferedReader openInput() throws IOException {

    int result = pickAFile.showOpenDialog( this );

    if ( result == JFileChooser.APPROVE_OPTION ) {
        return new BufferedReader(
                        new FileReader(
                            pickAFile.getSelectedFile()
                        ) );
    } else {
        return null;
    }
}
```

Figure 19.22 The openInput method

can either write the program as an application or as an extension of Controller. The only component in its main window should be a JLabel, in which you will display the file name after the user selects a file and clicks "Open" in the dialog box displayed by the JFileChooser. For example, the program should produce the display shown in Figure 19.25, if the user selected a file named default.html stored within a folder named Web Pages within the folder Document which was itself within the folder Mac HD of the folder Volumes.

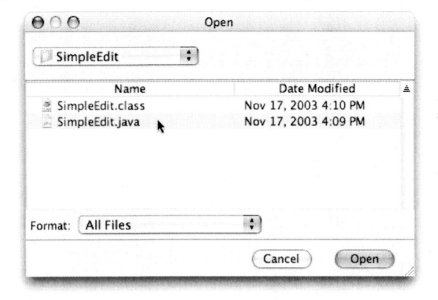

Figure 19.23 Dialog displayed by showOpenDialog

19.5 Sockets and Streams

In the introduction to this chapter, we explained that Java streams provide the means to transfer data between program variables and a variety of external sources and destinations. So far, however, all of our sources and destinations have been files. In this section, we will show how streams are used to send data through or to receive data from computer networks.

Network communication is almost always a two-way process. If you want to receive a web page from a remote web server, your browser first sends the server a message requesting the data that describes the web page. Then the web server sends the requested description back to your machine. When you read e-mail, your mail program sends your account identifier and password to your mail server, which responds by sending you any recently received mail.

As a result, streams used for network communications almost always come in pairs, one stream for sending data and one for receiving data. Because the relationship between the two streams in such a pair is important, the Java libraries include a class named Socket which can be used to construct a pair of streams for network communications as a single object. Associated with each Socket object are two methods named getInputStream and getOutputStream, which can be used to access the two streams that are the components of a Socket.

In this section, we will show how to create Sockets and how to use the streams associated with a Socket to send and receive data through the network. We will see that the actual use of the streams associated with a Socket is nearly identical to the use of streams associated with files. We will use the write method to send network messages and readLine to receive them. This illustrates the flexibility of streams. They make it possible for us to use a single programming

```
// Place the contents of text area in a selected file
private void saveText() {
    try {
        PrintWriter textFile = openOutput();

        if ( textFile != null ) {
            textFile.write( display.getText() );
            textFile.close();
        }

    } catch ( IOException e ) {
        warnings.setText( "Unable to save file" );
    }
}

// Use dialog box to let user select file to save
private PrintWriter openOutput() throws IOException {

    int result = pickAFile.showSaveDialog( this );

    if ( result == JFileChooser.APPROVE_OPTION ) {
            return new PrintWriter( new FileWriter(
                                    pickAFile.getSelectedFile() ) );
    } else {
        return null;
    }
}
```

Figure 19.24 Methods used by SimpleEdit to save files

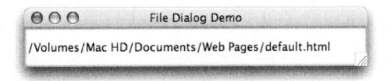

Figure 19.25 Screen displayed by program for Exercise 19.4.1

mechanism to manage two forms of communication we might have considered so different that they would require independent mechanisms.

19.5.1 Clients and Servers

All of the commonly used facilities of the Internet are based on the exchange of messages between machines functioning as clients and servers. A client machine requests a service. The request might be to deliver an e-mail message or to let the client view a web page. A server accepts requests and performs the desired services. A mail server accepts and then delivers outgoing messages. Web servers provide the contents of web pages.

It is actually somewhat misleading to talk about client machines and server machines. What makes a machine a client or a server is the software running on the machine rather than the physical characteristics of the machine. When you launch a web browser on your machine, it suddenly becomes a web client. When you click on a link in your web browser window, the code that is executed instructs the computer to send a request to a server, process the response that is returned, and then display it on your screen. It doesn't matter whether you use Internet Explorer, Netscape, Mozilla, Safari, or one of the many other web browsers that are available. They all instruct your computer to act as a client.

Similarly, there are many programs that instruct a computer to behave as a web server, including Apache, NCSA httpd, Alibaba, and MacHTTP. These programs just are not as well known as the browsers. If you do run a web server application on your machine, it waits to receive incoming requests, identifies the files requested, and sends them back to the client through the network.

While we have used web browsers and web servers as an example, the remarks we have made apply to many other Internet services, such as e-mail and instant messaging. By running a program like Microsoft Outlook Express, you can turn a computer into a mail client. Other programs, such as sendmail, are run on machines intended to act as mail servers.

19.5.2   Networking Protocols

As an example of the use of Java's mechanisms for network communication, we will construct a special-purpose web browser in this section. To prepare for this task, let us consider in more detail how a computer running a web browser interacts with a web server. There are very specific rules dictating the types and formats of the messages that clients send to servers and that servers send to clients. Such a collection of rules is called a network *protocol*. The rules that apply to web servers and clients are known as the *Hypertext Transfer Protocol* or simply HTTP.

You have probably noticed that almost all web browsers have a small field near the top of their windows in which the address or URL of the page being viewed in the browser window is displayed. Each time you click on a new link, this URL changes. For example, if you go to read the national news on the web site of the *New York Times*, you might find the address

        http://nytimes.com/pages/national/index.html

displayed at the top of the page.

An address like this actually has two components significant to our discussion. The text immediately following the "http://" prefix, nytimes.com, is the name of the server machine from which web pages provided by the *New York Times* can be fetched. The rest of the address, "/pages/national/index.html", is a path to a particular file stored on that computer.

To retrieve such a web page, the rules of HTTP state that the client program must send a message to the server requesting the specified file. The format of this request is quite simple. Most of the messages sent by clients and servers following the HTTP protocol are plain text, i.e., simple Java Strings. In particular, to request a file, the client must send a string containing the word GET and the name of the desired file to the server. Thus, to fetch the national news from the *New York Times*, a web browser sends the following line of text

        GET /pages/national/index.html

to the machine named nytimes.com. Once the server machine receives this request, it will verify that the requested file is available in its collection and will send messages containing the contents of the file back to the client which made the request.

This communication process is complicated by one issue. We have explained that the software running on a machine determines whether it is a server or a client. It is possible to run multiple applications at the same time on most computer systems. If both a web server application and a mail server application are running on a single computer at the same time, then that machine will be both a web server and a mail server. When a client request message such as

```
GET /pages/national/index.html
```

arrives at a server machine, the machine needs some simple way to determine whether the incoming message should be handled by the mail server application or by the web server application. As a result, it isn't enough for the client to specify that "nytimes.com" is the message's intended destination. The destination address must also somehow identify the server application to which the message should be delivered.

The Internet protocols depend on a mechanism called *port numbers* to provide this more specific form of destination address. A port number is somewhat like a telephone extension number. When you make a phone call to a large organization, you often have to enter the extension for the party or office you want to talk to after you have already entered the organization's main phone number. This enables the organization to list just a single number in the phone book while still making it possible for you to contact a particular individual within the organization. In the Internet, a machine address such as "nytimes.com" functions as an organization's phone number, and a port number is used like an extension number to specify a particular application on a machine to which a message should be delivered. One of the many communication details standardized by a protocol like HTTP is the port number that a server should be associated with. The HTTP protocol specifies that messages destined for port 80 on a machine should be delivered to the web server application running on that machine.

➡ EXERCISE 19.5.1

In this section, we gave a brief introduction to the Hypertext Transfer Protocol, HTTP. HTTP is just one of many protocols used on the Internet. There are distinct protocols for mail servers, file servers, chat systems, and many others. The details of most of these protocols are specified in documents called "Requests for Comment" or RFCs.

It isn't hard to find the RFC for a protocol. If you ask your favorite search engine to look for "HTTP RFC", it will almost certainly point you to an on-line copy of RFC 2616 very quickly. Reading and understanding the document may not be quite as easy.

To give you a feel for the process, we would like you to peruse one RFC looking for a few key details of an important protocol. The protocol we have in mind is named POP3, the Post Office Protocol. It is used by many mail clients to fetch mail.

We picked POP3 because it does something important and yet is relatively simple. The RFC that describes it is only about 20 pages long.

So, with the help of a search engine, answer the following questions:

a. *Which RFC describes the POP3 protocol?*
b. *What is the standard port number to which one should connect to talk to a POP3 server?*
c. *What is the format of the line a POP3 client should send to a POP3 server to retrieve a single email message?*

19.5.3 Creating and Using a Socket

When a Java client application wants to communicate with a server, it begins by creating a Socket that will provide the two streams necessary to communicate with the server. All messages sent through the output stream associated with this Socket will be addressed to the same remote server application. All these messages will go to the same port on the same machine. Therefore, rather than specifying this addressing information each time a message is sent, we provide it when we construct the Socket.

A Socket can be created using a construction in which we provide the name of the remote machine as a string and an integer port number. For example, to create a Socket to provide communications with the *New York Times* web site we might say

```
Socket timesConnection = new Socket( "nytimes.com", 80 );
```

When such a construction is executed, the system attempts to send network messages to the specified machine and port to ensure that the specified machine exists and that an appropriate server application is running on the machine. As a result, there are many ways in which such a construction can fail. For example, the construction may result in an UnknownHostException, if the machine name given does not correspond to any machine that can be found on the network at the moment, or an IOException, if it is not possible to communicate with the desired server application on the host. Accordingly, instructions that create Sockets should be placed in a try-catch construct that will respond to such errors.

Once a Socket has been created, the client program can use the Socket to access streams through which data can be sent to or received from the server. Two methods named getInputStream and getOutputStream make this possible. For example, if a connection to the *Times* web site were established by creating a Socket named timesConnection as shown above, then the initialized declaration

```
OutputStream toTheTimesStream = timesConnection.getOutputStream();
```

could be used to create a stream through which data could be sent to the *Times* web server.

Many network applications require the transmission of data other than text through the network. To provide the flexibility required by such applications, the streams returned by getInputStream and getOutputStream must be flexible enough to handle arbitrary binary data. As a result, these methods return objects of the InputStream and OutputStream classes rather than Readers and Writers. These streams can then be used to create objects of whatever stream class has the most appropriate interface for the type of data that is to be transmitted.

Since all the requests sent to a web server are strings, it is desirable to use the stream returned by getOutputStream to construct a stream of the Writer class which is specialized to process String data. This can be done using a class named OutputStreamWriter as in the following declaration:

```
Writer toTheTimes =
    new OutputStreamWriter( timesConnection.getOutputStream() );
```

With such a stream created, sending a request to the web server is quite simple. To request the document described by the national news section URL shown above, we would say

```
toTheTimes.write( "GET /pages/national/index.html" + "\n" );
```

The newline character must be included, since the protocol specifies that the server should only respond after a complete line has been received.

■➡ EXERCISE 19.5.2

In the code shown above to send a GET *request, we explicitly included a* "\n" *at the end of the line we sent to the server. An alternative would be to have used* println *instead of* write*. To do this, of course, we would need a* PrintWriter *associated with the stream that carries data to the server.*

Show how to modify the declaration/initialization of toTheTimes *so that it is a* PrintWriter *and then show the* println *that would be used to send the* GET *request.*   ❖

19.5.4   Receiving Information from a Server

To illustrate the use of stream classes in network communications, we will show how to write code that extracts a few tidbits of information from the text that describes a web page without displaying the web page as it might appear in an actual web browser. Such programs are not uncommon. There is a shareware application for the Macintosh named Simple Weather that displays a brief summary of current weather conditions in a window like the one shown in Figure 19.26. The program determines the current conditions by fetching the weather forecast for your area from the website www.weather.com. The program has to fetch all the data describing the web page from www.weather.com. This data provides much more information (including some advertisements) than is displayed by the interface of the Simple Weather program shown in Figure 19.26. The program extracts the essentials from the data the server sends in order to provide the information in a format some users find more convenient.

In this section, we will present the network components of another program that displays weather information extracted from a web page. During a recent spell of bitter cold weather in our area, we sought to obtain comfort from the fact that it was colder in Alaska than in Massachusetts. With this motivation, we constructed a program to draw a graph of the temperature in Fairbanks, Alaska, over the period of a day. An example of a graph produced by our program is shown in Figure 19.27.

Figure 19.26   Window displayed by the Simple Weather program

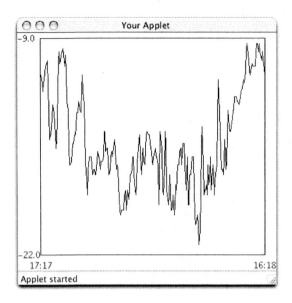

Figure 19.27   A temperature graph for Fairbanks from January, 2004

Constructing this program was fairly easy. We discovered that the Alaska Climate Reseach Center in Fairbanks provides a very nice web page that displays the local weather information and even includes a current photograph. An image of their web page is shown in Figure 19.28. The information we were interested in, the current time and temperature, can be found near the bottom of the page.

The URL for this web page is http://climate.gi.alaska.edu/ as shown in the top of the browser window. Accordingly, in order to display this web page, a web browser must send a request of the form

```
GET /
```

to port 80 on the web server climate.gi.alaska.edu. After receiving this request, the server will send back a description of the layout of the web page expressed in a notation called Hypertext Markup Language or HTML. The HTML description of the page bears little resemblance to the page shown in Figure 19.28. To start with, it is almost 340 lines of text. Most of it will make little sense to anyone who does not know HTML well.

It is easy to examine this text if you like. Most web browsers include a menu item with a name such as "View Source" or simply "Source", which will cause the browser to display the text of the HTML for the page it is displaying. Alternately, it is fairly easy to write Java code that displays the text of the HTML returned by the server. In fact, let us consider how we would write this code, before considering how to extract just the time and temperature information we need.

We will divide the code into three simple methods. The first, displayHTML, is shown in Figure 19.29. It begins by constructing a Socket to establish a connection to the server in Alaska. Since it wants to connect to a web server, port number 80 is specified as a parameter to the Socket constructor. It then invokes sendRequest, which sends a request through the Socket and displayResponse, which will use System.out.println to display all the data returned by the server in the console window.

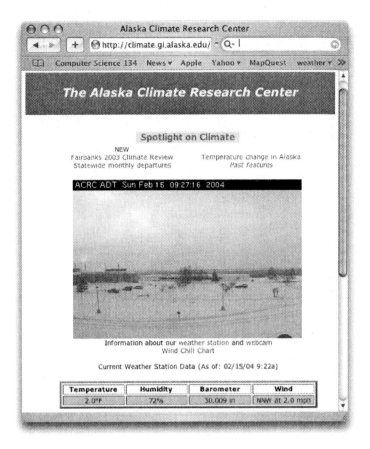

Figure 19.28   Website of the Alaska Climate Research Center

The sendRequest method is extremely simple. Its code is shown in Figure 19.30. It creates a Writer associated with the Socket's output stream and then uses the write method to send the request

    GET /

to the server. Finally, it tells Java to flush the Writer. This is necessary because the OutputStreamWriter class employs a technique called buffering to improve the efficiency with which data is transfered. Rather than sending data through the underlying stream each time the write method is invoked, an OutputStreamWriter saves the data it has been asked to write until a reasonable quantity has been collected, and only then does it send the collected data to the stream. Invoking flush forces the OutputStreamWriter to immediately send whatever data it has collected.

Finally, the displayResponse method is shown in Figure 19.31. This method's body contains a while loop that should look very familiar. It has the structure presented in Section 19.2 for a loop designed to process lines of text accessed through a Reader. When we described such loops, we were assuming that the data provided by the Reader came from a file. In this method,

```
public void displayHTML() {

    try {
        Socket server = new Socket( "climate.gi.alaska.edu", 80 );

        sendRequest( server );

        displayResponse( server );

        server.close();

    } catch ( IOException e ) {
        System.out.println( "Connection failed - "
                            + e.getMessage() ) ;
    }
}
```

Figure 19.29   A method to display the HTML of the Alaska Climate Center web page

```
private void sendRequest( Socket server ) throws IOException {

    Writer toWebServer = new OutputStreamWriter( server.getOutputStream()
                                                );

    toWebServer.write( "GET /" + "\n" );
    toWebServer.flush();
}
```

Figure 19.30   The sendRequest method

```
private void displayResponse( Socket server ) throws IOException {

    BufferedReader html = new BufferedReader(
                        new InputStreamReader( server.getInputStream() )
                                            );

    String curLine = html.readLine();

    while ( curLine != null ) {
        System.out.println( curLine );
        curLine = html.readLine();
    }
}
```

Figure 19.31   The displayResponse method

we instead create a BufferedReader associated with the Socket that connects to the server. Creating a BufferedReader is a three-step process. It first uses the Socker's getInputStream method to access the underlying stream. This is not a Reader, but is instead a steam designed for reading binary data. So it is necessary to first construct an InputStreamReader and then finally a BufferedReader to provide convenient access to the data.

After creating the BufferedReader, we read and print the lines sent through the connection by the server in response to our request.

⊫➡ EXERCISE 19.5.3

In an effort to keep our code very simple, we made the methods presented in this section less flexible than they really should be. Our displayHTML method always displays the HTML of the weather report from the Alaska Climate Research Center. It would be much more useful if it could retrieve any web page at all based on parameters passed to the method.

Show how to modify the code of our displayHTML, sendRequest, and displayResponse methods to provide such flexibility. Assume that displayHTML will take two String parameters: the name of the web server to contact and the path name of the file to retrieve. Add any parameters you feel are necessary to the definitions of the other two methods. ❖

19.5.5 Extracting Information from a Web Page

To create a graph of the temperature in Fairbanks, we have to extract just two pieces of information from the HTML: the time and the temperature. To do this, we have to examine each line of HTML a bit more carefully. We will still use a BufferedReader and a loop to access the lines sent by the server, but we will have to identify the lines that contain the interesting information and process them specially.

A sample of the most interesting section of the HTML we would see if we ran the program described above is shown in Figure 19.32. To make it easy for you to understand why this is an interesting portion of the HTML for this web page, we have displayed parts of two lines in bold font in the figure. The first of these is the fifth line of the HTML. This is the line that causes the current time to be included in the display of the web page. The other line is about halfway down. Buried in the middle of the line you will find the text "2.0F", the rather chilly temperature in the Fairbanks area.

We can extract the time and temperature by searching for these two lines in the file. The key observations are that the line containing the time turns out to be the only line in the HTML that contains the phrase "As of" and that the line containing the temperature is the only line that contains "F<". By searching for these lines, we can easily find the desired information.

We will focus on a method named getTemp designed to extract the time and temperature from a single copy of the web page. To draw a complete graph, we would have to invoke this method at regular intervals, collect the readings obtained in an array, and finally plot them. We will assume that the program uses a class named TempReading to represent a single reading. The constructor for this class will take two String parameters describing a time of day and a temperature. Our getTemp method will return a single TempReading object.

The code for the getTemp method is shown in Figure 19.33. This method depends on two methods named sendRequest and processResponse. The sendRequest used here will be identical to the method defined in Figure 19.30. It sends a GET request to the climate center's web server.

```
<TABLE BORDER=0 WIDTH=380 HEIGHT=77>
  <TR>
    <TD HEIGHT=17 BGCOLOR="#FFFFFF">
    <CENTER><FONT SIZE="-2" FACE="Verdana">Current Weather
    Station Data (As of: 02/15/04 9:22a)</FONT>

    <P><TABLE BORDER=3 CELLPADDING=0 WIDTH=400 HEIGHT=36 align=center>
     <TR>
        <TD WIDTH=100 BGCOLOR="#F0F8FF">
         <CENTER><FONT SIZE="-2" FACE="Verdana">
         <STRONG>Temperature</STRONG></FONT></CENTER>
        </TD>
        <TD WIDTH="25%" BGCOLOR="#F0F8FF">
         <CENTER><FONT SIZE="-2" FACE="Verdana"><B>Humidity</B></FONT></CENTER>
        </TD>
        <TD WIDTH="25%" BGCOLOR="#F0F8FF">
         <CENTER><FONT SIZE="-2" FACE="Verdana">
         <STRONG>Barometer</STRONG></FONT></CENTER>
        </TD>
        <TD WIDTH="25%" BGCOLOR="#F0F8FF">
         <CENTER><FONT SIZE="-2" FACE="Verdana"><B>Wind</B></FONT></CENTER>
        </TD>
     </TR>
     <TR>
        <TD WIDTH=100 BGCOLOR="#BBBBBB">
         <CENTER><FONT SIZE="-2" FACE="Verdana">2.0F</FONT></CENTER>
        </TD>
        <TD WIDTH="25%" BGCOLOR="#BBBBBB">
         <CENTER><FONT SIZE="-2" FACE="Verdana">74% </FONT></CENTER>
        </TD>
        <TD WIDTH="25%" BGCOLOR="#BBBBBB">
         <CENTER><FONT SIZE="-2" FACE="Verdana">30.029
         in</FONT></CENTER>
        </TD>
        <TD WIDTH="25%" BGCOLOR="#BBBBBB">
         <CENTER><FONT SIZE="-2" FACE="Verdana">WNW
         at 0.0 mph</FONT></CENTER>
        </TD>
     </TR>
    </TABLE>
```

Figure 19.32   A portion of the HTML for http://climate.gi.alaska.edu/

The processResponse method is a bit more involved. It depends on three auxiliary methods named getLineContaining, extractTime, and extractTemp. The processResponse and getLineContaining methods are shown in Figure 19.34. We have not included the code for extractTime or extractTemp, since these methods are simple String manipulation routines. They do not involve network or stream processing in any way.

The getLineContaining method is a BufferedReader processing method. Nothing about this method is specific to network communication. Although we will use this method to read from a stream associated with a network connection, it could be used just as easily to process data from a file. Given a BufferedReader and a String to search for, this method reads lines of

```
public TempReading getTemp( ) {

   Socket server;

   try {
      server = new Socket( "climate.gi.alaska.edu", 80 );

      sendRequest( server );
      TempReading reading =  processResponse( server );

      server.close();
      return reading;

   } catch ( IOException e ) {
      System.out.println( "Connection failed " + e.getMessage());
   }

   return null;
}
```

Figure 19.33 The getTemp method

```
private TempReading processResponse( Socket server )
                                        throws IOException  {

   BufferedReader html =
         new BufferedReader(
               new InputStreamReader(
                        server.getInputStream() ) );

   String timeLine = getLineContaining( "As of", html );
   String tempLine = getLineContaining( "F<", html );

   return  new TempReading( extractTime( timeLine ),
                     extractTemp( tempLine ) );
}

private String getLineContaining( String key, BufferedReader html )
                                        throws IOException  {

   String line;

   do {
      line = html.readLine();
   } while ( line != null && line.indexOf( key ) == -1);

   return line;
}
```

Figure 19.34 The processResponse and getLineContaining methods

text from the Reader until it finds a line containing the string it was asked to search for. Once it finds such a line, it returns the contents of the line. If no such line is found, it will return null.

The processResponse method accepts a Socket as a parameter, just like the sendRequest method. It first constructs a BufferedReader associated with the Socket. Once the BufferedReader has been constructed, the getLineContaining method is used to obtain the two interesting lines of text in the hundreds of lines the server will send in response to the GET request. These are the lines containing the time and temperature. Finally, the extractTime and extractTemp methods produce Strings that can be used to construct a TempReading object which the method will return. Since streams are the focus of this chapter, we do not show the details of the extractTime and extractTemp methods, which are both simple String processing methods.

The most important aspect of the code for this example is just how little of it explicitly depends on primitives for network access. In all of the methods other than getTemp itself, the uses of the getInputStream and getOutputStream methods are the only steps that depend on the fact that the data comes from the network rather than a file or any other form of stream. This illustrates the real flexibility of Java's stream classes.

> ### EXERCISE 19.5.4

The definition of the getLineContaining *method contains one of few uses of the* do-while *loop that appear in this text.*

a. *Show how to rewrite the method using the more familiar* while *loop.*

b. *In early examples, we have stressed the "standard" way of reading through the lines provided by a stream using a* while *loop. What is it about this method's function that made it possible/desirable to use a different approach?*

19.6   Summary

In this chapter we have seen how Java programs use streams to transfer information to and from data repositories such as disk files and network servers. If you look through all our stream examples, you may be surprised to discover that we only used four new methods in this chapter: readLine, write, flush, and close. This is not because we skipped most of the stream methods. There just aren't many stream methods. The methods we presented, together with the already familiar println method, are almost the only methods needed to write programs that manipulate files and perform network communication.

Furthermore, we have seen that these methods are normally used in simple, standard ways. To process data we obtain through a stream, we can almost always write a loop of the form

```
aString = aStream.readLine();
while ( aString != null ) {
      // Process data in aString
      ...
      aString = aStream.readLine();
}
aStream.close();
```

To send data through a stream, we will usually write a loop of the form:

```
while ( there is more data ) {
        // Arrange data in desired text form
        ...
        aStream.println( textdata );
    }
    aStream.close();
```

While we introduced very few stream methods, we introduced quite a few stream classes. Our examples involved objects and/or variables of nine different stream classes: `InputStream`, `InputStreamReader`, `FileReader`, `BufferedReader`, `OutputStream`, `Writer`, `OutputStreamWriter`, `FileWriter`, and `PrintWriter` together with the `Socket` class for network communications. In addition, there are many more stream classes, we could have discussed. Java provides a rich set of stream classes, so that a programmer can easily create a stream tailored to both the source or destination of the data and the ways in which the data will be processed.

We focused on stream classes specialized for handling text data, the `Reader` and `Writer` classes and their subclasses. We saw how to create objects of these classes to access text data, whether in a file or through the network. We saw how we could specialize these classes to allow us to use the convenient `println` and `readLine` methods by creating `BufferedReaders` and `PrintWriters` from simpler streams.

Finally, we introduced some aspects of Java that are not directly related to creating or manipulating streams but are important to writing programs that use streams. We showed how to construct a program that can be run as an application rather than an applet. We also explained how to create a dialog box through which a user could select a file for our program to read or write.

The mechanisms presented in this chapter are of great practical significance, since few useful programs can be written without the ability to save and retrieve data stored in files.

19.7 Chapter Review Problems

▶ EXERCISE 19.7.1

For each of the following classes introduced within this chapter:

* *Indicate whether the class is designed to support input, output, or both.*
* *Indicate whether the class is designed for working with files, for network communication, or for both (and possibly working with other types of streams as well).*

    a. `PrintWriter`
    b. `Socket`
    c. `FileReader`
    d. `BufferedReader`
    e. `InputStreamReader`
    f. `JFileChooser`

◗ EXERCISE 19.7.2

a. *Explain what happens if you attempt to create a* `FileReader` *using a construction such as*

  `new FileReader( "mybookmarks" )`

but the file named does not exist.

b. *Explain what happens if you attempt to create a* `FileWriter` *using a construction such as*

  `new FileWriter( "mybookmarks" )`

but the file named does not exist.   ❖

◗ EXERCISE 19.7.3

A loop that is similar to several loops we have used to process lines from a Reader *is shown below. This one prints all the lines sent through the stream.*

```
String curLine = source.readLine();
while ( curLine != null ) {
    System.out.println( curLine );
    curLine = source.readLine();
}
```

Many beginners are bothered by the fact that this approach to reading from a stream requires two distinct readLine*s. To appreciate the need for this apparent redundancy, we have written several loops that attempt to perform the same function as the loop above using only one* readLine*. None of these loops work. For each loop, explain what would go wrong if you attempted to use it in place of the standard loop.*

```
a. String curLine;
   while ( curLine != null ) {
       String curLine = source.readLine();
       System.out.println( curLine );
   }
b. String curLine = "";
   while ( curLine != null ) {
       String curLine = source.readLine();
       System.out.println( curLine );
   }
c. String curLine;
   do {
       curLine = source.readLine();
       System.out.println( curLine );
   } while ( curLine != null )
```
                                                                          ❖

◗ EXERCISE 19.7.4

Below you will find several code segments accompanied by brief descriptions of their intended purposes. Each segment contains one or more mistakes. Identify the mistake(s) and explain how to correct the code.

a. *The following method is intended to behave somewhat like the* indexOf *method for* Strings. *Given the name of a file and a* String *to look for, it should return the number of the first line that contains the search string or −1 if the string cannot be found. As with arrays and* Strings, *we will start numbering at 0. As shown, the code contains two errors that would be detected when the program was compiled. Explain what is wrong and show how to fix the problems.*

```java
private int fileIndexOf( String fileName, String toFind ) {

    BufferedReader source = new BufferedReader( filename );

    int lineNum = 0;
    String curLine = source.readLine();
    while ( curLine != null && curLine.indexOf( toFind ) ==
            -1 ) {
        lineNum++;
        curLine = source.readLine();
    }

    if ( curLine != null ) {
        return lineNum;
    } else {
        return -1;
    }

    source.close();
}
```

b. *The following method is supposed to store all the* Strings *in the array passed to it as its first parameter into the file whose name is provided as its second parameter. It contains an error that will be detected when the program is compiled. Identify the error and explain how to fix the program.*

```java
private void saveStringArray( String [ ] lines,
                              String fileName ) {

    try {
        FileWriter destination = new FileWriter( fileName );

        for ( int i = 0; i < lines.length; i++ ) {
            destination.println( lines[i] );
        }

        destination.close();
    } catch ( IOException e ) {
        System.out.println( "Error writing file" );
    }
}
```

c. *The method* `fileConcat` *is intended to concatenate two files to produce a third file. The names of the three files are provided as* `String` *parameters to the method. It uses a second method shown below named* `copyToDest` *to copy the contents of each of the two source files to the destination. The method* `fileConcat` *is supposed to work by first using* `copyToDest` *to copy the first source file to the destination and then using it again to copy the contents of the second source file to the destination. Unfortunately, when the program is run, the final contents of the destination file are not as expected. What is wrong with the program as shown? What is left in the destination file? How could it be fixed?*

```
private void fileConcat( String source1name, String source2name,
                         String destName) throws IOException {

    copyToDest( source1name, destname );
    copyToDest( source2name, destname );
}


private void copyToDest( String sourceName,
                         String destName ) throws IOException {

    BufferedReader source =
            new BufferedReader( new FileReader( sourceName ) );
    PrintWriter dest =
            new PrintWriter( new FileWriter( destName ) );

    String curLine = source.readLine();
    while ( curLine != null ) {
        dest.println( curLine );
        curLine = source.readLine();
    }

    source.close();
    dest.close();
}
```

❖

➡ EXERCISE 19.7.5

Each of the following methods is designed to perform an operation on one or more text files containing words stored one per line in alphabetical order. For each method, briefly explain what operation it performs.

a. `private void` `performOP1( BufferedReader source1,`
                          `BufferedReader source2,`
                          `PrintWriter destination )`
                          `throws IOException {`

```
    String line1 = source1.readLine();
    String line2 = source2.readLine();
```

```
        while ( line1 != null && line2 != null ) {

            if ( line1.compareTo( line2 ) < 0 ) {
                line1 = source1.readLine();
            } else {
                if ( line1.equals( line2 ) ) {
                    destination.println( line1 );
                    line1 = source1.readLine();
                }
                line2 = source2.readLine();

            }
        }
    }
```

b.
```
private void performOP2( BufferedReader source1,
                        PrintWriter destination )
                        throws IOException {

    String line1 = source1.readLine();
    String line2 = null;

    while ( line1 != null ) {
        if ( ! line1.equals( line2 ) ) {
            destination.println( line1 );
        }
        line2 = line1;
        line1 = source1.readLine();
    }
}
```

c.
```
private boolean performOP3( BufferedReader source1,
                           BufferedReader source2 )
                           throws IOException {

    String line1 = source1.readLine();
    String line2 = source2.readLine();

    while ( line1 != null && line2 != null &&
            line1.equals( line2 ) ) {
        line1 = source1.readLine();
        line2 = source2.readLine();
    }

    return line1 == null && line2 == null;
}
```

d. private boolean performOP4(BufferedReader source1,
                         BufferedReader source2)
                         throws IOException {

```
    String line1 = source1.readLine();
    String line2 = source2.readLine();

    while ( line1 != null && line2 != null ) {
        while ( line2 != null && line1.compareTo( line2 ) > 0 ) {
            line2 = source2.readLine();
        }
        if ( line2 != null && line2.equals( line1 ) ) {
            line1 = source1.readLine();
            line2 = source2.readLine();
        } else {
            return false;
        }
    }

    return line1 == null;
}
```

19.8   Programming Problems

▶ EXERCISE 19.8.1

In Exercise 19.2.2 we asked you to write a method to count the number of lines in a text file. Please write a complete program that counts not only the number of lines in a file, but also the total number of characters and the total number of words. For our purposes, a word is any sequence of nonblank characters that fall together on a single line.

When the program begins execution, it should display a blank JTextArea in its window and then use a JFileChooser to present a dialog box through which the user can select the file to be examined. The program should then count the lines, words, and characters in the file. When it is done, the results should be displayed in the JTextArea in a format similar to that shown in Figure 19.35.

▶ EXERCISE 19.8.2

No one likes to receive junk mail or spam, but someone has to send it! With this in mind, please write the following program, which would be very handy for compiling large mailing lists of addresses.

The program we have in mind will read in two text files containing lists of addresses. To keep things simple, you may assume the contents of each line is a single e-mail address. Also, assume

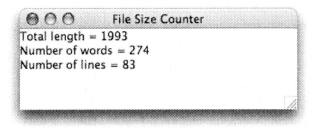

Figure 19.35 Output format desired for Exercise 19.8.1

that the addresses are sorted in alphabetical order. The goal of the program will be to create a
new file containing every address that appeared in either of the input files but no duplicates. You
may assume that there are no duplicates in an input file.

Your program should use a JFileChooser to let the user select both the input files and the
name of the destination file. Your program should be written as an application that extends JFrame
even though you will never display anything in its window. ❖

⬛➡ EXERCISE 19.8.3

The Internet Daytime Protocol is almost certainly the simplest of all Internet application protocols.
If a client machine creates a Socket connected to port 13 on a Daytime Protocol server, the server
sends back a description of the current date and time in text format. The client doesn't have to
send anything to the server. It just has to create the Socket. Internet protocols are described by
documents called RFCs (short for Request for Comment). A complete description of the Daytime
Protocol can be found in RFC 867 (which can be easily located by searching for "RFC 867" with
a good search engine).

Write a program that acts as a Daytime Protocol client. Your program should display a
JTextArea, a JTextField, and a JButton in its window. The user should enter the name
of a Daytime Protocol server in the JTextField. When the button is pressed, the program
should connect to the server and display any text sent back in the JTextArea. A sample of what
this might look like is shown in Figure 19.36.

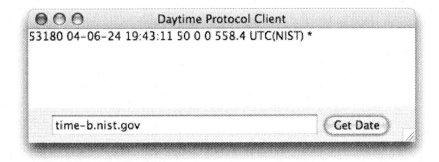

Figure 19.36 Sample output from program for Exercise 19.8.3

Network address	Geographical address
time-a.nist.gov	NIST, Gaithersburg, Maryland
time-b.nist.gov	NIST, Gaithersburg, Maryland
time-a.timefreq.bldrdoc.gov	NIST, Boulder, Colorado
time-b.timefreq.bldrdoc.gov	NIST, Boulder, Colorado
time-c.timefreq.bldrdoc.gov	NIST, Boulder, Colorado
utcnist.colorado.edu	University of Colorado, Boulder
time.nist.gov	NCAR, Boulder, Colorado
time-nw.nist.gov	Microsoft, Redmond, Washington
nist1.symmetricom.com	Symmetricom, San Jose, California
nist1-dc.glassey.com	Abovenet, Virginia
nist1-ny.glassey.com	Abovenet, New York City
nist1-sj.glassey.com	Abovenet, San Jose, California
nist1.aol-ca.truetime.com	TrueTime, AOL facility, Sunnyvale, California
nist1.aol-va.truetime.com	TrueTime, AOL facility, Virginia

Figure 19.37   Addresses of Daytime Protocol servers

When you are ready to test your program, try one of the Daytime Protocol servers listed in Figure 19.37. This list, like most things about the Internet, may become inaccurate with the passage of time. We obtained it from http://www.boulder.nist.gov/timefreq/service/its.htm, *where one is likely to be able to find an updated list.*

CHAPTER 20

Searching and Sorting

e all spend too much time searching for things and trying to arrange or sort our possessions so that it is easier to find them when they are needed. Computers spend lots of time searching and sorting as well. For example, consider a search engine like Google. First it must traverse all of the web pages it can find, keeping track of a variety of information. Then it must sort this information into some kind of order, so it is easier to search through it all when a user types in a query.

In this chapter we will look at the problems of searching and sorting. These operations are so important that efficient versions of these algorithms are typically supplied in software libraries. One important reason for examining these algorithms is to illustrate that very clever ones can be extremely efficient compared to naive ones. Another reason is to provide an example of how we can analyze an algorithm's complexity, which will help provide estimates on the comparative running time of different algorithms.

We begin by looking at linear and binary searches and their complexity. We then look at three sorting algorithms, the selection, insertion, and merge sorts. While there are many others, these three are sufficiently different to suggest the variety of algorithms possible.

20.1 Searching

Many of kinds of searches can be done on a computer. For example, one can look for the highest value in a list of numbers, or the most frequently occurring value in a list. We have seen examples of searches based on such global criteria in Chapter 14.

Other kinds of searches involve matching some specified external criterion. Examples include:

* Looking in a collection for a specific value (e.g., looking for your name in a list of prize winners).
* Looking for a value with a specific property (e.g., finding the object on a computer screen containing the mouse location).
* Looking for a record in a database (e.g., finding all CDs by a given artist).
* Searching for all occurrences of a value in a collection (e.g., finding all occurrences of the word "search" in this text).

In this section, we will focus on the first kind of search in this list, but exercises will investigate some of the other kinds of searches listed above.

20.1.1   Linear Searches

We begin with a very simple linear search of an array. For simplicity we will consider an array of `ints`, though it is easy to modify the code for arrays of values of other types. One place where such a search would be useful is in an example described in Section 14.6. There an array held the bib numbers of racers in the order in which they finished. By searching for a given bib number, we could determine the place in which that racer finished.

We will use the variable `key` for the element to be found. For this search we will simply start looking through the array from the beginning, returning the index in the array of the key if it is found and −1 if it is not. As in Section 14.6, we select −1 because that is not a legal index in the array, and hence will be clearly recognizable as an indication that `key` is not in the array. The method is shown in Figure 20.1.

The code for the method is straightforward, using a `for` loop to iterate through all of the elements of the array. Notice that we return the value of `index` as soon as we find a match. If we complete the `for` loop without finding `key` then −1 is returned.

20.1.2   Recursive Processing of Arrays

In Section 12.1.2 we wrote recursive classes representing lists of URLs. These classes included a recursive method `contains` that determined whether or not a given URL was in the list. We can

```
/*
 * Search for key in array.  Return the first index of key, or
 * -1 if it is not found.
 */
public int search( int[] array, int key ) {
  for ( int index = 0; index < array.length; index++ ) {
    if ( key == array[index] ) {
      return index;
    }
  }
  return -1;
}
```

Figure 20.1 Iterative version of linear search of an int array

```
/*
 * Search for key in array recursively. Return the first index of
 * key between array[start] and the end of the array,
 * or -1 if it is not in there.
 */
private int recSearch( int[] array, int key, int start ) {
    if ( start >= array.length ) {
        return -1;
    } else if ( key == array[start] ) {
        return start;
    } else {
        return recSearch( array, key, start + 1 );
    }
}
```

Figure 20.2 Recursive version of linear search

also write recursive methods on arrays, including one that will perform a linear search of a list. Because an array is not a recursively defined structure, this recursive method is more like those given in Section 12.2.

A method, recSearch, that performs a recursive version of linear search is shown in Figure 20.2. This recursive method takes three parameters rather than two. The extra parameter, start, indicates where in the array the method should begin the search.

The body of the method is quite simple. There are two base cases. The first is when start is beyond the end of the array. In that case, -1 is returned to indicate that the key is not in the array. The second base case is when key is at position start, in which case start is returned as the location of key. If both of those fail, then we recursively search starting from the next position in the array.

We can apply the rules listed in Section 12.2 in order to convince ourselves that this method works correctly. We've already seen that we have two base cases. We can measure the complexity of a recursive call by the number of elements between start and the end of the array. Each recursive call is simpler, because we begin one place farther along the array, and hence the number of elements left to be searched is one smaller.

Finally, if we assume that recSearch(array, key, start + 1) works correctly, then it is easy to argue that the method works correctly.

* If start is beyond the last element of the array, then key is clearly not in the array between array[start] and the end of the array, so returning -1 is appropriate.
* If key is equal to array[start], then start is clearly the index of first element equal to key between array[start] and the end of the array.
* Otherwise the method invocation returns the results of recSearch(array, key, start + 1). If recSearch(array, key, start + 1) returns -1, then, by our assumption on the correctness of that invocation, we know that key does not occur between array[start+1] and the end of the array, and hence does not occur between array[start] and the end of the array. On the other hand, if it returns the non-negative integer n, then we

know that n is the first index of `key` between `array[start+1]` and the end of the array. Because `array[start]` is not `key`, n must be the first index of `key` between `array[start]` and the end of the array.

This recursive version of search requires more parameters than nonrecursive versions. Generally we prefer to have the same parameters for calls to the recursive and nonrecursive versions of a method, as the user should not have to worry about whether the method body is recursive or iterative. We can accomplish this by providing an extra method whose only job is to make an initial call of the recursive method with the extra parameters. The method `recSearchStart` below is such a method.

```
/*
 * Search for key in array.  Return the first index of key, or
 * -1 if it is not found.
 */
public int recSearchStart( int[] array, int key ) {
    return recSearch( array, key, 0 );
}
```

All that it does is call `recSearch` with the `array` and `key` parameters as well as with a 0 as the initial value of the `start` parameter.

It follows from our discussion above that the call to `recSearch` will return the index of the first occurrence of `key` between `array[0]` and the end of the array. In other words, it will return the index of the first occurrence of `key` in the entire array. It returns -1 if it is not found. Thus this method has exactly the same description (and set of parameters) as the `search` method in Figure 20.1.

➡ EXERCISE 20.1.1

Suppose the array passed to the search methods only has relevant entries in the first `size` entries. How would you change the iterative and recursive search methods to accommodate this more restricted search? Notice that you will need to add a new parameter for the size.

➡ EXERCISE 20.1.2

Suppose you wish to find the index of the last entry of `key` in an array. How would you change the iterative and recursive search methods to accommodate this search?

➡ EXERCISE 20.1.3

Suppose that instead of searching an array of `int`s, you are to search an array of class C for a key of class K. Assume there is a method `getKey()` of C that returns a value of class K. How must you modify the code of the iterative and recursive search methods to handle these types of data?

20.1.3　Complexity of Linear Search

With operations like searching that may potentially be run on very large collections of data, it is often important to predict how much time the task may take. An obvious way to do this would be to time the operations on a wide variety of data. However, there are several problems with this.

Not surprisingly, different results will be obtained on different computers. A brand new top-end computer will run faster than an older computer. If the operation is running on a larger data set, it will usually take more time to finish. Moreover, running the same method on the same computer may not always result in the same time on data of the same size. Finding an element at the beginning of a long list will take much less time than looking for an element that is near the end or that is not there. Also, different times will be obtained depending on how many other tasks the computer is performing at the time the method is run.

As a result we generally prefer measures that will help predict relative timing, rather than provide an exact time in milliseconds. For searches, we are most interested in counting the number of comparisons with the key that must be made in a list of size n in order to find the key (or determine that it is not there). Of course, we may be lucky and find the key as the first element of the array, but that kind of "best-case" information is less useful than two other measures: "worst-case" and "average-case" behavior.

For the iterative search in Figure 20.1, it is easy to see that the key is compared with every element in the array until a match with the key is found. The largest number of comparisons ("worst-case") is obtained when the key either is not in the array or only occurs as the last element of the array. In that case n comparisons are made if the array has n elements. The same number of comparisons are made in the recSearch method, as it also compares the key with successive elements until it finds the key element.

Calculating the average number of comparisons made requires some assumptions on our part. First, we assume that the element being searched for occurs exactly once in the list. Second, we assume that the key element is equally likely to be in any of the places in the array. Under those assumptions, the key element is as likely to be in the first half as the second, so it is reasonable to assume that on average we will find it about halfway through the array, so roughly $n/2$ comparisons will be required on average.

20.1.4   Binary Searches

In this section we show how we can find elements with fewer comparisons if we assume that the array to be searched is in order. For simplicity, in the rest of this section we will assume that the array to be searched is in *nondecreasing order*. That is, successive elements either get larger or stay the same in moving from left to right through the array. Similar results can be obtained if the array is in nonincreasing order.

If the array is ordered, the intuitive analysis above on the average number of comparisons for a linear search can be extended to cases where the key does not occur in the list, because if we reach an element in the array that is larger than the key, then we know the key cannot possibly occur in the rest of the list. For example, suppose the key is 10 and the array holds the integers:

    2 4 8 11 15 22 24 25 34 42 47 53 54 72 93 97

Once we get to the 11 in the array, it is clear that 10 will not occur in the rest of the array. On the other hand, the knowledge that the list is in order does not really reduce the number of comparisons made with a linear search if the key is in the array. As a result, if the array is in order, the number of comparisons is roughly $n/2$ whether the key is in the array or not.

We can take advantage of the ordering of an array in a more clever way to greatly reduce the number of comparisons necessary to find a key. To illustrate, if you are interested in looking up someone's name in a large city's telephone directory, you would never consider using a linear search. Because we know the names in the directory are listed in alphabetical order, if we are looking for Sally Miller, we would open the phone book and start looking roughly in the middle of the book, rather than starting at the first listing on the first page. Of course, if the name was Joe Aardvark or Mary Zyzygy, we would start our search closer to the beginning or the end of the book. It turns out that we do not need even that amount of cleverness to search more efficiently in an ordered list.

To illustrate our strategy, let's examine the simple game of guessing a number in a given range. When a guess is made, the person who chose the number must respond with either yes (the guess is correct), too high (the actual number is smaller than the guess), or too low (the actual number is larger than the guess).

Suppose the game is being played by Alice and Bob, where Alice chooses a number between 1 and 7, inclusive, and Bob has to guess the number. In the absence of any other knowledge about how Alice chose the number, the optimal strategy is to always guess the middle of the range. Thus Bob's first guess should be 4, because there are three numbers above and three below 4 in the range of numbers. Suppose Alice responds that the guess is too low. Then Bob knows that her number is between 5 and 7. If Bob next guesses 6, then he either gets it right or reduces the range to only one remaining element. Thus in the worst case Bob can name the correct number by his third try. Notice that the same strategy works on all intervals of the same size. For example, if the range is from 9 to 15, then Bob can guess the number in at most three tries again. (The first guess is 11.)

It is easy to see that at most three guesses are necessary, no matter what number Alice chooses in that range. Now suppose Alice and Bob play a new game where the range of numbers is from 1 to 15. As before, Bob's strategy is to pick the number, 8, in the middle of the range. If he gets it right, then the game is over. If he gets it wrong, however, he will have reduced the range to 7 numbers. That is, if Alice says, "Too high," then he will know the number is in the range from 1 to 7, and if she says, "Too low," then he will know the number is in the range from 9 to 15. However, we saw above that if the range has size 7, then we can guess the number in at most 3 guesses. Thus after the first guess in this game, Bob will either have gotten it correct or will have reduced the range to one that he can solve with at most 3 guesses. Thus with a range of size 15 Bob can always win with at most 4 guesses.

It is easy to see that a range of size 31 (leaving ranges of 15 on either side after a first guess of 16) can be won with 5 guesses, a range of size 63 can be won in 6 guesses, and a range of size 127 can be won in 7 guesses. Jumping a bit farther ahead, a range of size 1023 can be won in 10 guesses. In general we can show that a number in a range of size at most $2^n - 1$ can always be found in at most n guesses.

We can write this in a slightly different way using logarithms base 2. Recall that $log_2 m = n$ if and only if $m = 2^n$. Let $k = 2^n - 1$. Then $n = log_2(k + 1)$. Substituting these into our answer above, we see that a number in a range of size at most k can always be found in at most $log_2(k + 1)$ guesses.

We will use exactly this strategy of searching by always guessing the middle element to find a key in an ordered array. In this case, we choose the middle element by choosing the element whose index is in the middle of the range of elements to be searched. This search strategy is called a *binary search* because it involves reducing the search range roughly in half after each guess. The general technique of dividing a problem into smaller pieces so that only problems whose size is a fraction of the original have to be solved is called a *divide-and-conquer* strategy.

```
/*
 * Recursive binary search for key in array. Return the index of key,
 * or -1 if it is not found.
 */
public int recBinarySearch( int[] array, int key ) {
    return binarySearch( array, key, 0, array.length - 1 );
}

/*
 * Recursive binary search for key in array[start..end]. Return the
 * index of key, or -1 if it is not found.
 */
private int binarySearch( int[] array, int key, int start, int end ) {
    if ( start > end ) {
        return -1;
    } else {
        int middleIndex = (start + end) / 2;
        if ( key == array[middleIndex] ) {
            return middleIndex;
        } else if ( key < array[middleIndex] ) {
            return binarySearch( array, key, start, middleIndex - 1 );
        } else {  // key > array[middleIndex]
            return binarySearch( array, key, middleIndex + 1, end );
        }
    }
}
```

Figure 20.3 Recursive binary search

We will provide both iterative and recursive methods to perform binary searches. This time we will begin with the recursive solution, as we believe it is easier to understand. The code for the recursive binary search is given in Figure 20.3. As before, we have a starter method that makes the initial call of the binarySearch method. In explaining this code, we informally use the shorthand array[start..end] to stand for the range of values between array[start] and array[end].

Let's ignore the first comparison between start and end for the moment and just focus on the else clause. We first calculate middleIndex as the index of the element halfway between start and end. If there are an odd number of elements in the range, it will be exactly the middle element. However, if there are an even number of elements, there is no middle element, so we will use the index of the element just below the halfway point.

As in the number-guessing game above, we then compare the key to the element in the middle of the array. If that element matches the key, then we return the index. If key is smaller than that element, then key cannot occur among the elements in array[middleIndex..end]. As a result, we return whatever index is obtained by doing a recursive binary search of array[start..middleIndex-1]. Similarly, if key is greater than the middle element, then we know that `key` cannot occur in the elements `array[start..middleIndex]`, so we return the index obtained by doing a binary search of `array[middleIndex+1..end]`.

For example, suppose that `key` is 22 and the array holds the integers shown below. To aid our explanation we place the indices of the array above the actual elements.

```
index:            0 1 2  3  4  5  6  7  8  9 10 11 12 13 14
array[index]:     2 4 8 11 15 22 24 25 34 42 47 53 54 72 93
```

We begin with `start` = 0 and `end` = 14. Then `middleIndex` = 7. Because 22 < `array[7]` which has the value 25, we evaluate `binarySearch( array, 22, 0, 6 )`. That is, `start` remains at 0, while `end` becomes 6. Now `middleIndex` is calculated as 3, and we find 22 > `array[3]` = 11. Thus we evaluate `binarySearch( array, 22, 4, 6 )`. With `start` = 4 and `end` remaining at 6, we calculate `middleIndex` = 5 and find 22 = `array[5]`. Thus 5 is returned through all of the method calls as the final answer.

Now, what happens if we look for something that is not in the array? For example, suppose we look for key 21 rather than 22. As above, we get to the call of `binarySearch( array, 21, 4, 6 )`, we calculate `middleIndex` = 5, but now we find 21 < `array[5]`. Thus we call `binarySearch( array, 21, 4, 4 )` (searching a range including only one value). We calculate `middleIndex` = 4 and find that 21 > `array[4]`. Thus we call `binarySearch ( array, 21, 5, 4 )`. But now the value of `start` is greater than the value of `end`, indicating that there are no elements left to search. Now we can understand why we have the initial comparison, `start` > `end`, at the beginning of the method body. If that comparison is `true`, then there is no hope of finding the key, and we return −1.

Because we are using exactly the same strategy as in the number-guessing game, the binary search of an array with k elements takes at most $2 * log_2(k + 1)$ comparisons, as one test for equality and one test for < is made for each calculation of the middle index. In particular, a binary search of 1000 elements takes at most 20 comparisons ($2 * log_2(1001) < 20$), while a binary search of one million elements takes at most 40 comparisons ($2 * log_2(1,000,001) < 40$). This is quite an improvement over the one million comparisons that would be needed with a linear search. When you consider that the Google search engine had cataloged about 4 billion web pages by the end of 2003, you can see that having a fast way of searching through a lot of data would be quite valuable.

It is also possible to write an iterative binary search algorithm by imitating what happens with the recursive version. The iterative algorithm is shown in Figure 20.4. In comparing this method with the recursive version we see that the two extra parameters, `start` and `end`, have been replaced by local variables with the same names. The outermost `if-else` statement testing if there are any elements left to be searched has been replaced with a `while` loop, where the code to be executed when no elements are left is now placed just after the end of the loop. Inside the `while` loop the logic is the same as before, but rather than placing recursive calls in the two `else` clauses, we simply update the variables corresponding to those that were changed for the recursive calls. For example, in the `else if` clause, the call of `return binarySearch ( array, key, start, middleIndex - 1 )` is replaced by an assignment updating `end`, the only parameter that was changed in the recursive call. Similarly, the call in the final `else` clause is replaced by an assignment to `start`, the only parameter changed in the corresponding recursive call. If you trace through the execution with our previous example of an array where we are looking for a key value of 22, you will see that essentially the same computations and comparisons are made as in the recursive case.

```
/*
 * Iterative binary search for key in array. Return the index of key,
 * or -1 if it is not found.
 */
public int iterBinarySearch( int[] array, int key ) {
    int start = 0;
    int end = array.length-1;
    while ( start <= end ) {
        int middleIndex = (start + end) / 2;
        if ( key == array[middleIndex] ) {
            return middleIndex;
        } else if ( key < array[middleIndex] ) {
            end = middleIndex - 1;
        } else {  // key > array[middleIndex]
            start = middleIndex + 1;
        }
    }
    return -1;
}
```

Figure 20.4 Iterative binary search

Table 20.1 Worst-case number of comparisons to search an array of size n

n	linear (unsorted)	binary (sorted)
7	7	6
15	15	8
31	31	10
127	127	14
1023	1027	20
1,048,575	1,056,783	40

In order to compare the relative efficiency of linear and binary search, we can use the calculations we made earlier of the number of comparisons necessary to search an array. Table 20.1 records the number of comparisons necessary in the worst case to do a linear search on an unsorted array and to do a binary search on a sorted array of size n. While the differences are minor for small arrays, when the array has size greater than 1000, the differences are significant. In general, doubling the size of the array only increases the number of comparisons by 2 for binary search versus doubling the number of comparisons for linear search.

EXERCISE 20.1.4

Show by example that the binary search algorithm will not return the correct answer if the array is not in order.

➠ EXERCISE 20.1.5

Suppose that instead of searching an array of ints, *you are to search an array of class* C *for a key of class* K. *Assume there is a method* getKey() *of* C *that returns a value of class* K. *You may also assume that* K *has a method:*

```
public int compareTo( K other )
```

where compareTo *returns a negative integer, zero, or a positive integer depending on whether the receiver is less than, equal to, or greater than* other. *How must you modify the code of the recursive binary search method to handle these types of data?*   ❖

20.2   Using Preconditions and Postconditions

Throughout this text we have followed the practice of writing comments before methods in order to provide informal specifications of what the methods do. However, to make it clearer to users under what conditions a method may be invoked and what the results of executing the method will be, it is useful to provide more formal comments in terms of *preconditions* and *postconditions*.

A precondition specifies the minimum conditions that must be true to guarantee that an invocation of the method will work correctly. For example,

```
// PRE: The elements of array are in nondecreasing order
```

would be the precondition for recBinarySearch. As in this example, the precondition is written as a comment that begins with PRE:. It is the responsibility of the caller to ensure that the precondition is true before calling the method. The precondition of a method typically mentions all of the parameters of the method and may also include information about the state (instance variables) of the object containing the method. The precondition for recBinarySearch does not mention the parameter key, because any integer value may be used for key.

A postcondition guarantees what will be true when a method has completed execution. The postcondition is only guaranteed to be true if the preconditions were satisfied before the method was called. A postcondition for the method recBinarySearch is:

```
// POST:  Returns -1 if key does not occur in array.  Otherwise
//          returns the index of an occurrence of key in array.
```

The programmer of the method is responsible for guaranteeing that the postcondition holds after the method execution if the precondition was true before the method began execution.

We typically put these together as the comments before the method declaration as follows:

```
/*
 * PRE: The elements of array are in nondecreasing order
 * POST:  Returns -1 if key does not occur in array.  Otherwise
 *          returns the index of an occurrence of key in array.
 */
public int recBinarySearch( int[] array, int key ) {...}
```

Sometimes there is no precondition necessary, and in that case the PRE clause can be omitted entirely. Notice that the method iterBinarySearch has exactly the same pre- and postconditions. Because they both also have exactly the same parameters, one can be substituted for the other in a program without affecting the program results.

You should think of the combination of precondition and postcondition as a contract between the caller and the provider of a method. If the caller guarantees that the preconditions are true before the method body begins execution, then the provider of the method guarantees that the postcondition will be true after the method execution completes. If the precondition is false before the method is invoked, then the method body is under no obligation to ensure that the postcondition will be true afterward.

This contract allows a clear division of labor and allows a programmer who wishes to use a method to clearly understand what is required and what the results will be of a method without needing to look at the code in the method. This makes the job of the programmer easier, because it is one less thing that she or he needs to worry about. For the rest of this chapter we will be careful to include preconditions and postconditions for all methods.

▶ EXERCISE 20.2.1

Write the precondition and postcondition for the method binarySearch that is called by recBinarySearch.   ❖

20.3 Sorting

In the last section we saw that the binary search algorithm was much more efficient than linear search if it was applied to an ordered array. In this section we examine three algorithms for sorting the elements in an array. The first two require approximately $n^2/2$ comparisons to sort the list, while the last requires significantly fewer. As before, we develop the algorithms for arrays of int, but it will be easy to change them to handle arrays of any type as long as the elements can be compared to each other.

The algorithms presented in this chapter will sort the elements of an array to be in nondecreasing order. It would be easy to change each of these algorithms to instead sort in nonincreasing order by replacing occurrences of < by > and vice versa. As a result, we won't show these variants.

20.3.1 Selection Sort

Probably the simplest way to think about sorting a collection of objects is to first find the smallest element and put it in the first available slot, then find the second smallest element and put it in the next slot, and so on. The *selection sort* works in exactly this way, with only two minor changes. First, we start with the 0th element, since that really is the first element in the array. Second, we wish to perform the sort in place. That is, rather than copying all of the data to a new array, we want to simply move data around the same array, using as little extra space as possible.

We present the iterative version of the selection sort first. It is shown in Figure 20.5. The method iterativeSelectionSort itself is quite simple, as we have pushed off most of the details into the helper methods. Let's talk about these first.

The method swap(i,j) simply interchanges the values in array[i] and array[j]. It uses a local variable, temp, to keep track of the value of array[i] temporarily so that it is not lost

```
// POST:  Elements of array have been rearranged into nondecreasing order.
public void iterativeSelectionSort( int[] array ) {
  for (int slotToFill = 0; slotToFill < array.length - 1; slotToFill++) {
    // INVARIANT: array[0..slotToFill-1] contains the slotToFill smallest
    // elements of the original array, sorted properly while the remaining
    // elements of the original array are in array[slotToFill..arrray.length-1].
    int smallestIndex = indexOfSmallest( array, slotToFill );
    swap( array, smallestIndex, slotToFill );
  }
}

/*
 * PRE: startIndex must be valid index for array
 * POST: returns an index of the smallest value in
 *       array[startIndex..array.length-1]
 */
private int indexOfSmallest( int[] array, int startIndex ) {
  int smallIndex = startIndex;
  for (int nextIndex = startIndex + 1;
      nextIndex < array.length;
      nextIndex++) {
    // INVARIANT: array[smallIndex] is the smallest element
    // of array[startIndex..nextIndex-1]
    if (array[nextIndex] < array[smallIndex]) {
      smallIndex = nextIndex;
    }
  }
  return smallIndex;
}

/*
 * PRE: i and j must be valid indices for array
 * POST: The values stored in array[i] and array[j] have been interchanged.
 */
private void swap( int[] array, int i, int j ) {
  int temp = array[i];
  array[i] = array[j];
  array[j] = temp;
}
```

Figure 20.5 Iterative selection sort and helping methods

when that variable is updated in the following statement. It is then associated with array[j] in the last line of the method.

➡ EXERCISE 20.3.1

Why does the following code not work for the body of swap?

```
array[i] = array[j];
array[j] = array[i];
```

Show what happens when you call swap(array, 0, 1) *with this alternative code when* array[0] = 5 *and* array[1] = 7. ❖

The method indexOfSmallest iterates through the indices of array[startIndex.. array.length-1], keeping track of which one corresponds to the smallest element seen so far. The comment inside the for loop of indexOfSmallest states that array[smallIndex] is the smallest element of array[startIndex..nextIndex-1]. This statement indicates an *invariant* of the method. An invariant is a statement that is true every time execution passes through that point.

Let's convince ourselves that the invariant is true every time execution passes through that point. We do this by essentially presenting an argument via mathematical induction, though we hope you will find the argument compelling even if you haven't seen proofs by mathematical induction.

The first time the invariant is encountered during execution is immediately after nextIndex is initialized with startIndex+1. Thus array[startIndex..nextIndex-1] only refers to the single element array[startIndex]. Because smallIndex was initialized with startIndex, the invariant is clearly true.

Next we see that if the invariant is true before executing the body of the loop, then the invariant will remain true at the end of the loop body. So, assume that array[smallIndex] is the smallest element of the array elements in array[startIndex..nextIndex-1]. Because we are going to execute the body of the loop again, we also know that nextIndex < array.length, and hence nextIndex is a valid index of array.

The body of the loop checks to see if array[nextIndex] is smaller than array[smallIndex], and if so, updates smallIndex with nextIndex. In this case, nextIndex was smaller than the smallest element of array[startIndex..nextIndex-1], so it is clearly the smallest element of array[startIndex..nextIndex]. On the other hand, if the condition is false, then array[nextIndex] is no smaller than array[smallIndex], so the latter element is the smallest in array[startIndex..nextIndex]. Either way, array[smallIndex] is the smallest in array[startIndex..nextIndex]. Thus when execution goes to the top of the for loop and nextIndex is increased by one, it will again be the case that array[smallIndex] is the smallest element in array[startIndex..nextIndex-1].

Every time execution returns to the top of the loop, the invariant will continue to be true. As a result, when the for loop finally terminates with nextIndex equal to array.length, we know that array[smallIndex] will be the smallest in array[startIndex.. array.length-1], as desired.

Now we are ready to see why iterativeSelectionSort correctly sorts the array. Each time through the for loop in iterativeSelectionSort, the index of the smallest remaining element in the unsorted part of the array—the elements in array[slotToFill..array.length-1]— is assigned to smallestIndex, and the element associated with smallestIndex is swapped with the element currently in array[slotToFill]. This results in the smallest remaining element being placed in array[slotToFill]. Because this is done for each slot in the array, starting with 0, at the end all of the array elements are placed in order.

Notice that the value of slotToFill during the last execution of the body of the for loop will be array.length-2. The reason is that after the second-to-last element is filled, there is only one element remaining, the largest element of the array, and it must be in the correct spot.

⊪➡ EXERCISE 2D.3.2

Give an argument like that used for the invariant in indexOfSmallest *to show that the invariant in the method* iterativeSelectionSort *is always true.*   ❖

Let's look at the operation of selection sort on the following array, elts, of 5 integers:

```
index:          0  1  2  3  4
elts[index]:    48 62 38 51 15
```

If we execute iterativeSelectionSort(elts), then slotToFill is initialized to 0 as we enter the for loop. We begin by finding the index, 4, of the smallest element, 15, in elts[0..4]. We then swap that element with the one in elts[0], leaving us with:

```
index:          0  1  2  3  4
elts[index]:    15 62 38 51 48
```

We have indicated with italics the portion of the array that has already been processed—in this case, just the element with index 0.

We next increment slotToFill so it has value 1. We find the index, 2, of the smallest element in elts[1..4]. Then elts[2] is swapped with elts[1], leaving:

```
index:          0  1  2  3  4
elts[index]:    15 38 62 51 48
```

We increment slotToFill again so it has value 2. We find the index, 4, of the smallest element in elts[2..4]. Then elts[2] is swapped with elts[4], leaving:

```
index:          0  1  2  3  4
elts[index]:    15 38 48 51 62
```

We increment slotToFill again so it has value 3. We find the index, 3, of the smallest element in elts[3..4]. Then elts[3] is swapped with elts[3], which has no effect.

```
index:          0  1  2  3  4
elts[index]:    15 38 48 51 62
```

When slotToFill is incremented again, it will be equal to 4, which is array.length-1, so the for loop will terminate and elts is now in order.

```
index:          0  1  2  3  4
elts[index]:    15 38 48 51 62
```

The development of an alternative, recursive method to perform a selection sort is straightforward. To sort the elements in a list, array, starting at the element with index start proceed as follows:

- If there are less than two elements in array starting with index start, then array is already sorted. You don't need to do anything.
- Otherwise, find the smallest element in the portion of array beginning with index start and swap it with array[start].
- Selection sort the elements in the array, starting with the element with index start+1.

```
public void sort( int[] array ) {
   recursiveSelectionSort( array, 0 );
}

/*
 * PRE: startIndex must be a valid index for array
 * POST: array[startIndex..array.length-1] has been rearranged and
 *        is in nondecreasing order.
 */
private void recursiveSelectionSort( int[] array, int startIndex ) {
   if (startIndex < array.length - 1) {
      // Find smallest element in rest of array
      int smallest = indexOfSmallest( array, startIndex );

      // Move smallest to index startIndex
      swap( array, smallest, startIndex );

      // Sort everything in the array after startIndex
      recursiveSelectionSort( array, startIndex + 1 );
   }
}
```

Figure 20.6 Recursive selection sort.

The Java code for two methods to accomplish the selection sort can be found in Figure 20.6. As with the searches, the first is a starter method that calls recursiveSelectionSort and specifies that the sort begins with the element at index 0. Notice that the code of recursiveSelectionSort follows the outline above and uses the methods indexOfSmallest and swap listed in Figure 20.5.

We can convince ourselves in the usual way that recursiveSelectionSort is correct. If startIndex >= array.length - 1, then there is at most one element to be sorted, and a list of size 1 (or 0) is already in order. For the recursive case, where the number of elements to be sorted is 2 or more, we assume that recursiveSelectionSort works properly on lists smaller than the current one. The method moves the smallest element of array[startIndex..array.length-1] to startIndex and then sorts array[startIndex+1.. array.length-1] through a recursive call. By assumption, that recursive call orders the elements of array[startIndex+1..array.length-1] properly. Moreover, the element at startIndex is less than or equal to all elements in the rest of the list. Thus all elements in array[startIndex..array.length-1] are in order.

⇒ EXERCISE 20.3.3

Suppose that instead of sorting an array of ints, *you are to sort an array of class* C *based on a key of class* K. *Assume there is a method* getKey() *of* C *that returns a value of class* K. *You may also assume that* K *has a method:*

```
public int compareTo( K other )
```

where compareTo *returns a negative integer, zero, or a positive integer depending on whether the receiver is less than, equal to, or greater than* other. *How must you modify the code of the iterative or recursive selection sort method to handle these types of data?* ❖

20.3.2 Complexity of Selection Sort

Because we are often interested in sorting large collections of data, it would be useful to have some indication of how long it would take to sort a large array using the selection sort. As with our searching methods, we calculate the total number of comparisons necessary to sort an array. Suppose the original array has n elements, where $n > 1$. It takes $n - 1$ comparisons to find the smallest element of the array (compare the first with the second, compare the smaller of those with the third, etc.). Once the smallest element has been placed in the first slot, we must find the smallest of the remaining $n - 1$ elements, which takes $n - 2$ comparisons. We continue with successively smaller arrays, with the searches requiring $n - 3$ comparisons, $n - 4$ comparisons, ..., all the way down to the last pass through the array, when there are only two elements and it takes only a single comparison to determine the smallest element.

If we add up all of these comparisons, we get $S = (n - 1) + (n - 2) + \cdots + 1$. We can calculate this sum by using the following clever observation. If we reverse the order of the terms on the right side of the sum and then add the two equations, we get:

$$
\begin{aligned}
S &= (n - 1) + (n - 2) + \cdots + \quad 1 \\
S &= \quad 1 \quad + \quad 2 \quad + \cdots + (n - 1) \\
\hline
2S &= \quad n \quad + \quad n \quad + \cdots + \quad n
\end{aligned}
$$

The right side of the equation consists of $n - 1$ copies of n added together, equaling $n(n - 1)$. Thus we get $2S = n(n - 1)$ and hence the total number of comparisons of elements to do a selection sort on an array of size n is given by:

$$
S = \frac{n(n - 1)}{2}.
$$

Notice that the number of comparisons of elements is the same regardless of the initial order of the elements. Thus the time for the average case is the same as for the worst case. In the next section we introduce a different sorting algorithm whose worst-case time is the same as that for selection sort, but whose average number of comparisons is half of that for selection sort.

20.3.3 Insertion Sort

Insertion sort is an algorithm that many people use when they need to sort a relatively small collection of cards or papers by hand. A very informal iterative explanation of the algorithm is as follows:

- Start with a single card in your hand.
- Take the second card and put it either before or after the first card so that the two cards are in order.
- Insert the third card into the ordered collection of the first two cards so that all three are now in order.
- Insert the fourth card in the appropriate place in the existing ordered collection of three cards so that all four are in order.
- Continue until all cards have been inserted properly.

```
/*
*    POST: array is sorted into nondecreasing order
*/
public void iterInsertionSort( int[] array ) {
    for (int index = 1; index < array.length; index++)  {
        // array[0..index-1] are in order
        insertNext( index, array );
    }
}


/* PRE: array[0..lastIndex-1] is in nondecreasing order and
*        lastIndex < array.length,
* POST: array[0..lastindex] contains the same elements as it did before
*        the execution of the method, but now is in nondecreasing order.
*/
private void insertNext( int lastIndex, int[] array ) {
    // Search for first elt (from rear) <=  array[lastIndex]
    int position = lastIndex-1; // index where element should be
                                // inserted
    while (position >= 0 && array[lastIndex] < array[position]) {
        position--;
    }
    position++;     // position is now where array[lastIndex] belongs

    // Move array[position .. lastIndex-1] to make room for
    // array[lastIndex] in array[position]
    int tempElt = array[lastIndex];
    for (int moveIndex = lastIndex-1;
        moveIndex >= position; moveIndex--) {
            array[moveIndex+1] = array[moveIndex];
    }
    // Insert element into proper position
    array[position] = tempElt;
    // Now array[0..lastIndex] are in order
}
```

Figure 20.7 Iterative insertion sort

The method iterInsertionSort in Figure 20.7 implements this approach to sorting. It follows the outline above, inserting the element in array[1] into the list consisting only of array[0], then inserting array[2] into the list consisting of array[0..1], and so on until finally, array[lastIndex] is inserted into array[0..lastIndex-1], where lastIndex is array.length - 1.

The precondition of the helper method insertNext states that array[0..lastIndex-1] is already in order. The first four lines of the method (up to and including the position++ statement) result in setting position to be the index where array[lastIndex] will be inserted. That is, array[position-1] <= array[lastIndex] < array[position]. In order to insert the new element there, we must move all of the elements in array[position..lastIndex-1] up one slot in the array. That is the purpose of the for loop. Finally, the new element, which has been saved in tempElt, is placed into array[position]. Because array[0..lastIndex-1] was in order before the sort, array[0..lastIndex] will be in order at the end.

 EXERCISE 20.3.4

Trace the operation of insertion sort on the following array, elts, *of 5 integers:*

index: 0 1 2 3 4
elts[index]:   48 62 38 51 15

❖

EXERCISE 20.3.5

What will the value of position *be after the* while *loop if* array[lastIndex] *is smaller than all elements of* array[0..lastIndex-1]*? Explain why this results in* array[lastIndex] *being inserted in the correct place in* array.

❖

EXERCISE 20.3.6

Determine invariants to be placed at the top of the while *and* for *loops in* insertNext. *Argue as we did with* indexOfSmallest *in Section 20.3.1 that each is always true when execution returns to the top of the loop.*

❖

A recursive description of insertion sort is even simpler. To do an insertion sort of a collection of *n* elements:

* If there are one or fewer items, stop, as you are done.
* Otherwise perform an insertion sort of the first $n - 1$ elements; then insert the *n*th element in order.

The implementation of the recursive insertion sort is in Figure 20.8. The code for the method recursiveInsertionSort is just as described above. The method iSort calls recursiveInsertionSort with the correct initial value for the parameter lastIndex.

EXERCISE 20.3.7

Provide an argument that the method recursiveInsertionSort *works correctly. You may assume that* insertNext *is correct. That is, if the preconditions are met before executing the method, then the postconditions will be true at the end.*

❖

20.3.4 Complexity of Insertion Sort

As with the searches and selection sort, we wish to compute the complexity of insertion sort. We will see that in the worst case, the number of comparisons necessary to perform an insertion sort on an array of size *n* is the same as for a selection sort. However, on average the insertion sort does only about half of the comparisons.

```
/*
 * POST: array is sorted into nondecreasing order
 */
public void iSort( int[] array ) {
    recursiveInsertionSort( array, array.length-1 );
}


/*
 * PRE: lastIndex must be valid index for array
 * POST: The elements originally in array[0..lastIndex] have been
 *       rearranged to be in nondecreasing order
 */
private void recursiveInsertionSort(int[] array, int lastIndex) {
    if (lastIndex >= 1) { // 2 or more elements
        // Sort everything in the array up to lastIndex
        recursiveInsertionSort( array, lastIndex - 1 );

        // Insert element at lastIndex into array[0..lastIndex-1]
        insertNext( lastIndex, array );
    }
}
```

Figure 20.8 Recursive insertion sort

Most of the complexity in the algorithm comes from the `insertNext` method. When
`insertNext` is called, there are `lastIndex` elements in the array before `lastIndex`. In the
worst case, the `while` loop will have to compare `array[lastIndex]` with every one of those
elements. On average, however, the new element will go in the middle of the list, so only half as
many comparisons will be needed.

If we look at the iterative version of the algorithm, we see that `insertNext` is called with
`index` starting out at 1 and increasing up to `array.length-1`. Thus, if `array.length` is
n, the total number of comparisons in the worst case is $1 + 2 + \cdots + (n-1) = n(n-1)/2$ as
before. However, in the average case, the number of comparisons in each call of `insertNext` is
half of the worst-case time, so the sum is as well. Thus in the average case, the total number of
comparisons is closer to $n(n-1)/4$.

EXERCISE 20.3.8

*We have been analyzing the worst-case behavior of methods, but it can also be interesting to look
at best-case behavior.*

a. *Suppose all of the elements in an array are already in order. How many comparisons are
necessary to perform an insertion sort?*

b. *Does the number of comparisons necessary to perform a selection sort depend the ordering
of the array?*

c. *Suppose a list is partially sorted. Which of the two sorts is likely to be much faster?* ❖

⟫ EXERCISE 20.3.9

Compare the number of assignment statements involving elements of the array that are executed in the selection sort with the number in the insertion sort. If we take those into consideration, how will that affect the comparison of the selection sort with the insertion sort? Run experiments on large randomly selected arrays to check the time complexity of each. ❖

20.3.5 Merge Sort

We've now seen two sorts whose worst-case complexity is $n(n - 1)/2$. We will see in this section that we can do significantly better if we try another divide-and-conquer strategy.

Before introducing this new sort, let's go back and think about how the recursive versions of the selection and insertion sorts worked on an array with n elements. With the selection sort we first did some work—found the smallest element, and then made a recursive call, performing a selection sort of the remaining $n - 1$ elements of the array. With the insertion sort we first made a recursive call, performing an insertion sort of the first $n - 1$ elements of the array, and then did some work—inserted the last element where it belonged in the already sorted elements. In each case the nonrecursive work involved roughly n comparisons, and roughly $n - 1$ recursive calls were made. Given this, it isn't surprising that the total number of comparisons for each sort was roughly a constant times n^2.

When we presented the recursive version of the linear and binary searches, we discovered that making recursive calls on half as many elements was much more efficient than making recursive calls with only one less element. We can use this idea to create more efficient sorts as well. We will design an algorithm so that successive recursive calls will be on half as many elements as the previous call. Of course, unlike the case of binary search where we essentially threw away half the elements after each comparison, we must sort all of the elements of the array. However, a divide-and-conquer strategy like this will reduce the depth of the recursion from n layers of calls to $log_2 n$.

The *merge sort* will be similar to the recursive insertion sort in that we make recursive calls and then do work to fix up things at the end. The general idea is as follows:

* If there are fewer than two elements to sort, you are done.
* Otherwise recursively (merge) sort the elements in the first half of the array and then sort the elements in the second half of the array.
* Merge the elements in the sorted first half with the elements in the sorted second half.

With the insertion sort, we were able to insert the last element after having sorted all but the last element. For the merge sort, because we have broken the list into two pieces, we must merge the two sorted sublists. For example, suppose we have two sorted sublists held in the same array:

```
index:          0  1  2  3  4     5  6  7  8  9
elts[index]:   15 38 48 51 62     7 12 23 49 88
```

We will merge them into a new array, `sorted`. We start by comparing the first elements of each half of `elts`, `elts[0]` and `elts[5]`. The smallest, `elts[5]`, is assigned to `sorted[0]`.

```
index:           0  1  2  3  4  5  6  7  8  9
sorted[index]:   7  -  -  -  -  -  -  -  -  -
```

Below we indicate the elements of elts that have been moved to sorted by writing them in italics:

```
index:           0   1   2   3   4        5  6   7   8   9
elts[index]:     15  38  48  51  62       7  12  23  49  88
```

We now compare the leftmost remaining elements of the halves of elts, elts[0] and elts[6], determining that elts[6] is the smallest. We move that into the next slot in sorted:

```
index:           0  1  2  3  4  5  6  7  8  9
sorted[index]:   7 12  -  -  -  -  -  -  -  -
```

The original array is now:

```
index:           0   1   2   3   4        5  6   7   8   9
elts[index]:     15  38  48  51  62       7  12  23  49  88
```

Comparing the remaining leftmost elements of elts, we determine that elts[0] should be moved next:

```
index:           0  1  2  3  4  5  6  7  8  9
sorted[index]:   7 12 15  -  -  -  -  -  -  -
```

The original array is now:

```
index:           0   1   2   3   4        5  6   7   8   9
elts[index]:     15  38  48  51  62       7  12  23  49  88
```

We leave it to the reader to finish this example of merging two lists. Notice that once one of the halves has been completed, the remaining elements of the other half must be moved into the remaining slots in sorted.

The Java code for the recursive merge sort can be found in Figure 20.9, and is essentially the same as that explained above. As before, the initial call to mergeSort will be made by the method sort, which adds parameters to indicate the beginning and end of the range of elements to be sorted, as well as a "helper" array that will be used when merging the two sorted lists together.

The merge method is presented in Figure 20.10. First, all of the elements from array are moved into tempArray in preparation for merging them together and placing them in the correct order in array. The indices indexLeft and indexRight keep track of the subscripts of the smallest unmerged elements in the left and right halves of the array. At each step in the first while loop the smallest of the two elements at indexLeft and indexRight is moved into array[target]. After the element has been moved, the index of the element that was moved is increased by 1 and the target index is also increased by 1.

This continues until all of the elements in one of the two halves has been used up. At that point, all of the remaining elements in the other half must be copied from tempArray into array. Because one of the halves has already been exhausted, only one of the last two while loops'

```
// POST: elts of array are rearranged in nondecreasing order
public void sort( int[] array ) {
    // Create tempArray for use in merging
    int[] tempArray = new int[array.length];
    mergeSort( array, 0, array.length-1, tempArray );
}

/*
 * PRE: left and right are valid indices of array with left <= right - 1.
 *       tempArray.length == array.length
 * POST: elts of array[left..right] are rearranged in nondecreasing order
 */
public void mergeSort( int[] array, int left, int right,
                       int[] tempArray ) {
    if (left < right) {
        int middle = (right + left) / 2;
        mergeSort( array, left, middle, tempArray );
        mergeSort( array, middle + 1, right, tempArray );
        merge( array, left, middle, right, tempArray );
    }
}
```

Figure 20.9   Recursive merge sort

bodies is actually executed. Whichever is executed simply copies the remaining elements from that half to array.

EXERCISE 20.3.10

Assuming that merge *does what it is supposed to, apply the rules presented in Section 12.2 to show that when the merge sort terminates, all of the elements will be in order.*

EXERCISE 20.3.11

As noted in the text, only one of the last two while *loop bodies is actually executed. Why is there not a conditional statement that selects which of the two* while *loops should be executed?*

EXERCISE 20.3.12

The merge *method is traditionally presented as an iterative method, as it was here. However, we could write it recursively. Write a recursive* merge *method. As usual, the new* merge *method should call the recursive method, which will need to be provided with extra parameters corresponding to* indexLeft *and* indexRight.

Hint: *The initial* for *loop and the final two* while *loops should be done in the main* merge *method, not the recursive method.*

```
/*
 * PRE: 0 <= left <= middle <= right < array.length, tempArray.length
 *      == array.length, and array[left..middle] and array[middle+1..right]
 *      are both in nondecreasing order.
 * POST: The two halves (array[left..middle] and array[middle+1..right])
 *       have been merged together so that array[left..right] is now in
 *       nondescending order
 */
private void merge( int[] array, int left, int middle, int right,
                    int[] tempArray ) {
  int indexLeft = left;          // Keeps track of next elements to be merged
  int indexRight = middle + 1; // from left and right halves.
  int target = left;             // Slot to put next element merged.

  // Copy both pieces into tempArray.
  for (int i = left; i <= right; i++) {
    tempArray[i] = array[i];
  }


  // Merge values while there are elements left in both halves.
  while (indexLeft <= middle && indexRight <= right) {
    if (tempArray[indexLeft] < tempArray[indexRight]) {
      array[target] = tempArray[indexLeft];
      indexLeft++;
    } else {
      array[target] = tempArray[indexRight];
      indexRight++;

    }
    target++;
  }


  // Move any remaining elements from the left half.
  while (indexLeft <= middle) {
    array[target] = tempArray[indexLeft];
    indexLeft++;
    target++;
  }


  // Move any remaining elements from the right half.
  while (indexRight <= right) {
    array[target] = tempArray[indexRight];
    indexRight++;
    target++;
  }
}
```

Figure 20.10 Merge method used in merge sort

20.3.6 Complexity of Merge Sort

Let's analyze the complexity of the merge sort algorithm by counting the number of comparisons of elements in the array. Notice that no comparisons of elements are performed in either the sort or mergeSort method. All comparisons are performed in the merge method.

During the merge method, every time we compare two elements of tempArray, we place one of them in the next slot in array. When we have exhausted all of the elements in one half of the array, the remaining elements in the other half are simply moved into array without any further comparisons being necessary. Thus merging the two halves of an array with a total of k elements takes at most $k - 1$ comparisons.

Let $T(n)$ be the function that will tell us how many comparisons must be made to perform a merge sort on an array of size n in the worst case. For example, $T(0) = T(1) = 0$, because no comparisons are necessary to sort an array of size ≤ 1. $T(2) = 1$, because only one comparison is necessary to merge sort an array of size 2.

Because merge sort is so regular, it is possible to write down a formula relating the number of comparisons to merge sort an array of size n with the number of comparisons to merge sort smaller arrays. Suppose n is even. Then to merge sort an array of size n, we must merge sort the two halves, which have size $n/2$, and then merge the two halves together. Thus,

$$T(n) \leq T(n/2) + T(n/2) + (n - 1) = 2 * T(n/2) + (n - 1)$$

The inequality arises because $n - 1$ is an upper bound on the number of comparisons to merge together the two halves of the array of size n. Because we are only computing upper bounds anyway, we can simplify the above formula to

$$T'(n) = T'(n/2) + T'(n/2) + n = 2 * T'(n/2) + n$$

by replacing the $n - 1$ by the even larger n and replacing the inequality by "=". $T'(n)$ thus represents an upper bound on the number of comparisons needed to merge sort an array of size n. As before, we will set $T'(0) = T'(1) = 0$.

Table 20.2 contains the values of $T'(n)$ for values of n that are powers of 2. Notice that the values calculated on the right-hand side can be rewritten in the form $n * (log_2 n)$, so it seems reasonable to hypothesize that

$$T'(n) = n * (log_2 n)$$

for n a power of 2. We could prove this using mathematical induction, but we omit that proof here. Instead we simply verify that with this formula, $T'(0) = T'(1) = 0$, as required, and that,

Table 20.2 Table of values of $T'(n)$ measuring the complexity of merge sort

n	$T'(n)$
$1 = 2^0$	$0 = 1 * 0$
$2 = 2^1$	$2 * T(1) + 2 = 2 = 2 * 1$
$4 = 2^2$	$2 * T(2) + 4 = 8 = 4 * 2$
$8 = 2^3$	$2 * T(4) + 8 = 24 = 8 * 3$
$16 = 2^4$	$2 * T(8) + 16 = 64 = 16 * 4$
$32 = 2^5$	$2 * T(16) + 32 = 160 = 32 * 5$
$\ldots$	$\ldots$
$n = 2^k$	$2 * T(n/2) + n = n * k = n * (log_2 n)$

if n is even,

$$2 * T'(n/2) + n = 2*(n/2) * (log_2 n/2) + n$$
$$= n * ((log_2 n) - (log_2 2)) + n$$
$$= n * ((log_2 n) - 1) + n$$
$$= n * (log_2 n)$$
$$= T'(n)$$

With some extra work, we could also show that $n * (log_2 n)$ is an upper bound on the number of comparisons in merge sorting an array of size n for all $n > 0$, including those that are not powers of 2.

━━▶ EXERCISE 20.3.13
━━━

In the binary search, the $log_2 n$ in the count of the total number of comparisons made arose because that is the number of times that an array of size n can be split in half. Give an intuitive explanation of why the $log_2 n$ factor appears in the complexity of merge sort. ❖

━━▶ EXERCISE 20.3.14
━━━

Write a merge sort program using the following approach:

   a. *Interchange the first and second elements if they are out of order, similarly with the third and fourth, fifth and sixth, etc.*
   b. *The first pair of elements are in order, as are the second pair. Merge those together so the first four elements are now in order. Do the same with the third and fourth pairs of elements, etc.*
   c. *The first four elements are in order, as is the second quadruple. Merge those into an ordered array of eight elements. Continue merging other quadruples in pairs.*
   d. *Continue merging successively longer groups until all of the elements are in order.*

One challenge in writing a method to do this is that you cannot easily merge runs of elements in place. Instead, you must merge them into another array. Use an array like `tempArray` *in the recursive merge sort to merge runs of elements. You can then interchange the roles of the original array and* `tempArray` *when you have finished a pass through the entire array.* ❖

20.4 Impact of the Complexity of Searching and Sorting

Table 20.3 lists the average number of comparisons necessary to sort an array of size n with the selection, insertion, and merge sorts. The selection sort always take the same number of comparisons, no matter what the initial ordering is of the array. On the other hand, the insertion and merge sorts depend on that initial ordering. As a result, we averaged the number of comparisons for several randomly chosen initial orderings of arrays to obtain the numbers for the insertion and merge sorts. The worst-case time for the insertion sort is the same as for the selection sort. In the

Table 20.3   Average number of comparisons
to sort an array of size *n*

n	Selection	Insertion	Merge
20	190	116	64
40	780	416	166
100	4,950	2,565	542
1000	499,500	245,132	8709

best case (for a previously sorted array) the number of comparisons is essentially equal to the size
of the array.

It is clear from the table that the average number of comparisons necessary using the insertion
sort is roughly half that for the selection sort. Because selection sort is of roughly n^2 complexity,
multiplying the size of the input by k results in multiplying the number of comparisons by k^2. For
example, doubling the size of the input (e.g., from 10 to 20) results in the number of comparisons
quadrupling. Similarly a tenfold increase in the size of the input (e.g., from 100 to 1000) results
in a hundredfold increase in the number of comparisons. Roughly the same increases hold for the
insertion sort.

Because the merge sort is an $n * (log_2 n)$ sort, the number of comparisons grows more slowly
than selection and insertion sorts. Thus when the array size doubles from 20 to 40, the number of
comparisons goes up by a factor of about 2.5. When the array size increases from 100 to 1000,
the number of comparisons goes up by a factor of 15. As a result, the number of comparisons
for merge sort grows much more slowly than that for selection and insertion sort. As a result,
selection sort on an array of size 1000 takes 50 times as many comparisons as a merge sort on an
array of the same size.

EXERCISE 20.4.1

Binary search is much faster than linear search, but binary search requires a sorted array.

  a. *Does it makes sense to merge sort an array and then do a binary search rather than doing
  a linear search? Provide the total number of comparisons to do each of these on an array
  of size n.*
  b. *How many searches must be made on the same array of size n to make the number of
  comparisons the same with either doing a series of linear searches or doing a single merge
  sort and then all binary searches?*
  c. *Given this information, why does the phone company sort all of the names in the phone
  book?*

20.5   Summary

In this chapter we examined linear and binary searches, as well as selection, insertion, and merge
sorts. For all algorithms aside from the merge sort we introduced both iterative and recursive
algorithms. We introduced the use of pre- and postconditions to specify the behavior of methods,
invariants to prove the correctness of algorithms, and we discussed the complexity of algorithms.

If an array has n elements, then roughly n comparisons are necessary to perform a linear search in the worst case, while $n/2$ are necessary on average if the element to be found is actually in the array. Binary searches only work on sorted arrays, but result in many fewer comparisons. Roughly $2 * log_2 n$ comparisons are required on a sorted array of size n.

Both the selection and insertion sorts require roughly $n^2/2$ comparisons on an array of size n in the worst case, while the merge sort requires $n * (log_2 n)$ comparisons on an array of size n.

20.6 Chapter Review Problems

EXERCISE 20.6.1

In Section 20.1.3, we claimed that the average number of comparisons to find the key using linear search was roughly n/2 under the assumption that key *occurs exactly once in* array *and that* key *is equally likely to be in any of the places in the array. A careful calculation of the average time complexity under the above assumptions would require us first to calculate the number of comparisons necessary for each of the n possible positions where* key *might occur, add these up, and then divide by n to compute the average. Use this to prove that the average number of comparisons to find the key using linear search is (n + 1)/2 if the array has n elements.* ❖

EXERCISE 20.6.2

Let elts *be an array of length 5 with values 89, 23, 15, 93, 7. Hand simulate each of the following sorts on the array* elts:

   a. *Iterative selection sort.*
   b. *Recursive selection sort.*
   c. *Iterative insertion sort.*
   d. *Recursive insertion sort.*
   e. *Recursive merge sort.* ❖

EXERCISE 20.6.3

Suppose that it takes 1 second to perform a selection sort on an array of 1000 elements. Approximately how long will it take to perform a selection sort on an array of 2000 elements? 5000 elements? 1,000,000? ❖

21

Introduction to Object-Oriented Design

By now you're probably fairly comfortable with class implementation. That is, given a description of a class that includes instance variables and method headers, you can fill in the necessary details to make the class usable. But how would you go about designing a class from scratch? If you were given the description of a problem, how would you determine what classes should be defined? This chapter will provide you with a methodology for analyzing problem descriptions so that you can begin to design classes of your own.

In this chapter we will discuss *object-oriented design*. We begin with a discussion of objects and their properties and show how entities in the real world can be mapped to Java objects. These objects provide *abstractions* of their real-world counterparts. We then introduce a simple programming problem and take you through the process of designing a program to solve it. Next we make that problem a bit more complex and discuss extensions to our original solution. Finally, we discuss the notion of *encapsulation* and illustrate its importance.

21.1 What Is Object-Oriented Design?

The design methodology that we introduce here is called *object-oriented design*. An important first step in object-oriented design is to recognize that very often our software is mimicking the real world. We can take inspiration from the real world to help us decompose a problem into objects. We can analyze the real-world objects to identify their properties and behavior, and we can then model those in our software. For example, recall the `Timer` object from Section 6.4. The timer object, `stopWatch`, behaved very much like a (simple) real stopwatch. Similarly, the `FallingBall` objects from Chapter 9 behaved very much like falling balls.

An object is an entity that provides an *abstraction* in our program. We call it an abstraction because we can use an object without knowing how it is implemented. That is, we abstract away the details and understand the object at a higher level. This follows naturally from the way we use objects in the real world. For example, you can use a real stopwatch (or a telephone, computer, car, etc.) without understanding exactly how it works.

A goal in object-oriented design is to define classes that provide this type of abstraction. A well-designed class will allow you (or another programmer) to construct and use objects without having to know precisely how they work.

21.2 Properties and Behaviors

As we just noted, entities in the real world often serve as the inspiration for objects in our programs. By analyzing real-world objects and carefully considering their properties and behaviors, we identify the specific aspects that we need to model in our programs. To illustrate this idea, we will take you through the process of designing the `Timer` class from Section 6.4.

21.2.1 Modeling Properties of Objects

We begin by considering the properties of the entity that we would like to model—in this case, a stopwatch. Typically a stopwatch has

* buttons that control various types of functionality, such as resetting, timing, stopping, and so on,
* a display area,
* internal memory to store the timing information to be displayed.

We can think of the properties of an object as the *nouns* and *adjectives* that describe it. That is, the properties include the various components of the object as well as its physical appearance.

Next we need to consider which of those properties really need to be modeled. We can go about this by considering the ways in which the object will be used. In the program from Section 6.4, a `Timer` is simply used to tell us whether we have clicked on a target object quickly enough. The stopwatch itself is never actually displayed. As a result, we need not worry about modeling a stopwatch's physical appearance. Instead, there's just one property of interest to us—the stopwatch's internal memory.

While a program provides a model of the real world, we always need to make decisions about how realistic our model should be. While we typically strive for some degree of realism, there is no need to model properties that are irrelevant to our application.

Once we have decided which properties to model, we need to decide how to model them. We model properties with instance variables and constants. Since the only information that we need to remember in the stopwatch's memory, elapsed time, is calculated by finding the difference between the current time (which is easily accessible) and some fixed start time, we only need to model the start time. So we declare a single instance variable, `startTime` to be of type `double`.

21.2.2   Modeling Behavior

In addition to having various properties, objects also have various behaviors. That is, they have certain types of functionality. For example, stopwatches can

- reset to zero,
- report elapsed time,
- stop,
- resume timing after being stopped.

We can think of behaviors as the *verbs* that describe an object's actions.

As with properties, we will want to model some of these behaviors, but not necessarily all of them. In our program, there is no need for the stopwatch to suspend timing or to resume from a suspended state. All we need to be able to do is report elapsed time and reset.

How do we model behavior? We define a method for each type of behavior that we want to allow. Therefore, we define one method to reset and another to report elapsed time. We call them `reset` and `elapsedMilliseconds`, respectively. We also define another method, `elapsedSeconds` to report elapsed time in seconds.

21.3   Design Fundamentals

Now that you have some basic understanding of the fundamental idea of modeling real-world objects by considering their properties and behaviors, let's step through a complete design process. In this section, we will aim to design and later implement a simple version of the shell game. The game works as follows: three cups are placed (upside-down) on a table. Player 1 places a marble under one of the cups, letting Player 2 see where it has been placed. The first player then shuffles the cups, while the second player watches. Player 2 then has to guess where the marble is.

Our simple program will work very much like this. We will assume there are two players. The game will begin with three cups drawn in a window, along with one marble, as shown in Figure 21.1. Player 1 will place the marble into one of the cups by dragging the marble on top of a cup. When the mouse is released, the marble has been dropped into the cup, so it is no longer visible. Player 1 then shuffles the cups by dragging them around the screen. When Player 1 stops moving the cups, Player 2 will guess which cup contains the marble. Clicking on a cup will result in the cup being raised and the marble being shown, if it's there.

21.3.1   Design Step 1: Identify the objects to be modeled

Given this specification of the desired program behavior, let's think about the classes that will be needed in our implementation. As discussed above, object-oriented design seeks to model the

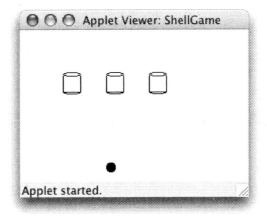

Figure 21.1 User interface for a simple shell game

world. So the entities described in the problem definition help to give us clues about the types of objects needed in the program. The description above mentions three types of objects: players, cups, and a marble. We do not need to model the players, since those will be the users of our software (though we'll certainly want to provide them with an interface). However, we do need to model the cups and the marble.

21.3.2 Design Step 2: List the properties and behaviors of each type of object

Next we need to list the properties and behaviors of each type of object we identified. We'll begin by analyzing the properties and behaviors that our cups need to have. Each cup has two important properties:

* It has an image on the screen that represents it.
* It is either empty or it contains a marble.

Of course, cups in the real world have these properties and more, but we only need to model the properties that are necessary for our program. Also, since we can get location information from the graphical image that represents a cup, we don't have to model the location separately.

Each cup also needs to behave in specific ways:

* A cup can be moved.
* A cup can have a marble placed in it.
* A cup can be raised to reveal its contents, if any.

An outline for the Cup class is shown in Figure 21.2. The first block of comments lists the properties to be modeled; the second block lists the behaviors.

We'll define a Cup class, modeling the cup properties with instance variables and the cup behaviors with methods. Before we do so, however, let's continue our analysis by considering the

```
// A class to represent a cup used in the Shell Game
public class Cup {

    // List of cup properties
    // Graphical image of the cup
    // Whether the cup contains the marble

    // List of cup behaviors
    // Move the cup
    // Place a marble in the cup
    // Reveal the contents of the cup; remove marble from cup,
    // if there
}
```

Figure 21.2   First level of design for a Cup class: properties and behaviors

marble. The marble has the following properties:

* It has an image on the screen that represents it.
* It is either in a cup or it is not.

Let's think about the second of these properties. There is certainly a relationship between the cups and the marble. A cup can contain the marble, and the marble can be contained in a cup. But do we really need to model this both from the cup's perspective and from the marble's perspective? It turns out that we do not need to. We will choose to model containment from the cup's perspective. That is, we will leave our design for the Cup class as in Figure 21.2. The only property of the marble that we will model is its image.[1]

Now let's consider the ways in which our marble must behave:

* A marble can be moved.
* A marble can be dropped into a cup.
* A marble can be removed from a cup.

As with the cup, we'll want a class that will allow us to model the marble properties and behaviors. An outline of the Marble class is given in Figure 21.3.

Before we go any further in filling in the details about cups and marbles, we need to consider one more class. We need to provide a user interface to allow our two players to play the shell game. We will define a controller class that will set up the program and that will allow the players to interact with it. The controller should allow a player to drag a cup or a marble. It should also allow a player to click on a cup to release its contents. Like cups and marbles, games have descriptive properties. If we think of the controller class as the game itself, we notice that it has an appearance—three cups and a marble on a canvas. In addition, the state of the game at any given time depends upon the position of the mouse and whether a player has currently selected a cup or the marble with the mouse.

---

[1] The reason for making this choice is that it seems more natural to us to think of cups as vessels that can either contain something or not.

```
// A class to represent a marble
public class Marble {
    // List of marble properties
    // Graphical image of the marble

    // List of marble behaviors
    // Move the marble
    // Place the marble in a cup
    // Remove the marble from a cup
}
```

Figure 21.3   First level of design for a Marble class: properties and behaviors

```
// Controller class for a simple Shell Game
public class ShellGame extends WindowController {

    // Properties that describe the shell game
    // Three cups
    // A marble
    // The current position of the mouse
    // Whether a marble or cup has been selected
    // Which object has been selected

    // Allowable game behaviors
    // Place three cups and a marble on the canvas
    // Move a cup or marble
    // Show contents of a cup
}
```

Figure 21.4   First level of design for a ShellGame class: properties and behaviors

The outline for the controller class, which needs to extend `WindowController`, is given in Figure 21.4.

21.3.3   Design Step 3: Model properties with instance variables

Now we can begin to refine our design. We start by thinking about the instance variables that will allow us to model the properties of each type of object. For a cup, we decided above that we wanted to have an image that would represent it in a window. If we intend to make the cups look like those in Figure 21.1, then we need several variables to represent the various components of the image. We will represent the outline of a cup with a `FramedRect` and two `FramedOvals`, one for the top and one for the bottom. The white interior will be represented by a `FilledRect` and two `FilledOvals`. We will name the instance variables `sideFrame`, `topFrame`, `bottomFrame`, cupSide, cupTop, and cupBottom, respectively. In addition to providing the right appearance for a cup, each of these graphical objects can be moved, which will allow us to implement the necessary functionality for a cup.

➡ EXERCISE 21.3.1

Why do we need all six instance variables to draw a cup? In particular, why do we need the three filled shapes? ❖

Next, we want to model whether a cup is empty or not. We can do this by declaring a variable, containsMarble, of type boolean. If the cup contains the marble, containsMarble will be true; it will be false otherwise.

Through this process, we refine our initial outline of the Cup class, as in Figure 21.5.

Now we go through the same process for the Marble class. The one property of a marble that we want to model is its appearance on the canvas. Since a marble is simply a filled circle, we will declare a variable, theMarble, to be of type FilledOval, as in Figure 21.6.

Next we turn to the ShellGame controller class. As shown in Figure 21.7, we declare three variables of type Cup and one of type Marble to keep track of the objects on the canvas.

We know that mouse positions are described by Locations, but when we think about the mouse position a bit more, we realize that we don't actually need to explicitly keep track of the current mouse position. The event-handling methods such as onMousePress and onMouseDrag, which will be essential for manipulating the objects on the canvas, already give us the current mouse location. We recall, however, that in order to drag an object on the screen, it is useful to know the previous mouse location. So we declare a variable, lastMousePos, of type Location

```
// A class to represent a cup used in the Shell Game
public class Cup {

    // List of cup properties

    // Graphical image of the cup
    private FilledRect cupSide;
    private FilledOval cupTop, cupBottom;
    private FramedRect sideFrame;
    private FramedOval topFrame, bottomFrame;

    // Whether the cup contains the marble
    private boolean containsMarble;

    // List of cup behaviors
    // Move the cup
    // Place a marble in the cup
    // Reveal the contents of the cup; remove marble from cup, if there
}
```

Figure 21.5 Second level of design for a Cup class modeling properties with instance variables

```java
// A class to represent a marble
public class Marble {

    // Marble properties
    // Graphical image of the marble
    private FilledOval theMarble;

    // Marble behaviors
    // Move the marble
    // Place the marble in a cup
    // Remove the marble from a cup
}
```

Figure 21.6   Second level of design for a Marble class: modeling properties with instance variables

```java
// Controller class for a simple Shell Game
public class ShellGame extends WindowController {

    // Properties that describe the shell game

    // Three cups
    private Cup cup1, cup2, cup3;

    // A marble
    private Marble theMarble;

    // The last position of the mouse
    private Location lastMousePos;

    // Whether a marble has been selected
    private boolean marbleSelected;

    // Which cup has been selected
    private Cup selectedCup;

    // Allowable game behaviors
    // Place three cups and a marble on the canvas
    // Move a cup or marble
    // Show contents of a cup
}
```

Figure 21.7   Second level of design for a ShellGame class: modeling properties with instance variables

and change the comment to reflect our decision. This illustrates an important part of the design process. While there is a well-defined set of steps to guide the process of design so that the decisions made at each step are logical, we still need to be open to the idea of modifying earlier decisions.

Next, we need to know which object, if any, has been selected by the player. Note that we need to keep track of a few different pieces of information here. First, we need to know whether an object has been selected. Second, we need to know which one, if any. There are many possibilities here. In order to make our design as simple as possible, we will define two variables. The first, the `boolean` variable `marbleSelected`, tells us whether the marble has been selected. Since there is only one marble, if the value of this variable is `true`, then we immediately know which object is selected. The second variable, `selectedCup`, tells us which, if any, cup has been selected. If `selectedCup` is not null, then we not only know that a cup is selected, but we also know which one.

21.3.4 Design Step 4: Model behaviors with methods

Next we turn to the behaviors that we need to model for each class of objects in our program. Remember that we will be modeling behaviors with methods. In this part of the design process, however, we won't concern ourselves with the details of those methods. Instead, we will focus on the method headers (or *signatures*), since they describe the interface between the various entities in our program.

Beginning with the Cup class, we see that we need three methods. The first should move a cup. Since we want the caller of this method to be able to specify the direction and distance of the movement, this method will take two parameters, a displacement in the x direction and a displacement in the y direction.

We also need a method that will drop a marble into the cup. Since a marble is being dropped into the cup, we should take that as a parameter. The next method should remove the marble that is in the cup, if any. There is no need for any parameters to this method. However, this method does point out that we are missing an instance variable. If the cup contains a marble, then that marble needs to become visible to the players of the game. In order to empty itself of a marble, the cup needs to keep track of the marble that was placed into it. So we add an instance variable, `theMarble` of type `Marble`. All of our modifications to the Cup class are shown in Figure 21.8.

At this point we have just about completed our abstraction of a cup. Before going on, however, we need to add one more important element—a constructor. A constructor tells us how to create the object and how to initialize its instance variables. The parameters passed to a constructor tell us how to distinguish one object from another one of the same type, if a distinction is to be made.

When a cup is created, it will appear on the canvas, so we have to think about the information that will be necessary for placing it on the screen. We will need to know a cup's dimensions; we also need to know the canvas on which it will be placed, as well as the location on that canvas. The canvas and location need to be passed to the constructor as parameters. But what about the dimensions? In the shell game, every cup should look the same. Otherwise, it's too easy to guess which one contains the marble. So in this case, we have a choice. We can define constants in the Cup class that specify the width and height of a cup, or we can get this information through parameters to the constructor. If we do the latter, then the class that sets up the shell game will be

```
// A class to represent a cup used in the Shell Game
public class Cup {

    // Graphical image of the cup
    private FilledRect cupSide;
    private FilledOval cupTop, cupBottom;
    private FramedRect sideFrame;
    private FramedOval topFrame, bottomFrame;

    // Whether the cup contains the marble
    private boolean containsMarble;

    // The marble contained in the cup, if any
    private Marble theMarble;

    // Construct a cup on the canvas.
    // upperLeft - the upper left corner of the cup
    // width, height - the desired width and height of the cup
    // canvas - canvas on which cup is to be drawn
    public Cup( Location upperLeft,
                double width, double height,
                DrawingCanvas canvas )

    // Move the cup
    // dx, dy - displacements in the x and y directions
    public void move( double dx, double dy )

    // Place a marble in the cup
    // aMarble - marble to be dropped in
    public void dropIn( Marble aMarble )

    // Reveal the contents of the cup; remove marble from cup, if there
    public void showContents()
}
```

Figure 21.8   Third level of design for a Cup class: modeling behaviors with methods

able to control the visual appearance of the game by specifying not only where the cups should be, but how large they should be. There are reasonable arguments for making either choice, but let's pick the one that allows the width and height to be specified as parameters. The header for the constructor is included in Figure 21.8.

We now go through a similar exercise for the Marble class. Earlier we determined that we wanted to model three behaviors for a marble, which means that we need three methods. The first needs to give the marble the ability to move. As with a cup (or any graphical object you've seen in this text), we will allow the caller to specify the x and y displacements for the move.

```
// A class to represent a marble
public class Marble {

    // Graphical image of the marble
    private FilledOval theMarble;

    // Move the marble
    // dx, dy - distance to move in the vertical and horizontal directions
    public void move( double dx, double dy )
}
```

Figure 21.9 Third level of design for a Marble class: modeling behaviors with methods

A second method needs to place the marble into a cup. This should cause us to think a bit more carefully, since we already determined that placing a marble into a cup should be a behavior provided by cups. Do we really want both marbles and cups to be responsible for the action of placing a marble in a cup? In this case, the answer is no. We'll leave this responsibility to the cup. In a sense, we will think of the marble as becoming part of the cup, once it's in there. (This makes sense, since interactions with a cup affect the marble contained within it.)

Our modifications to the Marble class are shown in Figure 21.9. At this point the design is incomplete, as we have not yet provided a constructor, but it gives us enough information to see that a Marble is nothing more than a FilledOval that can move. As a result, we determine that this class really isn't necessary after all. We can simply use a FilledOval throughout our program, rather than defining a specialized Marble class. There is some risk in taking this approach. Defining a separate Marble class would make it easier to add specialized behavior to our marble in some future, more sophisticated version of the program. In this case, however, giving up this potential benefit of abstraction seems justified to keep our design a bit simpler.

Next we consider the controller class for the game. We will set up the game, as we have throughout this text, in the begin method. We will control the rest of the game by handling mouse events. It is easy to see that the onMouseClick method will cause the contents of a cup to be displayed, if the cup is not empty. Selecting and moving cups and marbles will be a little harder, though, since it will involve more than a single mouse-event-handling method. In the onMousePress method, we will determine which object, if any, has been selected. In onMouseDrag, we will move the selected object. If a marble is dragged to a cup, then in onMouseRelease we need to drop the marble into that cup. These new design details are given in Figure 21.10.

You may have noticed that our analysis of the controller class has pointed out a deficiency in the Cup class. In the controller we need to determine which, if any, object has been selected during a mouse press. So a Cup needs to tell us whether it contains a given mouse location. Therefore, we add a contains method to that class, which will have the following specification:

```
// Returns true if the cup contains the given mouse location,
// mouseLoc; returns false otherwise
public boolean contains( Location mouseLoc )
```

```
// Controller class for a simple Shell Game
public class ShellGame extends WindowController {

    // Three cups
    private Cup cup1, cup2, cup3;

    // A marble
    private FilledOval theMarble;

    // The last position of the mouse
    private Location lastMousePos;

    // Whether a marble has been selected
    private boolean marbleSelected;

    // Which cup has been selected
    private Cup selectedCup;

    // Place three cups and a marble on the canvas
    public void begin()

    // Show contents of a cup
    public void onMouseClick( Location mousePos )

    // Select a cup or marble
    public void onMousePress( Location mousePos )

    // Move a cup or marble, if one has been selected
    public void onMouseDrag( Location mousePos )

    // Drop a marble into a cup
    public void onMouseRelease( Location mousePos )
}
```

Figure 21.10 Third level of design for a ShellGame class: modeling behaviors with methods

21.3.5 Design: The Process of Refinement

Before moving on to the implementation of our design, it is useful to reflect on the process of design. Designing software is a process of *refinement*. We never begin with implementation details. We always start with the highest level of abstraction. That is, we begin by considering the objects in the program in their most general sense, abstracting away the details of implementation. At each step in the design process, we *fill in more and more of the details*. That is, we make our plan less and less abstract.

There is a second sense in which refinement occurs during the process of design. In the last section you saw that, in filling out the details, we decided to make changes to our design. In working out the details, you will often find yourself *refining and changing earlier design decisions.* As you gain practice with design, you will likely find that you can develop the design of a small program, like our shell game, without having to make significant changes along the way. But even the most experienced software designers refine their original ideas when working on large projects.

21.3.6   Filling in the Details

We can now begin to fill in the implementation details for our shell game program. Basically, this phase involves filling in the bodies of the methods specified in our design. As we will see in this section, if a method is very simple, we can write the code for the method body right away. In some cases, however, it is useful to outline the method body before plunging into the process of writing actual Java statements.

We'll begin, as before, with the Cup class. First, we consider the constructor, in which we create the cup. Creating a cup that looks like the image in Figure 21.1 is not terribly difficult, but it does require a bit of thought. We need to construct the base first, then the side, and finally the top. We also need to determine the size of the top and bottom ovals, relative to the size of the cup itself. We'll say that the top and bottom will be one-tenth the size of the cup and will define a constant HEIGHTRATIO that represents the ratio of the full cup height to its top and bottom pieces, in this case, 10.

In addition to constructing the pieces of the cup, we need to remember to initialize containsMarble to false, to indicate that the cup is empty initially. In providing the details of the constructor, it is always useful to go through each instance variable, determining how it is to be initialized. The complete Cup constructor is shown in Figure 21.11.

➡ EXERCISE 21.3.2

Why do we need to construct the components of the cup in the order specified? What happens if we construct the top first?   ❖

In addition to the constructor, there are four methods that we need to provide. The move method is straightforward, as illustrated in Figure 21.12. Moving a cup simply involves moving the various graphical objects that together make up a cup. This notion of passing the work on to other objects is called *delegation.* In addition, we move the contents of the cup along with the cup. The contains method is similarly straightforward. We simply return whether the given location is contained in one of the graphical objects that represent the cup.

➡ EXERCISE 21.3.3

The contains method in the Cup class only checks for containment in the framed components. Why don't we need to check all the pieces of the cup?   ❖

The other two methods require a bit more thought. In the dropIn method there are several things we need to take care of. First, we need to note that the cup now contains a marble, i.e., that it is no longer empty. Visually, we also have some work to do. Once a marble is dropped

```java
// A class to represent a cup used in the Shell Game
public class Cup {

    // Ratio of the cup height to its top and bottom components
    private static final int HEIGHTRATIO = 10;

    // Graphical image of the cup
    private FilledRect cupSide;
    private FilledOval cupTop, cupBottom;
    private FramedRect sideFrame;
    private FramedOval topFrame, bottomFrame;

    // Whether the cup contains the marble
    private boolean containsMarble;

    // The marble contained in the cup, if any
    private FilledOval theMarble;

    // Construct a cup on the canvas.
    // upperLeft - the upper left corner of the cup
    // width, height - the desired width and height of the cup
    // canvas - canvas on which cup is to be drawn
    public Cup( Location upperLeft, double width, double height,
                DrawingCanvas canvas ) {
        double upperX = upperLeft.getX();
        double upperY = upperLeft.getY();

        cupBottom = new FilledOval( upperX, upperY+height-height/
                                    HEIGHTRATIO, width, height*2/
                                    HEIGHTRATIO, canvas );
        cupBottom.setColor( Color.WHITE );
        bottomFrame = new FramedOval( upperX, upperY+height-height/
                                    HEIGHTRATIO, width, height*2/
                                    HEIGHTRATIO, canvas );

        cupSide = new FilledRect( upperLeft, width, height, canvas );
        cupSide.setColor( Color.WHITE );
        sideFrame = new FramedRect( upperLeft, width, height, canvas );

        cupTop = new FilledOval( upperX, upperY-height/HEIGHTRATIO,
                                 width, height*2/HEIGHTRATIO, canvas );
        cupTop.setColor( Color.WHITE );
        topFrame = new FramedOval( upperX, upperY-height/HEIGHTRATIO,
                                 width, height*2/HEIGHTRATIO,
                                 canvas );

        containsMarble = false;
    }
```

Figure 21.11 Filling in the details for a Cup class: instance variables and constructor

```
// Move the cup
// dx, dy -- displacements in the x and y directions
public void move( double dx, double dy ) {
    cupSide.move( dx, dy );
    cupTop.move( dx, dy );
    cupBottom.move( dx, dy );
    sideFrame.move( dx, dy );
    topFrame.move( dx, dy );
    bottomFrame.move( dx, dy );

    if ( containsMarble ) {
        theMarble.move( dx, dy );
    }
}

// Returns true if the cup contains the given mouse location,
// mouseLoc; returns false otherwise
public boolean contains( Location mouseLoc ) {
    return cupSide.contains( mouseLoc ) || cupTop.contains( mouseLoc ) ||
                                cupBottom.contains(mouseLoc);
}

// Place a marble in the cup
// aMarble - marble to be dropped in
public void dropIn( FilledOval aMarble ) {
    // Note that the cup now contains a marble
    // Make the marble disappear into the cup
    // Remember the marble for later
}

// Reveal the contents of the cup; remove marble from cup, if there
public void showContents() {
    // If the cup actually contains a marble
        // Show the marble
        // Note that cup no longer contains a marble
    // Lift the cup
}
}
```

Figure 21.12 Filling in the details for a Cup class: methods

into a cup, it should no longer be visible on the canvas as a separate entity. We also need to remember the marble for later, because it is, in essence, now part of the cup. Rather than immediately writing out the Java code, we write these ideas as comments, as shown in Figure 21.12. Once we have done this, the process of translating into Java should be fairly easy. The method becomes:

```
// Place a marble in the cup
// aMarble - marble to be dropped in
public void dropIn( FilledOval aMarble ) {
    // Note that the cup now contains a marble
    containsMarble = true;
    // Make the marble disappear into the cup
    aMarble.hide();
    // Remember the marble for later
    theMarble = aMarble;
}
```

As you can see, this process of *iterative refinement* helps to make design and implementation simpler, by allowing us to look at a method in broad terms before worrying about details. But it also has a very convenient side effect. The ideas that we write as comments can serve as the documentation for our method. By the time we write our method, our comments are already there!

It is worthwhile to go through the same exercise for the showContents method. In this method we have to show the contents of the cup, if it is not empty. We also need to make note of the fact that the cup no longer contains anything. Once we fill in the details, the method looks like this:

```
// Reveal the contents of the cup; remove marble from cup, if there
    public void showContents() {
    // If the cup actually contains a marble
    if ( containsMarble ) {
        // Show the marble
        theMarble.show();
        // Note that cup no longer contains a marble
        containsMarble = false;
    }
    // Lift the cup
    move( 0, -LIFT_DIST );
}
```

Note that we have added the constant LIFT_DIST that specifies the distance to lift the cup.

EXERCISE 21.3.4

In our implementation of the method showContents *we first removed the marble from the cup and then lifted the cup. Why didn't we lift the cup before removing its contents?*

Turning to the controller class, ShellGame, we proceed similarly. If a method is fairly simple, we give its details immediately. If it is more complex, we first provide an outline in the form of comments. A first level of such details is shown in Figures 21.13 and 21.14.

The begin method sets up the game by putting three cups and a marble on the canvas. Since this method does initial set-up, as a constructor does, it is useful to ask ourselves whether any other

```
// Controller class for a simple Shell Game
public class ShellGame extends WindowController {

    // Three cups
    private Cup cup1, cup2, cup3;

    // A marble
    private FilledOval theMarble;

    // The last position of the mouse
    private Location lastMousePos;

    // Whether a marble has been selected
    private boolean marbleSelected;

    // Which cup has been selected
    private Cup selectedCup;

    // Place three cups and a marble on the canvas
    public void begin() {
        // Construct three cups
        // Construct the marble
        // Initially, nothing is selected
    }
```

Figure 21.13 Filling in the details for a ShellGame class: instance variables and begin method

instance variables need initialization here. In looking over the instance variables, we determine that we should set the boolean marbleSelected to false. The details of the begin method are as follows:

```
//  Place three cups and a marble on the canvas
public void begin() {
    // Construct three cups
    cup1 = new Cup( CUP1_LOC, CUP_WIDTH, CUP_HT, canvas );
    cup2 = new Cup( CUP2_LOC, CUP_WIDTH, CUP_HT, canvas );
    cup3 = new Cup( CUP3_LOC, CUP_WIDTH, CUP_HT, canvas );

    // Construct the marble
    theMarble = new FilledOval( MARBLE_LOC, MARBLE_SIZE, MARBLE_SIZE,
                                canvas );

    // Initially, nothing is selected
    marbleSelected = false;
}
```

```
// Show contents of a cup
public void onMouseClick( Location mousePos ) {
    // If a cup has been clicked
    // Show its contents
}


// Select a cup or marble
public void onMousePress( Location mousePos ) {
    // If a cup has been selected, remember it
    // else determine whether the marble has been selected
    // Remember the mouse location for any dragging that will be done

}


// Move a cup or marble, if one has been selected
public void onMouseDrag( Location mousePos ) {
    // If a cup has been selected
        // Move the selected cup
    // else if the marble has been selected
        // Move the marble
    // Remember the mouse position for further dragging

}


// Drop a marble into a cup
public void onMouseRelease( Location mousePos )  {
    // If the marble was selected and is currently positioned
    // over a cup
        // Drop the marble into that cup
    // Nothing is selected upon release of the mouse
}
}
```

Figure 21.14   Filling in the details for a ShellGame class: mouse-event-handling methods

Notice that each time we need to specify a value as a parameter, it indicates to us the need for a named constant.

With the game set up, we can now turn to the methods that control the game. In onMousePress we determine which, if any, object has been selected. We first consider the cups. If one of them contains the mouse location, we remember it; otherwise, we check whether the marble contains the mouse location. It is not an accident that we decided to check the cups first. Remember that at times the marble will be hidden inside a cup. We wouldn't want to pick up a hidden marble! Since we only want to pick up a marble that is visibly outside of a cup, we make that the last condition that we check:

```
// Select a cup or marble
public void onMousePress( Location mousePos ) {
    // If a cup has been selected, remember it
    if (cup1.contains( mousePos )) {
        selectedCup = cup1;
    } else if (cup2.contains( mousePos )) {
        selectedCup = cup2;
    } else if (cup3.contains( mousePos )) {
        selectedCup = cup3;
    }
    else { // else determine whether the marble has been selected
        marbleSelected = theMarble.contains( mousePos );
    }
    // Remember the mouse location for any dragging that will be done
    lastMousePos = mousePos;
}
```

Note that this decision works nicely for us, but it does have one other effect we should mention. If the mouse is positioned over two overlapping objects, only one can be selected.

The last statement in onMousePress remembers the location of the mouse. As you have seen in many examples throughout this text, when an item is to be dragged, we need to remember the initial location of the mouse in order to determine how far the item must be moved with each change in the mouse position.

If an object has been selected, then the onMouseDrag method causes that object to be dragged. First we check whether a cup has been selected. If so, we move it in the usual way. Otherwise we check the marble and move it, if it's appropriate to do so. We also remember the location of the mouse, so that we can continue to move the selected item properly:

```
// Move a cup or marble, if one has been selected
public void onMouseDrag( Location mousePos ) {
    // If a cup has been selected
    if ( selectedCup != null ) {     // Move the selected cup
        selectedCup.move( mousePos.getX()-lastMousePos.getX(),
                        mousePos.getY()-lastMousePos.getY() );
    }
    // else if the marble has been selected
    else if ( marbleSelected ) {      // Move the marble
        theMarble.move( mousePos.getX()-lastMousePos.getX(),
                        mousePos.getY()-lastMousePos.getY() );
    }
    // Remember the mouse position for further dragging
    lastMousePos = mousePos;
}
```

The onMouseRelease method takes care of dropping a marble into a cup. If the selected item is the marble, and if the point of release is over a cup, then the marble is dropped into that cup. Once the marble is released, we make sure that nothing is currently selected:

```
// Drop a marble into a cup
public void onMouseRelease( Location mousePos ) {
    // If the marble was selected and is currently positioned
    // over a cup drop the marble into that cup
    if ( marbleSelected ) {
        if (cup1.contains( mousePos ) ) {
            cup1.dropIn( theMarble );
        }
        else if (cup2.contains( mousePos ) ) {
            cup2.dropIn( theMarble );
        }
        else if (cup3.contains( mousePos ) ) {
            cup3.dropIn( theMarble );
        }
    }
    // Nothing is selected upon release of the mouse
    marbleSelected = false;
    selectedCup = null;
}
```

Finally, when the mouse is clicked on a cup, we show the contents of that cup:

```
// Show contents of a cup
public void onMouseClick( Location mousePos ) {
    // If a cup has been clicked
    // show its contents
    if ( cup1.contains( mousePos ) ) {
        cup1.showContents();
    } else if ( cup2.contains( mousePos ) ) {
        cup2.showContents();
    } else if ( cup3.contains( mousePos ) ) {
        cup3.showContents();
    }
}
```

21.3.7 Summary of the Design Process

As you have seen, the process of design is one of iterative refinement. We begin by thinking about the problem at its highest level of abstraction. At each step, we provide more and more details.

The process of object-oriented design can be summarized as follows:

1. Identify the objects to be modeled in your program.
2. For each type of object identified:
    a. List its properties.
    b. List its behaviors.
3. Model properties with instance variables.
4. Model behaviors with methods. *Don't forget that you will need a constructor for each class to set up objects of that type.* Focus on the method headers. What types of information need to be passed in as parameters? What will be the result of each method invocation?
5. Fill in implementation details.
    ◆ If a method is very simple, write the Java code.
    ◆ If a method is more complex, write comments that describe the steps that need to be implemented. These will allow you to organize your thoughts without becoming bogged down in details. They will also serve as your method documentation later. If it becomes clear at this point that the desired method will be very complex, it may be appropriate to add `private` methods to the design of the class to simplify its eventual implementation.

As you fill in the details, you might find that you need to modify your design somewhat. It is not uncommon for a design to change as it develops. If you follow this set of steps, it will help you to organize your ideas, so that any design changes along the way will probably be minimal.

21.4   Incremental Testing and Debugging

The process of design follows the idea that it is better to attack a large problem first by carefully planning and then by filling in the details a little at a time. The belief is that in doing this, the programmer will avoid getting confused by the details and will, therefore, be able to produce a more coherent and bug-free program.

We can also apply these ideas to the process of testing. Rather than testing a program only when it is completely written, we can test individual components as we develop them. This typically makes the process of debugging much easier for the following two reasons:

1. Testing smaller (and therefore simpler) pieces of code generally makes it easier to find bugs.
2. When we begin to test larger, more complex components, we can rely on the behaviors of the individual, smaller entities being correct.

In this section we revisit the shell game described in the previous section, discussing how we can test the code as we write it.

21.4.1   Developing and Testing Individual Classes

In writing our shell game program, we determined that we needed two classes, one to describe Cups and one to provide a user interface to the game, i.e., the controller class. This program structure is typical. That is, we can generally expect to have a class that controls the overall behavior of the program, as well as other classes that make up individual entities in the program.

As described above, it makes sense to test individual behaviors of the objects in the program before we put everything together. For the shell game, this means testing the behavior of Cups before writing and testing the ShellGame controller class. In fact, when testing the Cup class, we can focus first on the case where a cup is empty and then consider the case where a cup contains a marble.

Let's review the process of filling in the implementation details of the Cup class, so that we can explore how you can interleave development and testing. First we wrote the constructor. Then we wrote methods for familiar behaviors (i.e., those that allow us to drag an object around on the canvas). Finally, we wrote methods that were conceptually a bit more complex.

We can follow this same plan to test and debug the Cup class. As soon as we have written the constructor, we can write a test controller that simply constructs a cup in the begin method. Because a cup is meant to appear in a certain way on the canvas, we can check that the constructor works appropriately by making a cup (or, even better, several). If they appear as we expect them to, we can move on. If not, we can make corrections before attempting to do anything else with cups.

Now we can go on to the task of implementing the methods that will allow a cup to be dragged around on the canvas, i.e., contains and move. Once they are written, we can test that they work appropriately. Notice, however, that the move method shown in Figure 21.12 refers to the marble. In particular, if the marble is contained in a cup, we want to move it; otherwise we don't. This is clearly important functionality that we need to test, but first we can check that cups can be dragged appropriately by themselves. To test this, we can write simple onMousePress and onMouseDrag methods in the test controller as shown in Figure 21.15. As dragging a cup is really no different from dragging any other graphical object, the methods in Figure 21.15 should be quite familiar.

When testing that a cup can be dragged, try pressing the mouse in a variety of different places on the cup itself. Then try pressing the mouse outside the cup, to be sure that points outside it are not somehow considered to be contained in the cup.

If all is well when we test the dragging functionality, we can move on. Specifically, we test whether a cup will show its contents appropriately when we click on it. Remember that we're testing an empty cup at this point, so nothing should actually be revealed by the cup. The OnMouseClick method that we add to our test controller looks like this:

```
public void onMouseClick( Location mousePos ) {
    if (selected) {
        cup1.showContents();
    }
}
```

Once we are convinced that an empty Cup will do the right thing, we can test whether a Cup with a marble in it behaves appropriately as well. To do this, we construct a marble (i.e., a FilledOval) in our test controller. At this point, we could add code to allow a user to select a marble and drag it around the canvas so that it can be dropped into a cup. However, it is better to simply place the marble in cup1 and see whether it is dragged around with the cup and then dropped from it, as desired. We modify the test controller as in Figure 21.16. Notice that in the begin method, we construct a Cup and then a marble in the same location. This simulates the action of the marble being dropped into the cup.

```
// Test controller class for a simple Shell Game
public class ShellGame extends WindowController {

    // constant declarations omitted
    ...

    // A cup
    private Cup cup1;

    // Whether the cup is selected for dragging
    boolean selected;

    // The last position of the mouse
    private Location lastMousePos;

    // Place a cup on the canvas
    public void begin() {
        cup1 = new Cup( CUP1_LOC, CUP_WIDTH, CUP_HT, canvas );
    }

    // Select cup for dragging
    public void onMousePress( Location mousePos ) {
        selected = cup1.contains( mousePos );
        lastMousePos = mousePos;
    }

    // Move cup if it has been selected
    public void onMouseDrag( Location mousePos ) {
        if (selected) {
            cup1.move( mousePos.getX()-lastMousePos.getX(),
                       mousePos.getY()-lastMousePos.getY() );
            lastMousePos = mousePos;
        }
    }
}
```

Figure 21.15   A simple controller to test that a cup can be dragged

21.4.2 Putting the Pieces Together: Testing the Controller

As discussed above, the process of writing implementation details for a class can (and should be) interleaved with testing it. If there are multiple types of objects in a program, each individual class should be tested and debugged before all of the pieces are put together. At first this might seem to be too much extra work. However, if you follow this procedure, you will find that it is much easier to test and debug the controller class that coordinates all of the interactions, including those

```
// Test controller class for a simple Shell Game
public class ShellGame extends WindowController {

  // constant declarations omitted...
  ...

    // A cup
    private Cup cup1;

    // A marble
    private FilledOval theMarble;

    // Whether the cup is selected for dragging
    boolean selected;

    // The last position of the mouse
    private Location lastMousePos;

    // Place a cup on the canvas
    public void begin() {
        cup1 = new Cup( CUP1_LOC, CUP_WIDTH, CUP_HT, canvas );
        theMarble = new FilledOval( CUP1_LOC, MARBLE_SIZE, MARBLE_SIZE,
                                    canvas );
        cup1.dropIn( theMarble );
    }

    // Select cup for dragging
    public void onMousePress( Location mousePos ) {
        selected = cup1.contains( mousePos );
        lastMousePos = mousePos;
    }

    // Move cup if it has been selected
    public void onMouseDrag( Location mousePos ) {
        if ( selected ) {
            cup1.move( mousePos.getX()-lastMousePos.getX(),
                    mousePos.getY()-lastMousePos.getY() );
            lastMousePos = mousePos;
        }
    }

    // Show contents of cup
    public void onMouseClick( Location mousePos ) {
        if ( selected ) {
            cup1.showContents();
        }
    }
}
```

Figure 21.16 A simple controller to test that a cup with a marble can be dragged and its contents revealed

with the user. In the shell game, if the Cup class has been thoroughly tested and debugged before we write the details of ShellGame, we can expect the testing and debugging of ShellGame to go much more smoothly. This is because we can assume that any incorrect behavior is due to the new code.

With the ShellGame class, we begin in the same way that we did with the Cup class. We first implement and test the method that sets up everything—i.e., begin. Then we move on to test other functionality.

The begin method constructs three cups as well as a marble, this time in a location separate from any of the cups. It also sets two instance variables, the boolean marbleSelected and selectedCup, which is meant to refer to a Cup, if selected. Testing begin involves confirming that all is set up properly on the canvas.

Next we complete onMousePress and onMouseDrag. To test these, we can try dragging each of the three Cups around, as well as the marble. We should also test that dragging the mouse on the canvas (without selecting an object) does nothing to break the program.

The next method to be written is onMouseRelease, which is meant to drop the marble into a cup, if appropriate. Testing this method involves dragging the marble, moving it over a Cup and then releasing it. This should make the marble disappear. Now dragging the cup with the marble should move both objects together.

Finally, we write the method onMouseClick, which reveals the contents of a cup. To test this method, try clicking in a variety of different places—on the canvas, in an empty cup, in a cup containing a marble.

Again, this process of incremental testing should make it relatively easy to localize the source of any bugs. If you are confident that you are testing thoroughly, any new bugs are likely to be the result of the most recent code that was written. This is not a guarantee, of course, but it is a reasonable assumption in many cases.

21.5   Classes That Don't Model the Real World

When we introduced object-oriented design in Section 21.1, we said that a major idea behind the approach was the notion of modeling the real world. In thinking about a problem, we would first identify the objects to be modeled. For example, in the shell game, we defined a Cup class to model the cups used in the game. But not all classes model entities in the real world. In this section we will design a more interesting shell game to help illustrate some of the ways in which classes can be defined that don't model the real world.

21.5.1   An Animated Shell Game

Our earlier shell game provided an interface that would allow two or more people to play a simple game. Now let's consider a version in which a person plays against the computer. The game begins with three cups and a marble as before. As in the earlier version, a player will place the marble into a cup, by dragging it to a cup and then releasing it. All of the shuffling will be done by the computer, however. When the player moves the mouse off the canvas and then re-enters the canvas, the shuffling begins. Once the animation ends, the player guesses which cup contains the marble by clicking on that cup. As before, if a cup is clicked, it shows its contents.

The interface described in the animated version of the game is nearly identical to the first version. The only difference is that the player has no control over the movement of the cups. Since there are such strong similarities between the two versions of the shell game, we will see that we can reuse many of our earlier design ideas.

21.5.2 Identifying Classes That Don't Represent Entities in the Real World

Let's go through the entire process of design for this new version of the shell game. We can see from the program description that our design will need to model cups and marbles. As before, we will define a Cup class; in fact, we can reuse the earlier Cup class. A simple FilledOval is all we need to represent the marble. We will surely need a controller class to provide the interface to the players. While we will need to make some modifications, we will see that the earlier controller class will provide a good starting point for the new one.

Are there any other entities that we need to model? The only real objects in the program description are the cups, marble, and player, as we have already discussed. But there are certainly some things we haven't yet considered. In particular, we haven't figured out how we will model the animation process. In Chapter 9 you learned that animations could be created by writing classes that extend ActiveObject. That is precisely how we will construct the animation here.

In identifying the need for this new class, which we will call Shuffler, we have done something that was not discussed before. We have introduced a class that does not model any kind of real-world object. People can certainly shuffle cups, but we typically don't see machines that have cup shuffling as their purpose. While object-oriented design takes inspiration from the idea of modeling real-world objects and their relationships, there are times when this won't be quite enough, as in our animated shell game. In this case, it is not the process of modeling the real world but rather it is our knowledge of the techniques for creating animations in Java that motivates the inclusion of a class in our design.

21.5.3 Completing the Design for the Animated Shell Game

We have already identified the objects to be modeled in our program. As we saw earlier in this chapter, the next step in the design process is to identify the properties and behaviors of each type of object. The marble, as before, can be modeled simply with a FilledOval. The cups in the new shell game have identical properties to the earlier cups, and they have nearly identical behaviors. As will become obvious soon, the cups need to be able to do a bit more here. The three additional behaviors that we need to model for a cup are:

* the ability to move to a specific location;
* the ability to report where the cup is currently located;
* the ability to be lowered (for instance, after it has been raised to reveal a hidden marble).

The implemented methods that perform these are given in Figure 21.17.

Next, we need to identify properties and behaviors of a cup shuffler. Identifying properties of a shuffler might seem tricky, but certainly the needed behavior is obvious. The shuffler needs to provide an animation that moves three cups on the canvas. As shown in Figure 21.18, this will be

```
// Move to a specific location
// aLoc - the new cup location
public void moveTo( Location aLoc ) {
    // Determine how far to move to get to new location
    double dx = aLoc.getX()-cupSide.getX();
    double dy = aLoc.getY()-cupSide.getY();
    // Move dx and dy in horizontal and vertical directions
    this.move( dx, dy );
}

// Return the cup's current location
public Location getLocation() {
    return cupSide.getLocation();
}

// Lower the cup
public void lower() {
    move( 0, LIFT_DIST );
}
```

Figure 21.17   Extra methods required by the Cup class

```
// A class to animate shuffling in a Shell Game
public class Shuffler extends ActiveObject {

    // Three cups to be shuffled
    private Cup cup1, cup2, cup3;

    // Construct a shuffler

    // Shuffle the cups
    public void run()
}
```

Figure 21.18   High-level design for a Shuffler class

accomplished by the run method. We know that in addition to a run method, the Shuffler class will need a constructor. The constructor will set up all that is necessary to perform the animation of the shuffling that occurs in the run method.

Before we discuss the shuffling process in any more detail, let's think a bit more about the properties of a shuffler. Since there is no such thing as a cup shuffler in the real world, it's hard to imagine how we might describe one. But there is a way to handle this. Recall from Section 21.2.1 that we can think of properties as *nouns* and *adjectives*. We also know that these will be represented by instance variables. So what instance variables will be necessary for a shuffler?

Our description of shuffling gives us some clues: The shuffler needs to provide an animation that moves three cups on the canvas. If we look at the nouns in this description, we immediately identify that the shuffler will need three instance variables for the cups to be shuffled. While we will find later that we need more instance variables, this is certainly a good start.

We can use the close relationship between the constructor and the run method to help guide us in the next phase of design, where we outline what needs to be done by each of these. Let's begin by sketching out what needs to be done in the run method. There we need to swap two cups, then swap two more, and so on. We need to do this often enough that the player of the game will lose track of which cup contains the marble. We'll do twenty swaps, and we'll define a constant, SWAPS with this value.

Now let's think a bit more about the actual animation of the swap. When we select the two cups to be exchanged, we can't simply exchange their locations, because the swap won't be visible to the player. After all, the three cups look identical. So we'll make the shuffling look like the illustration in Figure 21.19. A cup is randomly selected and is moved aside, out of its current location. Another cup is then moved into its space. The first cup can now be moved into the space left free by the second cup. Then the process can begin all over again.

The run method will clearly need to know about all three cups in order to do any shuffling, so these will need to be passed in to the constructor as parameters, and the constructor will need to remember them in the instance variables cup1, cup2, and cup3. If shuffling is to proceed as just described, there needs to be a temporary location so that cups can be "moved out of the way". We could define a constant in the Shuffler class, but we'll choose to have the temporary location passed in to the constructor as a parameter. This way, the controller class will have control over the appearance of the game, just as in the earlier nonanimated version. The temporary location will need to be remembered in an instance variable, so we will need to add that to the high-level design that was shown in Figure 21.18. Finally, the run method will need something to help it randomly select cups for shuffling. One way to do this is to use a RandomIntGenerator. A RandomIntGenerator that can generate one of three choices is created in the constructor. Once the constructor has set up everything as described above, it simply starts the animation by invoking the start method. The design of the Shuffler class at this point, illustrating the ideas we just summarized, is shown in Figure 21.20.

Now that we have detailed designs for the Cup and Shuffler classes, we can complete our design of the controller class, AnimatedShellGame. The user interface for this version of the game is nearly identical to the earlier, nonanimated version, so we'll reuse ideas from the earlier controller. First, we can remove some of the functionality of the earlier version. After all, the player no longer has any control over the movement of the cups. Therefore, we can eliminate the need for the instance variable selectedCup, which was used for dragging a cup. We can also eliminate the statements in onMousePress and onMouseDrag that are concerned with selecting and dragging cups. These methods now only need to be concerned with the marble.

Now we can consider the onMouseEnter method. When the mouse enters the canvas, this should start the shuffling, but it only makes sense to do any shuffling if the marble is actually hidden in a cup. So we'll need some way to keep track of whether the marble is hidden or not. One obvious way to do so is to declare a boolean instance variable to keep track of this information. Initially the value of this variable should be false. In the case that the marble is dragged to a cup, we need to remember that the marble becomes hidden. Once the marble is revealed by a click of the mouse in a cup, we need to note that the marble is again visible. Figure 21.21 shows the new controller design just discussed.

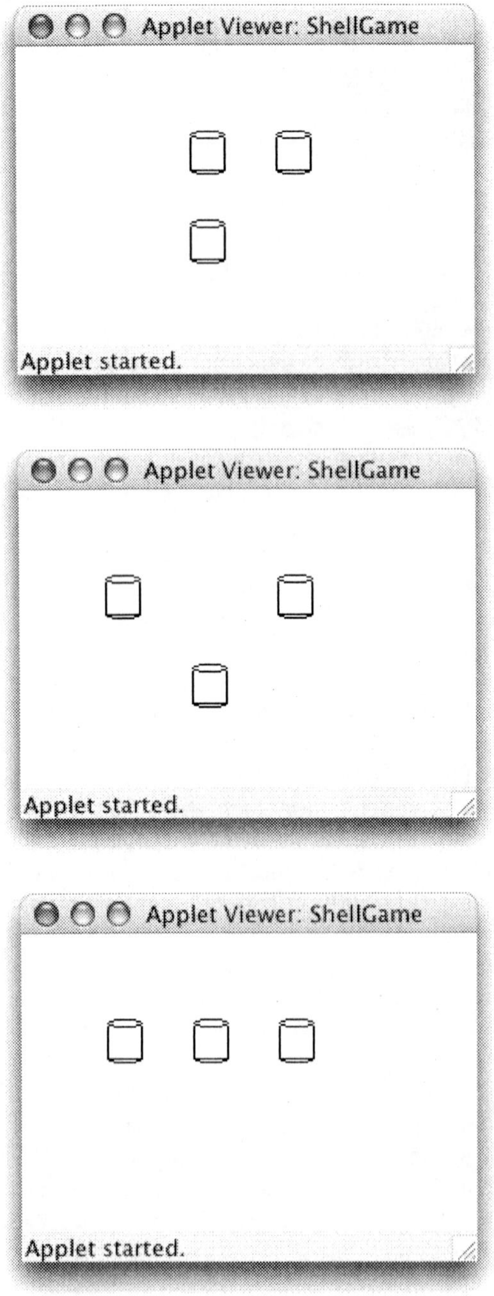

Figure 21.19 Animation of shuffling

```
// A class to animate shuffling in a Shell Game
public class Shuffler extends ActiveObject {

    // Number of times pairs of cups should be swapped
    private static final int SWAPS = 20;

    // Cups to be shuffled
    private Cup cup1, cup2, cup3;
    // A helper location for the shuffling
    private Location tempLocation;
    // Random int generator to select next cup for shuffling
    private RandomIntGenerator cupSelector;

    // Construct a shuffler
    // firstCup, secondCup, thirdCup - cups to be shuffled
    // aTempLocation - location to be used for moving cups out of
    // the way during shuffling
    public Shuffler( Cup firstCup, Cup secondCup, Cup thirdCup,
                     Location aTempLocation ) {
        // Remember the cups for shuffling
        // Remember the helper location for shuffling
        // Set up a RandomIntGenerator to help select next cup for shuffling
        // Start the shuffling animation
    }

    // Shuffle the cups
    public void run() {
        // Swap a cup out of one location and into another 20 times
            // Randomly select two cups
            // Move the first cup out of the way to a temporary location
            // Move the second cup to the location freed by the first
            // Move the first cup from the temporary location to the new
            // free space
    }
}
```

Figure 21.20 Filling in the design details for the Shuffler class

21.5.4 Filling in the Details for the Animated Shell Game

Filling in the details of our new shell game program is now quite easy. We simply have to follow the comments that we wrote, outlining our ideas. Again, these comments serve not only to help guide the implementation but to document our ideas to future readers of our classes.

The few additions that we needed to make to the Cup class were quite simple, so we don't have to concern ourselves with that class here. Instead, we can devote our attention to

```
public class AnimatedShellGame extends WindowController {
    ... // Details from earlier controller omitted

    // Whether the marble is hidden
    private boolean marbleHidden;

    // Place three cups and a marble on the canvas
    public void begin() {
        // Same as earlier controller
        // Marble is currently not hidden
        marbleHidden = false;
    }

    // Select the marble for dragging
    public void onMousePress( Location mousePos ) {
        // If the marble is not currently hidden and it contains the
        // mouse location
            // it is selected
        // Remember the mouse location for any dragging that will be done
    }

    // Move the marble, if it has been selected
    public void onMouseDrag( Location mousePos ) {
        // If the marble has been selected move the marble
    }

    // Drop a marble into a cup
    public void onMouseRelease( Location mousePos ) {
        // If the marble was selected and is currently positioned over a cup
            // Drop the marble into that cup
            // Remember that the marble is hidden

        // The marble is no longer selected upon release of the mouse
    }

    //  Show contents of a cup
    public void onMouseClick( Location mousePos ) {
    // If a cup has been selected and it contains the marble
        // Show the marble and remember that it is no longer hidden
    }

    public void onMouseEnter( Location mousePos ) {
        // If the marble is hidden, shuffle the cups
    }
}
```

Figure 21.21   Design of the controller class for the animated shell game

```
// A class to animate shuffling in a Shell Game
public class Shuffler extends ActiveObject {

    // Number of times pairs of cups should be swapped
    private static final int SWAPS = 20;

    // Cups to be shuffled
    private Cup cup1, cup2, cup3;
    // A helper location for the shuffling
    private Location tempLocation;
    // Random int generator to select next cup for shuffling
    private RandomIntGenerator cupSelector;

    // Construct a shuffler
    // firstCup, secondCup, thirdCup - cups to be shuffled
    // aTempLocation - location to be used for moving cups out of
    // the way during shuffling
    public Shuffler( Cup firstCup, Cup secondCup, Cup thirdCup,
                     Location aTempLocation ) {
        // Remember the cups for shuffling
        cup1 = firstCup;
        cup2 = secondCup;
        cup3 = thirdCup;

        // Remember the helper location for shuffling
        tempLocation = aTempLocation;

        // Set up a RandomIntGenerator to help select next cup for
        // shuffling
        cupSelector = new RandomIntGenerator( 1, 3 );

        // Start the shuffling animation
        start();
    }
```

Figure 21.22   Filling in the details of the Shuffler class: instance variables and constructor

the classes Shuffler and AnimatedShellGame. In fact, our design of the controller class, AnimatedShellGame is so detailed that the implementation of that class is quite straightforward and is left as an exercise. The Shuffler class is somewhat more interesting, so we'll devote the remainder of this section to that class.

Two elements of the Shuffler class require work. First, we need to write the code for the constructor, and then we will do the same for the run method. Implementing the constructor mainly involves remembering information passed in as parameters, such as the cups to be shuffled and the location to be used as a temporary holding spot. This is shown in Figure 21.22.

The implementation of the `run` method is more interesting, as it involves doing a bit of work to select cups for swapping. We could accomplish cup selection by selecting a random integer in the range 1 to 3, and then using that random number as follows:

```
int cupChoice = cupSelector.nextValue();
if (cupChoice == 1) {
    selectedCup = cup1;
} else if (cupChoice == 2) {
    selectedCup = cup2;
} else {
    selectedCup = cup3;
}
```

where `selectedCup` is of type Cup. The problem, however, is that we have to choose two cups. Using the code above to select two cups might cause us to pick the same one twice.

There are a number of ways we could handle this problem. One clever idea is to use the `RandomIntGenerator` to select the one cup that *won't be swapped*. If the selected random integer is 1, we will swap cups 2 and 3; if the random integer is 2, we will swap 1 and 3; if the random integer is 3, we will swap 1 and 2. The `run` method, which implements this idea, is shown in Figure 21.23.

As promised by the comments in the design, the `run` method selects a cup to be shuffled, moves it out of the way, and then selects another cup to be put in its place. There are a few interesting things to note in the implementation, however. First, before moving either randomly selected cup, we need to remember its old location. If we don't do this, we won't know where to move the cups when we're ready to actually swap them. Second, we need to pause between each move; if we didn't, the moves would happen so quickly that they wouldn't be visible to the player.

➡ EXERCISE 21.5.1

Complete the implementation of the `AnimatedShellGame` *controller class from the design given in Figure 21.21.*

Hint: *Our design is missing a useful piece of information. It is helpful to know which cup contains the marble.*   ❖

21.6   Guidelines for Writing Comments

When developing the designs in the previous sections, we wrote our ideas in the form of comments. We retained the comments after developing our code, since they described the various aspects of the classes we had written. While the design process outlined above should result in an appropriate level of documentation, the following guidelines will help you determine whether you have included all the information you need to include. Note that these are general guidelines and that your instructor might ask you to follow slightly different standards, such as the JavaDoc conventions, for commenting.

```java
// Time to wait between moves of cups
private static final double DELAY = 500;

// Shuffle the cups
 public void run() {
    Location firstLoc, secondLoc;
    Cup firstToSwap, secondToSwap;
    // Swap a cup out of one location and into another 20 times
    for (int count = 0; count < SWAPS; count++) {
        // Randomly select two cups
        int cupChoice = cupSelector.nextValue();
        if (cupChoice == 1) {
           firstToSwap = cup2;
           secondToSwap = cup3;
        } else if (cupChoice == 2) {
           firstToSwap = cup1;
           secondToSwap = cup3;
        } else {
           firstToSwap = cup1;
           secondToSwap = cup2;
        }
        // Move the first cup out of the way to a temporary location
        firstLoc = firstToSwap.getLocation();
        firstToSwap.moveTo( tempLocation );
        pause( DELAY );

        // Move the second cup to the location freed by the first
        secondLoc = secondToSwap.getLocation();
        secondToSwap.moveTo( firstLoc );
        pause( DELAY );

        // Move the first cup from the temporary location to the new
        // free space
        firstToSwap.moveTo( secondLoc );
        pause( DELAY );
    }
  }
}
```

Figure 21.23   Implementation of shuffling

* Each class should have a class comment. This should be placed at the top of the class and should include a description of the class as well as the author's name and the date.

```java
// A class to represent a cup for a shell game.
// Written by . . . , 2/14/04.
```

In the interest of saving space, we leave the author information out of all of the examples in the text.

* Each constant and variable should be commented. The comment associated with a constant or variable can be written either on the line before it, as follows:

```
// Whether the cup contains a marble
boolean containsMarble;
```

or can be written beside it:

```
boolean containsMarble;    // Whether the cup contains a marble
```

Note that the comment succinctly describes the purpose of the variable. If a group of variables serve a related purpose, they can be summarized by a single comment:

```
// The three cups
Cup cup1, cup2, cup3;
```

* Each constructor and method should have a comment that describes its purpose. The method comment should describe the parameters as well as the return value, if any:

```
// Construct a cup on the canvas.
// upperLeft - the upper left corner of the cup
// width, height - the desired width and height of the cup
// canvas - canvas on which cup is to be drawn
public Cup( Location upperLeft, double width, double height,
        DrawingCanvas canvas )

// Move the marble
// dx, dy - distance to move in the vertical and
// horizontal directions
public void move( double dx, double dy )
```

In the interest of succinctness in this text, we will abbreviate our method comments as follows:

```
// Construct a cup of the given width and height at the
// specified location on a canvas
public Cup(Location upperLeft, double width,
        double height, DrawingCanvas canvas)

// Move the cup dx pixels horizontally and dy vertically
public void move(double dx, double dy)
```

Note that the method comment should not describe how the method accomplishes its task. If it is important to describe the way a method works, such comments should be placed inside the method.

* Write comments describing how each method works. That is, write comments inside each method that explain what is happening. Short methods of five lines or less typically don't even require a comment, as they are generally simple enough to understand as they are. Comments should be detailed; on the other hand, overcommenting can be more distracting than helpful.

21.7 Encapsulation and Information Hiding

From the very beginning of this text, we have suggested that you make instance variables `private`. By doing so, you protect those variables from being inappropriately modified by other classes. If you want to provide access to those values, you can do so through accessor and mutator methods. This serves as a mechanism for providing exactly the type of access you want and no more. The idea of taking your variables and data structures and wrapping a shell around them in the form of a class definition is called *encapsulation*. The notion of hiding the details of your implementation as much as possible is called *information hiding*. These two related ideas are an important part of object-oriented design.

There are several reasons for designing and implementing classes this way. First, as already mentioned, it protects variables from being modified inappropriately by other classes. If several people are involved in a project, this allows them to proceed with the implementations of their individual classes without the fear that their variables will be "corrupted" by others. Even in the case when a single person is implementing an entire program, this notion provides protection from inadvertent modification of variables.

Second, this mechanism makes it possible to present classes to others for their use by simply specifying an interface. That is, it allows us to specify the functionality of a class of objects in terms of its methods, without giving any additional details. This is extremely beneficial to the user of that class, since he or she can create objects and invoke methods on them without needing to know anything about their implementation. The user can work with the *abstraction* in its simplest form.

It should be easy to convince you that this is useful. After all, this has been essential to your use of the objectdraw library. Once you were told the types of objects you could construct and the methods you could invoke, you could make use of those without needing to understand anything more about them. This is not just something that helps the novice programmer. The Java language consists of many class definitions that make it easier for programmers to do their jobs. In addition, programmers can share libraries, such as objectdraw, with others. The ability to make use of pre-existing classes means that programmers can focus on writing new classes with new functionality, rather than having to do everything from scratch.

Third, encapsulation and information hiding make it possible to change the details of a class definition without affecting others who might be using that class. During the time that we wrote this text, we modified the objectdraw library several times. Virtually all of those changes were completely transparent to users of our library. That is, they were invisible. While we improved the details of how things worked internally, the external interface remained the same, so old code did not "break" when new versions of the library were introduced.

In the remainder of this section we will look more closely at some examples that illustrate the utility of encapsulation and information hiding.

21.7.1 Nested Rectangles: A Graphical Object Class

Imagine for a moment that we have extended the objectdraw library to include a new type of graphical object called `NestedRects`. One of these is pictured in Figure 12.1. If you read Chapter 12 this will be familiar to you. A `NestedRects` object is constructed by specifying the *x* and *y* coordinates of the upper left corner, width and height of type `double`, and a `DrawingCanvas`. Once constructed, a `NestedRects` object can be moved to a particular location or it can be removed from the canvas. More specifically, the constructors and methods available for the `NestedRects` class are as follows:

```
// Constructs a collection of nested rectangles. Each interior
// rectangle is 8 pixels smaller in each dimension than its
// enclosing rectangle. x, y - the x and y coordinates of the
// upper left corner width, height - width and height of the
// bounding rectangle
// DrawingCanvas aCanvas - canvas on which the object is to be drawn
public NestedRects( double x, double y, double width,
                    double height, DrawingCanvas aCanvas )

// Move nested rectangles to the specified x and y coordinates
// x, y - new x and y coordinates of upper left
public void moveTo( double x, double y )

// Remove nested rectangles from the canvas
public void removeFromCanvas()
```

Given this new type of graphical object, let's write a simple program that does the following. It begins with a `NestedRects` object on the canvas. The `NestedRects` should be drawn at location (50,50); the width and height should be 19 and 21, respectively. When the user presses the mouse on the canvas, the `NestedRects` should move to the location of the press. When the mouse is released, the `NestedRects` that was just moved remains there, and a new one is constructed at (50,50), having width and height twice the size of the last one moved.

The program in Figure 21.24 does exactly what we have described. If you run this simple program, you will find that you can produce some interesting pictures, such as the one in Figure 21.25. But that isn't our reason for introducing it here.

Since we introduced the `NestedRects` class in Chapter 12, you probably imagine that the class we defined there was used together with the controller in Figure 21.24 to create the image in Figure 21.25, but that isn't the case. Instead, we used the `NestedRects` class definition shown in Figure 21.26. This alternate implementation makes use of an array of `FramedRects` to store the individual components of the `NestedRects` object. We are able to calculate exactly how big this array needs to be as long as we know the width and height of the object, as well as the size difference (in this case, eight) between successively smaller components of it.

The two implementations of the `NestedRects` class are equally valid. An array is a perfectly reasonable choice of data structure to represent the nested rectangles, as is a recursive structure. More importantly, the choice of one or the other is irrelevant to anyone making use of this class. There is no reason for a programmer to think of a `NestedRects` as "an array of rectangles" or as a "recursive structure of rectangles". A `NestedRects` object is simply a graphical object that can be created, moved, and removed from a canvas.

```
// Class to draw interesting pictures from nested rectangles
public class RectangleDrawer extends WindowController {

// x and y coordinates of each new NestedRects to be drawn
private static final double XPOSITION = 50;
private static final double YPOSITION = 50;

// Initial width and height of NestedRects
private static final double START_WIDTH = 19;
private static final double START_HEIGHT = 21;

// Width and height of NestedRects
private double width;
private double height;

// The most recently drawn NestedRects
private NestedRects theRect;

   // Draw a NestedRects on the canvas
   public void begin() {
      width = START_WIDTH;
      height = START_HEIGHT;
      theRect = new NestedRects( XPOSITION, YPOSITION,
                             START_WIDTH, START_HEIGHT, canvas );
   }

   // Move the most recent NestedRects to the location of the mouse press
   public void onMousePress( Location point ) {
      theRect.moveTo( point.getX(), point.getY() );
   }

   // Draw a new NestedRects twice the size of the last one
   public void onMouseRelease( Location point ) {
      width = width * 2;
      height = height * 2;
      theRect = new NestedRects( XPOSITION, YPOSITION, width, height,
                             canvas );
   }
}
```

Figure 21.24 A simple program to draw and move nested rectangles

21.7.2 The Important Relationship between Encapsulation and Abstraction

The NestedRects example illustrates the important relationship between encapsulation and abstraction. Encapsulating the details of an implementation in a class allows us to present an

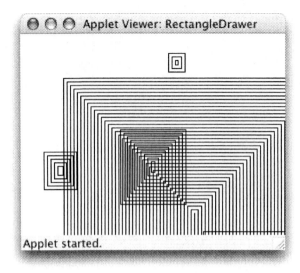

Figure 21.25   A sample drawing produced by running RectangleDrawer

abstraction to anyone using that class. As already mentioned, you have been taking advantage of these ideas from the beginning, when using the objectdraw library. Java programmers make use of these important concepts every day.

To summarize, encapsulation and its counterpart, information hiding, are important because:

- they allow the programmer to present a class to others for their use by simply specifying an interface. Thus the user can work with the abstraction in its simplest form.
- they protect variables from being modified inappropriately by other classes.
- they make it possible to change the details of a class definition without affecting others who might be using that class.

21.8   Summary

This chapter provided an introduction to object-oriented design. It discussed the important ideas of abstraction, encapsulation and information hiding. These concepts provide a foundation for object-oriented design techniques, but they are also of importance to many other aspects of computer science.

In this chapter we presented examples to illustrate the process of design, which we can outline as follows:

1. Identify the types of objects in the problem description that you will need to model with classes.
2. For each class, list the properties and behaviors that you want to model. If the class has a real-world counterpart, that can serve as inspiration for your ideas here, though you likely will not model every aspect of a real-world object.
3. Model each property as an instance variable.

```
// Class to represent a graphical structure composed of nested rectangles
public class NestedRects {

   // Size difference of successive rectangles
   private static final int SIZE_DIFF = 8;
   // Difference in x and y coordinates of upper left of successive rectangles
   private static final int INSET = 4;

   // The set of rectangles
   private FramedRect[ ] theRectangles;
   // The number of rectangles
   private int nestingDepth;

   // Construct a graphical object of nested rectangles
   // x, y - x and y coordinates of upper left
   // width, height - width and height of the outermost rectangle
   // canvas - canvas on which nested rects should be drawn
   public NestedRects( double x, double y, double width,
                       double height, DrawingCanvas canvas) {

      // Determine the number of rectangles in the nested structure
      nestingDepth =  (int) Math.min( width, height )/SIZE_DIFF + 1;
      theRectangles = new FramedRect[nestingDepth];

      // Construct the rectangular components
      for ( int i = 0; i < nestingDepth; i++ ) {
         theRectangles[i] = new FramedRect( x, y, width, height, canvas );
         x = x + INSET;
         y = y + INSET;
         width = width - SIZE_DIFF;
         height = height - SIZE_DIFF;
      }
   }

   // Move nested rects to specified location
   // x, y - new x and y coordinates of upper left
   public void moveTo( double x, double y ) {
      for (int i = 0; i < nestingDepth; i++) {
         theRectangles[i].moveTo( x + INSET*i, y + INSET*i );
      }
   }

   // Remove nested rects from the canvas
   public void removeFromCanvas() {
      for ( int i = 0; i < nestingDepth; i++ ) {
         theRectangles[i].removeFromCanvas();
      }
   }
}
```

Figure 21.26   An array-based NestedRects class

4. Model each behavior as a method. Specify only method headers, i.e., signatures, at this point in the design process.
5. Refine your design. If a method is very simple, you can refine the design by immediately writing the Java statements to implement it. If a method is more complex, write comments describing the steps to be followed.

Remember that design is a process of refinement. It involves refinement of high-level ideas into more and more concrete Java statements. It also involves refinement of the design plan itself.

21.9   Chapter Review Problems

▸ EXERCISE 21.9.1

What do we mean when we say that an object provides an abstraction in a program?   ❖

▸ EXERCISE 21.9.2

How do we model properties of objects? How do we model behaviors?   ❖

▸ EXERCISE 21.9.3

List the steps that we follow when doing object-oriented design.   ❖

▸ EXERCISE 21.9.4

We say that design is a process of refinement. Describe two ways in which refinement plays a role in the design process.   ❖

▸ EXERCISE 21.9.5

Write appropriate method comments for the following method of a `Circle` *class:*

```
public void resize( double sizeDiff )
```

This method resizes the circle by changing the size of the diameter by `sizeDiff`.   ❖

21.10   Programming Problems

▸ EXERCISE 21.10.1

In this exercise you will be asked to design and then implement an animation program. The program should draw a faucet and a glass on the canvas. The faucet should drip individual droplets of water into the glass until the glass is reasonably full. (It needn't be filled completely.) A picture of the canvas with the faucet and glass before any dripping has occurred is shown in Figure 21.27.

    a. *The first step in the design process is to identify the classes that will be needed. Suggest four classes that would be appropriate to model the objects mentioned in the problem description.*

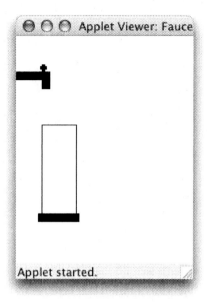

Figure 21.27   Leaky faucet and glass before the faucet drips

b. List the properties and behaviors that need to be modeled for each of the four classes included in your answer to part (a).

c. For each class, model the properties with instance variables.

d. For each class, model the behaviors with methods.

e. Fill in the implementation details for each class.

EXERCISE 21.10.2

In this exercise you will be asked to design and implement a Hangman program. The program should draw a text message on the canvas that contains a hyphen in the place of each letter of the word to be guessed. A list of all the letters the player has guessed so far should also be displayed. The player should guess a letter by selecting from a JComboBox. If the player guesses a letter that is in the target word, the word should be updated on the canvas. If the player guesses a letter that is not in the target word, an additional body part should be drawn. If the player guesses a letter that has already been guessed, the program should tell the player by displaying a message. A shapshot of such a program after several guesses is shown in Figure 21.28.

a. As always, the first step of the design process is to identify the classes that will be needed. List the classes you would include in this program's design. Don't place too much functionality in the controller class. In particular, we would expect you to include three or four classes in your design.

b. List the properties and behaviors that need to be modeled for each of the classes corresponding to the classes you included in your answer to part (a).

c. For each class, model the properties with instance variables.

d. For each class, model the behaviors with methods.

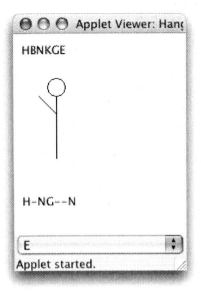

Figure 21.28   A Hangman game

e. *Fill in the implementation details for each class.*

APPENDIX A

Style Guidelines

he presentation of your program is just as important as its correctness. While good comments or good variable names will not affect the correctness of your program, they will make it easier to read your program.

Readability of code is important for several reasons. First, it is an important way for you to keep track of your thoughts as you design and write your program. The more careful you are about organizing your thoughts, the less likely it is for your code to be error prone. In the event that there are problems with your code, you will be able to debug it more easily if you can read and follow the work you have done. Second, it will allow others to better understand what you have written. This is particularly important if you are working on a team project or if you are writing code that will be modified over time.

This appendix outlines general rules of good programming style. There are many other sources of style guidelines that you might consult as well, including those at http://java.sun.com/docs/codeconv. While most style guides provide roughly the same advice, there are some places where they might differ. When in doubt, consult with your instructor to learn his/her style preferences.

A.1 Commenting

Comments are extremely important. Take some care to write accurate yet concise comments.

- Be specific with your comments. What happens when the mouse is pressed? What is the `FilledRect` used for? Your comments should describe the intent of the code. What are you trying to accomplish with this piece of code?
- Do not overcomment! Overcommenting can make the program hard to read just as much as undercommenting. Do not comment every line. If they are simple instructions, most people will understand them without your comments. If you think you need commenting, try commenting chunks of code under the same comment.
- Delete any code that is no longer used. In particular, if you have written and then commented out code, remove it.

You should write comments for:

1. **Class (Program)**: At the top of each class, you should write your name, date of creation, and a brief description of what the class is for.
2. **Methods**: Above each method heading there should be a brief description of what the method does. You should also describe what each parameter means and what the return result means. If the method code is simple, you do not need to comment in the method body. If the method body is complicated, you might want to add some comments to certain areas that you deem to be complicated. Be careful not to overcomment!
3. **Variables and constants**: In general, variables and constants should all have comments as to what the variable is used for. Occasionally several closely related variables or constants can be grouped together under the same comment.

A.2   Blank Lines

Blank lines are used to delineate different areas of the code. The instance variable declarations at the top of your program should be separated from the header of the class and the header of the first method. There should always be space between methods. It is advisable to break up long method bodies and long declarations into logical pieces. Always start a new line after the semicolon. Always leave a blank line before a comment line.

A.3   Names

You should always choose names that suggest the meanings of the things being named. If the purpose of a method is to draw a rectangle, then a good name for that method is `drawRect`. If there is a variable of type `FilledRect` that is used as the stem of a flower, then a good name would be `stem` or `stemRect`.

* Names that have nothing to do with the program are very bad names! For example: `FramedRect frodo`.
* Names that are not specific or descriptive enough are generally bad names. For example: `Line line` or `Line l` are not as good as `Line foulLine` if the line represents a foul line.
* Try not to name objects sequentially. You should only do this when the objects are related in some way that is not otherwise expressible. For example, `FramedRect box1`, `FramedRect box2`, `FramedRect box3` are not as good as `darksBasket`, `whitesBasket`, and `colorsBasket` if the rectangles represent laundry baskets for clothes of specific colors.

By convention, constants (indicated by "`static final`" in Java) are all capital letters, classes begin with capitals, variable and method names begin with lower-case letters, while capitals are used to start new words in multiword names.

Instance variables should never be declared to be public. Instance variables should only be used when a value must be saved for use after a constructor or method has been completed. Otherwise local variables should be used.

A.4   Format

Your program should be organized as neatly as possible. The structure of the text in the program should give the reader an overall sense of the program's logical organization. Indent the bodies of methods. Also indent the bodies of loops, as well as the `if` and `else` parts of conditional statements.

APPENDIX

●●●●■■■■■■■■■■■■■■■■■■■■■■■■■

Objectdraw API Summary

This appendix provides a brief outline of the public constructors and methods for the major classes in the objectdraw library. Much more information is available on-line in the Javadoc files for objectdraw at:

http://eventfuljava.cs.williams.edu/library/objectdrawJavadoc/.

B.1 WindowController

B.1.1 Methods to define in extensions of Controller or WindowController

void begin ()   Initialize the program.

B.1.2 Methods to define in extensions of WindowController

void onMouseClick(Location point)	Define actions to take when the mouse button is clicked.
void onMousePress(Location point)	Define actions to take when the mouse button is pressed.
void onMouseRelease(Location point)	Define actions to take when the mouse button is released.
void onMouseEnter(Location point)	Define actions to take when the mouse enters the window.
void onMouseExit(Location point)	Define actions to take when the mouse exits the window.
void onMouseDrag(Location point)	Define actions to take when the mouse is moved with the mouse button down.
void onMouseMove(Location point)	Define actions to take when the mouse is moved with the mouse button up.

B.1.3   Methods to call in classes extending `Controller` or `WindowController`

```
Image getImage( String fileName )
AudioClip getAudio( String fileName )
```
Loads a gif or jpeg file.
Loads an audio file.

B.2 ActiveObject

B.2.1   Methods to define in extensions of `ActiveObject`

```
void run()
```
The active behavior of the object.

B.2.2   Methods to call in classes extending `ActiveObject`

```
void start()
```
Results in the active object starting the execution of its run method.

```
void pause( double interval )
```
Causes active object to pause execution for `interval` milliseconds.

B.3 Drawable objects

B.3.1   Constructors for Drawable objects

```
FramedRect( double x, double y, double width,
            double height, DrawingCanvas canvas )
FramedRect( Location cornerLocation, double width,
            double height, DrawingCanvas canvas )
FramedRect( Location corner1Location, Location
            corner2Location, DrawingCanvas canvas )
FilledRect( double x, double y, double width,
            double height, DrawingCanvas canvas )
FilledRect( Location cornerLocation, double width,
            double height, DrawingCanvas canvas )
FilledRect( Location corner1Location, Location
            corner2Location, DrawingCanvas canvas )

FramedOval( double x, double y, double width,
            double height, DrawingCanvas canvas )
FramedOval( Location cornerLocation, double width,
            double height, DrawingCanvas canvas )
FramedOval( Location corner1Location, Location
            corner2Location, DrawingCanvas canvas )
FilledOval( double x, double y, double width,
            double height, DrawingCanvas canvas )
FilledOval( Location cornerLocation, double width,
            double height, DrawingCanvas canvas )
FilledOval( Location corner1Location, Location
            corner2Location, DrawingCanvas canvas )
```

The parameters to a rectangle or oval constructor describe the rectangle bounding the object to be drawn. You can either:

1. Specify the coordinates of the rectangle's upper left corner together with the width and height, or
2. Specify the coordinates of two opposite corners.

```
FramedRoundedRect( double x, double y, double width,
                   double height, double arcWidth,
                   double arcHeight, DrawingCanvas
                   canvas )
FramedRoundedRect( Location cornerLocation,
                   double width, double height,
                   double arcWidth, double arcHeight,
                   DrawingCanvas canvas )
FilledRoundedRect( double x, double y, double width,
                   double height, double arcWidth,
                   double arcHeight, DrawingCanvas
                   canvas )
FilledRoundedRect( Location cornerLocation,
                   double width, double height,
                   double arcWidth, double arcHeight,
                   DrawingCanvas canvas )
```

The arcHeight and arcWidth parameters refer to the height and width of ovals at corners.

```
FramedArc( double x, double y, double width,
           double height, double startAngle,
           double arcAngle, DrawingCanvas canvas )
FramedArc( Location cornerLocation, double width,
           double height, double startAngle,
           double arcAngle, DrawingCanvas canvas )
FilledArc( double x, double y, double width,
           double height, double startAngle,
           double arcAngle, DrawingCanvas canvas )
FilledArc( Location cornerLocation, double width,
           double height, double startAngle,
           double arcAngle, DrawingCanvas canvas )
```

The startAngle and arcAngle parameters refer to the starting angle of the arc and the total extent of the angle.

```
VisibleImage( Image image, double x, double y,
              DrawingCanvas c )
VisibleImage( Image image, Location origin,
              DrawingCanvas c )
VisibleImage( Image image, double x, double y,
              double width, double height,
              DrawingCanvas c )
VisibleImage( Image image, Location origin,
              double width, double height,
              DrawingCanvas c )
```

The parameters to a VisibleImage constructor require you to specify the upper left corner of the image, either using a Location object or a pair of values for x and y. You can also optionally resize the image by giving a width and height. If you do not specify a width and height, it will use the size that the Image itself has.

```
Text( String text, double x, double y,
      DrawingCanvas canvas )
Text( String text, Location cornerLocation,
      DrawingCanvas canvas )
```

The coordinates specify the upper left corner of the text.

```
Line( double startX, double startY,
      double endX, double endY,
      DrawingCanvas canvas )
Line( Location startLocation,
      Location endLocation,
      DrawingCanvas canvas )
```

A line is described by giving its end points.

B.3.2 Methods for all Drawable objects

boolean contains(Location someLocation)	If a line, determine if the line is within a few pixels of a point; if 2-D, determine if the object contains a point.
Color getColor() void setColor(Color someColor)	Access/change an object's color.
void move(double xOffset, double yOffset)	Move an object relative to its current position.
void moveTo(double x, double y) void moveTo(Location someLocation)	Move an object to point specified by coordinates.
void hide() void show() boolean isHidden()	Make an object invisible or visible on the display. Check if it is hidden.
void removeFromCanvas()	Permanently remove an object from the canvas.
void addToCanvas (DrawingCanvas c)	Add the object to a canvas. The object must have previously been removed from any canvas on which it was displayed.
void sendForward() void sendToFront() void sendBackward() void sendToBack()	Alter the stacking order that controls how overlapping objects appear.

B.3.3 Methods for Lines only

Location getStart()
Location getEnd()
void setStart(Location someLocation)
void setStart(double startX, double startY)
void setEnd(Location someLocation)
void setEnd(double startX, double startY)
void setEndPoints(Location startLocation,
                   Location endLocation)
void setEndPoints(double startX, double startY,
                   double endX, double endY)
	Access the coordinates of the starting or ending point of the line. Change either or both of a line's end points.

B.3.4   Methods for rectangles, ovals, VisibleImages, and Text objects

double getX() double getY() Location getLocation()	Access one or both coordinates of the upper left corner of an object's bounding rectangle.
double getWidth() double getHeight()	Access the dimensions of an object's bounding rectangle.
boolean overlaps(Drawable2DInterface item)	Returns true if the bounding rectangle of item overlaps with the bounding rectangle of the current object.

B.3.5   Methods for rectangles, ovals, and VisibleImages only

void setWidth(double width) void setHeight(double height) void setSize(double width, double height)	Change the width or height of a shape.

B.3.6   Methods for Text objects only

void setText(String text)	Change the characters displayed.
void setFontSize(int pointSize)	Change the font size used.
void setBold(boolean isBold) void setItalic(boolean isItalic)	Change the style in which text is displayed.
void setFont(Font someFont) void setFont(String fontName)	Change the font used.

B.4   Auxiliary Classes

B.4.1   Constructors for auxiliary objects

Location(double x, double y)	Builds a location corresponding to (x,y).
RandomIntGenerator(int min, int max)	Builds a random number generator that returns integers between min and max, inclusive.
RandomDoubleGenerator(double min, double max)	Builds a random number generator that returns doubles between min and max, inclusive.

B.4.2   Methods for Location objects

double getX()	Access x or y coordinate of a Location.
double getY()	
double distanceTo(Location other)	Determine the distance between two Locations.
void translate(double xDiff, double yDiff)	Translate a Location by given offsets.

B.4.3   Method for RandomIntGenerator objects

int nextValue()	Returns the next random integer.

B.4.4   Method for RandomDoubleGenerator objects

double nextValue()	Returns the next random double.

B.5   Type and Interface Hierarchies

In this section we describe the subclass and subinterface hierarchies involved in the objectdraw library. Indented classes and interfaces are extensions of their parents.

B.5.1   Subclass hierarchy for geometric objects

Drawable implements DrawableInterface

* Drawable2D implements Drawable2DInterface

    - Resizable2D implements Resizable2DInterface

        * Rectangular

            · Arc

                - FilledArc
                - FramedArc

            · Oval

                - FilledOval
                - FramedOval

            · Rect

                - FilledRect
                - FramedRect

            · RoundedRect

                - FilledRoundedRect
                - FramedRoundedRect

       · VisibleImage

   – Text

* Line implements Drawable1DInterface

   – AngLine

B.5.2 Subinterface hierarchy for geometric objects

DrawableInterface

* Drawable1DInterface
* Drawable2DInterface

   – Resizable2DInterface

B.5.3 Subclass hierarchy for controllers

Controller extends JApplet

* FrameController
* WindowController

   – FrameWindowController

APPENDIX C

Navigating Java APIs

In order to help us introduce Java programming concepts, we wrote the objectdraw library that you have been using throughout this text. Libraries like objectdraw, however, are not just teaching tools. They are an important part of the toolkit of any professional programmer. Libraries make it possible for programmers to write large complex programs without having to write everything from scratch.

An API, Application Programming Interface, specifies the details a programmer must know to use the resources a library provides. Conveniently, documentation for Java APIs can be automatically generated from comments (written in a special format) in the library code. This is nice for the library authors, but it is also useful for programmers who use libraries. Documentation generated by Javadoc, a tool from Sun Microsystems, Inc., has a consistent format. Once you are familiar with this format, you will feel comfortable looking at any Java API's documentation. To make things even more convenient, documentation generated by Javadoc can be read through a web browser. So as you are programming, you can have your browser open in a window right next to the code you're writing, just in case you need to find some information.

This appendix will show you how you might navigate the documentation of a Java API to find useful information. We will use the objectdraw API as our example. As you read through this appendix, you might want to have a web browser open, so that you can follow along with our example.

C.1 Introduction to objectdraw Documention

If you open your favorite web browser and type in the following URL:

```
http://eventfuljava.cs.williams.edu/library
```

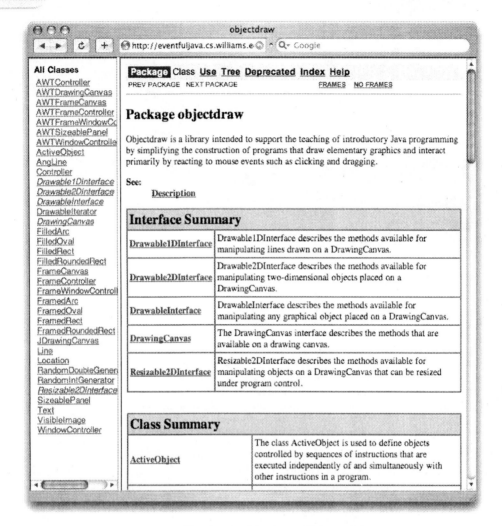

Figure C.1   Viewing the objectdraw API in a web browser

you will find a web page that describes our library and that contains a link to a detailed description of the features of the library. Clicking on this link will bring you to the main page of the documentation for the objectdraw API, which will look like the picture shown in Figure C.1.

At the left of the window, you will see a listing of all the available classes in the library. The remainder of the window provides a brief overview of the function of the library and summaries of all of the interfaces and classes it includes.

C.2   Getting Information about a Class

To get detailed information about any of the classes or interfaces included in objectdraw you can click on the name of the class or interface either in the listing on the left side of the window

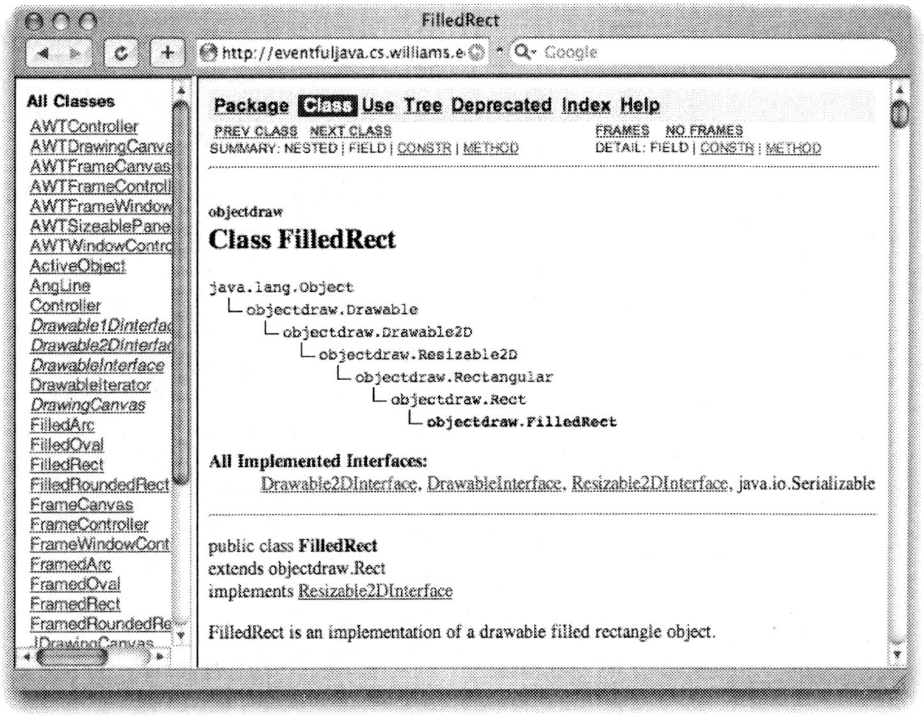

Figure C.2 Clicking on the FilledRect class gives information on FilledRects

or in the summary section. Find a link for the FilledRect class. If you click on it, you will now see information about the FilledRect class, as in Figure C.2. Let's explore some of this information. First, note that at the top of the window there is a panel. This will allow you to easily jump to various types of information. The PREV CLASS link, for example, will take you to the information about FilledOval, since that is the class that appears before FilledRect in the listing of all classes.

C.2.1 Summary Information about Constructors and Methods

Below the links to PREV CLASS and NEXT CLASS, you will see that you can access SUMMARY information or DETAIL information about things like constructors and methods for this class. Let's start out by looking at the summary information. Click on the CONSTR link, and you will see the information displayed in Figure C.3. Under the heading Constructor Summary you will see the headers for the three different FilledRect constructors. The first is the header for the constructor that takes as parameters an *x* coordinate, *y* coordinate, width, height, and canvas; the second is the header for the constructor that takes a Location, width, height, and canvas. The third is the header for a constructor that is probably new to you. It allows you to construct

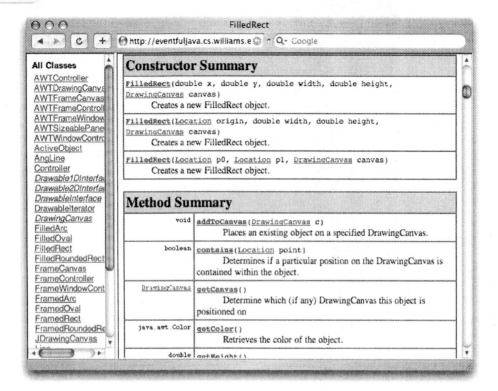

Figure C.3   A summary of constructors

a `FilledRect` by specifying `Location`s that are the endpoints of one of the diagonals of the rectangle.

Say that you wanted to know more about this third constructor. You could click on the `FilledRect` link in the constructor header, and the information in Figure C.4 would be displayed. It provides not only the constructor header, but a description of the constructor and its parameters. You have probably noticed that within the header parameter lists there are other links on which you can click. Whenever the name of an objectdraw class appears in the documentation, it is highlighted as a link so that you can quickly get information about it. For instance, you can click on the `Location` links in this constructor's header to get more information about the class to which these parameters must belong.

Now scroll back up to the top of the page. (Note that all the information about `FilledRect`s is on one page—some of the links simply get you to information on that page more quickly than scrolling through it.) Click on the METHOD link to get the summary information about methods. As in Figure C.5, you will see a summary of methods. There are too many methods associated with this class to fit in a typical browser window, so you will probably have to scroll to see all the method summaries. You can click on the name of a method to see a detailed description of its function. For example, if you scroll to find the `move` method and then click on its name, the browser will show you the information in Figure C.6.

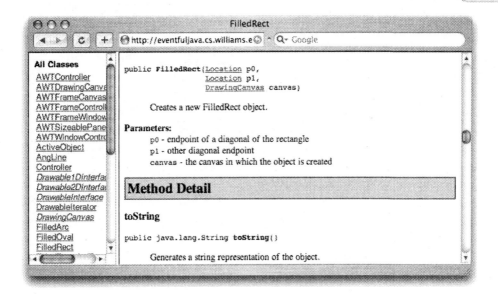

Figure C.4   Detail of a constructor

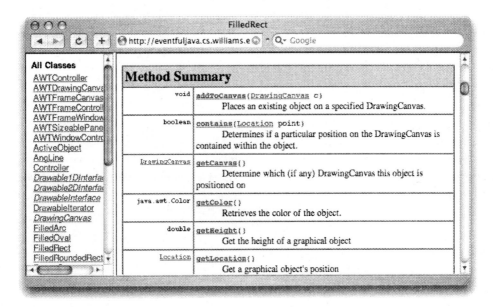

Figure C.5   Method summary for the FilledRect class

C.2.2   Detailed Information about Constructors and Methods

You can also find detailed information about methods and constructors by simply scrolling through the complete list of detailed descriptions. To do this, scroll back to the top of the page and click

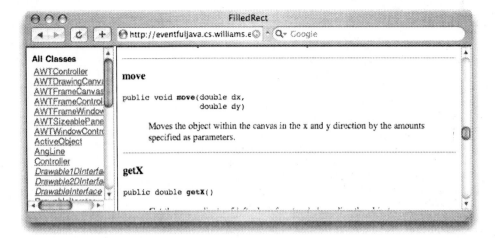

Figure C.6   Detail of a method

on the CONSTR link for DETAIL. This will take you to the documentation displayed in Figure C.7. You already saw detailed information about one of the FilledRect constructors. This shows you the same type of detail for all of the constructors. Similarly, you can view detailed information about any of the methods.

C.3   When Should I Refer to an API?

You might be asking yourself, "How do I know when I should look at an API?" There are two main reasons to read an API. First, you might simply need to remind yourself of something you already know. For instance, say that you have forgotten the order in which parameters should be passed to the constructor for Text. Or say that you simply want to review the methods available for Lines.

A second reason to browse an API is simply to learn about new things that you might use in your programs. For instance, did you know that the objectdraw library provides classes FilledRoundedRect and FramedRoundedRect? As their names imply, these allow you to construct and manipulate rectangles with rounded corners.

C.4   Other Java APIs

Many programmers have developed interesting Java libraries that they have made available to others. Perhaps more importantly, there is a vast collection of standard libraries that are part of the language itself. You can find these by going to

```
http://java.sun.com/apis.html
```

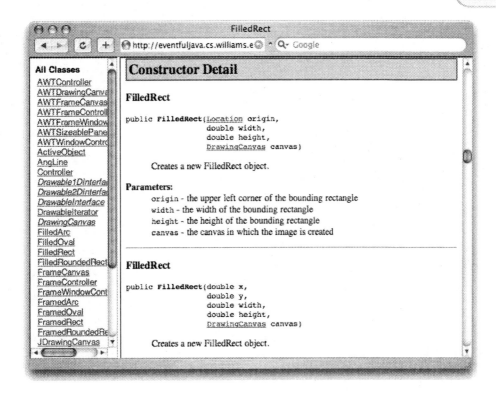

Figure C.7   Detail of all constructors for FilledRect

This page provides links to API documentation for many different versions of Java. For instance, you can click on the link to the J2SE 1.4.2 API Specification on whichever version you are using in class. If you do this, you will see an API in Javadoc format.

If you browse the classes at the left side of the window, you will be able to find, among others, Java's `String` class, and the various GUI component classes, such as `JButton` and `JComboBox`. You can see information about their constructors and methods by navigating the API exactly as you would the objectdraw API.

In addition, above the listing of all classes, you will see that you can get a listing of *packages* into which the classes are organized. So, for example, if you want to get information about all of the Java Swing classes, you can click on `javax.swing`. This will update the class listing so that it includes only the classes and interfaces in the `javax.swing` package.

APPENDIX D

Programming without objectdraw

$\mathcal{M}$ ost of the examples in this book depend on the use of the objectdraw library, a library designed by the authors to remove unnecessary syntactic overhead for novices. You are welcome to make copies of the library and to use it in any programs you write. However, it may be useful to understand how you can write programs that do not use the objectdraw library.

In this appendix we discuss how to write programs without the objectdraw library. We first discuss writing classes that extend JApplet rather than Controller or WindowController. We then go on to discuss how to use Java threads rather than active objects, and then how standard Java graphics works. Next we discuss random number generators in standard Java, before finishing with a discussion of applications in Java.

Most of the discussion below assumes that the reader is familiar with Chapter 11 on GUI components, while some parts assume that the reader is also familiar with Chapter 18 on exceptions.

D.1 Extending JApplet rather than Controller

In this text, you have been writing classes that extend WindowController or Controller, which are classes from the objectdraw library that extend JApplet. The class WindowController extends Controller by adding a canvas to the center of the window, being a listener for mouse actions, and adding default mouse-handling methods. We begin by explaining how to write classes that extend JApplet rather than Controller.

Rather than supporting a begin method, JApplet supports methods

```
public void init();
public void start();
```

The init method will generally be used to replace the begin method in Controller. It is the method called when the applet is created. The start method is called after the init method has completed. It is also called each time the applet is revisited when it is embedded in a web page. Thus start may be called several times during the execution of an applet. The method

```
public void stop();
```

is also supported by JApplet. That method is called when the web page containing the applet has been replaced by another page and also just before the applet is to be destroyed—for example, when the user quits the application running the applet.

As an example of how to change a class extending Controller to one extending JApplet, recall the class GUIApplet from Figure 11.18. To get this class to run as an applet we need only replace the following lines:

```
public class GUIApplet extends Controller implements
                                           ActionListener {
    ...
    public void begin() {
    ...
```

by

```
public class GUIApplet extends JApplet implements ActionListener {
    ...
    public void init() {
    ...
```

Two methods, getAudio and getImage, that can be used inside of Controller are only available in a slightly different form in JApplet. Our library allows you to call either of these with a String parameter representing the name of a file that is in the same directory as your program. However, the versions of these methods available in JApplet require parameters of type URL:

```
public AudioClip getAudioClip( URL url );
public Image getImage( URL url );
```

Notice that getAudio is replaced by getAudioClip, while getImage retains the same name. The easiest way to create a URL is by calling new URL(spec), where spec is a String representing a complete URL. If the image or audio clip is coming over the web, the URL will be of the form http://www.cs.williams.edu/..., for example. If it is being obtained from your computer, then it will be of the form file://*pathname*, where *pathname* is the complete specification of the path to the file.

The Controller class also ensures that when your program is stopped, all active threads generated by active objects are stopped. For example, if a program is running in a web browser and the user moves to a new page, then all active threads will be halted. If that were not the case, then these threads would continue executing in the background, and eventually your computer would react more and more slowly until you restarted your web browser. We discuss how to handle this in more detail in Section D.3.

D.2   Extending JApplet rather than WindowController

The class WindowController adds a great deal more to Controller. In particular, it adds a canvas to the center of the window. The canvas is an extension of JComponent that keeps track of what the user draws on the canvas and repaints it whenever necessary. For example, the canvas must be repainted when it is uncovered on the screen. We will discuss how graphics works in more detail in Section D.4.

The WindowController class implements both MouseListener and MouseMotion-Listener (see Section 11.7.2). It registers itself to be a mouse listener and a mouse motion listener for the canvas. Standard Java uses different names and parameter types for the mouse event handlers.

To handle mouse events in extensions of JApplet, you will need to use the following methods:

```
public void mouseClicked( MouseEvent e ); // MouseListener methods
public void mousePressed( MouseEvent e );
public void mouseReleased( MouseEvent e );
public void mouseEntered( MouseEvent e );
public void mouseExited( MouseEvent e );
public void mouseDragged( MouseEvent e ); // MouseMotionListener
                                          // methods
public void mouseMoved( MouseEvent e );
```

rather than the similarly named methods from WindowController.

The class Location is part of objectdraw and not part of standard Java. However, it is very similar to the standard Point class. Point represents a pair of integer *x* and *y* coordinates. The methods getX(), getY(), and translate(dx, dy) are all supported by Point. The only real difference between Location and Point is that Location represents coordinates held as doubles, while Point represents coordinates held as integers. While real screen coordinates are integers, we found it convenient not to have to worry about truncation problems when moving by fractions of a pixel.

The class MouseEvent supports methods getX(), getY(), and getPoint() that enable the programmer to determine where the mouse event occurred. Figure D.1 illustrates a simple program that prints a message determining where a user clicked in the content pane (interior) of the window. If a component (e.g., a JFrame) were serving as a canvas, then the listener would have been added to that component instead of the content pane. Note that we have omitted three methods that are required by MouseListener. If the programmer wishes to

```
// Print message when mouse pressed or clicked.
public class MouseApplet extends JApplet implements MouseListener {
    public void init() {
        Container contentPane = getContentPane();
        contentPane.addMouseListener( this );
        System.out.println( "starting" );
    }

    // Print message when mouse clicked
    public void mouseClicked( MouseEvent e ) {
        System.out.println( "User clicked at "+e.getPoint() );
    }

    // Print message when mouse pressed
    public void mousePressed( MouseEvent e ) {
        System.out.println( "User pressed mouse at "+e.getPoint() );
    }

    // mouseReleased, mouseEntered, mouseExited also required
}
```

Figure D.1   Handling mouse events in an extension of JApplet

have the program react to mouse moves or drags, then the class would also have to implement MouseMotionListener.

D.3   Java Threads Can Replace ActiveObject

The ActiveObject class in the objectdraw library is an extension of Java's Thread class. It does a lot of work in the background to manage active threads and make sure they are terminated properly when the applet is stopped. It is relatively easy to design your own concurrently executing processes using threads, but you must be responsible for stopping any executing threads when the applet stops.

You can define a class extending Thread in exactly the same way you would define a class extending ActiveObject, except that uses of the pause method should be replaced by Thread's sleep method. Because the sleep method throws an InterruptedException, you will need to surround it with a try-catch construct. Figure D.2 shows the general outline of a class extending Thread. Notice that, as with ActiveObjects, you must call start() in order to begin executing the run method in a separate thread.

The InterruptedException is thrown when another thread interrupts it by sending the thread an interrupt() message. The catch clause should gracefully terminate the thread or otherwise cause the thread to recover from the interruption.

```
public class ThreadExample extends Thread {
    // Constant and instance variable declarations

    public ThreadExample(...) {
        ...
        start();
    }

    public void run() {
        ...
        while (...) {
            ...
            try {
                sleep( PAUSE_TIME );
            } catch( InterruptedException e ) { ... }
            ...
        }
    }
}
```

Figure D.2   Extending a Thread instead of ActiveObject

When an applet is stopped, the stop() method of the applet should include code to stop any threads that may still be running. As usual, this is done by sending a message to the objects still running. The message should set a flag (e.g., a boolean variable done) that can be checked in the run method executed by the thread to terminate that method. When the thread detects that the flag has been changed, it can then terminate the thread.

D.4   Java Graphics

Standard Java graphics work differently from objectdraw graphics. Java graphics objects are created independently of a canvas and then are drawn on the canvas by a paint method that is called indirectly by the system every time a refresh is requested, either by the programmer or by the system.

Graphics classes are imported from package java.awt.geom. The classes closest to those used in the objectdraw library are Line2D.Double, Rectangle2D.Double, Ellipse2D.Double, and Arc2D.Double. In each case the parameters for the constructor are the same as in objectdraw, except that the parameter representing the canvas is omitted. For example, we can write:

```
Rectangle2D.Double rect = new Rectangle2D.Double( x, y, width,
                                                   height );
```

where x, y, width, and height are all of type double. Because the Location class is not part of standard Java, there is no constructor that takes an object representing the upper left-hand corner of the object.

Any Java component can be used as a canvas with standard Java graphics. Often the canvas is a JFrame, JPanel, or JApplet. Simply creating a graphical object does not place it on a canvas. Instead it must be *drawn* on the Graphics2D object corresponding to the canvas using either a draw or fill method. These drawing methods are usually placed in a paint method that can be invoked by the programmer's calling repaint() or by the system whenever any portion of the window needs to be redrawn (e.g., because a new portion of the window is revealed). It is important that the programmer *not* call the paint method directly. Calling repaint() schedules a call to the component's update() method. The default version of update draws the background of the component and then executes the paint method. (Note that the paint method is executed by the event-handling thread. If that thread is tied up, the paint will not occur!)

The program in Figure D.3 is based on an applet from Sun's Java Tutorial. It uses the applet itself as the canvas. There is nothing to be initialized, so the init and start methods are omitted. The paint method takes a parameter of type Graphics. When the system calls the paint method (either automatically or because the programmer has invoked repaint()), the system supplies the paint method with the appropriate Graphics for the component. That Graphics object plays a central role in painting a component, as all drawing is done by sending messages to the Graphics object.

The Graphics object sent to the paint method is actually an object of type Graphics2D. (The paint method continues to declare a parameter with type Graphics for compatibility with code written before Graphics2D was introduced.) However, we need methods that are only available in Graphics2D, so the first line in the paint method casts g to a Graphics2D object, g2. That cast will always succeed.

After calculating the starting positions and dimensions of the objects to be drawn and the strings describing them, the program begins drawing the graphics objects. It first creates an object, rect, of type Rectangle2D.Double, and then sends a draw message to g2 with rect as the parameter. This draws a framed rectangle in the applet window. A string is then drawn on the graphics by sending the drawString method. Notice that there is no Text object constructed.

In the next group of statements a Line2D.Double object is constructed and drawn, along with a descriptive string. The next group of code draws an ellipse (oval). In these cases the geometric objects are constructed and immediately passed as parameters to the draw method.

Finally, in the last group of commands, the paint attribute of the graphics is set to red; the rectangle referred to by rect is moved to a new location and then drawn with the fill method, which results in drawing a red-filled rectangle. Based on your experience with objectdraw, you might expect that the original rectangle that was drawn would also be moved to this new location, but once it has been drawn with the draw method, changes to the rectangle have no impact on what was already drawn on the screen. That is, the effect of sending a draw or fill message to the graphics with a geometric object as a parameter is to set some pixels to a particular color, but those pixels no longer have a connection to the geometric object.

Notice that the paint method is never called directly from within the applet. However, it is called by the system when the applet is first initialized, and then whenever an event occurs that requires the component to be repainted. For example, if the user changes the width or height of the applet by dragging the corner, the repaint method will be called, which will then eventually result in a call of the paint method.

Because the values of rectWidth and rectHeight depend on the width and height of the applet, the objects drawn will get stretched or shrunk along with the window size. If you run this

```java
public class StdGraphicsDemo extends JApplet {
    private final static Color fg = Color.BLACK;
    private final static Color red = Color.RED;

    public void paint( Graphics g ) {
        Graphics2D g2 = (Graphics2D) g;
        int gridWidth = getWidth() / 7;

        int x = 5;
        int y = 7;
        int rectWidth = gridWidth - 2*x;
        int stringY = getHeight() - 3;
        int rectHeight = stringY - y - 20;

        // Draw Rectangle2D.Double
        Rectangle2D.Double rect =
                    new Rectangle2D.Double( x, y, rectWidth,
                                           rectHeight );
        g2.draw( rect );
        g2.drawString( "Rectangle2D", x, stringY );
        x = x + gridWidth;

        // Draw Line2D.Double
        Line2D.Double line = new Line2D.Double( x, y+rectHeight-1,
                                               x + rectWidth, y );
        g2.draw( line );
        g2.drawString( "Line2D", x, stringY );
        x = x + gridWidth;

        // Draw Ellipse2D.Double
        g2.draw( new Ellipse2D.Double(x, y, rectWidth, rectHeight) );
        g2.drawString( "Ellipse2D", x, stringY );
        x = x + gridWidth;

        // fill Rectangle2D.Double (red)
        g2.setPaint( red );
        rect.setFrame( x, y, rectWidth, rectHeight );
        g2.fill( rect );
        g2.setPaint( fg );
        g2.drawString( "Filled Rectangle2D", x, stringY );
    }
}
```

Figure D.3   Example using standard Java graphics

program, you will notice that this happens smoothly, even though each time a repaint event is posted, the applet background is erased and then the new objects are drawn.

While this example did the drawing directly on the applet, it is possible to emulate the WindowController class by inserting a frame in the center of the applet and doing the drawing directly on the Graphics associated with that frame. The most straightforward way of doing this is to define a canvas class that extends JFrame, insert that in the center of the applet, and have the paint method of the canvas responsible for doing the actual drawing on the canvas.

There is much more involved in using graphics in standard Java—entire books are devoted to the subject—but we hope this quick introduction will give you a better understanding of the differences between the simple graphics of the objectdraw library and standard Java graphics.

D.5 Random Number Generators

Java includes a class Random that may be used to create objects that generate random numbers. The class Random is both more flexible and more limited than the classes RandomIntGenerator and RandomDoubleGenerator.

There are two constructors available for Random:

```
Random()
Random( long seed )
```

The first provides a different random number generator each time it is called. If the second construction is called multiple times with the same integer (or long) seed, then each of the generators will generate the same sequence of random numbers. This is especially useful when testing a program, as the behavior should then be more predictable.

While the class supports many methods, two that you will find most useful are:

```
public int nextInt( int n )
public double nextDouble()
```

The first method returns a randomly chosen int k such that $0 \leq k < n$. Notice that only integers between 0 and $n - 1$, inclusive, are in the range of this method. The second method always returns a double $0 \leq d < 1$.

Generators obtained from the Random class differ from those obtained from the classes RandomIntGenerator and RandomDoubleGenerator in several ways.

1. One generator can produce both ints and doubles upon request.
2. The nextInt method can return ints from several ranges, but only produces numbers less than the parameter.
3. The range of ints produced via nextInt always starts with 0.

If you wish to obtain a random integer k in the range $a \leq k \leq b$, for a and b integers, compute

```
myGen.nextInt( b-a+1 ) + a
```

where myGen is a variable of type RandomIntGenerator. The smallest value returned by nextInt(b-a+1) will be 0. Adding a to 0 will give a final result of a. The largest value returned by nextInt(b-a+1) will be $b - a$. Adding a to that will give a final result of b.

D.6   Applications vs. Applets

In this text, we have focused on writing applets rather than applications. Applets can be embedded in web pages or run in applet viewers, while applications can run on their own, and can even be made into "double-clickable" applications.

In this section we explore two alternatives for writing applications rather than applets in standard Java. In general, the only thing different about a class that will be run as an application is that it has a special main method with the following form:

```
public static void main( String[] args ) { ... }
```

When a class is executed as an application, the static method main will be executed. Any parameters supplied when execution is initiated are passed as the array of strings in args.

We won't discuss the args parameter further here. It is mainly useful if the program is being executed from a command line such as

```
java MyClass arg1 arg2 ...
```

We presume that you will generally not be supplying parameters when the program is initiated, but instead the user will be filling in needed values via a GUI interface.

The following is a trivial example of an application:

```
public class HelloWorld {
    public static void main( String[] args ) {
        System.out.println( "Hello world!" );
    }
}
```

When this program is compiled and executed, it will print out "Hello world!" (without the quotes) and then terminate.

While there are lots of programs that one can write that work well as applications, we will focus here on programs like those written in this text. That is, we will be interested in programs that pop up a window in which the user will interact with the program. We will first look at programs that do this directly, but later we will see how to embed an applet in an application.

D.6.1   Modifying an Applet to Be an Application

The example of the class MouseApplication in Figure D.4 is a slight variant of the class MouseApplet defined in Figure D.1. This new class creates an application that extends JFrame rather than an applet that extends JApplet but otherwise looks and behaves just like the earlier program.

```
// Modification of MouseApplet to be an application
public class MouseApplication extends JFrame implements MouseListener {

    // Constructor replaces the init method
    public MouseApplication() {
        super( "Mouse Application" );
        Container contentPane = getContentPane();
        contentPane.addMouseListener( this );
        System.out.println( "starting" );
        setSize( 300, 300 );                        // Set size of window
    }

    // print message when mouse clicked
    public void mouseClicked( MouseEvent e ) {
        System.out.println( "User clicked at "+e.getPoint() );
    }

    // Other methods exactly the same as for MouseApplet

    // Execute this method when class is executed as an application
    public static void main( String[] args ) {
        MouseApplication ma = new MouseApplication();
        ma.show();
    }
}
```

Figure D.4 Application with mouse event handling

The main differences between classes MouseApplication and MouseApplet are the following:

1. The class extends JFrame rather than JApplet. An object of class JFrame is a window that serves as a container for other GUI components, much as applets do.
2. The init method is replaced by a constructor for the class that executes the same code.
3. Rather than setting the size of the applet with an ".html" file or in the IDE, you instead set the size in the constructor with the setSize method.
4. You must include a main method in any application. The main method (with header exactly as given in MouseApplication) must include code to create the class extending JFrame being defined and show it. If you omit sending the show message, the window will not appear on the screen.

D.6.2 Running an Applet from within a JFrame

It is also possible to run an applet from within a JFrame. We suggest one way here. It is simply to add a main method to the applet that creates a special frame that will contain the applet.

The special frame can be an object from the class AppletFrame shown in Figure D.5. Class AppletFrame extends JFrame and includes methods that create a context in which an applet can

```java
// Class representing a frame that will hold an applet
public class AppletFrame extends JFrame implements AppletStub, AppletContext {
    JApplet app;    // Applet to be embedded in frame

    // Construct a frame with app inside
    public AppletFrame( JApplet app ) {
        Container contentPane = getContentPane();
        contentPane.add( app );
        this.app = app;
    }

    // Show the frame and start the applet going
    public void show() {
        super.show();
        app.init();
        app.start();
    }

    // These dummy methods are there to give the simplest possible response to
    // any queries from the applet running inside the frame. A better
    // solution would make these do something more intelligent.
    public boolean isActive() { return true; }

    public URL getDocumentBase() { return null; }

    public URL getCodeBase() { return null; }

    public String getParameter( String name ) { return ""; }

    public AppletContext getAppletContext() { return this; }

    public void appletResize( int width, int height ) { }

    public AudioClip getAudioClip( URL url ) { return null; }

    public Image getImage( URL url ) { return null; }

    public Applet getApplet( String name ) { return null; }
    public Enumeration getApplets() { return null; }

    public void showDocument( URL url ) { }
    public void showDocument( URL url, String target ) { }

    public void showStatus( String status ) { }

    public void setStream( String key, InputStream stream ) throws IOException { }
    public InputStream getStream( String key ) { return null; }
    public Iterator getStreamKeys() { return null; }
}
```

Figure D.5   Class that can contain an applet

be run. Notice that the constructor of `AppletFrame` adds the `JApplet` passed as a parameter to the content pane of the frame.

The large number of methods are required for the frame to behave as a context for running an applet. A smarter implementation would include more than just the simplest default behavior for these methods.

Suppose you wish to run applet `MyApplet` as an application. Just add the method:

```
public static void main( String[] args ) {
        AppletFrame frame = new AppletFrame( new MyApplet() );
        frame.setTitle( "MyApplet" );
        frame.setSize( 500, 500 );
        frame.setDefaultCloseOperation( JFrame.EXIT_ON_CLOSE );
        frame.show();
}
```

`MyApplet` can be any extension of `JApplet`, in particular, it can be an extension of `Controller` or `WindowController`. The `main` method creates a new object from the applet that is installed in a new `AppletFrame` object, `frame`. The frame's title and size are set; it is set to respond to a close operation by having the frame exit, and it is then shown on the screen. Notice that the `show` operation in `AppleFrame` not only shows the frame, but also executes the `init()` and `start()` methods of the applet. Because the applet is running inside the frame, it can be executed as an application, but it will behave just as if it were running as an applet.

Because we have included only the simplest default behavior for the methods required for the frame to serve as the context of an applet, some methods called in the applet won't work correctly. In particular, neither `getAudioClip` nor `getImage` will work correctly. If you wish to use those methods in your applet, then you will have to create a more capable version of `AppletFrame`.

If you are intending to write an application, you will probably find it easiest to write the main class directly as an extension of `JFrame`. However, if you already have an applet that you wish to run as an application, you may have luck in running it inside a `JFrame` as explained here. In particular, if you have an applet that extends `Controller` or `WindowController`, you can use this strategy and still be able to use all of the features of the objectdraw library.

Index